DAMRON
52nd Edition
MEN'S TRAVEL GUIDE

Publisher Damron Company

President
& Editor-in-Chief Gina M. Gatta

Editor at Large Erika O'Connor

Art Director Kathleen Pratt

In Memory of Bob Damron and Dan Delbex

How to Contact Us

Mail: 459 Fulton ST #301
San Francisco, CA 94102

Web: www.damron.com

Phone: 415/255-0404
[9am-5pm (PST) Mon-Fri]

Fax: 415/703-9049

Using this guide

Call first! Not because we haven't (in fact, we call several times a year!), but because every element of a listing, from hours to area codes, may have changed since we've hung up the phone.

Info Lines & Services This is the category for LGBT centers. At our web-site, www.damron.com, we extensively list hotlines, social or support groups as well as services like the state tourism board or the personal guide with a limo.

Accommodations Most accommodations (especially B&Bs) require advance reservations. It's a good idea to request a brochure ahead of time, and to be clear about deposit and cancellation policies when making reservations.

Bars & Nightclubs Many codes apply only a few nights a week, especially when we've noted "theme nights." You should call the bar to verify what is scheduled for which nights. Bars coded **BW** (beer/wine) might not serve both.

Restaurants All restaurants listed are gay-friendly; those with mostly gay/lesbian clientele are coded **MW**.

Cafes are casual hangouts serving coffee and pastries, but not full menus.

Entertainment & Recreation Something touristy, maybe a little kitschy, unusual, or commonly overlooked, that even your friends who've lived there all their lives won't mind doing with you.

Publications If you want to know what's new, get one when you get to town. They're usually free and distributed in many of the locations we list. Your best bet, however, is to go right to the local LGBT or alternative bookstore to get the latest issue and/or lowdown.

Gyms are workout facilities, not bathhouses. They're mostly straight, unless coded **MW** or **MO**.

Men's Clubs include sex clubs, bathhouses, playspaces, and sex-oriented groups.

Men's Services are mostly telephone-dating services.

Cruisy Areas In many cities, you're more likely to meet vice cops than partners at public grounds. Try the local bar or bathhouse instead if you're bent on picking up. To avoid entrapment.

Unconfirmed means we've called, several times, but no one answered. The phone still works but everything else may be different. Definitely call first.

Tour Operators A brief description of what kinds of tours the tour operator offers.

As Damron has done since 1964, we reward the best letters (those packed with new info of openings and closings we haven't already found) with a **FREE COPY** of next year's edition.

Key to the Codes

➤	an Advertiser – *please mention Damron when patronizing businesses that support us by advertising!*
★	very popular
$	cover charge
18+	must be **18** years or older (usually only on some nights)
A	Alternative music (modern rock, includes goth crowd)
AYOR	At Your Own Risk
B	Bears
BYOB	Bring Your Own Bottle
BW	Beer and/or Wine only
C	Cabaret
CW	Country/Western
D	Dancing (DJ spinning—usually Fri-Sat)
DS	Drag shows
E	live Entertainment (bands, comedy, spoken word, etc.)
F	hot Food served from a kitchen or grill
GF	Gay-Friendly (mostly straight)
GO	Gay-Owned and/or operated (includes Lesbian-owned)
GS	Gay/Straight
K	Karaoke (usually only on some nights)
L	Leather & fetish
LGBT	Lesbian/Gay/Bisexual/Transgender
M	mostly gay Men
MO	Men Only
MR	MultiRacial clientele
MR-A	mostly Asian-American
MR-AF	mostly AFrican-American
MR-L	mostly Latino/a-American
MW	gay men and lesbians (Men and Women)
N	Nudity permitted in some areas
NH	NeighborHood bar
NS	Non-Smoking building
OC	Older/more mature Crowd
P	Piano bar
PC	Private Club
R	Reservations required
S	Strippers & go-go dancers
SW	SWimming on-site or nearby
TG	TransGender-friendly
V	Videos shown
W	mostly Women (lesbians)
WC	WheelChair accessible (bathrooms too)
WI	WIFi
WO	Women Only
YC	Young/Collegiate types

Table of Contents

United States of America

Alabama	9
Alaska	10
Arizona	12
Arkansas	17
California	19
Colorado	65
Connecticut	69
Delaware	72
District of Columbia	73
Florida	77
Georgia	94
Hawaii	99
Idaho	103
Illinois	113
Indiana	113
Iowa	117
Kansas	120
Kentucky	121
Louisiana	124
Maine	130
Maryland	134
Massachusetts	135
Michigan	145
Minnesota	151
Mississippi	153
Missouri	154
Montana	158
Nebraska	159
Nevada	160
New Hampshire	163
New Jersey	164
New Mexico	166
New York	170
North Carolina	187
North Dakota	191
Ohio	192
Oklahoma	198
Oregon	201

Table of Contents

Pennsylvania 205
Rhode Island 213
South Carolina 214
South Dakota 217
Tennessee 217
Texas 220
Utah 230
Vermont 232
Virginia 235
Washington 237
West Virginia 243
Wisconsin 244
Wyoming 248

International

Canada 249
Caribbean 267
Mexico 273
Costa Rica 286
Argentina • Buenos Aires 289
Brazil • Rio de Janeiro 291
Chile • Santiago 294
Austria • Vienna 295
Czech Republic • Prague 297
Denmark • Copenhagen 300
England • London 301
France • Paris 307
Germany • Berlin 313
Ireland • Dublin 318
Italy • Rome 319
The Netherlands • Amsterdam 321
Scotland • Edinburgh 327
Spain • Madrid, Barcelona & Sitges 328
Japan • Tokyo 335
Thailand • Bangkok 337
Australia • Sydney 339

Travel/Tours

Tours & Tour Operators 342

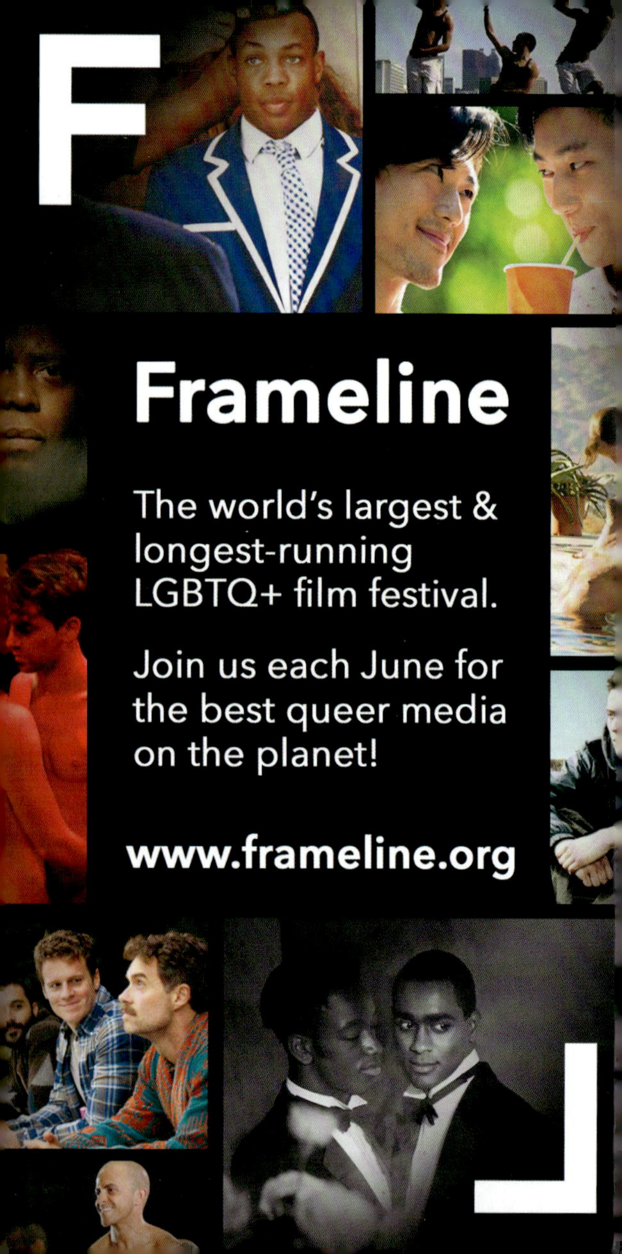
F
Frameline
The world's largest &
longest-running
LGBTQ+ film festival.
Join us each June for
the best queer media
on the planet!
www.frameline.org

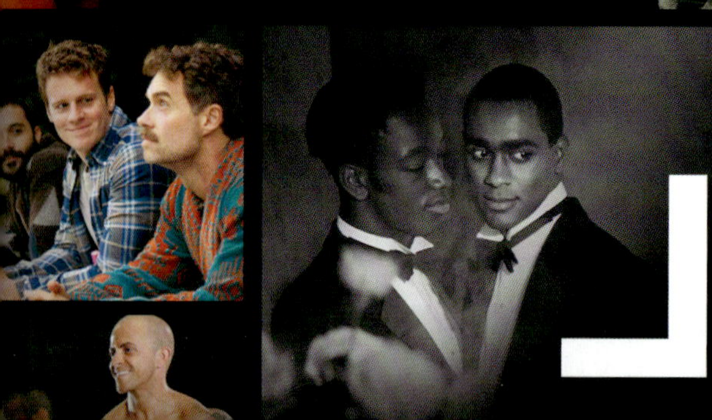

USA

ALABAMA

Statewide

PUBLICATIONS

Ambush Mag **504/522-8049** *LGBT newspaper for the Gulf South (TX through FL)*

Fake Listing To Test Ad Mark **504/522-8049** *this is a fake listing to test the ad marks*

Anniston

CRUISY AREAS

Cheaha Park [AYOR] Cheaha Scenic Dr *early evenings, head toward the walking trail (beware of cops!)*

Auburn

CRUISY AREAS

Rest Area [AYOR] Hwy 280 (30 miles E of Alexander City & 5 miles W of Auburn) *evenings*

Birmingham

ACCOMMODATIONS

Hampton Inn [GF,WI,WC] 2021 Park Pl N (at 21st St N) **205/322-2100** *also restaurant & lounge*

BARS

The Garage Cafe [GF,F,E] 2304 10th Terrace S (at 23rd St S) **205/322-3220** *11am-close, from 3pm Sun-Mon, great sandwiches, live music*

Our Place [M,NH,V,GO] **205/715-0077** *4pm-midnight, till 2am Fri-Sat*

Spike's [M,L] 620 S 27th St S **205/265-1496**

Wine Loft [GF] 2200 1st Ave N **205/323-8228** *5pm-close, clsd Sun-Mon, wine bar, light food served*

NIGHTCLUBS

Al's on 7th [MW,NH,D,DS,18+,PC] 2627 7th Ave S (at 27th St) **205/321-2812** *theme nights*

The Quest Club [M,K,D,DS,PC,WC,$] 416 24th St S (at 5th Ave S) **205/251-4313** *24hrs, [19+] Wed-Sun, patio*

CAFES

Chez Lulu [E] 1909 Cahaba Rd **205/870-7011** *lunch & dinner Tue-Sun, Sun brunch, clsd Mon, plenty veggie, also bakery*

RESTAURANTS

Bottega Cafe & Restaurant [WC] 2240 Highland Ave S (btwn 22nd & 23rd) **205/939-1000** *5:30pm-10pm, clsd Sun, full bar*

Highlands Bar & Grill [WC] 2011 11th Ave S (at 20th St) **205/939-1400** *5:30pm-10pm, clsd Sun-Mon*

John's City Diner [WC] 112 21st St N (btwn 1st & 2nd Ave N) **205/322-6014** *lunch weekdays & dinner Mon-Sat, clsd Sun, full bar*

Rojo 2921 Highland Ave S (at 30th St) **205/328-4733** *11am-10pm, clsd Mon, wknd brunch, Latin & American cuisine*

Silvertron Cafe 3813 Clairmont Ave S (at 39th St S) **205/591-3707** *11am-9pm, from 8am Sat, also full bar, more gay Mon*

Taj India 2226 Highland Ave S **205/939-3805** *lunch & dinner, Indian, plenty veggie*

ENTERTAINMENT & RECREATION

Terrific New Theatre 2821 2nd Ave S (in Dr Pepper Design Complex) **205/328-0868**

EROTICA

Alabama Adult Books 801 3rd Ave N (at 8th) **205/322-7323** *super-arcade*

Birmingham Adult Books 7610 1st Ave N (at 76th St) **205/836-1580** *booths*

CRUISY AREAS

Cahaba River Rd Park [AYOR] at Jefferson/ Shelby county line (on Hwy 280 E, exit before Cahaba River bridge & turn left) *follow trail; noon & late afternoon popular*

Dothan

Nightclubs

Dothan Dance Club [GF,DS,MR,C,PC,GO] 2563 Ross Clark Circle (at Hwy 52 West) **334/792-5166** *11pm Fri, from 6pm Sat-Sun, clsd Mon-Th*

Huntsville

Cruisy Areas

Monte Sano Scenic Overlook [AYOR] Governors Dr (on left before Monte Sano Blvd)

Mobile

Info Lines & Services

Pink Triangle AA Group 251/479-9994 (AA#), 251/438-7080 (church) *7pm Tue, Th & Sat, call for locations*

Accommodations

Berney Fly B&B [GF,SW,NS,WI] 1118 Government St **251/405-0949** *Victorian B&B, full brkfst, close to gay bars and restaurants*

Bars

Flipside Bar & Patio [MW,NH,NS] 54 S Conception St **251/431-8869** *open 4pm*

Gabriel's Downtown [MW,K,V,PC] 55 S Joachim St (off Government) **251/432-4900** *7pm-close, patio*

Midtown Pub [MW,NH,D,F,K] 153 S Florida St (at Emogene) **251/450-1555** *noon-2am*

Nightclubs

B-Bob's Downtown [M,D,B,DS,P,WC] 213 Conti St (at Joachim) **251/433-2262** *6pm-close, from 7pm Sat, 2-level multi-venue club, home den of Gulf Coast Bears, also gift shop*

Montgomery

Accommodations

The Lattice Inn [GS,SW,WI,WC,GO] 1414 S Hull St (at Clanton) **334/263-1414**

Nightclubs

Club 322 [MW,D,DS] 322 N Lawrence St **334/263-4322** *8pm-close, clsd Mon*

Cruisy Areas

Woodmere Park [AYOR] Woodmere Blvd (at Eastern)

Steele

Accommodations

Bluff Creek Falls [M,SW,PC,WI,GO] 1125 Loop Rd **256/538-0678, 205/515-7882** *secluded campground w/ waterfalls, bluffs, 50 minutes from Birmingham*

Tuscaloosa

Nightclubs

Icon [M,D,DS] 516 Greensboro Ave *9pm-2am, clsd Sun-Wed*

Cruisy Areas

Bowers Park [AYOR] from McFarland Blvd turn E onto 37th St, then turn N onto Bowers Park Dr

Jack Warner Pkwy Parks [AYOR] along Black Warrior River *formerly River Rd Parks, check out 4th park near boat ramp*

ALASKA

Statewide

Entertainment & Recreation

Out in Alaska [★] 1819 Dimond Dr, Fairbanks **907/339-0101** *adventure travel throughout Alaska for LGBT travelers*

Anchorage

Info Lines & Services

AA Gay/ Lesbian 336 E 5th Ave (at Community Center) **907/929-4528** *6pm Mon*

Identity, Inc 336 E 5th Ave **907/929-4528** *community center, newsletter*

Accommodations

A Wildflower Inn B&B [GS,NS,WI,GO] 1239 I St (at 13th) **907/274-1239, 877/693-1239** *convenient, downtown location*

Alaska Heavenly Lodge [GF,NS] 34950 Blakely Rd (at Mile 49 Sterling Hwy), Cooper Landing **907/599-0022, 866/595-2012** *hot tub, cedar sauna*

Arctic Fox Inn [GS,GO] 327 E 2nd Ct **907/272-4818, 877/693-1239** *also apts*

City Garden B&B [GS,NS,WI,GO] 1352 W 10th Ave (at N St) **907/276-8686** *beautiful views of Mt McKinley, 10-minute walk to downtown area*

Copper Whale Inn [GS,WI,NS,WC,GO] 440 L St (at 5th Ave) **907/258-7999, 866/258-7999** *downtown*

Inlet Tower Hotel & Suites [GS,WI,WC] 1200 L St (at 12th) **907/276-0110, 800/544-0786** *also bar & restaurant*

Renfro's Lakeside Retreat [GF,WI,GO] 27177 Seward Hwy, Seward **907/288-5059, 877/288-5059** *log cabins on Kenai Lake, seasonal*

Bars

Bernie's Bungalow Lounge [GF,F] 626 D St (at W 5th Ave) **907/276-8808** *cocktail lounge, patio, food served*

Mad Myrna's [MW,NH,D,F,K,DS] 530 E 5th Ave (at Fairbanks) **907/276-9762** *4pm-2:30am, till 3am Fri-Sat*

Raven [MW,NH,WC] 708 E 4th Ave **907/276-9672** *1pm-2:30am, till 3am wknds*

Restaurants

Bear Tooth Theatre Pub & Grill 1230 W 27th Ave **907/276-4200** *movie theater, pub & grill all in one*

China Lights 12110 Business Blvd, Eagle River **907/694-8080** *11:30am-10pm, till 10:30pm wknds*

Club Paris 417 W 5th Ave **907/277-6332** *11am-midnight, from 4pm Sun, perhaps the finest restaurant in town*

Garcia's 11901 Business Blvd #104 (next to Safeway), Eagle River **907/694-8600** *11am-midnight, from noon wknds, Mexican*

Ginger 425 W 5th Ave (at D St) **907/929-3680** *lunch Mon-Fri, dinner nightly, bar from 3pm, Pacific Rim/ Asian*

Marx Brothers Cafe 627 W 3rd Ave **907/278-2133** *5:30pm-10pm, clsd Sun-Mon, great food & views*

Simon & Seafort's 420 L St (btwn 4th & 5th) **907/274-3502** *lunch weekdays, dinner nightly, great view, full bar*

Snow City Cafe [★BW,WI] 1034 W 4th Ave (at L St) **907/272-2489** *7am-3pm, till 4pm wknds*

Entertainment & Recreation

Out North Contemporary Art House 3800 DeBarr Rd **907/279-3800** *community-based & visiting-artist exhibits, screenings & performances*

Bookstores

Title Wave Books 1360 W Northern Lights Blvd **907/278-9283, 888/598-9283** *10am-8pm, till 9pm Fri-Sat, 11am-7pm Sun, LGBT section*

Publications

Anchorage Press 907/561-7737 *alternative paper*

Fairbanks

Accommodations

All Seasons B&B Inn [GF,NS,WI,WC] 763 7th Ave (at Barnette St) **907/451-6649, 888/451-6649** *full brkfst*

Billie's Backpackers Hostel [GF,F] 2895 Mack Blvd **907/479-2034, 907/799-6120**

Cafes

Hot Licks Ice Cream 3453 College Rd **907/479-7813** *seasonal*

Homer

Accommodations

Sadie Cove Wilderness Lodge [GF,NS] Kachemak Bay State Park **907/235-2350, 888/283-7234** *tree planted for every guest to offset carbon emission, 3 full meals a day*

Cafes

Spit Sister Cafe [GS,WI] Homer Spit Rd (at Harbor View Boardwalk #5) **907/235-4921 (summer), 907/299-6868/ 6767 (winter)** *5am-4pm*

Juneau

Accommodations

Pearson's Pond Luxury Suites & Adventure Spa [GF,NS,WI] 4541 Sawa Circle **907/789-3772, 888/658-6328** *B&B resort & spa*

The Silverbow Inn [GF,NS,WI] 120 Second St **907/586-4146, 800/586-4146**

Restaurants

Hangar on the Wharf 2 Marine Way Ste 106 **907/586-5018** *lunch & dinner, full bar, great fish & chips*

Cruisy Areas

Cope Park [AYOR] *mornings & afternoons (summers)*

Ketchikan

Accommodations

Anchor Inn by the Sea [GF,NS,WI] 4672 S Tongass Hwy **907/247-7117, 800/928-3308**

Entertainment & Recreation

Southeast Sea Kayaks [GF] 3 Salmon Landing **907/225-1258, 800/287-1607**

McCarthy

Accommodations

McCarthy Lodge & Ma Johnson's Hotel [GF,F,NS] **907/554-4402** *inside Wrangell St Elias nat'l park*

Palmer

Accommodations

Alaska Garden Gate B&B [GS,NS,WI,GO] 950 S Trunk Rd **907/746-2333** *full brkfst, hot tub, lesbian-owned*

Seward

Entertainment & Recreation

Puffin Fishing Charters [GS] PO Box 606, 99664 **907/224-4653, 800/978-3346** *day fishing trips*

Sitka

Cafes

Backdoor Cafe 104 Barracks St (behind Old Harbor Books on Lincoln St, no street sign) **907/747-8856** *6:30am-5pm, till 2pm Sat, clsd Sun*

Entertainment & Recreation

Esther G Sea Taxi 215 Shotgun Alley **907/738-6481, 907/747-6481** *marine wildlife tours, transportation service*

Arizona

Bisbee

Accommodations

Casa de San Pedro B&B [GF,SW,NS,WI,WC,GO] 8933 S Yell Ln (at Hwy 92 & Palominas Rd), Hereford **520/366-1300, 888/257-2050** *full brkfst*

Copper Queen Hotel [GF,SW,NS,WC] 11 Howell Ave **520/432-2216** *restored historic landmark, restaurant*

Doublejack Guesthouse [M,NS,WI] **520/559-6708**

Eldorado Suites [GF,NS,WI] 55 OK St **520/432-6679**

Sleepy Dog Guest House [GF,NS,WI] 212A Opera Dr **520/432-3057, 520/234-8166 (cell)** *reclaimed miner's cabin*

Bars

St Elmo's [GF,E] 36 Brewery Ave **520/432-5578** *10am-2am, live bands Fri-Sat*

Bullhead City

includes Laughlin, Nevada

Cruisy Areas

Adult Theater Hwy 95 (S of town) *bookstores w/ arcade*

Karen's Adult Bookstore Hwy 95 (near Mohave Jct, S of town)

Flagstaff

Accommodations

Abineau Lodge [GS,NS,WI,GO] 1080 Mountainaire Rd **928/525-6212, 888/715-6386**

The Historic Hotel Monte Vista [GF,E,NS] 100 N San Francisco St (at Aspen) **928/779-6971, 800/545-3068** *full bar*

Inn at 410 [GF,WI,WC,GO] 410 N Leroux St **928/774-0088, 800/774-2008**

Motel in the Pines [GF,WC] 80 W Pinewood Blvd (exit 322), Pinewood **928/286-9699, 800/574-5080** *20 miles from Flagstaff*

Starlight Pines B&B [GS,NS,WI,GO] 3380 E Lockett Rd (at Fanning) **928/527-1912, 800/752-1912** *full brkfst*

Bars

Charly's Pub & Grill [GF,F,E,WC] 23 N Leroux St (at Weatherford Hotel) **928/779-1919** *8am-2am*

Monte Vista Lounge [GF,D,E,K] 100 N San Francisco St (at Hotel Monte Vista) **928/774-2403** *noon-2am, from 11am Fri-Sun*

Cafes

Macy's European Coffee House [F] 14 S Beaver St **928/774-2243** *6am-8pm, vegetarian/ vegan bakey*

Restaurants

Pasto [BW,WC] 19 E Aspen (at San Francisco) **928/779-1937** *lunch & dinner, clsd Sun*

Cruisy Areas

Rest Area [AYOR] off I-40 (17 miles W of Flagstaff)

Thorpe Park [AYOR]

Golden Valley

Erotica

Pleasure Palace Adult Bookstore 4150 US Hwy 68 (at Houck Rd) **928/565-5600**

Grand Canyon

Accommodations

Grand Canyon Lodge North [GF,F] end of Hwy 67, North Rim **877/386-4383** *at the North Rim of the Grand Canyon*

Grand Canyon Lodges [GF,F] **928/638-2631** *the only "in-park" lodging at the South Rim*

Jerome

Accommodations

Mile High Grill & Inn [GF,GO] 309 Main St **928/634-5094** *cool hotel, also restaurant*

Lake Havasu City

Info Lines & Services

Lake Havasu City AA 877/652-9005

Accommodations

Nautical Inn [GF,SW,WI] 1000 McCulloch Blvd N **928/855-2141, 800/892-2141**

Lake Powell

Accommodations

Dreamkatchers Lake Powell B&B [GS,WI,GO] **435/675-5828**

Phoenix

see also Scottsdale & Tempe

Info Lines & Services

Lambda Phoenix Center 2622 N 16th St (at Virginia Ave) **602/635-2090** *space for many 12-step programs*

Phoenix Pride LGBT Center 4442 North 7th Ave **602/712-0111** *10am-9pm, till 10pm Fri-Sat, till 4pm Sun, clsd Mon*

Accommodations

Arizona Royal Villa Complex [MO,SW,N,NS,WI,GO] 4312 N 12th St **602/266-6883, 888/266-6884** *hot tub*

Arizona Sunburst Inn [MO,R,SW,N,NS,WI,GO] 6245 N 12th Pl (at Rose Ln) **602/274-1474, 800/974-1474** *hot tub*

Best Western Plus Scottsdale Thunderbird Suites [GF,SW,NS,WI,WC] 7515 E Butherus Dr (at Scottsdale Rd), Scottsdale **480/951-4000, 800/951-1288**

Clarendon Hotel & Suites [GS,SW,WI,WC,GO] 401 W Clarendon Ave (at 3rd Ave) **602/252-7363**

FireSky Resort & Spa [GF,SW,WI,WC] 4925 N Scottsdale Rd, Scottsdale **480/945-7666, 800/528-7867**

Hotel San Carlos [GF,F,SW,WI] 202 N Central Ave **602/253-4121, 866/253-4121** *boutique hotel, rooftop pool, restaurant*

Maricopa Manor B&B Inn [GS,SW,WI,WC,GO] 15 W Pasadena Ave **602/274-6302, 800/292-6403**

Orange Blossom Hacienda [GF,SW,WI,GO] 3914 E Sunnydale Dr (btwn Recker & Hunt Hwy), Gilbert **480/755-4346, 877/589-8465**

The Saguaro [GF,SW,NS] 4000 N Drinkwater Blvd **480/308-1100** *hip boutique hotel*

ZenYard [GS,SW,NS,WI,GO] 830 E Maryland Ave **602/845-0830, 866/594-0242**

BARS

The Anvil [M,D,WC] 2424 E Thomas Rd (at 24th St) **602/682-5088** *3pm-2am Wed-Sun*

Bar 1 [★M,NH,K,WI] 3702 N 16th St (at E Clarendon) **602/266-9001** *10am-2am*

BS West [MW,D,K,S,WC] 7125 E 5th Ave (in the Kiva Center), Scottsdale **480/945-9028** *2pm-2am*

The Bunkhouse Saloon [M,NH,K] 4428 N 7th Ave (at Indian School) **602/200-9154** *8am-2am, from 10am Sun, patio*

Cash Inn Country [W,D,CW,K,WI,WC] 2140 E McDowell Rd (at 22nd St) **602/244-9943** *2pm-close, from noon wknds*

Charlie's [★M,D,CW,DS,WC] 727 W Camelback Rd (at 7th Ave) **602/265-0224** *2pm-2am, noon-4am Fri-Sat*

Cruisin' 7th [M,DS,K,TG,WC] 3702 N 7th St (near Indian School) **602/212-9888** *6am-2am, from 10am Sun, hustlers*

Dick's Cabaret [M,D,S,18+. BYOB] 3432 E Illini (off University) **602/274-3425** *7pm-3am, till 4am Fri-Sat "all male nude review," no alcohol*

Kobalt [MW,K,E] 3110 N Central Ave **602/264-5307** *11am-2am*

Nu Towne Saloon [★M,NH,WC] 5002 E Van Buren (at 48th St) **602/267-9959** *noon-2am, patio, cruisy*

Oz [MW,NH,V,WI,WC] 1804 W Bethany Home Rd (at 19th) **602/242-5114** *6am-2am*

Plazma [MW,NH,K,V] 1560 E Osborn Rd (at N 16th St) **602/266-0477** *4pm-1am*

The Rock/ La Roca [MW,NH,E,DS,TG,K] 4129 N 7th Ave (at Indian School) **602/248-8559** *2pm-2am, from 11am wknds*

Stacy's @Melrose [★MW,D] 4343 N 7th Ave **602/264-1700** *4pm-2am*

NIGHTCLUBS

Bar Smith [GS,D,F] **602/229-1265** *9pm-2am, till 3am Sat, clsd Sun*

Karamba [★M,D,MR-L,DS,WC] 1724 E McDowell (at 16th St) **602/254-0231** *9pm-close, clsd Mon-Wed, Latin wknds*

CAFES

Copper Star Coffee [WI] 4220 N 7th Ave (at Indian School) **602/266-2136** *6am-9pm, till 11pm Fri-Sat, coffee in a converted gas station*

RESTAURANTS

Alexi's [WC] 3550 N Central Ave #120 (in Valley Bank Bldg) **602/279-0982** *lunch Mon-Fri, dinner nightly, clsd Sun, int'l, full bar, patio*

AZ/88 7553 E Scottsdale Mall, Scottsdale **480/994-5576** *11:30am-1am, bar popular w/ gay men Fri-Sat evenings*

Barrio Cafe [E,GO] 2814 N 16th St **602/636-0240** *lunch Tue-Fri, dinner Tue-Sun, Sun brunch, clsd Mon, Mexican, live music*

Coronado Cafe 2201 N 7th St **602/258-5149** *lunch Mon-Sat, dinner Tue-Sat, clsd Sun*

DeFalco's Italian Deli 2334 N Scottsdale Rd **480/990-8660**

Dottie's True Blue Cafe [GO] 4151 N Marshall Way, Scottsdale **480/874-0303** *7:30am-3pm, clsd Mon, great brkfst*

Durant's 2611 N Central Ave **602/264-5967** *lunch Mon-Fri, dinner nightly*

FEZ 105 W Portland St (at Central) **602/287-8700** *11am-midnight, from 8:30am wknds, Moroccan influence, full bar, patio*

Green 2240 N Scottsdale Rd #8, Tempe **480/941-9003** *11am-9pm, clsd Sun, vegetarian/ vegan*

Los Dos Molinos 8684 S Central Ave **602/243-9113** *lunch & dinner, clsd Sun-Mon, Mexican*

MacAlpine's Soda Fountain 2303 N 7th St **602/262-5545** *11am-7pm, till 8pm Fri-Sat, great milkshakes*

Malee's 7131 E Main, Scottsdale **480/947-6042** *lunch & dinner, Thai, full bar*

Mi Patio 3347 N 7th Ave **602/277-4831** *10am-10pm, Mexican*

Persian Garden Cafe [WI] 1335 W Thomas Rd (at N 15th Ave) **602/263-1915** *lunch & dinner, dinner only Sat, clsd Sun-Mon,plenty vegan*

Rose & Crown 628 E Adams St **602/256-0223** *11am-2am, British pub*

Switch [WI] 2603 N Central Ave **602/264-2295** *11am-midnight, from 10am wknds, full bar*

Vincent on Camelback [WC] 3930 E Camelback Rd (at 40th St) **602/224-0225** *dinner Mon-Sat, clsd Sun, Southwestern*

Entertainment & Recreation

Soul Invictus 1022 NW Grand Ave (near W Van Buren St) **602/214-4344** *queer-friendly art gallery & cabaret*

Stray Cat Theatre 132 E 6th St (at Performing Arts Ctr), Tempe **480/634-6435** *off-the-beaten-path productions*

Bookstores

Changing Hands 6428 S McClintock Dr, Tempe **480/730-0205** *new & used, LGBT section*

Retail Shops

Off Chute Too 4111 N 7th Ave (at Indian School Rd) **602/274-1429** *9am-9pm, till 10pm Fri-Sat, 10am-6pm Sun, LGBT gift shop in Melrose District*

Publications

Echo Magazine 602/266-0550, 888/324-6624 *bi-weekly LGBT news-magazine*

Ion Arizona Magazine 602/308-4662 *entertainment guide for the AZ gay community*

Gyms & Health Clubs

Pulse Fitness 18221 N Pima Rd #H-130, Scottsdale **480/907-5900**

Men's Clubs

Chute [B,L,V,18+] 1440 E Indian School Rd **602/234-1654** *24hrs, private rooms, gym, steam room*

Flex Complex [SW,PC] 1517 S Black Canyon Hwy (btwn 19th Ave & I-17) **602/271-9011** *24hrs*

Erotica

Adult Shoppe 111 S 24th St (at Jefferson) **602/306-1130** *24hrs; several locations*

Castle Megastore 300 E Camelback (at Central) **602/266-3348** *11am-11pm, tll 2am Fri-Sat*

Fascinations 10242 N 19th Ave #1-7 **602/943-5859** *many locations*

International Bookstore 3640 E Thomas Rd (at 36th St) **602/955-2000**

Modern World 1812 E Apache (at McClintock Dr), Tempe **480/967-9052** *24hrs*

Pleasure World/ Book Cellar 4029 E Washington (at 40th St) **602/275-0015** *clsd 4am 6am, theatre*

Zorba's Adult Book Shop 2924 N Scottsdale Rd (N of Thomas), Scottsdale **480/941-9891** *24hrs, video rentals & arcade*

Cruisy Areas

Dreamy Draw Park [AYOR] Squaw Peak Pkwy (Hwy 51) (off Northern) *go E along the driveway to the back—popular w/ 9-5ers; be alert—major crackdown on cruising in Phoenix!*

Papago Park [AYOR] Galvin Pkwy (btwn McDowell Rd & Van Buren St) *be alert—major crackdown on cruising in Phoenix!*

Washington Park [AYOR] 21st Ave (at Glendale) *nights; be alert—major crackdown on cruising in Phoenix!*

Prescott

Accommodations

The Motor Lodge [GF,WI,GO] 503 S Montezuma St (at Leroux) **928/717-0157**

Cruisy Areas

Heritage Park [AYOR] Willow Creek Rd (3 miles S of Hwy 89)

Sedona

Accommodations

Apple Orchard Inn [GF,SW,NS,WC] 656 Jordan Rd **928/282-5328** *full brkfst*

El Portal Sedona [GF,NS,F,WI,WC] 95 Portal Ln **928/203-9405, 800/313-0017**

The Lodge at Sedona—A Luxury B&B Inn [GS,SW,NS,WI] 125 Kallof Pl **928/204-1942, 800/619-4467**

Sedona Rouge Hotel & Spa [GF,SW,NS,WI,WC] 2250 W Hwy 89-A **928/203-4111, 866/312-4111** *restaurant & bar*

Southwest Inn at Sedona [GF,SW,NS,WI] 3250 W Hwy 89-A **928/282-3344, 800/483-7422**

Cafes

Old Town Red Rooster Cafe 901 N Main St, Cottonwood **928/649-8100** *8am-4pm*

Restaurants

Judi's 40 Soldiers Pass Rd **928/282-4449** *lunch & dinner, clsd Sun, full bar*

Retail Shops

Sedona Green Gallery & Gifts 273 N Hwy 89A #K (btwn Jordan & Mesquite) **928/239-5353** *10-15% discount to self-identifying gay & lesbian customers*

Tucson

Info Lines & Services

AA Gay/ Lesbian 3269 N Mountain Ave **520/624-4183** *many mtgs*

Southern Arizona AIDS Foundation (SAAF) 375 S Euclid Ave **800/771-9054** *8am-5pm, clsd wknds*

Accommodations

Catalina Park Inn [GS,NS,WI,GO] 309 E 1st St (at 5th Ave) **520/792-4541, 800/792-4885**

Desert Trails B&B [GF,SW,NS] 12851 E Speedway Blvd **520/885-7295** *unique adobe territorial on 3 acres bordering Saguaro Nat'l Park*

Hacienda del Sol Guest Ranch Resort [GF,F,SW,NS,WI,WC] 5601 N Hacienda del Sol Rd **520/299-1501, 800/728-6514**

Hotel Congress [GS,F,E,WI] 311 E Congress St **520/622-8848, 800/722-8848** *cafe, full bar & club*

La Casita Del Sol [GS,NS,WI,GO] 407 N Meyer Ave (btwn Church Ave & Franklin Ave) **520/623-8882** *1880s adobe guesthouse*

Royal Elizabeth B&B Inn [GS,SW,NS,WI,GO] 204 S Scott Ave (at Broadway) **520/670-9022, 877/670-9022** *historic 1878 downtown mansion*

Bars

Club Congress/ The Tap Room [GF,NH,D,E,K] 311 E Congress (at Hotel Congress) **520/622-8848** *11am-2am, dance club from 9pm*

IBT's (It's About Time) [MW,D,K,S,WC] 616 N 4th Ave (at University) **520/882-3053** *noon-2am*

Venture-N [M,L,WI] 1239 N 6th Ave (at Stone) **520/882-8224** *noon-2am, from 9am Th-Fri, Sun BBQ, patio*

Cafes

Revolutionary Grounds [F,WI] 606 N 4th Ave (at E 5th St) **520/620-1770** *8am-8pm, also leftist bookstore*

Restaurants

Blue Willow 2616 N Campbell Ave (at Grant) **520/327-7577** *7am-9pm, from 8am wknds, brkfst served all day*

Cafe Poca Cosa 110 E Pennington St **520/622-6400** *11am-9pm, till 10pm Fri-Sat, clsd Sun-Mon, Mexican-influenced bistro, patio*

Entertainment & Recreation

The Loft Cinema [F,BW] 3233 E Speedway Blvd **520/795-0844, 520/322-5638** *Tucson's independent art house*

Bookstores

Antigone Books [WC] 411 N 4th Ave (at 7th St) **520/792-3715** *10am-7pm, till 9pm Fri-Sat, 11am-5pm Sun, LGBT*

Erotica

The Bookstore Southwest 5754 E Speedway Blvd **520/790-1550**

Caesar's Adult Shop 2540 N Oracle Rd (btwn Glen & Grant) **520/622-9479**

Continental Book Shop 2655 N Campbell Ave (at Grant) **520/327-8402** *private rooms, arcade*

Hydra 145 E Congress (at 6th) **520/791-3711** *vinyl, leather, toys, shoes*

Cruisy Areas

Tanque Verde Falls/ Reddington Pass *upper Tanque Verde Falls, clothing-optional, gay area is beyond straight area*

Arkansas

Batesville

Cruisy Areas

Riverside Park [AYOR]

Crosses

Cafes

Crosses Grocery & Cafe [★GO] 4223 Hwy 16 (E of Elkins, outside Fayetteville) **479/643-3307** *6am-8:30pm, on the Pig Trail*

Eureka Springs

Accommodations

The Grand TreeHouse Resort [GS,WI,GO] 350 W Van Buren (at Pivot Rock Rd) **479/253-8733**

Heart of the Hills Inn [GS,NS,GO] 5 Summit St (on Historic Loop) **479/253-7468, 800/253-7468**

Lookout Lodge [GF,NS,WI] 3098 E Van Buren **479/253-9335, 877/253-9335**

Magnetic Valley Resort [M,SW,WI,GO] 597 Magnetic Rd (at Passion Play Rd) **479/244-6821, 888/210-8401**

Out on Main [GS,NS,WI,GO] 269 N Main St (at Magnetic Rd) **479/253-8449** *3-room cottage, full kitchen*

Palace Hotel & Bath House [GF,NS,WI] 135 Spring St **479/253-7474, 866/946-0572** *historic bathhouse open to all*

Pond Mountain Lodge & Resort [GS,SW,NS,WC,GO] **479/253-5877, 800/583-8043** *mtntop inn on 150 acres*

Red Bud Manor Inn [GF,WI,WO] 7 Kingshighway **479/253-9649, 866/253-9649**

Roadrunner Inn [GF,R,NS,WI] 3034 Mundell Rd **479/253-8166, 888/253-8166** *guestrooms & log cabins, lake views*

Texaco Bungalow [GS,GO] 77 Mountain St **888/253-8093**

Tradewinds [GS,SW,WI,GO] 141 W Van Buren (at 23 N) **479/363-6189** *motel reminiscent of the motor inns of the '40s & '50s*

The Woods Cabins [MW,NS,GO] 50 Wall St (off Hwy 62) **479/253-8281** *cottages, kitchens, treehouse*

Bars

Chelsea's Corner Cafe [GF,E,D,WI] 10 Mountain St (at Center St) **479/253-6723** *11am-2am, till 10pm Sun, patio*

Eureka Live [GS,D,F,K] 35 N Main **479/253-7020** *11am-1:30am, clsd Mon-Tue*

Henri's Just One More [GS,NH,F,E,WI] 19 1/2 Spring St **479/253-5795** *noon-2am, clsd Tue, gay night Wed from 5pm*

Cafes

Mud Street Cafe 22G S Main St **479/253-6732** *8am-3pm, clsd Tue-Wed*

Restaurants

Ermilio's 26 White St **479/253-8806** *5pm-9pm, Italian, full bar*

Gaskins Cabin Steak House [GS,BW,R] 2883 Hwy 23 N (Hwy 187) **479/253-5466** *5pm-9pm, till 8pm Sun, clsd Mon-Tue*

Fayetteville

Info Lines & Services

AA Gay/ Lesbian 568 W Sycamore **479/443-6366 (AA#)**

Accommodations

Hilton Garden Inn Bentonville [GF,SW,WI,WC] 2204 SE Walton Blvd (Exit 85, off I-540), Bentonville **479/464-7300, 877/782-9444**

Restaurants

Bordinos 310 W Dickson St **479/527-6795** *dinner nightly, lunch Tue-Fri, clsd Sun, full bar*

Hugo's 25 1/2 N Block Ave **479/521-7585** *11am-10pm, clsd Sun*

Cruisy Areas

Flat Rock Beach [AYOR] 10 miles W of town *nude beach*

Helena

Accommodations

The Edwardian Inn [GF,NS,WI] 317 Biscoe **870/338-9155, 800/598-4749** *60 miles from Memphis*

Hot Springs

Accommodations

Park Hotel of Hot Springs [GS,WI] 211 Fountain St (at Central Ave) **501/624-5323, 800/895-7275**

Cruisy Areas

Degray Lake [AYOR] lakeside area *afternoon in the woods*

Rest Area [AYOR] off Hwy 70 (btwn Hot Springs & I-30)

Jonesboro

Cruisy Areas

Craighead Forest Park [AYOR] *seasonal (beware of cops!)*

Little Rock

Bars

Chaps [M,NH,B] 2769 Pike Ave, North Little Rock **501/313-2836** *7pm-2am, from 4pm Sun*

Discovery [GS,D,DS,S,V,PC,WC] 1021 Jessie Rd (btwn Cantrell & Riverfront) **501/664-4784** *9pm-5am Sat only*

Triniti Nightclub [MW,D,DS,S,V,18+,PC,WC] 1021 Jessie Rd (btwn Cantrell & Riverfront) **501/664-2744** *9pm-5am Fri only*

Restaurants

Bossa Nova 2701 Kavanaugh Blvd (at Ash St) **501/614-6682** *lunch & dinner, Sun brunch, clsd Mon, Brazilian, plenty veggie*

La Hacienda 3024 Cantrell Rd **501/661-0600** *lunch & dinner, Mexican*

Vino's Pizza [BW] 923 W 7th St (at Chester) **501/375-8466** *11am-close*

Entertainment & Recreation

The Weekend Theater [GO] 1001 W 7th St (at Chester) **501/374-3761** *plays & musicals on wknds*

Bookstores

Wordsworth Books & Co 5920 R St **501/663-9198** *9am-7pm, till 6pm Fri-Sat, noon-5pm Sun, independent*

Erotica

Adult Video 2923 W 65th St (off I-30 W) **501/562-4282** *24hrs, arcade*

Cupids 3920 W 65th St (off I-30, exit 135) **501/565-2020** *24hrs, arcade*

Cruisy Areas

Reservoir Park [AYOR] Cantrell Rd (2 miles E of I-430, exit 9)

Texarkana

Bars

The Chute [MW,D,K,DS] 714 Laurel St **870/772-6900** *7pm-2am Th-Sat*

CALIFORNIA

Amador City

Accommodations

Imperial Hotel [GF,NS] 14202 Hwy 49 (at Water St) **209/267-9172** *B&B, brick Victorian hotel, full brkfst, restaurant & bar*

Anaheim

see **Orange County**

Angeles Nat'l Forest

Cruisy Areas

Beach in the Upper Big Tujunga Canyon (UBTC) [AYOR] Hwy 2, exit Angeles Crest Hwy, head N, turn left to UBTC Rd, turn right (btwn marker 4.5 & 4.8) *little nude beach along creek*

Arcata

Info Lines & Services

Queer Humboldt PO Box 45 95518-0045 **707/502-2890** *"Humboldt County's online resource for the LGBT community," includes links & events calendar, check out www.queerhumboldt.org*

Bars

The Alibi [MW,NH,F,E,YC] 744 9th St **707/822-3731** *8am-2am, cocktail lounge w/ live music, also restaurant (8am-midnight)*

Cafes

Cafe Mokka [E] 495 J St (at 5th) **707/822-2228** *from noon, coffee & soups (bread bowls), live music, also Finnish sauna & hot tubs*

North Coast Co-op [WI] 811 I St **707/822-5947** *6am-9pm*

Restaurants

Wildflower Bakery & Cafe [★BW] 1604 G St **707/822-0360** *9am-3pm & 5:30pm-9:30pm, vegetarian*

Bookstores

Northtown Books 957 H St **707/822-2834** *10am-7pm, till 9pm Fri-Sat, noon-5pm Sun, LGBT section/ gay magazines*

Erotica

Pleasure Center 1731 G St #D **707/826-1708** *10am-midnight, till 2am Fri-Sat, till 10pm Sun*

Cruisy Areas

Aldergrove Marsh [AYOR] Alder Grove Rd (off West End Rd) *parking lot on left after Ericson Way*

Azalea State Reserve [AYOR] along Mad River (on N Bank Rd) *6 miles N of Arcata*

Bakersfield

Accommodations

The Padre Hotel [GS,F] 702 18th St **661/427-4900** *sleek hotel with nightclubs, bar, cafe, and fine dining room*

Bars

The Mint [GS,E] 1207 19th St (at M) **661/325-4048** *6am-2am, live music*

Nightclubs

The Casablanca Club [GS,NH,D,E,C,DS,V,WC] 1825 N St (at 19th St) **661/324-0661** *9pm-2am, clsd Mon-Wed*

Erotica

Cinema 19 [★] 1224 19th St (btwn L & M Sts, across from The Mint) **661/323-7711** *cruisy, arcade & theater*

Deja Vu 1524 Golden State Ave (at Chester Ave) **661/322-7300** *noon-2am, arcade*

Cruisy Areas

Gordon's Ferry [AYOR] Round Mountain Rd (at China Grade Loop), Oildale

Yokuts Park [AYOR] W of Hwy 99 (at Beach Park) *take W Truxtun Ave to Empire Dr entrance*

Benicia

Bookstores

Bookshop Benicia [WC] 636 First St **707/747-5155** *10am-7pm, 11am-5pm Sun*

Berkeley

see East Bay

Big Bear Lake

Accommodations

Grey Squirrel Resort [GS,SW,WI,GO] 39372 Big Bear Blvd **909/866-4335, 800/381-5569**

Big Sur

Accommodations

Lucia Lodge [GF,NS,WI] 62400 Hwy 1 **831/667-2708, 866/424-4787** *oceanview cabins, also restaurant & lounge*

Cambria

Accommodations

El Colobri [GF,WI] 5620 Moonstone Beach Dr **805/924-3003**

FogCatcher Inn [GF,SW,WI,WC] 6400 Moonstone Beach Dr **805/927-1400, 800/425-4121**

Cambria Pines [GF,SW,NS,WI,WC] 905 Burton Dr **805/927-4200** *resort on 25 acres above Cambria's East Village & lounge*

Bars

Mozzi's Saloon [GF,E] 2262 Main St **805/927-4767** *1pm-11pm, Fri-Sat till 2am, cowboy bar*

Restaurants

Robin's 4095 Burton Dr **805/927-5007** *great food, nice rooftop patio, pet friendly*

Sea Chest 6216 Moonstone Beach Dr **805/927-4514** *dinner only clsd Tue, local favorite, cash only*

Wild Ginger 2380 Main St **805/927-1001** *lunch & dinner, clsd Th, Pacific Rim & global menu*

Cruisy Areas

Fiscalini Ranch Preserve

Moonstone Beach Boardwalk

Carmel

see also Monterey

Accommodations

Carmel Mission Inn [GF,SW,NS] 3665 Rio Rd **831/624-1841, 800/348-9090** *pets ok, also restaurant & lounge*

Cypress Inn [GF,WI] Lincoln & 7th **831/624-3871, 800/443-7443** *pets very welcome, owned by Doris Day. also restaurant & lounge*

Restaurants

Flaherty's Seafood Grill & Oyster Bar [WC] 6th Ave (btwn Dolores and San Carlos) **831/625-1500** *open daily 11am*

Rio Grill 101 Crossroads Blvd **831/625-5436** *lunch and dinner daily, wknd brunch, full bar*

Cruisy Areas

Garland Ranch Regional Park [AYOR] Rte G16 (9 miles E of Carmel), Carmel Valley

Garrapata State Beach [AYOR] 10 miles S of crossroads (on right side of Hwy 1) *nude sunbathing*

Cayucos

Accommodations

Seaside Motel [GF,WI] 42 S Ocean Ave **805/995-3809**
, **800/549-0900** *conventional-looking '50s-style motel with immaculate rooms*

Bars

Old Cayucos Tavern and Cardroom [GF,E] 130 N Ocean Ave **805/995-3209** *10am-2am, liquor in the front, poker in the back*

Restaurants

Schooners Wharf 171 N Ocean Ave **805/995-3883** *lunch & dinner*

Chico

Info Lines & Services

Stonewall Alliance Center 358 E 6th St (at Flume) **530/893-3336** *HIV testing & counseling, recorded info, meetings*

Cruisy Areas

Deer Pens [AYOR] 8th & Forest Sts

Chino

Restaurants

Riverside Grill 5258 Riverside Dr (at Central) **909/627-4144** *8am-9pm*

Chula Vista

see also San Diego

Clearlake

includes major towns of Lake County

Accommodations

Blue Fish Cove Resort [GF,SW] 10573 E Hwy 20, Clearlake Oaks **707/998-1769** *lakeside resort cottages, boat facilities & rentals*

Edgewater Resort [GS,SW,NS,WI,GO] 6420 Soda Bay Rd (at Hohape Rd), Kelseyville **707/279-0208, 800/396-6224**

Featherbed Railroad B& B [GF,SW,WI] 2870 Lakeshore Blvd, Nice **707/274-8378**

Sea Breeze Resort [GS,SW,NS,WI,WC,GO] 9595 Harbor Dr, Glenhaven **707/998-3327** *lakefront cottages*

Cloverdale

see also Healdsburg

Accommodations

Kelley & Young Wine Garden Inn [GF,NS,WI] 302 N Main St (at 3rd) **707/894-4535** *Queen Anne mansion, full brkfst*

Restaurants

Hamburger Ranch & Bar-B-Que [BW] 31195 N Redwood Hwy **707/894-5616** *7am-9pm, patio*

Concord

see East Bay

Cupertino

Cruisy Areas

Stevens Creek Canyon Park [AYOR] Foothill Blvd *at first road, turn left below the dam, go down, then go up to the top parking area on the right*

Davis

see also Sacramento

Info Lines & Services

LGBTQIA Resource Center [WI,WC] Student Community Center, Ste 1400 **530/752-2452** *10am-6pm, till 5pm Fri, clsd wknds, info, referrals, meetings, library*

Cafes

Mishka's Cafe [★] 610 2nd St **530/759-0811** *7am-10pm*

Bookstores

The Avid Reader 617 2nd St **530/758-4040** *10am-10pm*

East Bay

includes major cities of Alameda and Contra Costa Counties: Alameda, Antioch, Berkeley, Concord, Danville, Fremont, Hayward, Lafayette, Newark, Oakland, Pleasant Hill, Richmond, San Leandro, Walnut Creek

Info Lines & Services

East Bay AA 510/839-8900 *variety of LGBT-friendly mtgs*

Oakland LBGTQ Community Center [WC] 3207 Lakeshore Ave (entrance on Rand Ave), Oakland **510/882-2286** *noon-5pm, clsd wknds*

Pacific Center for Human Growth [WC] 2712 Telegraph Ave (at Derby), Berkeley **510/548-8283** *10am to 8pm, till 2pm Sat, clsd Sun*

Rainbow Community Center of Contra Costa County 2118 Willow Pass Rd #500, Concord **925/692-0090** *10am-5pm Mon-Fri*

Accommodations

Graduate Berkeley [GS,F,NS,WI] 2600 Durant Ave, Berkeley **510/845-8981**

Washington Inn [GF,NS,WC] 495 10th St (at Broadway), Oakland **510/452-1776** *historic boutique hotel, also restaurant*

Waterfront Hotel [GF,SW,NS,WI,WC] 10 Washington St, Oakland **510/836-3800, 888/842-5333** *in Jack London Square*

Bars

The Alley [GS,K] 3325 Grand Ave (btwn Lake Park & Elwood Aves), Oakland **510/444-8505** *5pm-2am, dive bar, trivia nights & restaurant*

Cafe Van Kleef [GF,E,$] 1621 Telegraph Ave (at Broadway), Oakland **510/763-7711** *noon-2am, from 4pm Mon, from 7pm wknds, eclectic crowd & live-music scene—from cabaret to blue grass to jazz*

Club 21 [M,D,MR-L] 2111 Franklin St (at 21st St), Oakland **510/268-9425** *9pm-4am Fri-Sat*

Club BNB [★M,D,K,DS,P,S,YC,WC] 2120 Broadway, Oakland **510/444-2266** *4pm-2am*

The Port [MW] 2021 Broadway (next to the Paramount Theater), Oakland **510/823-2099** *5pm-midnight, till 2am Fri-Sat, from 3pm wknds*

White Horse [MW,D,K,WC] 6551 Telegraph Ave (at 66th), Oakland **510/652-3820** *3pm-2am, from 1pm wknds*

World Famous Turf Club [MW,D,K,DS,WI,WC] 22519 Main St (at A St), Hayward **510/881-9877** *4pm-2am, from noon Sat-Sun, sports bar, huge patio, BBQs, live music, 2 blks from BART*

Nightclubs

Club 1220 [MW,D,CW,K,WI,WC] 1220 Pine St (at Civic Dr), Walnut Creek **925/938-4550** *4pm-2am, theme nights*

Cafes

Caffe Strada [★WC] 2300 College Ave (btwn Way & Durant), Berkeley **510/843-5282** *6am-midnight, students, great patio*

The Chocolate Dragon bittersweet cafe & bakery 5427 College Ave (in Rockridge District), Oakland **510/654-7159** *9am-7pm, till 9pm Fri-Sat*

Cole Coffee 6255 College Ave (btwn 62nd & 63rd Sts), Oakland **510/985-1958** *7am-7pm, hip hide-away in lovely Rockridge*

Raw Energy [GO] 2050 Addison St (btwn Shattuck & Milvia), Berkeley **510/665-9464** *7:30am-7pm, 11am-4pm Sat, clsd Sun, organic juice cafe*

Restaurants

Arizmendi Bakery & Pizzeria 4301 San Pablo Ave (at 43rd St), Emeryville **510/547-0550** *7am-7pm, 8am-6pm Sun, clsd Mon, excellent pastries, breads & pizzas*

Au Coquelet Cafe [BW,WI] 2000 University Ave, Berkeley **510/845-0433** *7am-1:30am*

Banh Cuon Tay Ho [BW] 344-B 12th St (at Webster), Oakland **510/836-6388** *11am-9pm, clsd Mon, Vietnamese*

Cactus Taqueria 5642 College Ave (at Shafter, in Rockridge), Oakland **510/658-6180** *11am-10pm, till 9pm Sun*

César [★] 4039 Piedmont, Oakland **510/883-0222** *noon-10pm, Spanish tapas, full bar*

Connie's Cantina 3340 Grand Ave (btwn Lake Park Ave & Mandana Blvd), Oakland **510/839-4986** *10:30am-9pm, closed Sun, Mexican, plenty veggie, margaritas and sangria, patio*

Dopo [★] 4293 Piedmont Ave (btwn Glenwood & Echo), Oakland **510/652-3676** *lunch & dinner, clsd Sun-Mon, Italian, worth the wait*

Le Cheval [★BW,WC] 1007 Clay St, Oakland **510/763-8495** *11am-9pm, from 4pm Sun, Vietnamese,*

Lois the Pie Queen [★WC] 851 60th St (off Martin Luther King Jr Hwy), Oakland **510/658-5616** *8am-2pm, 7am-3pm wknds, Southern homecooking & killer desserts*

Mama's Royal Cafe [★BW,WC] 4012 Broadway (at 40th), Oakland **510/547-7600** *7am-2:30pm, from 8am wknds, come early for excellent wknd brunch*

Rockridge Cafe [★] 5492 College Ave (at Forest), Oakland **510/653-1567** *7:30am-3pm, great brkfsts, plenty veggie*

Zachary's Chicago Pizza [★BW] 5801 College Ave, Oakland **510/655-6385** *11am-10pm, pizza that is worth the crowds & the long wait!*

Bookstores

East Bay Booksellers 5433 College Avenue, Oakland **510/653-9965** *10am-9pm, till 10pm Fri-Sat, till 6pm Sun, independent*

Pegasus Books 5560 College Ave (at Oceanview), Oakland **510/652-6259** *9am-10pm, from 10am Sun, used books, great to browse while waiting for a table in Rockridge*

Men's Clubs

Steamworks [★WI,PC] 2107 4th St (at Addison), Berkeley **510/845-8992** *24hrs, call for recorded info*

Erotica

Good Vibrations [★WC] 2504 San Pablo Ave (at Dwight Wy), Berkeley **510/841-8987** *10am-9pm, till 10pm Fri-Sat*

Good Vibrations [★] 3219 Lakeshore Ave, Oakland **510/788-2389** *10am-9pm, till10pm Fri-Sat*

Not Too Naughty 15670 E 14th St, San Leandro **510/278-4944** *10am-10pm, till midnight Fri-Sat, noon-8am Sun, arcade*

Secrets 10601 San Pablo Ave (at Moeser Ln), El Cerrito **510/528-1569** *8am-1am, arcade*

Cruisy Areas

Aquatic Park [AYOR] Bolivar Dr (off I-80, at Ashby Ave exit), Berkeley

Bushrod Park [AYOR] Shattuck Ave (btwn 59th & 60th Sts), Oakland *near tennis courts*

Central Park (aka Lake Elizabeth) [AYOR] Paseo Padre Ave & Stevenson Blvd, Fremont *trails right of lake & parking lot*

Heather Farm Park [AYOR] Ygnacio Valley Rd, Walnut Creek *take Ygnacio Valley Rd for 2 miles E of Hwy 680, turn right into park on San Carlos Rd*

Hillcrest Park [AYOR] off Larkspur Dr, Antioch *take Hillcrest exit off Hwy 4, take left off Hillcrest Rd onto Larkspur Rd, park is on right after 6 blocks*

Keller Beach [AYOR] Miller-Knox Regional Park, Richmond *take Garrard Blvd exit of Hwy 580 after tunnel on Dornan Dr*

Lake Temescal Park [AYOR] Broadway Ave (at State Hwy 13), Oakland *afternoons*

Oyster Bay Park [AYOR] btwn San Leandro Marina & Oakland Airport (along the bay), San Leandro *take Doolittle to Williams, go W toward bay & make right when Williams ends*

Elk

Restaurants

Queenie's Roadhouse Cafe [GO] 6061 S Hwy 1 **707/877-3285** *8am-3pm, clsd Tue-Wed, fabulous all-day brkfsts*

Eureka

Accommodations

Carter House Inns [GF,NS,WC] 301 L St **707/444-8062, 800/404-1390** *enclave of 4 unique inns, full brkfst, restaurant, wine shop*

Trinidad Bay B&B [GF,NS,WI,GO] 560 Edwards St (at Trinity), Trinidad **707/677-0840** *full brkfst*

Bars

Lost Coast Brewery [GF,F,BW,WI,WC] 617 4th St (btwn G & H Sts) **707/445-4480** *11am-1am, kitchen open till midnight*

The Shanty [GS,NH,GO] 213 3rd St (at C St) **707/444-2053** *noon-2am*

Cafes

North Coast Co-op 25 4th St (at B St) **707/443-6027** *6am-9pm, co-op store w/ bakery, deli & espresso cafe*

Ramone's Cafe & Bakery 209 E St (Old Town) **707/445-2923** *7am-6pm*

Restaurants

Chalet House of Omelettes [WC] 1935 5th St (at U St) **707/442-0333** *6am-3pm*

Folie Douce [BW,R,WC] 1551 G St, Arcata **707/822-1042** *dinner only, clsd Mon, bistro*

Bookstores

Booklegger [WC] 402 2nd St (at E St) **707/445-1344** *10am-5:30pm, 11am-4pm Sun*

Erotica

Good Relations [WC] 223 2nd St **707/441-9570, 888/485-5063** *queer-owned/ run*

Cruisy Areas

Hilfiker Reserve [AYOR] off Hilfiker Ln *last parking lot & wood trails*

Fort Bragg

Accommodations

The Cleone Gardens Inn [GF,NS,WI,WC] 24600 N Hwy 1 (at Nameless Ln) **707/964-2788, 800/400-2189** *country garden retreat on 2.5 acres, cottages, hot tub*

The Weller House Inn [GF,NS,WI] 524 Stewart St (at Pine) **707/964-4415** *1886 Victorian, full brkfst*

Restaurants

Cowlick's 250B N Main St **707/962-9271** *delicious homemade ice cream, including mushroom ice cream (in-season)—it's actually quite good!*

Purple Rose [WC] 24300 N Hwy 1 **707/964-6507** *5pm-9pm, clsd Sun-Mon, Mexican*

Entertainment & Recreation

Skunk Train California Western foot of Laurel St **707/964-6371**

Fremont

see East Bay

Fresno

Info Lines & Services

Community Link 559/266-5465 *LGBT support, also publishes Newslink*

Fresno AA 559/221-6907

Accommodations

The San Joaquin Hotel [GF,SW,WI,WC] 1309 W Shaw Ave (at Fruit) **559/225-1309**

BARS

FAB Fresno [MW,D] 716 E Olive Ave **559/492-3911** *6pm-2am, from 4pm Fri, from noon wknds, clsd Mon*

Red Lantern [M,NH,CW,MR-L,WI,WC] 4618 E Belmont Ave (at Maple) **559/251-5898** *2pm-2am, Latin night Sat very popular, patio*

NIGHTCLUBS

Club Legends [GS,D,DS,SW] 3075 N Maroa Ave **559/222-2271** *4pm-2am*

RESTAURANTS

Don Pepe's 4582 N Blackstone Ave (at Gettysburg) **559/224-1431** *9am-9pm, Mexican*

Irene's Cafe [BW] 747 E Olive Ave (in Tower District) **559/237-9919** *8am-9pm, some veggie, good hamburgers*

Sequoia Brewing Company [E] 777 E Olive Ave (in Tower District) **559/264-5521** *11am-10pm, till midnight Fri-Sat, till 9pm Sun, micro-brewery w/ restaurant, live music*

Veni Vidi Vici [E,R] 1116 N Fulton (S of Olive Ave, in Tower District) **559/266-5510** *California fine dining, nightclub later*

EROTICA

Suzie's Adult Superstores 1267 N Blackstone Ave **559/497-9613** *10am-10pm, 11am-7pm Sun*

CRUISY AREAS

LA-SF Time Out [AYOR] US 99 (at Kingsburg, S of Fresno) *go to cheap motel next to rest area; rest stop activity discouraged*

Gaviota

CRUISY AREAS

Vista Point [AYOR] Hwy 101 S (1/2 S of Gaviota Beach) *parking lot & nearby woods*

Grass Valley

see also Nevada City

Gualala

ACCOMMODATIONS

Breakers Inn [GS] 39300 S Hwy 1 **707/884-3200**

North Coast Country Inn [GF,NS] 34591 S Hwy 1 **707/884-4537**

BOOKSTORES

The Four-Eyed Frog 39138 Ocean Dr (in Cypress Village) **707/884-1333**

Half Moon Bay

ACCOMMODATIONS

Mill Rose Inn [GF,NS,WI] 615 Mill St **650/726-8750, 800/900-7673** *classic European elegance by the sea, full brkfst, hot tub*

RESTAURANTS

Moss Beach Distillery [★WC] 140 Beach Wy (at Ocean) **650/728-5595** *lunch & dinner, Sun brunch, steak & seafood, patio, even own ghost*

Pasta Moon [E,WC] 315 Main St (at Mill) **650/726-5125** *lunch & dinner, Italian, full bar*

Sam's Chowder House 4210 N Cabrillo Hwy (S of Pillar Point Harbor) **650/712-0245** *lunch & dinner, great loster rolls and views*

Hayward

see East Bay

Healdsburg

see also Russian River & Sonoma County

Hemet

CRUISY AREAS

Gibbel Park [AYOR] 2500 W Florida Ave (at Kirby, enter here) *very discreet*

Idyllwild

ACCOMMODATIONS

The Rainbow Inn [GS,NS,WI,GO] 54420 S Circle Dr **951/659-0111** *full brkfst, patio, also conference center*

Strawberry Creek Inn B&B [GF,NS,WC,GO] 26370 Hwy 243 (at S Cir Dr) **951/659-3202** *relaxing getaway w/ sundeck, garden & hammocks*

RESTAURANTS

Cafe Aroma [E] 54750 North Circle **951/659-5212** *11am-9pm, from 7am wknds, great ambience & food*

Irvine

see Orange County

Joshua Tree

ACCOMMODATIONS

Kate's Lazy Desert [GF,NS,WI] 58380 Botkin Rd, Landers **845/688-7200** *love shack owned by Kate Pierson of the B-52s*

Joshua Tree Nat'l Park

ACCOMMODATIONS

The Desert Lily [GF,WI] PO Box 139, 92252-0800 **310/839-7290** *artist-owned adobe-style B&B on 5 acres; closed July-Aug*

Joshua Tree Highlands Houses [GS,NS,WI,WC,GO] **760/366-3636** *private, fully equipped rentals*

Sacred Sands [GS,NS,WI,GO] HC1 Box 1071 A, 63155 Quail Springs Rd (at Desert Shadows), Joshua Tree **760/424-6407**

Spin & Margie's Desert Hideaway [GF] 64491 29 Palms Hwy **760/366-9124** *hacienda-style B&B, suites w/ private patios*

Starland Retreat [M,N,18+] Yucca Valley **760/364-2069**

RESTAURANTS

The Crossroads Cafe & Tavern 61715 29 Palms Hwy **760/366-5414** *7am-8pm, till 9pm Fri-Sat,*

Kernville

ACCOMMODATIONS

Riverview Lodge [GS,NS,GO] 2 Sirretta St **760/376-6019** *resort on Kern River*

La Mirada

RESTAURANTS

Mexico 1900 11531 La Mirada blvd **562/941-2016** *lunch & dinner*

Laguna Beach

see Orange County

Lake Tahoe

see also Lake Tahoe, Nevada

ACCOMMODATIONS

Alpine Inn & Spa [GS,SW] 920 Stateline Ave (Lake Ave/ Hwy 50), South Lake Tahoe **530/544-3340, 800/826-8885**

Black Bear Inn [GS,NS,WI] **530/544-4451** *full brkfst, hot tub, fire-places*

The Cedar House Sport Hotel [GF,WI] 10918 Brockway Rd, Truckee **530/582-5655, 866/582-5655**

Spruce Grove Cabins [GF,NS] 3599-3605 Spruce Ave, South Lake Tahoe **530/544-0549**

Tahoe Valley Lodge [GF,SW,NS,WI] 2241 Lake Tahoe Blvd (at Tahoe Keys Blvd), South Lake Tahoe **530/541-0353, 800/669-7544** *motel*

RESTAURANTS

Driftwood Cafe [WC] 1001 Heavenly Vlg Way #1A **530/544-6545** *7am-3pm, homecooking*

CRUISY AREAS

El Dorado Beach [AYOR] btwn Rufus Allen Blvd & Lakeview, South Lake Tahoe

Private Beach [AYOR] off Pine St (near Park), South Lake Tahoe *private beach behind resorts*

Livermore

see East Bay

Lodi

EROTICA

Intimates & Adult Superstore [AYOR] 203 N Houston Ln **209/369-6191** *9am-10pm, also arcade*

Long Beach

Info Lines & Services

AA Gay/ Lesbian 2017 E 4th St (at Cherry, at Gay & Lesbian Center) **562/434-4455** *7pm Mon [MW] & 7pm Fri [M]*

The Gay & Lesbian Center of Greater Long Beach 2017 E 4th St (at Cherry) **562/434-4455** *10am-9pm, till 4pm Sat, clsd Sun, activities & support groups, HIV testing*

Accommodations

Beachrunners' Inn [GS,WI] 231 Kennebec Ave (at Junipero & Broadway) **562/856-0202, 866/221-0001** *B&B, near beach*

Hotel Current [GS,SW,WI,WC] 5325 E Pacific Coast Hwy **562/597-1341, 800/990-9991**

Hotel Maya [GS] 700 Queensway Dr **562/435-7676**

The Varden Hotel [GS,WI,NS,WC] 335 Pacific Ave (at 3rd St) **562/432-8950**

Bars

The Brit [M,NH,WC] 1744 E Broadway (at Cherry) **562/432-9742** *10am-2am, patio*

The Broadway [MW,NH,K,WC] 1100 E Broadway (at Cerritos) **562/432-3646** *10am-2am, [K] Fri-Sat*

The Crest [M] 5935 Cherry Ave (at South) **562/423-6650** *2pm-2am, from noon wknds*

Eagle 562 [M,D,B,L] 2020 E Artesia (at Cherry) **562/269-0313** *6pm-2am, from 2pm wknds, patio*

The Falcon [M,NH,WC] 1435 E Broadway (at Falcon) **562/432-4146** *8am-2am, from 7am wknds*

Flux [MW,NH,WI] 17817 Lakewood Blvd (at Artesia), Bellflower **562/633-6394** *noon-2am, patio, theme nights*

Mineshaft [★M,B] 1720 E Broadway (btwn Gaviota & Hermosa) **562/436-2433** *11am-2am*

Que Será [GS,D,A,E] 1923 E 7th St (at Cherry) **562/599-6170** *9pm-2am*

Silver Fox [M,K,V,WC] 411 Redondo (at 4th) **562/439-6343** *4pm-2am, from noon wknds, popular happy hour*

Sweetwater Saloon [M,NH,WC] 1201 E Broadway (at Orange) **562/432-7044** *10am-2am, popular days, cruisy*

Tidal Bay Beach Bar [GS,NH,F,E,K,GO] 3522 E Anaheim St **562/494-7564** *2pm-2am*

Nightclubs

Club Ripples [★M,D,MR,F,E,K,DS,S,V,YC] 5101 E Ocean (at Granada) **562/433-0357** *noon-2am, patio, theme nights, T-dance Sun, Bear Bar every 2nd Sat*

The Suite [★MW,D,E,WC] 3428 E Pacific Coast Hwy (at Redondo) **562/597-3884** *5pm-2am, 2pm-11pm Sun*

Cafes

Birdcage Coffee House [WC,GO] 224 W 4th Street **562/628-9835** *7am-6pm*

Hot Java [WI] 2101 E Broadway Ave **562/433-0688** *6am-11pm, also soups, sandwiches, salads*

The Library [WI] 3418 E Broadway **562/433-2393** *6am-midnight, till 1am Fri-Sat, from 7am wknds*

Restaurants

Cafe Sevilla 140 Pine St **562/495-1111** *dinner only, wknd brunch, Spanish, also music & dancing*

Egg Heaven 4358 E 4th St **562/433-9277** *7am-2pm, till 3pm wknds*

Hamburger Mary's [WI] 330 Pine Ave **562/436-7900** *11am-2am, full bar w/ theme nights*

Open Sesame 5215 E 2nd St **562/621-1698** *lunch & dinner, Lebanese*

Original Park Pantry [WC] 2104 E Broadway (at Junipero) **562/434-0451** *6am-10pm, till 11pm Fri-Sat, int'l*

Utopia 445 E 1st St **562/432-6888** *lunch Mon-Fri, dinner nightly, clsd Sun, seafood, California cuisine, plenty veggie*

Retail Shops

Hot Stuff [GO] 2121 E Broadway (at Junipero) **562/433-0692** *noon-8pm, 10am-6pm Sat-Sun, cards, gifts, and adult novelties, serving community since 1980*

Men's Clubs

1350 Club [18+] 510 W Anaheim St (at Neptune), Wilmington **310/830-4784** *24hrs*

Erotica

Love Stuff 5114 E 2nd St **562/439-9600** *10am-10pm, till midnight Fri-Sat*

The RubberTree 5018 E 2nd St (at Granada) **562/434-0027** *gifts for lovers, women-owned*

Cruisy Areas

Please Note: All cruisy areas for Long Beach have been removed by request of various LGBT community organizations.

Los Angeles

Los Angeles is divided into 8 geographical areas

LA—Overview
LA—West Hollywood
LA—Hollywood
LA—West LA & Santa Monica
LA—Silverlake
LA—Midtown
LA—Valley
LA—East LA & South Central

LA—Overview

Info Lines & Services

Alcoholics Anonymous 323/936-4343, 800/923-8722 *call or check web (www.lacoaa.org) for meetings*

LA Gay & Lesbian Center 1625 N Schrader Blvd (McDonald/Wright Building) **323/993-7400** *9am-9pm, till 1pm Sat, clsd Sun, wide variety of services*

LA Gay & Lesbian Center's Village at Ed Gould Plaza 1125 N McCadden Pl (at Santa Monica) **323/860-7302** *6am-10, 9am-5pm Sat, clsd Sun*

Restaurants

Hinterhof German Kitchen and Beer Garden [GO] 4939 York Blvd *all vegan menu*

Entertainment & Recreation

Bikes and Hikes LA 8743 Santa Monica Blvd **323/796-8555, 888/836-3710** *bike/hike tour company*

The Celebration Theatre 7051 Santa Monica Blvd (at La Brea) **323/957-1884** *LGBT theater, call for more info*

The Getty Center 1200 Getty Center Dr, Brentwood **310/440-7300** *10am-6pm, till 9pm Fri-Sat, clsd Mon, LA's shining city on a hill & world-class museum; of course, it's still in LA so you'll need to make reservations for parking (!)*

Griffith Observatory enter on N Vermont St (in Griffith Park) **213/473-0800** *noon-10pm, from 10am wknds, clsd Mon*

Highways 1651 18th St (at the 18th Street Arts Center), Santa Monica **310/315-1459** *"full-service performance center"*

Publications

Adelante Magazine 323/256-6639 *bilingual LGBT magazine*

Cruisy Areas

Beach in the Upper Big Tujunga Canyon (UBTC) [AYOR] Hwy 2, exit Angeles Crest Hwy, head N, turn left to UBTC Rd, turn right (btwn marker 4.5 & 4.8), Angeles Nat'l Forest *little nude beach along creek*

The Usual Suspects: Griffith Park, Elysian Park, Echo Park, Santa Fe Dam Regional Park, Whitsett Park [AYOR] *don't bother: LAPD & the rangers are waiting for you*

LA—West Hollywood

Accommodations

Andaz West Hollywood [GS,SW,NS,WI,WC] 8401 Sunset Blvd (at Kings Rd) **323/656-1234** *on the Sunset Strip, rooftop pool*

Chamberlain [GS,SW,WI,WC] 1000 Westmount Dr (near Holloway) **310/657-7400, 800/201-9652** *boutique hotel, rooftop pool, restaurant & lounge*

The Elan Hotel Los Angeles [GS,NS,WI,WC,GO] 8435 Beverly Blvd (at Croft) **323/658-6663, 866/203-2212** *hip & trendy, fitness room*

The Grafton on Sunset [GS,SW,WC] 8462 W Sunset Blvd (at La Cienega) **323/654-4600, 800/821-3660** *sundeck, panoramic views, located in heart of Sunset Strip*

Holloway Motel [GS,NS,WI] 8465 Santa Monica Blvd (at La Cienega) **323/654-2454, 888/654-6400** *centrally located*

Hotel Le Petit [GF,SW,WC] 8822 Cynthia St (at Larrabee) **310/854-1114** *all-suite hotel*

The Jeremy West Hollywood [GS,F,SW] 8490 W Sunset Blvd **310/424-1600, 800/301-0171** *newest kid on Sunset Strip, stunning panoramic views meet an LA chic aesthetic*

Le Parc Suite Hotel [GF,F,SW,WC] 733 N West Knoll Dr (at Melrose) **310/855-8888, 800/578-4837**

The London West Hollywood [GF,SW,WI] 1020 N San Vicente Blvd **866/282-4560** *luxury hotel*

Mondrian [GF] 8440 Sunset Blvd **323/650-8999** *home of trendy Skybar & Asia de Cuba restaurant*

Ramada Plaza Hotel—West Hollywood [GF,F,SW,WC] 8585 Santa Monica Blvd (at La Cienega) **310/652-6400**

SLS Hotel [GF,SW] 465 S La Cienega Blvd (at San Vicente) **310/247-0400** *luxury hotel, gym & spa*

Sunset Marquis Hotel & Villas [GS,SW,WI,WC] 1200 Alta Loma Rd (1/2 block S of Sunset Blvd) **310/657-1333** *full brkfst, sauna, hot tub*

Bars

The Abbey [★MW,F,WC] 692 N Robertson Blvd (at Santa Monica) **310/289-8410** *11am-2am, from 9am wknds, also restaurant, patio*

The Chapel [MW,WC] 696 N Robertson Blvd (at Santa Monica) **310/289-8410**

Fiesta Cantina [MW,F] 8865 Santa Monica Blvd (at San Vicente) **310/652-8865** *noon-2am, raucous Mexican restaurant & bar*

Flaming Saddles [M,CW,F,K] 8811 Santa Monica Blvd (at Larrabee St) **310/855-7501** *3pm-2am, from noon wknds*

Fubar [★M,D,K,S] 7994 Santa Monica Blvd (at Crescent Hts) **323/654-0396** *4pm-2am, theme nights*

Gold Coast [★M,NH,WC] 8228 Santa Monica Blvd (at La Jolla) **323/656-4879** *11am-2am, from 10am wknds*

Gym Sports Bar [GS,NH,WC] 8737 Santa Monica Blvd (at Hancock) **310/659-2004** *4pm-2am, from noon wknds*

Micky's [★M,D,F,V,YC,GO] 8857 Santa Monica Blvd (at San Vicente) **310/657-1176** *noon-2am, after-hours wknds, patio*

Mother Lode [★M,NH,K,WC] 8944 Santa Monica Blvd (at Robertson) **310/659-9700** *3pm-2am, beer bust Sun*

Revolver Video Bar [★M] 8851 Santa Monica Blvd (at Larrabee St) **310/694-0430** *4pm-2am, from noon wknds, a WeHo institution*

Trunks [M,NH,V,YC] 8809 Santa Monica Blvd (at Larrabee) **310/652-1015** *1pm-2am, from noon Sun*

Nightclubs

Plaza [M,D,MR-L,DS,$] 739 N La Brea Ave (at Melrose) **323/939-0703** *9pm-2am, from 8pm Fri-Sat, clsd Tue-Wed, shows nightly at 10:15pm & midnight*

Rage [★M,D,F,DS,V,18+,YC,WC] 8911 Santa Monica Blvd (at San Vicente) **310/652-7055** *noon-2am*

Cafes

Urth Caffe [F] 8565 Melrose Ave (btwn Robertson & La Cienega) **310/659-0628** *6:30am-midnight, organic coffees, teas & treats, plenty veggie & vegan, patio*

Restaurants

AOC 8700 W 3rd **323/653-6359** *dinner nightly, wine bar, eclectic, upscale*

Basix Cafe 8333 Santa Monica Blvd (at Flores) **323/848-2460** *7am-11pm, outdoor seating*

The Bayou [GO] 8939 Santa Monica Blvd (at Robertson) **310/273-3303** *4pm-2am, full bar*

Bossa Nova [BW,WC] 685 N Robertson Blvd (at Santa Monica) **310/657-5070** *11am-midnight,till 3am Fri-Sat, Brazilian, patio*

Cafe La Boheme [WC] 8400 Santa Monica Blvd (btwn Benecia Ave & Fox Hills Dr) **323/848-2360** *5pm-9:30pm, till 10:30 Fri-Sat, interior decor worthy of the opera, full bar, patio*

Canter's Deli [WC] 419 N Fairfax (btwn Melrose & Beverly) **323/651-2030** *24hrs, hip after-hours, full bar*

Cecconi's 8764 Melrose Ave **310/432-2000** *8am-midnight, classic Italian*

Hamburger Mary's Bar & Grill [MW,TG,E,K,DS,S,V,GO] 8288 Santa Monica Blvd **323/654-3800** *11am-1am, till 2am Fri-Sat*

Hedley's 640 N Robertson Blvd **310/659-2009** *lunch & dinner, also wknd brunch, clsd Sun night*

The Hudson 1114 N Crescent Heights Blvd **323/654-6686** *4pm-2am, from 10am Sat-Sun*

Il Piccolino Trattoria [WC] 350 N Robertson Blvd (btwn Melrose & Beverly) **310/659-2220** *lunch & dinner, clsd Sun, patio*

Joey's Cafe 8301 Santa Monica Blvd **323/822-0671** *8am-10pm, a little bit coffeehouse, a little bit diner, popular at lunch*

Lucques [WC] 8474 Melrose Ave (at La Cienega) **323/655-6277** *lunch Tue-Sat, dinner nightly, French, full bar, patio*

Marix Tex Mex [WC] 1108 N Flores (btwn La Cienega & Fairfax) **323/656-8800** *11:30am-11pm, from 11am wknds, great margaritas, patio*

Real Food Daily [BW,WC] 414 N La Cienega Blvd **310/389-9910** *11:30am-10pm, organic vegan*

St Felix 8945 Santa Monica Blvd (at Hilldale) **310/275-4428** *4pm-2am, Sun brunch, bar very gay*

Tart 115 S Fairfax Ave (at Farmer's Daughter Hotel) **323/556-2608** *7am-11pm, Southern*

Taste 8454 Melrose Ave (at La Cienega) **323/852-6888** *lunch & dinner, wknd brunch, upscale eclectic, full bar*

Versailles 1415 S La Cienega (at W Pico) **310/289-0392** *lunch & dinner, Cuban*

Wokcano 8000 Sunset Blvd, Santa Monica **323/450-9037** *11am-12:30am, till till 1am Fri-Sat, sushi bar & Chinese cafe*

Entertainment & Recreation

Comedy Store 8433 Sunset Blvd (at La Cienega) **323/650-6268** *8pm-2am, legendary stand-up club*

Bookstores

Book Soup 8818 W Sunset Blvd (at Larrabee) **310/659-3110** *9am-10pm, till 7pm Sun, LGBT section*

Retail Shops

665 Leather 8722 Santa Monica Blvd (at Huntley Dr) **310/854-7276** *11pm-7pm, till 10pm Fri-Sat,, custom leather & neoprene, also accessories & toys*

Marginalized Tattoo [GO] 4228 Melrose Ave (at Vermont) **213/422-4801** *featuring Dave Davenport (aka "Dogspunk"), named best gay tattoo artist*

Gyms & Health Clubs

24 Hour Fitness 8612 Santa Monica Blvd, West Hollywood **310/652-7440** *tres gay*

The Fitness Factory 650 N La Peer Dr (at Santa Monica) **310/358-1838** *6am-9pm, till 8pm Fri, 7am-4pm Sat, 8am-2pm Sun*

Men's Club

Slammer [18+,PC] 3688 Beverly Blvd (2 blocks E of Vermont) **213/388-8040** *8pm-4am, from 2pm wknds*

Erotica

Chi Chi LaRue's 8861 Santa Monica Blvd **323/337-9555** *10am-midnight, till 2am Th-Sun*

Pleasure Chest 7733 Santa Monica Blvd (at Genesee), N Hollywood **323/650-1022** *10am-midnight, till 1am Th-Sat*

Studs Theatre 7734 Santa Monica Blvd (at the Legendary Pussycat Theatre) *9am-3am, till 5am Fri-Sat*

LA—Hollywood

Accommodations

Hollywood Hotel - The Hotel of Hollywood [GF,SW,NS,WI,WC] 1160 N Vermont Ave (at Santa Monica) **323/473-5981**

Bars

Boardner's [GS,D,F,K] 1652 N Cherokee Ave **323/462-9621** *4pm-2am, "a Hollywood legend & best-kept secret since 1942", theme nights*

Faultline [★M,B,L,V,WC] 4216 Melrose Ave (at Vermont) **323/660-0889** *5pm-2am, from 2pm wknds, clsd Mon-Tue, patio*

Nightclubs

Avalon [GS,D,$] 1735 Vine St (at Hollywood Blvd) **323/462-8900** *one of LA's best dance music clubs, call for events*

Tempo [M,D,MR-L,E,S] 5520 Santa Monica Blvd (at Western) **323/466-1094** *9pm-2am, 7pm-3am Th-Sat, from 2pm Sun, live bands Sat, beer bust Sun*

TigerHeat [GS,D,TG,E,DS,V,18+,$] 1735 Vine (at Avalon) **323/467-4571** *9:30pm-3am Th only*

Restaurants

101 Coffee Shop 6145 Franklin Ave **323/467-1175** *7am-3am, diner*

La Poubelle [WC] 5907 Franklin Ave (at Bronson) **323/465-0807** *5pm-2am, from 4pm wknds, French, full bar*

Musso & Frank Grill 6667 Hollywood Blvd (near Las Palmas) **323/467-5123** *11am-11pm, clsd Sun-Mon, the grand-dame diner/ steak house of Hollywood: great pancakes, potpies & martinis!*

Off Vine [BW] 6263 Leland Wy (at Vine) **323/962-1900** *lunch & dinner, wknd brunch*

Prado [WC] 244 N Larchmont Blvd (at Beverly) **323/467-3871** *lunch & dinner, dinner only Sun, Caribbean*

Rockwell Table & Stage 1714 N Vermont Ave (at Prospect, enter in alley) **323/669-1550** *11am-midnight, brunch wknds*

Roscoe's House of Chicken & Waffles 1514 N Gower (at Sunset) **323/466-7453** *8:30am-midnight, till 4am Fri-Sat*

Bookstores

Skylight Books [★] 1818 N Vermont Ave (at Melbourne Ave) **323/660-1175** *10am-10pm, way cool independent in Los Feliz, great fiction & alt-lit sections*

Gyms & Health Clubs

Gold's Gym 1016 N Cole Ave (near Santa Monica & Vine) **323/462-7012** *5am-midnight, 7am-9pm Sat-Sun*

Men's Clubs

Flex [SW] 4424 Melrose Ave (btwn Normandie & Vermont) **323/663-7786** *24hrs, patio, steam*

The Zone [PC] 1037 N Sycamore Ave (at Santa Monica) **323/472-6495** *8pm-dawn, from 2pm Sun*

LA—West LA & Santa Monica

Accommodations

The Georgian Hotel [GF,F,WI,WC] 1415 Ocean Ave (btwn Santa Monica & Broadway), Santa Monica **310/395-9945, 800/538-8147**

Hotel Angeleno [GS,SW,NS,WI] 170 N Church Ln (at Hwy 405) **310/476-6411, 866/264-3536** *boutique hotel w/ landmark circular shape, gym*

Hotel Erwin [GS] 1697 Pacific Ave (at Venice Way), Venice Beach **800/786-7789**

Hotel Palomar [GS,SW,WC] **310/475-8711**

The Inn at Venice Beach [GF,WI,WC] 327 Washington Blvd (at Via Dolce), Marina Del Rey **310/821-2557** *European-style inn*

The Malibu Beach Inn [GF,F,WI] 22878 Pacific Coast Hwy, Malibu **310/651-7777** *balconies with views of the Pacific Ocean*

Shutters on the Beach [GF,SW,WI] 1 Pico Blvd, Santa Monica **310/458-0030, 866/527-6612**

W Los Angeles [GF,F,SW] 930 Hilgard Ave (at Le Conte) **310/208-8765, 800/421-2317** *suites, gym, day spa*

Bars

Artesia Bar [MW,NH,K,WC] 1995 Artesia Blvd (at Green Ln), Redondo Beach **310/318-3339** *7pm-2am, from 4pm Fri-Sun, patio*

The Birdcage [★MW,D] 2640 Main St (top floor of The Victorian), Santa Monica **310/392-4956** *8pm-2am, from 1pm Sun, clsd Mon, brunch Sun*

Roosterfish [★M,NH] 1302 Abbot Kinney Blvd (at Cadiz), Venice **310/977-8174** *4pm-2am, from 2pm Fri-Sun, patio*

Restaurants

Baja Cantina 311 Washington Blvd (at Sanborn), Marina Del Rey **310/821-2252** *10:30am-1am, also brunch wknds, full bar*

Cantalini's Salerno Beach Restaurant [★E,BW] 193 Culver Blvd (at Vista del Mar), Playa del Rey **310/821-0018** *lunch Mon-Fri, dinner nightly, Italian, homemade pastas, live music Sun nights*

Cora's Coffee Shoppe 1802 Ocean Ave (N of Pico Blvd), Santa Monica **310/451-9562** *7am-10pm, till 3pm Sun-Mon, organic*

Gjelina [BW] 1429 Abbot Kinney Blvd, Venice **310/450-1429** *pizzas & small plates*

Golden Bull 170 W Channel Rd (at Pacific Coast Hwy), Santa Monica **310/230-0402** *dinner only, clsd Mon, full bar*

Hamburger Habit [★] 11223 National Blvd (at Sepulveda) **310/478-5000** *10am-11pm, till midnight Fri-Sat*

The Novel Cafe 2507 Main St, Santa Monica **310/396-7700** *8am-9pm, till 4pm Tue*

Entertainment & Recreation

Muscle Beach Ocean Front Walk, Venice Beach *LOTS to see at this popular Venice Boardwalk beach!*

Santa Monica Pier Ocean Ave (at Colorado Ave), Santa Monica

Will Rogers State Beach Pacific Coast Hwy (at Temescal Canyon Rd) *gay beach*

Men's Clubs

Roman Holiday 12814 Venice Blvd (at Beethoven) **310/391-0200** *24hrs, rooms and lockers, sundeck, Jacuzzi, steam room, dry Finnish sauna*

Erotica

Pleasure Island 18426 Hawthorne Blvd (btwn Artesia & 190th), Torrance **310/793-9477** *11am-midnight, till 2am Fri-Sat*

LA—Silverlake

Bars

4100 Bar [GS,NH] 4100 Sunset Blvd (at Manzanita) **323/666-4460** *6pm-2am, from 8pm Mon-Wed*

AKBar [★GS,NH,D,WC] 4356 W Sunset Blvd (at Fountain) **323/665-6810** *7pm-2am, hip Silverlake hangout*

Cha Cha Lounge [GF,NH,GO] 2375 Glendale Blvd (at Silverlake) **323/660-7595** *5pm-2am, hipster lounge*

Eagle LA [★M,L,WC] 4219 Santa Monica Blvd (at Hoover) **323/669-9472** *4pm-2am, from 2pm wknds, uniform bar*

Good Luck Bar [GF] 1514 Hillhurst Ave (nr Hollywood Blvd) **323/666-3524** *7pm-2am, from 8pm wknds, stylish dive bar*

Silverlake Lounge [GS,E,DS] 2906 Sunset Blvd (at Silver Lake Blvd) **323/663-9636** *3pm-2am, rock 'n' roll club, drag shows wknds*

Nightclubs

The Echo [GS,D,E] 1822 W Sunset Blvd (at Glendale Blvd) **213/413-8200**

Restaurants

Casita Del Campo [★] 1920 Hyperion Ave **323/662-4255** *11am-midnight, till 2am Fri-Sat, Mexican, patio*

Cha Cha Cha [WC] 656 N Virgil Ave (at Melrose) **323/664-7723** *lunch & dinner, Caribbean*

Cliff's Edge 3626 Sunset Blvd (at Griffith Park Blvd) **323/666-6116** *dinner only, wknd brunch, plenty veggie, romantic, outdoor seating*

Home 1760 Hillhurst Ave, Los Feliz **323/669-0211** *9am-10pm, patio*

The Kitchen [GO] 4348 Fountain Ave (at Sunset Blvd) **323/664-3663** *5pm-1am, from 11am Sat, till 10pm Sun, cozy diner*

Michelangelo Pizzeria Ristorante 2742 Rowena **323/660-4843** *lunch & dinner*

Square One Dining 4854 Fountain Ave (at Vermont Ave) **323/661-1109** *8am-3pm, great brkfst*

Retail Shops

Rough Trade Gear 3915 Sunset Blvd **323/660-7956** *noon-10pm, 10am-midnight Fri-Sat, till 8pm Sun*

Erotica

Romantix Adult Superstore 3147 N San Fernando Rd **323/258-2867** *24hrs*

LA—Midtown

Accommodations

The Line [GS] 3515 Wilshire Blvd (in Koreatown) **213/381-7411** *restaurant and bar on site*

Luxe City Center [GS] 1020 S Figueroa St **213/748-1291** *2 other LA locations*

The NoMad Hotel Los Angeles [GS,F,SW,WC] 649 S Olive St **213/358 0000** *in the historic building, Giannini Place, great rooftop cafe*

O Hotel [GS,F,WI] 819 S Flower St **213/623-9904**

The Standard, Downtown LA [GS,SW,F,WI] 550 S Flower St **213/892-8080** *rooftop bar*

Bars

Bar Mattachine [M] 221 W 7th St (at Broadway) **213/278-0471** *5pm-2am, from 11am Sat, 2pm Sun,craft cocktails*

The New Jalisco Bar [M,DS] 245 S Main St **213/613-1802** *5pm-2am, Mexican dive bar, good tacos out front*

Precinct [M,H] 357 S Broadway **213/628-3112** *5pm-2am from 3pm wknds*

Redline Dtla [M,D,F] 131 E 6th St *5pm-2am, till midnight Tue, noon-midnight Sun, clsd Mon*

Restaurants

Bar & Kitchen LA 819 S Flower St (at O Hotel) **213/784-3048** *traditional american cuisine with local Californian farm to table influences*

Border Grill Downtown [E,WC] 445 S Figueroa St (at 5th St) **213/486-5171** *lunch & dinner, late-night cocktails*

Cassell's 3600 W 6th St (at Hotel Normandie) **213/387-5502** *8am-10pm, till midnight Fri-Sat, great burgers*

Louise's Trattoria [BW] (Hancock Park) 232 N Larchmont Blvd **323/962-9510** *11am-10pm, Italian, great foccacia bread*

Rossoblu 1124 San Julian St **213/749-1099** *dinner only, clsd Mon, beautiful Bolognese cooking to the most beautiful patio in the Arts District*

Men's Clubs

Klyt [MR-L] 132 E 4th St **213/972-9145** *24hrs, steam room & dry sauna*

Midtowne Spa—Los Angeles [SW] 615 S Kohler (at Central) **213/680-1838** *24hrs*

Erotica

The Stockroom 2408 S. Broadway Blvd **213/484-3882** *noon-11pm, leather and latex*

LA—Valley

includes San Fernando & San Gabriel Valleys

Bars

The Bullet [M,L,WC] 10522 Burbank Blvd (at Cahuenga), North Hollywood **818/762-8890** *noon-2am, patio*

Cobra [★M,D,MR-L,WC] 10937 Burbank Blvd (1 block E of Vineland), North Hollywood **818/760-9798** *9pm-2am, till 3am fri-Sat, clsd Sun-Wed*

Nightclubs

C Frenz [★MW,NH,D,MR,K,C,S,WC,GO] 7026 Reseda Blvd (at Sherman Way), Reseda **818/996-2976** *3pm-2am, till 3am Sat, patio, theme nights, beer bust Sun*

Club Coco Bongo [MW,D,MR-L,DS,S,18+] 19655 Sherman Wy (at Corbin Ave), Reseda **818/233-5322** *9pm-2am, clsd Mon-Wed*

Club Shine [MW,D] 12449 Ventura Blvd, Studio City **818/760-1002** *8pm-2am*

Oil Can Harry's [M,D,CW,S] 11502 Ventura Blvd (at Tujunga & Colfax), Studio City **818/760-9749** *7:30pm-2am, from 9pm Fri, from 8pm Sat, clsd Sun-Mon & Wed, dance lessons Tue & Th, classic disco Sat*

Rain [GS,D] 12215 Ventura Blvd, Studio City **818/755-9596** *9pm-2am Fri-Sat*

Cafes

Aroma 4360 Tujunga Ave, Studio City **818/508-0677** *6am-11pm, from 7am Sun*

Restaurants

Firefly Studio City 11720 Ventura Blvd, Studio City **818/762-1833** *5pm-2am, till midnight Sun, great beer braised mussels, full bar*

Men's Clubs

The North Hollywood Spa [M] 5636 Vineland (at Burbank) **818/760-6969, 800/772-2582** *24hrs, no membership required*

Roman Holiday 14435 Victory Blvd, Van Nuys **818/780-1320** *open 24hrs*

Erotica

Diamond Adult World 6406 Van Nuys Blvd (at Victory), Van Nuys **818/997-3665** *10am-10pm, till 11pm Fri-Sat*

Romantix Adult Superstore 21625 Sherman Wy (at Nelson), Canoga Park **818/992-9801**

Cruisy Areas

Chatsworth Park South [AYOR] 22360 Devonshire St, Chatsworth *parking lot & nearby woods*

LA—East LA & South Central

Bars

Chico Bar [M,D,MR-L,S] 2915 W Beverly Blvd (at Garfield), Montebello **323/721-3403** *9pm-2am, theme nights*

Restaurants

Pann's 6710 La Tijera Blvd **323/776-3770** *classic 1950s coffee shop for American fare from morning to night, plus weekend champagne brunch. Near LAX*

Manhattan Beach

see also LA–West LA & Santa Monica

Accommodations

Sea View Inn at the Beach [GF,SW,NS,WI] 3400 Highland Ave **310/545-1504**

Restaurants

The Local Yolk [WI,WC] 3414 Highland Ave (at Rosecranz) **310/546-4407** *6:30am-2:30pm*

Gyms & Health Clubs

Sand Spa 3408 Highland Ave **310/921-8231** *a modern spa experience to fit the everyday needs of any person*

Marin County

includes Corte Madera, Mill Valley, San Anselmo, San Rafael, Sausalito, Tiburon

Info Lines & Services

AA Gay/ Lesbian 415/499-0400 *check www.aasf.org for meeting times*

The Spahr Center [WC] 910 Irwin St, San Rafael **415/457-2487** *support and empower Marin's LBGTQ community*

Accommodations

Acqua Hotel [GF,NS,WI,WC] 555 Redwood Hwy, Mill Valley **415/380-0400**

Casa Madrona Hotel & Spa [GF,F] 801 Bridgeway, Sausalito **415/332-0502, 800/288-0502** *overlooks SF skyline*

The Lodge at Tiburon [GF,SW,NS,WI] 1651 Tiburon Blvd, Tiburon **415/435-3133, 800/762-7770** *also restaurant & bar*

Waters Edge Hotel [GS,NS,WI,WC] 25 Main St, Tiburon **415/789-5999**

Restaurants

Guaymas 5 Main St (at ferry dock), Tiburon **415/435-6300** *gourmet Mexican, great views of the Bay*

Terrapin Crossroads 100 Yacht Club Dr, San Rafael **415/524-2773** *4pm-9:30pm, from 11am wknds*

Entertainment & Recreation

Black Sand Beach heading to San Francisco: take last exit before Golden Gate Bridge, go right on Outlook Rd, look for dirt parking lot, Golden Gate Nat'l Rec Area *popular nude beach, look for trail*

Bookstores

Book Passage [★] 51 Tamal Vista Blvd, Corte Madera **415/927-0960, 800/999-7909** *9am-9pm, beloved independent which draws the biggest names to read*

Retail Shops

Cowgirl Creamery 80 4th St (at Tomales Bay Foods), Pt Reyes Station **415/663-9335** *10am-5pm Wed-Sun, handmade cheeses, picnic lunches to go*

Mendocino

Accommodations

Agate Cove Inn [GF,NS] 11201 N Lansing St **707/937-0551, 800/527-3111** *full brkfst, fireplaces*

The Alegria Quartet & Oceanfront Inn Cottages [GF,NS,WI] 44781 Main St **707/937-5150** *in the village, ocean views*

Blair House & Cottage [GF,NS] 45110 Little Lake St (at Ford St) **707/937-1800, 800/699-9296** *in former "home" of Jessica Fletcher of Murder, She Wrote*

Brewery Gulch Inn [GS,NS,WI] 9401 N Hwy 1 **707/937-4752** *oceanview B&B made of eco-salvaged redwood*

Cottages at Little River Cove [GS,WI] 7533 N Hwy 1, Little River **707/937-5339** *amazing ocean views*

Dennen's Victorian Farmhouse [GF,NS,WI] 7001 N Hwy 1 (at Hwy 128) **707/937-0697, 800/264-4723** *full brkfst*

Glendeven Inn [GF,NS,WI] 8205 N Hwy 1 (1.7 miles S of Mendocino), Little River **707/937-0083, 800/822-4536** *full brkfst& wine bar, farmhouse on the coast*

Hill House Inn [GS] 10701 Palette Dr **707/937-0554, 800/422-0554** *also restaurant*

The Inn at Schoolhouse Creek [GS,WI,WC] 7051 N Hwy 1, Little River **707/937-5525** *B&B w/ cottages & suites, full brkfst*

John Dougherty House [GF] 571 Ukiah St (at Kasten St) **707/397-0079**

Little River Inn Resort & Spa [GF,F,NS,WI] 7901 N Hwy 1, Little River **707/937-5942, 888/466-5683** *resort w/ spectacular ocean views*

MacCallum House Inn [GS,NS,WI,WC] 45020 Albion St (at Lansing) **707/937-0289, 800/609-0492** *also restaurant & Grey Whale bar & cafe*

Orr Hot Springs [GF,R,SW,N] 13201 Orr Springs Rd, Ukiah **707/462-6277** *mineral hot springs, yurts, cottages, and campsites, no pets*

Packard House [GF,NS,WI] 45170 Little Lake St (at Kasten St) **707/397-0079** *full brkfst*

Sea Gull Inn [GF,NS,WI,WC] 44960 Albion St **707/937-5204, 888/937-5204**

Stanford Inn by the Sea [GF,SW,NS,WI,WC] 44850 Comptche-Ukiah Rd (at Coast Hwy 1) **707/937-5615** *full brkfst, fireplaces*

RESTAURANTS

Cafe Beaujolais [R,WC] 961 Ukiah St **707/937-5614** *lunch & dinner*

BOOKSTORES

Gallery Bookshop Main & Kasten St S **707/937-2665** *9:30am-6pm, independent*

Menlo Park

see Palo Alto

Mill Valley

see Marin County

Modesto

see also Stockton

BARS

Brave Bull [MW,D,MR-L,E,K,S] 701 S 9th St **209/529-6712** *7pm-2am, clsd Mon-Tue*

Climax Bar & Nightclub [MW,D] 607 7th St (right of Hwy 99) **209/408-8659** *9pm-2am*

Tiki Lounge [MW,NH,D,MR,TG,K] 932 McHenry Ave (at Roseburg Ave) **209/577-9969** *5pm-2am*

CAFES

Deva Cafe [F,E,WC] 1202 J St **209/572-3382** *7am-3pm, 8am-noon Sun, patio*

Queen Bean 1126 14th St **209/521-8000** *7am-8pm, till 11pm wknds*

RESTAURANTS

Minnie's Restaurant 107 McHenry Ave **209/524-4621** *Chinese, lunch Tue-Fri, dinner Tue-Sun, clsd Mon, full bar*

RETAIL SHOPS

Mystical Body 121 McHenry Ave **209/527-1163** *noon-8pm, clsd Sun-Mon, body piercing*

EROTICA

L'Amour Shoppe 1507-B 9th St **209/521-7987**

Liberty Adult Book Store 1030 Kansas Ave **209/524-7603**

Suzie's Adult Superstores 115 McHenry Ave (at Needham) **209/529-5546** *9am-10pm, till midnight Th-Sat, arcade*

CRUISY AREAS

McHenry Ave Recreation Area [AYOR] River Rd (N of Modesto) *go N on McHenry to River Rd & turn left*

Tuolumne River Regional Park [AYOR] S Santa Cruz Ave *parking lot & nearby woods*

Monterey

ACCOMMODATIONS

Asilomar Conference Grounds [GF,F,SW,NS,WI] 800 Asilomar Blvd, Pacific Grove **831/372-8016, 888/635-5310** *Arts & Crafts-style buildings designed by Julia Morgan*

Gosby House Inn [GF,NS,WC] 643 Lighthouse Ave (at 18th), Pacific Grove **831/375-1287**

The Monterey Hotel [GF,WI] 406 Alvarado St **831/375-3184, 800/966-6490**

RESTAURANTS

Old Fisherman's Grotto 39 Fisherman's Wharf #1 **831/375-4604** *11am-10pm*

Tarpy's Roadhouse 2999 Monterey Salinas Hwy (at Canyon Dr) **831/647-1444** *lunch & dinner, Sun brunch, patios & gardens, full bar*

ENTERTAINMENT & RECREATION

Ag Venture Tours 831/761-8463

Monterey Bay Aquarium 886 Cannery Row **831/648-4800** *come for the otters, stay for the day*

Morro Bay

see also San Luis Obispo

Mountain View

Nightclubs

King of Clubs Nightclub [MW,NH,D,MR,TG,K] 893 Leong Dr (at Moffett Blvd) **650/968-6366** *8pm-2am, clsd Mon-Tue*

Napa Valley

Accommodations

Beazley House B&B Inn [GF,NS,WI,WC] 1910 First St, Napa **707/257-1649** *historic inn, full brkfst, pet-friendly*

Brannan Cottage Inn [GF,NS,WI] 109 Wapoo Ave (at Lincoln Ave), Calistoga **707/942-4200** *B&B in Victorian cottage, full brkfst*

The Chablis Inn [GF,SW,NS,WC] 3360 Solano Ave (Redwood Rd at Hwy 29), Napa **707/257-1944** *stylish motel*

The Chanric Inn [GS,SW,NS,WI,GO] 1805 Foothill Blvd, Calistoga **707/942-4535, 877/281-3671** *full brkfst*

Chateau de Vie [GS,SW,WI,NS,GO] 3250 Hwy 128, Calistoga **707/942-6446, 877/558-2513** *chateau w/ gardens, full brkfst, hot tub*

Embrace Calistoga [GS,WI,GO] 1139 Lincoln Ave (at Myrtle), Calistoga **707/942-9797** *on historic main street*

Hotel Yountville [GF,SW] 6462 Washington St, Yountville **707/967-7900** *luxury boutique hotel, spa & fitness center*

The Inn on First [GS,WI,GO] 1938 1st St, Napa **707/253-1331** *great corn dog omelets*

Meadowlark Country House [GS,SW,N,NS,WI,GO] 601 Petrified Forest Rd, Calistoga **707/942-5651, 800/942-5651** *clothing-optional mineral pool, sauna & hot tub, pets OK*

The Mount View Hotel & Spa [GF,SW,WI] 1457 Lincoln Ave, Calistoga **707/942-6877, 800/816-6877** *also cottages, full-service day spa*

Napa River Inn [GF,WI] 500 Main St (at 5th), Napa **707/251-8500** *luxury boutique hotel w/ spa, located in historic Napa Mill*

North Block Hotel [GS] 757 Washington Street, Yountville **707/944-8080** *modern boutique hotel with a restaurant & spa*

Restaurants

Brannan's [GO] 1374 Lincoln Ave (at Washington), Calistoga **707/942-2233** *lunch & dinner, brunch wknds, full bar, live jazz wknds*

Cindy's Backstreet Kitchen 1327 Railroad Ave, St Helena **707/963-1200** *11:30am-9:30pm*

Pizzeria Tra Vigne [R] 1050 Charter Oak Ave (Hwy 29), St Helena **707/963-4444** *11:30am-10pm, also wine bar*

Redd [R] 6480 Washington St, Yountville **707/944-2222** *lunch Mon-Sat, dinner nightly, Sun brunch, American*

SolBar 755 Silverado Trail (at the Solage Hotel), Calistoga **707/226-0850** *soul-food*

Entertainment & Recreation

Cameo Cinema 1340 Main St, St Helena **707/963-9779** *Cameo exists to entertain, inspire, educate and connect the community through the "art of storytelling"*

Bookstores

Copperfield's Books 1330 Lincoln Ave, Calistoga **707/942-1616** *9am-7pm, till 9pm Fri-Sat, 10am- 6pm Sun*

Cruisy Areas

Red Rock Beach [AYOR] Stinson Beach *nude beach 1 mile S of Stinson Beach, off Hwy 1*

Vista Point [AYOR] Rte 12/121 bridge over Napa River, Napa *parking lot & nearby woods N of bridge on E side*

Nevada City

Cafes

Java John's 306 Broad St **530/265-3653** *6:30am-4:30pm, from 7pm wknds*

Restaurants

Friar Tuck's [E,WC] 111 N Pine St (at Commercial) **530/265-9093** *dinner from 5pm, American/ fondue, full bar*

Cruisy Areas

Hoyt's Crossing [AYOR] Hwy 49 *take to Hoyt Trail & follow till crosses Yuba River, near upstream end of Miner's Tunnel, nude sunbathing*

Newport Beach

see Orange County

Oakland

see East Bay

Ontario

Restaurants

Hamburger Mary's Ontario 3550 E Porsche Way **909/944-9400** *5pm-2am, from 11am wknds*

Orange County

includes Anaheim, Costa Mesa, Garden Grove, Huntington Beach, Irvine, Laguna Beach, Newport Beach, Santa Ana

Info Lines & Services

AA Gay/ Lesbian Laguna Beach **714/556-4555**

The Center Orange County 1605 N Spurgeon St, Santa Ana **714/953-5428** *10am-9pm Mon-Fri or by appointment or event*

Accommodations

Best Western Plus Plus Laguna Brisas Spa Hotel [GS,SW,NS,WI,WC] 1600 S Coast Hwy (at Bluebird), Laguna Beach **949/497-7272, 888/296-6834** *resort hotel*

Best Western Raffles Inn & Suites [GF,SW,WI] 2040 S Harbor Blvd, Anaheim **714/750-6100, 800/308 -5278** *walk to Disneyland*

Casa Laguna Inn & Spa [GF,SW,WI,NS,GO] 2510 S Coast Hwy, Laguna Beach **949/494-2996, 800/233-0449** *inn & cottages overlooking the Pacific*

Laguna Beach House [★GF,SW,NS,WI,WC] 475 N Coast Hwy, Laguna Beach **949/497-6645, 800/297-0007** *easy beach access*

The St Regis Monarch Beach [GF,F,SW,NS,WI,WC] One Monarch Beach Resort, Dana Point **949/234-3426**

Surf & Sand Resort [GF,F,SW,WI] 1555 S Coast Hwy, Laguna Beach **949/497-4477, 877/741-5908**

Bars

Frat House [★MW,D,MR,DS,S,YC,WC] 8112 Garden Grove Blvd (at Beach Blvd), Garden Grove **714/373-3728** *4pm-2am*

Main Street Bar & Cabaret [MW,D,K,DS] 1460 S Coast Hwy, Laguna Beach **949/494-0056** *4pm-2am, upstairs dance bar Fri-Sat*

Tin Lizzie Saloon [M,NH,WC] 752 St Clair (at Bristol), Costa Mesa **714/966-2029** *noon-2am*

Velvet Lounge [★MW,D,F,K] 416 W 4th St, Santa Ana **714/232-8727** *11:30am-2am*

Nightclubs

Bravo [GS,D,A,MR-L,F,DS,S] 1490 S Anaheim Blvd, Anaheim **714/533-2291** *Latin music Wed & Fri-Sat, more gay Th & Sat night, goth & electronica Sun*

El Calor [GF,D,MR-L,DS] 2916 W Lincoln Ave (at E Beach Blvd), Anaheim **714/527-8873** *9pm-2am, Latin music, also restaurant*

Cafes

The Koffee Klatch [WI] 1440 S Coast Hwy (btwn Mountain & Pacific Coast Hwy), Laguna Beach **949/376-6867** *7am-11pm, till midnight Fri-Sat*

Zinc Cafe [BW,WC] 350 Ocean Ave (at Broadway), Laguna Beach **949/494-6302** *7am-4pm, also market till 6pm, patio*

Restaurants

Dizz's As Is 2794 S Coast Hwy (at Nyes Pl), Laguna Beach **949/494-5250** *open 5:30pm clsd Mon, full bar, patio*

Madison Square & Garden Cafe 320 N Coast Hwy, Laguna Beach **949/494-0137** *8am-3pm, clsd Tue, dog-friendly*

Nirvana Grille 303 Broadway St, Laguna Beach **949/497-0027** *5pm-9pm, clsd Mon, seasonal rooftop deck*

Three Seventy Common 370 Glenneyre St, Laguna Beach **949/494-8686** *dinner only, upscale American bistro & martini bar*

Entertainment & Recreation

San Onofre State Beach on I-5, S of San Clemente (exit at Basilone Rd), Laguna Beach

West St Beach Laguna Beach *gay beach*

Erotica

Garden of Eden 12061 Garden Grove Blvd, Garden Grove **714/534-9805** *24hrs*

Pink Kitty [GO] 17955 Sky Park Cir, Ste A, Irvine **949/660-4990** *10am-6pm*

Cruisy Areas

Calafia State Beach [AYOR] to the left, off the fwy (from Hwy 5 S), San Clemente

Eisenhower Park [AYOR] Orange

Fairview Park [AYOR] Costa Mesa

Fullerton Dam [AYOR] on Harbor Blvd, Fullerton *park*

Heisler Park [AYOR] N side of park, Laguna Beach *also take path to the ocean, then climb over the rocks to the right; beware cops (!)*

Santiago Park [AYOR] off I-5 (at Main St), Santa Ana *parking lot & nearby woods, early evenings*

William Mason Regional Park [AYOR] Culver St & University Ave, Irvine

Oxnard

Cruisy Areas

Oxnard Shores Beach [AYOR] 5th St (past Harbor Blvd) *head to sand dunes*

Pacifica

Restaurants

Nicks Seafood Restaurant [E] 100 Rockaway Beach Ave **650/359-3900** *11am-10pm, from 8am wknds*

Cruisy Areas

Grey Whale Cove Beach [AYOR] Hwy 1 *3 miles S of Pacifica on Devil's Slide, large parking lot on left, nude beach*

San Pedro Mountain Park [AYOR] Linda Mar & Odstaad Dr

Palm Springs

Info Lines & Services

AA Gay/ Lesbian 760/324-4880 *call for meeting schedule*

The LGBT Community Center of the Desert 1301 N Palm Canyon Dr, 3rd Fl **760/416-7790** *programs, education, recreation, social & counseling services*

Accommodations

Ace Hotel Palm Springs [GS,SW,F,WI] 701 E Palm Canyon Dr **760/325-9900**

All Worlds Resort [M,SW,N,WI,GO] 526 S Warm Sands Dr (at Ramon) **760/323-7505**

The Bearfoot Inn [MO,B,N,WI] 888 N Indian Canyon Dr (at El Alameda) **760/699-7641, 855/438-0414**

Caliente Tropics Resort [GS,F,SW,NS,WC,GO] 411 E Palm Canyon Dr **760/327-1391, 888/277-0999** *pet-friendly motor hotel, jacuzzi*

Canyon Club Hotel [M,SW,N,WI,GO] 960 N Palm Canyon Dr (btwn Tachevah & El Alameda) **760/778-8042, 877/258-2887** *clothing-optional, kitchens, hot tub & patios*

CCBC Resort Hotel [★M,SW,N,WC,GO] 68300 Gay Resort Dr (btwn Melrose & Palo Verde), Cathedral City **760/324-1350, 800/472-0836** *mention Damron for 25% off (holidays not included, JocKuzzi Spa, steam room, saltwater pool, waterfall & cave, jail & dungeon*

Chaps Inn [M,SW,WI,WC,GO] 312 E Camino Monte Vista **760/327-8222, 800/445-8916** *catering to leather & bears mostly*

Colt's Lodge [GS,SW,WI,WC,GO] 1586 E Palm Canyon Dr **760/323-2231** *11 room boutique inn, modern amenities and views of the San Jacinto Mountains*

Desert Paradise Resort Hotel [M,SW,N,NS,WI,GO] 615 S Warm Sands Dr (at Parocela) **760/320-5650, 800/342-7635**

The East Canyon Hotel & Spa [M,SW,NS,WI,GO] 288 E Camino Monte Vista **760/320-1928, 877/324-6835** *boutique hotel, day spa*

El Mirasol Villas [M,SW,N,NS,WI,GO] 525 Warm Sands Dr (at Ramon) **760/327-5913, 800/327-2985**

Escape [M,SW,N,NS,WI,GO] 641 E San Lorenzo Rd (at Random) **760/325-5269, 800/621-6973** *hot tub*

The Hacienda at Warm Sands [★M,V,SW,N,NS,WI,WC,GO] 586 Warm Sands Dr (at Parocela) **760/327-8111, 800/359-2007** *all-suite resort with spacious grounds, unparalleled views, friendly staff, concierge service, 2 beautifully situated pools and jacuzzi*

L' Horizon [GF,SW,WI] 1050 E Palm Canyon Dr **760/323-1858** *restaurant on site*

INNdulge Palm Springs [M,SW,N,NS,WI,GO] 601 Grenfall Rd (at Parocela) **760/327-1408**

La Dolce Vita Resort [M,SW,N,NS,WI,WC,GO] 1491 S Via Soledad (at Sonora & S Palm Canyon) **760/325-2686** *full brkfst, jacuzzi*

Rendezvous [GF,SW,WI] 1420 N Indian Canyon Dr **760/320-1178** *'50s chic*

Ruby Montana's Coral Sands Inn [GS,SW,WI,WC,GO] 210 W Stevens Rd (at N Palm Canyon) **760/325-4900** *resort, kitschy 1950s chic*

The Saguaro [GF,F,SW] 1800 East Palm Canyon Dr **760/323-1711** *hip boutique hotel*

Santiago Resort [M,SW,N,NS,WI,GO] 650 San Lorenzo Rd (at Mesquite) **760/322-1300, 800/710-7729**

The Skylark [GS,SW,WI,GO] 1466 N Palm Canyon Dr (at Monte Vista) **760/322-2267, 800/793-0063** *Modern twist on a California 50's classic*

The Three Fifty Hotel [GF,SW,WI] 350 S Belardo Rd (at Baristo) **760/323-3654** *pets ok*

Tortuga del Sol [M,SW,N,NS,WI,GO] 715 San Lorenzo **760/416-3111, 888/541-3777** *resort, jacuzzi*

Triangle Inn Palm Springs [M,SW,N,GO] 555 San Lorenzo Rd (at Random Rd) **760/322-7993** *hot tub, 2 sundecks*

Bars

The Barracks [M,L] 67-625 E Palm Canyon (at Canyon Plaza), Cathedral City **760/321-9688** *2pm-2am, Sun beer bust*

Chill Bar [M,D, K,DS] 217 E Arenas Rd **760/327-1079** *noon-2am, from 2pm wknds*

Georgie's Alibi [M,NH,F,V] 369 N Palm Canyon Dr **760/325-5533** *11am-close, from 10am Sun*

Hunter's Video Bar [★M,D,V] 302 E Arenas Rd (at Calle Encilia) **760/323-0700** *10am-2am, go-go boys Fri, theme nights*

Paul Bar/Food [GS] 3700 E Vista Chino (at Gene Autry Tr) **760/656-4082** *4pm-1am, clsd Tue, old school bar with small menu*

Quadz [M,NH,K,V] 200 S Indian Canyon Dr (at Arenas) **760/778-4326** *2:30-2am*

The Retro Room Lounge [M,K] 125 E Tahquitz Canyon Way #102 **760/656-8680** *2pm-2am, live entertainment in an intimate and retro atmosphere*

The Roost Lounge 68718 E Palm Canyon Dr, Cathedral City **760/507-8495**

Score [M,NH,V] 301 E Arenas Rd **760/327-0753** *6am-2am*

Stacy's @Palm Springs [GS,NH,E,P] 220 E Arenas Rd **760/620-5003** *10am-2am*

Streetbar [★M,NH,E,K,WC] 224 E Arenas Rd (at Indian) **760/320-1266** *10am-2am, patio*

Studio One 11 [M,D,S,K] 67-555 E Palm Canyon Dr #A-103, Cathedral City **760/328-2900** *3pm-2am, cocktail lounge with piano bar*

Tool Shed [M,NH,L] 600 E Sunny Dunes Rd (at Palm Canyon) **760/320-3299** *10am-2am, cruise bar*

Toucan's Tiki Lounge [MW,D,E,DS,S] 2100 N Palm Canyon Dr (at Via Escuela) **760/416-7584** *3pm-2am, from 1pm wknds, clsd Wed*

Trunks Bar [MW,NH,K] 36-737 Cathedral Canyon Dr (at 111), Cathedral City **760/321-0031** *10am-2am, patio*

Tryst [GS,NH] 188 S Indian Canyon Dr **760/832-6046** *2pm-2am, rockin juke-box*

Cafes

Palm Springs Koffi [★WI,GO] 515 N Palm Canyon Dr (at Alejo) **760/416-2244** *5:30am-7pm*

Restaurants

Billy Reed's [WC] 1800 N Palm Canyon Dr (at Vista Chino) **760/325-1946** *7am-9pm, till 10pm Fri-Sat*

Blackbook Bar & Kitchen [GO] 315 E Arenas **760/832-8497** *from noon weekdays, 11am wknds, small menu and tasty drinks*

Blue Coyote Grill 445 N Palm Canyon Dr **760/327-1196** *11am-10pm, till 11pm Fri-Sat, Southwestern*

Bongo Johnny's 214 E Arenas Rd **760/866-1905** *8am-10pm, till 3am Fri-Sat, burgers & sandwiches*

Brickworks 155 S Palm Canyon Dr (in Mercado Plaza, 2nd level) **760/778-6000** *4pm-10pm, till 11pm Fri-Sat*

Copley's 621 N Palm Canyon Dr (btwn E Tamarisk Rd & E Granvia Valmonte) **760/327-9555** *6pm-10pm, contemporary American, full bar*

El Gallito [BW] 68820 Grove St (at Palm Canyon), Cathedral City **760/328-7794** *10am-9pm, home-made Mexican*

Jake's 664 N Palm Canyon Dr **760/327-4400** *lunch & dinner, wknd brunch, clsd Sun night & Mon, American bistro*

John's 900 N Palm Canyon Dr **760/327-8522** *7am-9pm, til 8am Sun-Mon, great cheap brkfst*

Las Casuelas 368 N Palm Canyon Dr (btwn Amado & Alejo) **760/325-3213** *11am-10pm, Mexican*

Nature's Health Food & Cafe 555 S Sunrise Way #301 **760/323-9487** *7am-7pm, 8am-6pm wknds, vegan/vegetarian*

Oscar's Cafe & Bar 125 E Tahquitz Canyon Way #108 **760/325-1188** *4pm-9pm, till midnight Fri-Sat, from 9am wknds, popular T-dance Sun, patio*

Peppers Thai Cuisine 396 N Palm Canyon Dr **760/322-1259** *lunch & dinner*

Pinocchio in the Desert 134 E Tahquitz Canyon Way **760/322-3776** *7:30am-2pm, outdoor seating*

Pomme Frite 256 S Palm Canyon Dr **760/778-3727** *dinner nightly, Belgian beer & French food*

Rio Azul 350 S Indian Canyon Dr **760/992-5641** *dinner nightly, open for lunch Fri-Sun, drag bunch Sun from 10am, Mexican*

Shame on the Moon [R,WC] 69-950 Frank Sinatra Dr (at Hwy 111), Rancho Mirage **760/324-5515** *5pm-9:30pm, cont'l, full bar, patio*

Sherman's Deli & Bakery [★] 401 E Tahquitz Canyon Wy **760/325-1199** *7am-9pm, kosher-style deli*

Spencer's Restaurant [R] 701 W Baristo Rd **760/327-3446** *9am-2:30pm & 5pm-10pm, Sun brunch, upscale contemporary*

Tootie's Texas Barbeque 68-703 Perez Rd, Cathedral City **760/202-6963** *11am-7pm, clsd Sun, the name says it all*

Towne Center Cafe 44491 Town Center Wy, Palm Desert **760/346-2120** *5am-9pm, Greek diner*

Trio [★] 707 N Palm Canyon Dr **760/864-8746** *11am-10pm, till 11am Fri-Sat, from 10am wknds, also lounge*

The Tropicale Restaurant & Lounge 330 E Amado Rd **760/866-1952** *4pm-10pm, from 11am wknds, till 11pm Fri-Sat*

Wang's in the Desert 424 S Indian Canyon Dr (at E Saturnino Rd) **760/325-9264** *from 5:30pm, Chinese, full bar*

Zin American Bistro 198 S Palm Canyon (at Arenas) **760/322-6300** *lunch & dinner*

Bookstores

Q Trading Company 606 E Sunny Dunes Rd (at Indian Canyon) **760/416-7150** *10am-6pm, LGBT, also cards, gifts, videos*

Retail Shops

Bear Wear Etc 319 E Arenas Rd **760/323-8940** *11am-6pm, till 10pm Th-Sat, noon-6pm Sun, men's clothing, leather & resort wear*

GayMartUSA 305 E Arenas Rd (at Indian Canyon) **760/416-6436** *10am-midnight*

Greetings 301 N Palm Canyon Dr (at Amado) **760/322-5049** *9am-6pm, till 9pm Th-Sat*

Mischief 210 E Arenas Rd (at Indian Canyon) **760/322-8555**

Not So Innocent 2100 N Palm Canyon Dr **760/322-0999** *noon-10pm, clsd Wed, men's clothing & gear*

Off Ramp Leathers 650 E Sunny Dunes Rd #3 **760/778-2798** *11am-7pm, noon-4pm Sat, clsd Sun, custom motorcycle leathers*

Publications

Desert Daily Guide/ DDG Media Group 760/320-3237 *LGBT weekly*

Gyms & Health Clubs

WorkOUT Gym [GO] 2100 N Palm Canyon Dr #C100 **760/325-4600** *5am-8pm, 8am-6pm wknds*

World Gym Palm Springs [★M,WC,GO] 1751 N Sunrise Way (at Vista Chino) **760/327-7100** *5am-10pm, 6am-8pm wknds, day passes available, steam & sauna, club-quality sound system*

Erotica

Gear Leather & Fetish 650 E Sunny Dunes #1 (at S Calle Palo Fierro) **760/322-3363** *noon-7pm, till 9pm Fri-Sat*

Hidden Joy Book Shop 68-424 Commercial (at Cathedral Canyon), Cathedral City **760/328-1694** *24hrs, arcade*

Love Stuff 304 N Palm Canyon Dr **760/322-1444** *10am-10pm, till midnight Fri-Sat*

Perez Images 68-366 Perez Rd, Cathedral City **760/321-1033** *24hrs*

Cruisy Areas

Cahuilla Hills Park [AYOR] Palm Desert

Palo Alto

Accommodations

Creekside Inn [GS,SW,NS,WI,WC] 3400 El Camino Real (at Page Mill Rd) **650/493-2411** *restaurant & lounge*

Hotel Avante [GS,SW,NS,WI] 860 E El Camino Real, Mountain View **650/940-1000, 800/538-1600**

Nobu Hotel, Epiphany [GS,WI] 180 Hamilton Ave **800/224-6000** *luxury boutique hotel that caters to the region's tech-savvy travelers*

Bookstores

Books Inc 855 El Camino Real **650/321-0600** *9am-9pm*

Erotica

Good Vibrations [★WC] 534 Ramona St **650/422-2790** *10am-10pm, till 11pm Th-Sat*

Pasadena

Bars

The 35er [GS,NH,F] **626 /356-9315** *3pm-2am, from 12:30pm Fri, from 10am wknds*

The Boulevard Bar [M,NH,DS,K,P] 3199 E Foothill Blvd (at Sierra Madre Villa) **626/356-9304** *4pm-2am, from 3pm Fri-Sun*

Restaurants

Kings Row [E] 20 E Colorado Blvd **626/793-3010** *10:30m-1am, gastropub*

Entertainment & Recreation

The Huntington 1151 Oxford Rd, San Marino **626/405-2100** *art collection, botanical gardens*

Erotica

Romantix 45 E Colorado Blvd (at Raymond) **626/683-9468**

Paso Robles

Accommodations

Hotel Cheval [★GF,WI] 1021 Pine St **805/226-9995** *boutique luxury hotel just off town square*

The Oaks Hotel [GF,SW,WI,WC] 3000 Riverside Ave (at 24th St) **805/237-8700** *boutique-style hotel with many upscale amenities, bar & restaurant on site*

Entertainment & Recreation

River Oaks Hot Springs Spa 800 Clubhouse Dr **805/238-4600** *9am-9pm*

Petaluma

Accommodations

Sheraton Sonoma County [GF,SW,WC] 745 Baywood Dr **707/283-2888** *small dogs ok, restaurant and lounge*

Restaurants

Brixx [★E] 16 Kentucky St (in Lanmart Bldg) **707/766-8162** *dinner from 4pm, handmade pizzas, paninis*

Bookstores

Copperfield's Books 140 Kentucky St (btwn Western & Washington, downtown) **707/762-0563** *9am-9pm, 10am-6pm Sun*

Cruisy Areas

Lucchesi Park [AYOR]

Placerville

Accommodations

Rancho Cicada Retreat [M,SW,N,GO] 10001 Bell Rd, Plymouth **209/245-4841, 877/553-9481** *riverside retreat, campsites, tents & cabins*

Cruisy Areas

Lumsden Park [AYOR] Wiltse Rd *parking lots & woods*

Pleasant Hill

see East Bay

Point Reyes

Cruisy Areas

Hagmire Pond [AYOR] Hwy 1 (at milepost 20.53) *nude sunbathing & woods; walk right across meadow & look for pond on the right, walk up hill to right of pond*

Pomona

Bars

Alibi East & Back Alley Bar [M,D,K] 225 S San Antonio Ave (at 2nd) **909/623-9422** *noon-2am, till 3am Fri, smoking patio*

The Hookup [MW,F,K,V,WC,GO] 1047 E 2nd St (at Pico) **909/620-2844** *2pm-2am, beer bust Sun*

Nightclubs

340 [MW,D,F,DS] 340 S Thomas St **909/865-9340** *7pm--2am , clsd Mon-Wed*

Redding

Nightclubs

Club 501 [MW,D,YC] 1244 California St (at Center & Division, enter rear) **530/243-7869** *6pm-2am, from 3pm Th-Sun*

Erotica

Secrets, Hilltop Books 2131 Hilltop Dr **530/223-2675** *10am-midnight, till 2am Fri-Sat, till 10pm sun*

Cruisy Areas

Clear Creek Rd [AYOR] 13 miles W of Hwy 273 (4 miles W of old 99) *nude beach, summers*

Redlands

Cruisy Areas

Ford Park [AYOR] Ford St (at Parkford Dr) *take I-10 E & exit at Ford St, turn right & first street you come to (Prospect) turn right again; park begins where street stops; take sidewalk adjacent to tennis court that goes up hill*

Sylvan Park [AYOR] 601 N University St (exit 10 E at University St) *make left when going under bridge; weekdays only*

Redondo Beach

see also Los Angeles—West LA & Santa Monica

Riverside

see also San Bernardino

Nightclubs

Menagerie [MW,D,K,DS,WC] 3581 University Ave (at Orange) **951/788-8000** *4pm-2am*

VIP Nightclub & Restaurant [MW,D,F,K,DS,18+] 3673 Merrill Ave (at Magnolia) **951/784-2370** *5pm-2am*

Cruisy Areas

Fairmount Park [AYOR] off Rte 60 (at Market St exit)

Riverton

Cruisy Areas

Bull Creek Rd [AYOR] off Hwy 50 *trail along river*

Russian River

includes Cazadero, Forestville, Guerneville, Monte Rio, Occidental & Sebastopol

Info Lines & Services

AA Meetings in Sonoma County **707/938-8508, 707/546-2066** *call for meeting times*

Russian River Chamber of Commerce & Visitors Center 16209 First St (on the plaza), Guerneville **707/869-9000** *10am-5pm, till 4pm Sun*

Accommodations

Applewood Inn [GF,F,SW,NS,WI,WC] 13555 Hwy 116 (at Mays Canyon), Guerneville **707/869-9093**

Autocamp [GF] 14120 Old Cazadero Rd, Guerneville **888/405-7553** *polished aluminum Airstreams*

boon hotel & spa [GS,SW,NS,WI,GO] 14711 Armstrong Woods Rd, Guerneville **707/869-2721**

Fern Grove Cottages [GF,SW,NS,WI] 16650 River Rd, Guerneville **707/869-8105**

Guerneville Lodge [GS,NS,WI] 15905 River Rd (at Hwy 116), Guerneville **707/869-0102** *camping*

Highland Dell Resort [GF,F,WI] 21050 River Blvd (at Bohemian Hwy), Monte Rio **707/865-2300**

➤**Highlands Resort** [★MW,SW,N] 14000 Woodland Dr, Guerneville **707/869-0333** *country retreat on 4 wooded acres, hot tub*

Inn at Occidental [GF,NS,WC] 3657 Church St, Occidental **707/874-1047**

r3 Hotel [MW,E,F,V,SW,N,WC,GO] 16390 4th St (at Mill), Guerneville **707/869-8399** *bar & restaurant*

Rio Villa Beach Resort [GF,NS,WI,GO] 20292 Hwy 116 (at Bohemian Hwy), Monte Rio **707/865-1143, 877/746-8455**

Village Inn & Restaurant [GS,NS,WC,WI] 20822 River Blvd, Monte Rio **707/865-2304** *historic inn w/ restaurant & full bar*

West Sonoma Inn & Spa [GS,SW,NS,WI,WC] 14100 Brookside Ln (at Main St), Guerneville **707/869-2874** *6-acre resort*

The Woods Resort [M,SW,N,NS,WI,WC,GO] 16484 4th St (at Mill St), Guerneville **707/869-0600, 877/887-9218** *cottages, guest cabins & suites*

Bars

El Barrio [GO] 16230 Main St, Guerneville **707/604-7601** *4pm-9pm. till 11pm Fri-Sat, from noon wknds, clsd Tue*

Mc T's Bullpen [GS,NH,K,E,WI,WC] 16246 First St (at Church), Guerneville **707/869-3377** *10am-2am, sports bar, patio*

Rainbow Cattle Co [★GS,NH] 16220 Main St (at Armstrong Woods Rd), Guerneville **707/869-0206** *6am-2am, DJ Bruce Sat*

Cafes

Coffee Bazaar [★WI] 14045 Armstrong Woods Rd (at River Rd), Guerneville **707/869-9706** *6am-8pm, soups, salads & sandwiches*

Coffee Catz [E,WI,WC] 6761 Sebastopol Ave (at Hwy 116), Sebastopol **707/829-6600** *7am-6pm, till 8pm Th, till 10pm Wed & Fri-Sat*

Roasters Espresso Bar [E,WI] 6656 Front St (Hwy 116), Forestville **707/887-1632** *6am-6pm, from 7am Sat-Sun*

Restaurants

Betty Spaghetti 16390 4th St (at r3 Hotel), Guerneville **707/869-1400** *5:30pm-9pm, till 10pm Fri-Sat, clsd Mon-Tue*

boon eat + drink [BW] 16248 Main St (at Hwy 116), Guerneville **707/869-0780** *lunch & dinner,clsd Wed, modern California bistro*

Cape Fear Cafe [WC] 25191 Main St, Duncans Mills **707/865-9246** *9am-2:30pm & 5pm-9pm (clsd Wed & Th off-season)*

Chef Patrick's [BW,WC] 16337 Main St (at Hwy 116), Guerneville **707/869-9161** *dinner nightly*

Farmhouse Inn Restaurant [BW] 7871 River Rd, Forestville **707/887-3300, 800/464-6642** *dinner, clsd Tue-Wed*

Garden Grill 17132 Hwy 116, Guerneville **707/869-3922** *8am-8pm, clsd Tue-Wed, great burgers & sandwiches, some veggie, patio*

Main Street Station [C,BW] 16280 Main St (at Church St), Guerneville **707/869-0501** *11am-7pm, Italian restaurant & pizzeria*

River Inn Grill [★WC] 16141 Main St, Guerneville **707/869-0481** *8am-3pm, local favorite*

Seaside Metal Oyster Bar 16222 Main St, Guerneville **707/604-7250** *5pm-9pm, clsd Mon-Tue, a rustic seafood-based restaurant run by the duo behind SF's famous Bar Crudo*

Tahoe Chinese Restaurant 6492 Mirabel Rd, Forestville **707/887-9772** *lunch & dinner, dinner only Sat, clsd Sun*

Timberline At The River [GO] 16440 4th St, Guerneville **707/604-7617** *5pm-9pm, till 10pm Fri-Sat, bar open till midnight Fri-Sat*

Underwood Bar & Bistro 9113 Graton Rd, Graton **707/823-7023** *lunch & dinner, clsd Mon*

Willow Wood Market Cafe [★] 9020 Graton Rd, Graton **707/823-0233** *8am-9pm, brunch 9am-3pm Sun*

Entertainment & Recreation

The Nude Beach [AYOR] on Russian River at Wohler Bridge, Guerneville

Pegasus Theater Co [WC] 4444 Wood Rd (at Rio Nido Lodge, at Canyon Two Rd) **707/583-2343** *classic to contemporary plays*

Retail Shops

Sonoma Nesting Company [GO] 16151 Main St, Guerneville **707/869-3434** *antiques & home decorating*

Cruisy Areas

Steelhead Beach Regional Park [AYOR] 9000 River Rd, Forestville *beach & woods*

Sacramento

Info Lines & Services

Gay AA 916/454-1100 *24hr helpline*

Sacramento Gay & Lesbian Center 1927 L St **916/442-0185** *10am-6pm Mon-Fri*

Accommodations

The Citizen Hotel [GF,NS,WI,WC] 926 J Street **877/829-2429**

Governors Inn [GF,SW,NS,WI] 210 Richards Blvd (at I-5) **916/448-7224, 800/999-6689**

Inn & Spa at Parkside [GS,WI,WC,GO] 2116 6th St (at U St) **916/658-1818** *full brkfst, jacuzzi, also full-service spa*

Bars

The Bolt [M,NH,B,L] 2560 Boxwood St (at El Camino) **916/649-8420** *2pm-2am, patio, volleyball in summer*

The Depot [★M,NH,TG,E,S,V,WC] 2001 K St **916/441-6823** *4pm-2am, from 2pm wknds*

Dive Bar [★GS] 1016 K St **916 /737-5999** *4pm-2am, super cool water tank*

The Mercantile Saloon [★M,NH,WC] 1928 L St (at 20th St) **916/447-0792** *10am-2am*

Nightclubs

Badlands [M,D,S,V] 2003 K St **916/448-8790** *6pm-2am, from 2pm Fri-Sat, from 4pm Sun*

Faces [MW,D,K] 2000 K St (at 20th St) **916/448-7798** *4pm-2am, 3 bars w/ various theme nights, patio*

Restaurants

Ernesto's 1901 16th St **916/441-5850** *11am-11pm, from 9am wknds, Mexican*

Ink Eats & Drinks 2730 N St (at 28th) **916/456-2800** *lunch, dinner, late-night brkfst, wknd brunch, full bar, DJ wknds*

Jack's Urban Eats 1230 20th St (at Capitol Ave) **916/444-0307** *11am-8pm, till 9pm Wed Sat*

Paesanos 1806 Capitol Ave (at 18th) **916/447-8646** *11:30am-9:30pm, from noon wknds, Italian, funky artwork, patio, full bar; also 8519 Bond Rd, 916/690-8646*

Pizza Rock 1020 K St **916/737-5777** *11:30am-9pm, till 10pm Th, till 3am Fri-Sat*

Rick's Dessert Diner 2401 J St **916/444-0969** *10am-midnight, till 1am wknds, from noon Sun*

Thai Palace 3262 J St (33rd St) **916/447-5353** *lunch & dinner*

Zócalo 1801 Capitol Ave (at 18th St) **916/441-0303** *11am-10pm, Mexican, full bar*

Entertainment & Recreation

Lavender Library, Archives & Cultural Exchange of Sacramento 1414 21st St **916/492-0558** *4:30pm-8pm Th-Fri, noon-6pm wknds, clsd Mon-Wed*

Publications

Outword Magazine 916/329-9280 *statewide LGBT newspaper*

Men's Clubs

Sacs4men Men's Club 5940 Rosebud Ln #1 (at PolyUrbanStudios) **916/410-6550** *call for info & location; also over night room rentals*

Erotica

G Spot [★GO] 2007 J St (at 20th) **916/441-3200**

Goldies 201 N 12th St (at North B St) **916/447-5860** *10-midnight, till 4am Fri-Sat, till 10am Sun*

Kiss-N-Tell 4201 Sunrise Blvd (at Fair Oaks) **916/966-5477** *clean, well-lighted erotica store; also 2401 Arden Wy, 916/920-5477*

L'Amour Shoppe 2531 Broadway (at 26th) **916/736-3467** *9am-midnight, till 1am Fri-Sat*

Cruisy Areas

American River Access [AYOR] off La Rivera Dr, near Howe Ave & Watt Ave

Beach & levee on American River [AYOR] at end of N 10th St, off Richards Blvd

San Bernardino

see also Riverside

Info Lines & Services

AA Gay/ Lesbian 897 Via Lata, Colton **909/825-4700**

Cruisy Areas

Cajon Pass [AYOR] Cajon Pass (off Rte 138, W of I-15, in San Bernardino Nat'l Forest), Cajon Junction *parking lot & nearby woods*

San Diego

Info Lines & Services

Live & Let Live Alano Club 1730 Monroe Ave **619/298-8008** *see www.lllac.org for meetings*

San Diego LGBT Community Center 3909 Centre St (at University) **619/692-2077** *9am-10pm, till 7pm Sat, clsd Sun*

Accommodations

Andaz San Diego [GS,SW,WI] 600 F St **619/849-1234** *also restaurant & nighclub*

Blue Sea Beach Hotel [GF,SW,WC] 707 Pacific Beach Dr **858/488-4700** *beachfront hotel*

The Bristol Hotel [GS,WI,WC] 1055 First Ave **619/232-6141** *restaurant & bar, great collection of pop art*

Handlery Hotel & Resort [GF,SW,NS,WI,WC] 950 Hotel Circle N **619/298-0511, 800/676-6567** *restaurant and bar*

Inn at the Park [GF,WI] 525 Spruce St (btwn 5th & 6th) **619/291-0999** *1926 hotel, bar & 2 restaurants*

Keating House [GF,NS,WI,GO] 2331 2nd Ave (at Juniper) **619/239-8585** *Victorian B&B, full brkfst*

Lafayette Hotel & Suites [GF,F,SW,NS,WI,WC] 2223 El Cajon Blvd (btwn Louisiana & Mississippi) **619/296-2101** *also restaurant*

Pier South Resort [GS] 800 Seacoast Dr, Imperial Beach **619/621-5900** *steps from the ocean, restaurant on the beach*

Scripps Inn [GS] 555 Coast Blvd S (La Jolla) **888/976-2912** *14 room boutique B&B, short drive to Black's (gay)beach*

The Sofia Hotel [GS,F,WC] 150 W Broadway **619/234-9200, 800/826-0009** *boutique hotel with charm located a step away from the Gaslamp Quarter*

La Valencia Hotel [GS,SW] 132 Prospect St (La Jolla) **855/476-6870** *in the heart of downtown La Jolla, ask for a beach view room, pets ok*

Bars

The Brass Rail [MW,D,F,WC] 3796 5th Ave (at Robinson) **619/298-2233** *11am-2am. from 10am wknds, csld Tue-Wed, theme nights, Latin night Sat*

Brick Bar [GS] 1475 University Ave (at Herbert St) **619/291-8221** *4pm-midnight, from noon Fri-Sun,clsd Mon-Wed, sushi & wknds brunch*

The Caliph [M,E,F,K,P,OC,WC] 3100 5th Ave (at Redwood) **619/298-9495** *noon-2am, from 1pm wknds, piano bar*

Cheers [M,NH] 1839 Adams Ave (at Park) **619/298-3269** *11am-2am, patio*

Fiesta Cantina 142 University Ave **619/298-2500** *noon-2am, from 11am wknds, Mexican restaurant*

Flicks [★M,K,V,YC] 1017 University Ave (at 10th Ave) **619/297-2056** *4pm-2am, from noon wknds*

Gossip Grill [W,F,WC,GO] 1440 University Ave (at Normal) **619/260-8023** *2pm-close, also restaurant*

The Hole in the Wall [M] 2820 Lytton St (at Rosecrans) **619/996-9000** *4pm-2pm, from noon Sun*

The Loft [M,NH,WC] 3610 5th Ave (at Brookes) **619/296-6407** *11am-2am*

No 1 Fifth Ave (no sign) [M,NH,V] 3845 5th Ave (at University) **619/299-1911** *noon-2am, patio*

Pecs [M,NH,B,L,WC] 2046 University Ave (at Alabama) **619/296-0889** *noon-2am, from 10am Sun, patio, cruisy*

Redwing Bar & Grill [M,NH,K] 4012 30th St (at Lincoln, North Park) **619/281-8700** *11am-2am, patio*

San Diego Eagle [M,NH,L,WC] 3040 North Park Wy (at 30th) **619/295-8072** *4pm-2am, from 2pm Fri-Sun*

SRO Lounge [M,NH,TG,OC] 1807 5th Ave (btwn Elm & Fir) **619/232-1886** *10am-2am, cocktail lounge*

Nightclubs

Rich's [★M,D,V,S,YC] 1051 University Ave (at Vermont) **619/295-2195** *open Wed-Sun, theme nights, L.L. Bear [B,L] 3rd Sat*

Cafes

Babycakes [BW] 3766 5th Ave (at Robinson) **619/296-4173** *9am-11pm, till midnight Fri-Sat, patio*

The Big Kitchen [WC] 3003 Grape St (at 30th) **619/234-5789** *8am-2pm*

Extraordinary Desserts 2929 5th Ave **619/294-2132** *also store in Little Italy: 1430 Union, 619/249-7001, the name says it all*

Gelato Vero [WI] 3753 India St **619/295-9269** *7am-midnight, great desserts (yes, the gelato is truly delicious) & coffee*

Twiggs 4590 Park Blvd (at Madison Ave, University Heights) **619/296-0616** *7am-11pm*

Restaurants

2GOOD2B [GO] 204 N El Camino Real #H, Encinitas **619/942-4663** *7am-5pm, 8am-2pm Sun, clsd Mon, where everything is delicious, without gluten, corn or soy*

Arrivederci 3845 4th Ave **619/299-6282** *lunch & dinner*

Baja Betty's [★MW,WC] 1421 University Ave (at Normal St) **619/269-8510** *11am-midnight, till 1am Fri-Sat, Mexican, patio*

Cafe 222 222 Island Ave **619/236-9902** *7am-2pm, great brkfst*

Cody's La Jolla 8030 Girard Ave (at Coast Blvd S), La Jolla **858/459-0040** *brkfst & lunch daily, contemporary California cuisine*

The Cottage 7702 Fay (at Klein), La Jolla **858/454-8409** *7:30am-3pm*

Crazee Burger [BW] 4201 30th St (at Howard) **619/282-6044** *11am-10pm, till 11pm Fri-Sat*

Crest Cafe [WC] 425 Robinson (btwn 4th & 5th) **619/295-2510** *7am-midnight*

El Camino 2400 India St (at Kalmia, in Little Italy) **619/685-3881** *dinner nightly, Sun brunch, kitschy Mexican, live music, full bar*

Hash House A Go Go 3628 5th Ave **619/298-4646** *7:30am-2pm & 5:30pm-9pm, clsd Mon night, great brkfst*

Hillcrest Brewing Company [MW] 1458 University Ave (at Normal St) **619/269-4323** *3pm-midnight, world's first gay brewery*

insideOUT 1642 University Ave #100 **619/888-8623** *2pm-11pm, from 11am wknds, great ambience & full bar*

Jimmy Carter's Mexican Cafe 3172 5th Ave (at Spruce) **619/295-2070** *8am-9pm*

Juniper and Ivy 2228 Kettner Blvd **619/269-9036** *bar from 4pm, creative space with outdoor dining and famous Top Chef alum*

Kous Kous 3940 4th Ave, Ste 110 (beneath Martinis on Fourth) **619/295-5560** *5pm-10pm, clsd Mon, Moroccan*

Lips [DS] 3036 El Cajon Blvd **619/295-7900** *5pm-close, Sun gospel brunch, clsd Mon, "the ultimate in drag dining," Bitchy Bingo Wed, celeb impersonation Th*

Luna Grill 350 University Ave **619/296-5862** *11am-10pm, Near East & Mediterranean, plenty veggie/vegan*

Martinis Above Fourth [C,P,GO] 3940 4th Ave, Ste 200 (btwn Washington & University) **619/400-4500** *4pm-midnight, till 1am Fri-Sat, from 3pm Sun*

The Mission 3795 Mission Blvd (at San Jose), Mission Beach **858/488-9060** *7am-3pm*

The Prado 1549 El Prado (in Balboa Park) **619/557-9441** *lunch & dinner, Latin/Italian fusion*

Roberto's Taco Shop 2744 El Cajon Blvd **619/584-0377** *8am-11:30pm, the best rolled tacos & guacamole, multiple locations*

Rudford's [★] 2900 El Cajon Blvd (at Kansas St) **619/282-8423** *24hrs, homestyle cooking*

Rustic Root [E] 535 5th Ave **619/232-1747** *4pm-2am, from 9am wknds, Gaslamp's only rooftop restaurant, full bar*

Saigon on Fifth 3900 5th Ave, Ste 120 **619/220-8828** *11am-3am, Vietnamese*

Uptown Tavern 1236 University Ave (at Richmond) **619/241-2710** *4pm-2am, from 10:30 am wknds*

Urban Mo's [★MW,D,E,WC] 308 University Ave (at 3rd) **619/491-0400** *9am-1:30am, 3 full bars, patio*

Waffle Spot 1333 Hotel Circle S (at King's Inn) **619/297-2231** *7am-2pm*

West Coast Tavern 2895 University Ave **619/295-1688** *lunch & dinner, upscale, also lounge*

Entertainment & Recreation

Diversionary Theatre 4545 Park Blvd #101 (at Madison) **619/220-0097 (box office #), 619/220-6830** *LGBT theater*

Ocean Beach I-8 West to Sunset Cliffs Blvd *very dog-friendly*

Torrey Pines Beach State Park ("Blacks Beach") *popular nude beach, head north for the gay area*

Bookstores

Traveler's Depot 1655 Garnet Ave (btwn Jewell & Ingraham) **858/483-1421** *10am-6pm, 11am-5pm wknds, guides, maps & more*

Retail Shops

Auntie Helen's [WC] 4127 30th St (at Lincoln) **619/584-8438** *10am-6pm, clsd Sun, thrift shop benefits PWAs*

Manfest 1295 University Ave #1B **619/497-1970** *noon-9pm, till midnight Fri-Sat,*

Mankind [WI,GO] 1295 University Ave (at Richmond St) **619/497-1970** *noon-8am, till midnight Fri-Sat, favorite designer clothes, accessories, and adult goodies*

Publications

Blade California 562/314-7674

San Diego LGBT Weekly 1850 5th Ave (at Fir) **619/450-4288**

Gyms & Health Clubs

Last Real Gym 3148 University Ave (at Iowa St, North Park) **619/795-9712** *day passes*

Men's Clubs

Club San Diego [★PC] 3955 4th Ave (btwn Washington & University) **619/295-0850** *24hrs*

Erotica

Adult Emporium [GO] 3576 Main St (at San Diego) **619/239-1878** *24hrs*

Barnett Ave Adult Superstore 3610 Barnett Ave (near intersection of Barnett & Jessop Ln) **619/224-0187** *24hrs*

Barnett Ave Adult Superstore 3610 Barnett Ave (near intersection of Barnett & Jessop Ln) **619/224-0187** *24hrs*

Gemini Adult Books [WC] 5265 University Ave (at 52nd) **619/287-1402**

Pleasures & Treasures Adult/ Leather Shop [GO] 2525 University Ave (at Arnold) **619/822-4280** *11am-11pm, till 6pm Sun*

Romantix Adult Superstore 1407 University Ave (at Richmond) **619/299-7186**

Cruisy Areas

Please Note: All cruisy areas for San Diego have been removed because the SDPD aggressively polices these areas.

San Francisco

San Francisco is divided into 7 geographical areas:
SF—Overview
SF—Castro & Noe Valley
SF—South of Market
SF—Polk Street Area
SF—Downtown & North Beach
SF—Mission District
SF—Haight, Fillmore, Hayes Valley

SF—Overview

Info Lines & Services

AA Gay/ Lesbian 1821 Sacramento St **415/674-1821** *check www.aasf.org for meeting times*

The Center for Sex & Culture 1349 Mission St (btwn 10th & 11th St) **415/902-2071** *very queer-friendly classes, workshops, gatherings, events, readings & more*

The San Francisco LGBT Community Center 1800 Market St (at Octavia) **415/865-5555** *9am-8pm, till 5pm Fri-Sat, clsd Sun*

Strut 470 Castro St **415/437-3400** *10am-6pm, till 8pm Wed-Th, clsd Sun, center for gay men's health*

Nightclubs

Gus Presents [★M]

Restaurants

Beach Chalet Brewery & Restaurant [E] 1000 Great Hwy (at Fulton St) **415/386-8439** *great location, located above the Golden Gate Park Visitor's Center*

Entertainment & Recreation

Baker Beach Lincoln Blvd at Bowley, in the Presidio *popular nude beach*

Black Sand Beach first exit past Golden Gate Bridge (Alexander) (go left under fwy, right on Outlook Rd, look for dirt parking lot), Golden Gate Nat'l Rec Area *popular nude beach, look for trail*

Castro Theatre 429 Castro (at Market) **415/621-6120** *art house cinema, many LGBT & cult classics, live organ evenings*

Cruisin' the Castro Tours tour meets at the rainbow flag at Harvey Milk Plaza (corner of Castro & Market) **415/255-1821** *"a TOP city tour & walking w/ pride since 1989! Diverse, fun, informative & NO hills!"*

Frameline [★] **415/703-8650** *LGBT media arts foundation that sponsors annual SF Int'l LGBT Film Festival in June*

Golden Gate Bridge Beach/ Marshall Beach, aka "Nasty Boy Beach" [N,AYOR] Lincoln Blvd at Langdon Ct, in the Presidio *can get very crowded!*

The Intersection for the Arts [GF] 925 Mission St #109 **415/626-2787** *San Francisco's oldest alternative arts space (since 1965!) w/ plays, art exhibitions, live jazz, literary series, performance art & much more*

Local Tastes of the City Tours [GO] **888/358-8687** *explore history & culture of local neighborhoods as "we eat our way through San Francisco"*

The Marsh 1062 Valencia (at 22nd St) **415/826-5750, 415/282-3055** *queer-positive theater*

National AIDS Memorial Grove [WC] Golden Gate Park (on corner of Middle Drive East & Bowling Green Dr) **415/765-0497** *guided tours available 9am-noon every 3rd Sat*

New Conservatory Theatre Center 25 Van Ness Ave, Lower Lobby (at Market) **415/861-8972** *LGBT themed dramas, comedies & musicals, full bar*

QComedy Gay Comedy Showcase [★MW,$] **415/533-9133** *see www.qcomedy.com for location*

Steve Silver's Beach Blanket Babylon [★] 678 Beach Blanket Babylon Ave (formerly Green St) (btwn Powell & Columbus, in Club Fugazi) **415/421-4222** *the USA's longest running musical revue & wigs that must be seen to be believed; also restaurant & full bar*

Thanks Babs, the Day Tripper [GO] **702/370-6961**

Theatre Rhinoceros 1360 Mission St #200 **800/838-3006, 415/552-4100** *LGBT theater*

Victorian Home Walks [GO] **415/252-9485** *custom-tailored walking tours w/ San Francisco resident*

Yerba Buena Center for the Arts [GF] 701 Mission St (at 3rd St) **415/978-2787** *annual season includes wide variety of contemporary dance, theater & music, also film theater & gallery*

Publications

BAR (Bay Area Reporter) **415/861-5019** *the weekly LGBT newspaper*

Bay Times **415/503-1386** *bi-weekly*

Gloss Magazine **415/552-5070** *CA arts/ entertainment magazine, bi-weekly*

SF—Castro & Noe Valley

Accommodations

Beck's Motor Lodge [GF,WC] 2222 Market St (at Sanchez) **415/621-8212** *in the heart of the Castro (ie, cruisy)*

Inn on Castro [MW,NS,WI] 321 Castro St (btwn 16th & 17th) **415/861-0321** *full brkfst*

The Parker Guest House [★GS,NS,WI,GO] 520 Church St (at 17th) **415/621-3222** *guesthouse complex w/ gardens*

The Willows Inn [MW,NS,WI,GO] 710 14th St (at Church) **415/431-4770, 800/431-0277** *"amenities, comfort, great location"*

Bars

440 Castro [★M,NH,B,L] 440 Castro St **415/621-8732** *noon-2am, very cruisy*

Beaux [M,D] 2344 Market St (at Castro) *2pm-2am*

Blackbird [GS,NH,GO] 2124 Market St **415/503-0630** *3pm-2am*

The Cafe [MW,D,YC] 2369 Market St (at Castro) **415/861-3846** *5pm-2am, from 3pm Sat-Sun*

The Edge [M,NH,L] 4149 18th St **415/863-4027** *1pm-2am,from noon wknds, classic cruise bar*

Harvey's [★MW,NH,E,DS,WC] 500 Castro St **415/431-4278** *11am-11pm, 9am-2am wknds, also restaurant*

Hi Tops [MW,F] 2247 Market St **415/551-2500** *noon-2am, from 10am Sun*

Last Call Bar [M,NH] 3988 18th St **415/861-1310** *noon-2am*

The Lookout [★M,F] 3600 16th St (at Market) **415/431-0306** *3:30pm-2am, from 12:30pm wknds*

Martuni's [GS,NH,P] 4 Valencia St (at Market) **415/241-0205** *4pm-2am, lounge, great martinis*

Midnight Sun [★M,V] 4067 18th St (at Castro) **415/861-4186** *2pm-2am, from 1pm Sat-Sun*

The Mint [MW,K] 1942 Market St (at Buchanan) **415/626-4726** *3pm-2am, from 2pm wknds*

The Mix [M,NH] 4086 18th St **415/431-8616** *7am-2am, heated patio*

Moby Dick [M,NH,V] 4049 18th St (at Hartford) *noon-2am*

Pilsner Inn [★M,NH,YC] 225 Church St (at Market) **415/621-7058** *10am-2am, great patio*

Q Bar [★M,NH,D,WC] 456 Castro St **415/864-2877** *4pm-2am, from 2pm wknds, sidewalk patio*

SF Badlands [M,NH,D,V,WC] 4121 18th St (at Castro) **415/626-9320** *2pm-2am*

Swirl 572 Castro St (at 19th) **415/864-2262** *1:30pm-8pm, till 9pm Fri-Sat, from noon wknds, wine bar & wine store, tastings & events*

Twin Peaks Tavern [M,OC] 401 Castro St (at Market & 17th) **415/864-9470** *noon-2am, from 8am Th-Sun*

Cafes

Castro Country Club [MW] 4058 18th St (at Hartford) **415/552-6102** *alcohol- & drug-free space*

Duboce Park Cafe [F] 2 Sanchez St (at Duboce) **415/621-1108** *7am-8pm, outdoor seating*

Flore [★MW,WI] 2298 Market St (at Noe) **415/621-8579** *7am-2am, full bar, great patio to see & be seen, come early for a seat*

Restaurants

Anchor Oyster Bar [★BW] 579 Castro St (at 19th) **415/431-3990** *11:30am-10pm, from 4pm Sun*

Catch 2362 Market St **415/431-5000** *lunch & dinner, wknd brunch, seafood*

Chow [★] 215 Church St (at Market) **415/552-2469** *8am-11pm, till midnight wknds, patio*

Cove Cafe [★WC] 434 Castro St **415/626-0462** *8am-9pm, publisher's favorite*

Eric's Chinese Restaurant [★] 1500 Church St (at 27th St) **415/282-0919** *11am-9pm*

Finn Town Tavern [GO] 2251 Market St **415/626-3466** *5pm-11am, 10am-3pm wknds*

Firewood Cafe 4248 18th St (at Diamond St) **415/252-0999** *11am-11pm, rotisserie chicken, pastas, oven-fired pizzas, salads*

Hot Cookie 407 Castro St **415/621-2350** *11am-1am, hot cookies!*

Kasa Indian Eatery 4001 18th St (at Noe) **415/621-6940** *11am-10pm, till 11pm Fri-Sat, plenty veggie*

La Mediterranée [BW] 288 Noe (at Market) **415/431-7210** *11am-10pm, till 11pm Sat-Sun*

Mama Ji's 4415 18th St **415/626-4416** *11am-2:30pm & 5:30-9:30pm, from 9am wknds, great Dim sum in the Castro*

Orphan Andy's [GO] 3991 17th St **415/864-9795** *24hrs, diner*

Papi Rico 544 Castro St **415/655-3514** *from 4pm & 11am wknds, patio, full bar Cantina in the Castro*

Poesia Osteria Italiana 4072 18th St (at Collingwood) **415/252-9325** *dinner nighly, Italian, great food & full bar*

Takara Sushi 4243 18th St (at Diamond) **415/626-7864** *lunch & dinner, clsd Tue*

Woodhouse Fish Co 2073 Market St (at 14th) **415/437-2722** *noon-9:30pm, New England clam shack-style seafood, also 1914 Fillmore St*

Zuni Cafe [★] 1658 Market St (at Franklin) **415/552-2522** *lunch & dinner, clsd Mon, upscale SF classic spot, full bar*

Entertainment & Recreation

GLBT History Museum 4127 18th St (at Castro) **415/621-1107** *11am-7pm, noon-5pm Sun, clsd Tue*

Great Tan 329 Noe St **415/701-1080** *7am-9:30pm, till 6:30pm Sat-Sun, also at 2286 Union St*

Pink Triangle Park near Market & Castro *"in remembrance of LGBT victims of the Nazi regime"*

Bookstores

Aardvark Books 227 Church St **415/552-6733** *10:30am-10:30pm, mostly used, good LGBT section*

Retail Shops

HRC Action Center & Store 575 Castro St **415/431-2200** *10am-8pm, till 7pm Sun, Human Rights Campaign merchandise & info*

Kenneth Wingard 2319 Market St (btwn Castro & Noe) **415/431-6900**

Rolo [★] 2351 Market St **415/431-4545** *11am-7pm, till 6pm Sun, designer labels*

Gyms & Health Clubs

SF Fitness Castro 2301 Market St **415/348-6377** *day passes available*

Men's Clubs

The Academy [M,MR,E,BYOB,WI,PC] 2166 Market St **415/624-3429** *open Wed-Sat, membership-based social club and barbershop, out of town visitors are welcome to inquire about a special guest pass*

Eros [PC] 2051 Market St (btwn Church & Dolores) **415/864-3767** *noon-midnight, till 3am Fri-Sat, safer-sex club, theme nights, massage available, gay public bath house*

Erotica

Chaps 4057 18th St (btwn Castro & Hartford) **415/863-1699** *10am-11pm, till midnight Fri-Sat*

Rock Hard 518 Castro St (at 18th St) **415/437-2430** *9:30am-midnight, till 2am-Wed-Sat*

Cruisy Areas

Collingwood Park [AYOR] (btwn 18th & 19th Sts) *Castro merry-go-round, after bars close*

SF—South of Market

Accommodations

Holiday Inn Civic Center [GF,SW,WI,WC] 50 8th St (at Market) **415/626-6103, 800/972-3124** *great location for Folsom & Dore street fairs*

The Mosser Hotel [GS,NS] 54 4th St (btwn Market & Mission) **415/986-4400, 800/227-3804** *1913 landmark, also restaurant & full bar*

Park Central Hotel [GF,NS] 50 3rd St **415/974-6400** *sauna*

Proper Hotel [GS,NS,WI,WC] 45 McAllister St (at Market St) **415/735-7777** *1909 historical landmark building, lounge, restaurant*

Bars

Club OMG [GS,D] 43 6th St **415/896-64s3** *6pm-2am, gay bollywood events*

The Eagle Tavern [★M,L,E] 398 12th St (at Harrison) **415/626-0880** *2pm-2am, from noon wknds, great beer bust Sun, patio*

Hole in the Wall Saloon [★M,NH,L] 1369 Folsom (btwn 10th & Dore) **415/431-4695** *noon-2am, "a nasty little biker bar"*

Lone Star Saloon [★M,B,L] 1354 Harrison St (btwn 9th & 10th) **415/863-9999** *4pm-2am, from 2pm Sat, noon Sun*

Novela [GS,GO] 662 Mission St **415/896-6500** *4pm-1am, swank literary-themed late-night lounge*

Powerhouse [★M,NH,L] 1347 Folsom St (at Dore Alley) **415/552-8689** *4pm-2am, theme nights, popular wknds w/ DJ, patio, cruisy*

Nightclubs

Asia SF [★GS,D,MR-A,S,$] 201 9th St (at Howard) **415/255-2742** *10pm-close Wed-Sat, theme nights, go-go boys, also Cal-Asian restaurant w/ en-drag dinner service*

Bootie SF [★GF,D,E,$] 375 11th St (at Harrison, at DNA Lounge) **415/626-1409 (DNA info line)** *9pm-3am Sat,, mashups, bootlegs, bastard pop*

Cat Club [★GS,D] 1190 Folsom St (at 8th) **415/703-8965** *hosts many one-night clubs & events*

Endup [GS,D,MR] 401 6th St (at Harrison) **415/646-0999 (info line), 415/357-0827** *theme nights, popular Sun mornings*

Go BANG! [MW,D] 399 9th St (at The Stud) *1st Sat only, underground 70s-80s disco*

Honey Soundsystem [M,D,B] *check site for events, local DJ collective*

Mezzanine [GS,D,MR,TG,E,WC,$] 444 Jessie (at Mint) **415/625-8880** *9pm-close, live music, big name DJs, call for events*

Oasis [M,D,DS,E] 298 11th St **415/595-3725** *4pm-2am*

The Stud [★MW,D,YC] 399 9th St (at Harrison) **415/863-6623** *5pm-2am, theme nights*

Restaurants

Ananda Fuara 1298 Market St (at 9th) **415/621-1994** *8am-8pm, till 3pm Sun, clsd Mon, vegetarian*

Anchor & Hope 83 Minna St (at 2nd St) **415/501-9100** *lunch Mon-Fri, dinner nightly, seafood*

Don Ramon's Mexican Restaurant 225 11th St (btwn Howard & Folsom) **415/864-2700** *lunch Tue-Fri, dinner nightly, clsd Mon, some veggie, full bar*

Fringale [★WC] 570 4th St (btwn Bryant & Brannan) **415/543-0573** *lunch Tue-Fri & dinner nightly, French bistro*

Rocco's Cafe [★] 1131 Folsom St (at 7th) **415/554-0522** *brkfst & lunch daily, dinner Tue-Sat only, Italian*

The Slanted Door [★R] 1 Ferry Building #3 **415/861-8032** *lunch & dinner, Vietnamese, full bar*

Ted's 1530 Howard St (at 11th) **415/552-0309** *6am-6pm, 8am-5pm wknds, excellent deli sandwiches*

Tu Lan 8 6th St (at Market) **415/626-0927** *lunch & dinner, clsd Sun, Vietnamese, dicey neighborhood but delicious (& cheap) food*

Retail Shops

Mr S Leather & Fetters USA San Francisco 385 8th St (at Harrison) **415/863-7764, 800/746-7677** *11am-7pm, erotic goods, custom leather & latex*

Gyms & Health Clubs

SF Fitness [★] 1001 Brannan St (at 9th) **415/348-6377** *day passes available*

Men's Clubs

442 Natoma 442 Natoma (btwn 5th & 6th St) **415/936-5037** *play parties Fri-Mon, slings, glory holes, play beds, dark room, 2 levels*

Blow Buddies [★MO,L,V,PC,GO] 933 Harrison (btwn 5th & 6th) **415/777-4323** *open late Wed-Sun, clsd Mon-Tue*

SF Jacks 1349 Mission St **415/267-6999** *2nd & 4th Mon, doors open 7:30pm-8:30pm only, mandatory clothes check*

Erotica

Folsom Gulch 947 Folsom (btwn 5th & 6th) **415/495-6402** *10am-2am, 24hrs Fri-Sat, hot arcade action, serving the gay community for over 25 years!*

Good Vibrations [★WC] 899 Mission St (at 5th St) **415/513-1635, 800/289-8423** *10am-9pm, till 11pm Fri-Sat, clean, well-lighted sex toy store*

Cruisy Areas

Folsom St [AYOR] btwn 5th & 6th *late*

SF—Polk Street Area

Accommodations

Nob Hill Motor Inn [GF,NS,WI,WC] 1630 Pacific Ave (at Van Ness Ave) **415/775-8160, 800/343-6900** *walking distance to Fisherman's Wharf, free parking (!)*

The Phoenix Hotel [★GF,SW,WI] 601 Eddy St (at Larkin) **415/776-1380, 800/248-9466** *1950s-style motor lodge, fave of celebrity rockers*

Bars

The Cinch [M,NH,WI,WC] 1723 Polk St (at Clay) **415/776-4162** *9am-2am, from 6am wknds patio, lots of pool tables & no attitude, [D] Th-Sat, [DS] Fri*

Edinburgh Castle [GF,NH,E] 950 Geary St (at Polk) **415/885-4074** *5pm-2am, Scottish pub w/ single malts & authentic fish & chips (at shop around corner)*

Lush Lounge [GS,NH,WC] 1092 Post (at Polk) **415/771-2022** *3pm-2am, from 1pm wknds*

Nightclubs

Divas [M,NH,D,TG,DS] 1081 Post St (at Larkin) **415/474-3482** *7am-2am, TS/TVs & their admirers*

Restaurants

Grubstake II [BW] 1525 Pine St (at Polk) **415/673-8268** *5pm-4am, from 8am wknds, diner/ Portuguese*

Street 2141 Polk St (btwn Broadway & Vallejo) **415/775-1055** *dinner, clsd Mon, incredible hamburgers*

Bookstores

Books Inc Opera Plaza [★] 601 Van Ness Ave (at Turk) **415/776-1111** *8:30am-9pm, general, LGBT section, readings*

Erotica

Good Vibrations [★] 1620 Polk St (btwn Sacramento & Clay) **415/345-0400**

Cruisy Areas

Polk St [AYOR] btwn Geary & California Sts *hustlers*

SF—Downtown & North Beach

Accommodations

Adante Hotel [GS,NS,WC] 610 Geary St (at Jones) **415/673-9221, 888/423-0083** *in Union Square/ Theater District, kids ok*

Andrews Hotel [GF,NS,WI] 624 Post St (btwn Taylor & Jones) **415/563-6877, 800/926-3739** *Victorian hotel, also Italian restaurant*

Argonaut Hotel [GF,NS,WC] 495 Jefferson St (at Hyde) **415/563-0800, 800/790-1415** *boutique hotel in Fisherman's Wharf*

Cartwright Hotel [GF,WI,NS] 524 Sutter St (at Powell) **415/421-2865** *B&B-inn on Union Square*

Executive Hotel Vintage Court [GF,NS,WI,WC] 650 Bush St (at Powell) **415/392-4666, 888/388-3932** *also world-famous 5-star Masa's restaurant, French*

Galleria Park Hotel [GS,WI,NS,WC] 191 Sutter St (at Kearny) **415/781-3060, 800/792-9639** *boutique hotel*

Grand Hyatt San Francisco [GF,WI] 345 Stockton St (at Sutter) **415/398-1234** *restaurant & lounge, gym*

Handlery Union Square Hotel [GF,SW,WI,WC] 351 Geary St **415/781-7800, 800/995-4874** *steps from Union Square*

Harbor Court Hotel [GF,SW,WI,WC] 165 Steuart St (btwn Howard & Mission) **415/882-1300, 866/792-6283** *in the heart of the Financial District, gym*

Hilton San Francisco Financial District [GS] 750 Kearny St (at Clay) **415/433-6600**

Hotel Abri [GF,WI] 127 Ellis St (at Powell) **415/392-8800, 888/229-0677** *boutique hotel*

Hotel Adagio [GF,WC] 550 Geary St (at Shannon) **415/775-5000**

Hotel Carlton [GF] 1075 Sutter (at Larkin) **415/673-0242, 800/922-7586** *also restaurant*

Hotel Diva [GF,NS,WI] 440 Geary (at Mason) **415/885-0200, 844/592-4559** *hip hotel, gym*

Hotel Fusion [GS,NS,WI,WC] 140 Ellis St (at Powell St) **415/568-2525, 855/455-0755**

Hotel Griffon [GS,WI,WC] 155 Steuart St (at Mission) **415/495-2100, 800/321-2201** *also restaurant, bistro/cont'l*

Hotel Metropolis [GF,WI,NS] 25 Mason St (at Eddy) **415/775-4600, 877/628-4412** *near Union Square shopping*

Hotel Nikko San Francisco [GF,SW,NS,WC] 222 Mason St (at Ellis) **415/394-1111, 866/645-5673** *health club & spa, also ANZU restaurant*

The Hotel Rex [GF,WC] 562 Sutter St (at Powell) **415/433-4434, 800/433-4434** *full bar*

Hotel Triton [GF,WI,WC] 342 Grant Ave (at Bush) **877/793-9931** *designer theme rooms*

Hotel Union Square [GF,WI] 114 Powell St (at Ellis) **415/397-3000, 800/553-1900** *1930s art deco lobby*

Hotel Vitale [GF,NS,WI,WC] 8 Mission St (at Steuart) **415/278-3700, 888/890-8688** *4-star, full-service waterfront luxury hotel, rooftop spa, restaurant & bar*

Hotel Zeppelin [GF,NS,WI] 545 Post St (btwn Taylor & Mason) **415/563-0303, 888/539-7510** *small boutique hotel*

Hotel Zetta [GS,WI] 55 5th St **415/543-8555**

Hotel Zoe [GF,WC] 425 N Point St (at Mason) **415/561-1100, 888/648-4626**

Hyatt Regency San Francisco [GF,NS,WI] 5 Embarcadero Center (at California) **415/788-1234, 800/233-1234** *waterfront hotel*

The Inn at Union Square [GF,NS,WI] 440 Post St (at Powell) **415/397-3510** *complimentary breakfast and wine and cheese daily*

Kensington Park Hotel [GF,NS,WI] 450 Post St **415/788-6400** *on Union Square*

Nob Hill Hotel [GS,NS,WC] 835 Hyde St (btwn Bush & Sutter) **415/885-2987** *European-style hotel, jacuzzi*

Petite Auberge [GF,NS] 863 Bush St (at Taylor) **415/928-6000**

Serrano Hotel [GF,WI,WC] 405 Taylor St (at O'Farrell) **415/885-2500, 866/289-6561** *in Theater District*

Sir Francis Drake Hotel [GF,WI] 450 Powell St (at Sutter) **415/392-7755** *1928 landmark, also restaurant & Starlight Room*

Tilden Hotel [GF,WI,WC] 345 Taylor St (at Ellis) **415/673-2332, 877/854-4106** *restaurant*

The Touchstone Hotel [GF,WC] 480 Geary St (btwn Mason & Taylor) **415/771-1600** *in Theater District, full brkfst*

Vertigo Hotel [GS,NS,WI,WC] 940 Sutter St (at Leavenworth) **415/885-6800, 888/444-4605** *boutique hotel*

Villa Florence Hotel [GF,WI] 225 Powell St (at Geary) **877/564-2086** *Union Square boutique hotel, also Kuleto's restaurant, Italian*

Bars

Aunt Charlie's Lounge [M,NH,DS] 133 Turk St (at Taylor) **415/441-2922** *noon-2am, from 10am wknds, [DS] wknds*

Bourbon & Branch [GS,R] 501 Jones St (at O'Farrell) **415/931-7292** *in Prohibition-era speakeasy, drinks are worth the price*

Ginger's Trois [GS,GO] 246 Kearny St **415/989-0282** *open 5pm Thur-Sat*

CAFES

Caffe Trieste [★] 601 Vallejo St **415/392-6739** *get a taste of the real North Beach (past & present)*

RESTAURANTS

The Buena Vista 2765 Hyde St (at Beach) **415/474-5044** *9am-2am, from 8am wknds, the restaurant that introduced Irish coffee to America*

Le Colonial 20 Cosmo Pl (btwn Taylor & Jones) **415/931-3600** *dinner nightly, Vietnamese, full bar*

Mario's Bohemian Cigar Store Cafe [BW,WI] 566 Columbus Ave (at Union) **415/362-0536** *10am-close, great foccacia sandwiches*

ENTERTAINMENT & RECREATION

Feinstein's [★GS,C,WC] 222 Mason (at Nikko Hotel) **866/663-1063** *cabaret w/ world-class performers*

Sunday's A Drag@The Starlight Room [MW,E,$] 450 Mason St (at Sutter) **415/395-8595** *Sun brunch, noon & 2:30pm drag shows*

BOOKSTORES

Book Passage 1 Ferry Bldg #42 **415/835-1020** *10am-7pm, from 8am Sat, 10am-6pm Sun, independent*

City Lights Bookstore 261 Columbus Ave (at Pacific) **415/362-8193** *10am-midnight, historic beatnik bookstore, many progressive titles, LGBT section, whole floor dedicated to poetry*

SEX CLUBS

Power Exchange [GS] 220 Jones St **415/487-9944**

EROTICA

Good Vibrations [★W,WC] 189 Kearny St (at Sutter) **415/653-1364** *11am-8pm, till 6pm Sun*

Video Secrets 389 Bay St (at Mason) **415/391-9349** *10am-midnight, digital arcade that has a HOLE lot going on*

SF—Mission District

includes Bernal Heights

ACCOMMODATIONS

The Inn San Francisco [GF,NS,WI] 943 S Van Ness Ave (btwn 20th & 21st) **415/641-0188, 800/359-0913** *Victorian mansion*

Noe's Nest B&B [GF,NS] 1257 Guerrero St (btwn 24th & 25th Sts) **415/821-0751** *kitchens, fireplace*

BARS

El Rio [★GS,NH,MR,E] 3158 Mission St (at Cesar Chavez) **415/282-3325** *5pm-close Mon-Th, from 3pm wknds, patio*

Phone Booth [GS,NH] 1398 S Van Ness Ave (at 25th) **415/648-4683** *11am-2am*

Virgil's Sea Room [GS,GO] 3152 Mission St (at Precita) **415/829-2233** *4pm-2am,from 2pm wknds. patio*

Wild Side West [GS,WC] 424 Cortland, Bernal Heights (at Wool) **415/647-3099** *2pm-2am, patio, magic garden*

Zeitgeist [★GS,F] 199 Valencia St (at Duboce) **415/255-7505** *9am-2am, divey biker bar & beer garden*

NIGHTCLUBS

Hard French [MW,D,MR,F,$] *check www.hardfrench.com for events*

The Make-Out Room [GS,D,E] 3225 22nd St (at Mission) **415/647-2888** *6pm-2am*

Sundance Saloon [★MW,D,CW,GO,$] 550 Barneveld Ave (at space550, 2 blocks off Bayshore Blvd at Industrial) **415/820-1403** *5pm-10:30pm Sun (lessons at 5:30pm) & 6:30pm-10:30pm Th (lessons at 7pm)*

CAFES

Dolores Park Cafe [★F,E] 501 Dolores St (at 18th St) **415/621-2936** *7am-8pm, outdoor seating overlooking Dolores Park, live music Fri*

Farleys [E] 1315 18th St (at Texas St, Potrero Hill) **415/648-1545** *6:30am-9:30pm, from 7:30am wknds*

The Revolution Cafe [E] 3248 22nd St (btwn Mission & Bartlett) **415/642-0474** *9am-1am*

Tartine Bakery [★] 600 Guerrero St (at 18th St) **415/487-2600** *8am-7pm, from 9am Sun, French bakery w/ a line out the door*

Restaurants

Aslam's Rasoi 1037 Valencia St (at 21st) **415/695-0599** *5pm-11pm, Indian & Pakistani*

Delfina [★R] 3621 18th St (at Dolores) **415/552-4055** *5:30pm-10pm, excellent Tuscan cuisine, full bar, patio (summers)*

El Farolito [★] 2779 Mission St (at 24th) **415/824-7877** *10am-3am, delicious, cheap burritos & more*

Just For You [★MW] 722 22nd St (at 3rd St) **415/647-3033** *7:30am-3pm, Southern brkfst*

Moki's Sushi & Pacific Grill 615 Cortland Ave (at Moultine) **415/970-9336** *dinner nightly*

Pauline's Pizza Pie [★BW] 260 Valencia St (btwn 14th & Duboce) **415/552-2050** *5pm-10pm, clsd Sun-Mon, gourmet pizza*

Picaro [BW,WC] 3120 16th St (at Valencia) **415/431-4089** *5pm-10pm, from 9:30am wknds, Spanish tapas bar*

Pork Store Cafe [★BW] 3122 16th St (at Valencia) **415/626-5523** *8am-4pm daily & 7pm-3am Fri-Sat, American/ diner food, great breakfasts; also 1451 Haight St, 415/864-6981*

Entertainment & Recreation

Dolores "Beach" Church & 19th St (at the top corner of Dolores Park) *popular "beach" in Dolores Park, crowded on sunny days*

Bookstores

Dog Eared Books 900 Valencia St (at 20th) **415/282-1901** *10am-10pm, till 8pm Sun, new & used, good LGBT section*

Retail Shops

Black & Blue Tattoo [★TG] 381 Guerrero St (at 16th St) **415/626-0770** *noon-7pm, queer-, gender-fluid-, trans- & POC-friendly*

Body Manipulations 3234 16th St (btwn Guerrero & Dolores) **415/621-0408** *noon-7pm, piercing (walk-in basis), jewelry*

Erotica

Good Vibrations [★W,WC] 603 Valencia St (at 17th St) **415/522-5460, 800/289-8423** *10am-10pm, till11pm Fri-Satt, clean, well-lighted sex toy store*

SF—Haight, Fillmore, Hayes Valley

Accommodations

The Buchanan [GF,NS,WI] 1800 Sutter St (at Buchanan) **415/921-4000** *in Japantown, restaurant & bar*

The Chateau Tivoli B&B [GF,NS,WI] 1057 Steiner St (at Golden Gate) **415/776-5462, 800/228-1647** *historic SF B&B*

Hayes Valley Inn [GS,NS,WI] 417 Gough St (at Hayes) **415/431-9131** *European-style pension, shared baths*

Hotel Del Sol [★GS,NS,SW,WI,WC] 3100 Webster St (at Greenwich) **415/921-5520, 877/433-5765**

Hotel Drisco [GF,NS] 2901 Pacific Ave (at Broderick) **415/346-2880, 800/634-7277** *1903 luxury hotel in Pacific Heights*

Hotel Kabuki [GF,WC] 1625 Post St (at Laguna) **415/922-3200** *in Japantown*

Inn at the Opera [GF,F,WI,WC] 333 Fulton St (at Franklin) **415/863-8400, 866/729-7182**

Jackson Court [GF,NS,WI] 2198 Jackson St (at Buchanan) **415/929-7670**

The Laurel Inn [GF,NS] 444 Presidio Ave (at Sacramento) **415/567-8467, 800/552-8735** *'60s sophicate hotel in Pacific Heights*

Metro Hotel [GF,WI] 319 Divisadero St (at Haight) **415/861-5364** *European-style pension*

Queen Anne Hotel [GF,NS,WI,GO] 1590 Sutter St (at Octavia) **415/441-2828**

Stanyan Park Hotel [GF,NS,WC] 750 Stanyan St (at Waller) **415/751-1000** *historic Victorian*

Bars

Trax [M,NH] 1437 Haight St (at Masonic) **415/864-4213** *noon-2am*

Nightclubs

Cockblock [MW,D,MR] 155 Fell St (at Rickshaw Shop) *10pm 2am 2nd Sat*

Rickshaw Stop [★GS,F,E] 155 Fell St (btwn Van Ness & Franklin) **415/861-2011** *hipster bar, live bands*

Underground SF [GS,D,A] 424 Haight St (at Webster) **415/745-1921** *10pm-2am, clsd Sun, theme nights, call for events, more gay Sat*

Cafes

Blue Bottle Coffee Company [★] 315 Linden St (at Gough St) **510/653-3394** *7am6pm, from 8am wknds, organic coffee & treats from kiosk in front of artists' workshop—wonderful hidden treat*

Restaurants

Absinthe Brasserie & Bar 398 Hayes St (at Gough) **415/551-1590** *11:30-11pm, till midnight Fri-Sat, till 10pm Sun • upscale SF classic*

Alamo Square Seafood Grill 803 Fillmore (at Grove) **415/440-2828** *dinner only*

Burma Superstar [★] 309 Clement St **415/387-2147** *lunch & dinner, Burmese food that will rock your world*

Eliza's [★] 2877 California (at Broderick) **415/621-4819** *lunch Mon-Wed, dinner nightly, excellent Chinese food*

Ella's 500 Presidio Ave (at California) **415/441-5669** *brkfst & lunch Mon-Fri, popular wknd brunch*

Garibaldi's [WC,GO] 347 Presidio Ave (at Sacramento) **415/563-8841** *lunch weekdays, dinner nightly, Mediterranean, full bar*

Greens [★] Fort Mason, Bldg A (near Van Ness & Bay) **415/771-6222** *lunch Tue-Sat, dinner Mon-Sat, Sun brunch, gourmet vegetarian, spectacular view of the Golden Gate Bridge*

Memphis Minnie's BBQ 576 Haight St **415/864-7675** *11am-10pm, till 9pm Sun, clsd Mon*

Nopa 560 Divisadero St (at Hayes) **415/864-8643** *6pm-midnight, bar from 5pm, from 10:30am wknds, urban rustic*

Patxi's Chicago Pizza 511 Hayes St (at Octavia St) **415/558-9991** *11am-10pm, clsd Mon, Chicago-style deep dish pizza, also thin crust*

Suppenküche [BW,GO] 601 Hayes (at Laguna) **415/252-9289** *dinner, Sun brunch, German cuisine served at communal tables*

Thep-Phanom [BW] 400 Waller St (at Fillmore) **415/431-2526** *5:30pm-10:30pm, excellent Thai food, worth the wait!*

Bookstores

The Booksmith 1644 Haight St **415/863-8688** *cool independent, big-name author readings*

Retail Shops

Cold Steel America 1783 Haight St **415/621-7233** *noon-8pm, piercing & tattoo studio*

Flight 001 525 Hayes St (btwn Octavia & Laguna) **415/487-1001** *11am-7pm, till 6pm Sun, way cool travel gear*

Timbuk 2 Store 506 Hayes St **415/252-9860** *11am-7pm, noon-6pm Sun, messenger-style bags & backpacks*

Gyms & Health Clubs

Kabuki Springs & Spa 1750 Geary Blvd (at Fillmore) **415/922-6000** *10am-9:45pm, traditional Japanese bath w/ extensive menu of spa sevices*

Cruisy Areas

Buena Vista Park [AYOR] Haight St (btwn Baker & Central) *evenings in northern & highest part*

Land's End [AYOR] NW tip of SF *inquire locally*

San Jose

includes Campbell & Los Gatos; see also Cupertino, Santa Clara & Sunnyvale

Info Lines & Services

AA Gay/ Lesbian 408/374-8511 *24hr helpline, check www.aasanjose.org for meetings*

Billy DeFrank LGBT Community Center [WC] 938 The Alameda **408/293-3040** *4pm-9pm, from 6pm Fri, 1pm-4pm Sat*

Accommodations

Hotel De Anza [GF,F,E,WC,NS] 233 W Santa Clara St **408/286-1000, 800/843-3700** *art deco gem*

Moorpark Hotel [GF,SW,WC] 4241 Moorpark Ave **408/864-0300, 877/740-6622** *also bar & restaurant*

Bars

The Caravan Lounge [GS,NH,K] 98 S Almaden Ave **408/995-6220** *11am-2am*

Mac's Club [M,NH] 39 Post St (btwn 1st & Market) **408/288-8221** *noon-2am, patio*

Renegades [M,NH,B,L] 501 W Taylor St (at Coleman Ave) **408/275-9902** *4pm-2am, from 2pm wknds, clsd Mon, patio*

Nightclubs

Splash [M,D,K,DS,V,GO] 65 Post St (at 1st) **408/292-2222** *5pm-1:30am, from 4pm wknds*

Restaurants

Vin Santo 1346 Lincoln Ave **408/920-2508** *dinner nightly, clsd Mon, Northern Italian, wine bar*

Entertainment & Recreation

Tech Museum of Innovation 201 S Market St (at Park Ave) **408/294-8324** *10am-5pm, IMAX Dome Theater, a must-see for digital junkies*

Men's Clubs

Watergarden [★WI,18+,PC] 1010 The Alameda **408/275-1215** *24hrs, great outdoor patio & jacuzzi, Latino Th*

San Luis Obispo

Info Lines & Services

GALA/ Gay & Lesbian Alliance of the Central Coast 1060 Palm St (at Santa Rosa St) **805/541-4252** *8am-noon & 1pm-5pm , clsd wknds*

Accommodations

The Madonna Inn [GF,F,SW] 100 Madonna Rd **805/543-3000, 800/543-9666** *one-of-a-kind theme rooms*

The Palomar Inn [GS,NS,WI] 1601 Shell Beach Rd, Shell Beach **888/384-4004** *motel*

Sycamore Mineral Springs Resort [GF] 1215 Avila Beach Dr **805/595-7302, 800/234-5831** *hot mineral spring spa, integrative retreat center, also restaurant*

Bars

Legends [GF] 899 Main St, Morro Bay **805/772-2525**

The Library [GF,D,WC] 723 Higuera St **805/542-0199**

Cafes

Linnaea's Cafe [E,WI] 1110 Garden St (near Marsh) **805/541-5888** *6:30am-11pm*

Restaurants

Big Sky Cafe 1121 Broad St (btwn Higuera & Marsh Sts) **805/545-5401** *7am-10pm, 8am-9pm Sun-Th, plenty veggie/ vegan*

High Street Deli 350 High St **805/541-4738** *9am-5:30pm*

Novo 726 Higuera St **805/543-3986** *lunch & dinner*

Entertainment & Recreation

Pirate's Cove Beach [AYOR] 404 Front St, Avila Beach *nude beach*

Bookstores

Coalesce Bookstore 845 Main St, Morro Bay **805/772-2880** *10am-5:30pm, 11am-4pm Sun*

Volumes of Pleasure [WC,GO] 1016 Los Osos Valley Rd, Los Osos **805/528-5565** *10am-6pm, clsd Sun-Mon*

Publications

GALA News & Reviews **805/541-4252** *news & events for Central California coast*

Cruisy Areas

Embarcadero Boat Ramp [AYOR] Tidelands Park

Morro Bay Rock [AYOR] Coleman Dr

San Rafael

see Marin County

San Ramon

see East Bay

Santa Barbara

see also Ventura

Info Lines & Services

Pacific Pride Foundation 608 Anacapa St #A **805/963-3636** *social/ educational and support services, youth groups, HIV/AIDS services*

Accommodations

Autocamp [GF] 2717 De La Vina St **888/405-7553** *polished aluminum Airstreams*

Canary Hotel [GF,SW] 31 W Carrillo **805/884-0300** *Spanish colonial Santa Barbara boutique hotel gem, restaurant on site*

Inn of the Spanish Garden [GF,SW,NS,WC] 915 Garden St (at Carrillo) **805/564-4700** *luxury hotel*

Old Yacht Club Inn [GF,NS,WI] 431 Corona Del Mar Dr **805/962-1277** *only B&B on beach*

White Jasmine Inn [GS,NS,WI] 1327 Bath St (at Sola) **805/966-0589** *cottages, full brkfst, fireplaces*

Nightclubs

Wildcat Lounge [★GS,D] 15 W Ortega St **805/962-7970** *4pm-2am*

Restaurants

Joe's Cafe 536 State St **805/966-4638** *brkfst & dinner, full bar*

The Natural Cafe 508 State St **805/962-9494** *11am-9pm*

Opal Restaurant & Bar 1325 State St (at Sola St) **805/966-9676** *lunch (Mon-Sat) & dinner nightly, full bar*

Entertainment & Recreation

Santa Barbara Mission 2201 Laguna St **805/682-4713** *the "queen of the missions"; take a self-guided tour btwn 9am-4:30pm*

Bookstores

Chaucer's Books [★] 3321 State St (at Las Positas Rd, Loreto Plaza) **805/682-6787** *9am-9pm, till 8pm Sun*

Erotica

For Adults Only 223 Anacapa St **805/963-9922** *8am-4am*

The Riv 4135 State St (at Hwy 154 intersection) **805/967-8282** *10am-10pm till midnight wknds*

Santa Clara

Accommodations

Avatar Hotel [GS,WI,NS,WC] 4200 Great America Pkwy **408/235-8900, 800/586-5691** *hotspot in Silicon Valley*

Biltmore Hotel & Suites [GF,SW,WI] 2151 Laurelwood Rd (at Montague Expwy) **408/988-8411**

Erotica

L'Amour Shoppe 2329 El Camino Real **408/296-7076** *24hrs, arcade*

Santa Cruz

Info Lines & Services

AA Gay/ Lesbian **831/475-5782** *call or visit www.aasantacruz.org for meetings*

The Diversity Center [WI] 1117 Soquel Ave (at Cayuga) **831/425-5422** *open daily, call for events*

Accommodations

Chaminade Resort & Spa [GF,SW,NS,WC] 1 Chaminade Ln (at Soquel Ave) **831/475-5600, 800/283-6569**

Dream Inn [GS,F,SW,WI] 175 W Cliff Dr **831/740-8141, 844/510-1746**

Nightclubs

Blue Lagoon [GF,D,A,E,TG,V,WC] 923 Pacific Ave **831/423-7117** *3:30pm-2am, theme nights, live bands*

Restaurants

Betty Burgers 505 Seabright Ave (at Murray) **831/423-8190** *10am-10pm, retro burger joint, outdoor seating*

Cafe Limelight [TG,WC,GO] 1016 Cedar St (at Locust St) **831/425-7873** *lunch & dinner, clsd Mon, European*

Cilantros Mexican Restaurant 1934 Main St (in Town Center strip mall), Watsonville **831/761-2161** *lunch & dinner*

Crepe Place [E,WC] 1134 Soquel Ave (at Seabright, across from Rio Theater) **831/429-6994** *11am-midnight, from 9am Sat-Sun, full bar, garden patio*

Saturn Cafe [GO] 145 Laurel St (at Pacific) **831/429-8505** *9am-midnight, vegetarian diner*

Silver Spur 2650 Soquel Dr **831/475-2725** *6am-3pm, clsd Sun*

Entertainment & Recreation

Bonny Doon Beach [AYOR] Hwy 1 at Bonny Doon Rd (at milepost 27.6, N of Santa Cruz) *park in paved parking lot; nude side of beach to the north*

Bookstores

Bookshop Santa Cruz [WC] 1520 Pacific Ave **831/423-0900** *9am-10pm*

Gyms & Health Clubs

Kiva Retreat House Spa 702 Water St (at Ocean) **831/431-6385** *noon-11pm, till midnight Fri-Sat, check for women-only & men-only hours*

Erotica

Frenchy's Cruzin Books & Video 3960 Portola Dr (at 41st Ave) **831/475-9221** *arcade*

Cruisy Areas

Laguna Creek Beach [AYOR] 7 miles N of town

Santa Rosa

see Sonoma County

Sausalito

see Marin County

Sebastopol

see also Russian River & Sonoma County

Sonoma County

see also Russian River

Info Lines & Services

AA Meetings in Sonoma County **707/544-1300** *call or visit www.sonomacountyaa.org for meetings*

Sonoma County Tourism **707/522-5800, 800/576-6662**

Accommodations

An Inn 2 Remember [GF,NS,WI] 171 W Spain St (at First St W), Sonoma **707/938-2909** *located in Wine Country, whirlpool baths & fireplaces, free use of bikes*

Beltane Ranch [GF] 11775 Sonoma Hwy (Hwy 12), Glen Ellen **707/996-6501** *1892 New Orleans-style ranch house*

Best Western Dry Creek Inn [GS,SW,WI] 198 Dry Creek Rd, Healdsburg **707/433-0300, 800/222-5784**

Best Western Sonoma Valley Inn [GS,SW,WI] 550 W 2nd St, Sonoma **707/938-9200, 800/334-5784** *complimentary brkfst, gym, pets ok*

Camellia Inn [GF,SW,NS,WI] 211 North St (at Fitch), Healdsburg **707/433-8182** *Italianate Victorian, full brkfst*

The Gaige House [GF,SW,WI] 13540 Arnold Dr, Glen Ellen **707/935-0237, 800/935-0237** *in the Wine Country*

Grape Leaf Inn [GF,WI] 539 Johnson St, Healdsburg **707/433-8140, 866/433-8140** *Queen Anne Victorian, full brkfst*

Hyatt Vineyard Creek Hotel [GF,SW,WI,WC] 170 Railroad St (at Third St), Santa Rosa **707/284-1234** *cafe & bar*

Madrona Manor [GF,F,SW,NS,WC] 1001 Westside Rd, Healdsburg **707/433-4231** *also restaurant*

Magliulo's Rose Garden Inn [GF,WI,WC] 681 Broadway (at Andrieux), Sonoma **707/996-1031** *one of Wine Country's most romantic Victorian B&Bs*

Sonoma Chalet [GF] 18935 5th St W, Sonoma **707/938-3129, 800/938-3129**

Sonoma Coast Villa & Spa [GF,F] 16702 Hwy 1 (at Bodega Hwy), Bodega **707/876-9818, 888/404-2255** *organic Wine Country Cuisine and a lavish courtyard Spa*

Sonoma's Best Guest Cottages [GF,WI] 1190 E Napa St (at 8th St E), Sonoma **707/933-0340**

Cafes

A' Roma Roasters [MW,E,WC,GO] 95 5th St (Railroad Square), Santa Rosa **707/576-7765** *6am-close, from 7am Sat-Sun*

Coffee Catz [E,WI] 6761 Sebastopol Ave #300 (in Gravenstein Station), Sebastopol **707/829-6600** *7am-6pm, till 10pm Wed (open mic), till 10pm Fri-Sat (live bands), garden*

Screamin' Mimi's 6902 Sebastopol Ave (intersection of Hwy 12 & 116), Sebastopol **707/823-5902** *espresso drinks & homemade ice cream*

Sonoma's Best 1190 E Napa St (at 8th St E), Sonoma **707/996-7600** *7:30am-6pm, 8am-5pm Sun, local products, cheese, wine, olive oils & more*

Restaurants

Fig Cafe & Wine Bar 13690 Arnold Dr, Glen Ellen **707/938-2130** *dinner nightly, Sun brunch*

Mom's Apple Pie 4550 Gravenstein Hwy N, Sebastopol **707/823-8330** *pie worth stopping for on your way to & from Russian River!*

Singletree Cafe [GO] 165 Healdsburg Ave, Healdsburg **707/433-8263** *7am-3pm, good brkfsts, famous BBQ sandwiches, some veggie, local wines, outdoor seating*

Slice of Life 6970 McKinley St, Sebastopol **707/829-6627** *11am-9pm, from 9am Sat-Sun, clsd Mon, vegan & vegetarian*

Entertainment & Recreation

Out In The Vineyard [GO] **707/495-9732** *LGBT luxury wine event & tour company*

River's Edge Kayak & Canoe Company [GO] **707/433-7247** *river excursions*

Erotica

Secrets Santa Rosa 3301 Santa Rosa Ave (at Todd), Santa Rosa **707/542-8248**

Springville

Accommodations

Great Energy [MW,SW,NS] PO Box 473, 93265 **559/539-2382** *retreat in foothills of Sierra Nevada mtns*

Stockton

see also Modesto

Nightclubs

Paradise Club [MW,D,F,E,YC] 10100 N Lower Sacramento Rd (near Grider) **209/477-4724** *6pm-2am, from 3pm Sun*

Erotica

Suzie's Adult Superstores 3126 E Hammer Ln **209/952-6900** *24hrs, arcade*

Cruisy Areas

Oak Park [AYOR] Alpine Ave

Sunnyvale

see also San Jose

Accommodations

Wild Palms Hotel [GF,SW,WI,WC] 910 E Fremont Ave (at Wolfe Ave) **408/738-0500, 800/538-1600** *hot tub*

Sutter Creek

ACCOMMODATIONS

The Foxes Inn of Sutter Creek [GF,NS,WI] 77 Main St (at Keys St) **209/267-5882, 800/987-3344** *full brkfst*

Tiburon

see Marin County

Twentynine Palms

see Joshua Tree Nat'l Park

Ukiah

BARS

Perkins St Lounge [GF,D,E,K] 228 E Perkins St **707/462-0327** *3pm-2am*

Upland

EROTICA

Sensations Love Boutique 1656 W Foothill Blvd (at Mountain) **909/985-1654**

The Toy Box 1999 W Arrow Rte (at Central) **909/920-1135** *24hrs*

Vacaville

INFO LINES & SERVICES

Solano Pride Center 1234 Empire St #1560, Fairfield **707/207-3430** *provide relevant, fun, and innovative programs, services and support that meet the needs of the LGBTQI community of Solano County*

CRUISY AREAS

Lee Bell Park [AYOR] Travis Blvd (at Union Ave), Fairfield

Vallejo

includes Benicia

BARS

Town House Cocktail Lounge [GS,NH,E,K,GO] 401-A Georgia St (at Marin) **707/553-9109** *1pm-midnight, from 10am Sat, from noon Sun*

Ventura

see also Santa Barbara

INFO LINES & SERVICES

AA Gay/ Lesbian 805/389-1444

BARS

Paddy's [MW,D,F,E,K,GO] 2 W Main St (at Ventura) **805/652-1071** *2pm-2am*

EROTICA

Three Star Books 359 E Main St **805/653-9068** *24hrs*

CRUISY AREAS

Surfers Point [AYOR] N of the Ventura Pier (btwn fairgrounds & Ocean) *go N along beach to Hobo's Jungle*

Victorville

BARS

Ricky's [GS,D,F,K,DS,WC] 13728 Hesperia Rd #12 **760/951-5400** *3pm-2am*

CRUISY AREAS

Deep Creek Hot Springs [AYOR] Apple Valley *from I-15, take Bear Valley Cutoff & turn right onto Central Rd; go left onto Ocotillo Rd for 2 miles & turn right onto Bowen Ranch Rd (unmarked dirt road)*

Grady Trammel Park [AYOR] 3/4 mile N of West Side 15 bar (on Stoddard Wells Rd) *watch out for rangers (!)*

Visalia

INFO LINES & SERVICES

The Source LGBT Center 208 W Main St #B **559/429-4277** *3pm-6pm Tue-Fri*

Walnut Creek

see East Bay

Yosemite Nat'l Park

ACCOMMODATIONS

Highland House B&B [GF,WI] 3125 Wild Dove Ln (at Jerseydale Rd), Mariposa **559/696-3341**

The Homestead [GF,NS,WI] 41110 Rd 600, Ahwahnee **559/683-0495, 800/483-0495** *cottages & 2-bdrm house*

June Lake Villager [GF,WI] 2640 Hwy 158 (2.5 miles W of Hwy 395), June Lake **760/648-7712** *vintage motel; kids/ pets ok; organic, healthy breakfast; walking distance to lakes and trails; 20 minutes from Yosemite*

The Majestic Yosemite Hotel [GF,F,SW,NS] Yosemite Valley Floor **866/413-8869** *incredibly dramatic & expensive grand fortress*

Narrow Gauge Inn [GF,SW,NS] 48571 Hwy 41, Fish Camp **559/683-7720, 888/644-9050**

Queen's Inn by the River [GS,NS,WI,WC,GO] 41139 Hwy 41, Oakhurst **559/683-4354** *garden w/ river view, lesbian-owned*

Tenaya Lodge at Yosemite [GF,F,SW] 1122 Hwy 41, Fish Camp **559/683-6555, 866/771-9629**

Yosemite Big Creek Inn B&B [GS,NS,WI] 1221 Hwy 41, Fish Camp **559/641-2828**

Yosemite View Lodge [GF,SW,WC] 11136 Hwy 140, El Portal **209/379-2681, 888/742-4371** *3 pools, 2 restaurants & lounge*

Yosemite's Apple Blossom Inn B&B [GF,NS,WC] **559/642-2001, 888/687-4281**

Cruisy Areas

Rest Stop [AYOR] at turn to Glacier Point on road to valley

Colorado

Aspen

Accommodations

Aspen Mountain Lodge [GF,SW,NS] 311 W Main St **970/925-7650, 800/362-7736**

Hotel Aspen [GF,SW,NS,WI] 110 W Main St **970/925-3441, 800/527-7369** *hot tub, après-ski wine & cheese*

St Moritz Lodge [GF,SW,NS,WI,GO] 334 W Hyman Ave **970/925-3220, 800/817-2069**

Restaurants

Jimmy's 205 S Mill St (at Hopkins) **970/925-6020** *5:30pm-11pm, Sun brunch, also bar from 4:30pm, patio*

Bookstores

Explore Booksellers & Bistro [F,WI,WC] 221 E Main St (at Aspen) **970/925-5336, 800/562-7323** *10am-7pm, also nutritarian restaurant*

Beaver Creek

Accommodations

Beaver Creek Lodge [GF,SW,NS,WI,WC] 26 Avondale Ln (at Village Rd) **970/845-9800, 800/525-7280** *also restaurant, mtn chic, steam room, gym*

Boulder

Info Lines & Services

Out Boulder 2132 14th St **303/499-5777** *LGBT resource center*

Accommodations

The Briar Rose B&B [GF,NS,WI] 2151 Arapahoe Ave (at 22nd St) **303/442-3007, 888/786-8440** *full organic brkfst*

Cafes

Walnut Cafe [★WC] 3073 Walnut St (at 30th) **303/447-2315** *7am-3:30pm, patio*

Entertainment & Recreation

Boulder Area Bicycle Adventures [GO] **303/918-7062** *bike tours of Boulder & annual LGBT ride in June*

Cruisy Areas

Dream Canyon [SW,N] Lost Angel Rd (off Sugarloaf Mtn Rd) *inquire locally for detailed directions*

Colorado Springs

(includes Manitou Springs)

Accommodations

Blue Skies Inn B&B [GS,NS,WI,WC] 402 Manitou Ave (at Mayfair), Manitou Springs **719/685-3899, 800/398-7949**

Old Town Guesthouse [GF,NS,WI,WC] 115 S 26th St **719/632-9194, 888/375-4210** *full brkfst, hot tub*

Pikes Peak Paradise [GF,NS,WI,GO] 236 Pinecrest Rd, Woodland Park **719/687-6656, 800/728-8282** *full brkfst, hot tub, mansion w/ view of Pikes Peak*

Bars

Club Q [★M,NH,D,F,E,K,S,18+,WC,GO] 3430 N Academy Blvd (at N Carefree) **719/570-1429** *3pm-2am, till 4am Fri-Sat*

Restaurants

Dale Street Bistro Cafe 115 E Dale (at Nevada) **719/578-9898** *lunch and dinner, clsd Mon*

Men's Clubs

Buddies [PC,GO] 3430 N Academy Blvd (N Carefree) **719/591-7660** *3pm-4am, 24hrs wknds,, beer bust Sun*

Erotica

First Amendment Adult Bookstore 220 E Fillmore St (at Nevada) **719/630-7676** *8am-2am, till midnight Sun*

Cruisy Areas

Palmer Park [AYOR] *many undercover cops*

Denver

Info Lines & Services

Gay/ Lesbian AA 303/322-4440

The GLBT Center of Colorado (The Center) [WC] 1301 E Colfax **303/733-7743** *10am-8pm Mon-Fri, from noon Sat, extensive resources & support groups*

Accommodations

The Brown Palace [GF,WI] 321 17th St (at N Broadway) **303/297-3111, 800/321-2599** *sun in every room, also restaurant & spa*

Capitol Hill Mansion B&B [GF,NS,WI,GO] 1207 Pennsylvania St (at 12th) **303/839-5221, 800/839-9329** *full brkfst, hot tub*

Castle Marne B&B [GF,WI] 1572 Race St (at 16th Ave) **303/331-0621, 800/926-2763** *hot tubs on private balconies*

The Curtis-a DoubleTree by Hilton [GF,SW,WI] 1405 Curtis St **303/571-0300** *hip hotel, restaurant*

Hotel Monaco [GF,NS,WI] 1717 Champa St (at 17th) **303/296-1717, 800/990-1303** *gym, spa, also Italian restaurant*

Hotel Teatro [GF,NS,WI] 1100 14th St **303/228-1100, 888/727-1200** *luxury boutique hotel, 2 restaurants*

The Oxford Hotel [GF,F,WI] 1600 17th St **303/628-5400, 800/228-5838** *health club & spa, also restaurant & art deco lounge*

Bars

Blush & Blu [MW,WI,WC,GO] 1526 E Colfax (btwn Humboldt & Franklin) **303/484-8548** *11am-2am*

Boyztown [M,NH,S,WI] 117 Broadway (btwn 1st & 2nd Aves) **303/722-7373** *3pm-2am, from noon wknds, male dancers Tue-Sun*

Charlie's [★M,D,CW,K,DS,WC] 900 E Colfax Ave (at Emerson) **303/839-8890** *11am-2am, country bar & house music room*

The Compound Basix [★M,NH,D] 145 Broadway (at 2nd Ave) **303/722-7977** *7am-2am, [D] Fri-Sat*

Dazzle [GF,F,E] 930 Lincoln St (btwn 9th & 10th Aves) **303/839-5100** *from 4pm Sun-Th, from 11am Fri, also Sun brunch , jazz club & restaurant*

El Chapultepec [★GF,F,E,$] 1962 Market St (at 20th) **303/295-9126** *9am-2am, live jazz & blues, 1-drink minimum per set*

El Potrero [GS,DS,MR-L,E,F] 4501 E Virginia Ave, Glendale **303/388-8889** *Mexican restaurant from 3pm, Latino gay bar late, clsd Mon-Tue*

li'l Devil's [M,NH] 255 S Broadway **303/733-1156** *3pm-2am, from noon wknds*

Pride And Swagger [MW,D,DS] 450 E 17th Ave #110 **720/476-6360** *4pm-midnight, till 2am Th-Sat*

R&R Denver [MW,NH] 4958 E Colfax Ave (at Elm St) **303/320-9337** *3pm-2am, from 1pm Fri, from 11am wknds*

The Triangle Bar [MW,D,F] 2036 N Broadway **303/658-0914** *11am-2am*

X Bar [MW,D,F] 629 E Colfax Ave **303/832-2687** *3pm-2am, from noon Sun*

Nightclubs

Beta Nightclub [GS,D,$] 1909 Blake St (btwn 19th & 20th) **303/383-1909** *more gay Th*

Clocktower Cabaret [GF,F,E,C] 16th St Mall at Arapahoe (in historic D&F Tower) **303/293-0075** *upscale cabaret w/ variety of acts weekly, including drag & burlesque*

Tracks [GS,D,DS,MR] 3500 Walnut St (at 36th) **303/863-7326** *9pm-2am, clsd Sun-Wed, 2 rooms, theme nights*

Cafes

City, O City 206 E 13th Ave (at Sherman) **303/831-6443** *7am-2am, from 8am wknds, vegetarian/ vegan, also bar*

Jelly Cafe 600 E 13th Ave (at Pearl) **303/831-6301** *7am-2pm, a whole lotta Jelly filled fun*

The Market at Larimer Square 1445 Larimer Sq (btwn 14th & 15th) **303/534-5140** *6am-10pm, till 11pm Fri-Sat*

Restaurants

Annie's Cafe & Bar [★] 3100 E Colfax (at St Paul) **303/355-8197** *7am-9pm, from 8am Sat, till 8pm Sun, comfort food and cocktails*

The Avenue Grill 630 E 17th Ave (at Washington) **303/861-2820** *11am-10pm, till 11pm Fri-Sat*

Banzai Sushi 6655 Leetsdale Dr (E of Colorado Blvd) **303/329-3366** *lunch Mon-Fri, dinner nightly*

Barricuda's 1076 Ogden St (at E 11th) **303/860-8353** *10am-2am, from 8am wknd, also dive bar*

Beatrice & Woodsley [R] 38 S Broadway **303/777-3505** *one of America's top restaurants*

Benny's Restaurante y Tequila Bar 301 E 7th Ave (at Grant St) **303/894-0788** *lunch & dinner, patio*

The Corner Office Restaurant & Martini Bar 1405 Curtis St (at Curtis Hotel) **303/825-6500** *6am-11am, till midnight Fri-Sat, full bar*

Devil's Food: The Cookery at Myrtle Hill 1020 S Gaylord St (at E Tennessee) **303/733-7448** *7am-3:30pm, yummy desserts*

Duo 2413 W 32nd Ave (at Zuni) **303/477-4141** *dinner nightly, wknd brunch, hip, organic, creative American, full bar*

Euclid Hall Bar & Kitchen 1317 14th St **303/595-4255** *11:30am-2am, American tavern focuses on high quality and innovative pub food*

Fruition 1313 E 6th Ave **303/831-1962** *5pm-10pm, till 9pm Sun, contemporary French*

The Populist 3163 Larimer **720/432-3163** *5pm-10pm, clsd Sun-Mon, New American small plates*

Steuben's 523 E 17th Ave **303/830-1001** *11am-11pm, till midnight Fri-Sat from 10am wknds, comfort food, patio, full bar*

Sunny Gardens 6460 E Yale Avenue **303/691-8830** *Chinese, plenty veggie/ vegan*

Thai Pot Cafe 1550 S Colorado Blvd (at E Florida) **303/639-6200** *lunch & dinner*

Vesta 1822 Blake St (near 18th St) **303/296-1970** *5pm-10pm Sun-Th, till 11pm Fri-Sat, upscale*

WaterCourse Foods 837 E 17th Ave (at Clarkson) **303/832-7313** *7am-10pm, till 11pm Fri-Sat, vegetarian/ vegan*

Entertainment & Recreation

Rocky Mountain Rainbeaus **303/863-7739** *all-inclusive, all-levels, high-energy square dance club*

Bookstores

Tattered Cover Book Store [WC] 2526 Colfax Ave (at Elizabeth St) **303/322-7727, 800/833-9327** *9am-9pm, 10am-6pm Sun, independent, cafe; also 1628 16th St*

Retail Shops

CJ's Leather 135 Broadway **303/715-1157** *11am-9pm, from noon-5pm Sun*

Publications

Out Front Colorado 303/778-7900 *statewide bi-weekly LGBT newspaper, since 1976*

Men's Clubs

Denver Swim Club [MO,V,YC,SW,PC] 6923 E Colfax Ave (at Olive) **303/322-4023**

Midtowne Spa—Denver [PC] 2935 Zuni St (at 29th) **303/458-8902** *24hrs*

Erotica

Circus Cinema 5580 N Federal Blvd **303/455-3144** *24hrs*

Pleasure Entertainment Center 127 S Broadway (at Bayaud) **303/722-5852** *open 24hrs; also 3250 W Alameda, 303/934-2373 & 3490 W Colfax, 303/825-6505*

Romantix Adult Superstore 633 E Colfax Ave (at Washington) **303/831-8319**

Cruisy Areas

Cheesman Park [AYOR] near Pavilion *beware of undercover cops!*

Durango

Accommodations

Leland House B&B [GF,NS,WI,WC] 721 E 2nd Ave **970/385-1920**

Mesa Verde Far View Lodge [GF,NS,WI] 1 Navajo Hill, Mesa Verde National Park **800/449-2288** *inside nat'l park at 8250' elevation*

Rochester Hotel [★GF,NS,WC] 721 E 2nd Ave **970/385-1920** *Western-style house, full brkfst*

Restaurants

Palace Restaurant [WC,GO] 505 Main Ave (at 5th St) **970/247-2018** *11am-10pm, clsd Sun in winter, full bar, patio*

Estes Park

Accommodations

Stanley Hotel [GF,SW,WI] 333 Wonderview Ave **800/976-1377, 970/577-4000** *the inspiration for Stephen King's The Shining*

Fort Collins

Accommodations

Archer's Poudre River Resort [GF,GO] 33021 Poudre Canyon Hwy, Bellvue **970/881-2139, 888/822-0588** *cabins, tents, RV hookups, pets ok*

The Elizabeth Hotel [GF,E] 111 Chestnut St **970/490-2600** *modern luxury property is a musicians paradise, restaurant & bar*

Grand Junction

Restaurants

Leon's Taqueria 505 30th Rd **970/242-1388** *11am-9pm*

Erotica

24 Road Adult Emporium 639 24 Rd (at Mesa Mall) **970/243-4112** *10am-11pm*

Junction News 754 North Ave (at 7th St) **970/242-9702** *9am-11:30pm, till 1am Fri-Sat*

Cruisy Areas

Hawthorne Park [AYOR]

Walker Wildlife Area [AYOR] Hwy 6/50 W, past Mesa Mall (near the CO River) *in the woods*

Hotchkiss

Accommodations

Leroux Creek Inn & Vineyards [GF] 12388 3100 Rd **970/872-4746**

Restaurants

Pat's Bar and Grill [E] 140 W Bridge St **970/872-4215** *11am-8pm, bar open later, American/ Mexican*

Lamar

ACCOMMODATIONS

Sundance-High Plains RV Park and Cabins [GF,WI,GO] 29151 US Highway 287 **719/336-1031** *on the Old Santa Fe Trail in South Eastern Colorado, pets/kids ok*

Pueblo

BARS

Pirate's Cove [MW,NH,WC] 105 Central Plaza (off 1st & Union) **719/543-2683** *7pm-2am, clsd Mon*

CRUISY AREAS

City Park Pueblo Blvd & Thatcher *N side near gazebo*

Stratton

ACCOMMODATIONS

Claremont Inn & Winery [GS,F,WI,GO] 800 Claremont St (off exit 419, I-70) **000/201-0010** *2 hours from Denver, full brkfst*

Vail

RESTAURANTS

Larkspur Restaurant & Market [WC] 458 Vail Valley Dr (in the Golden Peak Lodge) **970/754-8050** *lunch & dinner, fine dining, also bar, patio, ski-in/ out*

Sweet Basil [WC] 193 E Gore Creek Dr **970/476-0125** *lunch & dinner, bar*

CONNECTICUT

Bethel

CAFES

Molten Java [E,GO] 213 Greenwood Ave **203/739-0313** *6am-9pm, till 10pm Fri-Sat, 8am-8pm Sat-Sun*

RESTAURANTS

Bethel Pizza House 206 Greenwood Ave **203/748-1427** *11am-11pm, till midnight Fri-Sat*

Bridgeport

RESTAURANTS

Bloodroot Restaurant & Bookstore 85 Ferris St (at Harbor Ave) **203/576-9168** *lunch Tue & Th-Sat, dinner Tue-Sat, brunch only Sun, clsd Mon, vegetarian*

EROTICA

Boston Book & Video 2053 Boston Ave **203/335-9705** *9am-2am, till 3am Fri-Sat*

Romantix Adult Superstore 410 North Ave **203/332-7129**

Bristol

CRUISY AREAS

Rockwell Park [AYOR] Rte 72

Colebrook

ACCOMMODATIONS

Rock Hall Luxe Lodging [GS,SW,NS,WI] 19 Rock Hall Rd **860/379-2230**

Danbury

ACCOMMODATIONS

Maron Hotel & Suites [GF,WI,WC] 42 Lake Ave Extension (off I-84) **203/791-2200, 866/811-2582** *kids/ pets ok*

RESTAURANTS

Sesame Seed 68 W Wooster St **203/743-9850** *lunch & dinner, clsd Sun, Lebanese*

Thang Long [BYOB] 56 Padanaram Rd (near North Street Shopping Center) **203/743-6049** *lunch & dinner, Vietnamese*

Enfield

EROTICA

Bookends 44 Enfield St/ Rte 5 **860/745-3988** *9am-10pm, till 11pm Fri-Sat, noon-8pm Sun*

Fairfield

NIGHTCLUBS

Trevi Lounge [M,D,E,K] 548 Kings Hwy Cutoff **203/255-0285** *7pm-1am, till 2am Fri-Sat*

Groton

Erotica

Amazing 591 Rte 12 #8 **860/448-0787**

Hartford

Info Lines & Services

Hartford Gay & Lesbian Health Collective 1841 Broad St (at New Britain Ave) **860/278-4163** *9am-8pm, till 4pm Fri, clsd Th & wknds*

True Colors 30 Arbor St (at Capital Ave) **860/232-0050** *support & mentoring for LGBT youth*

Accommodations

Butternut Farm [GS,NS,WI] 1654 Main St, Glastonbury **860/633-7197** *full brkfst*

Bars

Chez Est [★MW,D,F,K,DS] 458 Wethersfield Ave (at Main St) **860/525-3243** *5pm-1am, till 2am Fri-Sat, from 3pm Fri-Sun*

Cafes

Tisane Tea & Coffee Bar [F,K,WI] 537 Farmington Ave (at Kenyon) **860/523-5417** *8am-1am, till 2am Sat, also bar, men's night Tue*

Restaurants

Arugula [R,WC] 953 Farmington Ave, West Hartford **860/561-4888** *lunch & dinner, clsd Mon, Mediterranean*

Firebox 539 Broad St **860/246-1222** *11:30am-2:30pm & 5:30pm-10pm, 11am-4pm Sun, clsd Mon, contemporary American*

Peppercorns Grill 357 Main St **860/547-1714** *lunch Mon-Fri, dinner nightly, clsd Sun, Northern Italian*

Pond House Cafe [BYOB,WC] 1555 Asylum Ave, W Hartford **860/231-8823** *lunch & dinner Tue-Sat, wknd brunch, patio*

Trumbull Kitchen 150 Trumbull St (at Pearl St) **860/493-7417** *lunch Mon-Sat dinner nightly, global cuisine/ tapas*

Entertainment & Recreation

Real Art Ways [WI] 56 Arbor St **860/232-1006** *contemporary art, cinema, performance, also lounge*

Erotica

Erotic Zone [AYOR] 35 W Service Rd (at Hwy 91 N) **860/549-1896** *10am-10pm, til 2am Fri-Sat, till 8pm Sun*

Very Intimate Pleasures 100 Brainard Rd (exit 27, off I-91) **860/246-1875**

Cruisy Areas

Bushnell Park [AYOR] S of Asylum Ave (downtown exit off I-84)

Meriden

Cruisy Areas

Hubbard Park [AYOR]

Mystic

Accommodations

House of 1833 B&B Resort [GF,SW,NS,WI,GO] 72 N Stonington Rd **860/536-6325, 800/367-1833**

The Mare's Inn B&B [GF,NS,WC,GO] 333 Colonel Ledyard Hwy, Ledyard **860/572-7556** *great birding, near casinos, full brkfst, lesbian-owned*

Mermaid Inn of Mystic [GS,WI,NS,GO] 2 Broadway **860/536-6223, 877/692-2632**

The Old Mystic Inn [GF,NS,WI,GO] 52 Main St (at Rte 27), Old Mystic **860/572-9422**

New Britain

Cruisy Areas

Martha Hart Park [AYOR] off Corbin Ave

New Haven

Info Lines & Services

New Haven Pride Center [WC] 84 Orange , West Haven **203/387-2252** *3pm-6pm Tue-Th*

Accommodations

Omni New Haven Hotel at Yale [GF,WI,WC] 155 Temple St (at Chapel) **203/772-6664**

Bars

168 York St Cafe [MW,GO] 168 York St **203/789-1915** *3pm-1am, till 2am Fri-Sat, also restaurant, patio*

The Bar [GS,D,E,F,WC] 254 Crown St (at College) **203/495-8924** *11:30am-1am, from 5pm Mon-Tu, more gay Tue*

Partners [MW,D,L,K,DS] 365 Crown St (at Park St) **203/776-1014** *8pm-1am, till 2am Fri-Sat, from 5pm Fri*

Nightclubs

Empire Nightclub/ Gotham City Cafe [★GS,D,DS,18+,WC] 84 Orange **203/498-2484** *9pm-4am, clsd Sun-Wed, more gay Sat*

Cafes

Atticus Bookstore/ Cafe 1082 Chapel St (at York St) **203/776-4040** *7am-9pm*

Restaurants

116 Crown 116 Crown St **203/777-3116** *5pm-1am, clsd Sun-Mon, great cocktails*

Claire's Corner Copia [WI,WC] 1000 Chapel St (at College St) **203/562-3888** *8am-9pm, till 10pm Fri-Sat, vegetarian*

Mezcal 14 Mechanic St (at Lawrence) **203/782-4828** *lunch Tue-Sun, dinner nightly, authentic Mexican*

Miya Sushi 58 Howe St (at Chapel St) **203/777-9760** *lunch & dinner, clsd Sun-Mon*

Soul de Cuba 238 Crown St **203/498-2822** *lunch & dinner, full bar*

Erotica

Fairmount Theatre 33 Main St Annex **203/467-3832** *10am-10pm, till midnight Fri-Sat*

Very Intimate Pleasures 170 Boston Post Rd, Orange **203/799-7040**

Cruisy Areas

East Rock State Park [AYOR] lower parking lot *days*

New London

Bars

O'Neill's Brass Rail [M,K,DS,WI] 52 Bank St **860/443-6203** *1pm-1am, till 2am Fri-Sat*

Norwalk

Info Lines & Services

Triangle Community Center 650 West Ave **203/853-0600** *10am 6pm, clsd wknds*

Bars

Troupe 429 [MW,D,E,K,DS,WC] 3 Wall St *4:29pm-1am, till 2am Fri-Sat*

Cruisy Areas

Merritt Pkwy Park & Ride [AYOR] Rte 15, exit 38 (Rte 123, New Canaan Ave) *main lot, turn right*

Ridgefield

Cruisy Areas

Riverside on Rte 7 [AYOR] opposite Ridgefield Motor Inn

Stamford

Cruisy Areas

Cove Island Park [AYOR] intersection of Cove Rd & Weed Ave

Waterbury

Erotica

Video Book of Waterbury 90 S Main St **203/573-1066** *10am-11pm*

Cruisy Areas

Lakewood Park/ Twin Lakes Annex [AYOR] Farmwood Rd *days*

Westport

Entertainment & Recreation

Sherwood Island State Park Beach left to gay area *popular gay beach*

DELAWARE

Rehoboth Beach

INFO LINES & SERVICES

Camp Rehoboth Community Center 37 Baltimore Ave **302/227-5620** *9am-5:30pm Mon-Fri, 10am-4pm wknds, community center, HIV testing & counseling*

Gay & Lesbian AA 302/856-6452 *noon Th*

ACCOMMODATIONS

At Melissa's B&B [GS,NS,WI] 36 Delaware Ave (btwn 1st & 2nd) **302/227-7504, 800/396-8090**

Bellmoor Inn [GF,SW,WI] 6 Christian St (at Delaware) **866/227-5800** *upscale inn & spa*

Bewitched & BEDazzled B&B [GS,NS,WI,WC,GO] 67 Lake Ave (at Rehoboth Ave) **302/226-3900, 866/732-9482**

Canalside Inn [GS,SW,NS,WI,WC,GO] Canal at 6th **302/226-2006, 866/412-2625**

The Homestead at Rehoboth B&B [GF,NS,WI,WC,GO] 35060 Warrington Rd (at Old Landing Rd) **302/226-7625** *small-dog-friendly, "country charm at the beach"*

Lazy L at Willow Creek [GS,SW,WI,GO] 16061 Willow Creek Rd (at Hwy 1), Lewes **302/644-7220**

Rehoboth Guest House [MW,NS,WI,GO] 40 Maryland Ave (btwn 1st & 2nd Sts) **302/227-4117, 800/564-0493**

Shore Inn at Rehoboth [MO,WI,N,GO] 37239 Rehoboth Ave (across from Double L Bar) **302/227-8487**

BARS

The Blue Moon [★MW,E,DS,K] 35 Baltimore Ave (btwn 1st & 2nd) **302/227-6515** *6pm-2am, clsd Jan, also restaurant*

Dogfish Head Brewings & Eats [GF,F,E] 320 Rehoboth Ave (at 4th) **302/226-2739**

Double L Bar [M,D,L,B,D,E] 622 Rehoboth Ave (at Church) **302/227-0818** *3pm-2am, patio*

The Pond Bar & Grill [GF,NH,F,E,K] 3 S 1st St (near Rehoboth Ave) **302/227-2234** *11am-1am*

Rigby's Bar & Grill [GS,F,E,K] 404 Rehoboth Ave (at State St) **302/227-6080** *3pm-1am, from 10am Sun*

CAFES

The Coffee Mill [WI,GO] 127B Rehoboth Ave **302/227-7530** *7am-11pm, till 5pm (off-season)*

Honey's Farm Fresh 329 Savannah Rd, Lewes **302/644-8400** *8am-3pm, clsd Tue-Wed*

Lori's Cafe [GO] 39 Baltimore Ave (at 1st) **302/226-3066** *seasonal, call for hours, courtyard*

RESTAURANTS

Aqua Grill [E] 57 Baltimore Ave **302/226-9001** *seasonal, deck, full bar*

Back Porch Cafe 59 Rehoboth Ave **302/227-3674** *lunch & dinner, Sun brunch, seasonal*

Buttery [R] 102 2nd St, Lewes **302/645-7755** *lunch, dinner, Sun brunch*

The Cultured Pearl 301 Rehoboth Ave (2nd flr) **302/227-8493** *dinner only, pan-Asian/ sushi, cocktail lounge*

Dos Locos [★] 208 Rehoboth Ave (across from Fire Company) **302/227-3353** *11:30am-10pm, till 11pm Fri-Sat, Mexican*

Eden [★WC] 23 Baltimore Ave **302/227-3330** *dinner Wed-Sun, full bar*

Fins 243 Rehoboth Ave **302/226-3467** *dinner nightly, lunch Sat-Sun, fish house & raw bar*

Go Fish! 24 Rehoboth Ave **302/226-1044** *11:30am-9:30pm (in-season), authentic British fish & chips*

Iguana Grill 52 Baltimore Ave **302/727-5273** *lunch & dinner (summers), Southwestern, full bar, patio*

Jerry's Seafood 108 2nd St, Lewes **302/645-6611** *lunch & dinner daily, "home of the crab bomb"*

Mariachi [WC] **302/227-0115** *10am10pm, till 11pm Fri-Sat, Tex-Mex*

Purple Parrot Grill [K,DS,WC] 134 Rehoboth Ave **302/226-1139** *lunch & dinner daily, brunch Sun, karaoke & drag shows wknds*

Entertainment & Recreation

Cape Henlopen State Park Beach [AYOR] 42 Cape Henlopen Dr, Lewes **302/645-8983** *8am-sunset, beware of cops*

Poodle Beach S of boardwalk at Queen St *popular gay beach*

Retail Shops

Leather Central 36983 Rehoboth Ave **302/227-0700** *leather uniforms, toys, accessories*

Publications

Letters from Camp Rehoboth **302/227-5620** *newsmagazine w/ events & entertainment listings*

Wilmington

Nightclubs

Crimson Moon Tavern [M,D,DS,V] 1909 W 6th St (at Union St) **302/654-9099** *6pm-2am, from 7pm Sat, clsd Sun-Tue*

Restaurants

Eclipse 1020 Union St **302/658-1588** *lunch Mon-Fri, dinner nightly, upscale*

The Green Room [E] 11th & Market St (at Hotel Dupont) **302/594-3154** *brkfst, lunch & dinner, Sun brunch, full bar*

Mrs Robino's [WC] 520 N Union St (at Pennsylvania) **302/652-9223** *11am-9pm, till 10pm Fri-Sat, family-style Italian, full bar*

District of Columbia

Washington

Info Lines & Services

➤Kasper's Livery Service [GO] 201 Eye St SW **202/554-2471, 800/455-2471** *limousine service serving DC, MD & VA*

Triangle Club **202/659-8641** *various 12-Step groups, call for times*

Accommodations

Beacon Hotel & Corporate Quarters [GF,F,WC] 1615 Rhode Island Ave NW (at 17th) **202/296-2100, 800/821-4367**

The Carlyle Suites Hotel [GS,F,WI,WC] 1731 New Hampshire Ave NW (btwn R & S Sts) **202/234-3200, 800/964-5377** *art deco*

Donovan House [GS,WI] 1155 14th St NW (at Massachusetts Ave NW) **202/737-1200** *stylish hotel, rooftop bar*

Glover Park Hotel [GF,WI,WC] 2505 Wisconsin Ave NW (near Georgetown) **202/337-9700, 877/219-2970** *also restaurant*

Hamilton Crowne Plaza Hotel [GF,NS,WC] 14th & K St, NW **202/682-0111**

Hotel George [GF,WI] 15 E St NW **202/347-4200, 800/576-8331**

Hotel Monaco Washington DC [GF,WC,WI] 700 F St NW (at 7th) **202/628-7177, 800/649-1202** *boutique hotel*

Hotel Palomar [GF,F,SW,WI,WC] 2121 P St NW (at 21st St) **202/448-1800, 866/866-3070** *in Dupont Circle*

Hotel Rouge [GF,WI,WC] 1315 16th St NW (at Rhode Island) **202/232-8000, 800/738-1202** *also restaurant & bar*

Kalorama Guest House [GS,NS,WI] 2700 Cathedral Ave NW (off Connecticut Ave) **202/588-8188**

Kimpton Mason & Rook Hotel [GF,WC,NS,WI] 1430 Rhode Island Ave NW **202/742-3100, 800/706-1202** *on a residential, tree-lined street in the NW quadrant, restaurant and rooftop bar*

The Line [GS] 1770 Euclid St NW (in Adams Morgan) **202/588-0525** *housed inside a historic church, restaurants and bars on site*

Madison Hotel [GF,WI] 1177 15th St NW (at M St NW) **202/862-1600** *luxury hotel, also restaurant & spa*

Morrison-Clark Historic Hotel & Restaurant [GF,WI] 1015 L St NW (at Massachusetts Ave NW) **202/898-1200, 800/322-7898** *hotel in 2 Victorian town houses w/ very popular restaurant*

The River Inn [GF,WI,WC] 924 25th St NW (at K St) **202/337-7600** *also Dish + Drinks restaurant*

Topaz Hotel [GF,WI,WC] 1733 N St NW (at Massachusetts Ave NW) **202/393-3000** *also restaurant & bar*

Bars

Back Door Pub [M,MR-AF,S,WC] 1104 8th St SE, 2nd flr (at L St) **202/546-5979** *5pm-2am, till 3am Fri-Sat*

The Black Cat [GS,D,E,WC] 1811 14th St NW (at the Black Cat) **202/667-4490** *many queer events, live music, dance parties, also cafe*

DC Bear Crue [M,D,B,K] *Fri nights and Sun beer bust, check dcbearcrue.com for details*

DC Eagle [★M,L,WC] 3701 Benning Rd NE **202/347-6025** *4pm-2am, till 3am Fri-Sat, 2pm-2am Sun*

DIK Bar/ Windows [M,D,K,OC] 1637 17th St NW (at R St NW, upstairs) **202/328-0100** *4pm-2am, aka Dupont Italian Kitchen*

The Dirty Goose [MW,F] 913 U St NW **202/629-1462** *5pm-1am, till 3am Fri-Sat from 1pm wknds*

The Fireplace [M,NH,MR,V,WC] 2161 P St NW (at 22nd St) **202/293-1293** *1pm-2am, till 3am Fri-Sat*

Green Lantern [M,NH,D,B,K,V,WC] 1335 Green Court NW (in alley L St, btwn 13th & 14th) **202/347-4533** *4pm-2am, till 3am wknds*

JR's [★M,NH,F,V,YC] 1519 17th St NW (at Church) **202/328-0090** *4pm-2am, till 3am Fri, 1pm-3am Sat, 1pm-2am Sun*

Larry's Lounge [MW,NH,F,WC,GO] 1840 18th St NW (at T St) **202/483-1483** *4pm-1am, till 2am Fri-Sat, patio*

Mr Henry's Capitol Hill [GF,MR,E,NS,WC] 601 Pennsylvania Ave SE (at 6th St) **202/546-8412** *11:30am-midnight, also restaurant*

Nellie's Sports Bar [M,NH,K] 900 U St NW (at 9th) **202/332-6355** *5pm-midnight, 3pm-2am Fri, from 11am wknds*

Number Nine [MW,NH] 1435 P St NW (at 15th St NW) **202/986-0999** *5pm-close, from 2pm wknds*

Pitchers DC [MW] 2317 18th St NW **202/733-2568** *5pm-midnight, till 2am Tue-Sat, from noon wknds, clsd Mon, sports bar*

POV Roof Terrace Bar [GF,F] 515 15th Street NW (at W Hotel) **202/661-2400** *11am-2am, pricey cocktails; superior views of the White House & Lincoln Memorial*

UpRoar Lounge & Restaurant [M,B,F] 639 Florida Ave NW **202/462-4464** *5pm-midnight, till 2am wknds*

Wisdom [GS,F] 1432 Pennsylvania Ave SE **202/543-2323** *5:30pm-midnight, till 2am Fri-Sat, till 11pm Sun*

Nightclubs

Bachelors Mill [★M,D,MR-AF,K,S,WC] 1104 8th St SE (downstairs at Back Door Pub) **202/546-5979** *11pm-3am Th-Sat only*

Cobalt/ 30 Degrees Lounge [★M,D,E,DS] 1639 R St NW (at 17th) **202/232-4416** *5pm-2am, till 3am Fri-Sat*

Mixtape [MW,D] *2nd Sat only, alternative queer dance party, check mixtapedc.com for info*

Secrets [M,D,DS,S] 1824 Half St SW **202/863-0670** *9pm-close Th-Sun, [DS] downstairs, strippers upstairs*

Cafes

Cosi [★WI] 1647 20th St NW **202/332-6364** *7am-11pm, till midnight Fri-Sat, 8am-10pm Sun, full bar from 4pm, make your own s'mores*

Jolt 'n' Bolt [★] 1918 18th St NW (at Florida) **202/232-0077** *7am- 8:30pm, patio*

Soho Tea & Coffee [WI,WC] 2150 P St NW (at 21st St) **202/463-7646** *7am-11pm, patio*

Restaurants

2 Amys Pizza [WC] 3715 Macomb St NW **202/885-5700** *lunch & dinner*

Acadiana [R] 901 New York Ave NW **202/408-8848** *lunch Mon-Fri, dinner nightly, brunch Sun, Cajun, great bourbon selection*

Annie's Paramount Steak House [WC] 1609 17th St NW (at Corcoran) **202/232-0395** *11am-10pm, till 11pm Fri-Sat, from 9am Sun, full bar*

Banana Cafe & Piano Bar [E,P,GO] 500 8th St SE (at E St) **202/543-5906** *11am-10:30pm, till 11pm Fri-Sat, Puerto Rican/ Cuban,, famous margaritas*

Bar Pilar 1833 14th St NW (at Swann St) **202/265-1751** *dinner nightly, wknd brunch, new American*

Beacon Bar & Grill [★] 1615 Rhode Island Ave NW (at 17th, at Beacon Hotel) **202/872-1126** *brkfst, lunch & dinner, popular Sun brunch, patio*

Busboys & Poets [E,WI,WC] 2021 14th St NW (at V St) **202/387-7638** *8am-midnight, till 2am Fri-Sat, 10am-midnight Sun, also bookstore, live jazz & poetry*

Cafe Saint Ex/ Gate 54 1847 14th St NW **202/265-7839** *lunch, dinner, Sun brunch, modern American, also Gate 54 club downstairs, popular Th [GF,D]*

Duplex Diner [★] 2004 18th St NW (at Ave U) **202/265-7828** *6pm-11pm, till 2am Th-Sat, from 11am wknds, American comfort food, full bar*

Dupont Italian Kitchen & Bar [WC] 1637 17th St NW (at R St) **202/328-3222, 202/328-0100** *11am-11pm, bar 4pm-2am*

Floriana [GO] 1602 17th St NW (at Q St NW) **202/667-5937** *dinner nightly, Italian, full bar, patio*

Food For Thought [WC] 1811 14th St NW (at the Black Cat) **202/667-4490** *8pm-1am, 7pm-2am Fri-Sat, mostly vegan/ veggie, indie/ punk music shows, readings*

Guapo's [WC] 4515 Wisconsin Ave NW (at Albemarle) **202/686-3588** *lunch & dinner, Mexican, full bar*

Jaleo [E,WC] 480 7th St NW (at E St) **202/628-7949** *lunch & dinner, tapas, full bar, Sevillanas dancers Wed*

Level One 1639 R St NW (at 17th) **202/745-0025** *dinner nightly, wknd brunch*

Logan Tavern [GO] 1423 P St NW **202/332-3710** *lunch & dinner, wknd brunch, American comfort food, also bar*

Occidental Grill 1475 Pennsylvania Ave NW (btwn 14th & 15th) **202/783-1475** *lunch Mon-Sat, dinner nightly, clsd Sun, upscale, political player hangout*

Perry's 1811 Columbia Rd NW (at 18th) **202/234-6218** *5:30pm-11:30pm, popular drag Sun brunch, contemporary American & sushi, full bar*

Pizza Paradiso 2003 P Street NW **202/223-1245** *11am-11pm, till midnight wknds,Gluten-Free Crust*

Rasika [WC] 633 D St NW **202/637-1222** *lunch Mon-Fri, dinner Mon-Sat, clsd Sun, Indian*

Rice 1608 14th St NW (at 'Q') **202/234-2400** *lunch & dinner, Thai*

Rocklands 2418 Wisconsin Ave NW (at Calvert) **202/333-2558** *11am-10pm, till 9pm Sun, BBQ & take-out*

Sala Thai 1301 U St NW (at 13th) **202/462-1333** *lunch & dinner*

Smoke & Barrell [E] 2471 18th St NW **202/319-9353** *beer, bbq & bourbon*

Thaitanic 1326 14th St NW (at Rhode Island Ave) **202/588-1795** *lunch & dinner, Thai, plenty veggie*

Zaytinia 701 9th Street NW (at G St) **202/638-0800** *lunch & dinner, Greek/ Mediterranean*

Entertainment & Recreation

Anecdotal History Tours [GF] **301/294-9514** *guided tours, by appt only*

Bike & Roll Washington DC [GF] 1100 Pennsylvania Ave NW (off 12th St, at Old Post Office Pavilion) **202/842-2453**

Capital Bikeshare 877/430-2453 *look for the red bikes at parking stations around the city; join for 24hrs or longer*

Hillwood Museum & Gardens [R] 4155 Linnean Ave NW (at Tilden St NW) **202/686-5807** *10am-5pm Tue-Sat, Fabergé, porcelain, furniture & more*

Phillips Collection 1600 21st St NW (at Q St) **202/387-2151** *clsd Mon, America's first museum of modern art, near Dupont Circle*

Bookstores

G Books [GO] 1520 U St NW, bassment (btwn 15th St & U St) **202/986-9697** *4pm-10pm, used gay books, mags, movies, pride items*

Kramerbooks & Afterwords Cafe & Grill [E,F,WC] 1517 Connecticut Ave NW (at Q St) **202/387-1400** *7:30am-1am, 24hrs wknds, also cafe & bar*

Publications

Metro Weekly 202/638-6830 *LGBT newsmagazine, extensive club listings*

Washington Blade 202/747-2077 *LGBT newspaper*

Men's Clubs

Crew Club 1321 14th St NW (at Rhode Island) **202/319-1333** *24hrs*

Glorious Health Club 2120 W Virginia Ave NE **202/269-0226** *24hrs*

Erotica

Bite the Fruit 1723 Connecticut Ave NW (btwn R & S Sts) **202/299-0440** *11am-11pm, till 18pm Sun*

Cruisy Areas

Rock Creek Park [AYOR] Beach Dr N of Military Rd *area behind Francis swimming pool*

FLORIDA

Statewide

PUBLICATIONS

HOTSPOTS! Magazine **954/928-1862** *"South Florida's largest gay publication"*

Bonifay

CRUISY AREAS

Wayside Park Hwy 79 *parking lot & woods 6 miles N of Bonifay at Holmes Creek bridge*

Boynton Beach

see also West Palm Beach

Bradenton

see also Sarasota

Cape Coral

see Fort Myers

Clearwater

see also Dunedin, New Port Richey, Port Richey & St Petersburg

BARS

Pro Shop Pub [★M,NH,B,GO] 840 Cleveland St (at Prospect) **727/447-4259** *1pm-2am*

RETAIL SHOPS

Skinz 2027 Gulf to Bay Blvd (aka State Rd 60, at Hercules Rd) **727/441-8789** *10am-6pm, clsd Sun*

Cross City

ACCOMMODATIONS

Southern Comfort Campground [M,SW,NS,WI,WC,GO] 50 SE 74th Ave (at Hwy 19) **352/498-0490**

Daytona Beach

ACCOMMODATIONS

Mayan Inn [GF,SW,WI,WC] 103 S Ocean

BARS

Streamline Lounge [GF,D,E,WI] 140 S Atlantic Ave (at Streamline Hotel) **386/947-7470** *11am-3am, penthouse lounge*

CAFES

Java Joint & Eatery 2201-E N Oceanshore Blvd, Flagler Beach **386/439-1013** *7am-2pm*

RESTAURANTS

Anna's Trattoria [BW] 304 Seabreeze Blvd **386/239-9624** *5pm-10pm, clsd Sun-Mon, Italian*

Frappes North [E,WC] 123 W Granada Blvd (at S Yonge St), Ormond Beach **386/615-4888** *lunch Tue-Fri, dinner nightly, clsd Sun*

Hamburger Mary's [MW,DS] 180 N Beach St **386/256-2564** *11am-1am, till 8pm Sun, clsd Mon*

PUBLICATIONS

Watermark Online 407/481-2243 *bi-weekly LGBT newspaper*

EROTICA

Fantasy Shoppe 701 N Ridgewood Ave **386/252-7399** *9am-1am, till 3am Fri-Sat*

X-Mart Boutique 2591 W International Speedway Blvd **386/252-8707** *24hrs*

Dunedin

see also St Petersburg

NIGHTCLUBS

Blur Nighclub [M,D,K,DS] 325 Main St **727/736-2587** *3pm-2am*

RESTAURANTS

Kelly's 319 Main St **727/736-5284** *8am-9:30pm, also Chic a Boom Room Martini Bar*

CRUISY AREAS

Honeymoon Island State Recreation Area [AYOR] end of Causeway Blvd *nude sunbathing & beach*

Fort Lauderdale

Info Lines & Services

Fort Lauderdale LGBT Visitors Center 2300 NE 7th Ave, Wilton Manors **954/523-3500** *10am-6pm, clsd wknds*

Greater Fort Lauderdale Convention & Visitors Bureau 101 NE 3rd Ave Ste 100 **954/765-4466**

Lambda South [WC] 1231-A E Las Olas Blvd *meeting space for LGBT in recovery*

The Pride Center at Equality Park [WC] 2040 N Dixie Hwy, Wilton Manors **954/463-9005** *10am-10pm, noon-5pm wknds, outreach*

Accommodations

Alcazar Resort [MO,SW,N,NS,WI,GO] 555 N Birch Rd (at Terramar) **954/563-6819, 800/445-7036** *at the beach*

The Atlantic Hotel & Spa [GS,SW,WI] 601 N Fort Lauderdale Beach Blvd **954/567-8020** *gym, restaurant & bar*

The Cabanas [M,SW,NS,WI,GO] 2209 NE 26th St **954/564-7764** *riverfront, kayaks available, clothing-optional jacuzzi, spa*

Calypso Inn [M,SW,WI,GO] 2520 NE 6th Ave (at NE 26th St), Wilton Manors **954/605-3561** *tropical compound surrounds a heated lagoon pool*

Cheston House [MO,SW,N,NS,WI,GO] 520 N Birch Rd (at Viramar) **954/566-7950**

Courtyard Fort Lauderdale Beach [GF,SW,NS,WI] 440 Seabreeze Blvd **954/524-8733** *sundeck bar, fitness center, beach across street*

Ed Lugo Resort [★GF,SW,WI,GO] 2404 NE 8th Ave (Wilton Manors) **954/275-8299**

The Grand Resort & Spa [MO,SW,N,NS,WI,WC,GO] 539 N Birch Rd (at Windamar) **954/630-3000, 800/818-1211** *sundeck, spa, gym*

Inn Leather Guesthouse [MO,L,SW,N,WI,GO] 610 SE 19th St (at SW 1st Ave) **954/467-1444, 877/532-7729** *sling in each room & dungeon*

Island Sands Inn [GS,SW,WI,GO] 2409 NE 7th Ave **954/990-6499**

Las Olas Guesthouse [GS,SW,N,WI,WC] 908 NE 15th Ave (at Sunrise) **954/683-6250** *Key West-style guesthouse*

Manor Inn [MO,SW,N,NS,WI,GO] 2408 NE 6th Ave (at NE 24th St), Wilton Manors **954/566-8223, 866/682-7456**

Marriott Harbor Beach Resort [GF,SW] 3030 Holiday Dr **954/525-4000** *also restaurant & spa, private beach access*

Pelican Grand Beach Resort [GS,SW] 2000 N Ocean Blvd **954/568-9431, 800/525-9431** *waterfront resort with restaurant, spa & ice cream parlour*

Pineapple Point Guest House [★MO,SW,N,NS,WI,WC,GO] 315 NE 16th Terr (at NE 3rd Ct) **954/527-0094, 888/844-7295** *luxury guesthouse, gym*

Riverside Hotel [GS,SW,WI] 620 E Las Olas Blvd **954/467-0671** *restaurant & bar on site, near the riverwalk and minutes from the beaches, pets ok*

Time in Paradise Coral Woods B&B [MO,SW,WI,GO] 3548 NE 18 Ave, Oakland Park **305/333-5735** *relaxing and peaceful*

Villa Venice Men's Resort [MO,SW,NS,WI,GO] 2900 Terramar St (at Orton) **954/563-6819, 800/445-7036** *2 blocks to beach*

W Fort Lauderdale [GS,SW,F,WI,WC] 401 N Fort Lauderdale Beach Blvd **954/414-8200** *restaurant & lounge*

Westin Beach Resort [GF,SW,WC] 321 N Fort Lauderdale Beach Blvd (A1A) **954/467-1111** *beachfront hotel with sports deck, gym, restaurant & lounge*

The Worthington Guest House [★MO,SW,NS,WI,GO] 543 N Birch Rd (at Terramar) **954/563-6819, 800/445-7036** *resort, clothing-optional hot tub*

Bars

Alibi [MW,F,V,NS,WI,WC] 2266 Wilton Dr (at NE 4th Ave) **954/565-2526** *11am-2am*

Boardwalk [★M,NH,S,18+] 1721 N Andrews Ave **954/463-6969** *3pm-2am, till 3am Fri-Sat, strippers from 5pm*

Le Boy [M,S] 1243 NE 11th Ave **954/368-8786** *2pm-2am, clsd Mon, patio*

Chardees Lounge [MW,E] 2440 Wilton Dr, Wilton Manors **954/533-4916** *4pm-1am, from 1pm wknds*

Corner Pub [GS,NH,GO] 1915 N Andrews Ave **954/564-7335** *11am-2am, till 3am Fri-Sat, from 8am Fri-Sun*

Cubby Hole [M,NH,B,F,WI] 823 N Federal Hwy (at 8th St) **954/728-9001** *11am-2am, till 3am Fri-Sat*

G Spot [W,D] 2031 Wilton Dr, Wilton Manors **954/368-2724** *5pm-3am*

Gym Sports Bar [M] 2287 Wilton Dr **954/368-5318** *11am-2am*

Hunter's [★M,D,E,K,DS,V,GO] 2232 Wilton Dr, Wilton Manors **954/630-3556** *4pm-2am, from 2pm wknds, till 3am wknds, T-dance Sun*

Infinity Lounge [M] 2184 Wilton Dr **754/223-3619** *3pm-2am*

Johnsons [M,S,$] 2340 Wilton Dr **954/908-1272** *6pm-2am, till 3am Fri-Sat, clsd Mon-Tue*

LeBoy Tonight [M,D,S] 1243 NE 11 Ave **954/368-8786** *4pm-2am,till 3am, wknds, clsd Mon*

The Manor Complex [MW,D,F,E,C] 2345 Wilton Dr, Wilton Manors **954/626-0082** *11am-11pm, also Epic nightclub, also restaurant & cafe*

Matty's Wilton Park [M,V] 2100 Wilton Dr **954/900-3973** *2pm-2am, from noon wknds*

Mona's [M,NH,K] 502 E Sunrise Blvd (at 5th Ave) **954/525-6662** *noon-2am, till 3am wknds*

Monkey Business [M,NH,C,DS] 2740 N Andrews Ave **954/514-7819** *7am-2am*

Naked Grape [GF] 2163 Wilton Dr (at NE 20th St), Wilton Manors **965/563-5631** *4pm-midnight, clsd Sun-Mon, wine bar & tapas*

The Pub [M,NH,DS,WI] 2283 Wilton Dr **754/200-5244** *11am-2am, till 3am Fri-Sat*

Ramrod [★M,B,L] 1508 NE 4th Ave (at 16th St) **954/763-8219** *3pm-2am, till 3am wknds, cruisy, patio, also LeatherWerks leather store*

Rumors [M,NH,F,WC] 2426 Wilton Dr, Wilton Manors **954/565-8853** *11am-2am, till 3am Fri-Sat*

Scandals [M,D,CW,B,E,F,K,OC,WC] 3073 NE 6th Ave, Wilton Manors **954/567-2432** *noon-2am, patio*

Smarty Pants [M,NH,F,E,K,DS,WC] 2400 Oakland Park Blvd **954/561-1724** *9am-2am, till 3am Fri-Sat, noon-2am Sun*

Nightclubs

Southern Nights [M,D,DS,WC] 2209 Wilton Dr (off NE 23rd St) **754/312-5722** *5pm-2am, from 8pm Sat, clsd Sun-Mon*

Cafes

Cafe Emunah 3558 N Ocean Blvd **954/561-6411** *clsd Fri-Sat, sushi menu & extensive tea offerings that adhere to kosher laws*

Java Boys [★WI] 2230 Wilton Dr, Wilton Manors **954/564-8828** *7am-11pm*

Jimmies Chocolates & Cafe 148 N Federal Hwy, Dania Beach **954/921-0688** *opens 11am, lunch & dinner Wed-Sat, bistro w/ fresh fare & wine*

Storks [WC] 2505 NE 15th Ave (at NE 26th St, Wilton Manors) **954/567-3220** *6:30am-midnight*

Restaurants

La Bonne Crêpe 815 E Las Olas Blvd **954/761-1515** *7am-9:30pm, till 11:30pm Fri-Sat, patio*

Canyon 1818 E Sunrise Blvd **954/765-1950** *artisanal cuisine with Asian, South and Central American undertones, full bar*

Courtyard Cafe [GO] 2211 Wilton Dr **954/563-2499** *7am-11pm, 24hrs Th-Sat*

Flip Flops 3051 NE 32nd Ave **954/567-1672** *11:30am-9pm, till 10pm Fri-Sat, clsd Mon, casual waterfront dining*

The Floridian [WC] 1410 E Las Olas Blvd **954/463-4041** *24hr diner*

Galanga 2389 Wilton Dr, Wilton Manors **954/202-0000** *dinner nightly, lunch weekdays, Thai, also sushi*

J Marks Restaurant [GO] 1245 N Federal Hwy **954/390-0770** *11am-10pm, till 11pm Fri-Sat, full bar*

Jaxson's Ice Cream Parlor 128 S Federal Hwy, Dania Beach **954/923-4445** *noon-11pm, American fare served at this old-fashioned parlor with memorabilia*

Kitchenetta [WC] 2850 N Federal Hwy **954/567-3333** *dinner nightly, clsd Mon*

La Bamba [WC] 4245 N Federal Hwy **954/568-5662** *more gay Mon night*

Lester's Diner [★WC] 250 State Rd 84 **954/525-5641** *24hrs, more gay late nights*

Lips [K,DS] 1421 E Oakland Park Blvd (at Dixie Hwy) **954/567-0987** *6pm-close, from noon Sun, clsd Mon, "the ultimate in drag dining"*

Mason Jar Cafe [GO] 2980 N Federal Hwy **954/568-4100** *lunch & dinner, clsd Sun, comfort food*

Mind Your Manors Bar & Grill 2045 Wilton Dr, Wilton Manors **754/223-2172** *noon-10pm, till midnight Fri-Sat*

Mojo [E] 4140 N Federal Hwy **954/568-4443** *open 5pm, clsd Sun, full bar*

New York Grilled Cheese 2207 Wilton Dr **954/564-6887** *11am-11pm, till 3am Th-Sun*

Le Patio [GO] 2401 NE 11th Ave **954 /530-4641** *lunch & dinner, clsd Mon, comfort food*

Rosie's Bar & Grill [★] 2449 Wilton Dr, Wilton Manors **954/563-0123** *11am-11pm*

Shooters Waterfront 3033 NE 32nd Ave **954/566-2855** *11am-10pm, till midnight wknds, laid-back spot on the Intracoastal, great from brunch from 10am wknds*

Tequila Sunrise Mexican Grill [E] 4711 N Dixie Hwy **954/938-4473** *11:30am-10pm, till 11pm Th-Sat, 1pm-10pm Sun*

Entertainment & Recreation

Stonewall National Museum & Archives 1300 E Sunrise Blvd **954/763-8565** *houses LGBT books, periodicals & archival materials*

World AIDS Museum and Educational Center 1201 NE 26th St #111, Wilton Manors **954/390-0550** *noon-6pm, clsd Mon-Tue, interactive experiences and education that document the history, deepen the understanding and remove the stigma of HIV and AIDS*

Bookstores

Pride Factory 850 NE 13th St **954/463-6600** *10am-9pm, 11am-7pm Sun*

Retail Shops

LeatherWerks [GO] 1226 NE 4th Ave (at 13th St) **954/761-1236** *10am-8pm, till 9pm Fri-Sat, 11am-7pm Sun, also inside the Ramrod*

Out of the Closet 2097 Wilton Dr, Wilton Manors **954/358-5580** *10am-7pm, till 6pm Sun*

The Poverello Center 2056 N Dixie Hwy **954/561-3663** *thrift store to support the purchase of food for people living w/ HIV/AIDS in Broward County*

To The Moon [GO] 2205 Wilton Dr (at 6th Ave), Wilton Manors **954/564-2987** *10am-11pm, pride gifts, cards & candy candy candy!*

Men's Clubs

321 Slammer [BYOB,PC] 321 W Sunrise Blvd **954/524-2625** *5pm-3am, till 5am Fri-Sat*

Club Fort Lauderdale [★SW,18+,PC] 110 NW 5th Ave (at Broward) **954/525-3344** *24hrs*

Clubhouse II [V,PC] 2650 E Oakland Park Blvd **954/566-6750** *24hrs, gym, [L] Tue*

Erotica

Cross-Dress 10145 NW 46th St, Sunrise **954/748-5855** *10am-2pm, clsd Sun, cross dressing emporium*

Fetish Factory 855 E Oakland Park Blvd **954/563-5777** *noon-9pm, noon-6pm Sun*

Love Stuff 2075 S Federal Hwy **954/524-2888**

Rock Hard 2205-A Wilton Dr, Wilton Manors **954/318-7625** *11am-2am. till 3:30am Fri-Sat*

Tropixxx Video 1514 NE 4th Ave (at NE16th St), Wilton Manors **888/464-5988** *10am-2am, till 3am Fri-Sat*

Cruisy Areas

Beach at Sebastian St [AYOR]

Fort Lauderdale Beach [AYOR] opposite 18th St NE (btwn Oakland Park & Sunrise Blvds) *dune area cruisy all night & gay beach during the day*

Holiday Park [AYOR] Sunrise Blvd (on right side at Federal Hwy) *exit I-95 at Sunrise Blvd & head E toward beach, open 5am-midnight*

Pompano Beach [AYOR] 16th St & A1A (N of Atlantic)

Fort Myers

Info Lines & Services

Gay AA Lambda Drummers [WC] 3049 McGregor Blvd (at St John the Apostle MCC) **239/275-5111** *8pm Tue & Sat in social hall*

Accommodations

Cape Paradise Resort [MO,SW,WI,GO] 1508 SW 47th St, Cape Coral **239/246-5808** *B&B in private home*

Bars

Rascals [M,D,DS,K] 3758 Cleveland Ave (at US 41) **239/931-9976** *noon-2am*

Restaurants

McGregor Grill [GO] 15675 McGregor Blvd, Ste 24 **239/437-3499** *11am-2am, from 4pm Sun, pub fare, some outdoor dining*

The Oasis [BW,WC] 2260 Dr Martin Luther King Blvd **239/334-1566** *breakfast, lunch & dinner*

Cruisy Areas

Bowditch Point Recreational Park [AYOR] 50 Estero Blvd (at end of street), Fort Myers Beach

Bunche Beach [AYOR] John Morris Pkwy *S end of beach*

Horton Park [AYOR] Everest Pkwy (go E on Del Prado to end), Cape Coral *open sunrise to sunset*

Fort Pierce

Erotica

Lion's Den 7100 Okeechobee Rd (exit 129 off I-95) **772/466-6323**

Gainesville

Info Lines & Services

Free to Be AA 3131 NW 13th St (The Pride Center) **352/372-8091 (AA#)** *7:30pm Sun, LGBT AA group*

Pride Community Center 3131 NW 13th St #62 **352/377-8915** *3pm-7pm, noon-4pm Sat, clsd Sun*

Bars

The University Club [★MW,D,K,DS,S,YC,WC] 18 E University Ave (enter rear) **352/378-6814** *5pm-2am, 3 levels, patio*

Entertainment & Recreation

Ponte Vedra LGBT Beach *Go N from Gainesville on Waldo Rd to N 301, then E on I-10. I-10 becomes 95. Go S on 95, then take a left. Go E onto Butler Blvd, which ends at A1A. Turn right onto A1A & then drive 5 to 7 minutes looking for Guana Boat Landing parking lot on the right.*

Cruisy Areas

Bolen's Bluff Dock [AYOR] US 441 S (past Praynes Prairie, on the right) *days*

Hollywood

ACCOMMODATIONS

Rooftop Resort [GS,SW,N,WI] 1215 N Ocean Dr **954/925-0301** *the premier nudist swinger resort hotel in S Florida*

EROTICA

Pleasure Emporium 1321 S 30th Ave **954/927-8181**

CRUISY AREAS

Holland Park [AYOR] Johnson St (at Intracoastal)

Inverness

ACCOMMODATIONS

Camp David [MO,SW,N] 2000 S Bishop Point Rd **352/344-3445** *camping/ RV retreat, membership req'd*

Islamorada

ACCOMMODATIONS

Casa Morada [GF,SW] 136 Madeira Rd **305/664-0044, 888/881-3030** *luxury all-suite hotel w/ private island*

Jacksonville

INFO LINES & SERVICES

Free to Be LGBT AA 634 Lomax St **904/399-8535** *6:30pm Mon & Fri*

ACCOMMODATIONS

Hilton Garden Inn Jacksonville JTB/ Deerwood Park [GF,SW,WI,WC] 9745 Gate Pkwy (at Southside Blvd) **904/997-6600**

Spring Hill Suites Jacksonville [GF,SW,NS,WI] 4385 Southside Blvd (at J Turner Butler Blvd) **904/997-6650**

BARS

Bos Coral Reef [MW,NH,D,DS] 201 5th Ave N (at 2nd St), Jacksonville Beach **904/246-9874** *2pm-2am*

In Cahoots [M,D,MR,E,K,DS,WC] 711 Edison Ave (btwn Riverside & Park) **904/353-6316** *6pm-2am, clsd Mon*

The Metro [★MW,D,DS,P,S,V,WC] 859 Willow Branch Ave **904/388-8719** *2pm-2am, till 4am Fri-Sat*

The New Boot Rack Saloon [M,CW,K,BW,WI,WC] 4751 Lenox Ave (at Cassat Ave) **904/384-7090** *3pm-2am, patio*

Park Place Lounge [MW,NH,D,WC] 931 King St (at Post) **904/389-6616** *noon-2am*

RESTAURANTS

Al's Pizza 1620 Margaret St, Ste 201 **904/388-8384** *in Riverside/ Little 5 Points area*

Biscotti's [★] 3556 Saint Johns Ave (Talbot Ave) **904/387-2060** *10:30am-10pm, till midnight Fri-Sat, from 8am Sat-Sun*

Bistro Aix 1440 San Marco Blvd **904/398-1949** *11am-10pm, till 11pm Fri, 5pm-11pm Sat, 5pm-9pm Sun*

European Street Cafe [★BW,WC,GO] 2753 Park St (at King) **904/384-9999** *10am-10pm, deli, patio*

Mossfire Grill 1537 Margaret St **904/355-4434** *lunch & dinner, full bar*

MEN'S CLUBS

Club Jacksonville [SW,PC,WI] 1939 Hendricks Ave (at Atlantic Blvd) **904/398-7451** *24hrs*

CRUISY AREAS

Willowbranch Park [AYOR] Park St (btwn Willow Branch Ave & Cherry St) *take Roosevelt Blvd to McDuff Ave & head toward river*

Key Biscayne

CRUISY AREAS

Bear Cut Park [AYOR] in Crandon Beach Park *head W on beach; beware cops (even undercover)!*

Key West

INFO LINES & SERVICES

Gay & Lesbian Community Center [WI] 513 Truman Ave **305/292-3223** *many meetings & groups*

Keep It Simple (Gay/ Lesbian AA) **305/296-8654** *8pm Mon-Sat, 5:30pm Sun*

Accommodations

Alexander Palms Court [GF,SW,WC,GO] 715 South St (at Vernon) **305/296-6413, 800/858-1943**

Alexander's Guest House [★MW,SW,N,WI,WC,GO] 1118 Fleming St (at Frances) **305/294-9919, 800/654-9919**

Ambrosia House Tropical Lodging [GF,SW,WI,WC] 615 & 618-622 Fleming St (at Simonton) **305/296-9838**

Andrews Inn [GF,SW,NS,WI] Zero Whalton Ln (at Duval) **305/294-7730, 888/263-7393**

The Artist House [GS,NS,WI] 534 Eaton St (at Duval) **305/296-3977**

Avalon B&B [GF,SW,WI] 1317 Duval St (at United) **305/294-8233, 800/848-1317**

Curry House [GS,SW,NS,WI] 806 Fleming St (at William) **305/294-6777** *full brkfst, patio*

Cypress House & Guest Studios [GF,SW,NS,WI,WC] 601 Caroline (at Simonton) **305/294-6969, 800/549-4430**

Equator Guest House [MO,SW,N,NS,WI,WC,GO] 822 Fleming St (at William) **305/294-7775, 800/278-4552**

The Grand Guesthouse [MW,WI,NS,GO] 1116 Grinnell St **305/294-0590, 888/947-2630**

Heron House Court [GF,SW,NS,WI,WC] 412 Frances St (at Eaton) **305/294-9227** *luxury guesthouse, hot tub, sundeck*

Island House Key West [★MO,F,SW,N,NS,WI,GO] 1129 Fleming St (at White) **305/294-6284, 800/890-6284** *cafe & bar, very cruisy*

Key West Harbor Inn B&B [GS,SW,NS,WI] 219 Elizabeth St (at Greene) **305/296-2978, 800/608-6569**

Knowles House B&B [GS,SW,N,NS,GO] 1004 Eaton St (at Grinnell) **305/296-8132, 800/352-4414**

La Te Da [★MW,S,21+,SW,WI,WC,GO] 1125 Duval St (at Catherine) **305/296-6706, 877/528-3320**

Marquesa Hotel [GF,SW,NS,WI,WC] 600 Fleming St (at Simonton) **305/292-1919, 800/869-4631** *also Cafe Marquesa 6pm-10:30pm, full bar*

The Mermaid & the Alligator—A Key West B&B [GF,SW,NS,WI] 729 Truman Ave (at Windsor Ln) **305/294-1894, 844/308-0008** *full brkfst, located in the heart of Old Town, walking distance to world-famous Duval St*

The New Orleans House Guesthouse [M,SW,N,WI,GO] 724 Duval St (at Petronia) **305/293-9800, 888/293-9893** *sundeck, hot tub, garden bar, play areas*

Seascape Inn [GF,SW,NS,WI] 420 Olivia St (at Duval) **305/296-7776, 800/765-6438**

Simonton Court Historic Inn & Cottages [GF,SW,NS,WI] 320 Simonton St (at Caroline) **305/294-6386, 800/944-2687**

The Southernmost Inn [GS,SW,NS,WI,WC] 525 United St (at Duval) **888/525-0037** *all-welcome historic inn offering guesthouse ambiance & resort*

Tropical Inn [GF,SW,WI] 812 Duval St (near Petronia) **305/294-9977, 888/611-6510** *hot tub, sundeck*

Bars

The 801 Bourbon Bar [★MW,NH,D,K,C,DS,P,S] 801 Duval St (at Petronia) **305/294-4737** *10am-4am, from noon Sun, also Saloon One [M,L]*

Bobby's Monkey Bar [M,NH,E,K,WI,WC] 900 Simonton St (at Olivia) **305/294-2655** *noon-4am*

Bourbon Street Pub [★M,S,V,SW,WC] 724 Duval St (at Petronia) **305/293-9800** *11am-4am, from noon Sun, popular daytime bar*

Garden of Eden [GS,D,E,N] 224 Duval St **305/296-4565** *10am-4am, from noon Sun*

Hog's Breath Saloon [GF,F,E] 400 Front St **305/296-4222** *10am-2am*

La Te Da [★MW,F,C,P,WC,GO] 1125 Duval St (at Catherine) **305/296-6706**

Nightclubs

Aqua [★MW,D,E,K,DS,V,WC,GO] 711 Duval St **305/294-0555** *3pm-2am*

Bottle Cap Lounge [GS,D,E] **305/296-2807** *noon-4am*

Cafes

Croissants de France [BW] 816 Duval St **305/294-2624** *bakery 7:30am-6pm, restaurant open till 10pm, patio*

Restaurants

Antonia's Restaurant [★] 615 Duval St (at Southard) **305/294-6565** *lunch & dinner, Italian, full bar*

Azur 425 Grinnell St **305/292-2987** *Mediterranean*

Blue Heaven [E] 729 Thomas St **305/296-8666** *great brkfst, also lunch & dinner*

Bo's Fish Wagon [★] 801 Caroline (at William) **305/294-9272** *lunch & dinner, "seafood & eat it"*

Cafe Sole 1029 Southard St (at Frances) **305/294-0230** *dinner nightly, romantic, candlelit backyard*

Camille's 1202 Simonton (at Catherine) **305/296-4811** *brkfst, lunch & dinner, bistro, hearty brkfst*

El Meson de Pepe [E] 410 Wall St (in Mallory Sq) **305/295-2620** *lunch & dinner, Cuban*

The Flaming Buoy Filet Co [WC] 1100 Packer St (at Virginia) **305/295-7970** *open daily at 6pm*

Grand Cafe Key West 314 Duval St **305/292-4740** *lunch & dinner*

Half Shell Raw Bar 231 Margaret St **305/294-7496** *11am-10pm, waterfront*

Hurricane Hole 305/294-8025 *11am-11pm, dockside bar*

Jack Flats [WC] 509 Duval St **305/294-7955** *11am-2am, sports bar*

La Trattoria Venezia 524 Duval St (at Fleming) **305/296-1075** *5pm-10:30pm*

Louie's Backyard [★] 700 Waddell Ave (at Vernon) **305/294-1061** *11:30am-1am, deck*

Mangia Mangia [BW] 900 Southard St (at Margaret St) **305/294-2469** *dinner only, fresh pasta, patio*

Michaels 532 Margaret St **305/295-1300** *dinner only, steakhouse*

New York Pasta Garden 1075 Duval St (Duval Square) **305/292-1991** *11am-10pm*

Nine One Five 915 Duval St **305/296-0669** *11:30am-11pm Wed-Sun,from 5pm Mon-Tue, tapas, full bar*

Sarabeth's 530 Simonton St **305/293-8181** *8am-9pm,clsd Mon, American*

Seven Fish [★] 921 Truman **305/296-2777** *6pm-10pm, clsd Tue*

Entertainment & Recreation

BluQ Sailing [M,GO] 200 Margaret St **305/923-7245** *all-gay sails*

Fort Zachary Taylor Beach *more gay to the right*

Gay & Lesbian Trolley Tour 305/294-4603

Schooner Hindu Bight Marina **305/509-1771** *a beautiful wooden sailboat for daytime or sunset sails Nov-Jun*

Venus Charters [★GO] Garrison Bight Marina **305/304-1181**

Bookstores

Key West Island Books 513 Fleming St (at Duval) **305/294-2904** *10am-9pm, till 6pm Sun*

Retail Shops

Fausto's Food Palace 522 Fleming St (at Duval) **305/296-5663** *8am-8pm, till 7pm Sun, cruisy grocery store*

In Touch Gay Pride Store 706-A Duval St (at Angela) **305/294-1995** *9am-9pm, gay gifts*

Erotica

Fairvilla Megastore 520 Front St **305/292-0448**

Leather Master 418 Appelrouth Ln **305/292-5051** *11am-10pm, noon-8pm Sun*

Truman Adult Books & Video 922 Truman Ave **305/295-0120** *24hrs, arcade*

Cruisy Areas

Higgs Beach [AYOR] on White St

Little Hamaca Park [AYOR] on Government Rd *from downtown, go E on Flagler Rd, turn right on Government, and follow past airport to park at end of road*

Lake Park

Retail Shops

Eurotique 804 US Hwy 1 Ste 2 **561/791-6386** *11am-6pm, till 5pm Sat, clsd Sun, corsets, lingerie, clothing, bondage gear, and novelty items for your convenience*

Lake Worth

see also West Palm Beach

Info Lines & Services

Compass LGBT Community Center [WC] 201 N Dixie Hwy **561/533-9699** *9am-9pm, till 7pm Fri, 3pm-7pm Sat, clsd Sun*

Bars

The Mad Hatter Bar & Grill [M,NH,V,OC,GO] 1532 N Dixie Hwy (16th Ave) **561/547-8860** *1pm-2am, noon-midnight Sun*

Lakeland

Bars

The Pub [M,NH,DS] 2523 Broadway St **863/213-9602** *4pm-2am, till midnight Sun*

Cruisy Areas

Lake Morton [AYOR] *beware cops (including undercover)!*

Lantana

Bars

Pennys At The Duke [MW,NH,D,K,GO] 902 N Dixie Hwy **561/370-3954** *2pm-2am, noon-midnight Sun*

Largo

Bars

Quench Lounge [M,D,K,S] 13284 66th St N **727/754-5900** *2pm-2am*

Erotica

Buddies of Largo 13801 66th St **727/539-7979** *noon-midnight*

Madison

Accommodations

The Mystic Lake Manor [MO,SW,N,WI,WC,GO] **850/973-8435** *full brkfst, hot tub*

Marathon

Accommodations

Tropical Cottages [GF,V,NS] 243 61st St Gulf **305/743-6048**

Entertainment & Recreation

Bahia Honda State Park & Beach 12 miles S of Marathon

Melbourne

Accommodations

Beach Bungalow [GF,NS,WI] 312 Wavecrest Ave, Indialantic by the Sea **321/984-1330** *beachfront town homes with private patios and spas. pets ok*

Crane Creek Inn B&B [GS,SW,NS,WI] 907 E Melbourne Ave **321/768-6416**

Erotica

Hot Flixx 3369 Sarno Rd (Bldg A) **321/752-8805** *9am-2am*

Miami

Miami is divided into 3 geographical areas:

Miami–Overview

Miami–Greater Miami

Miami–Miami Beach/ South Beach

Miami—Overview

Info Lines & Services

Greater Miami CVB 305/539-3000, 800/933-8448 *plan your Miami vacation!*

Jewish Community Services of South Florida (JCS) 305/576-6550 *24hrs, gay-friendly info & referrals for Dade County*

LGBT Visitor Center 1130 Washington Ave, 1st flr N (at 11th St), Miami Beach **305/397-8914** *9am-8pm, 11am-4pm wknds*

Entertainment & Recreation

Sailboat Charters of Miami 3400 Pan American Dr (at S Bayshore Dr) **305/772-4221** *private sailing charters aboard all-teakwood 46-foot clipper to Bahamas & the Keys*

Miami—Greater Miami

Bars

Jamboree [M,NH,DS] 7005 Biscayne Blvd (at NE 70th) **305/759-3413** *7pm-2am, dive bar, patio*

Nightclubs

Azucar [MW,D,MR-L,DS] 2301 SW 32nd Ave (at Coral Wy) **305/443-7657** *10:30pm-5am Th-Sat, 8pm-3am Sun, clsd Mon-Wed*

Club Boi [M,D,MR,18+] 1437 Washington Ave (at Score) **786/617-4746** *11pm-close Tue & Fri-Sat*

Floppy Rooster [GS,S] 7018 NW 72nd Ave (south side of The Vivid Live complex) **786/766-0778** *8pm-5am Fri-Sat, all male nude dancers*

Space Miami [GF,D] 34 NE 11th St (at NE 1st Ave) **305/375-0001** *popular club w/ int'l visiting DJs*

Cafes

Gourmet Station 646 NE 79th St **305/762-7229** *11:30am-9pm, till 4pm Sun. clsd Mon*

Restaurants

Area 31 [WC] 270 Biscayne Blvd Way (at the Epic Hotel) **305/424-5234** *brkfst, lunch & dinner, amazing view*

Jimmy's Eastside Diner [WC] 7201 Biscayne Blvd **305/754-3692** *7am-4pm*

Joey's 2506 NW 2nd Ave **305/438-0488** *lunch & dinner, clsd Mon, Italian, patio*

Ortanique on the Mile 278 Miracle Mile (at Salzedo), Coral Gables **305/446-7710** *Caribbean, full bar*

Ristorante Fratelli Milano [WC] 213 SE 1st St (at 2nd Ave) **305/373-2300** *11am-10pm, clsd Sun*

Royal Bavarian Schnitzel Haus 1085 NE 79th St **305/754-8002** *6pm-11pm, German fare*

Soyka 5556 NE 4th Ct **305/759-3117** *lunch & dinner, wknd brunch, full bar*

Wynwood Kitchen & Bar 2550 NW 2nd Ave **305/722-8959** *5:30pm-midnight, Latin, great art*

Retail Shops

Creative Male 3227 NE 2nd Ave **305/573-3080** *noon-8pm, till 6pm Sun*

Men's Clubs

Club Aqua Miami [MO,SW,PC] 2991 Coral Wy (at S Red Rd) **305/448-2214** *24hrs*

Erotica

Miami Playground 2657 NW 36th St **305/638-4957** *24hrs*

Tokyo Valentino 8330 Biscayne D **305/758-1330** *24hrs*

Cruisy Areas

Matheson Hammock Beach [AYOR] on Old Cutler Rd (S of Kendall Dr) *also Indian Hammocks Park on 117 Ave in Kendall*

Miami – Miami Beach/ South Beach

Accommodations

The Angler's [GS,SW,WI] 660 Washington Ave **305/534-9600, 866/729-8800** *restaurant & lounge*

Beacon South Beach Hotel [GS,WI] 720 Ocean Dr **305/674-820, 800/997-9814**

Blue Moon Hotel [GF,SW,WI] 944 Collins Ave **305/673-2262** *Mediterranean-style hotel, also bar & restaurant*

The Century [GF,F,NS,WI,WC] 140 Ocean Dr **305/674-8855**

Chesterfield Hotel, Suites & Day Spa [GS] 855 Collins Ave **305/531-5831, 877/762-3477**

Circa 39 Hotel [GF,SW,NS,WI,WC] 3900 Collins Ave (at 39th St) **305/538-4900, 877/824-7223**

The Colony Hotel [GF,F,WI,WC] 736 Ocean Dr (at 7th St) **305/673-0088**

Crest Hotel Suites [GF,F,SW,WI] 1670 James Ave **877/531-0321** *boutique hotel completely restored*

Delano Hotel [GF,F,SW,WC] 1685 Collins Ave **305/672-2000**

The Hotel [GF,F,SW,NS,WI,WC] 801 Collins Ave **305/531-2222**

Hôtel Gaythering [M] 1409 Lincoln Rd **786/284-1176** *Miami Beach's only "straight friendly" hotel*

Hotel Ocean [GS,F,WI,WC] 1230-38 Ocean Dr **305/672-2579, 844/319-3854**

Island House South Beach [GS,GO] 1428 Collins Ave **305/864-2422, 800/382-2422**

The National Hotel [GS,F,SW,WI,WC] 1677 Collins Ave **305/532-2311, 800/327-8370** *luxury hotel on the beach*

Penguin Hotel [GS,F,WI,WC] 1418 Ocean Dr **305/534-9334**

The Raleigh, Miami Beach [GF,SW,WI,WC] 1775 Collins Ave (at Ocean Front) **305/534-6300, 800/848-1775**

The Savoy Hotel [GS,F,SW,NS,WI,WC] 425 Ocean Dr (at 5th St) **305/532-0200, 800/237-2869** *art-deco-meets-eclectic-boutique hotel, kids ok*

South Seas [GF,F,SW,WI] 1751 Collins Ave **305/538-1411, 800/345-2678**

The Tides [GS,F,SW,WI] 1220 Ocean Dr (at 12th St) **305/604-5070** *private beach area*

The Winterhaven [GS,WI,WC] 1400 Ocean Dr **305/531-5571**

Bars

Palace Bar & Grill [MW,F,DS,GO] 1052 Ocean Dr **305/531-7234** *11am-1am, till 2am Fri-Sat*

Nightclubs

Score [★MW,D,K,DS,V] 1437 Washington Ave **305/535-1111** *lounge opens 3pm, dance club 10pm-5am Tue & Th-Sat*

Twist [★M,D,K,DS,S,V,WC] 1057 Washington Ave (at 11th) **305/538-9478** *1pm-5am*

Cafes

News Cafe 800 Ocean Dr (at 8th St) **305/538-6397** *24hrs, gift shop and bar*

Restaurants

11th Street Diner 1065 Washington (at 11th) **305/534-6373** *24hrs, full bar*

Balans 1022 Lincoln Rd (btwn Michigan & Lennox) **305/534-9191** *8am-midnight*

Big Pink 157 Collins (at 2nd St) **305/531-0888** *8am-midnight*

Juice & Java [WC] 1346 Washington Ave (at 14th St) **305/531-6675** *9am-9pm, 10am-6pm Sun, healthy fast food*

Larios on the Beach [WC] 820 Ocean Dr (at 8th) **305/532-9577** *11:30am-midnight, Cuban*

Nexxt Cafe 700 Lincoln Rd (at Euclid Ave) **305/532-6643** *11:30am-11pm*

Spiga 1228 Collins Ave (at 12th St) **305/534-0079**

ENTERTAINMENT & RECREATION

Fritz's Skate & Bike 1620 Washington Ave **305/532-1954** *rentals, in pedestrian mall*

The Gay Beach/ 12th St Beach 12th St & Ocean *where the boys are*

Lincoln Rd Lincoln Rd (btwn Bay Rd & Collins Aves) *pedestrian mall*

South Beach Bike Tours [GO] **305/673-2002**

GYMS & HEALTH CLUBS

Crunch 1259 Washington Ave **305/674-8222**

EROTICA

Sensations Video 1317 Washington Ave **305/534-2330** *24hrs*

CRUISY AREAS

Haulover Beach Park [AYOR] North Miami Beach *popular nude beach, N of station #27; beware of cops (even undercover)!*

Mt Dora

ACCOMMODATIONS

Adora Inn [GS,NS,WI,GO] **352/735-3110** *full brkfst*

Naples

see also Fort Myers

BARS

Bambusa Bar & Grill [GF,NH,F,V,GO] 600 Goodlette Rd N (at 5th Ave N) **239/649-5657** *4pm-midnight*

CAFES

Sunburst Cafe [WC] 2340 Pine Ridge Rd (at Airport Pulling Rd) **239/263-3123** *7am-3pm*

RESTAURANTS

Caffe dell'Amore [BW,R,WC,GO] 1400 Gulf Shore Blvd N (at Banyan Blvd) **239/261-1389** *dinner only, clsd Sun in summer, Italian*

Patric's [WI,GO] 2091 Pine Ridge Rd **239/596-7708** *brkfst & lunch, animal friendly*

The Real Macaw 3275 Bayshore Dr **239/732-1188** *occasionally have gay events*

New Port Richey

BARS

Wena's [M,D,DS,WC] 6153 Massachusetts Ave **727/807-7022** *3pm-2am, clsd Mon*

Ocala

BARS

The Copa [M,D,DS,F] 2330 S Pine Ave **352/351-5721** *7pm-1am, till 2am Fri-Sat, clsd Mon*

Orlando

INFO LINES & SERVICES

GLBT Community Center of Central Florida 946 N Mills Ave **407/228-8272** *9am-9pm, noon-5pm Sat-Sun*

ACCOMMODATIONS

B Resort & Spa [GS,F,SW,WI,WC] 1905 Hotel Plaza Blvd, Lake Buena Vista, DC **407/828-2828**

Eo Inn & Spa [GS,F,NS,WI] 227 N Eola Dr (at Robinson) **407/481-8485** *boutique hotel, rooftop terrace, hot tub*

Four Points by Sheraton Studio City [GF,SW,WI,WC] 5905 International Dr (at Kirkman) **407/351-2100, 866/716-8105** *bar & restaurant*

Grand Bohemian Hotel Orlando [GF,SW,NS,WI,WC] 325 S Orange Ave **407/313-9000, 866/663-0024**

Hyatt Residency Grand Cypress [GF,SW,WI,WC] 1 Grand Cypress Blvd **407/239-1234** *1,500 acre resort, private lake, golf*

The Parliament House Resort [MW,D,MR,F,S,YC,SW,WC,GO] 410 N Orange Blossom Tr **407/425-7571** *also 6 bars (open at 8pm)*

The Point Orlando Resort [GF,SW,WC] 7389 Universal Blvd **407/956-2000, 866/994-6309** *all-suite luxury boutique hotel, gym, bar & grill*

Wyndham Orlando Resort [GF,SW,WC] 8001 International Dr **407/351-2420**

Bars

Bar Codes [M,NH,B,L,BW] 4453 Edgewater Dr (at Thistledown Dr) **407/412-6917** *noon-2am, patio*

Bear's Den [M,B] 410 N Orange Blossom Tr (at Parliament House) **407/425-7571** *6pm-2am, from noon wknds, also restaurant*

Copper Rocket [GF,BW,WC] 106 Lake Ave (at 17-92), Maitland **407/645-0069** *4pm-2am, also restaurant*

Hank's [M,NH,BW,WC] 5026 Edgewater Dr (at Lee Rd) **407/291-2399** *noon-2am, patio*

Savoy [M,S] 1913 N Orange Ave (at Berkshire) **407/898-6766** *5pm-2am, male dancers nightly*

Stonewall Bar [M,D,F,K,S,WC,GO] 741 W Church St (at Glenn Ln) **407/373-0888** *5pm-2am*

Nightclubs

Parliament House Resort [★MW,D,MR,F,S,V,18+,SW,WC,GO] 410 N Orange Blossom Tr **407/425-7571** *10:30am-3am, 6 bars*

Southern Nights [MW,D,MR,DS] 375 S Bumby Ave (at South St) **407/412-5039** *4pm-2:30am, from 9pm Sun-Mon*

Cafes

Pom Pom's 67 N Bumby Ave **407/894-0865** *11am-10pm, 24hrs Fri-Sat, tea & sandwiches*

White Wolf Cafe & Antique Shop [E,BW,WC] 1829 N Orange Ave (at Princeton) **407/895-9911** *8am-9pm, till 3pm Sun-Tue*

Restaurants

Dandelion Communitea Cafe [BW] 618 N Thornton Ave (at Colonial) **407/362-1864** *11am-10pm, till 3pm Mon, till 5pm Sun, vegetarian/ vegan*

Dexter's Thornton Park [E] 808 E Washington St **407/648-2777** *lunch & dinner, also Winter Park & Lake Mary locations*

Ethos Vegan Kitchen [WI,WC] 601-B New York Ave (at Fairbanks) **407/228-3898** *11am-10pm, 10am-3pm Sun*

Hamburger Mary's Orlando [E,K,V,WC,GO] 110 W Church St (at Garland) **321/319-0600** *11am-midnight, till 1am Th-Sat, full bar*

The Rainbow Cafe at Parliament House **407/425-7571** *7am-11pm*

Soco 629 E Central Blvd (at N Summerlin Ave) **407/849-1800** *dinner nightly and wknd brunch, full bar*

Retail Shops

Fairvilla's Sexy Things 7631 International Blvd **407/826-1627** *gifts, adult toys*

Publications

Hotspots 954/928-1862 *weekly entertainment guide*

Watermark PO Box 533655 32853 **407/481-2243** *digital LGBT news for Central FL*

Men's Clubs

Club Orlando [SW,PC] 450 E Compton St (at Delaney Ave) **407/425-5005** *24hrs*

Erotica

Fairvilla Megastore 1740 N Orange Blossom Tr **407/425-6005** *9am-2am*

Midnight News at Parliament House **407/425-7571** *6pm-2am*

Cruisy Areas

Mead Botanical Gardens [AYOR] Denning Rd & Garden St, Winter Park *take I-4 to Fairbanks exit & go E to Denning Rd, turn right & go 1 mile, on left*

Split Oak Park [AYOR] Narcoossee Rd *Take Narcoossee Rd, 5 miles S of 417, to Clapp Sims Duda Rd & turn left. Go for 1.5 miles to park*

Turkey Lake Rest Area [AYOR] *take FL Turnpike N from I-4 to milepost 263 btwn exits 259 & 265*

Palm Beach

Accommodations

The Chesterfield Hotel [GF,SW] 363 Coconut Row **561/659-5800**

Restaurants

Ta-boo [WC] 221 Worth Ave **561/835-3500** *11:30am-10pm, till 11pm Fri-Sat, cont'l*

Erotica

Adult Video Warehouse 501 Northlake Blvd, North Palm Beach **561/331-4196** *9am-2am*

Panama City

Accommodations

Casa de Playa [MW,SW,NS,GO] 20304 Front Beach Rd, Panama City Beach **850/381-1351** *guesthouse, steps from Gulf of Mexico*

Wisteria Inn [GS,SW,NS] 20404 Front Beach Rd, Panama City Beach **850/234-0557** *tropical inn,pets ok*

Bars

Splash Bar [M,NH,DS,S,V,18+,YC,WC,GO] 6520 Thomas Dr, Panama City Beach **850/236-3450** *6pm-2am, till 4am Th-Sat, also pride shop*

Cruisy Areas

Tyndall Bridge [AYOR] on Tyndall Pkwy (toward Air Force base) *parking lot*

Pensacola

Info Lines & Services

GLBT AA Group 2001 E Lloyd St **850/433-4191** *7:30pm Tue, Th & Fri*

Bars

The Cabaret [MW,E,K,WC] 101 S Jefferson St **850/607-2020** *3pm-3am*

The Round-Up [★M,NH,B,L,V,WC] 560 E Heinberg St **850/433-8482** *2pm-3am, patio*

Cafes

End of the Line Cafe [★E,WI,WC] 610 E Wright St **850/429-0336** *10am-10pm, 11am-5pm Sun, clsd Mon, vegetarian*

Cruisy Areas

The Bluffs [AYOR] Scenic Dr *beware of cops!*

Pompano Beach

Restaurants

J Marks Restaurant [E,WC,GO] 1490 NE 23th St (at Federal Hwy/ US1) **954/782-7000** *11am-10pm, till 11pm Fri-Sat, full bar*

Sarasota

Info Lines & Services

Gay AA 7225 N Lockwood Ridge Rd (in Pierce Hall, Church of the Trinity MCC) **941/355-0847 (church #)** *7pm Sun & 7pm Th*

Accommodations

Turtle Beach Resort [GF,SW,WI,WC] 9049 Midnight Pass Rd **941/349-4554**

Bars

Purple Rhino [MW,F, DS,18+] 2920 Beneva Rd **941/735-6553** *check www.thepurplerhino.org for hours, a non-profit organization providing a place for fellowship to the LGBT*

Restaurants

Caragiulos 69 S Palm Ave **941/951-0866** *lunch & dinner, Italian-American*

Cruisy Areas

Gravel Pit Lake [AYOR] Honore Ave (N of 17th St at Cooper Creek Park) *road has no sign, turn right after passing power lines*

South Beach

see Miami Beach/ South Beach

St Augustine

see also Jacksonville

Accommodations

Bayfront Marin House [GF,WI] 42 Avenida Menendez **904/824-4301** *laid-back inn located right in the historic district with great water views, full brkfst , pets & kids okk*

Casa Monica [GF,SW,NS,WC] 95 Cordova St **904/827-1888, 888/213-8903**

The Inn at Camachee Harbor [GF,F,WI] 201 Yacht Club Dr (at May St) **904/825-0003, 800/688-5379**

Our House B&B [GS,WI,GO] 5 Cincinnati Ave **904/347-6260**

Restaurants

Collage [R] 60 Hypolita St **904/829-0055** *dinner nightly, "artful global dining"*

Cruisy Areas

Riverdale Park [AYOR] CR 13 (at SR 207) *take Hwy 207 to CR 305, follow through Racey Point & then Riverdale, days*

Vilano Beach Walkway [AYOR] *go N on A1A 2 miles, 2nd crosswalk over A1A, beachside*

St Petersburg

see also Tampa

Accommodations

Bay Palms Waterfront Resort [GF,SW,NS,WI] 4237 Gulf Blvd, St Petersburg Beach **727/360-7642, 800/257-8998**

Changing Tides Cottages [GS,NS,WI,GO] 225 Boca Ciega Dr, Madeira Beach **727/397-7706** *fully furnished rental cottages on harbor, pets ok*

Cordova Inn [GS,NS,WI] 253 2nd Ave N (at 2nd St) **727/822-7500, 800/735-6607**

Dicken's House B&B [GS,WI,GO] 335 8th Ave NE **727/822-8622**

Flamingo Resort [M,E,SW,K,DS,WI,WC] 4601 34th St South **727/321-5000** *hotel with 6 theme bars & restaurant*

GayStPete House [M,SW,N,NS,WI,WC,GO] 4505 5th Ave N (at 45th) **727/365-0544** *centrally located; close to bars, beaches & downtown, pets ok*

The Hotel Zamora [GS,F,SW] 3701 Gulf Blvd **727/456-8900** *new Mediterranean boutique luxury with a great rooftop bar*

Plaza Beach Resort [GF,SW,WI] 4506 Gulf Blvd, St Petersburg Beach **727/367-2792** *beachfront on the Gulf of Mexico, pets ok*

Postcard Inn on the Beach [GF,F,SW,WI] 6300 Gulf Blvd **727/367-2711, 800/237-8918**

Watergarden Inn at the Bay B&B [GF,NS,WI,WC] 126 4th Ave NE (at 1st St) **727/822-1700** *full brkfst*

Bars

Dog Bar St Pete [GS,F,GO] 2300 Central Ave, Saint Petersburg **727/317-4968** *4pm-2am, from noon wknds*

Enigma [GS,D,K,DS] 1110 Central Ave **727/235-0867** *noon-3am*

Gran Central Garage [M,D,K,DS] 2729 Cental Ave **727/253-9086** *4pm-3am, patio*

Lucky Star Lounge [M,NH] 2760 Central Ave (at 28th St) *noon-3am*

Pro Shop Pub [★M,NH] 840 Cleveland St (at Prospect), Clearwater **727/447-4259** *noon-3am, cruise bar*

Restaurants

Bella Brava 204 Beach Dr NE **727/895-5515** *11:30-10pm, till 11pm Fri-Sat, new world trattoria*

The Oyster Bar 249 Central Ave **727/897-9728** *11am-midnight, till 3am Fri-Sat*

Parkshore Grill 300 Beach Dr NE **727/896-3463** *11am-10pm, till 11pm Fri-Sat, from 10am Sun, local favorite*

Sea Porch Cafe 3400 Gulf Blvd (at Don Cesar Hotel) **727/360-1884** *7am-10pm, beach views*

Sea Salt 183 2nd Ave N **727/873-7964** *fine dining*

Skyway Jack's 2795 34th St S **727/867-1907** *5am-3pm, Southern cooking (diner-style)*

Entertainment & Recreation

Bedrocks Beach/ Sunset Beach W Gulf Blvd (at S end of Treasure Island, Sunset Beach) *popular park*

Dali Museum 1 Dali Blvd **727/823-3767, 800/442-3254**

Fort DeSoto Park Pinellas Bayway S

Erotica

XTC Adult Supercenter 4800 34th St S **727/865-6977** *8am-2am, arcade*

Cruisy Areas

Fort DeSoto Park [AYOR] Pinellas Bayway S *days, beautiful beach, after leave North Beach parking lot & cross rainbow bridge*

North Shore Park [AYOR]

Tallahassee

Info Lines & Services

The Family Tree 850/222-8555 *LGBT community information*

Erotica

Rick's Toy Box 618 W Tennessee St **850/577-9000** *10am-2am*

X-Mart Adult Supercenter [AYOR] 2962 Apalachee Pkwy **850/575-2169** *24hrs, arcade*

Tampa

see also St Petersburg

Accommodations

Gram's Place Hostel [GS,N,NS,WI] 3109 N Ola Ave **813/221-0596**

Hampton Inn & Suites [GS,SW,WI,WC] 1301 East 7th Ave **813/247-6700** *walking distance to all things gay*

Sawmill Camping Resort [M,D,E,K,SW,N,GO] 21710 US Hwy 98, Dade City **352/583-0664** *RV hookups, cabins, tent spots*

Bars

Bradley's on 7th [M,D,DS] 1510 E 7th Ave, Ybor City **831/241-2723** *4pm-3am*

Centro Cantina [GS] 1600 E 8th Ave **813/241-8588** *11am-9pm, till midnight Th, till 2am Fri-Sat, Tex Mex, great balcony*

City Side [MW,D,NH,K,WI] 3703 Henderson Blvd (at Dale Mabry) **813/350-0600** *11am-3am, patio*

Reservoir Bar [GS,NH,WC] 1518 E 7th Ave **813/248-1442** *5pm-3am*

Nightclubs

The Castle [GS,D] 2004 N 16th St **813/247-7547** *10:30pm-3am, clsd Sun-Wed, theme nights*

Crowbar [GS,D,E,K] 1812 N 17th St **813/241-8600** *9pm-3am*

Southern Nights [MW,D,DS] 1401 E 7th Ave **813/599-8625** *8pm-3am, from 4pm Fri-Sat, clsd Sun-Tue*

Steam Fridays [★M,D,DS,18+] 1507 E 7th Ave (at the Honey Pot) **813/247-4663** *10pm Fri only, 3 flrs*

Cafes

The Bunker [E] 1907 19th St N **813/247-6964** *8am-8pm, 10am-4pm Sun*

Restaurants

Bernini 1702 E 7th Ave **813/242-9555** *11:30am-10pm, Italian*

Columbia 2117 E 7th Ave **813/248-4961** *11am-close, Cuban & Spanish*

Crabby Bill's 401 Gulf Blvd, Indian Rocks Beach **727/595-4825** *inexpensive seafood joint*

Gaspar's Grotto [E,K,WI] 1805 E 7th Ave **813/248-5900** *7am-3am, from 10:30 Sun, patio*

Hamburger Mary's [E,K,WC,GO] **813/241-6279** *11am-11pm*

The Queen's Head [E] 2501 Central Ave, St Petersburg **727/498-8584** *5pm-10pm, from 11am wknds clsd Mon, full bar*

Entertainment & Recreation

Picnic Island Picnic Island Blvd (across from the military base, on E side) *gay beach at end of park*

Retail Shops

King Corona Cigars 1523 E 7th Ave **888/248-3812** *local, handmade cigars.also cafe & bar*

Publications

Watermark 813/655-9890, 877/926-8118 *LGBT digital news for Central FL*

Men's Clubs

Rainbow Cabaret [AYOR,WI] 4421 N Hubert Ave (behind Playhouse Theatre) **813/877-7585** *24hrs*

Tampa Men's Club 4061 W Crest Ave (at Hillsborough & Lois) **813/876-6367** *24hrs*

Erotica

Buddies Video 4322 W Crest Ave (at Hillsborough) **813/876-8083** *9am-midnight*

Planet X 9921 Adamo Dr **813/740-8484** *8am-2am*

Playhouse Theatre [AYOR] 4421 N Hubert Ave (at Alva) **813/873-9235** *24hrs*

Tres Equis 6220 Adamo Dr (behind Goldrush topless bar) **813/740-8664** *24hrs*

Cruisy Areas

Al Lopez Park [AYOR] N Himes Ave (1 blk S of Hillsborough), West Tampa *take I-275 N toward Ocala, take Hillsborough exit, then go W on Hillsborough Ave for 2 1/2 miles, turn left on Himes Ave*

Picnic Island [AYOR] Picnic Island Blvd (across from the military base, on E side) *gay beach at end of park, past the last parking lot & beyond the mangroves*

Venus

Accommodations

Camp Mars [M,SW,N,GO] 326 Goff Rd **863/699-6277** *campground w/ cabins, tents, RV hookups, 2 hours from Fort Lauderdale & Miami*

West Palm Beach

Accommodations

Grandview Gardens B&B [GF,SW,NS,WI,WC,GO] 1608 Lake Ave (at Palm) **561/833-9023**

Hotel Biba [GF] 320 Belvedere Rd **561/832-0094** *mid-century chic motor lodge*

Scandia Lodge [GS,SW,NS] 625 S Federal Hwy (at 6th Ave), Lake Worth **561/586-3155**

Bars

Fort Dix [M,D,NH,WC] 6205 Georgia Ave (at Colonial) **561/533-5355** *noon-3am, till 4am Fri-Sat, patio*

Rooster's [★M,NH,F,K,DS,S,WC] 823 Belvedere Rd (btwn Parker & Lake) **561/832-9119** *3pm-3am, till 4am Fri-Sat*

Nightclubs

Respectable Street [GF,D,A,E,18+] 518 Clematis St **561/832-9999** *9pm-3am, till 4am Fri-Sat, clsd Sun-Tue, retro & new wave nights*

Restaurants

Rhythm Cafe [BW] 3800-A S Dixie Hwy **561/833-3406** *5:30pm-10pm*

Thai Bay 1900 Okeechobee Blvd (in Palm Beach Market Pl) **561/640-0131** *lunch & dinner, clsd Sun*

Entertainment & Recreation

MacArthur Beach Singer Island, N Palm Beach

Erotica

Redlight Adult Video Outlet 3900 Byron Dr **561/629-7331** *9am-2am, till 3am Fri-Sat*

Cruisy Areas

Jupiter Beach [AYOR] Jupiter *going S on A1A, it's the 3rd catwalk past Jupiter Key on the left*

Wilton Manors

see Fort Lauderdale

Georgia

Athens

Accommodations

Ashford Manor B&B [GF,SW,NS,WI,GO] 5 Harden Hill Rd (at Main St), Watkinsville **706/769-2633**

Nightclubs

Forty Watt Club [GF,E,WC] 285 W Washington St (at Pulaski) **706/549-7871** *call for events, live music venue*

Cafes

Jittery Joe's Coffee [WI,WC] 297 E Broad St (at Jackson) **706/613-7449** *7am-11pm, from 8am wknds*

Restaurants

Globe 199 N Lumpkin St (at Clayton) **706/353-4721** *11am-2am, till midnight Sun, 40 single-malt scotches*

The Grit [WC] 199 Prince Ave **706/543-6592** *11am-10pm, great wknd brunch 10am-3pm*

Cruisy Areas

Ben Burton Park [AYOR] Mitchell Bridge Rd (just before Oconee River Bridge)

Kangaroo Truck Stop [AYOR] Hwy 29 N

Atlanta

Info Lines & Services

Galano Club 585 Dutch Valley Rd (at Monroe) **404/881-9188** *meetings throughout the day, LGBT recovery club*

Accommodations

The Georgian Terrace Hotel [GF,SW,WI,WC] 659 Peachtree St NE (at Ponce de Leon) **404/897-1991, 800/651-2316** *hosted Gone w/ the Wind world-premier reception in 1939*

Glenn Hotel [GS,WI] 110 Marietta St NW (at Spring) **404/521-2250, 888/717-8851** *boutique hotel, also restaurant & rooftop lounge*

Hotel Indigo [WI] 683 Peachtree St NE (at 3rd) **404/874-9200, 800/863-7818** *cozy, stylish no-frills hotel, workout room, also restaurant*

In the Woods Campground & Resort [M,N,SW,GO] 142 Casey Ct (at Hwy 327 & Hwy 51), Canon **706/246-0152** *campground w/ 36+ campsites & 20+ RV hookups*

Le Méridien Atlanta Perimeter Hotel [GF,SW,NS,WI,WC] 111 Perimeter Center W (at Ashford Dunwoody Rd) **770/396-6800** *also restaurant*

Stonehurst Place Bed & Breakfast [GS,NS,WI,GO] 923 Piedmont Ave NE (at 8th St) **404/881-0722** *luxury green B&B 1896 shingle-style house, a few minutes walk to the Midtown gay scene, full brkfst, lesbian-owned*

W Atlanta Midtown [GS,WI,SW] 188 14th St NE (at Juniper St NE) **404/892-6000** *stylish hotel, convenient location*

Bars

Amsterdam [GS,D,F,V] 502 Amsterdam Ave NE **404/892-2227** *11:30am-close, video & sports bar*

Atlanta Eagle [★M,D,B,L,GO] 306 Ponce de Leon Ave NE (at Argonne) **404/873-2453** *7pm-3am, from 5pm Sat, clsd Sun, also leather store*

BJ Roosters [M,NH,WC,GO] 2043 Cheshire Bridge Rd NE **404/634-5895** *2:30pm-3am, till midnight Sun, go-go boys*

Blake's on the Park [★MW,NH,F,K,S,V] 227 10th St (at Piedmont) **404/892-5786** *3pm-3am, from 1pm Fri-Sun, till midnight Sun*

Bulldogs [★M,NH,D,L,MR-AF] 893 Peachtree St NE (btwn 7th & 8th) **404/872-3025** *4pm-3am, 12:30pm-midnight Sun*

The Daiquiri Factory [MW] 889 W Peachtree St (at 7th) **404/881-8188** *11am-2:30am, the name says it all*

Eddie's Attic [GS,E] 515-B N McDonough St (at Trinity Place), Decatur **404/377-4976** *5pm-close Mon-Th, till 2am Fri-Sat, open 1 hr before showtime Sun, live music, comedy, also restaurant, rooftop deck*

Felix's on the Square [M,F,K,WC] 1510-G Piedmont Ave NE (Ansley Square) **404/249-7899** *2pm-2:30am, from noon Sat, 12:30pm-midnight Sun*

Friends on Ponce [MW,NH,V,WI,WC] 736 Ponce de Leon NE (at Ponce de Leon Pl) **404/817-3820** *2pm-3am, from noon Sat, till midnight Sun, rooftop patio*

The Hideaway [M,NH,OC,WC] 1544 Piedmont Ave NE #124 (at Monroe, in Ansley Mall) **404/874-8247** *2pm-2am Mon-Th, till 3am Fri-Sat, 12:30pm-midnight Sun*

Mary's [★MW,NH,D,K,V,WC] 1287B Glenwood Ave (at Flat Shoals) **404/624-4411** *5pm-2:30am*

Mixx [M,NH,D,K,P,B,F] 1492-B Piedmont Ave NE (at Monroe, in Ansley Square) **404/228-4372** *4pm-3am, till midnight Sun. cl;sd Mon-Tue*

Model T [M,NH,F,K,DS,OC,WC] 699 Ponce de Leon NE #11 (at Barnett) **404/872-2209** *9am-3am, till midnight Sun, cruisy*

Opus I [M,NH,WC] 1086 Alco St NE (at Cheshire Bridge) **404/634-6478** *11am-3am, 12:30pm-midnight Sun*

Oscar's Video Bar [M,S] 1510-C Piedmont Ave NE (in Ansley Mall) **404/815-8841** *2pm-2:30am, clsd Sun*

Sister Louisa's Church of the Living Room & Ping Pong Emporium [MW,K,NS] 466 Edgewood Ave SE **404/522-8275** *5pm-3am, Church, as it's commonly called, is a quirky spot religious art, killer organ karaoke Wed, and super-gay patio parties*

Woofs on Piedmont [★M,NH,B,F,GO] 2425 Piedmont Rd NE (at Lindbergh) **404/869-9422** *noon-2am, sports bar*

Nightclubs

The Heretic [★M,D,L,F,S,WC] 2069 Cheshire Bridge Rd (at Piedmont) **404/325-3061** *9am-3am, clsd Sun, till 11pm Mon-Tue, patio, theme nights, also Heretic Leathers store*

Swinging Richard's [M,S,$] 1400 Northside Dr NW (btwn I-75 & Northside Dr) **404/352-0532** *6:30pm-close, from 8:30pm Mon, clsd Sun, gay strip club, nude dancers*

Cafes

Apache Cafe [MR,F,E] 64 3rd St NW **404/876-5436** *food served, poetry readings, events, gallery*

Aurora Coffee 468 Moreland Ave **404/523-6856** *6:30am-8pm*

Intermezzo [WI] 1845 Peachtree Rd NE **404/355-0411** *7:30am-2am, full bar, great desserts*

Restaurants

Allora [R] 361 17th St **404/961-7370** *brkfst, lunch & dinner, Italian*

Apres Diem 931 Monroe Dr #C-103 **404/872-3333** *11:30am-midnight, till 2am Fri-Sat, from 11am wknds, brunch Sat-Sun, French bistro, live jazz Wed, full bar*

Aria 490 E Paces Ferry **404/233-7673** *dinner only, clsd Sun*

Buckhead Diner 3073 Piedmont Rd NE **404/262-3336** *lunch Mon-Sun, dinner nightly, Sun brunch, upscale diner fare*

Cafe Sunflower 2140 Peachtree Rd NW (at Bennett St NW) **404/352-8859** *lunch & dinner, clsd Sun, vegetarian*

The Colonnade 1879 Cheshire Bridge Rd NE **404/874-5642** *dinner nightly, lunch wknds, traditional Southern*

Cowtippers [TG,WC] 1600 Piedmont Ave NE (at Monroe) **404/874-3751** *11am-11pm, till midnight Fri-Sat, steak house*

Ecco [R,WC] 40 7th St NE **404/347-9555** *5:30pm-10pm, till 11pm Fri-Sat, till 10pm Sun, Italian*

Einstein's [★WC] 1077 Juniper St (at 12th) **404/876-7925** *11am-11pm, till midnight Fri-Sat, from 9am Sun, wknd brunch, full bar, patio*

The Flying Biscuit Cafe [★BW,WC] 1655 McLendon Ave (at Clifton) **404/687-8888** *7am-10pm, healthy brkfst all day; multiple locations*

Fresh To Order 860 Peachtree St NE (at 7th St NE) **404/593-2333** *11am-10pm, patio, healthy fast food, patio*

Frogs 931 Monroe Dr NE **404/607-9967** *11am-10pm, till 11pm wknds, Mexican*

Hobnob [WC] 1551 Piedmont Ave NE (at Monroe) **404/968-2288** *11am-11pm, till 3pm Sun*

Joe's On Juniper 1049 Juniper St NE **404/875-6634** *11am-2am, till midnight Sun, patio*

Las Margaritas [E,WC] 1842 Chesire Bridge Rd **404/873-4464** *11am-10pm, from 4pm Tue-Wed, clsd Mon, Latin fusion*

Little Star Provisions 1198 Howell Mill Rd NW **404/365-0410** *10am-6pm*

Majestic Diner [★AYOR,WC] 1031 Ponce de Leon Ave (at Highland) **404/875-0276** *24hrs, diner right from the '50s, cantankerous waitresses included*

Mi Barrio Restaurante Mexicano [WC] 571 Memorial Dr SE **404/223-9279** *lunch Tue-Sat, dinner nightly, clsd Sun*

Murphy's [★WC] 997 Virginia Ave NE (at N Highland Ave) **404/872-0904** *11am-10pm, till midnight Fri-Sat, from 8am wknds*

No Más! Cantina [GO] 180 Walker St **404/574-5678** *lunch & dinner daily, wknd brunch, Mexican, also huge furniture & gift store*

Pastries A Go Go [WC] 235 Ponce De Leon Place (at Commerce), Decatur **404/373-3423** *7:30am-4pm, clsd Tue, delicious baked goods*

R Thomas Deluxe Grill [BW,WC] 1812 Peachtree Rd NW (btwn 26th & 27th) **404/872-2942, 404/881-0246** *24hrs, healthy Californian/ juice bar, popular late night*

Ria's Bluebird Cafe [★BW,TG,WC] 421 Memorial Dr (at Cherokee) **404/521-3737** *8am-3pm, gourmet brunch in quaint old diner in Grant Park*

Roxx Tavern & Diner [WC] 1824 Cheshire Bridge Rd NE (at Manchester) **404/892-4541** *lunch & dinner, Sun brunch, patio*

The Shed at Glenwood 475 Bill Kennedy Way **404/835-4363** *dinner nightly, Sun brunch, also bar*

Swan Coach House 3130 Slaton Dr NW **404/261-0636** *11am-2:30pm, clsd Sun, also gift shop & art gallery*

Table 1280 1280 Peachtree St NE (at Woodruff Arts Center) **404/897-1280** *lunch & dinner, wknd brunch, clsd Mon, also lounge, upscale American & tapas*

TWO urban licks [E,R] 820 Ralph McGill Blvd **404/522-4622** *dinner nightly, brunch Sun, great grill, full bar, live blues*

The Vortex 438 Moreland Ave NE (at Euclid) **404/688-1828** *11am-midnight, till 3am wknds, biker ambiance, great burgers*

Watershed [WC] 1820 Peachtree St **404/809-3561** *5:30pm-10pm, bar till 11pm Fri-Sat, clsd Sun-Mon*

Entertainment & Recreation

AIDS Memorial Quilt/ NAMES Project 117 Luckie St **404/688-5500** *This 2,500 square foot storefront space sits proudly between the Center for Civil and Human Rights (just down the hill) and Ebenezer Baptist Church (just down the street).*

Joining Hearts, Inc Piedmont Park Pool **678/318-1446** *great dance/ pool party in July, 100% of every dollar raised is donated*

Little 5 Points, Moreland & Euclid Ave S of Ponce de Leon Ave *hip & funky area w/ too many restaurants & shops to list*

Martin Luther King, Jr Center for Non-Violent Social Change 449 Auburn Ave NE **404/526-8900** *includes King's birth home, the church where he preached in the '60s & his gravesite*

Piedmont Park [AYOR] NE of Piedmont at 10th *hilltop sunbathing*

Bookstores

Brushstrokes [GO] 1510 Piedmont Ave NE (near Monroe) **404/876-6567** *10am-10pm, till 11pm Fri-Sat, LGBT variety store*

Retail Shops

The Boy Next Door 1447 Piedmont Ave NE (btwn 14th & Monroe) **404/873-2664** *10am-8pm, noon-6pm Sun, clothing*

The Junkman's Daughter [WC] 464 Moreland Ave NE (at Euclid) **404/577-3188** *11am-7pm, till 8pm Fri, till 9pm Sat, from noon Sun, hip stuff*

Publications

Fenuxe 404/835-2016 *the voice of Atlanta's Gay Community*

Georgia Voice 404/815-6941 *bi-weekly LGBT publication*

Peach Atlanta 404/835-2016 *gay entertainment magazine*

Gyms & Health Clubs

Gravitee Fitness 2201 Faulkner Rd (off Cheshire Bridge Rd) **404/486-0506** *day passes available*

Urban Body Fitness 500 Amsterdam Ave **404/885-1499**

Men's Clubs

The Den [MO,MR-AF,PC] 2135 Liddell Dr (at Cheshire Bridge) **404/292-7746**

Flex [SW,WI] 76 4th St NW (at Spring St) **404/815-0456** *24hrs*

Manifest4u 2103 Faulkner Rd NE (off Cheshire Bridge Rd) **404/549-2815** *opens 8pm Wed, 9pm Th-Sun, clsd Mon-Tue, theme nights, also yoga classes*

Qi Clay Sauna Men's Spa 7130 Buford Hwy #A-107, Doraville **770/733-0988** *11am-midnight, till 2am Fri-Sun*

Erotica

Southern Nights Videos 2205 Cheshire Br Rd (at Woodland Ave NE) **404/728-0701** *24hrs*

Starship 2275 Cheshire Bridge Rd **404/320-9101** *24hrs, many locations in Atlanta*

Tokyo Valentino Boutique 1739 Cheshire Bridge Rd **404/875-9200** *24hrs*

Cruisy Areas

Piedmont Park [AYOR] 10th St (at Monroe)

Augusta

Accommodations

The Executive Inn [GS,WI] 1238 Gordon Hwy **706/722-1155** *in the Metropolis Complex of bars*

Metropolis Complex [GS,GO] 1250 Gordon Hwy **706/722-1155** *resort complex on 12 acres of beautifully landscaped grounds featuring 2 motels, 2 bars and an RV Park*

Parliament Resort [★MO,L,V,18+,SW,WI,PC,GO] 1250 Gordon Hwy **706/722-1155** *24hrs, motel complex w/ hot tub, video lounge, maze, novice dungeon*

Bars

Capri Lounge [GS] 1238 Gordon Hwy **706/724-3351** *4pm-midnight, from 3pm wknds, retro piano bar*

Edge [M,D,DS] 1258 Gordon Hwy **706/804-2882** *9pm-close Wed-Sat only*

Cartersville

Erotica

Lion's Den 33 Kent Dr (exit 296, off I-75) **770/607-5113** *24hrs*

Dahlonega

Accommodations

Mountain Laurel Creek Inn [GS,NS,GO] 202 Talmer Grizzle Rd (at Hwy 19 & McDonald Rd) **706/867-8134** *spa & pub*

Dewy Rose

Accommodations

The River's Edge [M,F,E,SW,N,NS,WC] 2311 Pulliam Mill Rd **706/213-8081** *cabins, camping, RV*

Lake Lanier

Entertainment & Recreation

Gay Cove btwn Athens Park Rd & Frank Boyd Rd (Channel Marker 21) *a rainbow rendezvous for the pleasure-boating crowd—look for the rainbow flag*

Macon

Cruisy Areas

Central City Park [AYOR] Walnut St (at 7th)

Rest Area [AYOR] I-475 bypass (off I-75, after Mercer University Dr)

Marietta

Erotica

Tokyo Valentino 345 Cobb Pkwy **678/701-9647** *10am-2am*

Savannah

Accommodations

The Azalea Inn & Gardens [GF,SW,NS,WI] 217 E Huntingdon St (at Abercorn St) **912/236-6080** *19th-c Italianate, vintage gardens, full Southern brkfst*

Catherine Ward House Inn [GS,WI,NS] 118 E Waldburg St (at Abercorn) **912/234-8564, 800/327-4270** *full brkfst*

The Galloway House [GS,GO] 107 E 35th St **912/658-4419** *furnished apts, cont'l brkfst*

Kehoe House [GF,WI] 123 Habersham St **912/232-1020, 800/820-1020** *full brkfst*

Mansion on Forsyth Park [GF,SW,NS,WI,WC] 700 Drayton St **912/238-5158, 888/213-3671**

Statesboro Inn [GF,WI] 106 S Main, Statesboro **912/489-8628** *full brkfst*

Thunderbird Inn [GF,NS,WI,GO] 611 W Oglethorpe Ave (at MLK Blvd) **912/232-2661**

Bars

Chuck's Bar [GS,NH,K] 305 W River St **912/232-1005** *8pm-2am, clsd Sun*

Nightclubs

Club One [MW,D,F,K,C,DS,S,V] 1 Jefferson St (at Bay) **912/232-0200** *5pm-3am, till 2am Sun*

Cafes

Joe's Homemade Café & Bakery [GO] 5515 Waters Ave (at 70th St) **912/349-0251** *10:30am-5:30pm, 11am-4pm Sat, clsd Sun*

The Sentient Bean 13 E Park Ave (at Bull St) **912/232-4447** *7am-10pm, food served, vegetarian/ vegan, shows at night*

Wright Square Cafe [★GO] 21 W York St **912/238-1150** *7:30am-5pm, from 9am Sat, clsd Sun, patio*

Restaurants

The 5 Spot 4430 Habersham St **912/777-3021** *8am-11pm, till 10pm Sun*

B Matthews [WC] 325 E Bay St **912/233-1319** *8am-9pm, till 10pm Fri-Sat, till 3pm Sun, casual bistro*

Bar Food [WI,WC,GO] 4523 Habersham St **912/355-5956** *3pm-1am, from 10am wknds, full bar*

Churchill's Pub 13 W Bay St **912/232-8501** *5pm-1am*

Clary's Cafe 404 Abercorn (at Jones) **912/233-0402** *7am-4pm, from 8am Sat-Sun, country cookin*

The Distillery [WC] 416 W Liberty St **912/236-1772** *11am-1am, till 3am Fri-Sat, noon-9pm Sun*

Fannie's on the Beach [D,E] 1613 Strand Ave (at Silver Ave), Tybee Island **912/786-6109** *noon-11pm, till 2am wknds*

Green Truck Neighborhood Pub [BW,WC,GO] 2430 Habersham St **912/234-5885** *11am-11pm, clsd Sun*

Local 11 Ten 1110 Bull St **912/790-9000** *dinner nightly, upscale dining in a restored 1950s bank; also Perch rooftop bar*

Mellow Mushroom [WC] 11 W Liberty St **912/495-0705** *11am-10pm, pizza & beer*

Olde Pink House [E] 23 Abercorn St **912/232-4286** *upscale Southern dining upstairs, cozy bar downstairs, live jazz*

Rocks on the Roof 102 W Bay St (on the roof of The Bohemian Hotel) **912/721-3900** *7am-10pm, till 11pm wknds, fantastic views*

Soho South Cafe 12 W Liberty St **912/233-1633** *11am-3pm, from 10am wknds*

Entertainment & Recreation

Savannah Walks, Inc 912/385-0577, 888/238-0542 *walking tours of downtown Savannah*

Unadilla

Erotica

Lion's Den 790 Pine St (Exit 121, off I-75) **478/627-2782** *24hrs*

Valdosta

Cruisy Areas

Langdale Park [AYOR] N Valdosta Rd *days*

Hawaii

Please note that cities are grouped by islands:
Hawaii (Big Island)
Kauai
Maui
Molokai
Oahu (includes Honolulu)

Hawaii (Big Island)

Captain Cook

Accommodations

Aloha Guest House [GS,N,NS,WI,WC,GO] 84-4780 Mamalahoa Hwy **808/328-8955, 800/897-3188**

Horizon Guest House [GS,SW,NS,WI,WC,GO] **808/938-7822**

Ka'awa Loa Plantation [GS,NS,WI,GO] 82-5990 Napoopoo Rd 96704 **808/323-2686** *plantation-style B&B on 5-acre start-up coffee farm*

Kealakekua Bay B&B [GS,NS] **808/328-8150, 800/328-8150**

Hilo

Restaurants

Cafe Pesto [E] 308 Kamehameha Ave **808/969-6640** *pizzas, salads, pastas*

Entertainment & Recreation

Richardson Beach at end of Kalanianaole Ave (Keaukaha)

Cruisy Areas

Reeds "Gay" Bay Tearooms [AYOR] Banyan Dr *1st beach S of the hotels*

Honaunau-Kona

Accommodations

Dragonfly Ranch Healing Arts Center [GS,NS,WI] 1 1/2 miles down City of Refuge Rd **808/328-2159** *eco-spa; luxuriously rustic upscale treehouse*

Kailua-Kona

Accommodations

1st Class B&B Kona Hawaii [GF,NS,WI] 77-6504 Kilohana St **808/329-8778, 888/769-1110**

Holualoa Inn [GF,WI] 76-5932 Mamalahoa Hwy **808/324-1121**

KonaLani Hawaiian Inn & Coffee Plantation [MW,NS,WI,GO] 76-5917 Hookahi St **808/324-0793**

Royal Kona Resort [GF,F,E,SW,NS,WI,WC] 75-5852 Ali'i Dr **808/329-3111, 800/222-5642**

Bars

The Mask-querade [MW,NH,D,B,E,K,GO] 75-5660 Kopiko St **808/329-8558** *noon-2am*

My Bar [GF,K] 74-5606 Luhia St (btwn Kaiwi & Eho St) **808/331-8789** *11am-2am, from 10am wknds*

Restaurants

Buzz's Original Steak House [WC] 413 Kawailoa Rd **808/261-4661** *across from beach, great Mai Tais*

Huggo's [E,K] 75-5828 Kahakai Rd (on Kailua Bay) **808/329-1493** *dinner only, also bar, patio*

Moke's Bread & Breakfast 27 Ho'olai St **808/261-5565** *6:30am-2pm, clsd Tue, great brkfst*

Bookstores

Kona Stories 78-6831 Ali'i Dr #142 (in the Keauhou Shopping Ctr) **808/324-0350** *bookstore that hosts PFLAG meetings & other LGBT groups*

Cruisy Areas

67 Beach Old Puako Rd *take Rte 19 N to Puako Beach Rd, take 1st right onto Old Puako Rd, look for telephone pole #67, then go north for about 0.5 miles. You drive to the shore on an unpaved lane & walk to the water*

Honokohau Beach [AYOR] 5 miles S of airport, Kailua-Kona *far N end of beach*

Kahaluu Beach Park [AYOR]

Old Airport Park *the beach area just north of the end of the parking area, which is the old airport runway*

Pahoa

Accommodations

Isle of You Naturally Farm & Retreat [M,NS,GO] **808/965-1639** *cabin & yurts on naturist farm retreat*

Kalani [GS,F,SW,N,NS,WI,WC,GO] **808/965-7828, 800/800-6886**

Entertainment & Recreation

Kehena Beach off Hwy 137 (trailhead at 19-mile marker phone booth) *lava rock trail to clothing-optional black-sand beach*

Cruisy Areas

Steam Vents [AYOR] 3 miles S of Pahoa on Keaau-Pahoa Rd *early evenings*

Volcano Village

Accommodations

The Artist Cottage at Volcano Garden Arts [GF,WI] 19-3834 Old Volcano Rd (at Wright Rd) **808/967-7261**

The Chalet Kilauea Collection [GF,NS,WI] 19-4178 Wright Rd **808/967-7786**

Hale Ohia Cottages [GS,NS,WI,GO] **808/967-7986, 800/455-3803**

Cafes

Ono Cafe 19-3834 Old Volcano Rd (at Wright St, at Volcano Garden Arts) **808/985-8979** *11am-2pm, clsd Mon*

Kauai

Hanalei

Nightclubs

Tahiti Nui [GF,D,F,E,K,WC] 5-5134 Kuhio Hwy (near Hanalei Center) **808/826-6277** *11am-2am, 4pm-11pm Sun, also restaurant*

Kapaa

Accommodations

17 Palms Kauai [GS,NS,WI,WC,GO] **888/725-6799** *2 secluded cottages 200 steps from beach*

Fern Grotto Inn [GS,WI,NS] 4561 Kuamoo Rd (at Kuhio Hwy) **808/821-9836**

Plantation Hale Suites [GF,SW,WI,WC] 525 Aleka Loop **808/822-4941, 800/775-4253**

Restaurants

Caffe Coco [E,BYOB,WC] 4-369 Kuhio Hwy **808/822-7990** *lunch Tue-Fri, dinner nightly, clsd Mon*

Cruisy Areas

Coconut Marketplace 484 Kuhio Hwy (NW corner)

Donkey Beach [AYOR] off Hwy 56, N of Kapaa (btwn 11 & 12-mile markers) *walk along cane field, down through ironwood trees & then to the right on the dirt road to the beach*

Kilauea

Cruisy Areas

Secret Beach [AYOR] *inquire locally*

Lihue

Accommodations

Kauai Beach Resort [GF,SW,NS,WI] 4331 Kauai Beach Dr **808/245-1955, 866/536-7676** *also restaurant/ bar*

Entertainment & Recreation

Lydgate State Park Beach off Hwy 56 btwn Lihue & Kapaa (S of Wailua River) *gay beach btwn the condos & the golf course*

Waimea

Accommodations

Waimea Plantation Cottages [GF,SW,WI] **808/338-1625, 877/997-6667**

Maui

Info Lines & Services

Maui Pride *LGBT community resources & events*

Hana

Accommodations

Hana Accommodations [GS,NS,GO] **808/248-7868, 800/228-4262** *studios & tropical cottages, hot tub*

Kaanapali

Accommodations

The Royal Lahaina Resort [GF,F,SW,WC] 2780 Kekaa Dr **808/201-2926**

Kihei

Accommodations

Eva Villa [GF,SW,WI,WC] 815 Kumulani Dr **808/874-6407, 800/884-1845** *near Wailea beaches*

Pineapple Inn Maui [GS,GO] 3170 Akala Dr **808/298-4403**

Bars

Diamond's Ice Bar & Grill [GF,F,E] 1279 S Kihei Rd **808/874-9299** *11am-2am, from 7am Sun*

Nightclubs

Vibe [GS,D,E,WC] 1913 S Kihei Rd #H (in Kihei Kalama Village) **808/891-1011** *6pm-2am*

Cafes

Cafe at La Plage [WI,WC] 2395 S Kihei Rd (at Kam Beach I) **808/875-7668** *7am-5pm, till 3pm Sun*

Restaurants

Jawz Tacos [WC] 41 E Lipoa St (in the Lipoa Center) **808/874-8226** *11am-9pm*

Gyms & Health Clubs

Maui Massage for Men [GO] **808/280-7175**

Erotica

The Love Shack 1913 S Kihei Rd (in Kalama Vlg) **808/875-0303**

Cruisy Areas

Kalama Park [AYOR]

Kula

Accommodations

The Upcountry B&B [GF,NS,WI,WC] 4925 Lower Kula Rd (at Copp St) **808/878-8083**

Lahaina

Restaurants

Betty's Beach Cafe [★] 505 Front St **808/662-0300** *8am-10pm, more gay at bar till midnight, great views*

Lahaina Coolers [WC] 180 Dickenson St **808/661-7082** *8am-1am, patio*

Cruisy Areas

Front St [AYOR] along Beach Walk

Makawao

Accommodations

Aloha Cottage [GS,WI,GO] **808/575-9228, 800/782-6105** *designed for comfort, style, charm & seclusion, outdoor soaking tub*

Hale Ho'okipa Inn B&B [GF,NS,WI] 32 Pakani Pl **808/572-6698, 877/572-6698** *gracious old Hawaiian plantation home*

Restaurants

Casanova Restaurant & Deli [D,E] 1188 Makawao Ave **808/572-0220** *lunch & dinner, Italian, full bar till 2am, live music*

Makena

Entertainment & Recreation

Little Beach at Makena [MW] *Pilani Hwy S to Wailea, right at Wailea Ike Dr, left on Wailea Alanui Dr to public beach, then take trail up hill at right end of beach*

Wailuku

Info Lines & Services

AA Gay/ Lesbian 1910 S Kihei Rd (Kalama Park) **808/244-9673** *7:30am Sun*

Molokai

Kaunakakai

Restaurants

Kanemitsu Bakery & Coffee Shop [★] 79 Ala Malama St **808/553-5855** *5:30am-5pm, clsd Tue, great sweet bread*

Oahu

Honolulu

Info Lines & Services

Gay/ Lesbian AA 808/946-1438

Accommodations

Aqua Oasis Hotel [GF,SW,NS,WI,WC] 320 Lewers St (at Kalakaua Ave, Waikiki) **808/441-7781** *boutique hotel, near beach*

Aqua Palms Waikiki [GF,SW,NS,WI,WC] 1850 Ala Moana Blvd (at Kalia & Ena) **808/954-7424 , 866/970-4165** *boutique hotel w/ retro-Hawaiian style, in heart of Waikiki, full spa, each room with private lanai or balcony*

Aston Waikiki Circle Hotel [GF,NS,WI] 2464 Kalakaua Ave (at Uluniu St, Waikiki) **808/923-1571, 877/997-6667**

Hotel Renew [GF,NS,WI] 129 Paoakalani Ave (at Lemon Rd, Waikiki) **808/687-7700**

Bars

Amnesia [GS,D,F] 2256 Kuhio Ave, 2nd flr (at Seaside, Waikiki) **808/922-1422** *noon-2am*

Bacchus Waikiki [MW,NH,] 408 Lewers St **808/926-4167** *noon-2am*

Bar Leather Apron [GS] 745 Fort St Mall #12 **808/524-0808** *4pm-midnight, from 5pm Sat. closd Sun-Mon*

Chiko's Tavern [GS,NH,F,K] 930 McCully St (at Algaroba St) **808/949-5440** *5pm-2am*

In Between [M,NH,K] 2155 Lau'ula St (off Lewers, across from Planet Hollywood, Waikiki) **808/926-7060** *noon-2am*

Tapa's Restaurant & Lanai Bar [GS,E,F,K,GO] 407 Seaside, 2nd flr (at Kuhio Ave) **808/921-2288** *2pm-2am, from 9am wknds, lanai bar, also restaurant for dinner & Sun brunch*

Wang Chung's [MW,K,WC] 2424 Koa Ave (at Kaiulani) **808/921-9176** *5pm-2am*

Nightclubs

District [GS,D,MR-A,S,YC,WC] 1349 Kapiolani Blvd **808/949-1349** *9pm-4am, [DS] Sat*

Hula's Bar & Lei Stand [★M,D,TG,F,S,V,YC,WI] 134 Kapahulu Ave (2nd flr of Waikiki Grand Hotel) **808/923-0669** *10am-2am, near gay beac, weekly catamaran sails*

Scarlet Honolulu [MW,D,DS] 80 S Pauahi St *8pm-2am Fri-Sat only*

Cafes

Leonard's Bakery 933 Kapahulu Ave **808/737-5591** *5:30am-10pm, till 11pm Fri-Sat, irresistible malasadas & doughnuts*

Mocha Java Cafe [WI,WC] 1200 Ala Moana Blvd (in Ward Center) **808/591-9023** *7am-9pm, til5pm Sun, outdoor seating*

Restaurants

Alan Wong's 1857 S King St (at Pumehana St) **808/949-2526** *dinner only, upscale*

Arancino [★] 2552 Kalakaua Ave (in Waikiki Beach Marriott) **808/931-6273** *brkfst,lunch & dinner, Italian*

Cafe Sistina [WC] 1314 S King St **808/596-0061** *lunch Mon-Fri, dinner nightly, northern Italian, full bar*

Cheeseburger in Paradise 2500 Kalakaua Blvd **808/923-3731** *7am-11pm, full bar*

Chef Chai [E] 1009 Kapiolani Blvd **808/585-0011** *4pm-10pm, clsd Mon*

Chuck's Cellar 50 Ka'iulani Ave **808/923-4488** *prime rib, fresh seafood and its famous all-you-can-eat salad bar*

Eggs 'n' Things 343 Saratoga Rd (at Kalakaua Ave) **808/926-3447** *6am-2pm, 4pm-10pm*

House Without A Key 2199 Kalia Rd (at Lewers St, at Halekulani Hotel) **808/923-2311** *7am-9pm, stunning sunset views, Hawaiian music nightly*

Hula Grill [E] 2335 Kalakaua Ave (in Outrigger Hotel) **808/923-4852** *oceanview dining*

La Cucaracha 2446 Koa Ave **808/924-3366** *noon-11pm, Mexican, full bar*

Liliha Bakery [WC] 515 N Kuakini St (at Liliha St) **808/531-1651** *open 24hrs, till 8m Sun, clsd Mon, diner fare & baked goods*

Lulu's [E] 2586 Kalakaua Ave **808/926-5222** *7am-2am, full bar*

Rock Island Cafe 131 Kaiulani Ave (off Kalakaua, in King's Village Waikiki) **808/923-8033** *old-fashioned soda fountain*

Tiki's Grill & Bar [E] 2570 Kalakaua Ave (in ResortQuest Hotel) **808/923-8454** *hip, open-air restaurant with retro South Pacific design & experience*

Entertainment & Recreation

Diamond Head Beach [GS] *take road from lighthouse to beach; some nude sunbathing*

Honolulu Gay/ Lesbian Cultural Foundation 1670 Makaloa St #204 **808/675-8428** *Honolulu Rainbow Film Festival*

Queen's Surf Beach Kapiolani Park (off Kalakaua) *popular gay beach at far end of Kuhio Beach*

Rainbow Sailing Charters [MW,GO] **808/347-0235** *day & overnight sailing adventures*

Erotica

Velvet Video 2155 Lau'ula St, 2nd flr (above In Between, Waikiki) **808/924-0868** *24hrs, booths, toys*

Cruisy Areas

Ala Moana Beach Park [AYOR] *near Waikiki Yacht Club*

Alan Davis Beach Rte 27 *turn past Sandy Beach but before Makapuu Point Lighthouse*

Diamond Head Road [AYOR] *on trails across the street from the lighthouse*

IDAHO

Boise

Info Lines & Services

The Community Center 1088 N Orchard St **208/336-3870** *volunteer staff*

Accommodations

Bed & Buns [MO,N,NS,WI,GO] **208/631-4004, 208/362-1802** *B&B, hot tub*

Hotel 43 [GS,F,WI] 981 W Grove St (at 10th & Front) **800/243-4622** *upscale boutique hotel in the heart of downtown*

The Modern Hotel & Bar [GF,WI] 1314 W Grove St **208/424-8244, 866/780-6012**

Bars

The Lucky Dog [M,NH,B,L,WI] 2223 W Fairview Ave (at 23rd) **208/333-0074** *2pm-2am, from noon wknds, patio*

Neurolux [★GF,D,E] 111 N 11th St (at W Idaho) **208/343-0886** *noon-2am, live music*

Nightclubs

The Balcony Club [★MW,D,K,WC,GO] 150 N 8th St #226 (at Idaho) **208/336-1313** *4pm-2am, theme nights*

Cafes

Flying M Coffeehouse [WI] 500 W Idaho St (at 5th St) **208/345-4320** *6:30am-11pm, from 7:30am wknds, till 6pm Sun*

River City Coffee 5517 W State St **208/853-9161** *6am-5pm, till 4pm Sun*

Restaurants

Lucky 13 Pizza 3662 S Eckert Rd **208/344-6967** *11am-9pm, till 10pm wknds, full bar, patio*

Entertainment & Recreation

The Flicks [F,E,BW,WC] 646 Fulton St **208/342-4222** *opens 4pm, from noon Fri-Sun, 4 movie theaters, patio*

Visual Arts Collective 3638 Osage St **208/424-8297** *noon-6pm Sat, performance and music venue in Garden City with a full bar*

Retail Shops

The Record Exchange [E] 1105 W Idaho St (at 11th) **208/344-8010** *9am-9pm, till 7pm Sun, also cafe*

Erotica

The O!Zone 1615 Broadway Ave (at Howe) **208/395-1977**

Pleasure Boutique 5022 Fairview Ave (at Orchard) **208/433-1161**

Vixen Video [GO] 5777 W Overland Rd **208/672-1844**

Cruisy Areas

Ann Morrison Park [AYOR] near baseball fields

Coeur d'Alene

see also Spokane, Washington

Lava Hot Springs

see also Pocatello

Accommodations

Aura Soma Lava [GS,SW] 196 E Main St **208/776-5800, 800/757-1233** *also retail store*

Moscow

Bookstores

Bookpeople 521 S Main (btwn 5th & 6th) **208/882-2669** *10am-6pm, till 4pm Sun*

Nampa

Cafes

Flying M Coffee Garage [E] 1314 2nd St S **208/467-5533** *7am-11pm, till 6pm wknds*

Pocatello

Nightclubs

Club Charleys [MW,D,E,DS,K,WC] 331 E Center St **208/232-9606** *5pm-2am, clsd Sun*

Cafes

Main Stream Coffee & Desserts 234 N Main St (btwn Lander & Clark) **208/234-9834** *8:30am-5:30pm, till 2pm wknds*

Cruisy Areas

Ross Park [AYOR] *upper level*

Powell

Cruisy Areas

Jerry Johnson Hot Springs [AYOR] US 12 *days*

Twin Falls

Restaurants

Pizza Planet 720 Main St (at 8th St), Buhl **208/543-8560** *11am-8pm, clsd Sun*

Cruisy Areas

City Park [AYOR] Shoshone & 4th Ave E

Rock Creek Park [AYOR] W on Hwy 30 *days*

Illinois

Alton

see also St Louis, Missouri

Nightclubs

Bubby & Sissy's [MW,D,DS,K,F,WC] 602 Belle St (at 6th) **618/465-4773** *3pm-2am, till 3am Fri-Sat, clsd Mon*

Cruisy Areas

Rock Springs Park [AYOR] College Ave (at Rock Springs Dr)

Arlington Heights

see Chicago

Bloomington

Cafes

Coffee Hound [WI] 407 N Main St **309/827-7575** *6:30am-6pm, 8am-5pm Sun*

Kelly's Bakery & Cafe [WC] 113 N Center St **309/820-1200** *7am-6pm, till 2pm Sat, clsd Sun*

Blue Island

see also Chicago

Nightclubs

Club Krave [MW,NH,TG,F,K,C,DS,S,WI,WC] 13126 S Western Ave (at Grove) **708/597-8379** *8pm-2am, till 3am Fri-Sat, from 6pm Mon*

Calumet City

Cruisy Areas

Clayhole Woods, Shabonna Woods & Sandridge Forest Preserves [AYOR]

Carbondale

Cruisy Areas

Crab Orchard Lake [AYOR] Cambria Neck Ln *exit off Rte 13 onto Cambria Rd, drive 1 mile N, on right side of Cambria Rd is side road called Cambria Neck Ln, turn right onto it*

Centreville

see also St Louis, Missouri

Nightclubs

Boxers 'n' Briefs [M,D,F,DS,18+,WC,$] 55 Four Corners Ln **618/332-6141** *7pm-4am, till 6am Fri-Sat, till 3am Sun, clsd Mon, nude dancers*

Champaign/ Urbana

Accommodations

Sylvia's Irish Inn [GF,NS,WI] 312 W Green St, Urbana **217/384-4800**

Bars

Seven Saints [GS,F] 32 E Chester St, Champaign **217/351-7775** *11am-2am, patio*

Nightclubs

Chester Street [MW,D,DS,GO] 63 Chester St (at Water St), Champaign **217/356-5607** *5pm-2am*

Cafes

Aroma Cafe 118 N Neil St, Champaign **217/356-3200** *7am-10pm, from 8am wknds*

Cafe Kopi [WI] 109 N Walnut (at University), Champaign **217/359-4266** *7am-11pm, espresso bar with sandwiches*

Espresso Royale 602 E Daniel St (at 6th St), Champaign **217/328-1112** *7am-midnight*

Pekara Bakery & Bistro 116 N Neil St, Champaign **217/359-4500** *7am-8pm, from 8am Sun*

Restaurants

The Courier Cafe 111 N Race St, Urbana **217/328-1811** *7am-11pm*

Dos Reales [WC] 1407 N Prospect Ave, Champaign **217/351-6879** *11am-10pm, Mexican*

Farren's Pub & Eatery [WC] 308 N Randolph St, Champaign **217/359-6977** *11am-10pm, till 11pm Fri-Sat, from 4pm Sun, full bar*

Fiesta Cafe [E,GO] 216 S 1st St (at E Clark), Champaign **217/352-5902** *11am-11pm, bar till 1am, Mexican, full bar*

Radio Maria 119 N Walnut St, Champaign **217/398-7729** *11am-2am, till 5pm Mon, eclectic Mexican cuisine*

Silvercreek [E] 402 N Race St, Urbana **217/328-3402** *lunch & dinner, brunch Sun*

Gyms & Health Clubs

Refinery 2302 W John St, Champaign **217/355-4444**

Erotica

Illini Video Arcade 33 E Springfield Ave (S Neil exit, off I-74), Champaign **217/359-8529** *24hrs*

Lovers Playground 3604 N Cunningham Ave (Cunningham exit off I-74 E), Urbana **217/328-1199** *24hrs, video booths*

Cruisy Areas

Crystal Lake Park [AYOR] at Park & University Sts, Urbana

Chicago

Chicago is divided into 5 geographical areas:
Chicago—Overview
Chicago—North Side
Chicago—Boystown/ Lakeview
Chicago—Near North
Chicago—South Side

Chicago—Overview

includes some listings for Greater Chicagoland; please check individual cities like Oak Park as well

Info Lines & Services

AA/ New Town Alano Club 909 W Belmont Ave, 2nd flr (btwn Clark & Sheffield) **773/529-0321** *for meeting times check, www.newtownalanoclub.org*

The Center on Halsted 3656 N Halsted St (at Waveland) **773/472-6469** *8am-9pm, LGBT center, theater, gym, technology center*

Entertainment & Recreation

Chicago Neighborhood Tours **312/819-5363** *the best way to make the Windy City your kind of town*

Heartland Cafe 7000 N Glenwood Ave (in Rogers Park) **773/465-8005** *cafe w/ full bar, theater, lots of live music*

Leather Archives & Museum 6418 N Greenview Ave **773/761-9200** *11am-7pm Th-Fri, till 5pm Sat-Sun, membership required (purchase at door)*

Second City [GF,E] 1616 N Wells St (at North) **312/337-3992**, **312/337-3992** *legendary comedy club, call for reservations*

Publications

boi magazine 773/975-0264 *slick glossy w/ bar listings, articles, photos & circuit dish*

Nightspots 773/871-7610 *weekly LGBT nightlife magazine*

Windy City Times 773/871-7610 *weekly LGBT newspaper & calendar guide*

Cruisy Areas

Humboldt Park [AYOR] North Ave & Sacramento *near pavilion & bushes*

Marquette Park [AYOR] 7100 S Kedzie Avenue (at 71st Street W) *use S entrance*

Chicago—North Side

Accommodations

House 5863 B&B [GS,NS,WI,GO] 5863 N Glenwood (at Admore) **773/682-5217**

Lang House B&B [GS,WI,GO] 7421 N Sheridan Rd (at Jarvis) **773/764-9851** *on the Lake Michigan beach block*

Bars

The Anvil [M,NH,V] 1137 W Granville (E of Broadway) **773/973-0006** *9am-2am*

Big Chicks [MW,NH,D,B,F,V,WI,WC] 5024 N Sheridan (btwn Foster & Argyle) **773/728-5511** *4pm-2am, from 10am wknds for brunch, Bear Den on Th*

The Call [MW,D,CW,DS,V,WC] 1547 W Bryn Mawr (at Clark) **773/334-2525** *4pm-2am*

Elixir Lounge Andersonville [M] 1509 W Balmoral Ave **773/654-1751** *6pm-2am, till 4am Fri-Sat, 4pm-midnight Sun, swank cocktails*

The Glenwood [MW,NH,E,WC] 6962 N Glenwood Ave (at Morse) **773/764-7363** *3pm-2am, from noon Sun, sports bar*

Green Mill [★GS,E] 4802 N Broadway Ave (at Lawrence) **773/878-5552** *noon-4am, noted jazz venue, hosts the Uptown Poetry Slam*

Marty's [GF,F] 1511 W Balmoral Ave (at Clark) **773/321-7481** *5pm-2am, upscale wine & martini bar*

Scot's [M,NH] 1829 W Montrose Ave (at Damen) **773/528-3253** *3pm-2am, 1pm-3am Sat, from 11am Sun*

The Sofo Tap [M,NH,V,WC] 4923 N Clark St (at W Argyle) **773/784-7636** *5pm-2am, from 3pm Fri, from noon wknds, backyard beer garden*

Spyner's Pub [W,NH,K] 4623 N Western Ave (at W Eastwood) **773/784-8719**

Touché [★M,L] 6412 N Clark St (at Devon) **773/465-7400** *5pm-4am, 3pm-5am Sat, noon-4am Sun*

Nightclubs

Atmosphere [MW,D,DS,C,S,WI,GO] 5355 N Clark St (at W Balmoral Ave) **773/784-1100** *6pm-2am, clsd Mon-Tue*

Cafes

Coffee Grind [F,WI,WC] 5256 N Broadway St (btwn Berwyn & Foster) **773/784-1305** *7am-9pm, from 8am wknds*

KOPI: A Traveler's Cafe [E,F,WC] 5317 N Clark St **773/989-5674** *8am-11pm*

Metropolis Coffee [★WI] 1039 W Granville Ave (at Kenmore) **773/764-0400**

Restaurants

A Taste of Heaven [GO] 5401 N Clark St **773/989-0151** *brunch, dinner and delicious. savory and sweet items*

Andie's [WC] 5253 N Clark (btwn Berwyn & Farragut) **773/784-8616** *4pm-11pm, from 11am Fri-Sun, eastern Mediterranean, full bar*

Anteprima [WC] 5316 N Clark St (at Summerdale) **773/506-9990** *dinner nightly, Italian*

Fat Cat [WC] 4840 N Broadway (at Lawrence Ave) **773/506-3100** *4pm-2am, from 10am wknds, full bar*

Fireside [WI,WC] 5739 N Ravenswood (at Rosehill) **773/561-7433** *11am-4am, Cajun & pizza, patio, full bar*

Hamburger Mary's [E,K,DS,WC] 5400 N Clark St (at Balmoral) **773/784-6969** *11:30am-midnight, till 2am Wed-Sun, from 10:30am wknds, also full bar*

Hot Woks Cool Sushi 30 S Michigan Ave (at Madison) **312/345-1234** *11am-9pm, sushi/ Thai*

Jin Ju [WC] 5203 N Clark St (at Summersdale) **773/334-6377** *dinner only, clsd Mon, Korean, also bar*

Pauline's [WC] 1754 W Balmoral (at Ravenswood) **773/561-8573** *7am-3pm, hearty brkfsts*

Svea Restaurant [WC] 5236 N Clark (btwn Berwyn & Farragut) **773/275-7738** *7am-2pm, till 3pm wknds, Swedish/ American comfort food*

Tedino's [★WC] 5335 N Sheridan Rd (at Broadway) **773/275-8100** *11am-midnight, from 3pm Mon, pizza, full bar*

Thai Pastry & Restaurant [WC] 4925 N Broadway St, Unit E (at Argyle) **773/784-5399** *11am-10pm, till 11pm Fri-Sat*

Tweet [WI] 5020 N Sheridan Rd (at Argyle) **773/728-5576** *9am-3pm, brkfst & brunch, cash only*

Entertainment & Recreation

Hollywood /Osterman Beach [★] at Hollywood & Sheridan Sts *"the" gay beach*

Retail Shops

Enjoy, An Urban General Store 4727 N Lincoln Ave (Lincoln Square) **773/334-8626** *10am-7pm, till 6pm Sun, pride items*

Full Kit Gear 5021 N Clark St **773/657-8000** *noon-9pm, leather, latex, fetish-wear*

Leather 6410 [GO] 6410 N Clark St (at Devon, btwn Jackhammer & Touché) **773/508-0900** *10am-3:30am. till 4:30am Sat, from noon Sun*

GYMS & HEALTH CLUBS

Cheetah Gym 5248 N Clark St (at Foster) **773/728-7777, 866/961-6840**

Sir Spa [GO] 5151 N Clark St **773/271-7000** *11am-9pm, till 8pm wknds*

EROTICA

Banana Video 4923 N Clark St (at Argyle, 2nd flr) **773/561-8322** *4pm-2am, till 4am Fri-Sat, from noon wknds, arcade*

CRUISY AREAS

Hollywood Beach [AYOR] along lake (at 5700 N)

Lincoln Park [AYOR] E of Lake Shore Dr (btwn Foster & Montrose)

Chicago—Boystown/ Lakeview

ACCOMMODATIONS

Best Western Plus Hawthorne Terrace [GF,WI,WC] 3434 N Broadway St (at Hawthorne Pl) **773/244-3434** *in heart of Chicago's gay community, gym*

City Suites Hotel [GF,WI] 933 W Belmont Ave (btwn Clark & Sheffield) **773/404-3400** *European style*

Hotel Lincoln [GS] 1816 N Clark St **312/254-4700** *great location and fabulous rooftop restaurant & bar*

Majestic Hotel [GF,NS,WI] 528 W Brompton Ave (at Addison) **773/404-3499**

The Willows [GS,NS,WI] 555 W Surf St (at Broadway) **773/528-8400, 800/916-0767**

BARS

Beat Kitchen [GF,F,E] 2100 W Belmont (btwn Hoyne & Damen) **773/281-4444** *4pm-2am, from 11:30am Sat-Sun, till 3am Sat, live bands, also grill*

Blues [GF,E] 2519 N Halsted St (at Lill Ave) **773/528-1012,** / *8pm-2am, till 3am Sat, classic Chicago blues spot*

Bobby Love's [MW,NH,K,WC] 3729 N Halsted St (at Waveland) **773/525-1200** *3pm-2am, from noon wknds, till 3am Sat*

Cell Block [M,B,L,WC] 3702 N Halsted St (at Waveland) **773/665-8064** *4pm-2am, from 2pm wknds, till 3am Sat, back bar wknds from 10pm*

Charlie's [M,D,CW,K] 3726 N Broadway St (btwn Waveland & Grace) **773/871-8887** *3pm-4am, till 5am Sat, club music after 1am*

The Closet [★MW,NH,K,DS,V] 3325 N Broadway St (at Buckingham) **773/477-8533** *4pm-4am, from noon wknds*

D.S. Tequila Company [GS,E,WI] 3352 N Halsted St (at Roscoe) **773/697-9127** *11am-midnight, till 2am Fri, 3am Sat, good burgers and tacos*

Elixir [M] 3452 N Halsted St (at Cornelia) **773/975-9244** *6pm-2am, till 4am Fri-Sat,4pm-midnight Sun, swank cocktails*

Little Jim's Tavern [M,NH] 3501 N Halsted St (at Cornelia) **773/871-6116** *11am-4am, till 5am Sat, till midnight Sun*

The Lucky Horseshoe Lounge [M,NH,S] 3169 N Halsted St (at Briar) **773/404-3169** *3pm-2am, from 1pm wkndst*

Manhandler Saloon [M,NH,V] 1948 N Halsted St (at Armitage) **773/871-3339** *noon-4am, till 5am Sat, patio*

Minibar [MW,F,WC] 3341 N Halsted St (at Roscoe) **773/871-6227** *5pm-2am, from 11am wknds*

The North End [M,NH,WC] 3733 N Halsted St (at Grace) **773/477-7999** *2pm-2am, from 11am Fri-Sun, sports bar*

Progress Bar [MW,D] 3359 N Halsted **773/697-9268** *4pm-2am, from 3pm Fri, 2pm-3am Sat, from 1pm Sun*

Replay [M,NH] 3439 N Halsted St (btwn Cornelia & Newport) **773/975-9244** *3pm-2am, from noon wknds, till 3am Sat, queer arcade & great beer garden*

Roscoe's [★MW,NH,D,F,K,DS,S,V] 3354-56 N Halsted St (at W Roscoe) **773/281-3355** *4pm-2am, from 3pm Fri, from 2pm Sat, patio*

Scarlet [M,D] 3320 N Halsted St (at Aldine) **773/348-1053** *6pm-2am, from 2pm wknds*

Shakers [GS,E,WC,GO] 3160 N Clark St (at Belmont) **773/327-5969** *3pm-2am, from noon wknds*

Sidetrack [★MW,NH,V,WC] 3349 N Halsted St (at Roscoe) **773/477-9189** *3pm-2am, till 3am Sat*

Nightclubs

Berlin [★MW,D,TG,S,V,WC] 954 W Belmont (at Sheffield) **773/348-4975** *5pm-4am, from 10pm Sun-Tues*

Fantasy [M,D,MR,S] 3641 N Halsted St (at Addison) **773/325-2233** *9pm-4am, till 5am Sat, clsd Mon-Wed, Latin nights Th & Sun (T-dance)*

Hydrate [★GS,D,E,DS,S] 3458 N Halsted St (at Cornelia) **773/975-9244** *8pm-4am, till 5am Sat, opens earlier in summer*

Planet Earth [GS,D] 3534 W Belmont (at Late Bar) **773/267-5283** *10pm-5am Sat, New Wave*

Smart Bar [★GF,D,A,E] 3730 N Clark St (downstairs at the Metro) **773/549-0203** *10pm-4am, till 5am Sat, clsd Mon-Tue, theme nights*

Stardust Thursdays [W,D,DS] 954 W Belmont (at Berlin) **773/348-4975**

Urbano/SX Chicago [M,D,MR-AF,MR-L] 3641 N Halsted St (at Addison) **773/814-1246**

Cafes

The Coffee & Tea Exchange 3311 N Broadway St (at Roscoe) **773/528-2241** *7am-8pm, till 7pm Sat, 9am-6pm Sun*

Restaurants

Angelina Ristorante [WC] 3561 N Broadway St (at Addison) **773/935-5933** *5pm-10pm, wknd brunch, Italian, full bar*

Ann Sather's [★] 909 W Belmont Ave (at Sheffield) **773/348-2378** *7am-3pm, till 4pm Sat-Sun, Swedish diner & Boystown fixture*

Cesar's [WI] 2924 N Broadway (at Oakdale) **773/296-9097** *"home of the killer margaritas"*

Chicago Diner [BW] 3411 N Halsted St (at Roscoe) **773/935-6696** *11am-10pm, from 10am wknds, till 11pm Fri-Sat, hip & vegan*

Home Bistro [★BYOB,WC] 3404 N Halsted St (at Roscoe, btwn Addison & Belmont) **773/661-0299** *dinner only, clsd Mon*

J Parker 1816 N Clark St (at Hotel Lincoln) **312/254-4747** *5pm-1am, from 4pm Fri-Sun, most spectacular views in all of Chicago, cocktail bar and small plate menu*

Joy's Noodles & Rice [BYOB,WC] 3257 N Broadway St (at Melrose) **773/327-8330** *11am-10pm, till 11pm Fri-Sat, Thai, patio*

Kit Kat Lounge & Supper Club [C,DS,GO] 3700 N Halsted St (at W Waveland Ave) **773/525-1111** *5:30pm-2am, brunch Sun*

Kitsch'n On Roscoe 2005 W Roscoe (at Damen) **773/895-5790** *8:30am-3pm, dinner served in summer, full bar*

Las Mananitas [★WC] 3523 N Halsted St (at Cornelia) **773/528-2109** *11am-11pm, till midnight Fri-Sat, strong margaritas*

Mon Ami Gabi 2300 N Lincoln Park W (at Belden) **773/348-8886** *dinner & Sun brunch, French bistro*

Nookie's Tree [★BYOB,WC] 3334 N Halsted St (at Roscoe) **773/248-9888** *7am-3;30pm*

Orange 2413 N Clark St **773/549-7833** *8am-3pm, popular brunch spot*

Panino's Pizzeria [WC] 3702 N Broadway (at Waveland) **773/472-6200** *4pm-10pm, from 11am wknds, full bar*

Pick Me Up Cafe 3408 N Clark St (at Roscoe) **773/248-6613** *11am-2am, from 9am wknds, vegan*

Pingpong [WC] 3322 N Broadway St **773/281-7575** *11am-midnight, Asian fusion, patio*

Stella's Diner 3042 N Broadway St **773/472-9040** *7am-10pm*

Yoshi's Cafe [★WC] 3257 N Halsted St (at Melrose) **773/248-6160** *dinner Tue-Sun, also Sun brunch, Asian-inspired French*

Bookstores

Unabridged Books [★] 3251 N Broadway St (at Aldine) **773/883-9119** *10am-9pm, till 7pm wknds, LGBT section*

Retail Shops

Brown Elephant 5404 N Clark St **773/271-9382** *11am-6pm, all purchases benefit Howard Brown general health center; also in Lakeview and Oak Park*

Men's Clubs

Steamworks Men's Gym/ Sauna [WI] 3246 N Halsted St (N of Belmont) **773/929-6080** *24hrs*

Erotica

Batteries Not Included 3704 N Halsted St **773/935-9900** *11am-midnight, till 1am Fri, 10am-2am Sat*

Cupid's Treasures 3519 N Halsted St (at Cornelia) **773/348-3884** *11am-midnight*

The Pleasure Chest 3436 N Lincoln Ave (at Newport) **773/525-7152** *10am-midnight, till 11pm Sun*

The Ram Bookstore 3511 N Halsted St (at Addison) **773/525-9528**

Cruisy Areas

Belmont Rocks [AYOR]

Chicago—Near North

Accommodations

ACME Hotel Company Chicago [GF,WI,WC] 15 E Ohio St (at State St) **312/894-0900**

The Alise Hotel [GF,NS,WI] 1 W Washington St (at State) **312/940-7997, 800/886-6416**

Allegro Chicago [GF,F,E,WI,WC] 171 W Randolph St (at LaSalle) **312/236-0123, 866/672-6143**

Dana Hotel & Spa [GF,F,NS,WC] 660 N State St (at Erie) **312/202-6000**

Hotel Indigo Chicago Gold Coast [GF,WI,WC] 1244 N Dearborn Pkwy (btwn Goethe & Division) **312/787-4980, 866/521-6950**

Hotel Monaco [GF,WI,NS] 225 N Wabash (at S Water & Wacker Pl) **312/960-8500, 800/397-7661**

Millennium Knickerbocker Hotel [GF,F,WC] 163 E Walton Pl (Michigan Ave) **312/751-8100, 866/866-8086**

Palmer House Hilton [GF,SW] 17 E Monroe St (at State St) **312/726-7500**

W Chicago—Lakeshore [GF,SW,NS,WI,WC] 644 N Lake Shore Dr (at Ontario) **312/943-9200**

Bars

Davenport's [GS,C,P] 1383 N Milwaukee (in Wicker Park) **773/278-1830** *7pm-midnight, till 2am Fri-Sat, till 11pm Sun, clsd Tue*

Second Story Bar [M,NH] 157 E Ohio St (at Michigan Ave) **312/923-9536** *1pm-2am, till 3am Sat*

Slippery Slope [GS,D] 2357 N Milwaukee Ave **773/799-8504** *7pm-2am, dive bar, more gay on the 3rd Th*

Wang's [GS,E] 3317 N Broadway St **773/296-6800** *4pm-11pm, till 2am Fri-Sat, frpm 6pm Fri-Sat, more gay men late night*

Nightclubs

Baton Show Lounge [MW,DS,WC] 436 N Clark St (btwn Illinois & Hubbard) **312/644-5269** *showtimes at 8:30pm, 10:30pm, 12:30am, clsd Mon-Tue, reservations advised, since 1969!*

Restaurants

Blackbird 619 W Randolph St (at Des Plaines) **312/715-0708** *lunch Mon-Fri, dinner nightly*

Catch 35 35 W Wacker Dr (at Dearborn) **312/346-3500, 312/346-3535** *lunch Mon-Fri, dinner nightly, steak & seafood*

Fireplace Inn 1448 N Wells St (at North Ave) **312/664-5264, 312/664-5264** *lunch & dinner, BBQ, full bar open late*

Girl and the Goat [GO] 809 W Randolph St **312/492-6262** *4:30pm-11pm*

Hot Chocolate [WC] 1747 N Damen Ave (in Wicker Park) **773/489-1747** *lunch, dinner & dessert, wknd brunch, clsd Mon*

Kiki's Bistro [WC] 900 N Franklin St (at Locust) **312/335-5454** *lunch Mon-Fri, dinner nightly, clsd Sun, French, full bar*

Lou Mitchell's 565 W Jackson Blvd (at Jefferson) **312/939-3111** *great brkfst*

Manny's [WC] 1141 S Jefferson St (at Roosevelt) **312/939-2855** *7am-8pm, till 3pm Sun-Mon, killer corned beef*

Nacional 27 325 W Huron (at N Orleans) **312/664-2727** *dinner nightly, clsd Sun, Nuevo Latino, also lounge open late*

Park Grill 11 N Michigan Ave (in Millennium Park) **312/521-7275** *11am-10pm*

Shaw's Crab House [E,WC] 21 E Hubbard St (at State St) **312/527-2722** *lunch & dinner, full bar*

Topolobampo 445 N Clark St (btwn Illinois & Hubbard) **312/661-1434** *lunch & dinner, clsd Sun-Mon*

Vermilion [★WC] 10 W Hubbard St (at State) **312/527-4060** *lunch Mon-Fri, dinner nightly, Latin-Indian fusion, full bar, patio*

Bookstores

After-Words New & Used Books [WI] 23 E Illinois St (btwn State & Wabash) **312/464-1110** *10:30am-10pm, till 11pm Fri-Sat, noon-7pm Sun*

Quimby's Bookstore [WC] 1854 W North Ave (at Wolcott, in Wicker Park) **773/342-0910** *noon-9pm, 11am-10pm Sat, noon-7pm Sun*

Erotica

Lover's Playground [WC] 1246 W Randolph (at Elizabeth) **312/226-5222** *24hrs*

Lovers Playground 872 N State St (at Delaware) **312/337-9190** *24hrs*

Wells Books 178 N Wells (at Lake) **312/263-9266**

Chicago—South Side

Bars

Club Escape [MW,D,DS,MR-AF,F] 1530 E 75th St (at Stoney Island Ave) **773/599-9372** *4pm-2am, till 3am Sat*

Inn Exile [M,D,V,WI,WC] 5758 W 65th St (at Menard, near Midway Airport; 1 mile W of Midway hotel center at 65th & Cicero) **773/582-3510** *8pm-2am, till 3am Sat*

Jeffery Pub [★MW,D,MR-AF,DS,WC] 7041 S Jeffery Blvd (at 71st) **773/363-8555** *noon-4am, till 5am Sat, clsd Mon*

Bookstores

57th St Books 1301 E 57th St, Hyde Park (at Kimbark St) **773/684-1300** *10am-8pm*

Powell's Bookstore [★] 1501 E 57th St **773/955-7780** *9am-11pm*

De Kalb

Erotica

Lovers Playground 157 E Lincoln Hwy (at 2nd) **815/758-8061**

Decatur

Restaurants

Robbie's Grill 122 N Merchant St **217/423-0448** *11am-10pm, till 3am Sat, clsd Sun, full bar*

Erotica

Romantix Adult Superstore 2015 N 22nd St **217/362-0105** *booths*

Cruisy Areas

Fairview Park [AYOR] in the back

Elk Grove Village

see also Chicago

Cruisy Areas

Busse Woods Forest Preserve [AYOR]

Forest View

Bars

Forest View Lounge [W,F,E] 4519 S Harlem Ave (at 46th St) **708/484-3067** *11am-midnight, till 2am wknds, clsd Sun*

Galesburg

Men's Clubs

Hole in the Wall [PC,WC,GO] 1438 Knox Hwy 9 (off I-74 at Exit 51) **309/289-2375** *11am-6pm, till 7pm Tue, till 10pm Fri, clsd Mon*

Erotica

Romantix Adult Superstore 595 N Henderson St (at Losey) **309/342-7019**

Hoffman Estates

Cruisy Areas

Beverly Lake Forest Preserve [AYOR] Rte 72 (btwn 25 & 59)

Ina

Cruisy Areas

Rend Lake [AYOR] off I-57 (S of Mt Vernon, N of Carbondale) *near boat ramp, beware of cops*

Joliet

Info Lines & Services

Community Alliance & Action Network [WI] 68 N Chicago St #401 (at Jefferson) **815/726-7906** *by appointment, LGBT community center*

Nightclubs

Maneuvers & Co [MW,D,TG,DS] 118 E Jefferson (at Chicago) **815/727-7069** *8pm-2am, till 3am Fri-Sat, patio, frequent events*

Cruisy Areas

Hammill Woods [AYOR] Rte 59 (2 miles N of Hwy 52) *beware of cops*

Kankakee

Cruisy Areas

Kankakee River State Park [AYOR] Rte 102 *across from main entrance, Dan Uze Area*

LaGrange

Cruisy Areas

Possum Hollow Woods [AYOR] 31st St (W of LaGrange Rd)

Leroy

Cruisy Areas

Moraine View State Park [AYOR] *around Dawson Lake & Timber Point*

Monticello

Restaurants

The Brown Bag 212 W Washington St **217/762-9221** *9am-7pm, till 8pm Tue & Fri, till 4pm Sat, clsd Sun*

Morris

Erotica

Forty-Seven Video 50 Gore Rd (N of exit 112, off I-80) **815/942-8309** *24hrs*

Normal

Cafes

Coffeehouse & Deli [E,WI] 114 E Beaufort St **309/452-6774** *7am-10pm, vegetarian/ vegan*

Oak Park

see also Berwyn & Chicago

Oakwood

Erotica

Oasis Books & Video 504 N Oakwood St (off I-74) **217/354-4820** *24hrs, arcade*

Ottawa

Erotica

Brown Bag Video 3042 N State Rte 71 (at I-80, exit 93) **815/313-4125** *24hrs*

Cruisy Areas

Matthiessen State Park [AYOR] 1 mile E of I-39 (at Exit 54) *river area*

Peoria

Accommodations

Peoria Marriott Pere Marquette [GF,WI] 501 Main St **309/637-6500** *bar and restaurant, fitness center*

Cafes

One World [WI,WC] 1245 W Main St (at University) **309/672-1522** *7am-11pm, from 8am wknds*

Restaurants

Two 25 225 NE Adams St (at Mark Twain Hotel) **309/282-7777** *lunch Mon-Fri, dinner nightly, clsd Sun*

Erotica

The Green Door 2610 W Farmington Rd (near Sterling Ave) **309/674-4337**

Lovers Playground 335 SW Adams (at Harrison) **309/676-9275**

Quincy

Erotica

Chelsea Entertainment 4804 Gardner Expwy **217/224-7000** *9:30am-10pm., till midnight Fri-Sat*

Cruisy Areas

Parker Heights Park [AYOR] *parking lot by archery range*

Rockford

Nightclubs

The Office Niteclub [★MW,D,E,K,DS,S,V] 513 E State St (btwn 2nd & 3rd) **815/965-0344** *noon-2am*

Restaurants

Lucerne's Fondue & Spirits [R,WC] 845 N Church St (at Whitman) **815/968-2665** *5pm-11pm, clsd Mon*

Schiller Park

Cruisy Areas

Schiller Woods [AYOR] Irving Park Rd (btwn N Cumberland Ave & River Rd)

Springfield

Info Lines & Services

The Phoenix Center 109 E Lawrence Ave **217/528-5253** *8:30am-4:30pm, clsd wknds*

Bars

The Station House [MW,NH,D,WC] 304-306 E Washington (btwn 3rd & 4th Sts) **217/525-0438** *4pm-3am, from noon wknds, till midnight Sun*

Retail Shops

New Age Tattoos & Body Piercings 2915 S MacArthur Blvd **217/546-5006** *11am-8pm, till 6pm Sun*

Cruisy Areas

Douglas Park [AYOR] MacArthur & Mason

Riverside Park [AYOR] Peoria Rd N, past river

Waukegan

Cruisy Areas

Green Belt Forest Preserve Hwy 120 E, right on Green Bay Rd

INDIANA

Bloomington

Bars

The Back Door [MW,D,DS,K] 207 S College Ave (down the alley), IN **812/333-3123** *4pm-2am, from 7pm Fri-Sun*

Cafes

Soma Coffee House [WI] 322 E Kirkwood Ave (below Laughing Planet) **812/331-2770** *6am-9pm, from 7am wknds*

Restaurants

Laughing Planet Cafe 322 E Kirkwood Ave (enter on Grant) **812/323-2233** *11am-9pm, vegan/veggie, outdoor seating*

Village Deli 409 E Kirkwood **812/336-2303** *7am-6pm, 8am-6pm wknds*

Erotica

Lover's Playground 1013 N College Ave (at 14th) **812/332-5160** *24hrs*

Cruisy Areas

Cascades Park [AYOR] *beware of cops late evenings!*

Columbus

Cruisy Areas

Nobblitt Park [AYOR] 17th St (1 1/2 blocks W of Washington) *walk to train bridge*

Elkhart

see also South Bend

Evansville

Nightclubs

Someplace Else [MW,D,K,DS] 930 Main St (at Sycamore) **812/424-3202** *4pm-3am*

Erotica

Boudoir Noir 4605 Washington Ave **812/401-7399** *10am-midnight, noon-10pm Sun*

Fulton Ave Adult Books 201 S Fulton Ave (at 2nd) **812/421-0222** *10am-midnight, till 2amFri-Sat, noon-10pm Sun*

Lovers Playground 519 N Main (by Lucky Lady) **812/423-2011** *24hrs*

Cruisy Areas

Mesker Park [AYOR] *police patrols are heavy*

Fort Wayne

Nightclubs

After Dark [M,D,B,K] 112 E Masterson Ave **260/456-6235** *3pm-3am, from 6pm Sat-Sun*

After Dark/Babylon [M,D,K,DS,S,WC,GO] 112 E Masterson Ave **260/456-6235** *noon-3am, 6pm-12:30am Sun*

Cafes

Firefly [E,WI] 3523 N Anthony Blvd **260/373-0505** *6:30am-8pm, from 8am wknds*

Restaurants

The Loving Cafe [WC] 7605 Coldwater Rd **260/489-8686** *10am-8pm, clsd Sun, vegetarian/ vegan*

Retail Shops

Boudoir Noir 512 W Superior St **260/420-0557** *10am-midnight, noon-8pm Sun, gifts, toys, leather*

Cruisy Areas

Swinney Park [AYOR] *be alert—major crackdown on cruising in Fort Wayne*

Gary

see also Chicago, Illinois

Erotica

Romantix Adult Superstore 8801 W Melton Rd/ US 20 (at Ripley Rd) **219/938-2194** *24hrs*

Goshen

see also South Bend

Cafes

The Electric Brew [E] 136 S Main St **574/533-5990** *6am-10pm, noon-7pm Sun*

Hammond

Bars

Dick's R U Crazee? [M,NH,K,DS] 1221 E 150th St **219/852-0222** *8pm-3am, from 9pm Fri-Sat*

Hebron

Erotica

Lion's Den 18010 Colorado St (exit 240, off I-65) **219/696-1276** *24hrs*

Indianapolis

Info Lines & Services

AA Gay/ Lesbian 317/632-7864 *check www.indyaa.org for meeting times & locations*

Accommodations

The Alexander [GF] 333 S Delaware St **855/200-3002** *boutique-style art hotel*

The Fort Harrison State Park Inn [GF,NS,WC] 5830 N Post Rd **317/638-6000** *luxury inn in historic Fort Harrison in NE Indianapolis*

Stone Soup Inn [GS,WI] 1304 N Central Ave (at 13th St) **866/639-9550** *in the heart of the historic Old Northside*

The Villa [GS,WI] 1456 N Delaware St (at 15th) **317/916-8500** , **866/626-8500** *spa and restaurant*

Wyndham Indianapolis West [GF,SW] 2544 Executive Dr (off Airport Expy) **317/248-2481** *WI] in lobby, restaurant & lounge*

Bars

Downtown Olly's [M,NH,K,V,WC] 822 N Illinois St (at St Clair) **317/636-5597** *open 24hrs, sports & video bar, brkfst, lunch, dinner*

Metro Nightclub & Restaurant [★MW,F,K,P,WC] 707 Massachusetts Ave (at College) **317/639-6022** *3pm-3am, from noon wknds, patio, also restaurant*

Zonie's Closet [GS,K,DS] 1446 E Washington St (at Arsenal) **317/266-0535** *3pm-2am, cld Mon Tue*

Nightclubs

Greg's [★M,D,DS,CW,V,WC] 231 E 16th St (at Alabama) **317/638-8138** *4pm-3am, patio*

Cafes

Bee Coffee 5510 Lafayette Rd (at 56th St) **317/280-1236** *6am-5pm, 7am-3pm Sat, clsd Sun*

Henry's Coffee Bistro [★WI,GO] 627 N East St **317/951-0335** *7am-4pm, from 11am Mon, 8am-3pm wknds*

Hubbard & Cravens [F,WI] 4930 N Pennsylvania St (in Broad Ripple) **317/251-5161** *6am-7pm, 7am-3pm Sun*

Hubbard & Cravens [F,WI] 4930 N Pennsylvania St **317/251-5161** *6am-7pm, 7am-5pm Sun*

Moe & Johnny's [F,WI] 5380 N College Ave **317/255-6376** *6am-10pm, from 7am Sat, till 9pm Sun, also full bar*

Monon Coffee Company 920 E Westfield Blvd (at Guilford) **317/255-0510** *6:30am-8pm, till 10pm Fri, from 7am Sat, 8am-8pm Sun*

Restaurants

Bazbeaux Pizza 329 Massachusetts Ave **317/636-7662** *lunch & dinner*

English Ivy's [WI,WC] 944 S Alabama (at 10th) **317/822-5070** *11am-2am from 10am Sun, also full bar*

India Garden [WC] 830 Broad Ripple Ave (btwn Carrollton & Guilford) **317/253-6060** *lunch & dinner, Indian; also 207 N Delaware St, 317/634-6060*

King David Dogs 15 N Pennsylvania St *clsd wknds, great hot dogs*

La Piedad 6524 Cornell Ave **317/475-0988** *lunch & dinner, Mexican*

Mama Carolla's [★WC] 1031 E 54th St (at Winthrop) **317/259-9412** *dinner only, clsd Sun-Mon, traditional Italian*

Naked Tchopstix [★BW] 6253 N College Ave (in Broad Ripple) **317/252-5555** *lunch & dinner, Korean, Japanese, Chinese cuisine, also sushi bar*

Oakley's Bistro [★WC] 1464 W 86th St (at Ditch Rd) **317/824-1231** *lunch & dinner, clsd Sun-Mon, gourmet cont'l, reservations suggested*

Pancho's Taqueria [WC] 9658 Allisonville Rd, Fishers **317/585-8427** *11am-9pm, authentic Mexican*

Sawasdee [WC] 1222 W 86th St (at Ditch Rd) **317/844-9451** *lunch Mon-Sat, dinner nightly, Thai, some veggie*

Three Sisters Cafe 6360 N Guilford Ave (at Main St) **317/257-5556** *8am-4pm, plenty veggie and vegan, popular Sun brunch*

Yats [★WC] 885 Massachusetts Ave **317/423-0518** *11am-9pm, till 10pm Fri-Sat, till 7pm Sun, Cajun; also also 5363 N College Ave*

Entertainment & Recreation

Indy Indie Artist Colony 26 E 14th St **317/295-9302** *noon-5pm Th-Sat, largest artist community in the city with 72 artist live/work spaces*

Retail Shops

All My Relations 7218 Rockville Rd **317/227-3925** *noon-6pm, till 7pm Wed-Th, 10am-6pm Sat, New Age/metaphysical store, also classes*

Metamorphosis 828 Broad Ripple Ave (at Carrollton) **317/466-1666** *1pm-9pm, till 5pm Sun, tattoo & piercing parlor*

Publications

Nuvo 317/254-2400 *Indy's alternative weekly*

Men's Clubs

Club Indianapolis [18+,SW,PC] 620 N Capitol Ave (at North & Walnut) **317/635-5796** *24hrs, steam, sauna, gym, outdoor patio*

The Works [WI,PC,GO] 4120 N Keystone Ave (at 38th) **317/547-9210** *24hrs*

Erotica

Adultmart 6767 E 38th St (at Massachusetts) **317/549-3522** *9am-midnight, till 2am Fri-Sat*

Cruisy Areas

Damron does not list here as there are 9 cops to every 1 cruiser [AYOR]

Kokomo

Cruisy Areas

Highland Park [AYOR] near "Old Ben"

Lafayette

Info Lines & Services

Pride Lafayette, Inc 640 Main St #218 **765/423-7579** *community center 6pm-8pm, support/ social activities*

Erotica

Fantasy Gift Shop 2315 Concord Rd (at Teal) **765/474-2417** *10am-1am*

Logansport

Cruisy Areas

Spencer Park [AYOR] near tennis courts & trails along Eel River

Madison

Cruisy Areas

Clifty St Park [AYOR] btwn poplar & oak groves

Vaughn Dr [AYOR] along river

Marion

Erotica

After Dark 1311 W Johnson St **765/662-3688** *10am-11pm, till midnight Fri-Sat, noon-10pm Sun*

Michigan City

Accommodations

Duneland Beach Inn & Restaurant [GF] 3311 Pottawattomie Trail (at Duneland Beach Dr) **219/874-7729, 800/423-7729** *also restaurant &bar, 1 block away from Lake Michigan, private beach, 60 miles from Chicago*

Tryon Farm Guest House [GF,NS,WI] 1400 Tryon Rd (at Hwy 212) **219/879-3618** *full brkfst, hot tub*

Mishawaka

see also South Bend

Accommodations

The Beiger Mansion [GF,SW,NS,WI,GO] 317 Lincolnway E **574/255-6300, 800/437-0131** *B&B in 4-level neo-classical limestone mansion*

Morgantown

Accommodations

Camp Buckwood [MO,SW,GO] 8670 Spearsville Rd **812/597-2450** *lodge w/ tents & RV sites, cabins, play areas*

Muncie

Bars

Mark III Tap Room [MW,NH,DS,K] 107 E Main St **765/216-1327** *5pm-2am, till 3am wknds*

Cruisy Areas

McCulloch Park [AYOR] on Broadway (past the Muncie Mall)

New Albany

Nightclubs

Pride Bar & Lounge [MW,D,K] 504 State St **812/329-0519** *7pm-midnight, till 2am Fri-Sat, clsd Sun*

Richmond

Erotica

Roxxy's 12 S 11th St **765/935-5827** *9am-midnight, noon-10pm Sun*

South Bend

Accommodations

Innisfree B&B [GF,NS] 702 W Colfax **574/318-4838** *1892 Queen Anne minutes from Notre Dame, full brkfst*

Bars

Jeannie's Tavern [GS,NH,TG,GO] 621 S Bendix (at Ford St) **574/288-2962** *6pm-2am, clsd Mon*

Vickies Inc [GS,NH,TG,F,GO] 112 W Monroe St (at S Michigan St) **574/232-4090** *2pm-2am, football party every Sat in season*

Entertainment & Recreation

GLBT Resource Center of Michiana **574/254-1411** *5pm-8pm Mon & 11am-2pm Sat*

Erotica

Romantix Adult Superstore 2715 S Main St (at Eckman St) **574/291-1899**

Cruisy Areas

Rum Village Park [AYOR] W Ewing Ave

Terre Haute

Nightclubs

Zimmarss Nightclub [MW,D,TG,DS,S,GO] 1500 Locust St (at 15th St) **812/232-3026** *8pm-3am, 7pm-12:30am Sun, clsd Mon-Tue*

Cruisy Areas

Deming Park [AYOR]

Fairbanks Park [AYOR] S 1st Ave

Valparaiso

Accommodations

Inn at Aberdeen [GF,NS,WI,WC] 3158 S State Rd 2 **219/465-3753, 866/761-3753** *1880s Queen Anne, full brkfst*

Vincennes

Cruisy Areas

George Rodgers Clark Memorial Park [AYOR]

IOWA

Ames

Restaurants

Bar La Tosca 400 Main St (at Burnett) **515/232-8484** *lunch & dinner, clsd Sun, full bar*

Erotica

Romantix Adult Superstore 117 Kellogg St (at Lincoln Wy) **515/232-7717** *9am-4am*

Boone

Cruisy Areas

Roadside Park [AYOR] 1 mile W on US-30

Burlington

Accommodations

Arrowhead Motel [GF,WI,WC,GO] 2520 Mt Pleasant St **319/752-6353**

Bars

Steve's Place [GS,F,K,WC,GO] 852 Washington St (at Central Ave) **319/754-5868** *4am-2am, from 2pm Sat,clsd Sun, full menu*

Erotica

Lovers Playground 421 Dry Creek Ave, West Burlington **319/753-5455** *8am-midnight, 24hrs Th-Sat*

Cruisy Areas

Hunt Woods [AYOR] 1 mile S of town *days*

Cedar Falls

see also Waterloo

Cedar Rapids

Nightclubs

Belle's Basix [MW,D,L,TG,DS,GO] 3916 1st Ave NE (btwn 39th & 40th) **319/363-3194** *4pm-2am*

Cafes

Blue Strawberry 118 2nd St SE **319/247-2583** *6:30am-4pm, 7am-11am Sat, clsd Sun*

ENTERTAINMENT & RECREATION

CSPS Arts Center 1103 3rd St SE **319/364-1580** *many LGBT events*

EROTICA

Adult Shop 630 66th Ave SW (at 6th St) **319/362-4939** *9am-midnight*

Adult Shop North 5539 Crane Ln NE **319/294-5360** *24hrs*

Clinton

EROTICA

18 and Beyond 135 5th Ave S **563/242-7687**

Council Bluffs

see also Omaha, Nebraska

RESTAURANTS

Dixie Quick's [R] 157 W Broadway **712/256-4140** *lunch & dinner, brunch from 9am wkds, clsd Mon, Southern*

EROTICA

Romantix Adult Superstore 3216 1st Ave (at Broadway) **712/328-2673** *24hrs*

Davenport

ACCOMMODATIONS

Hotel Blackhawk [GF] 200 East 3rd St **563/322 5000, 888/525-4455**

BARS

Mary's on 2nd [MW,NH,D,E,V,WC] 832 W 2nd St (btwn Warren & Brown) **563/884-8014** *4pm-2am, patio*

EROTICA

TR Video 3727 Hickory Grove Rd (at Fairmont & Hickory Grove) **563/386-7914** *8am-3am, til 4am Fri-Sat*

Venus News 902 W 3rd St (at Warren) **563/322-7576** *10am-midnight, till 4am Fri-Sat*

CRUISY AREAS

Credit Island Park [AYOR] W River Dr (W end) *daytime*

Davenport Levee [AYOR] under the Centennial Bridge *dusk*

Le Clair Park [AYOR] on riverfront from Main to Ripley *late*

Des Moines

ACCOMMODATIONS

The Renaissance Savery Hotel [GF,F,SW,WI,WC] 401 Locust St (at 4th) **515/244-2151**

BARS

The Blazing Saddle [★M,D,L,DS,S,WI,WC] 416 E 5th St (btwn Grand & Locust) **515/246-1299** *2pm-2am, from noon wknds*

Buddy's Corral [GF,K] 418 E 5th St (btwn Grand & Locust) **515/244-7140** *noon-2am*

NIGHTCLUBS

The Garden [MW,D,K,S,V,YC,WC] 112 SE 4th St **515/243-3965** *5pm-2am, from 8pm Sat, clsd Mmdnight Sun, patio*

CAFES

Java Joe's [E,NS,WI,WC] 214 4th St (at Court Ave) **515/288-5282** *7am-11pm, till midnight Th-Sat, till 10pm Sun*

Ritual Cafe 1301 E Locust St **515/288-4872** *7am-5pm, till 6pm Fri-Sat, clsd Sun*

Zanzibar's Coffee Adventure [WC] 2723 Ingersoll Ave (at 28th St) **515/244-7694** *6:30am-8pm, till 9pm Fri-Sat, 8am-6pm Sun*

RESTAURANTS

Drake Diner [F,WC] 1111 25th St (btwn University & Cottage Grove) **515/277-1111** *7am-11pm, try the cake shake, patio, also full bar*

ENTERTAINMENT & RECREATION

First Friday Breakfast Club, Inc [M,R] 1501 Woodland (Hoyt Sherman Place) **515/288-2500, 515/284-0880** *7am-8:15am 1st Fri, gay & bisexual men, cont'l brkfst, guest speakers, call to reserve*

Retail Shops

Liberty Gifts 333 E Grand Ave, Ste 105 (entrance on E 4th St) **515/508-0825** *10am-8pm, 11am-7pm Sun pride store*

Erotica

Lovers Playground 1000 Cherry St (at 10th) **515/244-2916**

Minx Love Boutique 1510 NE Broadway **515/266-2744** *also Minx Show Palace*

Romantix Adult Superstore 1401 E Army Post Rd (at SE 14th St) **515/256-1102** *24hrs*

Romantix Adult Superstore 2020 E Euclid Ave (at Delaware) **515/266-7992** *24hrs*

Cruisy Areas

West River Dr [AYOR] N of downtown, by the river (off 2nd Ave N)

Dubuque

Cruisy Areas

Julien Dubuque Monument Park [AYOR]

Fort Dodge

Erotica

Romantix Adult Superstore 15 N 5th St (on the square) **515/955-9756**

Iowa City

Info Lines & Services

AA Gay/ Lesbian 500 N Clinton (at church) **319/338-9111 (AA#)** *5pm Sun*

Bars

Deadwood Tavern [★GF,NH,WC] 6 S Dubuque St **319/351-9417** *11am-2am, mostly straight, college crowd*

Studio 13 [MW,D,DS,S,19+,GO] 13 S Linn St (in the alley btwn Linn & Dubuque Sts) **319/338-7185** *8pm-2am, from 7pm Fri-Sun, clsd Mon*

Restaurants

The Mill [E] 120 E Burlington St **319/351-9529** *lunch & dinner, wknd brunch, live music*

Bookstores

Prairie Lights Bookstore [WC] 15 S Dubuque St (at Washington) **319/337-2681, 800/295-2665** *9am-9pm, till 6pm Sun, also cafe & wine bar*

Retail Shops

New Pioneer Co-op & Bakehouse [GF,WC] 22 S Van Buren (at Washington) **319/338-9441** *7am-11pm, health food store & deli; also Coralville location at 1101 2nd St*

Erotica

Romantix Adult Superstore 315 Kirkwood Ave (at Gilbert) **319/351-9444** *8am-4am*

Newton

Erotica

Lion's De 7717 Hwy F 48 West (Exit 159, off I-80) **641/792-9301** *24hrs*

Ottumwa

Cruisy Areas

Greater Ottumwa Park [AYOR]

Sioux City

Erotica

Romantix Adult Superstore 511 Pearl St **712/277-8566** *8am-4am, noon-2am Sun*

Waterloo

Nightclubs

Kings & Queens Knight Club [GS,D,TG,DS,V,YC,WC] 304 W 4th St (at Jefferson) **319/232-3001** *6:30pm-2am, clsd Mon*

Erotica

Adult Cinema 16 315 E 4th St (at Mulberry) **319/234-7459** *9am-10pm, till midnight Fri-Sat*

Romantix Adult Superstore 1507 La Porte Rd (at Lock) **319/234-9340** *24hrs*

Kansas

Statewide

Publications

The Liberty Press 316/652-7737 *Kansas statewide LGBT newspaper*

Abilene

Erotica

Lion's Den 2349 Fair Rd (exit 272 off I-70) **785/263-9898**

Great Bend

Cruisy Areas

Fort Zarah Rest Area [AYOR] on Santa Fe Trail (on Hwy 56) *2 miles E of Great Bend*

Hutchinson

Cruisy Areas

Carey Park [AYOR] Main St (at the very S end)

Kansas City

see also Kansas City, Missouri

Cruisy Areas

Pierson Park [AYOR] Wyandotte County (off Nieman Rd) *Mon-Fri*

Lawrence

Nightclubs

Granada [GS,D,E,NS,WC] 1020 Massachusetts (at 11th) **785/842-1390** *hours vary, live bands*

Jazzhaus [GF,E,K,WI] 926-1/2 Massachusetts St **785/749-3320, 785/749-1387** *8pm-2am, clsd Sun*

Cafes

Henry's [★WI] 11 E 8th St (btwn Massachusetts St & New Hampshire St) **785/331-3511** *7am-2am, cafe downstairs, bar from 5pm upstairs*

Java Break [GO] 17 E 7th St (at New Hampshire) **785/749-5282** *24hrs, sandwiches, desserts*

Restaurants

Merchants Pub & Plate [WC] 746 Massachusetts St (at 8th) **785/843-4111** *11am-midnight, till 2am Th-Sat, serving rich Midwestern harvest with over 30 craft beers*

Bookstores

The Dusty Bookshelf [GO] 708 Massachusetts St **785/749-4643** *10am-8pm, till 10pm Fri-Sat, noon-6pm Sun, LGBT section*

Cruisy Areas

Memorial Drive [AYOR] E of Jayhawk Blvd

Riverfront Park [AYOR] Hwy 24/40 (at N 2nd St)

Manhattan

Cruisy Areas

Tuttle Creek Park [AYOR]

Olathe

Cruisy Areas

Cedar Lake [AYOR] on Lone Elm Rd

Overland Park

Accommodations

Hawthorn Suites [GF,SW,NS,WI,WC] 11400 College Blvd **913/624-3981**

Salina

Cruisy Areas

Thomas Park [AYOR] 1/2 mile S of I-70 (at 9th St exit)

Topeka

Info Lines & Services

Freedom Group AA 1100 SW Wanamaker Rd **785/235-2226** *8pm Fri*

Cruisy Areas

Gage Park [AYOR] *beware of cops!*

Shunga Park [AYOR] 29th St & Fairlawn Rd

Wichita

Info Lines & Services

One Day at a Time Gay AA 156 S Kansas Ave (at MCC, enter on English) **316/684-3661** *8pm Tue & Th*

Accommodations

Hawthorn Suites [GF,WI,WC] 2405 N Ridge Rd **316/729-5700** *brkfst buffet*

Bars

Club Boomerang [MW,D,F,DS,K] 1400 E 1st **316/247-0350** *5pm-2am, from 11am Sun, clsd Mon-Tue*

J's Lounge [MW,E,K,C,WC] 513 E Central Ave (at N Emporia St) **316/262-1363** *4pm-2am, cabaret, patio, "an upscale dive"*

Kirby's Beer Store [MW,NH,E] 3210 E Osie **316/239-7990** *3pm-2am*

Rain Cafe & Lounge [★MW,D,F,K] 518 E Douglas (btwn St Francis & Emporia) **316/261-9000** *11am-2am, from 10:30am Sun, full menu till 9pm, full bar, DJ on wknds*

Rockys Bar [MW,K] 604 S. Topeka **316/440-4979** *2pm-2am*

XY Bar [★GS,D,E,DS] 235 N Mosley (in Old Town) **316/201-4670** *4pm-2am*

Cafes

The Vagabond [WI] 614 W Douglas Ave **316/303-1110** *7am-2am, also art gallery & bar, theme nights*

Restaurants

Moe's Sub Shop 2815 S Hydraulic St (at Wassall) **316/524-5511** *11am-8pm, clsd Sun*

Oh Yeah! China Bistro [WC] 3101 N Rock Rd **316/425-7700** *lunch & dinner*

Old Mill Tasty Shop 604 E Douglas Ave (at St Francis) **316/264-6500** *11am-3pm, from 8am Sat, clsd Sun, old-fashioned soda fountain*

River City Brewing Company 150 N Mosley St **316/263-2739** *11am-10pm, till 2am wknds, also live music*

Riverside Cafe 739 W 13th St (at Bitting) **316/262-6703** *6am-8pm, till 2pm Sun*

Entertainment & Recreation

Mosley Street Melodrama [F,$] 234 N Mosley St (btwn 1st & 2nd St) **316/263-0222** *melodrama, homestyle buffet & full bar!*

Wichita Arts 334 N Mead **316/462-2787** *promotes visual & performing arts; ArtScene publication has extensive cultural calendar*

Publications

The Liberty Press 316/652-7737 *statewide LGBT newspaper*

Erotica

Adult Superstore 5858 S Broadway **316/522-9040**

Circle Cinema 2570 S Seneca St (at Crawford St) **316/263-0587** *24hrs*

Fetish Lingerie 2150 S Broadway St (btwn E Clark & E Kinkaid Sts) **316/264-7800** *11:30-7pm, clsd Sun-Mon*

Patricia's 6143 W Kellogg (at Dugan) **316/942-1244** *9am-midnight, 1pm-10pm Sun*

Xcitement Video 3909 W Pawnee St **316/942-0200** *24hrs*

Cruisy Areas

Chisholm Trail Park [AYOR] Oliver & 29th St *days*

Kentucky

Ashland

Cruisy Areas

Central Park [AYOR] *beware of cops on bikes!*

Campbellsville

Cruisy Areas

Green River Dam [AYOR] Hwy 55 (below dam)

Covington

see also Cincinnati, Ohio

Bars

Bar 32 [GF,NH,D,F,E,K] 701 Bakewell St (at 7th St) **859/431-7011** *3pm-1am, from 1pm Sun*

Rosie's Tavern [GS,NH,GO] 643 Bakewell St (at 7th St) **859/291-9707** *3pm-2:30am*

Cruisy Areas

Devou Park [AYOR] Covington exit, off Rte 75

Jamestown

Cruisy Areas

Kendall Recreation Area [AYOR] below Wolf Creek Dam (10 miles S on Hwy 127) *also pull-off areas & overlook above dam*

Lexington

Info Lines & Services

Gay/ Lesbian AA 859/225-1212

Pride Community Services Organization 389 Waller Ave #100 **859/253-3233** *1pm-5pm Tue-Fri, 11am-3pm Sat, clsd Sun-Mon*

Accommodations

GuestHouse Inn & Suites [GF,SW,NS,WI,WC] 2261 Elkhorn Rd (off I-75) **859/294-7375**

Hyatt Regency Lexington [GF,F,SW,WC] 401 W High St **859/253-1234**

Bars

The Bar Complex [★MW,D,DS,S,WI,WC] 224 E Main St (at Esplanade) **859/255-1551** *4pm-midnight, till 2:30am Th-Sat*

Crossings [M,NH,K,L,S,WC] 117 N Limestone St **859/233-7266** *4pm-2am*

Soundbar [GS,D,K] 208 S Limestone **859/523-6338** *4:30pm-close*

Cafes

Third Street Stuff 257 N Limestone **859/255-5301** *6:30am-11pm, from 8am Sun, salads & sandwiches, also funky boutique*

Restaurants

Alfalfa Restaurant [E] 141 E Main St **859/253-0014** *lunch & dinner, brunch wknds, healthy multi-ethnic, folk music wknds*

Bookstores

Joseph-Beth [WI,WC] 161 Lexington Green Circle (at Nicholasville Rd) **859/273-2911, 800/248-6849** *9am-10pm, till 11pm Fri-Sat, 11am-9pm Sun, also cafe*

Sqecial Media 371 S Limestone St (btwn Pine & Winslow) **859/255-4316** *10am-8pm, noon-6pm Sun, also pride items*

Publications

LinQ 859/253-3233 *local news & calendar*

Erotica

Hook Novelty 940 Winchester Rd **859/252-2093**

Romantix Adult Superstore 933 Winchester Rd (at Liberty Rd) **859/252-0357** *24hrs*

Cruisy Areas

Jacobson Park [AYOR] Richmond Rd (3 miles W of Lexington) *take 3 rights inside park to sunbathing area*

Woodland Park [AYOR] E High St

London

Accommodations

The Bear & Boar B&B Resort [MO,SW,WI,GO] Wood Creek Lake **606/862-6557** *also camping, theme parties*

Louisville

Info Lines & Services

Gay AA 502/582-1849

Accommodations

21c Museum Hotel Louisville [★GF] 700 W Main St **502/217-6300** *boutique hotel w/ museum*

The Brown Hotel [GF,WI,NS] 335 W Broadway (at 4th) **502/583-1234** *also restaurant & bar*

Columbine B&B [GF,NS,WI,GO] 1707 S 3rd St (near Lee St) **502/635-5000, 800/635-5010** *1896 Greek Revivial mansion, full brkfst*

Galt House Hotel & Suites [GF] 140 N 4th St (at W Main) **502/589-5200, 800/843-4258** *waterfront hotel*

Louisville Bourbon Inn [GF,NS,WI] 1332 S 4th St (at Park Ave) **502/638-0045** *restored mansion, full brkfst*

Bars

Big Bar Louisville [M,DS] 1202 Bardstown Rd **502/618.2237** *4pm-4am from 2pm wknds*

Chill BAR Highlands [★M.NH] 1117 Bardstown Rd **859/913-8679** *4pm-2am, from 2pm Fri-Sun*

The Levee [GS,NH,D,K,WI] 1005 W Market, Jeffersonville, IN **812/284-4759** *4pm-3am*

Magnolia Bar [GF,NH] 1398 S 2nd St (at Magnolia) **502/637-9052** *3pm-4am*

Purrswaytions [W,K] 2235 S Preston St **502/409-8487** *2pm-1am, till 4am Fri-Sat*

Teddy Bears Bar & Grill [M,NH,WC] 1148 Garvin Pl (at St Catherine) **502/589-2619** *11am-4am, from 1pm Sun*

Tryangles [M,K,S,WC] 209 S Preston St (at Market) **502/583-6395** *4pm-4am, from 1pm Sun*

Nightclubs

Play Louisville [M,DS] 1101 E Washington St **502/882-3615** *9pm-4am, from 6pm Sun, clsd Mon-Tues*

Restaurants

Cafe Mimosa 1543 Bardstown Rd (at Stevens Ave) **502/458-2233** *lunch & dinner, Vietnamese, Chinese & sushi*

El Mundo [★WC] 2345 Frankfort Ave **502/899-9930** *11:30am-10pm, full bar till 2am Th-Sat, clsd Sun-Mon, Mexican*

Havana Rumba 4115 Oechsli Ave (off State Hwy 1447) **502/897-1959** *lunch & dinner, Cuban*

Jack Fry's [WC] 1007 Bardstown Rd **502/452-9244** *lunch & dinner, steak/ Southern, live jazz*

Mayan Cafe 813 E Market St **502/566-0651** *lunch Mon-Fri, dinner nightly, clsd Sun, Mayan/ Mexican*

Porcini 2730 Frankfort Ave (at Bayly) **502/894-8686** *dinner nightly, clsd Sun, Italian*

Proof on Main 702 W Main St (at 7th, at 21c Hotel) **502/217-6360** *brkfst & lunch Mon-Fri, dinner nightly, wknd brunch, American w/ Tuscan influence*

Ramsi's Cafe on the World [WC] 1293 Bardstown Rd **502/451-0700** *4pm-1am, 11am-2am Fri-Sat, from 10am Sun eclectic menu & full bar*

Vietnam Kitchen [WC] 5339 Mitscher Ave **502/363-5154** *clsd Wed, plenty veggie*

Zen Garden [WC] 2240 Frankfort Ave **502/895-9114** *lunch & dinner, clsd Sun, Asian, vegetarian*

Entertainment & Recreation

Pandora Productions PO Box 4185 40204 **502/216-5502** *LGBT-themed productions*

Bookstores

Carmichael's 1295 Bardstown Rd (at Longest Ave) **502/456-6950** *8am-9pm, till 10pm Fri-Sat*

Men's Clubs

Vapor [SW] 227 E Breckinridge St **502/785-0818** *24hrs, rooftop deck*

Erotica

Blue Movies 140 W Jefferson St (at 2nd) **502/585-4627** *9am-1am, till 5am wknds*

Campus Video 2822 7th St (at Arcade) **502/637-8388** *6am-4am*

Louisville Manor 4600 Dixie Hwy (at San Jose Ave) **502/449-1443** *6am-4am*

Metro Station 4948 Poplar Level Rd **502/968-2353** *6am-4am*

Showboat Adult Bookstore 3524 S 7th St (at Berry Blvd) **502/361-0007** *hustlers*

Theatair X 4505 Hwy 31 E (1/2 mile N of I-65), Clarksville, IN **812/282-6976** *24hrs*

Madisonville

Cruisy Areas

Grapevine Lake [AYOR]

Madisonville City Park [AYOR] Park Ave (off Pennyrile Pkwy) *go W thru 3 traffic lights, go left & drive 1 mile*

Morehead

Cruisy Areas

Cave Run State Park [AYOR]

Daniel Boone Campground [AYOR]

Newport

see also Cincinnati, Ohio

Bars

The Crazy Fox Saloon [GS,NH,E] 901 Washington Ave (at 9th) **859/261-2143** *3pm-2:30am, patio*

Cruisy Areas

James Taylor Park [AYOR] on Newport Levee

Paducah

Erotica

Romantix/Tammy's 5 243 Brown (at Irvin Cobb Dr) **270/442-5584**

Somerset

Cruisy Areas

Alpine Rest Area [AYOR] S Hwy 27 Daniel Boone Nat'l Forest

Upton

Erotica

Lion's Den 2833 Weldon Loop (exit 76 off I-65) **270/369-8171**

Whitesburg

Cruisy Areas

Carr Creek Dam [AYOR] Hazard

LOUISIANA

Alexandria

Erotica

Alexandria Adult Emporium 3117 Masonic Dr (across from Bringhurst Park) **318/561-0306** *24hrs*

Capri Video #3 1820 N MacArthur Dr (off Hwy 1) **318/767-1669** *10am-midnight, clsd Sun, arcade*

Cruisy Areas

Bringhurst Park [AYOR] 3016 Masonic Dr

Baton Rouge

Info Lines & Services

Freedom of Choice/ Gay AA 7747 Tom Dr (at MCC) **225/930-0026** *8pm Mon*

Bars

George's Place [★MW,NH,K,S,V,WC] 860 St Louis **225/387-9798** *3pm-2am, from 5pm wknds*

Hound Dogs [MW,NH,WC] 668 Main St (at 7th) **225/344-0807** *4pm-2am*

Nightclubs

Splash [★MW,D,DS,18+,WC] 2183 Highland Rd **225/242-9491** *9pm-2am, clsd Sun-Wed*

Restaurants

Drusilla Seafood 3482 Drusilla Ln (at Jefferson Hwy) **225/923-0896, 800/364-8844** *11am-10pm*

Mestizo 2323 Acadian Thruway (just off I-10) **225/387-2699** *lunch & dinner, Louisiana-Mexican fusion*

Ralph & Kacoo's [WC] 6110 Bluebonnet Blvd (off I-10 & Perkins) **225/766-2113** *11am-9:30pm, till 10:30pm Fri-Sat, Cajun, full bar*

Erotica

Grand Cinema Station 10732 Florida Blvd **225/272-2010**

Cruisy Areas

Capitol Lakes Park [AYOR] New Orleans *also adjacent area*

Manchac Park [AYOR] Hwy 73 (N of Bayou Manchac)

Breaux Bridge

Accommodations

Maison des Amis [GF,WI] 111 Washington St (at Bridge St) **337/507-3399**

Egan

Erotica

Lion's Den 191 Bocage Rd (exit 72 off I-10) **337/783-5000** *24hrs*

Lafayette

Info Lines & Services

AA Gay/ Lesbian 115 Leonie St **337/991-0830 (AA#)** *call for times & locations*

Cruisy Areas

Acadiana Park, Beaver Park & Moore Park [AYOR]

Lake Charles

Accommodations

Aunt Ruby's B&B [GS,WI] 504 Pujo St (at Hodges) **337/430-0603** *full brkfst*

Nightclubs

Crystal's [MW,D,CW,F,DS,WC,GO] 112 E Broad (at Ryan) **337/433-5457** *9pm-2am, till 4am Fri*

Restaurants

Pujo St Cafe [GO] 901 Ryan St (at Pujo) **337/439-2054** *11am-9pm, till 10pm Fri-Sat, 10am-2pm Sun, full bar*

Cruisy Areas

Pindarosa Park [AYOR] Sampson St, Westlake

Prien Lake Park & Tuten Park [AYOR]

Metairie

see New Orleans

Monroe

Nightclubs

Club Pink [M,NH,D,K,18+,WC,GO] 1914 Roselawn Ave **318/654-7030** *9pm-2am, from 7pm Th, clsd Sun-Wed*

Cruisy Areas

Forsythe Park [AYOR] Forsythe Ave (at Riverside Dr)

Natchitoches

Accommodations

Judge Porter House B&B [GS,WI,GO] 321 Second St **800/441-8343**

New Iberia

Erotica

Leisure Time Entertainment 7600 Hwy 90 W **337/364-1883** *24hrs, arcade*

New Orleans

Info Lines & Services

AA Lambda Center 1024 Elysian Fields Ave **504/838-3399 (general AA office #)** *daily meetings, call for schedule*

LGBT Community Center of New Orleans [WC] 2727 S Broad St #101 **504/945-1103**

Accommodations

1896 O'Malley House B&B [GS,NS,WI,GO] 120 S Pierce St (at Canal St) **504/488-5896, 866/226-1896**

Aaron Ingram Haus [GS,WI,GO] 1012 Elysian Fields Ave (btwn N Rampart & St Claude) **504/949-3110** *guesthouse, apts, courtyard*

Andrew Jackson Hotel [GF,WI,NS] 919 Royal St (btwn St Philip & Dumaine) **504/561-5881** *historic inn*

Antebellum Guest House [GS,N,NS,WI,GO] 1333 Esplanade Ave (at Marais St) **504/943-1900** *full brkfst*

Ashton's B&B [GF,NS,WI] 2023 Esplanade Ave (at Galvez) **504/942-7048**

Auld Sweet Olive B&B [★GS,NS,WI] 2460 N Rampart St (at Spain) **504/947-4332, 877/470-5323**

B&W Courtyards B&B [GF,NS,WI,GO] 2425 Chartres St (btwn Mandeville & Spain) **504/322-0474, 800/585-5731**

Blue 60 [GF,NS,WI] 1008 Elysian Fields Ave (at Rampart St) **504/324-4311**

Bon Maison Guest House [GS,NS,GO] 835 Bourbon St (btwn Lafitte's & Bourbon Pub) **504/561-8498**

Bourbon Orleans Hotel [GF,F,SW,WI,NS] 717 Orleans (at Bourbon St) **504/523-2222, 866/513-9744**

Bourgoyne Guest House [★MW] 839 Bourbon St (at Dumaine St) **504/524-3621, 504/525-3983** *1830s Creole mansion furnished w/ antiques, courtyard*

The Burgundy B&B [GS,NS,WI,GO] 2513 Burgundy St (at St Roch) **504/261-9477** *1890s "double shotgun" in Faubourg Marigny, near French Quarter*

Canal Street Inn [GS,NS,WI] 3620 Canal St (at Telemachus) **504/483-3033**

Chez Palmiers B&B [GS,NS,WI] 1744 N Rampart St (at St Anthony) **504/324-4059**

The Chimes B&B [GF,NS,WI] 1146 Constantinople St (in Garden District) **504/899-2621**

The Cornstalk Hotel [GF,WI] 915 Royal St **504/523-1515**

Crescent City Guest House [GS,N,NS,WI,GO] 612 Marigny St (at Chartres) **504/944-8722** *near French Quarter, hot tub*

The Frenchmen Hotel [GS,SW,NS,WI,WC] 417 Frenchmen St (where Esplanade, Decatur & Frenchmen intersect) **504/945-5453**

The Green House Inn [MW,SW,NS,WI,GO] 1212 Magazine St (at Erato) **504/525-1333** *gym, hot tub*

Harrah's Casino [GF,F,WC] 228 Poydras St **504/533-6000, 800/847-5299**

Hotel Monteleone [GF,WI,SW] 214 Royal St (at Iberville) **504/523-3341, 866/338-4684**

La Dauphine, Residence des Artistes [GS,NS,WI,GO] 2316 Dauphine St (btwn Mandeville & Marigny) **504/948-2217**

La Maison Marigny B&B on Bourbon [GS,NS,WI,GO] 1421 Bourbon St (at Esplanade) **504/948-3638, 800/570-2014** *on the quiet end of Bourbon St*

Lafitte Guest House [GS,NS,WI] 1003 Bourbon St (at St Philip) **504/581-2678** *elegant French manor house*

Lamothe House Hotel [GS,SW,NS,WI,GO] 621 Esplanade Ave (btwn Royal & Chartres) **800/535-7815**

Maison de Ville [GS,WI] 727 Toulouse St **504/324-4888**

Maison Dupuy Hotel [GF,SW,WI] 1001 Toulouse St **504/586-8000, 800/535-9177**

The Old No. 77 & Chandlery [GS,WI] 535 Tchoupitoulas St **504/527 5271, 866/226 4727** *vintage building, excellent bar and restaurant worth a visit, pets ok*

The Olivier House Hotel [GF,SW,WI,WC] 828 Toulouse (at Bourbon) **504/525-8456**

Pierre Coulon Guest House [GS,NS,WI,GO] **504/250-0965** *quiet apt*

Royal Street Courtyard [GS,WI] 2438 Royal St (at Spain) **504/943-6818** *historic 1850s guesthouse*

W New Orleans—French Quarter [GF,SW,WI,WC] 316 Chartres St **504/581-1200** *also Bacco restaurant*

Bars

700 Club [MW,V,F,WC] 700 Burgundy (at St Peter) **504/561-1095** *noon-4am*

Big Daddy's [MW,NH,WC] 2513 Royal St (at Franklin) **504/948-6288** *24hrs*

Bourbon Pub & Parade [★MW,D,DS,S,V,18+,YC,WI] 801 Bourbon St (at St Ann) **504/529-2107** *11am-3am, till 5am Fri-Sat, theme nights, Sun T-dance*

Cafe Lafitte in Exile/ The Balcony Bar [★M,D,S,V] 901 Bourbon St (at Dumaine) **504/522-8397** *24hrs*

The Corner Pocket [★M,NH,DS,S] 940 St Louis (at Burgundy) **504/568-9829** *noon-2am, 24hrs Fri-Sat, male dancers nightly*

Country Club [★GS,F,V,K,S,SW,N,WI] 634 Louisa St (at Royal) **504/945-0742** *11am-1am, not your father's country club!*

Cutter's [MW,NH,E,WI,WC] 706 Franklin Ave (at Royal) **504/948-4200** *3pm-3am, from 11am wknds*

The Double Play [M,NH,TG] 439 Dauphine (at St Louis) **504/523-4517** *24hrs*

The Four Seasons [M,NH,E,DS,GO] 3229 N Causeway Blvd (at 18th), Metairie **504/784-8322** *5pm-close, also the Out Back Bar summers, patio*

The Friendly Bar [M,NH,WC] 2301 Chartres St (at Marigny) **504/943-8929** *11am-3am*

Good Friends Bar [M,NH,K,WC] 740 Dauphine (at St Ann) **504/566-7191** *also Queens Head Pub upstairs Fri-Sun, popular piano sing-along 4pm-8pm*

GrandPre's [MW,NH,DS,WC] 834 N Rampart (at Dumaine) **504/267-3615** *9:30am-2am, 24hrs Fri-Sun, patio*

Mag's 940 [★M,D,E,DS] 940 Elysian Fields Ave (at N Rampart) **504/948-1888** *3pm-2am, from noon wknds*

Napoleon's Itch [★MW,E] 734 Bourbon (at St Ann) **504/237-4144** *noon-2am, till 4am Fri-Sat, wine & martini bar*

Phoenix [★M,NH,B,L,F,GO] 941 Elysian Fields Ave (at N Rampart) **504/945-9264** *24hrs, cruise room, beer busts, also The Eagle [D] 9pm-5am*

Rawhide 2010 [M,NH,D,A,B,L,V] 740 Burgundy St (at St Ann) **504/525-8106** *24hrs*

The Spotted Cat Music Club [GF,E,D,WC] 623 Frenchmen St *4pm-2am, excellent live jazz in the Faubourg Marigny*

Tubby's Golden Lantern [M,NH,K,DS,S] 1239 Royal St (at Barracks) **504/529-2860** *8am-2am*

Nightclubs

All Ways Lounge & Theater [M,NH,D,CW,E,WI] 2240 St Claude Ave (at Marigny) **504/218-5778** *open 6pm, clsd Mon,*

Oz [★M,D,E,DS,S,V,YC,WC] 800 Bourbon St (at St Ann) **504/593-9491** *24hrs*

Cafes

Cafe Rose Nicaud [WI] 632 Frenchmen St (btwn Royal & Chartres) **504/949-3300** *7am-6pm*

CC's Coffee House [WI] 941 Royal St **504/581-6996** *7am-9pm*

Croissants d'Or [WC] 617 Ursulines St **504/524-4663** *6am-3pm, clsd Tue, delicious pastries*

The Orange Couch [F,E,WI,WC] 2339 Royal St **504/267-7327** *7am-9pm, ultra mod cafe*

Royal Blend Coffee & Tea House 621 Royal St **504/523-2716** *6am-8pm, till midnight wknds, on a quiet, hidden courtyard, also salads & sandwiches*

Z'otz [E] 8210 Oak St **504/861-2224** *7am-1am, coffee shop & art space*

Restaurants

13 Monaghan's [WC] 517 Frenchmen St **504/942-1345** *11am-4am, brkfst, lunch & dinner all the time, full bar*

Acme Oyster House 724 Iberville St (at Royal) **504/522-5973** *11am-10pm, till 11pm wknds, long line moves quickly, worth the wait!*

Bayona 430 Dauphine St **504/525-4455** *lunch Wed-Sat, dinner night, clsd Sun, creative Louisiana fare in a charming old cottage with a lush courtyard*

Brennan's [R] 417 Royal St (at Conti) **504/525-9711** *brkfst, lunch & dinner, upscale*

Cafe Amelie 912 Royal St (in Princess of Monaco Courtyard) **504/412-8965** *lunch & dinner, Sun brunch, clsd Mon-Tue, Creole*

Cafe Negril [E,D,WC] 606 Frenchman St (at Chartres St) **504/944-4744** *6pm-2am, from 4pm Fri-Sat, Caribbean*

Casamento's [WC] 4330 Magazine St (at Napoleon Ave) **504/895-9761** *best oyster loaf in city*

Clover Grill [★] 900 Bourbon St (at Dumaine) **504/598-1010** *24hrs, diner fare*

Commander's Palace [★R,WC] 1403 Washington Ave (at Coliseum St, in Garden District) **504/899-8221** *lunch Mon-Fri, dinner nightly, jazz brunch wknds, upscale Creole, dress code*

Coquette [WC] 2800 Magazine St (at Washington Ave) **504/265-0421** *lunch Wed-Sat, dinner Mon-Sat*

The Court of Two Sisters 613 Royal St **504/522-7261** *daily jazz brunch buffet 9am-3pm, dinner nightly, Creole*

Dante's Kitchen [WC] 736 Dante St (at River Rd) **504/861-3121** *dinner nightly, wknd brunch, clsd Tue, Cajun*

EAT New Orleans 900 Dumaine St (at Dauphine) **504/522-7222** *lunch & dinner, Sun brunch, clsd Mon, Cajun/Creole, some veggie, cute waiters*

Elizabeth's 601 Gallier St **504/944-9272** *8am-2:30pm &5pm-10pm, clsd for dinner Sun, one of the best brunch's in the city*

Feelings Cafe 535 Franklin Ave **504/446-0040** *3pm-midnight*

Fiorella's Cafe 1136 Decatur St **504/605-4816** *5pm-10pm, from 11am Fri-Sun, awesome Fried Chicken*

Gumbo Shop 630 St Peter St (at Chartres) **504/525-1486** *award-winning gumbo*

Herbsaint 701 St Charles Ave **504/524-4114** *lunch & dinner, bistro menu afternoons, clsd Sun, French/Southern*

Marigny Brasserie 640 Frenchmen St **504/945-4472** *lunch Mon-Fri, dinner nightly, wknd brunch, French*

Meauxbar Bistro 942 N Rampart St (at St Philip) **504/569-9979** *dinner nightly, wknd brunch*

Mona Lisa [BW,GO,WC] 1212 Royal St (at Barracks) **504/522-6746** *11am-10pm, Italian*

Mona's 504 Frenchmen St **504/949-4115** *10am-9pm, till 10pm Fri-Sat, noon-9pm Sun, cheap Middle Eastern eats*

Napoleon House [WC] 500 Chartres St **504/524-9752** *lunch daily, dinner only Mon, clsd Sun, po' boys & muffulettas*

Orleans Grapevine [WC] 718-720 Orleans Ave **504/523-1930** *4pm-10:30pm, till 11:30pm Fri-Sat, wine bar & bistro*

Phillips [WC,GO] 733 Cherokee St (at Maple) **504/865-1155** *4pm-2am*

Praline Connection [E] 542 Frenchmen St (at Chartres) **504/943-3934** *11am-10pm, soul food*

Restaurant August [WC] 301 Tchoupitoulas St (at Gravier St) **504/299-9777** *lunch Mon-Fri, dinner nightly, upscale French/ Mediterranean*

Stanley 547 St Ann St (at Chartres) **504/587-0093** *7am-7pm, upscale diner fare*

The Upperline Restaurant [WC] 1413 Upperline St **504/891-9822** *dinner Wed-Sun, Creole, fine dining, full bar*

Willa Jean [GO] 611 O'Keefe Ave **504/509-7334** *7am-close, great brkfst*

Entertainment & Recreation

Cafe du Monde [WC] 800 Decatur St (at St Ann, corner of Jackson Square) **504/525-4544, 800/772-2927** *till you've had a beignet—fried dough, powdered w/ sugar, that melts in your mouth—you haven't been to New Orleans & this is "the" place to have them 24hrs a day*

Haunted History Tour **504/861-2727** *guided 2-1/2-hour tours of New Orleans' most famous haunts, including Anne Rice's former home*

Mardi Gras World 1380 Port of New Orleans Pl **504/361-7821** *tour this year-round Mardi Gras float workshop*

Pat O'Brien's [GF,F,WC] 718 St Peter St (btwn Bourbon & Royal) **504/525-4823, 800/597-4823** *more than just a bar—come for the Hurricane, stay for the kitsch*

Preservation Hall [NS,$] 726 St Peter St (btwn Bourbon & Royal) **504/522-2841, 888/946-5299** *come & hear the music that started jazz: New Orleans-style jazz!*

St Charles Streetcar St Charles St (at Canal St) **504/248-3900** *it's not named Desire, but you should still ride it, Blanche, if you want to see the Garden District*

Bookstores

Garden District Book Shop 2727 Prytania St (at Washington) **504/895-2266** *10am-6pm, till 4pm Sun*

Kitchen Witch Cook Books [GF] 1452 N Broad St #C **504/528-8382** *10am-7pm, clsd Tue, cookbooks from rare to campy*

Retail Shops

Angela King Gallery [GO] 241 Royal St **504/524-8211** *10am-5pm, from 11am Sun*

Bourbon Pride 909 Bourbon St (at Dumaine) **504/566-1570** *10am-8pm, till 11pm wknds, LGBT cards, gifts*

Fleurty Girl 1627 St Charles Ave **504/309-3944** *great Louisiana-made souvenirs and housewares*

Hit Parade 741 Bourbon St **504/524-7700** *3pm-11pm, 11am-2am Fri-Sat, 11am-midnight Sun, gift and clothing store*

Queork [GO] 838 Chartres **504/481-2585** *10am-6pm, sustainable home accessories, also at 3005 Magazine St*

Publications

Ambush Mag 504/522-8049 *LGBT newspaper for the Gulf South (TX through FL)*

Flame Magazine 1905 Washington Ave #A **504/507-0970** *Louisiana's Premier LGBT Lifestyle & Entertainment Magazine*

Erotica

Airline Adult Books 1404 26th St (off Bainbridge), Kenner **504/468-2931** *super-arcade w/ 30 rooms*

Mr Binky's 107 Chartres St (off Canal St) **504/302-2095** *24hrs*

Shreveport

Accommodations

Twenty-Four Thirty-Nine Fairfield [GF,WI] 2439 Fairfield Ave **318/424-2424** *1905 Victorian*

Bars

Korner Lounge II [M,NH,K] 800 Louisiana Ave (near Cotton) **318/222-9796** *4pm-2am*

Nightclubs

Central Station [★MW,D,K,DS,TG,WC] 1025 Marshall St (btwn Fairfield & Creswell) **318/222-2216** *5pm-close, till 4am Fri-Sat*

Erotica

Fun Shop Too 9434 Mansfield Rd **318/688-2482** *clsd Sun-Mon, adult, novelty & gag gifts & toys*

Slidell

Bars

Anything Geauxs [MW,D,DS,TG.E,K] 1540 W Lindberg Dr (at Gause Blvd) **504/722-2101** *6pm-2am, clsd Mon-Wed*

Billy's [MW,NH,K,DS,WI] 2600 Hwy 190 W **985/847-1921** *6pm-1am*

MAINE

Albion

ACCOMMODATIONS

Twin Ponds Lodge [MO,SW,N,WI] 96 York Town Rd (at Libby Hill Rd) **207/437-2200** *clothing optional resort for adult men, day passes available*

Aroostook County

ACCOMMODATIONS

Magic Pond Wildlife Sanctuary & Guest House [MW,NS,GO] Blaine 215/287-4174

Augusta

ACCOMMODATIONS

Annabessacook Farm [GS,SW,NS,WI,GO] 192 Annabessacook Rd, Winthrop **207/377-3276** *restored 1810 farmhouse, full brkfst*

Maple Hill Farm Inn [GS,NS,WI,WC,GO] Hallowell **207/622-2708, 800/622-2708** *historic Victorian farmhouse, full brkfst*

RESTAURANTS

Slates [E] 163 Water St (Franklin), Hallowell **207/622-9575, 207/622-4104** *lunch Tue-Fri, dinner Mon-Sat, brunch wknds, also bakery*

Bangor

CRUISY AREAS

Valley Avenue Park [AYOR] along river bank

Bar Harbor

ACCOMMODATIONS

Aysgarth Station [GF,NS,WI] 20 Roberts Ave (at Cottage St) **207/288-9655** *10-minute drive from Acadia, cats on premises*

Manor House Inn [GF,NS,WI] 106 West St (near Bridge St) **207/288-3759, 800/437-0088** *open April-Oct, 1887 Victorian mansion, full brkfst, some rooms w/ whirlpools*

The Otter Creek Inn & Market [GS,WI,WC] Rte 3, Otter Creek, Mt Desert Island **207/288-5151 , 800/845-5852** *located in Acadia National Park , kids/pets ok, seasonal*

RESTAURANTS

Cafe This Way 14 1/2 Mt Desert St **207/288-4483** *brkfst & dinner, seasonal*

Mama DiMatteo's [GO] 34 Kennebec Pl (at Firefly Ln) **207/288-3666** *4:30pm-10pm, full bar*

ENTERTAINMENT & RECREATION

ImprovAcadia 15 Cottage St (2nd flr) **207/288-2503** *live improvised theater*

CRUISY AREAS

Lake Wood [AYOR] off Crooked Rd (1 mile from Hulls Cove) *follow trail to the "Ledges"*

Thompson Island [AYOR] Mt Desert Island *beware of cops!*

Bath

ACCOMMODATIONS

The Inn at Bath [GS,NS,WC] 969 Washington St (at North St) **207/443-4294, 800/423-0964** *1810 Greek Revival B&B, full brkfst*

Boothbay Harbor

ACCOMMODATIONS

Topside Inn [GS,WI,GO] 60 McKown St **207/633-5404, 888/633-5404**

Bucksport

ACCOMMODATIONS

Williams Pond Lodge B&B [GS,WI,GO] **207/460-6064**

Corea

ACCOMMODATIONS

The Black Duck Inn on Corea Harbor [GS,NS,WI,GO] **207/963-2689** *full brkfst, restored farmhouse on harbor, also cottages*

Deer Isle

Restaurants

Fisherman's Friend 5 Atlantic Ave, Stonington **207/367-2442** *seasonal, 11am-9pm, till 10pm Fri-Sat*

Dexter

Accommodations

Brewster Inn [GF,NS,WI,WC] 37 Zion's Hill Rd (at Dexter St) **207/924-3130** *historic mansion, full brkfst*

Farmington

Bookstores

Devany, Doak & Garrett Booksellers 193 Broadway (at High St) **207/778-3454** *10am-5pm, till 5:30pm Th, till 6:30pm Fri, 9am-5pm Sat, noon-3pm Sun, LGBT section*

Freeport

Accommodations

The Royalsborough Inn [GF,NS,WI] 1290 Royalsborough Rd, Durham **207/353-6372, 800/765-1772** *full brkfst, spa services, massage, also alpaca farm*

Restaurants

Harraseeket Lunch & Lobster Co 36 Main St (at Harraseeket Rd), S Freeport **207/865-4888, 207/865-3535** *open May-Oct*

Greenville

Accommodations

Greenville Inn at Moosehead Lake [GS,WI,GO] 40 Norris St **207/695-2206** *private suites, cottages & historic inn rooms, full brkfst, one block from town and lake, also restaurant*

Kennebunkport

Accommodations

Grace White Barn Inn & Spa [GF,SW,F,NS,WI] 37 Beach Ave **207/967-2321** *also restaurant*

Hidden Pond Maine [GF] 354 Goose Rocks Rd **207/967-9050, 888/967-9050**

Restaurants

Nunan's Lobster Hut 9 Mills Rd **207/967-4362** *seasonal*

Kittery

see also Portsmouth, New Hampshire

Erotica

Amazing 92 Rte 236 N (1 mile from traffic circle), Eliot **207/439-6285**

Lewiston

Erotica

Paris Adult Book Store 297 Lisbon St (at Chestnut) **207/783-6677** *9am-8pm, 11am-4pm Sun*

Ogunquit

Accommodations

2 Village Square Inn Ogunquit [M,SW,NS,WI,GO] 14 Village Square Ln (at Main St) **207/646-5779, 800/674-9149** *open May-Oct, Victorian w/ ocean views, hot tub*

Abalonia Inn [GS,SW,WI,GO] 268 Main St (at Berwick Rd) **207/646-7001** *pets ok*

Beauport Inn [GS,SW,WI,GO] 339 Clay Hill Rd, Cape Neddick **207/361-2400** *full brkfst, complimentary bikes*

Beaver Dam Campground [GF,SW] 551 School St, Rte 9, Berwick **207/698-2267** *campground on 20-acre spring-fed pond*

Belm House Vacation Units [MW,WI,GO] **207/641-2637** *rental units w/ kitchens*

Black Boar Inn [MW,NS,WI,GO] 277 Main St (at Ogunquit Rd) **207/646-2112** *weekly rentals only*

Bourne Bed & Breakfast [GS,NS,WI] 13 Bourne Ln (at Main St) **207/646-3891**

Leisure Inn [GF,NS,WI] 73 School St (at Main St) **207/646-2737** *seasonal*

Meadowmere Resort [GF,SW,NS,WI,WC] 74 S Main St (at Rte 1) **207/646-9661, 800/633-8718** *health club & spa*

Moon Over Maine B&B [MW,NS,WI,GO] Berwick Rd **207/646-6666** *hot tub*

Ogunquit Beach Inn [MW,WI,GO] 67 School St **207/646-1112** *5 minutes walk to beach*

The Ogunquit Inn [MW,NS,WI,GO] 17 Glen Ave **207/646-3633, 866/999-3633** *Victorian B&B*

Rockmere Lodge B&B [GS,NS,GO] 150 Stearns Rd **207/646-2985, 888/646-2985** *Maine shingle cottage, near beach*

Twenty Shore [GS] 20 Shore Rd **207/200-3303** *exclusive collection of four luxury guest suites*

Yellow Monkey Guest Houses & Motel [GS,WC,GO] 280 Main St **207/646-9056** *seasonal*

Bars

Front Porch Cafe [GS,F,P] 9 Shore Rd (at Beach St) **207/646-4005** *seasonal, lunch & dinner*

Nightclubs

Maine Street [★MW,D,F,K,C,GO] 195 Main St/ US Rte 1 **207/646-5101** *5pm-1am, T-dance from 3pm wknds, seasonal*

Cafes

Bread & Roses 246 Main St **207/646-4227** *7am-7pm, seasonal*

Restaurants

Angelina's Ristorante 655 Main St **207/646-0445** *dinner, Italian*

Backyard Coffeehouse & Eatery [WO] Rte 1 **207/251-4554** *7am-8pm*

Beachfire Bar & Grill 658 Main St **207/646-8998** *dinner nightly, wknd brunch, outdoor fire pit*

Clay Hill Farm [P] 220 Clay Hill Rd (off Logging Rd), Cape Neddick (York) **207/361-2272** *dinner only, seafood, also piano bar*

Five-0 50 Shore Rd **207/646-5001** *5pm-midnight, martini bar & restaurant, full bar*

Jonathan's [E,WC] 92 Bourne Ln **207/646-4777** *dinner nightly, steak/ seafood, full bar*

The Lobster Shack 110 Perkins Cove Rd **207/646-2941** *11am-9pm, gluten-free chowder*

La Pizzeria [BW,GO] 239 Main St **207/646-1143** *open April-Dec, lunch & dinner*

Wild Blueberry Cafe & Bistro [E] 82 Shore Rd **207/646-0990** *brkfst, lunch & dinner, jazz brunch 10am-1pm Sun*

Entertainment & Recreation

Ogunquit Playhouse 10 Main St **207/646-5511** *summer theater, some LGBT-themed productions*

Cruisy Areas

Ogunquit Beach [AYOR] off Rte 1 *200 yds N of beach entrance*

Portland

Accommodations

The Chadwick B&B [GS,WI,GO] 140 Chadwick St **207/774--5141**

The Inn at St John [GS,NS,WI,GO] 939 Congress St **207/773-6481, 800/636-9127**

The Inn by the Sea [GF,SW,NS,WC] 40 Bowery Beach Rd, Cape Elizabeth **207/799-3134**

The Percy Inn [GF,WI,NS] 15 Pine St (at Longfellow Square) **207/871-7638, 888/417-3729**

The Pomegranate Inn [GF,NS,WI] 49 Neal St (at Carroll St) **207/772-1006**

Sea View Inn [GS,SW,NS,WI,WC] 65 W Grand Ave (at Atlantic Ave), Old Orchard Beach **207/934-4180** *motel*

West End Inn [GF,NS,WI] 146 Pine St (at Neal St) **800/338-1377**

Wolf Cove Inn [GF,WI] 5 Jordan Shore Dr, Poland Spring **207/998-4976**

Bars

Blackstones [M,NH,WC] 6 Pine St (off Longfellow Square) **207/775-2885** *4pm-1am, from 3pm wknds, [L] 3rd Sat, theme nights*

Cafes

Coffee by Design 1 Diamond St **207/874-5400** *6:30am-6pm*

Restaurants

The Back Bay Grill 65 Portland St **207/772-8833** *opens 5pm, clsd Sun-Mon, quiet, contemporary spot in an out-of-the-way location*

Becky's [WC] 390 Commercial St (at High St) **207/773-7070** *4am-10pm, great brkfst & chowdah*

Eventide Oyster Co. 86 Middle St **207/774-8538** *11am-midnight, pristine shellfish and a fresh take on classic New England fare*

Grace 15 Chestnut St **207/828-4422** *fine dining in renovated old church*

Katahdin 27 Forest Ave **207/774-1740** *5pm-11pm, clsd Sun-Mon, American menu, bar*

Street & Co [★BW,WC] 33 Wharf St (btwn Dana & Union) **207/775-0887** *5:30pm-9:30pm, till 10pm Fri-Sat, seafood*

Walter's Cafe [WC] 2 Portland Sq (at Union) **207/871-9258** *comfortable dining room, coupled with our vibrant bar scene and inventive bar menu*

Entertainment & Recreation

Reel North Fly Fishing [GO] **207/200-8829** *casting lessons, half & full day river trips*

Bookstores

Longfellow Books 1 Monument Way **207/772-4045** *9am-7pm, till 6pm Sat, 9:30am-5pm Sun, LGBT section*

Retail Shops

The Corner General Store 154 Middle St (at Market) **207/253-5280** *8am-1am, great wine selection*

Erotica

Amazing Intimate Essentials 666 Congress St (at State) **207/774-1377**

CS Boutique 424 Fore St (at Union) **207/871-0356, 877/871-0356** *10am-8pm, till 9pm Th, till 10pm Fri-Sat, till 6pm Sun*

Cruisy Areas

Cutter Street [AYOR] *at the foot of the street on the Eastern Promenade*

Rockland

Accommodations

Lindsey Hotel [GF,NS,WI,WC] 5 Lindsey St **207/596-7950** *sophisticated boutique hotel*

The Old Granite Inn [GF,NS,WI] 546 Main St **207/594-9036, 800/386-9036** *1880s stone guesthouse, full brkfst*

Rockport

Restaurants

Lobster Pound [WC] Rte 1, Lincolnville Beach **207/789-5550** *11:30am-8pm May-Oct, full bar, patio*

Tenants Harbor

Accommodations

Eastwind Inn [GF,F] **207/372-6366, 800/241-8439** *clsd Dec-April, full brkfst, rooms & apts*

Upper Kennebec Valley

Accommodations

The Sterling Inn B&B [GF,WI,GO] 1041 US Route 201, Caratunk **207/672-3333** *mention Damron for special rates*

Waterville

Erotica

Treasure Chest II [GO] 5 Sanger Ave (at Main) **207/873-7411**

Video 54 [GO] 18 Water St (at Sherwin St) **207/873-4201** *10am-9pm, noon-7pm Sun*

Western Mtns

Accommodations

Mountain Village Farm B&B [GF,NS,WI] 164 Main St, Kingfield 04947 **207/265-2030** *working farm & B&B, full brkfst*

York Harbor

Restaurants

York Harbor Inn 480 York St **207/363-5119** *lunch Mon-Sat, dinner nightly, Sun brunch, also the Cellar Pub, also lodging*

MARYLAND

Annapolis

INFO LINES & SERVICES

AA Gay/ Lesbian 199 Duke of Gloucester St (at St Anne's Parish) **410/268-5441** *8pm Tue*

ACCOMMODATIONS

Two-O-One B&B [GS,NS,WI,GO] 201 Prince George St (at Maryland Ave) **410/268-8053** *full brkfst*

RESTAURANTS

Cafe Sado 205 Tackle Cir (at Castle Marina Rd), Chester **410/604-1688** *lunch & dinner, sushi/ Asian fusion*

Baltimore

INFO LINES & SERVICES

AA Gay/ Lesbian 410/663-1922 *call for times and locations*

The GLCCB 2530 N Charles St 3rd Fl ( ) **410/777-8145** *10am-10pm, till 6pm Mon, clsd wknds, many groups and services, may be moving*

ACCOMMODATIONS

Hotel Monaco Baltimore [GS,WI,WC] 2 N Charles St **443/692-6170, 888/752-2636** *also restaurant*

Lord Baltimore Hotel [GS,F,WI,WC] 20 W Baltimore St **410/539-8400, 855/539-1928** *historic, landmark hotel*

Pier 5 Hotel [GS,F,WI,WC] 711 Eastern Ave (at President) **410/539-2000**

BARS

Baltimore Eagle [M,L,WC] 2022 N Charles St (enter on 21st) **410/200-9858** *6pm-2am, leather & video store, patio*

Club Bunns [MW,D,MR-AF,S] 608 W Lexington St (at Greene St) **410/234-2866** *5pm-2am, 7pm-1am Sun*

The Drinkery [M,NH,K,MR-AF] 205 W Read St (at Park) **410/225-3100** *11am-2am*

G•A•Y Lounge [M,D,F] 518 N Charles St *4pm-midnight, till 2m Th-Sat from 11am Sun drag brunch*

The Gallery Bar & Studio Restaurant [MW,MR-AF,WC] 1735 Maryland Ave (at Lafayette) **410/539-6965** *6pm-1am, dinner Mon-Fri*

Grand Central [★MW,D,F,K,DS,V,18+] 1001 N Charles St (at Eager) **410/752-7133** *4pm-close, 3 bars*

Leon's [MW,NH,B,F,WI,WC] 870 Park Ave (at Chase) **410/539-4993, 410/539-4850** *4pm-2am, also Singer's restaurant*

Mixers [MW,NH,D,E,K] 6037 Belair Rd (at Glenarm Ave) **410/483-6011** *5pm-2am*

The Rowan Tree [GS,K] 1633 S Charles St (at E Heath) **410/468-0550** *11am-2am, "where diversity is our name"*

Ziascoz [GS,NH,K,MR-AF] 1313 E Pratt St (at Eden) **410/276-5790** *7pm-2am*

NIGHTCLUBS

Club Orpheus [GS,D] 1003 E Pratt St **410/276-5599**

Factory 17 [GS,D,MR,18+,PC] 1722 N Charles St (at Lafayette) **410/547-8423** *afterhours club, Fri-Sat only, 1:45am-close, BYOB*

CAFES

Station North Arts Cafe 1816 N Charles St **410/625-6440** *8am-3pm, from 10am Sat, clsd Sun, also art gallery, events*

RESTAURANTS

Aldos [★WC] 306 S High St **410/727-0700** *dinner nightly, Italian*

Alonso's [NS,WC] 415 W Cold Spring Ln (at Keswick Rd) **410/235-3433** *4pm-10:30pm, from 11:30am Fri-Sat, full bar*

Cafe Hon [WC] 1002 W 36th St (at Roland) **410/243-1230** *11am-9pm, from 9am-close wknds*

The Dizz 300 W 30th St **443/869-5864** *10am-midnight, full bar*

Golden West Cafe 1105 W 36th St **410/889-8891** *brkfst, lunch & dinner, New Mexican, also bar, live bands*

Jerry D's Saloon 7804 Harford Rd, Parkville **410/665-0525** *11am-11pm, from 9am wknds, selection of seafood, including raw bar*

Mount Vernon Stable & Saloon 909 N Charles St (btwn Eager & Read) **410/685-7427** *11:30am-midnight, till 1am Fri-Sat, Sun brunch, also bar*

Woodberry Kichen [WC] 2010 Clipper Park Rd #126 **410/464-8000** *dinner nightly, organic & sustainable, full bar*

XS Baltimore 1307 N Charles St **410/468-0002** *7am-midnight, till 2am Fri-Sat, sushi restaurant, cafe & lounge*

Publications

Baltimore OUTloud 410/802-1310 *Mid Atlantic's premier independent voice of the LGBTQ community*

Erotica

Sugar [TG,GO] 1001 W 36th St (at Roland) **410/467-2632**

Cruisy Areas

Druid Hill Park [MR-AF,YC,AYOR] W side of town (near Park Cir)

Lake Montebello Park [AYOR] Lake Montebello Terr (at Harford Rd) *in the woods*

Wyman Dell Park [AYOR] Charles St (btwn 29th & 33rd) *hustlers on the sidewalk, cruising on the Wyman Park Dr side*

Edgewood

Erotica

Bush River Books & Video 3909 Pulaski Hwy (Rte 40), Abingdon **410/676-9051** *24hrs*

Frederick

Cruisy Areas

Gambrill State Park [AYOR] W of Frederick (off I-70) *go to the summit, turn left*

Greenbelt

see also Washington, District of Columbia

Cruisy Areas

Greenbelt Park [AYOR]

Hagerstown

Nightclubs

The Lodge [M,D,DS,MR,K,TG,GO] 21614 National Pike, Boonsboro **301/591-4434** *9pm-2am, 7:30-midnight Wed-Th, clsd Sun-Tue*

Laurel

see also Washington, District of Columbia

Erotica

Route 1 News 106 Washington Blvd (at Main) **410/880-4253**

Rock Hall

Accommodations

Tallulah's on Main [GS,NS,WC,GO] 5750 Main St (at Sharp St) **410/639-2596** *small suite hotel*

Rockville

see also Washington, District of Columbia

Cruisy Areas

Lake Needwood [AYOR] N of Rte 28 (off Avery Rd)

Salisbury

Erotica

Salisbury News Agency 616 S Salisbury Blvd (near Vine) **410/543-4469**

Snow Hill

Accommodations

River House Inn [GF,SW,WI,GO] 201 E Market St (at Green St) **410/632-2722**

MASSACHUSETTS

Amherst

see also Northampton

Bookstores

Amherst Books 8 Main St **413/256-1547, 800/503-5865** *6:30am-9pm, till 5pm Sun, independent, LGBT section*

Barre

ACCOMMODATIONS

Jenkins Inn & Restaurant [GF,F,NS,WI,GO] **978/355-6444** *also restaurant & full bar*

Berkshires

ACCOMMODATIONS

The Barrington [GF,NS,WI,GO] 281 Main St (at Church), Great Barrington **413/528-6159**

Gateways Inn [GF,NS,WI] 51 Walker St (at Church St), Lenox **413/637-2532** *also bar & restaurant*

Guest House at Field Farm [GF,TG,NS,SW,WI] 554 Sloan Rd, Williamstown **413/458-3135**

River Bend Farm B&B [GF,NS] 643 Simonds Rd, Williamstown **413/458-3121**

The Rookwood Inn [GS,NS,WI] 11 Old Stockbridge Rd (at Walker St/ Rte 183), Lenox **413/637-9750, 800/223-9750** *Victorian inn near Tanglewood & skiing*

Topia Inn [GS,NS,WI,WC,GO] 10 Pleasant St (at Rte 8), Adams **413/743-9600, 888/868-6742**

Windflower Inn [GF,SW,NS,WI] 684 S Egremont Rd, Great Barrington **413/528-2720** *country inn in the Berkshires, full brkfst*

RESTAURANTS

Allium Restaurant + Bar 42 Railroad St (at Main), Great Barrington **413/528-2118** *5pm-9pm, till 10pm Fri-Sat, bar open late*

Cafe Lucia 80 Church St (at Tucker), Lenox **413/637-2640** *dinner only, clsd Mon, seasonal*

Mezze Bistro + Bar 777 Cold Spring Rd, Williamstown **413/458-0123** *5pm-9pm, till 9:30 Fri-Sat*

ENTERTAINMENT & RECREATION

Tanglewood [E] 197 Rte 183, Lenox **888/266-1200** *summer home of the Boston Symphony/ Pops*

Williamstown Theatre Festival just E of Rte 2 & Rte 7 junction, Williamstown **413/597-3400, 413/458-3200** *call for season calendar*

EROTICA

Amazing Intimate Essentials 1575 W Housatonic St, Pittsfield **413/464-7890**

CRUISY AREAS

Onota Lake [AYOR] parking lot near woods, Pittsfield

Boston

INFO LINES & SERVICES

Fenway Health 1340 Boylston St (Ansin Building) **617/267-0900** *medical & HIV services, LGBT health resources*

Gay AA 617/426-9444

GLBT Helpline 617/267-9001, 888/340-4528 *6pm-11pm*

ACCOMMODATIONS

463 Beacon St Guest House [GS,NS,WI,GO] 463 Beacon St **617/536-1302**

Beacon Hill Hotel & Bistro [GS,F,WI] 25 Charles St (at Chestnut St) **617/723-7575**

The Charles Hotel [GF] 1 Bennett St (at Eliot), Cambridge **617/864-1200, 800/882-1818**

Clarendon Square Inn [GS,NS,WI,GO] 198 W Brookline St (btwn Tremont & Columbus) **617/536-2229**

Encore B&B [GF,NS,GO] 116 W Newton St (at Tremont) **617/247-3425** *19th-c town house in Boston's South End*

Fifteen Beacon Hotel [GF,F,WI] 15 Beacon St (at Somerset) **617/670-1500, 877/982-3226**

Hotel 140 [GS,NS,WC] 140 Clarendon St (at Stuart St) **617/681-8861, 800/714-0140**

Hotel Onyx [GF,WI,NS] 155 Portland St (at Causeway) **617/557-9955, 866/660-6699**

The Liberty Hotel [GF,NS,WI,WC] 215 Charles St (at Cambridge St) **617/224-4000, 866/507-5245** *in the former Charles St Jail, restaurant, bar & patio*

Nine Zero Hotel [GF,WI,NS,WC] 90 Tremont St (at Bosworth) **617/772-5800, 800/546-7866** *luxury hotel, full brkfst, jacuzzi*

Oasis Guest House [★GS,NS,WI,WC,GO] 22 Edgerly Rd (at Westland) **617/267-2262, 800/230-0105** *in Back Bay*

The Verb Hotel [GS,WI] 1271 Boylston St **617/566-4500** *great Fenway location, restaurant & bar on site*

Whitman House Inn [GS,NS,WI,GO] 17 Worcester St (at Norfolk St), Cambridge **617/945-5350**

Bars

The Alley [★M,NH,D,B,K,WC,GO] 14 Pi Alley (at 275 Washington St) **617/263-1449** *2pm-2am, 2 floors, cruisy*

Bella Luna Restaurant & Milky Way Lounge [GS,F,E,K] 284 Amory St, Jamaica Plain **617/524-3740** *5pm-1am, live music, also restaurant*

Boston Eagle [M,NH,WC] 520 Tremont St (near Berkeley) **617/542-4494** *4pm-2am, from noon Sun*

Boston Ramrod [★M,D,B,L,WC] 1254 Boylston St (at Ipswich, 1 block from Fenway Park) **617/266-2986** *noon-2am*

Cathedral Station [MW,NH,F] 1222 Washington St **617/338-6060** *2pm-2am, from noon wknds, sports bar & pub*

Club Cafe Restaurant, Nightclub & Cabaret [★MW,D,F,E,K,P,V,WC] 209 Columbus Ave (at Berkeley St) **617/536-0966** *11am-2am, incredible Sunday brunch buffet along with lunch other days*

Jacque's [★M,TG,C,DS,$] 79 Broadway (at Stuart) **617/426-8902** *11am-midnight, from noon Sun*

Ryles [GS,F,E] 212 Hampshire St (at Cambridge St, in Inman Square), Cambridge **617/876-9330** *great wknd jazz brunch*

Trophy Room [GS] 26 Chandler St **617/482-3450** *4pm-2am, brunch wknds, American bistro & bar*

Nightclubs

dbar [GS,D,WC] 1236 Dorchester Ave (at Hancock St), Dorchester **617/265-4490** *5pm-midnight, till 2am wknds, also restaurant, dinner nightly*

Machine [★M,D,V,S,YC,WC] 1254 Boylston St (at Park, below Boston Ramrod) **617/536-1950** *10pm-2am*

The Middle East & ZuZu [GF,A,F,E,YC,$] 472 Massachusetts Ave (in Central Square), Cambridge **617/864-3278** *11am-1am, till 2am wknds, live music*

Napoleon Cabaret [★E,F,P,OC,WC] 209 Columbus Ave (at Club Cafe) **617/536-0966** *nightly piano & vocals*

Paradise [M,D,S] 180 Massachusetts Ave, Cambridge **617/868-3000** *9pm-1am, 7pm-2am Fri-Sat*

Cafes

1369 Cafe 757 Massachusetts Ave (in Central Square), Cambridge **617/576-4600** *7am-11pm*

Berkeley Perk [F,WC,GO] 69 Berkeley St (at Chandler) **617/426-7375** *6:30am-4:30pm, from 7:30am Sat, clsd Sun*

Diesel Cafe [WC,GO] 257 Elm St (in Davis Square), Somerville **617/629-8717** *6am-11pm, from 7am wknds*

Fiore's Bakery [GO] 55 South St (at Bardwell), Jamaica Plain **617/524-9200** *7am-7pm, from 8am wknds, some vegan*

South End Buttery [WC] 314 Shawmut Ave (at Union Park St) **617/482-1015** *cupcakes! also brkfst, lunch & dinner, full bar*

Restaurants

BarLola [E] 160 Commonwealth Ave (at Dartmouth) **617/266-1122** *4pm-midnight*

Casa Romero 30 Gloucester St (at Commonwealth) **617/536-4341** *Mexican, also bar*

Charlie's Sandwich Shoppe [WC] 429 Columbus Ave (at Pembroke St) **617/536-7669** *7am-3pm, great brkfst*

City Girl Cafe [BW,GO] 204 Hampshire St (at Inman), Cambridge **617/864-2809** *seasonal hours, Italian, great sandwiches*

Club Cafe [★E,P,V,WC] 209 Columbus Ave (adjacent to Club Cafe) **617/536-0966** *dinner & Sun brunch, also 3 bars*

My Thai Vegan Cafe 3 Beach St, 2nd flr (at Washington) **617/451-2395** *11am-10pm*

Rabia's [WC] 73 Salem St (at Cross St) **617/227-6637** *11am-10:30pm, fine Italian*

Ristorante Lucia [WC] 415 Hanover St (at Harris) **617/367-2353** *great North End pasta*

Stella [WI,WC] 1525 Washington St (at W Brookline) **617/247-7747** *dinner & Sun brunch, full bar till 2am, also cafe 7am-3pm*

Sweet Cheeks Q [GO] 1381 Boylston St **617/266-1300** *11:30am-11pm, American south north of the Mason Dixon*

Trattoria Pulcinella 147 Huron Ave (at Concord), Cambridge **617/491-6336** *5pm-10pm, clsd Mon, fine Italian*

Veggie Galaxy 450 Massachusetts Ave, Cambridge **617/661-1513** *11:30am-10:30pm*

Entertainment & Recreation

Freedom Trail 617/357-8300 *start at the Visitor Information Center in Boston Common (at Tremont & West Sts), the most famous cow pasture & oldest public park in the US, then follow the red line to some of Boston's most famous sites*

New Repertory Theatre 321 Arsenal St, Watertown **617/923-8487** *one of the Boston area's premiere theatre companies*

Urban AdvenTours 103 Atlantic Ave (at Richmond St) **617/670-0637** *guided bike tours & bike rentals*

Bookstores

Trident Booksellers & Cafe [F,BW,WI,WC] 338 Newbury St (off Mass Ave) **617/267-8688** *8am-midnight*

Publications

Bay Windows 617/464-7280 *LGBT newspaper*

The Rainbow Times 617/444-9618 *bi-weekly LGBT news magazine for MA, northern CT & southern VT*

Erotica

Good Vibrations [★WC] 308 Harvard St ((rear entrance)), Brookline **617/264-4400** *10am-9pm, till 10pm Th-Sat*

Hubba Hubba 2 Ellery St, Cambridge **617/492-9082** *fetish & drag gear*

Cruisy Areas

Carson Beach [AYOR] William J Day Blvd

Charles River Esplanade [AYOR] across foot bridge at end of Dartmouth St, near lagoon *go to the right*

The Fens (FenwayVictory Gardens) [AYOR] near the Ramrod bar

Cambridge

see Boston

Cape Cod

see also Provincetown listings

Info Lines & Services

Gay/ Lesbian AA 508/775-7060 *call for info*

Accommodations

Lamb & Lion Inn [GF,NS,SW,WI] 2504 Main St (Rte 6A), Barnstable **508/362-6823, 800/909-6923**

Woods Hole Passage [GF,NS,WI] 186 Woods Hole Rd, Falmouth **508/548-9575, 800/790-8976** *full brkfst, near beaches*

Cruisy Areas

Boardwalk [AYOR] Jarvis St (off 6-A, exit 1), Sandwich *nights*

Crow's Pasture [AYOR] N on 6-A to South St, past cemetery, Dennis *in dunes*

Kalmus Park Beach [AYOR] end of Ocean St, Hyannis *behind parking lot*

Ryder Woods Conservation Area [AYOR] Rte 130 to Cotuit Rd (toward Mashpee for 3.5 miles), Sandwich *trails along the lake*

Skaket Beach [AYOR] Dennis *off to the right*

Chelsea

see Boston

Greenfield

Accommodations

Brandt House [GF,NS,WI] 29 Highland Ave **413/774-3329** *16-rm estate on hill, full brkfst, formal garden*

Restaurants

Hope & Olive 44 Hope St **413/774-3150** *lunch & dinner, clsd Mon*

Bookstores

World Eye Bookshop 156 Main St (at Miles St) **413/772-2186** *9:30am-6:30pm, 9am-5pm Sat, 11am-4pm Sun, LGBT section*

Haverhill

Bars

Phoenix [MW] 103 Washington St (2nd Fl of Chit Chat Lounge) **978/374-9710** *5pm-1am, till 2am Fri, clsd Mon-Tue*

Cafes

Wicked Big Cafe [WI,WC,GO] 19 Essex St (at Wingate) **978/556-5656** *6am-6pm, 7am-5pm Sat, 8am-3pm Sun*

Ipswich

Cruisy Areas

Crane's Beach [AYOR] 1/2 mile to the right

Lowell

Erotica

Tower News 101 Gorham St **978/452-8693**

Martha's Vineyard

Accommodations

Martha's Vineyard Surfside Motel [GF,NS,WI,WC] 7 Oak Bluffs Ave, Oak Bluffs **508/693-2500**

Restaurants

The Black Dog Tavern [WC] Beach St Extension #21 (at Water St) **508/693-9223** *brkfst, lunch & dinner, seasonal*

Bookstores

Bunch of Grapes 23 Main St, Vineyard Haven **508/693-2291, 800/693-0221** *9am-6pm, some LGBT titles*

Medford

Erotica

Amazing 423 Mystic Ave/ Rte 38 **781/391-7438**

New Bedford

Bars

Le Place [★MW,D,K] 20 Kenyon St (at Belleville Ave) **508/990-1248** *2pm-2am*

Erotica

Amazing 10 Sconticut Neck Rd/Rte 6, Fairhaven **508/991-8191**

Northampton

see also Amherst

Accommodations

The Hotel Northampton [GF,NS,WI,WC] 36 King St (near Bridge St) **413/584-3100, 800/547-3529** *cafe & historic tavern*

Starlight Llama Solar B&B [GS] 940 Chesterfield Rd, Florence **413/584-1703** *award winning green inn*

Nightclubs

Pearl Street [GS,D,E,YC] 10 Pearl St (at Main) **413/586-8686** *7pm-1am, live music*

Cafes

Haymarket Cafe [★F,WC] 185 Main St **413/586-9969** *7am-10pm, till 11pm Fri-Sat, also restaurant*

Restaurants

Bela [WC,GO] 68 Masonic St **413/586-8011** *noon-8:30pm, clsd Sun-Mon, vegetarian, cash only*

Blue Heron Restaurant [GO] 112 N Main St, Sunderland **413/665-2102** *5pm-9pm, till 10pm Fri-Sat, clsd Sun-Mon*

Bueno Y Sano 134 Main St (at Center St) **413/586-7311** *11am-10pm, till 9pm Sun, Mexican*

The Old Creamery Co-op [GO] 445 Berkshire Trail, Cummington **413/634-5560** *7:30am-7:30pm, from 8:30am wknds, delicious, quality, home-made deli and bakery foods; abundant fresh produce, try the Spicy Maddow (hint hint)*

Paul & Elizabeth's [BW,WC] 150 Main St (in Thorne's Marketplace) **413/584-4832** *lunch & dinner, Sun brunch, seafood*

Entertainment & Recreation

The Iron Horse 20 Center St (at Main) **413/586-8686** *5:30pm-close, live music, all ages*

Retail Shops

Oh My A Sensuality Shop 122 Main St (at Center) **413/584-9669** *noon-7pm, till 8pm Fri-Sat, noon-5pm Sun*

Cruisy Areas

Northampton Meadows [AYOR] next to the Connecticut River (dirt roads) *not far from I-91 rest areas*

Pulaski Park [AYOR] Main St *summer nights*

Provincetown

see also Cape Cod listings

Info Lines & Services

Provincetown Business Guild 508/487-2313

Accommodations

8 Dyer Hotel [MW,SW,GO] 8 Dyer St **508/487-0880** *yummy full brkfst*

A Secret Garden Inn [MW,NS] 300-A Commercial St **508/487-9027**

Admiral's Landing [MW,NS,WI] 158 Bradford St (btwn Conwell & Pearl) **508/487-9665**

Aerie House & Beach Club [MW,WI,GO] 184 Bradford St (at Miller Hill) **508/487-1197, 800/487-1197**

Anchor Inn Beach House [GS,NS,WC] 175 Commercial St (at Winthrop) **508/487-0432** *private beach*

Atlantic Light Inn [GS,NS,WI,GO] 11 Pearl St (at Bradford) **508/487-0302** *historic 1850's house with bay views*

Awol [GS,SW,NS,WI] 59 Provincelands Rd **508/930-2098** *motel, across from Nat'l Seashore Province Lands, seasonal*

Bayberry Accommodations [MW,NS,WI,GO] 16 Winthrop St (at Commercial) **508/487-4605, 800/422-4605**

Bayshore [GS,WI,NS,GO] 493 Commercial St (at Howland) **508/487-9133** *apts, private beach, pets ok*

Beaconlight Guest House [M,NS,WI,GO] 12 Winthrop St (at Bradford) **508/487-9603, 800/696 9603**

Benchmark Inn [MW,SW,NS,WI,WC,GO] 6 Dyer St **508/487-7440**

Boatslip Resort [★M,SW,GO] 161 Commercial St **508/487-1669, 877/786-9662** *seasonal, also several bars & popular T-dance*

The Bradford Carver House [MW,NS,WI,GO] 70 Bradford St **508/487-0728, 800/826-9083** *restored mid-19th-c home, centrally located*

Brass Key Guesthouse [M,SW,NS,WI,WC,GO] 67 Bradford St (at Carver) **508/487-9005, 800/842-9858**

Cape Colony Inn [GS,SW,WI] 280 Bradford St **508/487-1755** *15 minute walk from town, pets ok*

Captain's House B&B [M,B,NS,WI,GO] 350-A Commercial St (at Center) **508/487-9353**

Carl's Guest House [MO,N,NS,WI,GO] 68 Bradford St (at Court St) **508/487-1650** *sundeck*

Carpe Diem Guesthouse & Spa [MW,NS,WI,GO] 12 Johnson St **508/487-4242, 800/487-0132**

Charm [GS,WI,GO] 156 Bradford St **508/487-0085** *breakfast dropped off at your door in the morning*

Chicago House [MW,NS,WI,GO] 6 Winslow St (at Bradford) **508/487-0537** *rooms & apts*

Christopher's by the Bay [MW,NS,WI,GO] 8 Johnson St (at Commercial) **508/487-9263** *some shared baths, patio*

Crown & Anchor [MW,SW,NS,WI,GO] 247 Commercial St **508/487-1430** *also cabaret & poolside bars*

Crowne Pointe Historic Inn & Shui Spa [MW,SW,NS,WI,WC,GO] 82 Bradford St **508/487-6767, 877/276-9631** *also restaurant*

Eastwood At Provincetown [SW,SW,WI] 324 Bradford St **508/487-0760** *apts & studios*

Eben House [MW,NS,WI,GO] 90 Bradford St **508/487-0386** *parking*

Enzo [GS,WI] 186 Commercial St (at Court) **508/487-7555** *also home to Grotto Bar & Local 186*

The Foxberry Inn [GS,WI,GO] 29 Bradford Street Ext **508/487-8583** *12 room inn on the west end with great brkfst*

The Gaslamp [MW,N,WI,GO] 97 Bradford St (btwn Gosnold & Masonic) **508/487-6636, 877/487-6636** *hot tub*

Gifford House Inn [MW,WI,GO] 11 Carver St **508/487-0688, 800/434-0130** *seasonal, also several bars & restaurant*

Howards End [GS,GO] 5 Winslow St **508/487-0169**

Inn at 7 Central [GS,WI,GO] 7 Central St (at Commercial) **508/487-8855** *contemporary hotel-style guesthouse*

The Inn at Cook Street [GF,NS,GO] 7 Cook St (at Bradford) **508/487-3894, 888/266-5655**

John Randall House [MW,NS,WI,GO] 140 Bradford St (at Center) **508/487-3533, 800/573-6700**

Land's End Inn [GS,NS,WI] 22 Commercial St **508/487-0706**

Lotus Guest House [MW,WI,GO] 296 Commercial St (at Standish) **508/487-4644** *seasonal, decks, garden*

The Masthead Resort [GS,WI] 31-41 Commercial St **508/487-0523** *beach-front cottages, motel rooms or apts, pets ok*

Moffett House [MW,GO] 296-A Commercial St (at Ryder) **508/487-6615, 800/990-8865**

Prince Albert Guest House [M,NS,WI,GO] 164 Commercial St (at Central) **508/487-1850**

Provincetown Hotel at Gabriel's [★MW,NS,WI,GO] 102 Bradford St **508/487-3232** *B&B inn w/ beautiful suites & gardens, pets/kids ok*

Queen Vic Bed & Beverage [GS,GO] 166 Commercial St 02657 **508/487-8425** *great front yard & fire pit*

Ravenwood Guest House [MW,NS,WC,GO] 462 Commercial St (at Cook) **508/487-3203** *private beach*

The Red Inn [GF,NS,WC,GO] 15 Commercial St (at Point) **508/487-7334**

Revere Guesthouse [MW,NS,GO] 14 Court St (btwn Commercial & Bradford) **508/487-2292, 800/487-2292**

Rose & Crown Guest House [GS,GO] 158 Commercial St (at Central) **508/487-3332**

Roux [GS,WI,GO] 210 Bradford St **508/487-1717** *restored Victorian property on the East End*

Sage Inn & Lounge [GS,WI,WC] 336 Commercial St **508/487-6424**

Salt House Inn [MW,NS,WI,GO] 6 Conwell St (at Railroad) **508/487-1911** *sundeck*

Sandcastle Resort and Club [GS,SW,WI] 929 Commercial St **508/487-9300**

Seaglass Inn & Spa [GS,SW,WI] 105 Bradford Street Ext **508/487-1286** *four acre hilltop property with 57 rooms*

Snug Cottage [GS,NS,WI,GO] 178 Bradford St **508/487-1616**

Somerset House [MW,NS,WI,GO] 378 Commercial St (at Pearl) **508/487-0383, 800/575-1850**

Sunset Inn [MW,N,NS,WI,GO] 142 Bradford St (at Center) **508/487-9810, 800/965-1801**

Surfside Hotel & Suites [GS,SW,NS,WI] 543 Commercial (at Kendall Ln) **508/487-1726** *seasonal, waterfront hotel w/ lots of amenities, private beach*

The Tucker Inn [MW,NS,WI,GO] 12 Center St (at Bradford) **508/487-0381, 800/477-1867**

The Waterford [GS,WI] 386 Commercial St (at Pearl) **508/487-6400, 800/487-0784** *deck w/ full bar, also restaurant*

Watermark Inn [GS,NS,WI] 603 Commercial St **508/487-0165** *suites with kitchens, beachside*

Watership Inn [M,WI,GO] 7 Winthrop St (at Commercial St) **508/487-0094, 800/330-9413**

West End Inn [GF,WI,NS,GO] 44 Commercial St **508/487-9555** *seasonal*

White Porch Inn [M,WI] 7 Johnson St **508/364-2549**

White Wind Inn [MW,WI,GO] 174 Commercial St (at Winthrop) **508/487-1526**

Bars

The Boatslip Resort [★MW,D,F,YC] 161 Commercial St **508/487-1669, 877/786-9662** *seasonal, popular T-dance 4pm daily, special events, outdoor/ waterfront grill*

Governor Bradford [GF,F,E,K,DS] 312 Commercial St (at Standish) **508/487-2781** *11am-1am, from noon Sun, also restaurant in summer*

The Monkey Bar [GS,F] 149 Commercial St **508/487-2879** *noon-1am*

PiedBar [★MW,D,F,E,P,S,WC] 193-A Commercial St (at Court St) **508/487-1527** *seasonal May-Oct, noon-1am, mostly men 6:30pm-9:30pm at After Tea T-Dance*

Porchside Lounge [M,NH,P] 11 Carver St (in the Gifford House) **508/487-0688** *5pm-1am, Lobby Bar from 10pm, also restaurant*

Shipwreck Lounge [MW] 10 Carver St (at Brass Key) **508/487-1472** *upscale lounge, outdoor seating w/ fire pit*

The Underground Bar [GS,D] 293 Commerical St (downstairs) **508/413-9648** *5pm-1am, from 1pm wknds*

Vault [MO,B,L] 247 Commercial St (downstairs in the Crown & Anchor) **508/487-1430** *9pm-1am Th-Sun only*

Wave Video Bar [MW,NH,K] 247 Commercial St (in the Crown & Anchor) **508/487-1430** *from 6pm, from noon wknds*

Nightclubs

Atlantic House (The "A-House") [★M,D] 6 Masonic Pl **508/487-3169** *10pm-1am, 3 bars, weekly theme parties, also The Little Bar [M,NH] & the Macho Bar [M,L]*

Club Purgatory [MW,D,L] 9-11 Carver St (at Bradford St, in the Gifford House) **508/487-8442** *opens 7pm, from 9pm Sun (in season)*

Paramount [★MW,D,E,C,DS,$] in the Crown & Anchor **508/487-1430** *10pm-1am wknds, seasonal*

Cafes

Post Office Cafe Cabaret [E] 303 Commercial St (upstairs) **508/487-3892** *8am-11pm, seasonal hours*

Restaurants

1620 Brewhouse 214 Commerical St **774/593-5180** *11:30-10pm, try the chowdah fries & burgers*

Bayside Betsy's [WC] 177 Commercial St **508/487-6566** *lunch & dinner, bar till 10pm, on waterfront*

Big Daddy's Burritos 205 Commercial St **508/487-4432** *11am-10pm (May-Oct)*

Bubala's by the Bay [★] 183-185 Commercial **508/487-0773** *lunch & dinner, bar till 1am, patio*

Cafe Heaven 199 Commercial St **508/487-9639** *8am-2pm & 6pm-10pm*

Ciro & Sal's [R] 4 Kiley Ct (btwn Bangs St & Lovett's Ct) **508/487-6444** *dinner from 5:30pm, Northern Italian*

Fanizzi's [★WC] 539 Commercial St (at Kendall Lane) **508/487-1964**

Front Street Restaurant [BW] 230 Commercial St **508/487-9715** *seasonal, bistro 6pm-10:30pm, bar till 1am*

Liz's Cafe, Anybody's Bar 31 Bradford St **508/413-9131** *serving breakfast, lunch, and dinner, historic maritime decor by Ken Fulk*

Lobster Pot [WC] harborside (at 321 Commercial St) **508/487-0842** *11:30am-10pm (April-Nov)*

The Mews Restaurant & Cafe [★E,WC] 429 Commercial St (at Bangs St) **508/487-1500** *dinner, seasonal Sun brunch, waterfront dining*

Napi's Restaurant [WC] 7 Freeman St **508/487-1145, 800/571-6274** *dinner (lunch Oct-April), int'l/ seafood*

Patio Grill & Bar 328 Commercial St 02657 **508/487-4003** *11am-10pm, till 11:30pm Fri-Sat*

Pepe's Wharf 371 Commercial St 02657 **508/487-8717** *11:30am-5pm, till 10:30pm Fri-Sun, great waterfront views*

The Point 82 Bradford St (at Crown Point) **508/487-2365** *5:30pm-9:30pm,clsd Mon-Tue, bar from 4:30 daily*

The Red Inn [GF,NS,WC,GO] 15 Commercial St (at Point) **508/487-7334, 866/473-3466** *dinner nightly, brunch Th-Sun, clsd Jan-April, full bar*

Relish [★] 93 Commercial St **508/487-8077** *yummy baked goods, pick up a sandwich on the way to the beach!*

Sal's Place [★] 99 Commercial St **508/487-1279** *seasonal, clsd Tue, seafood/ Italian (publisher's choice: cheese and butter pasta), deck, on the water*

Spindler's 386 Commercial St (at The Waterford) **508/487-6400** *French-style cuisine with Italian soul*

Spiritus Pizza [★] 190 Commercial St **508/487-2808** *noon-2am, great espresso shakes & late-night hangout for a slice*

Stangers & Saints 404 Commercial St **508/487-1449** *5pm-10pm, till 11:30pm Fri-Sat, clsd Tue-Wed*

Tin Pan Alley [E] 269 Commercial St **508/487-1648** *11:30am-11:30pm, till 12:30am Fri-Sat*

Waydowntown [E] 265 Commercial St **508/487-8800** *10am-1am, seaside dining, full bar and live shows, seasonal*

Yolqueria 401 1/2 Commercial Street **508/487-0600** *8am-2pm for brunch & 6pm-10pm for tacos*

Entertainment & Recreation

Art House Theatre & Cafe 214 Commercial St **508/487-9222**

Art's Dune Tours [GO] 4 Standish St **508/487-1950, 800/894-1951** *day trips, sunset tours & charters through historic sand dunes & Nat'l Seashore Park*

Dolphin Fleet Whale Watch [GF,WC] 305 Commercial St **508/240-3636, 800/826-9300** *3-hr day & evening cruises*

Herring Cove Beach

Ptown Bikes [GO] 42 Bradford **508/487-8735** *9am-6pm, rentals*

Schooner Hindu MacMillan Pier **508/542-2996** *a beautiful wooden sailboat for daytime or sunset sails June-Oct*

Spaghetti Strip *nude beach, 1.5 miles S of Race Point Beach*

Retail Shops

Adam's Nest 379a Commercial St **508/487-6600** *11am-9pm, queer and visible; politically engaged with a social conscience store*

Full Kit Gear 192 Commercial St **508/413-9676** *leather, latex, fetish-wear*

HRC Action Center & Store 209-211 Commercial St **508/487-7736** *Human Rights Campaign merchandise & info*

Publications

Provincetown Magazine **508/487-1000** *seasonal, Provincetown's oldest weekly magazine*

Wicked Local Provincetown 167 Commercial St **508/487-7400** *newspaper*

Gyms & Health Clubs

Mussel Beach Health Club 35 Bradford St (btwn Montello & Conant) **508/487-0001** *6am-9pm, till 8pm in winter*

Provincetown Gym 82 Shank Painter Rd (at Winthrop) **508/487-2776**

Cruisy Areas

Dick Dock [AYOR] behind Boatslip Beach Club *late*

Herring Cove Beach [AYOR]

Quincy

see also Boston

Raynham

Erotica

Video Xtra **508/821-7800** *8am-10pm, from 10am Sun*

Springfield

Bars

Pure [M,NH,F,WC] 234 Chestnut St (E of Main) **413/205-1483** *1pm-2am*

Nightclubs

Oz Nightclub [M,NH,D,K] 397 Dwight St (at Taylor) **413/732-4562** *9pm-2am, from 7pm Fri-Sat, clsd Sun-Mon*

The X Room [M,D,S] 395 Dwight St **413/732-4562** *7pm-2am, from 2pmTh-Sun, nude dancers*

The X Room [M,D,S] 87 Taylor St *4pm-2am, from 1pm Sun, nude dancers*

Stoneham

Cruisy Areas

Sheep's Fold Conservation Area [AYOR] Rte I-93 exit 33 (off Rte 28) *top of the hills*

Taunton

Bars

Bobby's Place [MW,D,F,K,DS] 62 Weir St (at Route 44, 138 & 140, at Taunton Green) **508/824-9997** *5pm-1am, till 2am Fri-Sat, from 2pm Sun*

Worcester

Bars

MB Lounge [MW,NH,WI,WC,GO] 40 Grafton St (at Franklin) **508/799-4521** *5pm-2am*

Michigan

Statewide

Publications

Out Post **313/702-0272** *bi-weekly nightlife guide for SE Michigan*

Albion

Erotica

Lion's Den 2101 N Concord Rd (exit 127, off I-94) **517/531-5051** *24hrs*

Ann Arbor

Info Lines & Services

The Jim Toy Community Center 319 Braun Ct **734/995-9867** *LGBT resource center, HIV testing 5pm-7pm Sun*

Lesbian/ Gay AA **734/482-5700**

Bars

\'aut\ Bar [★MW,NH,F,WC] 315 Braun Ct (at Catherine) **734/994-3677** *4pm-2am, from 11am Sat, 10 am Sun, clsd Mon, patio*

Nightclubs

The Necto [GS,D,V,18+,YC] 516 E Liberty (at Maynard) **734/994-5436** *9pm-2am, theme nights, gay night Fri*

Cafes

Cafe Verde [★F] 214 N Fourth Ave (at Catherine St) **734/994-9174** *7am-9:30pm, 9am-8pm Sun, fair trade & organic coffee & tea*

Restaurants

Dominick's [BW,WC] 812 Monroe St (at Tappan Ave) **734/662-5414** *10am-10pm, clsd Sun, Italian, full bar*

The Earle [BW,WC] 121 W Washington (at Ashley) **734/994-0211** *5:30pm-9pm, till 11pm Fri-Sat, 5pm-8pm Sun*

Mani Osteria & Bar 341B E Liberty **734/769-6700** *11:30am-10pm, clsd Mon, great pizza*

Seva 2541 Jackson Ave (at 5th Ave) **734/662-1111** *11am-9pm, vegetarian, also cafe & wine bar*

Zingerman's Delicatessen [GO] 422 Detroit St (at Kingsley) **734/663-3354, 888/636-8162** *7am-10pm, also ship food worldwide*

Entertainment & Recreation

The Ark [GF,E] 316 S Main St (btwn William & Liberty) **734/761-1818, 734/761-1800** *concert house*

Bookstores

Common Language [WC] 317 Braun Ct (at 4th) **734/663-0036** *11am-6pm,till 9pm Th, till10pm Fri-Sat, LGBT*

Crazy Wisdom Books & Tea Room 114 S Main St (btwn Huron & Washington) **734/665-2757** *11am-9pm, till 11pm Fri-Sat, 11am-8pm Sun*

Battle Creek

Nightclubs

910 "The Underground" [MW,D,K,S,V,WC] 910 North Ave (at Morgan) **269./964-7276** *7pm-2am, clsd Mon*

Erotica

Romantix Adult Superstore 690 W Michigan Ave (at Grand) **269/964-3070**

Bellaire

Accommodations

Applesauce Inn B&B [GF,WI] 7296 S M-88 **231/533-6448** *B&B in 100-year-old farmhouse*

Bellaire B&B [GS,WI,GO] 212 Park St (at Antrim) **231/533-6077, 800/545-0780** *stately 1879 home, full brkfst*

Big Rapids

Erotica

Fantasies Unlimited 13480 Northland Dr (at Arthur Rd) **231/792-8052** *10am-8pm, tll 10pm Fri-Sat, noon-8pm Sun*

Detroit

Info Lines & Services

Affirmations Community Center 290 W 9 Mile Rd (at Planavon), Ferndale **248/398-7105** *9am-9pm, clsd Sun, helpline line 4pm-9pm*

Affirmations Community Center 290 W Nine Mile , Ferndale **248/398-7105** *9am-9pm, clsd Sun*

Accommodations

The Atheneum Suite Hotel [GF,WI,WC] 1000 Brush Ave (at Lafayette) **313/962-2323, 800/772-2323**

Detroit Marriott at the Renaissance Center [GF,WC] 400 Renaissance Center Dr **313/568-8000**

Honor & Folly [GS,WI] 2138 Michigan Ave (above Slows BBQ) *design-focused B&B, honorandfolly.com*

Bars

Adam's Apple [M,NH,K,GO] 18931 W Warren Ave (at Artesian) **313/240-8482** *3pm-2am, from noon wknds*

Briggs Detroit [MW,D,WC] 519 E Jefferson **313/656-4820** *11am-midnight, till 2am Fri-Sat, sports bar with a great roof deck*

Centaur Bar [GS,F] 2233 Park Ave (at W Montcalm St) **313/963-4040** *4pm-2am*

Club Gold Coast [★M,D,DS,S,WI,WC] 2971 E 7 Mile Rd (at Conant) **313/366-6135** *7pm-2am, male dancers nightly*

Gigi's [M,D,TG,K,DS,S,GO] 16920 W Warren (at Clayburn, enter rear) **313/584-6525** *noon-2am, from 2pm wknds*

Hayloft Saloon [M,NH,B,L,OC,WI,WC] 8070 Greenfield Rd (S of Joy Rd) **313/581-8913** *2pm-2am*

Menjo's [★M,D,K,V,YC] 928 W McNichols Rd (at Hamilton) **313/863-3934** *1pm-2am, popular happy hour*

Pronto [★MW,F,V] 608 S Washington (at 6th St), Royal Oak **248/544-7900** *11am-2am, patio*

Soho [MW,K] 205 W 9 Mile (at Woodward), Ferndale **248/542-7646** *4pm-close, from 2pm wknds*

The Woodward Video Bar & Grill [★M,D,MR,F,K,V] 6426 Woodward Ave (at Milwaukee, rear entrance) **313/872-0166** *4pm-2am*

The Works Detroit [GS,D,V] 1846 Michigan Ave (at Rosa Parks) **313/961-1742** *10pm-3am Th, till 5am Fri-Sat*

Nightclubs

Escape [MW,NH,F,DS,GO] 19404 Sherwood (at 7 Mile) **313/892-1765** *10pm-5am*

Leland City Club [GF,D,A,18+] 400 Bagley St (at Leland Hotel) **313/962-2300** *10pm-4:30am Fri-Sat, goth/ alternative crowd*

Luna [GF,D,A] 1815 N Main St (at 12 Mile), Royal Oak **248/589-3344** *from 9pm, clsd Sun-Tue, theme nights*

Temple [GS,D,MR-AF,TG,WC] 2906 Cass Ave (btwn Charlotte & Temple) **313/832-2822** *1pm-2am, popular wknds*

Cafes

Avalon International Breads [GO] 422 W Willis (at Cass) **313/832-0008** *6am-6pm, 8am-4pm Sun,*

Coffee Beanery Cafe [WI] 300 Renaissance Center, Berkley **248/568-1040** *7am-11pm*

Five 15 [E,WI,GO] 515 S Washington St, Royal Oak **248/515-2551** *11am-8pm till 6pm Sun, 10am-9:30pm Fri-Sat, Drag Bingo Th-Sat, performances, art shows*

Restaurants

Amici's [GO] 3249 12 Mile Rd (at Gardner Ave), Berkley **248/544-4100** *gourmet pizza & martinis*

Cacao Tree Cafe 204 W 4th St, Royal Oak **248/336-9043** *8am-8pm, gourmet raw food/ vegan*

Cass Cafe [WI] 4620 Cass Ave (at Forest) **313/831-1400** *11am-2am, 5pm-1am Sun, full bar*

Elwood Bar & Grill 300 Adams (at Brush, by Comerica Park) **313/962-2337** *11am-8pm, till 2pm Mon, clsd Sun (unless there's a Tiger's game); Art Deco diner*

Inn Season 500 E 4th St (at Knowles), Royal Oak **248/547-7916** *lunch & dinner, Sun brunch, clsd Mon, organic vegetarian/ vegan*

La Dolce Vita [MW,WC] 17546 Woodward Ave (at McNichols) **313/865-0331** *lunch & dinner, Sun brunch, clsd Mon, Italian, patio*

Mercury Burger & Bar 2163 Michigan Ave **313/964-5000** *11am-midnight, till 1am Fri-Sat*

One-Eyed Betty's [GO] 175 W Troy, Ferndale **248/808-6633** *4pm-2am, from 9am wknds*

Red Star 13944 Michigan Ave, Dearborn **313/581-1451** *11am-10pm • Chinese, plenty veggie/ vegan*

Roast 1128 Washington Ave (at State St) **313/961-2500** *dinner nightly, steakhouse*

Seva 66 E Forest **313/974-6661** *11am-9pm, till 11pm Fri-Sat, vegetarian*

Traffic Jam & Snug [WC] 511 W Canfield St (at SE corner of 2nd Ave) **313/831-9470** *11am-10:30pm, till midnight Fri-Sat, till 9pm Sun, also full bar, bakery, dairy & brewery*

Vivio's [WC] 2460 Market St (at Napoleon St) **313/393-1711** *lunch & dinner, clsd Sun, full bar*

Wolfgang Puck Grille 1777 3rd St (at the MGM Grand Hotel) **313/465-1648** *5pm-10pm, array of grilled steaks, shellfish, and roasted whole fresh fish offerings*

Entertainment & Recreation

Charles H Wright Museum of African American History 315 E Warren Ave (at Cass) **313/494-5800**

Motown Historical Museum 2648 W Grand Blvd **313/875-2264**

Retail Shops

Royal Oak Tattoo 820 S Washington Ave (at Lincoln), Royal Oak **248/398-0052** *tattoo & piercing studio*

Publications

Between the Lines 734/293-7200 *statewide LGBT weekly*

Metra Magazine PO Box 71844, Madison Heights 48071 **248/543-3500** *covers IN, IL, MI, OH, PA, WI & Ontario, Canada*

Men's Clubs

Body Zone Health Club [MO,V,18+,PC,GO] 1617 E McNichols (at I-75) **313/366-9663** *24hrs*

Erotica

Escape Adult Bookstore 18728 W Warren Ave (8 blocks W of Southfield) **313/336-6558** *10am-midnight, from noon Sun*

Noir Leather [WC] 124 W 4th St (btw S Main St & S Washington), Royal Oak **248/541-3979** *11am-9pm, till 10pm Fri-Sat, noon-7pm Sun*

Uptown Book Store 16541 Woodward Ave (at 6 Mile Rd), Highland Park **313/869-9477**

Douglas

see Saugatuck

Flint

Bars

Pachyderm Pub [MW,NH,D,MR,TG,K,F,WI,GO] G-1408 E Hemphill Rd (btwn I-475 & Saginaw St), Burton **810/744-4960** *3pm-2am, from 5pm wknds, patio*

Cafes

The Good Beans Cafe [E,WI,WC,GO] 328 N Grand Traverse (at 1st Ave) **810/237-4663** *7:30am-4pm, till 7:30am-4pm, till 8pm Fri, open some wknds*

Frankfort

Accommodations

Wayfarer Lodgings [GF,NS,WI] 1912 S Scenic Hwy (M-22) **800/735-8564**

Grand Rapids

Info Lines & Services

Grand Rapids Pride Center 343 Atlas Ave SE (behind Spirit Dreams in Eastown) **616/458-3511** *9am-6pm, till 5pm Fri, clsd wknds,*

Accommodations

The Grand River Hotel [GF,NS,SW,WI,WC] 270 Ann St NW (at Turner Ave) **616/363-9001**

Bars

Apartment Lounge [M,NH,WC] 33 Sheldon NE (at Library) **616/451-0815** *1pm-2am, from noon wknds*

Nightclubs

Rumors Nightclub [MW,D,DS,K,S,V,WC,GO] 69 S Division Ave (at Oakes St) **616/454-8720** *4pm-2am*

Restaurants

Brandywine 2844 E Beltline Ave NE **616/363-1723** *7am-8pm, till 2:30pm wknds*

Cherie Inn [WC] 969 Cherry St SE (at Lake Dr) **616/458-0588** *7am-3pm, from8am wknds, clsd Mon*

Men's Clubs

Diplomat Health Club [PC] 2324 Division Ave (at Whithey) **616/452-3754** *24hrs*

Kalamazoo

Info Lines & Services

Kalamazoo Gay/ Lesbian Resource Center 340 S Rose St **269/349-4234** *9am,-5pm, clsd wknds*

Lansing

Bars

Esquire [MW,NH,K] 1250 Turner St (at Clinton) **517/487-5338** *3pm-2am*

Nightclubs

Spiral [M,D,S,DS,18+,WC] 1247 Center St (at Clinton) **517/371-3221** *9pm-2am, clsd Mon-Wed, theme nights*

Bookstores

Everybody Reads 2019 E Michigan Ave **517/346-9900** *11am-7pm, 10am-4pm Sun, cool general bookstore, also coffeehouse*

Erotica

Fantasies Unlimited 3208 S MLK Blvd (at Southland Ave) **517/393-1159** *10am-2am, till 4am Fri-Sat, 11am-10pm Sun*

Marquette

Accommodations

The Landmark Inn [GF,NS,WI] 230 N Front St (at Ridge St) **906/228-2580, 888/752-6362** *historic boutique hotel overlooking Lake Superior, restaurant & bar*

Cruisy Areas

Presque Isle Point [AYOR]

Mount Pleasant

Cruisy Areas

Mission Creek Park [AYOR] Harris St *summers*

Pontiac

Bars

Liberty Bar [MW,D,F] 85 N Saginaw **248/758-0771** *11:30am-2am, from 6pm wknds, till 7pm Mon*

Cruisy Areas

Hawthorne Park [AYOR] N Telegraph Rd (at Dixie Hwy)

Port Huron

Cruisy Areas

Pine Grove Park [AYOR]

Saugatuck

Accommodations

Beechwood Manor Inn & Cottage [GS,NS,WI,GO] 736 Pleasant St (at Allegan) **269/857-1587**

Bella Vita Spa & Suites [GF,WI] 119 Butler St **269/857-8482** *also day spa*

The Belvedere Inn & Restaurant [GF,NS,WI,GO] 3656 63rd St **269/857-5777, 877/858-5777** *European-style boutique inn in restored 1913 mansion, full brkfst*

Campit Outdoor Resort [MW,SW,WI,GO] 6635 118th Ave, Fennville **269/543-4335, 877/226-7481** *seasonal, campsites & RV hookups, membership required*

Douglas House B&B [GS,NS,GO] 41 Spring St (at Wall St), Douglas **269/857-1119** *near gay beach*

The Dunes Resort [MW,D,TG,F,E,DS,SW,WC,GO] 333 Blue Star Hwy, Douglas **269/857-1401**

Hidden Garden Cottages & Suites [GF,NS,WI] 247 Butler St **269/857-8109, 888/857-8109**

Hillby Thatch Cottages [GS,NS] 1438-1440 71st St, Glenn **847/274-9004**

The Kingsley House B&B [GF,NS,WI] 626 West Main St, Fennville **269/561-6425, 866/561-6425** *full brkfst*

Maple Ridge Cottages [GS,NS,GO] 713-719 Maple **269/857-5211** *quaint cottages, hot tubs*

The Park House Inn B&B [GF,NS,WI] 888 Holland St **269/857-4535** *B&B in one of Saugatuck's oldest residences*

The Pines Motor Lodge & Cottages [GS,NS,WI,GO] 56 Blue Star Hwy (at Center St), Douglas **269/857-5211** *boutique retro motel, also retro gift gallery*

The Spruce Cutter's Cottage [GS,GO] 6670 126th Ave (at Blue Star Hwy & M-89), Fennville **800/493-5888**

Bars

Dunes Disco [MW,D,TG,E,C,DS,GO] 333 Blue Star Hwy (at the Dunes Resort) **269/857-1401** *9am-2am*

Cafes

Uncommon Grounds [WI] 127 Hoffman (at Water) **269/857-3333** *7am-7pm, coffee & juice bar*

Restaurants

Back Alley Pizza Joint 22 Main St (at Center), Douglas **269/857-7277** *11am-10pm, till 11pm Fri-Sat*

Everyday People Cafe [E,WC] 11 Center St (at Main), Douglas **269/857-4240** *call for hours*

Marro's Italian [E] 147 Water St (at Mason St) **269/857-4248** *dinner only, clsd Mon-Tue, lounge till 2am Fri-Sat*

Phil's Bar & Grille 215 Butler St (at Mason) **269/857-1555** *11:30am-9:30pm, till 10:30pm Fri-Sat, patio*

Scooters 322 Culver St (at Griffith) **269/857-1041** *noon-9:30, till 11pm wknds, till 8pm Sun, great pizza*

Wicks Park [E,WC] 449 Water St **269/857-2888** *dinner nightly, live music wknds*

Wild Dog Grill 24 W Center St (at Spring), Douglas **269/857-2519** *dinner nightly, from noon wknds, clsd Tue-Wed*

Entertainment & Recreation

Oval Beach consult local map for driving directions, Douglas *popular beach on Lake Michigan*

Tulip Time Festival Holland **800/822-2770** *May, go Dutch without leaving the country*

Retail Shops

Amaru Leather 322 Griffith St (at Hoffman St) **269/857-3745** *"original & custom creations in leather by two resident designers"*

Groovy! Groovy! Retro Gift Gallery [GO] 56 Blue Star Hwy (at Center St), Douglas **269/857-2171** *seasonal hours, antiques, funky gifts & goods*

Saugatuck Drug Store 201 Butler St (at Mason) **269/857-2300** *seasonal, old-fashioned corner drug store, including actual soda fountain!*

Gyms & Health Clubs

Pump House Gym 6492 Blue Star Hwy (at 135th) **269/857-7867** *day passes*

Cruisy Areas

Oval Beach [AYOR] *walk north*

South Haven

Accommodations

Yelton Manor B&B [GS,NS,WI,WC] 140 North Shore Dr (at Dyckman) **269/637-5220** *full brkfst*

St Ignace

Accommodations

Budget Host Inn & Suites [GF,SW,WI,WC] 700 N State St **906/643-9666, 800/872-7057**

Traverse City

Info Lines & Services

Polestar LGBT+ Community Center **231/715-9203** *currently Polestar is a virtual center,check www.tcpolestar.org for social media links*

Accommodations

Neahtawanta Inn [GF,SW,NS,WI,WC] 1308 Neahtawanta Rd (at Peninsula Dr) **231/223-7315, 800/220-1415** *member based/community supported property*

Nightclubs

Side Traxx [MW,D,V,GO] 520 Franklin St (at E 8th) **231/935-1666** *5pm-2am, cruise bar*

Bookstores

The Bookie Joint 124 S Union St (btwn State & Front) **231/946-8862** *10am-5pm, clsd Sun, pride gifts, used books*

Cruisy Areas

Westend Beach Hwy 31 (N of Munson Hospital)

Union Pier

Accommodations

Blue Fish Guest House & Cottage [GS,NS,GO] 10234 Community Hall Rd **269/469-0468 x112** *cottages & guesthouses*

Fire Fly Resort [GS,NS,GO] 15657 Lakeshore Rd **269/469-0245** *1- & 2-bdrm units*

Ypsilanti

see also Ann Arbor

Minnesota

Bemidji

Cruisy Areas

Diamond Point Park [AYOR] *summers*

The Indian Trail [AYOR] below Lake Blvd (btwn 10th & 12th St)

Duluth

see also Superior, Wisconsin

Accommodations

The Olcott House B&B Inn [GF,NS,WI,GO] 2316 E 1st St (at 23rd Ave) **218/728-1339**

Bars

Duluth Flame [MW,D,E,K,DS] 28 N 1st Ave W **218/727-2344** *3pm-2:30am*

Restaurants

At Sara's Table Chester Creek Cafe [E,WI,WC] 1902 E 8th St (at 19th) **218/724-6811** *7am-8pm*

Men's Clubs

Duluth Family Sauna 18 N 1st Ave E **218/726-1388** *noon-10pm*

Erotica

Wabasha Books 114 E 1st St **218/723-1980**

Lanesboro

Accommodations

Stone Mill Hotel & Suites [GS,NS,WI,WC,GO] 100 E Beacon St (at Parkway Ave) **507/467-8663**

Mankato

Cafes

The Coffee Hag [E,WC] 329 N Riverfront Dr **507/387-5533** *7am-10pm, till 11pm Fri-Sat*

Erotica

Pure Pleasure 2102 N Riverfront Dr **507/388-6871** *24hrs*

Minneapolis/ St Paul

Info Lines & Services

AA Intergroup 952/922-0880

OutFront Minnesota 310 E 38th St #204, Minneapolis **612/822-0127, 800/800-0350** *info line w/ 24hr pre-recorded visitor info*

Quatrefoil Library 1220 East Lake St, Minneapolis **612/729-2543** *7pm-9pm, 10am-5pm Sat, 1pm-5pm Sun, LGBT resource center*

Accommodations

The Depot Renaissance Minneapolis [GF,F] 225 3rd Ave S, Minneapolis **612/375-1700**

Hotel 340 [GF,SW,WI] 340 Cedar St **651/280-4120**

Le Meridien Chambers [GF,WI,WC] 901 Hennepin Ave, Minneapolis **612/767-6900, 866/961-2861** *art-filled hotel; also restaurant & bar*

Water Street Inn [GF,WI,WC] 101 S Water St, Stillwater **651/439-6000** *also restaurant & pub*

Bars

19 Bar [M,NH,WC] 19 W 15th St (at Nicollet Ave), Minneapolis **612/871-5553** *3pm-2am, from 1pm wknds*

Bev's Wine Bar [GF,F,WC] 250 3rd Ave N #100 (at Washington Ave), Minneapolis **612/337-0102** *4:30pm-1am, patio*

Brass Rail [★M,F,K,S,V,WC] 422 Hennepin Ave (at 4th), Minneapolis **612/332-7245** *4pm-2am, from noon Fri-Sun*

Bryant Lake Bowl [GF,F,E,WC] 810 W Lake St (near Bryant), Minneapolis **612/825-3737** *8am-2am, bar, theater & bowling alley*

Camp Bar [★M,D,F,K,DS,S,V,WC] 490 N Robert St (at 9th St), St Paul **651/292-1844** *3pm-2am*

Eagle Bolt Bar [M,B,L,F] 515 Washington Ave S (btwn Portland & 5th Ave), Minneapolis **612/338-4214** *4pm-2am, from 10am Sat-Sun, beer bust Sun, also Bolt underground dance bar*

Jetset [MW,D,K] 115 N First St (at 1st Ave N), Minneapolis **612/339-3933** *7pm-close,from 6pm Fri, from 6pm Sat, clsd Sun-Mon*

Lush Food Bar [MW,D,C,DS,F] 990 Central Ave (at Spring St), Minneapolis **608/208-0358** *4pm-midnight, till 2am Th-Sat from 10am wknds*

The Town House [★MW,D,E,F,K,C,DS,P,GO] 1415 University Ave W (at Elbert), St Paul **651/646-7087** *3pm-1am, till 2am Wed, Fri-Sat, from noon wknds*

Nightclubs

Gay 90s [★MW,D,MR,F,E,K,DS,18+,WC] 408 Hennepin Ave (at 4th St S), Minneapolis **612/333-7755** *8am-2am (dinner Wed-Sun), also Men's Room [MO,L]*

Ground Zero [★GS,D,S,WC] 15 NE 4th St (at Hennepin), Minneapolis **612/378-5115** *10pm-2am Th-Sat only, more gay Sat for Bondage-A-Go-Go*

Kitty Cat Klub [GF,F,E] 315 14th Ave SE (at SE University Ave) **612/331-9800** *lounge w/ eclectic decor, live bands*

The Saloon [★M,D,F,S,YC,WC,GO] 830 Hennepin Ave (at 9th), Minneapolis **612/332-0835** *noon-2am, from 11am Sun*

Cafes

Black Dog Coffee & Wine Bar [BW,F] 308 Prince St (at Broadway), St Paul **651/228-9274** *7am-10pm, till 11pm Fri-Sat, 8am-8pm Sun*

Blue Moon [WI,GO] 3822 E Lake St, Minneapolis **612/721-9230** *7am-10pm, from 8am wknds*

Cahoots [WI,WC] 1562 Selby Ave (at Snelling), St Paul **651/644-6778** *6:30am-10:30pm, from 7am wknds*

Cuppa Java [BW,WI] 400 Penn Ave S, Minneapolis **612/374-4806** *6am-10:30pm, from 7pm wknds*

Moose & Sadie's [WI,WC] 212 3rd Ave N (at 2nd St), Minneapolis **612/371-0464** *7am-8pm, 9am-2pm wknds*

Quixotic Coffee [WI] 769 Cleveland, St Paul **651/699-5448** *7am-9pm, till 7pm Sun*

Uncommon Grounds 2809 Hennepin Ave (at W 28th St), Minneapolis **612/872-4811** *11am-11pm, till midnight Fri-Sat, till 10pm Sun, patio*

The Urban Bean [WI,WC] 822 W Lake St, Minneapolis **612/824-6611** *6:30am-10pm*

Restaurants

Al's Breakfast [★] 413 14th Ave SE (at 4th), Minneapolis **612/331-9991** *6am-1pm, 6pm-1am Fri-Sat, from 9am Sun, great hash*

Alma: Cafe, Hotel and Restaurant 528 University Ave SE, Minneapolis **612/379-4909** *dinner nightly, cafe opens at 7am, organic New American*

Barbette 1600 W Lake St (at Irving), Minneapolis **612/827-5710** *8am-midnight, till 1am Fri-Sat*

Birchwood Cafe [WI,WC] 3311 E 25th St, Minneapolis **612/722-4474** *7am-9pm, from 8am Sat, 9am-8pm Sun, veggie/ vegan*

Brasa Premium Rotisserie [BW,WC] 600 E Hennepin, Minneapolis **612/379-3030**

French Meadow [BW] 2610 Lyndale Ave S, Minneapolis **612/870-7855** *7am-9pm, till 10pm Fri-Sat organic & local, plenty veggie/ vegan*

Hard Times Cafe [WI] 1821 Riverside Ave, Minneapolis **612/341-9261** *6am-4am, vegan/ vegetarian, punk rock ambiance*

Hell's Kitchen 80 9th St S, Minneapolis **612/332-4700** *7:30am-10pm, till 2am Fri-Sat, great brkfst & free music wknds 11am-2pm*

Monte Carlo [WC] 219 3rd Ave N, Minneapolis **612/333-5900** *lunch & dinner, bar till 1am*

Murray's 26 S 6th St (at Hennepin), Minneapolis **612/339-0909** *lunch Mon-Fri, dinner nightly*

Namaste Cafe 2512 Hennepin Ave S, Minneapolis **612/827-2496** *11am-10pm, full bar, great Indian & Napali food*

Nye's Polonaise [E,P] 112 E Hennepin Ave, Minneapolis **612/379-2021** *4pm-2am, from 11am Fri-Sat*

Psycho Suzi's Motor Lounge [F,WC] 2519 Marshall St NE, Minneapolis **612/788-9069** *11am-2am, pu-pu's & pizza*

Punch Neapolitan Pizza [WC] 704 Cleveland Ave S, St Paul **651/696-1066** *11am-9:30pm; also at 210 E Hennepin Ave*

Red Stag Supperclub [E,WC] 509 1st Ave NE (at 5th St), Minneapolis **612/767-7766** *11am-2am, from 9am wknds*

Seward Cafe [WC] 2129 E Franklin Ave, Minneapolis **612/332-1011** *7am-6pm, from 8am wknds, clsd Tue, vegetarian/ vegan*

Wilde Cafe & Spirits [BW,WC,GO] 65 Main St SE (at Hennepin Ave), Minneapolis **612/331-4544** *7am-10pm, till 11pm Fri-Sat, till 9pm Sun*

Entertainment & Recreation

Calhoun 32nd Beach 3300 E Calhoun Pkwy (33rd & Calhoun Blvd), Minneapolis **612/230-6400**

Twin Lake Beach [N] in Wirth Park (33rd & Calhoun Blvd), Minneapolis *popular gay beach, aka Hidden Lake, hard to find, inquire locally*

Retail Shops

The Rainbow Road [WC] 109 W Grant St (at LaSalle), Minneapolis **612/872-8448** *10am-10pm, LGBT*

Publications

Lavender Magazine 612/436-4660, 877/515-9969 *LGBT newsmagazine for IA, MN, ND, SD, WI*

Scene 612/886-3151 *LGBTQA Twin Cities publication*

Erotica

Lickety Split 251 3rd Ave S, Minneapolis **612/333-0599** *10am-2am, till 3am Fri-Sat*

SexWorld 241 2nd Ave N (at Washington), Minneapolis **612/672-0556** *24hrs*

The Smitten Kitten [TG,GO] 3010 Lyndale Ave S, Minneapolis **612/721-6088**

Cruisy Areas

"Bare Ass" Beach [AYOR] E bank of the Mississippi (btwn the Franklin Ave & I-94 bridges), Minneapolis *especially summer afternoons*

Loring Park [AYOR] 15th St (near 35 W & I-94 exchange), Minneapolis

Moorhead

see also Fargo, North Dakota

Bars

Sanctuary Bar and Bistro [MW,F,K] 9816 21st St N **218/303-8994** *11:30am-2am, full menu*

Owatonna

Erotica

Lion's Den 1178 W Frontage Rd (exit 42B, off I-35) **507/214-3900** *24hrs*

MISSISSIPPI

Biloxi

Bars

Just Us Lounge [MW,NH,D,E,K,DS,S] 906 Division St (at Caillavet) **228/374-1007** *24hrs*

Veaux Bar & Grill [M,D,DS] 834 Howard Ave **228/207-3271**

Cruisy Areas

Hiller Park [AYOR] off Pass Rd

Gulfport

Bars

Sipps [GS,DS] 2218 25th Ave **228/206-7717** *open 5pm*

Hattiesburg

Info Lines & Services

The Spectrum Center 210 S 25th Ave **601/909-5338** *noon-5pm, LGBTQ+ community center*

Bars

The Thirsty Hippo [GS,F,E] 309 McLeod St **601/583-9188** *a music venue, restaurant and bar located in a 1930's warehouse in downtown*

Nightclubs

Klub Xclusive [MW,MR-AF,DS] 5729 Hwy 49 South **601/270-7953** *check www.facebook.com/KlubXclusive for events*

Jackson

Info Lines & Services

Lambda AA 5400 Old Canton Rd (at Saint Phillips Episcopal Church) **601/624-4858** *6:30pm Mon, eastern wing in the lower level*

Bars

Metro Reloaded [MW,D] 4670 Hwy 80 West **601/259-0661** *10:30pm-4am, ladies night Fri, boys night Sat, clsd Sun-Th*

Nightclubs

Wonderlust [GS,D,DS] 3911 Northview Dr **337/378-9003** *from 8pm Th-Sat*

Cruisy Areas

Battlefield Park [AYOR] Terry Rd (at Hwy 80) *afternoons*

Natchez

Accommodations

Historic Oak Hill Inn B&B [NS,WI,GO] 409 S Rankin St (at Orleans St) **601/446-2500** *antebellum mansion near the Mississippi*

Oxford

Cruisy Areas

Pat Lamar Park [AYOR]

Tupelo

Cruisy Areas

Chickasaw Village & Old Town Site Scenic Overlooks [AYOR] Natchez Trace Pkwy *closes at sunset*

Confederate Grave Site [AYOR] Hwy 78-Natchez Trace Pkwy interchange (5 miles N)

Vicksburg

Cruisy Areas

Rest Stop I-20 E (2nd rest stop)

Water Valley

Bookstores

Violet Valley Bookstore 303 N Main Street **662/506-2750** *10am-4pm Fri-Sat, an LGBTQ feminist bookstore*

Missouri

Ava

Accommodations

Cactus Canyon Campground [MO,N,GO] 16 miles E of Ava on Hwy 14 (N 1 mile on County 223) **417/683-9199**

Boonville

Men's Clubs

Megaplex Health Club & Spa [MO,V] 11674 Old Hwy 40 (off I-70 exit 98) **660/882-0008**

Erotica

Passions Video 17701 Old Five Dr (off I-70 exit 103) **660/882-9426** *8am-midnight*

Branson

see also Springfield & Eureka Springs, Arkansas

Cruisy Areas

Table Rock Lake Dam [AYOR] Fish Hatchery area

Cape Girardeau

Nightclubs

Independence Place [MW,D,TG,DS] 5 S Henderson St (at Independence, at Holiday Happenings) **573/334-2939** *8:30pm-1:30am, from 7pm Fri-Sat, clsd Sun*

Cruisy Areas

Capaha Park [AYOR]

Clinton

Cruisy Areas

Sparrowfoot Park [AYOR] 4 miles S off Hwy 13 Lithuania *swimming & boat launch area at Truman Lake*

Columbia

Bars

The Arch & Column Pub [M,NH,K,WC,GO] 1301 Business Loop 70 E (at College) **573/441-8088** *5:30pm-1am, clsd Sun*

Cafes

Ernie's Cafe 1005 E Walnut St (at 10th) **573/874-7804** *6:30am2pm*

Uprise Baker/ RagTag Cinema [BW] 10 Hitt St (Broadway) **573/256-2265, 573/441-8504** *6:30am-8pm, clsd Sun, independent & alternative cinema, also theater, music & dance*

Restaurants

Main Squeeze [WI,WC] 28 S 9th St (at Cherry St) **573/817-5616** *8am-8pm, till 5pm Sun, local organic ingredients, vegetarian*

Bookstores

The Peace Nook 804 C East Broadway (btwn 8th & 9th) **573/875-0539** *10am-9pm, noon-6pm Sun, LGBT section, books, pride products*

Erotica

Bocomo Bay 1122-A Wilkes Blvd **573/443-0873** *smoke shop too*

Olde Un Theatre/ Midwest Adult Book Store 101 E Walnut St (at 1st) **573/442-6622** *7am-midnight*

Venus [GO] 1010 Old Hwy 63 N **573/442-4319** *10am-midnight*

Cruisy Areas

Cosmopolitan Park [AYOR] W side of town (off Business Loop 70)

Hannibal

Accommodations

Garden House B&B [GF,WI,NS,GO] 301 N 5th St (at Bird) **573/221-7800**

Rockcliffe Mansion B&B [GF,NS,WI,GO] 1000 Bird St (at 10th St) **573/221-4140**

Restaurants

LaBinnah Bistro [BW,GO] 207 N 5th St (at Center) **573/221-8207** *dinner only, clsd Sun-Mon, in a Victorian home*

Joplin

Info Lines & Services

Joplin Pride Community 401/595-0061

Kansas City

see also Kansas City & Overland Park, Kansas

Info Lines & Services

Kansas City Center for Inclusion 3911Main St **816/753-7770** *1pm-5pm, LGBT community center founded by country music star, Chely Wright*

Accommodations

Hotel Phillips [GF,WI] **816/221-7000** *art deco landmark in downtown KC*

The Raphael [GF,F,WI] 325 Ward Pkwy (at Wornall Rd) **816/997-9267**

Bars

Buddies [M,NH] 3715 Main St (at 37th) **816/561-2600** *6am-3am, clsd Sun*

Missie B's/ Bootleggers [MW,NH,D,L,TG,K,DS,S] 805 W 39th St (at SW Trafficway) **816/561-0625** *noon-3am*

Sidekicks [MW,D,CW,DS,WC] 3707 Main St (at 37th) **816/931-1430** *1pm-3am*

Sidestreet Bar [M,NH,GO] 413 E 33rd St (at Gillham Rd) **816/531-1775** *10am-1:30am*

Cafes

Broadway Cafe 4106 Broadway (at Westport) **816/531-2432** *7am-9pm*

Restaurants

Beer Kitchen [E] 435 Westport Rd (at Pennsylvania) **816/389-4180** *11am-3am, from 10am wknds, gastro pub, live music*

Bistro 303 [★WC,GO] 303 Westport Rd **816/753-2303** *open 3pm, from 11am Sat-Sun, patio*

Blue Bird Bistro [WC] 1700 Summit St (at W 17th St) **816/221-7559** *7am-9pm, 10am-2pm Sun, organic fare*

Cafe Trio/ Starlet Lounge [GO] 4558 Main St **816/756-3227** *11am-10pm. till 11pm Sat, 4pm-9pm Sun, piano bar*

Chubby's [WC] 3756 Broadway St (at 38th) **816/931-2482** *6am-3pm, 24hrs Th-Sat, popular late nights, diner fare*

Classic Cup Cafe [WC] 301 W 47th St (at Central) **816/753-1840** *brkfst, lunch, dinner, Sun brunch*

Grand Street Cafe [NS,WC] 4740 Grand St (at 47th St) **816/561-8000** *lunch & dinner, Sun brunch, patio seating*

Hamburger Mary's KC [K,F,E] 3700 Broadway Blvd **816/842-1919** *11am-1:30am, clsd Mon, juicy burgers w/ a side of camp*

Le Fou Frog 400 E 5th St (at Oak St) **816/474-6060** *dinner only, French bistro*

McCoy's Public House 4057 Pennsylvania Ave **816/960-0866** *11am-3am, till midnight Sun, huge patio*

The Mixx [WC] 4855 Main St (at W 48th) **816/756-2300** *lunch & dinner, fast & healthy, huge selection of salads*

Tannin Wine Bar **816/842-2660** *11:30am-1:30am, from 4pm wknds, wine & cheese flights, patio seating*

YJ's Snack Bar [WC] 128 W 18th St (at W Baltimore Ave) **816/472-5533** *8am-10pm, 24hrs Th-Sat*

Entertainment & Recreation

First Fridays Art Walk Crossroads District (Baltimore & 20th) **816/994-9325** *5pm-10pm 1st Fri, art gallery walk, also live music & vendors*

Nelson-Atkins Museum 4525 Oak St **816/751-1278** *American Indian galleries*

Erotica

Erotic City 8401 E Truman Rd (off I-435, at Alice Ave) **816/252-3370**

Video Mania [GO] 208 Westport Rd **816/561-6397** *11am-10pm, noon-8pm Sun*

Moberly

Cruisy Areas

Rothwell Park [AYOR]

Nelson

Erotica

Lion's Den RR1 Hwy J Box 163 (Exit 84, off I-70) **660/859-2741**

Overland

Erotica

Patricia's 10210 Page Ave (E of Ashby) **314/423-8422**

Springfield

Info Lines & Services

AA Gay/ Lesbian 417/823-7125

Gay & Lesbian Community Center of the Ozarks [WC] 518 E Commercial St **417/869-3978** *many groups, newsletter*

Bars

Martha's Vineyard [MW,NH,D,DS,18+,WC,$] 219 W Olive St (at S Patton) **417/864-4572** *7pm-1:30am, from 2pm Sun, clsd Mon patio*

Mud Lounge [GF,F] 321 E Walnut **417/865-6964** *4pm-1:30am, clsd Sun*

Nightclubs

Mix Ultralounge [MW,D,K] 1221 E Saint Louis St **417/866-7166** *5pm-1:30am, 6pm-midnight Sun*

Cafes

Mudhouse 323 South Ave **417/832-1720** *7am-midnight, 9am-8pm Sun*

Erotica

Patricia's 1918 S Glenstone (at E Cherokee) **417/881-8444**

Cruisy Areas

Lake Springfield Park [AYOR] *NW side, north of power plant, days*

Phelps Grove Park [AYOR]

St Joseph

Cruisy Areas

Riverfront Park [AYOR] downtown

St Louis

Accommodations

The Cheshire [GS,SW,WI] 6300 Clayton Rd **314/647-7300**

Dwell 912 B&B [GF,NS,WI,GO] 912 Hickory St (at S 9th St) **314/599-3100**

Grand Center Inn [GS,WI,NS,GO] 3716 Grandel Sq (at N Grand Blvd) **314/533-0771**

Bars

Bar: PM [MW,D,DS,E] 7109 S Broadway (at Blow St) **314/835-7251** *5pm-1:30am*

Club Escapades [MW,D,DS,F,K,S,WI] 133 W Main St (at 2nd), Belleville, IL **618/222-9597** *6pm-2am, clsd Sun-Tue*

Grey Fox Pub [MW,NH,TG,DS,S] 3503 S Spring (at Potomac) **314/772-2150** *2pm-1:30am, noon-midnight Sun, patio*

JJ's Clubhouse & Bar [★M,NH,B,L,WC] 3858 Market St (at Vandeventer) **314/535-4100** *3pm-3am*

Just John [★MW,NH,D,K,V] 4112 Manchester Ave **314/371-1333** *3pm-3am, from noon-1am Sun*

Keypers Piano Bar [MW,NH,P,F] 2280 S Jefferson (at Shenandoah) **314/664-6496** *2pm-1:30am, noon-midnight Sun, patio*

The Monocle & Emerald Room [MW,DS] 4510 Manchester Ave **314/932-7003** *5pm-midnight, till 1:30am Fri-Sat, clsd Sun-Mon*

Rehab Bar & Grill [GS,NH,DS] 4052 Chouteau Ave (at Boyle) **314/652-3700** *11am-1am, noon-9pm Sun*

Rosie's Place [GS,NH] 4573 Laclede Ave **314/361-6423** *11am-1:30am*

Soulard Bastille [M,NH] 1027 Russell Blvd (at Menard) **314/664-4408** *11am-1:30am*

Sub Zero Vodka Bar [GS,F] 308 N Euclid Ave **314/367-1200** *11:30am-1:30am, sushi and burgers*

Nightclubs

Atomic Cowboy [GS,F,E,WI] 4140 Manchester Ave (btwn Kentucky & Talmadge) **314/775-0775** *11am-3am, from 5pm Sat-Sun, also Fresh-Mex Mayan grill*

The Back Door [W,D,K] 9212 St Charles Rock Rd (lower level of O.T.Saloon, enterance is at rear of building) **314/426-9990** *4pm-midnight Wed, 6pm-1:30am Fri-Sat. noon-8pm Sun*

Bubby & Sissy's [MW,D,E,F,K,DS,V,WC] 602 Belle St (at 6th St), Alton, IL **618/465-4773** *3pm-2am, till 3am Fri-Sat*

Cafes

Coffee Cartel [★F,WI,WC] 2 Maryland Plaza (at Euclid) **314/454-0000** *24hrs*

MoKaBe's [★E,WC] 3606 Arsenal (at S Grand) **314/865-2009** *8am-midnight, from 9am Sun*

Soulard Coffee Garden Cafe [F,WI,WC] 910 Geyer Ave (btwn 9th & 10th) **314/241-1464** *6:30am-4pm, from 8am wknds*

Restaurants

Billie's Fine Food [WC] 1802 S Broadway **314/621-0848** *5am-2:30pm, till 1:30pm wknds*

Cafe Osage 4605 Olive St (at Boxwood Farms) **314/454-6868** *7am-2pm, till 5pm Th-Sat, from 9am Sun*

City Diner [★WC] 3139 S Grand Blvd **314/772-6100** *7am-11pm, 24hrs Fri-Sat, till 10pm Sun*

Crafted [WI,WC] 3200 Shenandoah (at Compton) **314/865-3345** *4pm-midnight, till 1:30am Fri-Sat, 10am-2pm Sun, full bar*

Dressel's [E,WC] 419 N Euclid (at McPherson) **314/361-1060** *11am-1am, till midnight Sun, great Welsh pub food, full bar*

Eleven Eleven Mississippi 1111 Mississippi **314/241-9999** *lunch Mon-Fri, dinner nightly, clsd Sun, wine country bistro*

Joanie's Pizza 2101 Menard St **314/865-1994** *11am-11pm, till midnight wknds*

Mango 1101 Lucas Ave **314/621-9993** *11am-10pm, bar till 1:30am Fri-Sat, 4pm-9pm Sun, Latin American/ Peruvian*

Meskerem 3210 S Grand Blvd **314/772-4442** *lunch & dinner, Ethiopian, plenty veggie*

Molly's in Soulard [E] 816 Geyer Ave **314/241-6200** *11am-9pm, full bar till 1:30am, old-world New Orleans charm, huge patio*

Pappy's Smokehouse 3106 Olive St **314/535-4340** *11am-8pm, till 4pm Sun, excellent BBQ*

Ted Drewes Frozen Custard [★WC] 6726 Chippewa (at Jameson) **314/481-2652, 314/352-7376** *11am-10pm, seasonal, a St Louis landmark; also 4224 S Grand Blvd, 314/352-7376*

Three Monkey's 153 Morgan Ford Rd **314/772-9800** *11am-1:30am, full bar*

Tony's [R,WC] 410 Market St (at Broadway) **314/231-7007** *dinner only, clsd Sun-Mon, Italian fine dining*

Vin de Set [WC] 2017 Chouteau Ave (at S 21st St) **314/241-8989** *lunch & dinner, dinner only wknds, clsd Mon, rooftop bar & bistro*

The Wild Flower Restaurant & Bar [WC] 4590 Laclede Ave (at Euclid) **314/367-9888** *lunch and dinner, wknd brunch, bar till 1am*

BOOKSTORES

Left Bank Books [★] 399 N Euclid Ave (at McPherson) **314/367-6731** *10am-10pm, 11am-6pm Sun*

RETAIL SHOPS

TRX [WC] 3209 S Grand Blvd (at Wyoming St) **314/664-4011** *alternative shopping, body piercing, tattoos*

PUBLICATIONS

Vital Voice 314/256-1196 *bi-weekly news & features publication*

MEN'S CLUBS

Club St Louis [PC,SW,18+] 2625 Samuel Shepard Dr (at Jefferson) **314/533-3666** *24hrs*

EROTICA

Patricia's 3552 Gravois Ave (at Grand) **314/664-4040**

CRUISY AREAS

Creve Coeur Park [AYOR] Dorset Rd W (off Hwy 2-70)

Steele

EROTICA

Lion's Den 36 E Outer Rd (exit 8, off I-55) **573/695-7294**

Waynesville

EROTICA

Lion's Den 25965 Hwy 17 (Exit 153, off I-44) **573/774-9957**

MONTANA

Billings

BARS

The Loft [MW,D,E,K,WC] 1123 1st Ave N (at 12th) **406/259-9074** *10am-2am*

EROTICA

Lovers Playground 1203 1st Ave N (at 12th St) **406/259-0051** *9am-3am, 10am-2am Sun*

The Victorian [P] 2019 Minnesota Ave (at 21st) **406/245-4293** *noon-midnight, clsd Sun-Mon, also HIV & Hep B/C testing*

Bozeman

Accommodations

Lehrkind Mansion Inn [GS,NS,WI,GO] 719 N Wallace Ave **406/585-6932**

Cafes

The Nova Cafe 312 E Main St (at Rouse Ave) **406/587-3973** *7am-2pm*

Butte

Restaurants

Four Seasons 3030 Elm St **406/723-3888** *11am-9:30pm,from noon wknds, Chinese*

Matt's Place 2339 Placer St (btwn Montana & Rowe) **406/782-8049** *11:30am-7pm, clsd Sun-Mon, (clsd winter) classic soda-fountain diner*

Pork Chop John's 2400 Harrison Ave **406/782-1783** *10:30am-10:30pm,clsd Sun; also 8 W Mercury, 406/782-0812*

Uptown Cafe [WC] 47 E Broadway **406/723-4735** *lunch weekdays & dinner nightly, bistro, full bar*

Great Falls

Info Lines & Services

LGBTQ Center 600 Central Ave #323 **406/290-7338** *3pm-7pm, 9am-1pm Wed, 1pm-5pm Sun*

Missoula

Info Lines & Services

KISMIF Gay/ Lesbian AA 405 University Ave (at church) **406/543-0011** *7pm Mon*

Western Montana Gay/ Lesbian Community Center 127 N Higgins Ave #202 **406/543-2224** *LGBT resource center*

Bars

The Oxford [★GF] 337 N Higgins Ave (at Pine) **406/549-0117** *8am-2am, 24hr cafe & casino*

Cafes

The Catalyst 111 N Higgins **406/542-1337** *7am-3pm*

Restaurants

Montana Club [WC] 2620 Brooks **406/543-3200** *6am-10pm, till 11pm Fri-Sat, casino open till 2am*

Bookstores

Fact & Fiction [WC] 220 N Higgins **406/721-2881** *9am-6pm, 10am-5pm Sat, noon-4pm Sun*

Retail Shops

Jeannette Rankin Peace Center 519 S Higgins Ave **406/543-3955** *10am-6pm, noon-4pm Sun, fair trade gift store; also peace resource center*

Cruisy Areas

McCormick Park [AYOR] W side of Orange St Bridge

Swan Valley

Accommodations

Holland Lake Lodge [GF,WI,WC,GO] 1947 Holland Lake Rd (at Hwy 83) **406/754-2282** *resort w/ lakefront cabins, restaurant & bar*

NEBRASKA

Columbus

Cruisy Areas

Pawnee Park [AYOR]

Lincoln

Info Lines & Services

Rainbow Group Gay/ Lesbian AA 2325 S 24 St (at Sewell, at St Matthew's) **402/438-5214** *7:30pm Mon*

Bars

Panic [MW,E,WI,WC,GO] 200 S 18th St (at N St) **402/435-8764** *3pm-1am, from 1pm wknds, till midnight Sun, patio*

Cruisy Areas

15th St [AYOR] from A St to State Capitol

Pioneers & Van Dorn Parks [AYOR]

Norfolk

Cruisy Areas

Tahazooka Park [AYOR]

Omaha

Info Lines & Services

AA Gay/ Lesbian 851 N 74th St (at Presbyterian Church) **402/556-1880** *8:15pm Fri*

Accommodations

Castle Unicorn [GS,NS,WI,GO] 57034 Deacon Rd (at Hwy 34 & I-29), Pacific Jct, IA **712/527-5930** *medieval-style B&B*

The Cornerstone Mansion Inn [GF,NS,WI] 140 N 39th St (at Dodge) **402/558-7600, 888/883-7745**

Bars

The Omaha Mining Company [M,D,K,DS,WC] 1715 Leavenworth St (btwn 17th & 18th) **402/449-8703** *4pm-2am, very cruisy*

Nightclubs

Flixx Lounge [M,D,C,DS] 1019 S 10th St **402/408-1020** *4pm-2am*

The Max [★M,D,DS,S,V,WC,$] 1417 Jackson St (at 15th St) **402/346-4110** *4pm-2am, patio*

Restaurants

The Boiler Room [WC] 1110 Jones St **402/916-9274** *dinner only, clsd Sun, full bar*

California Tacos & More [BW,WC] 3235 California St **402/342-0212** *11am-9pm, clsd Sun*

The Flatiron Cafe [WC] 1722 St Marys Ave **402/344-3040** *dinner only, clsd Sun, full bar*

Cruisy Areas

Glen Cunningham Lake [AYOR] along W side

Scottsbluff

Cruisy Areas

Riverside Zoo Park [AYOR]

Nevada

Carson City

Accommodations

West Walker Motel [GF,WI] 106833 Hwy 395, Walker, CA **530/495-2263** *in Toiyabe Nat'l Forest near West Walker River*

Elko

Cruisy Areas

Elko City Park [AYOR]

Lake Tahoe

see also Lake Tahoe, California

Las Vegas

Info Lines & Services

Alcoholics Together 900 E Karen, 2nd flr #A-202 (at Sahara, in Commercial Center) **702/598-1888** *12:15pm & 8pm daily*

The Gay/ Lesbian Community Center of Southern Nevada 401 S Maryland Pkwy **702/733-9800** *10am-8pm, clsd wknds*

Accommodations

Alexis Park [GS,F,SW,WC] 375 E Harmon Ave **702/796-4334, 800/582-2228** *three minutes from The Strip, pets ok, downscale but occasionally has gay pool parties*

Delano [GF,SW] 3950 Las Vegas Blvd S **702/632-9444** *great property*

El Cortez [GF] 600 Fremont St (at 7th St) **702/385-5200, 800/634-6703** *recently renovated, old-style Vegas glamour Downtown*

Paris, Las Vegas Resort & Casino [GF] 3655 Las Vegas Blvd S **877/796-2096**

Vdara Hotel & Spa [GF,SW,NS] 2600 W Harmon Ave **702/590-2767, 866/745-7767**

Bars

Badlands Saloon [M,NH,D,CW,WC,GO] 953 E Sahara #22 (in Commercial Center) **702/792-9262** *24hrs*

Bastille on 3rd [M,NH] 1402 S 3rd St (at Imperial) **702/385-9298** *10am-2am, in the Arts District*

Charlie's Las Vegas [★M,D,DS,CW,WC] 5012 S Arville St (at Tropicana) **702/876-1844** *24hrs, dance lessons 7pm-9pm Mon, Th-Sat*

Flex [MW,D,DS,S,WC] 4347 W Charleston (at Arville) **702/878-3355** *24hrs*

Freezone [MW,NH,D,TG,F,K,DS,S,YC,GO] 610 E Naples **702/794-2300** *24hrs, also restaurant*

Fun Hog Ranch [M,D,B,L] 495 E Twain (off Paradise) **702/791-7001** *24hrs*

The Garage [M,NH,F,B,WC] 1487 E Flamingo Rd #C (at Maryland) **702/440-6333** *24hrs*

The Las Vegas Eagle [M,L,K] 3430 E Tropicana (at Pecos) **702/458-8662** *24hrs, DJ Wed & Fri*

Las Vegas Lounge [GF,NH,TG] 900 E Karen Ave (at Maryland Pkwy) **702/737-9350** *24hrs*

Phoenix Bar & Lounge [MW,K,WC,GO] 4213 W Sahara Ave **702/826-2422** *noon-4am*

Quadz [★M,B,V,WC] 4640 Paradise Rd #11 (at Naples) **702/733-0383** *24hrs*

The Spotlight Lounge [M,NH,WI] 975 E Sahara (at Commercial Center's entrance) **702/431-9775** *24hrs*

Nightclubs

Don't Tell Mama [M,E,WC] 517 Fremont St #A (downtown) **702/207-0788** *8pm-3am, clsd Mon, great piano bar*

Downtown Cocktail Room [GS] 111 Las Vegas Blvd S **702/880-3696** *4pm-2am, clsd Sun, speakeasy with a warm bohemian-chic décor*

Inspire [GS] 107 Las Vegas Blvd S **702/910-2388** *opens 5pm, clsd Mon-Tue, also rooftop lounge*

The Light Las Vegas [GS,D] 3950 Las Vegas Blvd S (Mandalay Bay Las Vegas) **702/693-8300** *open Wed, Fri-Sat, nightclub by Cirque du Soleil*

Piranha [MW,D,WC] 4633 Paradise Rd (at Naples) **702/791-0100** *opens 10pm nightly*

Restaurants

Bootlegger Bistro [E] 7700 S Las Vegas Blvd (btwn Windmill & Robindale) **702/736-4939** *24hrs, a Vegas classic, Italian*

Border Grill 3950 Las Vegas Blvd S (at the Mandalay Bay Resort & Casino) **702/632-7403** *11:30am-close, Mexican, full bar, patio*

Chicago Joe's 820 S 4th St (at Gass Ave) **702/382-5637** *11am-10pm, from 5pm Sat, clsd Sun-Mon, old-school Italian, in downtown arts district*

Cupcakery 7175 W Lake Mead **702/835-0060** *also at 9680 South Eastern Ave*

Downtown Terrace 707 Fremont St (in the Container Park) **702/854-1418** *11am-9pm, from 9am wknds, full bar*

Eat [★GO] 707 Carson (at 7th) **702/534-1515** *8am-3pm, till 2pm wknds*

The Egg & I [★WC] 4533 W Sahara Ave (near Arville) **702/364-9686** *6am-3pm*

Firefly [WC] 3900 Paradise Rd #A **702/369-3971** *11:30am-1am, tapas, also bar*

Grand Lux Cafe 3355 Las Vegas Blvd S (at the Venetian) **702/414-3888** *open 24hrs, generous portions*

Lindo Michoacan [★] 2655 E Desert Inn Rd (near Eastern) **702/735-6828** *10am-11pm, till midnight wknds, Mexican*

Lotus of Siam [★WC] 953 E Sahara Ave #A-5 (in Commercial Center) **702/735-3033** *lunch Mon-Fri, dinner nightly, Thai*

Mingo Kitchen & Lounge [GO] 1017 S First St #180 (in the heart of the Arts District) **702/685-0328** *11am-10pm, till midnight Fri-Sat, Latin chic menu*

Mon Ami Gabi [WC] 3655 Las Vegas Blvd S (at Paris Las Vegas) **702/944-4224** *7am-11pm, classic bistro serving up everyday French, with an unbeatable view of the Vegas Strip*

Park on Fremont [★] 506 Fremont St **702/834-3160** *8am-11pm, till 1am Fri-Sat, great outdoor comfort food dining*

Stir Krazy Mongolian Gril [GO] 4503 Paradise Rd (across from the Hard Rock) **702/998-9994** *11:30am-9pm, till 10pm Fri-Sat, Asian Cuisine Stir-Fry*

Entertainment & Recreation

18b Arts District [★] bounded by Commerce St, Hoover Ave, Fourth St and Las Vegs Blvd (at Charleston and Colorado Ave)

Cupid's Wedding Chapel [GS] 827 Las Vegas Blvd S (1 block N of Charleston) **702/598-4444, 800/543-2933** *commitment ceremonies*

Erotic Heritage Museum 3275 Sammy Davis Jr Dr **702/369-6442** *11am-7pm, till 10pm Th-Sun*

Frank Marino's Divas Las Vegas [DS] 3535 Las Vegas Blvd S (at the Imperial Palace) **888/777-7664** *show at 7:30pm, Frank Marino & friends impersonate the divas, from Joan Rivers to Tina Turner*

Las Vegas Urban Adventures [GO] **702/370-6961** *a new style of travel experience for those who want to get off the beaten path and really connect with a destination*

Thanks Babs, the Day Tripper [GO] **702/370-6961**

Viva Las Vegas Wedding Chapel [GO] 1205 Las Vegas Blvd **800/574-4450**

Retail Shops

Get Booked 4640 S Paradise Rd #15 (at Naples) **702/737-7780** *10am-midnight, till 2am Fri-Sat, LGBT*

Just You 3400 W Desert Inn Rd #2 **702/697-1800** *clsd Sun, large-size dresses, wigs, etc*

Gyms & Health Clubs

The Las Vegas Athletic Club [GF] 2655 S Maryland Pkwy **702/734-5822** *day passes*

Men's Clubs

Entourage Vegas [SW] 953 E Sahara Ave #A19 (near Paradise & Maryland, at Commercial Center entrance) **702/650-9191** *24hrs*

Hawks Gym [MO,PC,AYOR,GO,$] 953 E Sahara (at SE corner of Commercial Center) **702/731-4295** *24hrs wknds*

The Studios [TG,18+,$] 5150 S Pecos Rd **702/443-3732** *play space open to hetero, gay, bi, trans, men & women; cover charge for men*

Erotica

Adult World/ Mini Theaters 3781 Meade Ave (at Valley View) **702/579-9735** *24hrs*

Fantasy World Arcade/ Theaters 6760 Boulder Hwy (btwn Sunset & Russell) **702/433-7577** *24hrs*

Tropicana Adult Superstore 3850 W Tropicana (at Valley View) **702/798-0144** *24hrs, cruisy theaters*

Cruisy Areas

Jaycee Park [AYOR] Eastern & St Louis (N of Sahara)

Sunset Park [AYOR]

Reno

Info Lines & Services

Our Center 1745 S Wells Ave **775/624-3720** *2pm-8pm, noon-9pm Fri, 9am-6pm Sat, clsd Sun-Mon*

Accommodations

Boomtown Hotel & Casino [GF,E,F,WI,WC] 2100 Garson Rd, Verdi **775/345-6000, 800/648-3790** *great live shows*

Silver Legacy Resort & Casino [GF,F,SW] 407 N Virginia St **775/325-7401, 800/687-8733**

Whitney Peak Hotel [GS,F] 255 N Virginia St **775/398-5400, 888/776-9551** *downtown Reno's only non-gaming, non-smoking boutique hotel*

Bars

Cadillac Lounge [MW,NH] 1114 E 4th St (at Sutro) **775/324-7827** *noon-2am*

Carl's Saloon [M,NH,] 3310 S Virginia St (at Moana) **775/829-8886** *10am-2pm, patio*

Carl's The Saloon [MW,NH,E] 3310 S Virginia St **775/829-0099** *noon-2am, till 4am Fri-Sat*

Chapel Tavern [GS,E] 1099 S Virginia St (at Vassar) **775/324-2244** *2pm-4am, from 10am wknds*

Five Star Saloon [GS,NH,D,TG,WI,WC] 132 West St (at 1st) **775/499-5655** *5pm-5am*

Nightclubs

Splash Reno [MW,D,V] 340 Kietzke Ln (btwn Glendale & Mill)

Restaurants

4th Street Bistro 3065 W 4th St **775/323-3200** *dinner nightly, clsd Sun-Mon, upscale, extensive wine list*

Brasserie Saint James 901 S Center St **775/348-8888** *11am-10pm, till midnight Fri-Sat, till 9pm Sun, full bar & great roof deck*

The Daily Bagel 495 Morill Ave # 102 **775/786-1611** *6am-4pm, 7am-2pm Sun*

M&M Southern 820 Holman Way , Sparks **775/356-1070** *11am-7pm, till 8pm Fri-Sat, clsd Sun-Mon*

Old Granite Street Eatery 243 S Sierra St **775/622-3222** *11am-11pm, from 10am wknds, full bar*

Stone House Cafe 1907 S Arlington Ave **775/284-3895** *7am-9pm, till 8pm Sun-Mon*

Entertainment & Recreation

Brüka Theatre 99 N Virginia St **775/323-3221** *alternative theater & performance space*

Bookstores

Sundance Books 121 California Ave **775/786-1188** *9am-9pm, 9am-5pm wknds, independent*

Publications

Reno Gay Page **775/453-4058** *monthly, bar & resource listings, community events, arts & entertainment*

Men's Clubs

Steve's Bathouse [PC] 1030 W 2nd St (at Keystone) **775/323-8770** *24hrs, co-ed Sunday noon-8am Mon*

Erotica

Suzie's 195 Kietzke Ln (at E 2nd St) **775/786-8557** *10am-10pm, till midnight Fri-Sat, 11am-7pm Sun*

Cruisy Areas

Crissie Caughlin Park [AYOR] W end of the park *days*

Winnemucca

Bars

Cheers [GF,NH,F] 320 S Bridge St, Winnemuca **775/623-2660** *10am-3am*

Cruisy Areas

Button Point [AYOR] I-80, exit 187 (3 miles E of Winnemuca), Winnemuca

NEW HAMPSHIRE

Concord

Cruisy Areas

Rollings Park [AYOR] S end of town

Manchester

Bars

The Breezeway [MW,NH,D,C,DS,GO] 14 Pearl St **603/621-9111** *4pm-1am, theme nights*

Doogie's Bar & Grill [M,NH,F,D,WC.GO] 37 Manchester St **603/232-0732** *4pm-1am, patio*

Element Lounge [MW,D,F,K,DS] 1055 Elm St **603/627-2922** *3pm-1am, from noon Sun,clsd Mon*

Nashua

Accommodations

Radisson Hotel [GF,SW,WI,WC] 11 Tara Blvd **603/888-9970**

Newfound Lake

ACCOMMODATIONS

The Inn on Newfound Lake [GS,SW,NS,WI,GO] 1030 Mayhew Tpke Rte 3-A, Bridgewater **603/744-9111, 800/745-7990** *private beach on cleanest lake in NH, also restaurant, full bar*

Portsmouth

ACCOMMODATIONS

Ale House Inn [GF,WI,GO] 121 Bow St (at Market St) **603/431-7760**

The Hotel Portsmouth [GF,WI,WC,GO] 40 Court St **603/433-1200** *downtown boutique hotel*

CAFES

Breaking New Grounds [WI] 14 Market Square **603/436-9555** *6:30am-11pm*

RESTAURANTS

The Mombo [WC] 66 Marcy St (at State St) **603/433-2340** *dinner only, clsd Mon*

EROTICA

Moonlight Reader 940 Rte 1 Bypass N **603/436-9622**

White Mtns

ACCOMMODATIONS

Beal House [GF,WI] 2 W Main St, Littleton **603/444-2661** *also restaurant*

The Horse & Hound Inn [GF,F,NS,WI,GO] 205 Wells Rd, Franconia **603/823-5501, 800/450-5501** *also restaurant*

The Inn at Bowman [GS,SW,WI,WC,GO] 1174 Rte 2 (Presidential Hwy), Randolph **603/466-5006**

Inn at Crystal Lake [GS,NS,WI,GO] 2356 Eaton Rd (at Rte 16), Eaton **603/447-2120, 800/343-7336**

The Notchland Inn [GS,F,NS,GO] 2 Morey Rd, Hart's Location **603/374-6131, 800/866-6131**

Wildcat Inn & Tavern [GF,E,NS] Rte 16A, Jackson Village **603/383-4245, 855/532-7727**

RESTAURANTS

Polly's Pancake Parlor 672 Rte Sugar Hill Rd (exit 38 off 93 N), Sugar Hill **603/823-5575** *7am-2pm, till 3pm wknds, winter clsd Tue-Th*

The Red Parka Steakhouse & Pub [E] Rte 302, Glen **603/383-4344** *open from 3pm, also bar*

CRUISY AREAS

Scenic Rest Area [AYOR] on left of Rte 16 N, Chocorua

NEW JERSEY

Statewide

PUBLICATIONS

Out in Jersey 743 Hamilton Ave, Trenton 08629 **609/213-9310** *bimonthly glossy magazine for all of New Jersey's LGBT community*

Asbury Park

ACCOMMODATIONS

Asbury Hotel [GF,SW] 210 5th Ave **732/774-7100** *rrock n roll theme property, rooftop bar*

Empress Hotel [GF,SW,WI] 101 Asbury Ave **732/774-0100** *also Empress Lobby Lounge on wknds*

BARS

Georgie's [MW,NH,F,K,DS] 812 5th Ave (at Main) **732/988-1220** *2pm-2am*

NIGHTCLUBS

Paradise [MW,D,E,P,SW] 101 Asbury Ave (at Ocean Ave) **732/988-6663** *4pm-2am, from 2pm Sat, from noon Sun, 2 dance flrs, also piano bar & tiki/ pool bar in summer*

RESTAURANTS

Moonstruck [E] 517 Lake Ave (at Grand) **732/988-0123** *dinner only, clsd Mon-Tue, also bar, live music wknds*

Atlantic City

ACCOMMODATIONS

The Carisbrooke Inn [GF,NS,WI] 105 S Little Rock Ave, Ventnor **609/822-6392** *on a beach block*

Ocean House [MO,V,N,GO] 127 S Ocean Ave **609/345-1964**

Tropicana Casino & Resort [GF,SW] 2831 Boardwalk (at Brighton) **609/340-4000, 800/345-8767**

Bars

Rainbow Room [M,NH,WI,WC] 55 S Bellevue Ave **609/317-4593** *9pm-2am, from 4pm Fri-Sun*

Restaurants

Dock's Oyster House [WC] 2405 Atlantic Ave **609/345-0092** *5pm-10pm, till 11pm Fri-Sat*

White House Sub Shop 2301 Arctic Ave (at Mississippi) **609/345-1564** *10am-8pm, till 9pm Fri-Sat*

Belmar

Cruisy Areas

Belmar Beach [AYOR] *under fishing pier*

Berlin

Erotica

The Berlin News Agency 520 Berlin Kresson Rd **856/767-6003** *9am-midnight, from noon Sun, also cinema*

Red Barn 597 N State (Rte 73 W) **856/767-1525** *9am-midnight, from noon Sun*

Camden

Entertainment & Recreation

The Walt Whitman House 30 Mickle Blvd (btwn S 3rd & S 4th Sts) **856/964-5383** *the last home of America's great & controversial poet*

Cape May

Accommodations

Congress Hall [GF,SW,WI] 251 Beach Ave **609/884-8421, 888/944-1816**

Highland House [GF,NS] 131 N Broadway (at York) **609/898-1198**

The Virginia Hotel [GF,WI] 25 Jackson St (btwn Beach Dr & Carpenter's Ln) **609/884-5700, 800/732-4236** *also The Ebbitt Room restaurant*

Cruisy Areas

Cape May Promenade [AYOR] Beach Ave (btwn Broadway & 2nd)

Higbee Beach [AYOR]

Cherry Hill

Cruisy Areas

Cooper River Park [AYOR] Cuthbert Blvd S (off Rte 70)

Cliffwood

Cruisy Areas

Cliffwood Beach [AYOR]

East Hanover

Restaurants

Penang Malaysian & Thai Cuisine [WC,GO] 200 Route 10 West **973/887-6989** *11am-10pm, full bar*

Hammonton

Nightclubs

The Central [GS,D,E,K,GO] 19 N Egg Harbor Rd (at Orchard Ave) *6pm-midnight Th, 7pm-3am Fri-Sat, clsd Sun-Wed*

Highland Park

Info Lines & Services

Pride Center of New Jersey 85 Raritan Ave (at S 1st Ave) **732/846-2232** *7pm-10pm*

Jamesburg

Restaurants

Fiddleheads [BYOB,GO] 27 E Railroad Ave **732/521-0878** *lunch & dinner, Sun brunch, clsd Mon-Tue, upscale bistro*

Jersey City

Info Lines & Services

Hudson Pride Connections Center 32 Jones St **201/963-4779** *"serving the LGBT communities & all people living w/ HIV, since 1993"*

Accommodations

Hyatt Regency Jersey City [GF,SW,NS,WC] 2 Exchange Pl (on the Hudson) **201/469-1234** *luxury waterfront hotel, short ride to NYC*

Bars

Pint [M,NH] 34 Wayne St **201/367-1222** *4:30pm-2am*

Morristown

Info Lines & Services

GAAMC (Gay Activist Alliance in Morris County) 21 Normandy Hts Rd (at Columbia Rd, Unitarian Fellowship) **973/285-1595** *provides social, educational, and outreach programs*

New Brunswick

Restaurants

The Frog & the Peach [WC] 29 Dennis St (at Hiram Square) **732/846-3216** *lunch Mon-Fri, dinner nightly, full bar, upscale*

Sophie's Bistro 700 Hamilton St (at Douglas), Somerset **732/545-7778** *dinner nightly, lunch Tue-Fri, clsd Mon , patio*

Stage Left Steak [★WC,GO] 5 Livingston Ave (at George) **732/828-4444** *full bar*

Newark

Erotica

Little Theatre 562 Broad St **973/623-5177** *10am-10pm*

Ocean City

Cruisy Areas

58th St Pavilion [AYOR] *late*

Princeton

Cruisy Areas

Herrontown Woods Park [AYOR] off Snowden Ln, btwn mailbox 586 & 603 (no sign, entrance looks like private driveway) *beware of cops!*

River Edge

Nightclubs

Feathers [★M,D,F,K,S,V,YC,WC] 77 Kinderkamack Rd (at Grand) **201/342-6410** *9pm-2am, till 3am Sat, clsd Mon-Tue*

Cruisy Areas

Park & Ride [AYOR] off Rte 4 (across the street from Feathers nightclub)

Sandy Hook

Entertainment & Recreation

Gunnison Nude Beach Beach G parking lot (near Gunnison Park, S end) *at the beach go right (all the way) to the gay section, cruisy area year-round*

Toms River

Cruisy Areas

Winding River [AYOR] Rte 37 (near Garden State Pkwy)

New Mexico

Alamogordo

Cruisy Areas

Alameda Park [AYOR] off White Sands Blvd *nights*

Foothills Park [AYOR] 1st St E (past Scenic Dr) *days*

Albuquerque

includes Bernalillo, Corrales, Placitas & Rio Rancho

Info Lines & Services

AA Gay/ Lesbian [NS,WC] **505/266-1900 (AA#)**

Common Bond 505/636-0845 *serve at-risk sectors of the LGBTQ population*

Accommodations

Bottger Mansion of Old Town B&B [GF,TG,WI] 110 San Felipe (at Central Ave) **505/243-3639** *n Old Town Albuquerque*

Brittania & W E Mauger Estate B&B [GF,NS,WI] 701 Roma Ave NW (at 7th) **505/242-8755, 800/719-9189**

Casa Manzano B&B [GS,GO] 103 Forest Rd 321 (at State Rte 55), Tajique **505/384-0689**

Casas de Suenos [GS] 310 Rio Grande Blvd SW (btwn York & Alhambra) **505/767-1000, 800/665-7002**

The Hotel Blue [GS,SW,WI,WC] 717 Central Ave NW (at 8th St) **505/924-2400, 877/878-4868** *central location walking distance to restaurants, bars, nightlite, pets ok*

The Nativo Lodge [GF] 6000 Pan American Fwy NE **505/798-4300, 866/505-7829**

Sheraton Albuquerque Airport Hotel [GF,F,SW] 2910 Yale Blvd SE (at Gibson) **505/843-7000, 888/625-4937**

Bars

Albuquerque Social Club [★MW,D,PC] 4021 Central Ave NE (at Morningside, enter rear) **505/262-1088** *3pm-2am, noon-midnight Sun*

Sidewinders Ranch [M,D,CW,B,K,WC] 8900 Central SE (at Wyoming) **505/554-2078** *3pm-2am, noon-midnight Sun*

Nightclubs

Effex [MW,D] 420 Central SW (at 5th) **505/842-8870** *9pm-2am Th-Sat*

Cafes

Cafe Cubano at Laru Ni Hati [GO] 3413 Central Ave NE (btwn Tulane & Amherst) **505/255-1575** *10am-9pm, till 8pm Sat, noon-5pm Sun, clsd Mon, cigars & cheap Cuban food, also unisex hair salon*

Java Joe's 906 Park Ave SW **505/765-1514** *6:30am-3:30pm, coffee & pastries, monthly art shows*

Restaurants

Artichoke Cafe [WC] 424 Central Ave SE (at Arno St) **505/243-0200** *lunch Mon-Fri, dinner nightly, full bar*

Copper Lounge [K, WC] 1504 Central Ave SE (at Maple) **505/242-7490** *11:30am-2am, clsd Sun, pizza, burgers, full bar*

El Patio [★BW,WC] 142 Harvard St SE (at Central) **505/268-4245** *8am-9pm, from 11am Sun, plenty veggie*

El Pinto 10500 4th St NW (at Roy Ave) **505/898-1771** *lunch & dinner, Sun brunch, Mexican*

Flying Star Cafe [WI,WC] 3416 Central Ave SE (2 blocks W of Carlisle) **505/255-6633** *6am-10pm, till 11pm Fri-Sat*

Frontier 2400 Central Ave SE (at Cornell) **505/266-0550** *5am-1am, good breakfast burritos*

The Original Garcia's Kitchen [WC] 1113 4th St NW (at Mountain) **505/247-9149** *7am-2pm, awesome little down home place*

Romano's Macaroni Grill [WC] 2100 Louisiana NE (at Winrock Mall) **505/881-3400** *11am-10pm, Italian*

Sadie's Cocinita [★WC] 6230 4th St NW (near Osuna) **505/345-5339** *11am-10pm, 10am-9pm Sun, New Mexican*

Zinc Wine Bar & Bistro [E,R] 3009 Central Ave NE (at Dartmouth) **505/254-9462** *lunch & dinner, brunch wknds, also Blues Cellar till 1am Mon-Sat, live music*

Entertainment & Recreation

Bio Park Botanic Garden 2601 Central Ave NW (at New York Ave) **505/768-2000** *an oasis in the desert: native & exotic plants, butterflies*

Bookstores

Page One 5850 Eubank Blvd NE #B41 **505/294-2026, 800/521-4122** *10am-7pm, "New Mexico's Largest Independent Bookstore"*

Erotica

Castle Megastore 5110 Central Ave SE (at San Mateo) **505/262-2266**

Self Serve [GO] 3904-B Central Ave SE (at Morningside) **505/265-5815** *noon-7pm, till 8pm Fri, till 6pm Sun*

Video Maxxx 810 Comanche NE (at I-25) **505/341-4000** *leather, novelties, books, etc*

Chimayo

Accommodations

Casa Escondida B&B [GF,NS,WI] **505/351-4805** *full brkfst, hot tub*

Clovis

Cruisy Areas

Main St [AYOR] btwn 2nd & 7th

Las Cruces

Accommodations

Hotel Encanto de Las Cruces [GF,SW] 705 S Telshor Blvd **575/522-4300, 866/383-0443** *on-site restaurant and bar*

Retail Shops

Spirit Winds Gifts & Cafe [E,F,WI,WC] 2260 S Locust St (at Thomas Dr) **575/521-0222** *7am-7pm, 8am-6pm Sun, patio*

Cruisy Areas

Burn Lake [AYOR] btwn W Amador & Westgate

Madrid

Bars

Mineshaft Tavern [GF,F,E] 2846 State Hwy 14 **505/473-0743** *11:30am-close, also restaurant*

Cafes

Java Junction [WI] 2855 State Hwy 14 **505/438-2772** *7am-4pm, till 5pm wknds, also giftshop & B&B*

Ramah

Accommodations

El Morro RV Park, Cabins & Cafe [GS,NS,WI,GO] 4018 Hwy 53 **505/783-4612** *in Zuni Mtns, full brkfst, lesbian-owned*

Ruidoso

Cruisy Areas

Cedar Creek [AYOR] off Mechem Dr

Santa Fe

Info Lines & Services

AA Gay/ Lesbian 311 E Palace Ave **505/982-8932** *6pm Fri*

Accommodations

Alexander's Inn [GS,NS,WI] 106 Faithway St **505/986-1431, 888/321-5123** *vacation rentals w/ kitchens, pets/kids ok*

El Farolito B&B [GS,NS,WI,GO] 514 Galisteo St (at Paseo de Peralta) **505/988-1631, 888/634-8782** *adobe compound w/ casitas*

Four Kachinas Inn [GS,NS,WI,WC,GO] 512 Webber St **505/982-2550, 888/634-8782** *near the Plaza*

Hacienda Nicholas [GS,NS,WI,WC] 320 E Marcy St **505/986-1431, 888/284-3170** *full brkfst*

Hotel Chimayó de Santa Fe [GF,WC] 125 Washington Ave **505/988-4900, 855/752-9273** *private balconies, view of Sangre de Cristo Mtns, also restaurant & lounge*

Inn at Vanessie [GF,NS,WI,WC] 427 W Water St **505/984-1193, 800/646-6752** *historic adobe inn, also restaurant & live music club*

The Inn of the Five Graces [GF] 150 E DeVargas St **505/992-0957 , 866/992-0957**

Inn of the Turquoise Bear B&B [MW,NS,WI,GO] 342 E Buena Vista St (at Old Santa Fe Tr) **505/983-0798**

Inn on the Alameda [GF,WI,WC] 303 E Alameda (at Canyon Rd) **505/984-2121, 888/984-2121** *afternoon wine reception, hot tubs*

Las Palomas [GF,NS,WI,WC] 460 W San Francisco St **505/982-5560, 855/982-5560** *luxury hotel 3 blocks from historic Plaza*

The Madeleine Inn [GS,NS,WI] 106 Faithway St **505/982-3465, 888/877-7622** *Queen Anne Victorian, full brkfst, hot tub, also spa*

Rosewood Inn of the Anasazi [GF,WI,NS,WC] 113 Washington Ave **505/988-3030** *luxury hotel 1/2 block from historic Plaza, also restaurant*

Restaurants

Anasazi Restaurant [WC] 113 Washington Ave (at Inn of the Anasazi) **505/988 3236** *brkfst, lunch, dinner & wknd brunch*

Cafe Pasqual's [★BW,WC] 121 Don Gaspar Ave (at Water St) **505/983-9340, 800/722-7672** *brkfst, lunch, dinner & Sun brunch, Southwestern*

The Compound Restaurant [★GS,NS,R,WC] 653 Canyon Rd (at Delgado) **505/982-4353** *lunch Mon-Sat & dinner nightly, upscale, Southwestern, patio*

Cowgirl BBQ 319 S Guadalupe St (at Aztec) **505/982-2565** *11am-11pm, till midnight Fri-Sat, great margaritas*

El Farol 808 Canyon Rd **505/983-9912** *Spanish/ tapas, live music*

Garbo's [OC,WC] 500 Rodeo Rd (at the Montecito Santa Fe) **505/428-7777** *7:30-7:30pm, full bar, located at retirement home*

Geronimo [WC] 724 Canyon Rd (at Camino del Monte Sol) **505/982-1500** *dinner nightly, eclectic gourmet, full bar from 11am-11pm*

Harry's Roadhouse 96 Old Las Vegas Hwy **505/989-4629** *7am-9:30pm, patio, popular brunch*

Pink Adobe 406 Old Santa Fe Trl **505/983-7712** *steak & seafood, also Dragon Room bar*

Santacafe [WC] 231 Washington Ave **505/984-1788** *lunch & dinner, patio*

Tune Up Cafe [BW,WC] 1115 Hickox St (at Cortez) **505/983-7060** *7am-10pm, from 8am wknds, New Mexican*

Entertainment & Recreation

Ten Thousand Waves [N] 3451 Hyde Park Rd (4 miles out of town) **505/982-9304** *Japanese health spa & lodging, clothing-optional*

Bookstores

Downtown Subscription [WC] 376 Garcia St (at Acequia Madre) **505/983-3085** *7am-6pm, newsstand & coffee shop*

Retail Shops

The Ark 133 Romero St (at Agua Fria) **505/988-3709** *10am-6pm, 11am-5pm Sun, spiritual*

Queork [GO] 203 W Water St **505/316-0286** *10am-6pm, sustainable home accessories*

Silver City

Restaurants

Diane's Restaurant & Bakery [BW] 510 N Bullard **575/538-8722** *lunch and dinner*

Taos

Accommodations

Blue Sky Retreat [GS,SW,NS,WI,WC] 1101 Witt Rd (off Kit Carson) **575/751-3776** *full brkfst, hot tub & massage available*

Casa Benavides Inn [GF,NS,WI,WC] 137 Kit Carson Rd (at Paseo del Pueblo Sur) **575/758-1772** *fireplaces, hot tubs, extensive gardens, mtn views, full brkfst*

Casa Gallina [GS,NS,WC,GO] 613 Callejon Rd **575/758-2306** *3 adobe casitas in pastoral setting*

Dreamcatcher B&B [GF,NS,WI,WC] 416 La Lomita Rd (at Valverde) **575/758-0613** *full brkfst, hot tub*

The Historic Taos Inn [GF] 125 Paseo del Pueblo Norte (at Bent St) **575/758-2233** *several adobe houses date from the 1800s, pueblo-style fireplaces, also restaurant & bar*

Touchstone Inn B&B [GF,WI] 110 Mable Dodge Ln (at Hail Creek Rd) **575/779-8712**

Restaurants

Sabroso [E,WC] 470 State Hwy 150, Arroyo Seco **575/776-3333** *5pm-10pm, clsd Tue, American & Mediterranean, also full bar, patio*

Entertainment & Recreation

Llama Trekking Adventures **800/758-5262** *day hikes & multiday llama treks in Sangre de Cristo Mtns & Rio Grande Gorge*

New York

Adirondack Mtns

Accommodations

The Cornerstone Victorian [GF,WI] 3921 Main St (Rte 9), Warrensburg **518/623-3308** *gourmet brkfst*

The Doctor's Inn [FG] 304 Trudeau Rd (at Bloomingdale Ave), Saranac Lake **518/304-3763**

Secluded Retreat Cabin [MW,NS] Lake Luzerne **518/361-2375** *secluded, rustic cabin*

Tea Island Resort [GF] 3020 Lake Shore Dr, Lake George **518/668-2776**

Albany

see Capital District

Angelica

Accommodations

Jones Pond Campground [MO,SW,N,WI,GO] 9835 Old State Rd **585/567-8100** *May-Oct 15, theme wknds, campsites & RV, guesthouse & log cabins*

Binghamton

see also Scranton, Pennsylvania

Info Lines & Services

AA Gay/ Lesbian 607/722-5983

Bars

Squiggy's [MW,NH,D,K,DS] 34 Chenango St (at Court) **607/722-2299** *7:30pm-1am, till 3am Fri-Sat. 4:30pm-11pm Sun, clsd Mon*

Cafes

Lost Dog Cafe [★E,K,WC] 222 Water St (at Henry) **607/771-6063** *11:30am-10pm, clsd Sun*

Restaurants

The Whole in the Wall 43 S Washington St **607/722-5138** *11am-9pm, clsd Sun-Wed, veggie/ vegan*

Erotica

North Street Bookshop 17 Washington Ave (at North), Endicott **607/785-1588**

Buffalo

Info Lines & Services

Lesbian/ Gay AA 18 Trinity Pl (at AIDS Comm Svc) **716/852-7743** *8pm Mon & Wed*

Pride Center of Western NY 206 S Elmwood Ave **716/852-7743** *meetings, resources & more*

Accommodations

The Mansion on Delaware [GS,WI,WC] 414 Delaware Ave **716/886-3300**

Bars

Cathode Ray [M,NH,K,WC] 26 Allen St (at N Pearl) **716/884-3615** *1pm-4am*

Fugazi [GS,V] 503 Franklin St (near Allen St) **716/881-3588** *5pm-2am, cocktail lounge*

Q Bar [MW,NH] 44 Allen St **716/332-2223** *3pm-4am, from noon wknds*

The Underground [M,NH,D,K] 274 Delaware Ave (at Johnson) **716/853-0092** *noon-4am*

Nightclubs

Club Marcella [MW,D,DS,WC,18+] 622 Main St **716/847-6850** *10pm-4am, clsd Mon-Wed*

Cafes

Cafe 59 [WI,GO] 62 Allen St **716/883-1880** *8am-10pm, till midnight Fri, 10am-11pm Sat, noon-9pm Sun*

Restaurants

Allen Street Hardware Cafe [E] 245 Allen St (at College) **716/882-8843** *from 5pm daily, full bar, live music, art*

Anchor Bar 1047 Main St **716/886-8920** *11am-10pm, till midnight Fri-Sat, home of the original Buffalo Chicken Wing*

Mothers 33 Virginia Pl (at Virginia St) **716/882-2989** *4pm-3am, from 1pm Sun, full bar*

Tempo 581 Delaware Ave (at Allen St) **716/885-1594** *dinner only, clsd Sun, upscale Italian/ American*

Towne Restaurant 186 Allen St **716/884-5128** *7am-10pm, till 1am Th, till 3am Fri-Sat, classic American breakfasts as well as Greek classics*

Entertainment & Recreation

Babeville 341 Delaware Ave (at W Tupper) **716/852-3835** *Ani Di Franco's rehabbed church performance space, also Hallwalls Arts Center*

Bookstores

Talking Leaves 951 Elmwood Ave **716/884-9524** *10am-9pm, till 6pm Sat-Sun*

Erotica

Adult Mart 1871 Elmwood Ave, Kenmore **716/874-1045** *10am-midnight, from 8am Fri-Sun*

Video Liquidators 1770 Elmwood Ave **716/874-7223** *24hrs*

Cruisy Areas

South Park Lake [AYOR] 15 minutes from downtown *best btwn 5pm & midnight*

Capital District

includes Albany, Cohoes, Salem, Schenectady & Troy

Info Lines & Services

Capital District Lesbian/ Gay Community Center 332 Hudson Ave, Albany **518/462-6138** *social & human service programs; also Rainbow Cafe 6pm-9pm*

Accommodations

The Morgan State House [GF,NS,WI] 393 State St, Albany **518/427-6063, 888/427-6063** *Ultimate Urban Inn*

Bars

Clinton Street Pub [MW,NH,D,E,K] 159 Clinton St, Schenectady **518/377-8555** *11am-2am*

Oh Bar [MW,NH,MR,K,V,WC] 304 Lark St (at Madison), Albany **518/463-9004** *2pm-4am*

Rocks [MW,NH,K,GO] 77 Central Ave (at Elk), Albany **518/472-3588** *2pm-4am*

Waterworks Pub [M,NH,D,F,E,K,18+,WC] 76 Central Ave (btwn Lexington & Northern), Albany **518/465-9079** *1pm-4am, garden bar, DJ wknds*

Nightclubs

Fuze Box [GS,D,E,GO] 12 Central Ave, Albany **518/703-8937** *8pm-4am Th-Sat, swing dancing*

Restaurants

Bomber's Burrito Bar [GO] 258 Lark St, Albany **518/463-9636** *11am-2am, till 3am wknds, plenty veggie*

Bomber's Burrito Bar [E] 447 State St, Schenectady **518/374-3548** *11am-2am, till 3am wknds*

Cafe Hollywood 275 Lark St, Albany **518/472-9043** *3pm-3am, bar & grill sidewalk seating*

El Loco Mexican Cafe 465 Madison Ave (btwn Lark & Willett), Albany **518/436-1855** *lunch Wed-Sat, dinner nightly, clsd Mon, full bar*

Yono's [E,WC] 25 Chapel St (at Sheridan), Albany **518/436-7747** *5:30pm-10pm, clsd Sun*

Retail Shops

Romeo's Gifts 299 Lark St (at Madison), Albany **518/434-4014** *noon-9pm, till 5pm Sun*

Men's Clubs

River Street Club [MO,V,N,NS,PC,WC,GO] 540 River St (at corner of River & Hoosick St), Troy **518/272-0340** *7am-10pm, from 10am wknds,*

Cruisy Areas

Empire State Plaza [AYOR] Albany

Catskill Mtns

Info Lines & Services

Out in the Catskills 845/747-4449, 800/882-2287 *organization & bulletin board for bringing LGBT of Sullivan County together*

Accommodations

Beds on Clouds [GS] 5320 Main St/ Rte 23 (at CR21), Windham **518/734-4692** *1854 mansion features suites and famous artwork*

Bradstan Country Hotel [GF,C,P] 1561 Rte 17-B, White Lake **845/583-4114** *also piano bar & cabaret from 9pm-1am Fri-Sat*

Clark House [GS,NS] 3292 Rte 23A, Palenville **518/678-5649** *Victorian guesthouse, full brkfst, hot tub*

Country Suite [GF,NS,GO] Rte 23, Windham **518/734-4079** *B&B, Victorian-style farmhouse, full brkfst, antique shop*

Cuomo's Cove [GF,NS] 33 Cumo's Cove Rd (at South St), Windham **518/734-5903**

ECCE B&B [GS,NS,WI,GO] 19 Silverfish Rd, Barryville **845/557-8562, 888/557-8562** *above Upper Delaware River, full brkfst*

The Emerson Resort [GF] 5340 Route 28, Mt Tremper **845/688-2828** *activity packages and great spa, pets ok*

Fairlawn Inn [GF,WI,GO] 7872 Main St, Hunter **518/263-5025**

Hasbrouck House [GF,SW] Rte 209, Stone Ridge **845/687-0736** *restaurant open Wed-Sun, bar on site*

Kate's Lazy Meadow Motel [GF,NS,WI] 5191 Rte 28, Mt Tremper **845/688-7200** *love shack owned by Kate Pierson of the B-52s*

The Roxbury, Contemporary Catskill Lodging [GS,NS,WI,WC,GO] 2258 County Hwy 41 (at Bridge St), Roxbury **607/326-7200** *hip country motel, kids ok*

The Woodstock Inn on the Millstream [GF,NS,WI,WC] 48 Tannery Brook Rd, Woodstock **845/679-8211** *swimming hole*

Bars

Public Restaurant & Lounge [GF] 2318 City Hwy 41 (Bridge St), Roxbury **607/326-4026**

Restaurants

Catskill Rose 5355 Rte 212, Mt Tremper **845/688-7100** *5pm-close Th-Sun, full bar, patio, also lodging*

Hollowbrook Inn & Restaurant 10616 Country Route 32, Greenville **518/966-4683** *lunch & dinner, clsd Mon-Tue & Dec-April*

Bookstores

Golden Notebook [WC] 29 Tinker St, Woodstock **845/679-8000** *10am-6pm, till 7pm Fri-Sat*

Cherry Creek

Accommodations

The Cherry Creek Inn [GF] 1022 West Rd (CR68) (at Center Rd) **716/296-5105** *B&B, full brkfst*

Cooperstown

Accommodations

Cobblescote on the Lake [GF,WI,F,GO] 6515 State Hwy 80 **607/437-1146** *spectacular views at refurbished water-front resort*

Corning

Accommodations

Black Sheep Inn [GS,WI] 8329 Pleasant Valley Rd (Rte 54), Hammondsport **607/569-3767**

Rufus Tanner House B&B [GS,NS,WI,WC] 60 Sagetown Rd, Pine City **607/732-0213** *full brkfst, hot tub*

Elmira

Erotica

Deluxe Books 123 Lake St **607/734-9656** *10am-midnight, till 2am Fri-Sat*

Fire Island

see also Long Island

Info Lines & Services

AA 631/669-1124 *call for meeting times*

Accommodations

➤Belvedere Guest House for Men [MO,SW,WC,GO] **631/597-6448** *Venetian-style palace, hot tub, jacuzzi, gym*

Dune Point Guesthouse [GF,NS,WC] **631/597-6261** *hot tub*

Grove Hotel [M,SW,N,WC,GO] 1 Ocean Walk, Cherry Grove **631/597-6600** *nonsmoking room available, also 4 bars*

Hotel Ciel [M,F,SW,WC] Harbor Walk **631/597-6500** *also restaurant*

The Madison Fire Island Pines [M,SW,NS,WI,GO] 22 Atlantic Walk **631/597-6061** *near beach, roof deck, hot tub*

Pines Bluff Overlook [M,SW] **631/597-3064** *B&B in the Pines*

Bars

Blue Whale [★MW,D,F,WC] Harbor Walk, The Pines **631/597-6500** *seasonal, popular Low Tea dance*

Cherry's On the Bay [★MW,D,F,E,DS,P] 158 Bayview Walk, Cherry Grove **631/597-7859** *seasonal, noon-4am, patio, also restaurant*

Pines Bistro & Martini Bar [M,D,E,P] 36 Fire Island Blvd, The Pines **631/597-6862** *seasonal, opens 6pm*

Sip • n • Twirl [M,D,E] 36 Fire Island Blvd, The Pines **631/597-3599** *seasonal, noon-4am*

Nightclubs

Ice Palace [MW,D,DS,WC] Bayview Walk, Cherry Grove **631/597-6600** *hours vary*

The Pavilion [★M,D,WC] Harbor Walk, The Pines **631/597-6500** *seasonal, popular High Tea dance*

Restaurants

Cherry Grove Pizza 197 Ocean Walk, Cherry Grove **631/597-6766** *seasonal, 11am-10pm*

Marina Meat Market Harbor Walk, The Pines **631/597-4040** *great sandwiches*

Pines Pizza 36 Fire Island Blvd, The Pines **631/597-3597** *seasonal, 11am-11pm*

Sand Castle 140 Lewis Walk, Cherry Grove **631/597-4174** *seasonal, lunch & dinner, also bar*

Entertainment & Recreation

Cherry Grove Beach *nude beach*

Invasion of the Pines The Pines dock (July 4th wknd) *come & enjoy the annual fun as boatloads of drag queens from Cherry Grove arrive to terrorize the posh Pines*

The Pines Beach [M] *nude beach*

Gyms & Health Clubs

Pool Deck & Gym Harbor Walk, The Pines *noon-5pm, till 10pm Fri-Sun, DJ wknds*

Cruisy Areas

Meat Rack [AYOR] trail btwn Cherry Grove & W end of Pines *where the boys of Fire Island really work out*

Geneva

Accommodations

Belhurst [GF,F] 4069 Rte 14 S (near Snell Rd) **315/781-0201** *fireplaces, also restaurant*

Glens Falls

Accommodations

Glens Falls Inn [GF,WI] 25 Sherman Ave **518/743-9365** *Victorian B&B, full brkfst*

Hamptons

see Long Island—Suffolk/ Hamptons

Hudson Valley

Hudson Valley includes Catskill, High Falls, Highland, Hudson, Hyde Park, Kinderhook, Kingston, New Paltz, Poughkeepsie, Rhinebeck & Saugerties

Accommodations

Barclay Heights B&B [GF,NS] 158 Burt St (at Trinity Place), Saugerties **845/246-3788** *full brkfst*

Hotel Tivoli [GS] 53 Broadway, Tivoli **845/757-2100** *amazing design, restaurant and pets ok*

Hudson City B&B [GS,WI,GO] 326 Allen St (at Rte 9-G/ 3rd St), Hudson **518/822-8044** *18th-c Victorian*

Rondout Inn [GS,GO] 79 Broadway, Kingston **845/339-2902** *also own antique store Mezzanine*

Van Schaack House [GF,NS,GO] 20 Broad St (at Albany Rd), Kinderhook **518/758-6118** *B&B, full brkfst*

Restaurants

Armadillo Bar & Grill 97 Abeel St, Kingston **845/339-1550** *lunch wknds, dinner nightly, clsd Mon*

Home/Made [GO] 119 Warren St, Hudson **203/496-1169**

Terrapin 6426 Montgomery St, Rhinebeck **845/876-3330** *lunch & dinner, bistro, also bar, patio*

The Would Restaurant [GO] 120 North Rd (off Rte 9 W), Highland **845/691-9883** *dinner nightly, clsd Sun-Mon, full bar, patio*

Entertainment & Recreation

Big Gay Hudson Valley *check out www.biggayhudsonvalley.com*

Dia:Beacon Riggio Galleries 3 Beekman St (at Rte 9D), Beacon **845/440-0100** *modern art museum*

Erotica

Ulster Video & Gifts 584 Ulster Ave, Kingston **845/331-6023**

Ithaca

Info Lines & Services

AA Gay/ Lesbian 607/273-1541

Accommodations

Juniper Hill B&B [GF,NS,WI,GO] 16 Elm St (at Main St), Trumansburg **607/387-3044** *full brkfst*

William Henry Miller Inn [GF,WI] 303 N Aurora St (at E Buffalo St) **607/256-4553, 877/256-4553**

Cruisy Areas

Stewart Park [AYOR]

Jamestown

Bars

Sneakers [MW,WC] 100 Harrison (at Institute) **716/484-8816** *3pm-2am, clsd Mon*

Entertainment & Recreation

The Lucille Ball/ Desi Arnaz Center 2 W 3rd St (at Main) **716/484-0800, 877/582-9326** *for those who love Lucy*

Long Island

Long Island is divided into 2 geographical areas:
Long Island—Nassau
Long Island—Suffolk/ Hamptons

see also Fire Island

Long Island—Nassau

Info Lines & Services

Long Island GLBT Center 400 Garden City Plaza #110, Garden City **516/323-0011** *Long Island GLBT services network*

Bars

NuBar: Booze & Bites [M,NH,K,E,S] 47 Boundary Ave, South Farmingdale **516/694-6906** *5pm-4am, from 3pm Sun*

Restaurants

RS Jones 153 Merrick Ave (off Sunrise), Merrick **516/378-7177** *dinner, clsd Mon-Tue, Tex-Mex*

Entertainment & Recreation

Jones Beach walk E from Field #6, Wantagh

Pride for Youth 2050 Bellmore Ave, Bellmore **516/679-9000** *serves LGBTQ youth through age 30*

Long Island—Suffolk/ Hamptons

Info Lines & Services

The Center at Bay Shore 34 Park Ave, Bay Shore **631/665-2300** *drop-in lounge w/ cybercenter, events*

The Hamptons GLBT Center 44 Union St, Sag Harbor **831/899-4950** *Long Island GLBT services network*

Accommodations

The Atlantic [GF,SW,WC] 1655 Country Rd 39, Southampton **631/283-6100**

Mill House Inn [GF,NS,WI,WC] 31 N Main St (at Newtown Lane), East Hampton **631/324-9766** *full brkfst, kids/ dogs ok*

Stirling House B&B [GF,NS,WI,GO] 104 Bay Ave, Greenport **631/477-0654, 800/551-0654** *full brkfst, jacuzzi*

Sunset Beach [GF,F] 35 Shore Rd, Shelter Island **631/749-2001** *seasonal*

Restaurants

Babette's 66 Newtown Ln, East Hampton **631/329-5377** *seasonal, brkfst, lunch & dinner, healthy*

Erotica

Sugar Bush 290A Knickerbocker Ave (btwn Sunrise & Vets Hwy), Bohemia **631/567-9779** *10am-11pm, till midnight Fri-Sat*

Cruisy Areas

Fowler Beach [AYOR] Southampton *go right*

Smith Point Park [AYOR] Fire Island Nat'l Seashore (at end of William Floyd Pkwy), Shirley

Middletown

Accommodations

Best Western Inn at Hunt's Landing [GF,SW,WI] 120 Rtes 6 & 209, Matamoras, PA **570/491-2400** *restaurant & bar, pets ok*

Montgomery

Accommodations

The Borland House B&B [GF,WI] 130 Clinton St **845/457-1513**

New York City

New York City is divided into 9 geographical areas:
NYC–Overview
NYC–Soho, Greenwich & Chelsea
NYC–Downtown
NYC–Midtown
NYC–Uptown
NYC–Brooklyn
NYC–Queens
NYC–Bronx
NYC–Staten Island

NYC—Overview

Info Lines & Services

AA Gay/ Lesbian Intergroup at Lesbian/ Gay Community Center **212/647-1680**

LGBT Community Center [WC] 208 W 13th (at 7th Ave) **212/620-7310** *tons of groups & resources, museum*

Entertainment & Recreation

Gay and Lesbian History: Before Stonewall meet: Washington Square Arch (at Big Onion Walking Tours) **212/439-1090**

Publications

Gay City News 646/452-2500 *LGBT newspaper, weekly*

Get Out Magazine 646/761-3325 *content from the hottest gay and gay-friendly spots in New York*

MetroSource 212/315-0800 *LGBT lifestyle magazine & resource directory*

NYC—Soho, Greenwich & Chelsea

Info Lines & Services

Audre Lorde Project [TG] 147 W 24th St **212/463-0342** *1pm-7pm Tue-Th only, LGBT center for people of color, events, resources, HIV services*

Accommodations

Ace Hotel [GF] 20 W 29th St (at Broadway) **212/679-2222** *hip hotel near Flatiron District*

Chelsea Mews Guest House [MO,NS,GO] 344 W 15th St (btwn 8th & 9th Aves) **212/255-9174** *some shared baths*

Chelsea Pines Inn [MW,WI,GO] 317 W 14th St (btwn 8th & 9th Aves) **212/929-1023, 888/546-2700**

The Chelsea Savoy Hotel [GS,WI,WC] 204 W 23rd St (at 7th Ave) **212/929-9353, 866/929-9353**

➤**Colonial House Inn** [★MW,N,NS,GO] 318 W 22nd St (btwn 8th & 9th Aves) **212/243-9669, 800/689-3779** *1850 brownstone in Chelsea, rooftop patio*

Crosby Street Hotel [GF,WI] 79 Crosby St (at Spring) **212/226-6400** *each of the 86 rooms are one-of-a-kind, afternoon tea served, bar, restaurant and gym*

The Evelyn [GF,WI] 7 E 27th St (at 5th Ave) **212/545-8000, 888/468-3501** *s*

Eventi [GF] 851 6th Ave (at 30th St) **212/564-4567, 866/996-8396**

Hotel 17 [GF] 225 E 17th St **212/475-2845** *"East Village chic" budget hotel, shared baths*

Hotel Henri [GF,WI,WC] 37 W 24th St **844/277-9123**

Incentra Village House [GS,NS,WI] 32 8th Ave (at W 12th St) **212/206-0007** *in 2 red-brick buildings built in 1841*

The Jane [GS,WI] 113 Jane St (at Hudson River Pk) **212/924-6700** *inspired by luxury train cabins, some shared baths*

Riff Chelsea [GS,WI] 300 W 30th St (at 8th Ave) **212/ 244-7827, 877/827-6969** *budget friendly accommodations with decor inspired by the NYC Party Scene*

Roxy Hotel [GS,WI] 2 Ave of the Americas **212/519-6600**

Soho Grand Hotel [GF,WI,WC] 310 W Broadway (at Canal St) **212/965-3000, 800/965-3000** *big, glossy, over-the-top hotel*

The Standard Hotel [GF,SW,WI] 848 Washington St (at W 13th) **212/645-4646** *ultra-modern, luxe hotel straddling the High Line*

Washington Square Hotel [GF,F,WI] 103 Waverly Pl (at MacDougal St) **212/777-9515, 800/222-0418** *on historic Washington Square Park*

Bars

Bar 13 [GS,D] 35 E 13th St (btwn Broadway & 5th Ave) **212/979-6677** *3pm-4am, ,bar snacks and rooftop bar*

Barracuda [★M,S] 275 W 22nd St (at 8th Ave) **212/645-8613** *4pm-4am, live DJs*

Beauty Bar [GS,D,E] 231 E 14th St (at 3rd Ave) **212/539-1389** *5pm-4am, from 2pm wknds*

The Boiler Room [M,NH,WI] 86 E 4th St (at 2nd Ave) **212/254-7536** *4pm-4am*

Boxers NYC [M,NH,F,V,WC] 37 W 20th St (at 6th Ave) **212/255-5082** *4pm-2am, from 1pm wknds*

Club Cumming [★GS,D,S,WC] 505 E 6th St (at Ave A) **917/265-8006** *5pm-4am*

The Cock [M,K,S,$] 93 2nd Ave **212/473-9406** *4pm-4am, a "sleazy rock 'n' roll bar," live DJs*

Cubbyhole [MW,NH] 281 W 12th St (at 4th St) **212/243-9041**

Duplex [GF,C,P,$] 61 Christopher St (at 7th Ave) **212/255-5438** *4pm-4am, piano bar from 9pm*

The Eagle [★M,L] 554 W 28th St (btwn 10th & 11th) **646/473-1866** *10pm-4am*

Gym Sports Bar [M,NH] 167 8th Ave (btwn 18th & 19th) **212/337-2439** *4pm-close, from 1pm wknds*

The Hangar [M,DS,S] 115 Christopher St (at Bleecker) **212/627-2044** *3pm-4am*

Julius' [M,NH,F] 159 W 10th St **877/746-0528** *11am-4am, noon-3am Sun, good burgers*

Marie's Crisis [MW,P] 59 Grove St (at 7th Ave) *4pm-4am, piano bar from 9:30pm*

➤**The Monster** [★M,D,C,P,WC] 80 Grove St (at W 4th St, Sheridan Square) **212/924-3558** *4pm-4am, from 2pm wknds, piano bar, T-dance Sun*

Nowhere [MW,NH,TG] 322 E 14th St (btwn 1st & 2nd) **212/477-4744** *3pm-4am*

Phoenix [MW,NH] 447 E 13th (at Ave A) **212/477-9979** *3pm-4am, patio*

Pieces [M,NH,D,K,DS] 8 Christopher St (btwn 6th & 7th) **212/929-9291** *2pm-4am*

Rockbar [M,NH,DS,WC] 185 Christopher St (at Weehawken St) **212/242-9113** *4pm-4am*

The Rust Knot [GS,NH,F,WC] 425 West St (at 11th St) **212/645-5668** *4pm-2am, from 2pm wknds, LGBT Sunday Tea dance*

Stonewall Inn [MW,NH,D,DS,B,E] 53 Christopher St (at 7th Ave) **212/488-2705** *2pm-4am*

Ty's [M,NH,L,B,GO] 114 Christopher St (btwn Bleecker & Hudson) **212/741-9641** *3pm-4am*

Nightclubs

Alegria [★M,D] *sexy dance parties held during holiday weekends and the Black Party in March*

Big Apple Ranch [MW,D,CW,BW,$] 39 W 19th St, 5th flr (btwn 5th & 6th, at Dance Manhattan) *8pm-1am Sat only, two-step lessons*

BRUT [★M,D] 96 Lafayette St (Santos Party House) *monthly leather party, check www.brutparty.com for event dates*

Eleven Eleven [M,D] 244 E Houston St (at Essex, at Open House) *11pm Fri, dancing, drag & debauchery*

Hot Rabbit [W,D] *facebook.com/BoyWonderEvents*

Pyramid [GS,D] 101 Ave A (at 7th St) **212/228-4888** *theme nights*

Sea Tea [M,D,MR,F,P,S,GO,$] leaves from Pier 40 (West Side Hwy at Houston St) **212/675-2971** *6pm-10pm Sun (June-Sept)*

Restaurants

Agave 140 Seventh Ave (btwn 10th St & Charles) **212/989-2100** *noon-close, Southwestern, popular brunch*

Awash 338 E 6th (btwn 1st & 2nd Aves) **212/982-9589** *11am-11pm, Ethiopian*

Benny's Burritos 113 Greenwich (at Jane) **212/633-9210** *11am-11pm, till midnight Fri-Sat, cheap and huge*

Big Gay Ice Cream Shop 125 E 7th St (at 1st Ave) **212/533-9333** *noon-10pm, till midnight Fri-Sat; also Big Gay Ice Cream Truck from May-Oct*

Blue Ribbon [WC] 97 Sullivan St (at Spring St) **212/274-0404** *4pm-4am, cont'l/ American, chef hangout*

Cowgirl Hall of Fame 519 Hudson St (at W 10th) **212/633-1133** *lunch, dinner, wknd brunch*

Crispo 240 W14th St (at 7th) **212/229-1818** *dinner only, great caramelized cauliflower & carbonara*

The Dish 201 8th Ave (btwn 20th & 21st) **212/352-9800** *7am-midnight, from 8am wknds, also bar*

Elmo 156 7th Ave (at 20th St) **212/337-8000** *lunch & dinner, also lounge*

Intermezzo 202 8th Ave (at 21st St) **212/929-3433** *noon-11pm,till 4pm Sun, Italian, great wknd brunch*

LaVagna 545 E 5th St (btwn Aves A & B) **212/979-1005** *dinner nightly, lunch wknds*

The Meatball Shop [★] 200 9th St **212/257-4363** *6pm-midnight, till 1am Fri-Sat, also on 84 Stanton, 64 Greenwich & 170 Bedford*

Omai 158 9th Ave (at 19th St) **212/633-0550** *dinner nightly, Vietnamese*

Parm [★] 248 Mulberry St **212/993-7189** *11:30am-10pm, till 11pm Fri-Sat, old-school Italian*

Philip Marie 569 Hudson St (at 11th St) **212/242-6200** *noon-11pm, clsd Mon*

Red Bamboo 140 W 4th St (at MacDougal) **212/260-1212** *noon-midnight, vegetarian/ vegan*

Sacred Chow [WC] 227 Sullivan St (btwn W 3rd St & Bleecker) **212/337-0863** *11am-10pm, till 11pm Fri-Sat, from 4:30 Mon, gourmet vegan*

Sigiri 91 1st Ave (btwn 5th & 6th Sts) **212/614-9333** *lunch & dinner, Sri Lankan*

Trattoria Pesce Pasta 262 Bleecker St (at 6th Ave) **212/645-2993** *noon-midnight*

Veselka 144 2nd Ave (at 9th St) **212/228-9682** *24hrs, Ukrainian, great pierogi*

Entertainment & Recreation

Dixon Place 161 Chrystie St (at Delancey) **212/219-0736** *many gay-themed productions; also HOT Festival of queer performance in July*

High Line Gansevoort & W 30th St (btwn 9th & 11th Ave) **212/500-6035** *elevated railway converted to beautiful urban park*

La Mama 74 E 4th St **212/352-3101** *experimental theater*

Leslie/ Lohman Gay Art Foundation & Gallery 26 Wooster St (btwn Grand & Canal) **212/431-2609** *noon-6pm, clsd Sun-Mon*

PS 122 150 1st Ave (at E 9th St) **212/477-5829, 212/352-3101 (tickets)** *it's rough, it's raw, it's real New York performance art*

Retail Shops

Flight 001 96 Greenwich Ave (btwn Jane & 12th) **212/989-0001, 877/354-4481** *11am-7pm, noon-6pm Sun, way cool travel gear*

Nasty Pig 259 West 19th St **212/691-6067** *11am-7pm*

Men's Clubs

HandsomeNYC.com [MO,BYOB] 250 W 26th St (btwn 7th & 8th, at Paddles) **212/366-9339** *8pm Wed only, dungeon party*

➤**West Side Club** [★M,PC] 27 W 20th St, 2nd flr (at 6th Ave) **212/691-2700** *24hrs*

Erotica

Leather Man 111 Christopher St (at Bleecker) **212/243-5339** *noon-8pm*

Pleasure Chest 156 7th Ave S (at Charles) **212/242-2158** *10am-midnight*

Purple Passion [GO] 211 W 20th St (at 7th Ave) **212/807-0486** *fetishwear*

NYC—Downtown

Accommodations

Gild Hall, A Thompson Hotel [GS,WC] 15 Gold St (at Platt) **212/232-7700** *high-tech boutique hotel, also restaurant & lounge*

Restaurants

La Flaca [WC] 384 Grand St **646/692-9259** *noon-4am, Mexican, full bar*

NYC—Midtown

Accommodations

Archer [GS] 45 W 38th St **212/719-4100, 855/437-9100** *filled with quirky, curated luxuries, restaurant and rooftop bar*

Chambers Hotel [GF] 15 W 56th St (at 5th Ave) **212/974-5656** *upscale boutique hotel; fabulous art collection*

Distrikt Hotel [GF,WI] 342 W 40th St (at 9th Ave) **212/706 6100** *upscale boutique hotel*

Hotel 57 [GF,NS,WI,WC] 130 E 57th St (at Lexington) **212/753-8841, 866/240-8604**

The Hotel Metro [GF,WI,WC] 45 W 35th St (at 5th Ave) **212/947-2500, 800/356-3870**

Hotel Shocard [★GS,WI] 206 W 41st St **212/703-8600** *reside amid the old glamour and bright lights of Broadway's Theater District*

Hudson Hotel [GF,WI,WC] 356 W 58th St (at 9th) **512/554-6000, 800/697-1791** *magical hotel w/ trendy bars*

Ink48 [GF,WI] 653 11th Ave (at 48th St) **212/757-0088, 877/843-8869** *luxe hotel in former printing house*

The MAve [GF,WI] 61 Madison Ave (at 27th St) **844/325-4256**

The Pod Hotel [NS,WI,WC] 230 E 51st Street (near 2nd Ave) **844/763-7666** *compact rooms, rooftop lounge*

Room Mate Grace [GF,SW,NS,WI,WC] 125 W 45th St (near Sixth Ave) **212/354-2323**

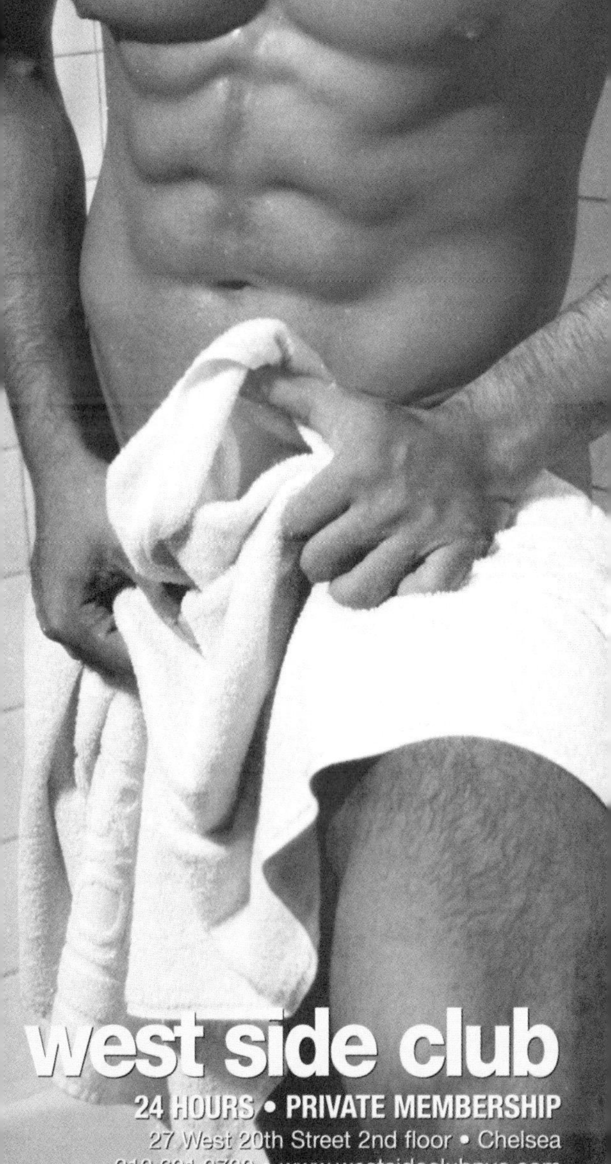
west side club
24 HOURS • PRIVATE MEMBERSHIP
27 West 20th Street 2nd floor • Chelsea
212.691.2700 • www.westsideclubnyc.com

Travel Inn [GF,SW,WC] 515 W 42nd St (at 10th Ave) **212/695-7171, 800/869-4630**

The Tuscany [GS,WI,WC] 120 E 39th St (at Park Ave) **212/686-1600**

Bars

9th Avenue Saloon [M,NH,K] 656 9th Ave (at 46th St) **212/307-1503** *noon-4am*

Adonis [M,S,$] 221 E 58th St (at Evolve) **845/536-3323** *7pm-1am Wed, M4M Weekly Strip Show*

Atlas Social Club [M] 753 9th Ave (btw 59th & 51) **212/262-8527** *4pm-4am, decorated like an old school boxing gym*

Bar Centrale [GS] 324 W 46th St (at 8th Ave) **212/581-3130** *5pm-close, celebs a-plenty*

Barrage [M] 401 W 47th St (at 9th Ave) **212/586-9390** *5pm-4am*

Don't Tell Mama [★GF,C,P,YC,$] 343 W 46th St (at 9th Ave) **212/757-0788** *4pm-4am, cover + 2-drink minimum for [C]*

Evolve [M,E,DS,S,TG,GO] 221 E 58th St (at 2nd Ave) **212/355-3395** *4pm-4am, theme nights*

Fairytail Lounge [M,NH] 500 W 48th St **929/445-8245** *5pm-2am, tiny, trippy lounge*

Flaming Saddles Saloon [MW,D,CW] 793 9th Ave **212/713-0481** *3pm-2am, from noon wknds*

Hardware [M] 697 10th Ave (at 48th) **212/924-9885** *4pm-2am*

Industry [★M,DS] 355 W 52nd St (at 9th Ave) **646/476-2747** *4pm-4am*

Posh Bar & Lounge [M,NH] 405 W 51st St (at 9th Ave) **212/957-2222** *3pm-4am, popular happy hour, DJ nightly*

Rise Bar [M,E] 859 9th Ave (nr Columbus Circle) **646/892-3313** *4pm-2am, fun happy hour & good musice*

The Ritz [M,D,DS] 369 W 46th St (btwn 8th & 9th Aves) **212/333-2554** *4pm-4am, great place for a drink pre- or post-theater*

Therapy [MW,F,E,C] 348 W 52nd St (at 9th) **212/397-1700** *5pm-4am*

Townhouse Bar [M,E,C,P] 236 E 58th St (btwn 2nd Ave & 3rd Ave) **212/754-4649** *4pm-3am, till 4am Fri-Sat, upscale*

Uncle Charlie's [M,E,K,C,P] 139 E 45th St (btwn 3rd & Lexington) **212/661-9097** *4pm-4am, piano bar Wed-Sun*

Restaurants

44 & X Hell's Kitchen [WC,GO] 622 10th Ave (at 44th St) **212/977-1170** *lunch & dinner*

44 1/2 [WC,GO] 626 10th Ave (btwn 44 & 45) **212/399-4450** *5:30pm-close, brunch wknds*

Arriba Arriba [★] 762 9th Ave (at 51st) **212/489-0810** *noon-midnight, till 1am wknds, Mexican, great margaritas*

Bann 350 W 50th St (btwn 8th & 9th Aves) **212/582-4446** *noon-10pm, Korean*

Lips [DS] 227 E 56th St (at 3rd Ave) **212/675-7710** *6pm-midnight, till 1:30am Fri-Sat, gospel brunch Sun, clsd Mon, full bar, "the ultimate in drag dining"*

Lucky Cheng's [★K,DS] 605 W 48th Street **212/995-5500** *5:30pm-midnight, Asian/fusion, full bar, drag shows*

Entertainment & Recreation

Ars Nova 511 W 54th St (at 10th Ave) **212/489-9800** *many gay-themed productions*

Sex & the City Hotspots Tour [R] 5th Ave, in front of the Pulitzer Fountain (at 58th St) **212/913-9780** *3 hours, reservations a must!*

Men's Clubs

➤**East Side Club** [★PC] 227 E 56th St, 6th flr (btwn 2nd & 3rd) **212/888-1884** *24hrs*

NYC—Uptown

ACCOMMODATIONS

710 Guest Suites [GF] 710 St Nicholas Ave (at 145th) **212/491-5622** *modern, chic apt suites*

Bubba and Bean Lodges [GS,NS,WI,GO] 1598 Lexington Ave (btwn 101st & 102nd) **917/345-7914** *private rooms w/ private kitchens*

Hotel Newton [GS,NS,WC] 2528 Broadway (btwn 94th & 95th) **212/678-6500, 800/643-5553** *nearest hotel to Columbia University*

BARS

Brandy's Piano Bar [MW,P] 235 E 84th St (at 2nd Ave) **212/650-1944** *4pm-4am, piano from 9:30pm*

Suite [M,NH,K,DS] 992 Amsterdam (at 109th St) **212/222-4600** *5pm-4am*

Tool Box [M,NH,E,K] 1742 2nd Ave (at 91st St) **212/348-1288** *4pm-4am, from 3pm wknds*

NIGHTCLUBS

Alibi [GS,MR-AF] 2376 Adam Clayton Powell *6pm-2am, till 4am Fri-Sat, clsd Mon, elegant place uptown*

RESTAURANTS

B2 Harlem [GO] 271 W 119th St (at St Nicholas Ave) **212/280-2248** *5pm-10pm, till 11pm Fri-Sat, from 11am Sun, clsd Mon, a new seafood concept for Harlem, full bar*

Joanne Trattoria 70 W 68th St (btw Columbus & Central Park W), New York **212/721-0068** *owned by Lady Gaga's parents*

EROTICA

Les Hommes 217-B W 80th St, 2nd flr (btwn Broadway & Amsterdam) **212/580-2445** *10am-2am, till 3am Fri Sat*

Pleasure Chest 1150 2nd Ave (at E 60th) **212/355-6909** *10am-10pm, till midnight Th-Sat*

CRUISY AREAS

The Rambles [AYOR] in Central Park

NYC—Brooklyn

INFO LINES & SERVICES

Audre Lorde Project [TG] 85 S Oxford St **718/596-0342** *1pm-7pm Tue-Th only, LGBT center for people of color*

Brooklyn Community Pride Center 1360 Fulton St, Brooklyn **347/889-7719** *noon-8pm, clsd wknds*

ACCOMMODATIONS

Hotel Le Bleu [GF,WI] 370 4th Ave **718/625-1500**

Hotel Le Jolie [GF] 235 Meeker Ave **718/625-2100, 866/526-4097**

NU Hotel - Brooklyn [GF] 85 Smith St **718/852-8585**

BARS

The Abbey [GS,NH] 536 Driggs Ave (btwn N 7th & 8th), Williamsburg **718/599-4400** *3pm-4am*

Alligator Lounge [GS,F,K] 600 Metropolitan Ave (at Lorimer) **718/599-4440** *3pm-4am, from 1pm wknds, free pizza from 6pm*

Branded Saloon [GS,NH,E,K,GO] 603 Vanderbilt Ave (at Bergen) **718/484-8704**

Excelsior [MW] 653 5th Ave (btwn 6th & 7th) **718/788-2710** *6pm-4am, from 2pm wknds, patio*

Ginger's Bar [MW,NH,E] 363 5th Ave (btwn 5th & 6th Sts, in Park Slope) **718/788-0924** *5pm-4am, from 2pm wknds, patio*

Happyfun Hideaway [GS] 1211 Myrtle Ave, Brooklyn **917/999-9982** *4pm-4am*

Macri Park [MW,DS,K,V] 462 Union Avenue, Brooklyn **718/599-4999** *3pm-4am*

Metropolitan [MW,NH,D,WI] 559 Lorimer St (at Metropolitan Ave), Williamsburg **718/599-4444** *3pm-4am, comfy bar w/ fireplaces & patio*

Secret Project Robot [GS] 1186 Broadway, Brooklyn *4pm-4am, an artist run art space with music, performance art, DJ's and a bar called Cloud Cuckoo Land*

Nightclubs

Club Langston [M,D,MR-AF] 1073 Atlantic Ave (btwn Franklin & Classon) **718/622-5183** *11pm-4am Th-Sun*

Sutherland NY [GS,D] 260 Meserole St (at Three Dollar Bill), Brooklyn *10pm-6am Fri-Sat only, queer nightclub located in East Williamsburg, check www.sutherlandny.com for events*

Xstasy [M,D,MR-L] 758 5th Ave, Brooklyn *5pm-4am*

Cafes

Outpost [MW,YC,BW,GO] 1014 Fulton St (at Downing) **718/636-1260** *7:30am-midnight, 9am-11pm wknds, also lounge, art gallery*

Restaurants

Alma 187 Columbia St (at Degraw) **718/643-5400** *dinner nightly, wknd brunch, upscale Mexican, outdoor rooftop seating w/ view of Manhattan, also B61 Bar downstairs*

Bogota Latin Bistro [E,GO] 141 5th Ave (at St John's Pl) **718/230-3805** *dinner nightly, wknd brunch, clsd Tue*

Johnny Mack's [E] 1114 8th Ave (btwn 11th & 12th) **718/832-7961** *4pm-2am, from noon wknds*

Santa Fe Grill [WC] 62 7th Ave (at Lincoln) **718/636-0279** *5pm-close, from noon wknds, also bar*

Superfine [E,GO] 126 Front St (at Pearl St) **718/243-9005** *11:30am-3am, 2pm-11pm Sat, 11am-10pm Sun, clsd Mon, also bar*

Erotica

Babeland 462 Bergen St (at 5th Ave) **718/638-3820** *noon-9pm, till 7pm Sun*

NYC—Queens

Bars

Albatross [GS,NH,GO] 36-19 24th Ave (at 37th), Astoria **718/204-9045** *6pm-4am, more gay wknds*

Bungalo Astoria [GS,F] 32-03 Broadway (at 32nd St) **718/204-7010** *5pm-4am, from 3pm Fri-Sat, dress code*

The Deep End [M,D,F,E] 1080 Wyckoff Ave, Ridgewood **347/689-4996** *6pm-4am, clsd Mon*

Friend's Tavern [M,NH,MR-L] 78-11 Roosevelt Ave, Jackson Hts **718/397-7256** *4pm-4am, DJ Wed-Sun*

Hombres Lounge [M,NH,K] 85-25 37th Ave #206, Jackson Heights **718/930-0886** *6pm-4pm*

Icon [M,D,K,DS] 31-84 33rd St, Astoria **917/832-6364** *5pm-4am*

Music Box [M,MR-L,DS] 40-08 74th St (at Roosevelt Ave), Jackson Hts **718/424-8612** *4pm-4am, theme nights*

Sorry Not Sorry Restaurant Bar & Lounge [GS,D,F] 70-15 Austin St, Forest Hills **718/263-7743** *4pm-4am*

True Colors [M,NH,D,MR-L] 79-15 Roosevelt Ave (btwn 79th & 80th Sts, Jackson Hts) **718/672-7505** *4pm-4am*

Nightclubs

Evolution [MW,D,MR-L,DS] 76-19 Roosevelt Ave (at 77th St), Jackson Hts **718/457-3939** *5pm-4am*

Restaurants

Monika's Cafe Bar 3290 36th St, Astoria **718/204-5273** *10am-2am, till 4am Fri-Sat*

Men's Clubs

Northern Men's Sauna [PC] 3365 Farrington St, Flushing **718/445-9775** *11am-10pm, run-down*

Rochester

Info Lines & Services

Out Alliance 100 College Ave #100 **585/244-8640** *events, education, SAGE & youth services*

Rochester Gay Men AA 17 Fitzhugh St (St Lukes & Simon Church) **585/232-6720 (AA#)** *8pm Sun*

Accommodations

Silver Waters Bed & Breakfast [GS,GO] 8420 Bay St (at Lummis), Sodus Point **315/483-8098**

Bars

140 Alex Bar & Grill [MW,D,E,K,DS,V,GO] 140 Alexander St (at Broadway) **585/256-1000** *5pm-2am, from 12:30pm Sun*

Avenue Pub [★M,NH,D] 522 Monroe Ave (at Goodman) **585/244-4960** *4pm-2am, patio*

The Bachelor Forum [M,B,L] 670 University Ave (at Atlantic) **585/271-6930** *2pm-2am*

Nightclubs

Vertex [GS,D] 169 N Chestnut St **585/232-5498** *10pm-2am Wed-Sat, goth club*

Cafes

Equal Grounds 750 South Ave (at Caroline) **585/256-2362** *7am-midnight, from 10am wknds*

Little Theatre Cafe [★E,BW,WC] 240 East Ave **585/258-0400** *5pm-10pm, till 11pm Fri-Sat, till 8pm Sun*

Publications

Empty Closet 585/244-8640 *LGBT newspaper, resource listings*

Men's Clubs

Rochester Spa & Body Club [PC] 109 Liberty Pole Way **585/454-1074** *24hrs*

Saratoga Springs

Accommodations

The Mansion [GF,NS,WC,GO] 801 Rte 29, Rock City Falls **518/885-1607** *1860 Victorian mansion, full brkfst, also supperclub*

Bars

Desperate Annie's [GF,NH] 12 Caroline St (off Broadway) **518/587-2455** *4pm-close*

Restaurants

Esperanto [★] 6 1/2 Caroline St (off Broadway) **518/587-4236** *11am-close, doughboys!*

Little India [BW] 60 Court St **518/583-4151** *lunch & dinner*

Sharon Springs

Accommodations

American Hotel [GS,F,NS,WI,WC,GO] 192 Main St **518/284-2105** *1847 Nat'l Register hotel, also restaurant & bar*

Edgefield [GS,NS,GO] 153 Washington St **518/284-3339** *well-appointed English Country house*

The TurnAround Spa Lodge [MW,F,NS,GO] 105 Washington St **518/284-9708** *small hotel & health spa, full brkfst, hot tub*

Syracuse

Info Lines & Services

AA Gay/ Lesbian 315/463-5011 *call for meeting schedule*

Bars

Rain Lounge [M,NH,MR,TG,E,K,GO] 103 N Geddes St **315/218-5951** *4pm-2:30am*

Wolf's Den [MW,NH,K] 617-619 Wolf St **315/560-5637** *4pm -2am, till midnight Sun-Tue, from noon Sun for brunch*

Nightclubs

Trexx [M,D,DS,S,V,18+WC] 319 N Clinton St (exit 18, off Rte 81) **315/474-6408** *8pm-2am, till 4am Fri-Sat, clsd Sun-Wed, go-go dancers*

Men's Clubs

Red Gym Men's Club [WI] 448 E Brighton Ave (at Thurber) **315/472-0380** *noon-9pm, till 4am Fri-Sat*

Erotica

Boulevard Books 2576 Erie Blvd E (at Seeley) **315/446-1595** *24hrs*

Salt City Book & Video 2807 Brewerton Rd **315/454-0629** *24hrs*

Cruisy Areas

Thornden Park [AYOR] pink triangle rock

White Plains

Info Lines & Services

The LOFT 252 Bryant Ave **914/948-2932, 914/948-4922 (helpline)** *LGBT community center, call for hours, also newsletter*

North Carolina

Asheville

Info Lines & Services

Lambda AA 9 Swan St (at Cathedral of All Souls Episcopal Church) **828/254-8539 (AA#), 800/524-0465** *7pm Mon, Wed & Sat, 8pm Fri*

Accommodations

1889 WhiteGate Inn & Cottage [GS,NS,WI,GO] 173 E Chestnut St **828/253-2553**

The 1900 Inn on Montford [GF,NS,WI] 296 Montford Ave **828/254-9569, 800/254-9569**

Bear and Butterfly B&B [M,WI,GO] 649 Morgan Hill Rd, Fairview **828/628-4588**

Biltmore Village Inn [GF,NS,WI,GO] 119 Dodge St (at Irwin) **828/274-8707, 866/274-8779**

Cedar Crest Inn [GS,GO] 674 Biltmore Ave **828/252-1389**

North Lodge on Oakland B& B [GS,WI,GO] 84 Oakland Rd (at Victoria Rd) **828/252-6433**

Bars

O Henry's/ The Underground [M,NH,D,B,L,DS,WC] 237 Haywood St **828/254-1891** *4pm-2am; Underground from 10pm Fri-Sat only*

Tressa's [GS,D,E] 28 Broadway **828/254-7072** *from 7pm, clsd Sun, jazz/ cigar bar*

Nightclubs

Scandals [MW,D,DS,V,18+,PC,WC] 11 Grove St (at Patton) **828/252-2838** *10pm-3am Th-Sun*

Cafes

Biltmore's [WC] 67 Biltmore Ave **828/252-1500** *8am-6pm, clsd Sun*

Restaurants

Avenue M 791 Merrimon Ave (at Graclyn Rd) **828/350-8181** *5pm-late, clsd Mon-Tuen, full bar*

Barley's Taproom & Pizzeria [E] 42 Biltmore Ave **828/255-0504** *11:30am-until, till 2am Fri-Sat, live jazz, bluegrass & Americana*

Charlotte Street Grill & Pub [WI,GO] 157 Charlotte St **828/252-2948** *noon-2am*

Early Girl Eatery 8 Wall St **828/259-9292** *7:30-3pm, till 9pm Thur-Sun*

Laughing Seed Cafe [BW,WC] 40 Wall St (at Haywood) **828/252-3445** *11:30am-9pm, till 10pm Fri-Sat, Sun brunch from 10am, clsd Tue, vegetarian/ vegan, patio*

Table 48 College St **828/254-8980** *11am-2:30pm Wed-Fri & 5:30pm-11pm nightly, brunch wknds*

Tupelo Honey Cafe 12 College St **828/255-4404** *9am-10pm*

Entertainment & Recreation

LaZoom Tours [BYOB] 90 Biltmore Ave **828/225-6932** *city-wide comedy tours of Asheville, afternoons & evenings*

Bookstores

Firestorm Cafe & Books [E,WI] 610 Haywood Rd **828/255-8115** *10am-8pm, clsd Sun-Mon, vegetarian*

Malaprop's Bookstore/ Cafe [E] 55 Haywood St (at Walnut) **828/254-6734, 800/441-9829** *9am-9pm, till 7pm Sun*

Erotica

BedTyme Stories 2334 Hendersonville Rd, Arden **828/684-8250** *8am-midnight, till 3am Fri-Sat*

Cruisy Areas

The Blue Ridge Parkway [AYOR] Sleepy Gap & Chestnut Cove overlooks (at mile marker 397 & 398)

Blowing Rock

Accommodations

Victorian Inn [GF,NS,WI] 242 Ransom St (at US 321) **828/295-0034**

North Carolina • *USA*

Brevard

Accommodations

Ash Grove Mountain Cabins & Camping [GS,NS,WI,GO] 749 E Fork Rd **828/885-7216** *camping & cabins*

Charlotte

Info Lines & Services

Acceptance Group Gay/ Lesbian AA 2830 Dorcester Pl (at St. Paul United Methodist Church) **704/377-0244, 877/233-6853** *8pm Fri*

Accommodations

VanLandingham Estate [GF,NS,WI,GO] 2010 The Plaza (at Belvedere) **704/334-8909, 888/524-2020**

Bars

Bar Argon [MW,D,V] 4544 South Blvd #H **703/525-7787** *6pm-2am, clsd Mon*

The Bar At 316 [★MW,NH,V,PC] 316 Rensselaer Ave (at South Blvd) **704/910-1478** *5pm-2am, from 3pm Sun*

Boulevard 1820 [M,DS,F] 1820 South Blvd **980/498-1892** *drag dining and restaurant*

Petra's Piano Bar [GS,E,K,WI] 1917 Commonwealth Ave (at Thomas) **704/332-6608** *5pm-2am, clsd Mon*

Sidelines Sports Bar & Billiards [GF,NH,F,WI,PC,WC,GO] **704/525-2608** *4pm-2am, from noon wknds*

The Woodshed [M,NH,B,L,PC,WC] 4000 Queen City Dr (at Little Rock) **704/394-1712** *5pm-2am, from 3pm Sun, also patio bar*

Nightclubs

Chasers [M,D,S,DS,PC,WC] 3217 The Plaza (at 36th) **704/339-0500** *9pm-2am*

The Nickel Bar [MW,D,MR-AF] **704/916-9389** *9pm-2am, from 5pm Sun, clsd Mon-Wed*

Scorpio's [★MW,D,MR,DS,V,18+,PC,WC] 2301 Freedom Dr (at Berryhill Rd) **704/373-9124** *9pm-3am Wed & Fri-Sun*

Cafes

Amelie's French Bakery 2424 N Davidson St **704/376-1781** *open 24hrs*

Smelly Cat Coffee 514 E 36th St **704/374-9656** *6:30-8pm, till 10pm Fri-Sat, till 3pm Mon-Tue*

Restaurants

300 East [WC] 300 East Blvd (at Cleveland) **704/332-6507** *11am-10pm, Sun brunch, full bar*

Alexander Michael's 401 W 9th St (at Pine) **704/332-6789** *lunch & dinner, clsd Sun, full bar*

Dish 1220 Thomas Ave (at Central) **704/344-0343** *11am-10pm, clsd Sun, patio*

Lupie's Cafe [★] 2718 Monroe Rd (near 5th St) **704/374-1232** *11am-10pm,from noon Sat, clsd Sun*

Entertainment & Recreation

One Voice Chorus [GO] PO Box 9241 28299

Bookstores

Paper Skyscraper [WC] 330 East Blvd (at Euclid Ave) **704/333-7130** *10am-7pm, till 6pm Sat, noon-5pm Sun, books & funky gifts*

White Rabbit Books 920 Central Ave (at E 10th) **704/377-4067** *10am-9pm, noon-6pm Sun, LGBT, also magazines, T-shirts, DVDs, novelties*

Publications

Q Notes 704/531-9988 *bi-weekly LGBT newspaper for North Carolina*

Men's Clubs

Qi Clay Sauna Men's Spa 5101-D Nations Ford Rd **980/322_8685** *6pm-6am*

Erotica

Carolina Adult Source 8829 E Harris Blvd (at Albemarle Rd) **704/566-9993**

Cruisy Areas

Freedom Park [AYOR]

Fayetteville

Erotica

Cupid's Boutique 137 N Reilly Rd (at Morganton) **910/860-7716**

Priscilla McCall's 3800 Sycamore Dairy Rd (at Bragg Blvd) **910/860-1776**

Greensboro

Info Lines & Services

Guilford Green Foundation's LGBTQ Center 1205 W Bessemer Ave #226 **336/790-8419** *creates unity through programming and philanthropy that advances equality and inclusion for LGBTQIA communities*

Live & Let Live AA 1205 W Bessemer Ave (LGBTQ Center) **336/854-4278** *7pm Th*

Accommodations

Biltmore Greensboro Hotel [GS,NS,WI,GO] 111 W Washington St (at Elm St) **336/272-3474, 800/332-0303**

O Henry Hotel [GF,SW,WC] 624 Green Valley Rd (at Benjamin Pkwy) **336/854-2000, 800/965-8259** *bar/ restaurant popular w/ local gay community*

Bars

The Q [MW,NH,D,18+,WI] 708 W Market St **336/272-2587** *6pm-close, from 2pm Sun, patio, patio*

Nightclubs

Chemistry [M,D,K,DS] 2901 Spring Garden St **336/617-8571** *8pm-2:30am, clsd Mon-Tue*

Erotica

New Vision Video & News [PC,$] 507 Mobile St (off Randleman Rd) **336/274-6443** *10am-8pm*

Greenville

Cruisy Areas

Green Springs Park [AYOR] 5th St (behind Pizza Hut)

Hickory

Nightclubs

Club Cabaret [MW,D,S,WI,PC,WC] 101 N Center St (at 1st Ave) **828/322-8103** *8pm-2am, from 9pm Fri-Sat, clsd Mon-Wed*

Cafes

Taste Full Beans [GO] 29 2nd St NW **828/325-0108** *7am-7pm, till 9pm Fri-Sat, clsd Sun, art exhibits*

Jacksonville

Erotica

Priscilla McCall's 113-A Western Blvd **910/355-0765**

Little Switzerland

Accommodations

La Petite Chalet [GS,GO] 38 Orchard Ln (at Hwy 226A) **888/828-1654**

Mooresville

Restaurants

Pomodoro's Italian American Cafe [BW,WC,GO] 168 Norman Station Blvd **704/663-6686** *11am-10pm, till 11pm Fri-Sat*

Raleigh/Durham/Chapel Hill

Info Lines & Services

Common Solutions Gay/ Lesbian AA Crownwell Bldg, East Campus (at Duke University), Durham **919/286-9499** *6:30pm Mon*

LGBT Center of Raleigh 324 S Harrington St, Raleigh **919/832-4484**

LGBTQ Center of Durham 114 Hunt St, Durham **919/827-1436** *2pm-8pm, noon-6pm wknds*

Accommodations

Heartfriends Inn B&B [GS,WI,WC,GO] 4389 Siler City/Snow Camp Rd (at Ed Clapp Rd), Siler City **919/663-1707**

The King's Daughters Inn [GF] 204 N Buchanan Blvd, Durham **919/354-7000**

Bars

Flex [★M,B,E,K,DS,PC] 2 S West St (at Hillsborough), Raleigh **919/832-8855** *8pm-close, from 5pm Sun*

Hibernian Restaurant & Pub [GF,F,E] 311 Glenwood Ave (at W Lane St), Raleigh **919/833-2258** *11am-2am*

Nightclubs

The Bar [MW,D,E,K,PC,GO] 711 Rigsbee Ave, Durham **919/956-2929** *4pm-2am, from 2pm wknds, clsd Mon-Tue*

Legends Nightclub Complex [MW,D,DS,S,YC,PC,WC] 330 W Hargett St (at S Harrington St), Raleigh **919/831-8888** *5pm-2am, from 9pm Sun*

The Pinhook [GS,E] 117 W Main St, Durham **991/667-1100** *5pm-2am, 6pm-midnight Sun, patio*

Ruby Deluxe [GS,D,DS,PC] 415 S Salisbury St (basement), Raleigh **919/900-8194** *8pm-2am, from 5pm wknds*

Cafes

Bean Traders 105W NC Hwy 54 #249, Durham **919/484-2499** *6am-8pm, from 8am wknds*

Caffe Driade [E,BW] 1215 E Franklin St #A (at Elizabeth St), Chapel Hill **919/942-2333** *7am-11pm*

Third Place [F] 1811 Glenwood Ave (at W Whitaker Mill Rd), Raleigh **919/834-6566** *6am5pm*

Restaurants

Blu Seafood & Bar 2002 Hillsborough Rd (at 9th St), Durham **919/286-9777** *lunch & dinner, clsd Sun*

Crooks Corner [WC] 610 Franklin St (at Merritt Mill Rd), Chapel Hill **919/929-7643** *dinner nightly, Sun brunch, clsd Mon, Southern cooking, full bar*

Elmo's Diner 776 9th St (in the Carr Mill Mall), Durham **919/416-3823** *6:30am-10pm*

Five Star 511 W Hargett St (at West St), Raleigh **919/833-3311** *5:30pm-2am, Asian-fusion*

Humble Pie 317 S Harrington St (at Martin), Raleigh **919/829-9222** *5pm-11pm, bar open late, brunch only Sun*

Irregardless Cafe [E] 901 W Morgan St (at Hillsborough), Raleigh **919/833-8898** *lunch Tue-Fri, dinner Tue-Sat, Sun brunch, clsd Mon*

Lantern 423 W Franklin St, Chapel Hill **919/969-8846** *dinner nightly, clsd Sun, Asian, also cocktail lounge till 2am*

The Mad Hatter's Bakeshop & Cafe [WI] 1802 W Main St (at Broad), Durham **919/286-1987** *7am-9pm, 8am-3pm Sun*

The Pit 328 W Davie St (at S Dawson), Raleigh **919/890-4500** *11am-10pm, till 11pm wknds, upscale BBQ*

Rue Cler 401 E Chapel Hill St (at Mangum St), Durham **919/682-8844** *lunch & dinner, wknd brunch, clsd Mon, French*

Solas **919/755-0755** *dinner, Sun brunch, upscale dining, dress code, also rooftop lounge & nightclub*

Spotted Dog 111 E Main St (at N Greensboro St), Carrboro **919/933-1117** *11:30am-11pm, till midnight Fri-Sat*

Sunrise Biscuit Kitchen 1305 E Franklin St, Chapel Hill **919/933-1324** *great brkfst, drive-thru only*

Vivace 4209 Lassiter Mill Rd #115 (at Pamlico Dr), Raleigh **919/787-7747** *lunch & dinner, Sun brunch, Italian, patio seating, full bar*

Weathervane Cafe [WC] 201 S Estes Dr (in the University Mall), Chapel Hill **919/929-9466** *9am-9pm, till 3pm Sun, patio, full bar, great brunch*

Bookstores

Quail Ridge Books 4209-100 Lassiter Mill Rd, Raleigh **919/828-1588** *9am-9pm, 10am-6pm Sun, LGBT section*

The Regulator Bookshop 720 9th St (btwn Hillsborough & Perry), Durham **919/286-2700** *10am-9pm, noon-6pm Sun*

RETAIL SHOPS

Boxer & Brief 330 W Hargett St (at S Harrington St), Raleigh **919/323-1300** *10m-3am Fri-Sat, men's underwear boutique located within Legends Nightclub Complex*

EROTICA

Capitol Blvd News 2236 Capitol Blvd, Raleigh **919/831-1400** *9am-6am*

Castle Video & News 1210 Capitol Blvd, Raleigh **919/836-9189** *24hrs*

Cherry Pie [18+] 1819 Fordham Blvd, Chapel Hill **919/928-0499** *10am-midnight*

Frisky Business Boutique 1720 New Raleigh Hwy, Durham **919/957-4441**

Washington

CAFES

Back Water Jack's Tiki Bar [WC] 1052 E Main St (at Havens St) **252/975-1090** *lunch & dinner, clsd Mon, also bar*

Wilmington

ACCOMMODATIONS

Best Western Coastline Inn [GS,NS,WC,WI,GO] 503 Nutt St **910/763-2800**

Blue Heaven B&B [GF,NS,WI] 517 Orange St **910/772-9929** *1800s historic home, full brkfst, pets ok*

Rosehill Inn B&B [GF,NS,WI] 114 S 3rd St (at Dock St) **910/815-0250, 800/815-0250**

The Taylor House Inn [GS,NS] 14 N 7th St **910/763-7581, 800/382-9982**

NIGHTCLUBS

Ibiza [M,D,K,DS,S,YC,PC,WC,GO] 118 Market St (rear) **910/251-1301** *8pm-3am Wed-Sun only*

ENTERTAINMENT & RECREATION

Thalian Hall 310 Chestnut St ( ) **910/632-2285** *classic, foreign & notable films*

Winston-Salem

EROTICA

New Vision Video & News 1045 N Cherry St (at N Huff) **336/725-8034**

NORTH DAKOTA

Fargo

INFO LINES & SERVICES

The Fargo Moorhead Pride Collective and Community Center 1105 1st Ave S **218/287-8034** *referrals, support/ social groups*

ACCOMMODATIONS

The Hotel Donaldson [GS,F,WI] 101 Broadway **701/478-1000**

CAFES

Atomic Coffee [F,WI] **701/478-6160** *7am-11pm, 8pm-10pm Sun*

RESTAURANTS

Fargo's Fryn' Pan [★WC] 300 Main St (at 4th) **701/293-9952** *24hrs*

Mom's Kitchen 1322 Main St **701/235-4460** *6am-10pm, full bar*

RETAIL SHOPS

Zandbroz Variety 420 N Broadway **701/239-4729** *9am-8pm, noon-5pm Sun, books & gifts*

EROTICA

Romantix Adult Superstore 417 N Pacific Ave **701/235-2640** *9am-3am*

CRUISY AREAS

Island Park [AYOR] near pool

Grand Forks

EROTICA

Romantix Adult Superstore 102 S 3rd St (at Kittson) **701/772-9021**

Mandan

EROTICA

Risque's II 2113 Memorial Hwy **701/663-9013**

Minot

Erotica

Risque's 1514 S Broadway **701/838-2837**

Cruisy Areas

Rest Area [AYOR] Hwy 2 (10 miles E of town)

Ohio

Akron

Info Lines & Services

AA Intergroup 330/253-8181 (AA#)

Bars

Akron City Tavern [GF,NH,MR,P,WI,WC] 778 N Main St (at Cuyahoga Falls Ave) **330/230-6656** *11am-10pm, till midnight Fri-Sat, from 4pm sat, clsd Sun*

Cocktails [M,D,DS] 33 W Mapledale Ave **330/376-2625** *3pm-2:30am*

Tear-Ez [MW,NH,DS,WI,WC] 360 S Main St (near Exchange St) **330/376-0011** *11am-2:30am, from noon Sun*

Nightclubs

Interbelt [MW,D,DS,S,V] 70 N Howard St (near Perkins & Main) **330/253-5700** *9pm-2:30am, clsd Tue-Wed, patio*

Square [M,D,E,K,WC,GO] 820 W Market St (near Portage Path) **330/374-9661** *5pm-2:30am, from 7pm wknds*

Cafes

Angel Falls Coffee Company [WC,WI,GO] 792 W Market St (btwn S Highland & Grand) **330/376-5282** *7am-10pm, patio*

Restaurants

Aladdin's Eatery 782 W Market St (at Grand) **330/535-0110** *11am-10pm, Middle Eastern*

Bricco [GO] 1 W Exchange St (at S Main St) **330/475-1600** *11am-11pm, also bar*

Men's Clubs

Akron Steam & Sauna [PC] 41 S Case Ave (near River Rd) **330/252-2791** *noon-midnight, 24hrs wknds*

Bowling Green

Bars

Uptown Downtown Sports Grill [GS] 162 N Main St **419/352-9310** *4pm-2:30am, dancing/DJ Fri-Sat*

Brunswick

see also Akron & Cleveland

Canton

Nightclubs

Crew [MW,D,K,DS] 304 Cherry Ave NE (at 3rd) **330/575-5748** *6pm-2:30am, from 9pm Sat-Sun*

Cincinnati

Info Lines & Services

AA Gay/ Lesbian 328 W McMillan St (enter at 445 Herman St), Corryville **513/351-0422** *7pmTue, Th, Fri & Sat*

Accommodations

Cincinnatian Hotel [GF,NS,WI,WC] 601 Vine St (at 6th St) **513/381-3000, 800/942-9000** *restaurant & lounge*

Crowne Plaza [GF,SW,WI,WC] 5901 Pfeiffer Rd (at I-71) **513/793-4500, 800/468-3597**

First Farm Inn [GF,NS,WI,WC] 2510 Stevens Rd, Petersburg, KY **859/586-0199** *20 minutes from Cincinnati*

Millennium Hotel Cincinnati [GF,SW,WI,WC] 150 W 5th St **513/352-2100, 800/876-2100** *outdoor rooftop pool & sundeck*

Weller Haus B&B [GF,NS,WI] 319 Poplar St, Bellevue, KY **859/391-8315, 800/431-4287**

Bars

Below Zero Lounge [★GS,D,DS,E,K,WI] 1120 Walnut St (at E Central Pkwy) **513/421-9376** *4pm-2am, from 1pm wknds*

Junkers Tavern [GF,NH,K,E] 4158 Langland St (at Chase) **513/541-5470** *9am-1am, live bands*

The Main Event [GS,NH,DS] 835 Main St (at 9th) **513/421-1294** *6am-2:30am, from 11am Sun*

Milton's [GF,NH] 301 Milton St (at Sycamore) **513/784-9938** *4pm-2:30am*

Nightclubs

The Cabaret [M,DS] 1122 Walnut St (at E Central Pkwy) **513/284-2050** *10pm-2am Th-Sat, from noon Sun brunch*

The Dock [★MW,D,DS,MR-AF,19+,WC] 603 W Pete Rose Wy (near Central) **513/241-5623** *10pm-3am, till 4am Fri-Sat, clsd Mon-Wed*

Cafes

College Hill Coffee Co [E,WI,WC] 6128 Hamilton Ave (at North Bend Rd) **513/542-2739** *6:30am-6:30pm, till 10pm Fri, 8:30am-10pm Sat, till 4pm Sun, clsd Mon*

Restaurants

Boca [WC] 114 E 6th Street, Oakley **513/542-2022** *dinner only, clsd Sun, full bar*

The Loving Hut 6227 Montgomery Rd (at Woodmont) **513/731-2233** *11am-7pm, clsd Sun-Mon, vegetarian/ vegan*

Melt Eclectic Deli 4165 Hamilton Ave (at Lingo St) **513/818-8951** *11am-8pm, till 10pm Fri-Sat, 10am-2pm Sun, plenty veggie*

Tucker's [WC] 1637 Vine St (at Green) **513/721-7123** *great brkfst hole in wall, vegan too*

Entertainment & Recreation

Know Theatre 1120 Jackson St (at Central Pkwy) **513/300-5669** *contemporary multicultural theater*

Cleveland

Info Lines & Services

AA Gay/ Lesbian 6600 Detroit Ave (at LGBT Center) **216/241-7387, 800/835-1935**

LGBT Community Center [WC] 6600 Detroit Ave **216/651-5428** *1pm-8pm, clsd wknds*

Accommodations

Clifford House [GS,NS,WI,GO] 1810 W 28th St (at Jay) **216/589-0121** *near downtown*

Radisson Hotel Cleveland—Gateway [GF,WI,WC] 651 Huron Rd (at Prospect) **216/377-9000, 800/967-9033** *also restaurant*

Stone Gables B&B [GS,WI,WC] 3806 Franklin Blvd (at W 38th) **216/961-4654, 877/215-4326** *full brkfst, sauna*

Bars

ABC The Tavern [GF,NH,F] 1872 W 25th St **216/861-3857** *4pm-2:30am, from noon wknds, dive bar w/ great food*

Cocktails Cleveland [★M,D,L,B,K,S,V,WI] 9208 Detroit Ave (at W 93rd St) **216/961-3115** *4pm-2:30am, patio*

The Hawk [MW,NH,WC] 11217 Detroit Ave (at 112th St) **216/521-5443** *noon-2:30am, from 1pm Sun*

Leather Stallion Saloon [★M,NH,B,L,F] 2205 St Clair Ave (near E 21st St) **216/589-8588** *4pm-2am, DJ Sun, patio*

Now That's Class [GF,NH,F,E,TG,WC] 11213 Detroit Ave (at 112th St) **216/221-8576** *4pm-close, punk & metal bands*

Twist [★MW,NH,D,P] 11633 Clifton (at 117th St) **216/221-2333** *11:30am-2:30am, from noon Sun*

Vibe [MW,NH,E,K] 11633 Lorain Ave (at W 117th St) **216/476-1970** *5pm-2:30am, from 3pm Sat, patio*

Cafes

Grumpy's Cafe 2621 W 14th St **216/241-5025** *7am-9pm, till 3pm Sun-Mon*

Gypsy Beans & Baking Co [WI,WC] 6425 Detroit Ave (at W 65th St, next to Cleveland Public Theatre) **216/939-9009** *7am-9pm, till 11pm Fri-Sat, fresh-baked gourmet pastries, soups, sandwiches*

Lucky's Cafe [WI,WC] 777 Starkweather Ave (at Professor Ave) **216/622-7773** *7am-5pm, 8am-3pm wknds, clsd Tue, popular wknd brunch, cafe & bakery, outdoor seating*

Phoenix Coffee [★E,WI,WC] 2287 Lee Rd (at Essex), Cleveland Heights **216/932-8227** *6am-10pm, till 11pm Fri, from 7am Sat, 7am-7pm Sun, great sandwiches, patio*

Restaurants

Bar Cento [BW,WC] 1948 W 25th St (at Lorain Ave) **216/274-1010** *4:30pm-2am, from 11am wknds, great pizza*

Battiste & Dupree Cajun Grill & Bar [WC] 1992 Warrensville Ctr Rd (at Wyncote) **216/381-3341** *lunch & dinner, clsd Sun-Mon*

Cafe Tandoor [WC] 2096 S Taylor Rd (at Cedar), Cleveland Heights **216/371-8500** *lunch & dinner, 3pm-9pm Sun, Indian*

The Coffee Pot 12415 Madison Ave (at Robin), Lakewood **216/226-6443** *6am-2pm, clsd Mon, diner*

Crop Bistro & Bar 2537 Lorain Ave (at 25th) **216/696-2767** *lunch & dinner, innovative American*

Flying Fig 2523 Market Ave (at W 25th St) **216/241-4243** *lunch Wed-Fri & dinner nightly, wknd brunch, clsd Tue*

The Greenhouse Tavern 2038 E 4th St **216/241-5025** *11am-9pm, till 11pm Fri-Sat*

Hecks [★WC] 2927 Bridge Ave (at W 30th) **216/861-5464** *lunch & dinner, brunch Sun, gourmet burgers*

Hodge's 668 Euclid Ave **216/771-4000** *11:30am-10pm, from 4pm wknds, global comfort food*

The Inn on Coventry [WC] 2785 Euclid Heights Blvd (at Coventry), Cleveland Heights **216/371-1811** *7am-2pm, 8am-2:30pm wkndss, homestyle, popular Bloody Marys*

Johnny Mango World Cafe & Bar 3120 Bridge Ave (btwn Fulton & W 32nd, in Ohio City) **216/575-1919** *11am-10pm, till 11pm Fri-Sat, healthy world food & juice bar, also full bar till 1am*

Luchita's [★] 3456 W 117th St (at Governor) **216/252-1169** *lunch & dinner, clsd Mon, Mexican, full bar*

Luxe [E,WC] 6605 Detroit Ave (at W 65th St) **216/920-0600** *5pm-10pm, till midnight Fri-Sat, from 10am wknds, gourmet comfort food, also lounge*

Momocho [WC] 1835 Fulton Rd (at Woodbine Ave) **216/694-2122** *5pm-close, from 4pm Sun, clsd Mon, modern Mexican, also bar*

My Friend's Deli & Restaurant [WI,BW] 11616 Detroit Ave (at W 117th) **216/221-2575** *24hrs*

Pearl of the Orient [WC] 19300 Detroit Rd (in Beachcliff Market Sq), Rocky River **440/333-9902** *lunch & dinner, pan-Asian, some veggie, also restaurant on East Side*

Tommy's [WI,WC] **216/321-7757** *9am-9pm, till 10pm Fri, 7:30am-10pm Sat, plenty veggie, great milkshakes*

Entertainment & Recreation

Rock & Roll Hall of Fame 1100 Rock & Roll Blvd (at E 9th & Lake Erie) **216/781-ROCK** *even if you don't like rock, stop by & check out IM Pei's architectural gift to Cleveland*

Bookstores

Loganberry Books 13015 Larchmere Blvd, Shaker Heights **216/795-9800** *10am-6pm, till 8:30pm Wed-Th, noon-4pm Sun, used & rare books*

Mac's Backs 1820 Coventry Rd (next to Tommy's), Cleveland Heights **216/321-2665** *10am-9pm, till 10pm Fri-Sat, 11am-8pm Sun, great new & used, 3 floors, reading series, some LGBT titles*

Retail Shops

The Dean Rufus House of Fun 1422 W 29th St (at Detroit) **216/348-1386** *1pm-midnight, till 2:30am Fri-Sat, clsd Mon, clothing, DVDs*

Men's Clubs

Flex [★MR,SW,V,PC] 2600 Hamilton Ave **216/812-3304** *24hrs*

Erotica

Adult Mart 16700 Brookpark Rd (at W 150th) **216/267-9019** *8pm-midnight*

Adult Mart 19121 Neff Rd **216/738-0133**

Bank News 4025 Clark Ave (at W 41st St) **216/281-8777** *11am-8pm, clsd Sun-Mon, general magazine store with section for adult videos, magazines, toys*

Rocky's Entertainment & Emporium 13330 Brookpark Rd (at W 130th) **216/267-4659**

Columbus

Info Lines & Services

AA Gay/ Lesbian 614/253-8501, 800/870-3795 (in OH)

Stonewall Columbus Community Center/ Hotline [WC] 1160 N High St (at E 4th Ave) **614/299-7764** *10am-5pm, clsd wknds*

Accommodations

The Blackwell [GF,F,WI] 2110 Tuttle Park Pl (at Lane Ave) **614/247-4000, 866/247-4003** *on OSU campus*

Harrison House B&B [GF,NS,WI] 313 W 5th Ave (at Neil Ave) **614/421-2202**

The Lofts Hotel [GF,SW,WI] 55 E Nationwide Blvd (at High St) **614/461-2663** *in the heart of Columbus*

The Westin Columbus [GF,F] 310 S High St (at Main) **614/223-3800** *beautiful old 100+ year old hotel, great location, pets ok*

Bars

AWOL [M,NH,K,WC] 49 Parsons Ave (at Oak) **614/621-8779** *2pm-2:30am, from noon wknds*

Boscoe's [M,DS] 1224 S High St **614/826-3758** *3pm-2:30am*

Bossy Grrl's Pin Up Joint [GS,F,BW] 2598 N High St **614/725-5402** *4pm-2:30am, till midnight Sun*

Cavan Irish Pub [GF,E,K] 1409 S High St (at Jenkins) **614/725-5502** *2pm-2:30am, from noon wknds*

Club Diversity [MW,E,K,P,WI] 863 S High St (at Whittier) **614/224-4050** *4pm-midnight, till 2:30am Fri-Sat*

The Highball Tavern [M,DS] 1071 Parsons Ave **614/972-7746** *noon-2:30am*

O'Connors Club 20 [M,NH,K] 20 E Duncan (at N Pearl) **614/447-9173** *4pm-2am, from noon wknds, patio*

Slammers Bar & Pizza kitchen [W,D,F,E,WI,WC] 202 E Long St (at N 5th St) **614/221-8880** *11am-midnight, till 2am Fri-Sat, clsd Mon, patio*

The South Bend Tavern [MW,NH,DS,WC] 126 E Moler St (at 4th St) **614/444-3386** *noon-2:30am*

The Toolbox Saloon [M,NH,D,DS] 744 Frebis Ave **614/670-8113** *8am-2:30am*

Tremont [M,NH,OC] 708 S High St (at Frankfort) **614/444-2041** *1pm-2:30am*

Union Cafe [★MW,F,V,WI,WC] 782 N High St (at Hubbard) **614/421-2233** *11am-2:30am*

Nightclubs

Axis [★M,D,C,DS,S,18+,WC,GO] 775 N High St (at Hubbard) **614/291-4008** *m-2:30am Fri-Sat, from 6pm Sun*

Cafes

Stauf's Coffee Roasters 627 S 3rd St (at Sycamore) **614/221-1563** *7am-9pm, till 8pm Sun*

Restaurants

Banana Leaf [WC] 816 Bethel Rd (at Olentangy River Rd) **614/459-4101** *11:30am-9:30pm, vegetarian/ vegan Indian*

Cap City Diner 1299 Olentangy River Rd (at W 5th) **614/291-3663** *11am-10pm, till 11pm Fri-Sat, till 9pm Sun*

Lemongrass [★R] 641 N High (at Russell) **614/224-1414** *lunch & dinner, clsd Sun-Mon, Asian*

Northstar Cafe [★] 951 N High St (at W 2nd Ave) **614/298-9999** *9am-10pm, plenty veggie*

Tip Top Kitchen & Cocktails 73 E Gay St (at 3rd St) **614/221-8300** *11am-2am*

Bookstores

The Book Loft of German Village 631 S 3rd St (at Sycamore) **614/464-1774** *10am-11pm, till midnight Fri-Sat, LGBT section*

Retail Shops

Hausfrau Haven 769 S 3rd St (at Columbus) **614/443-3680** *10am-7pm, noon-5pm Sun, cards, wine & gifts*

Piercology [GO,WC] 190 W 2nd Ave (at Hunter Ave) **614/297-4743** *noon-8pm*

Schmidt's Fudge Haus 220 E Kossuth St (in Historic German Village) **614/444-2222** *noon-close, old fashioned fudge & candy, gifts*

Men's Clubs

The Club Columbus [SW] 795 W 5th Ave (at Olentangy River Rd) **614/291-0049** *gym, steam, sauna*

Erotica

The Garden 1174 N High St (btwn 4th & 5th Ave) **614/294-2869** *11am-3am, noon-midnight Sun*

Lion's Den 4315 Kimberly Pkwy (off Hamilton Rd) **614/861-6770** *6am-midnight*

Dayton

Info Lines & Services

Greater Dayton Lesbian/ Gay Center 117 E 3rd St **937/274-1776**

Bars

Argos Bar [MO,NH,L,GO] 301 Mabel Ave (near Linden & I-35) **937/252-2976** *8pm-2am Fri-Sat only*

MJ's on Jefferson [M,D,K,S] 20 N Jefferson St **937/223-3259** *3pm-2:30am, deck*

Right Corner [MW,E] 105 E 3rd St **937/228-2033** *1pm-2:30am*

Stage Door [M,WC] 44 N Jefferson St (at 2nd) **937/223-7418** *3pm-2:30am*

Nightclubs

Masque [★M,D,DS,S,18+] 34 N Jefferson St (btwn 2nd & 3rd) **937/228-2582** *8pm-2:30am, till 5am wknds*

Restaurants

The Spaghetti Warehouse 36 W 5th St (at Ludlow) **937/461-3913** *11am-10pm, till 11pm wknds, more gay Tue w/ Friends of the Italian Opera*

Bookstores

Books & Co 4453 Walnut St (in Greene Shopping Ctr) **937/429-2169** *10am-10pm, 9am-11pm Fri-Sat, till 9pm Sun*

Publications

Gay Dayton 937/623-1590 *monthly LGBT publication*

Erotica

Adultmart [M] 6388 N Dixie Dr (at Needmore Ave) **937/454-9999**

Fairlawn

Restaurants

Bruegger's Bagels 3737 W Market St **330/665-1050** *5:30am-5pm*

Findlay

Erotica

Findlay Adult Books & Video 623 Trenton Ave (at I-75, exit 159) **419/422-1301**

Kent

Bars

The Zephyr Pub [GF,E,K] 106 W Main St (at Water St) **330/678-4848** *3pm-2am*

Lima

Nightclubs

Somewhere in Time [MW,D,DS,K,S] 804 W North St (at Baxter) **419/227-7288** *5pm-2:30am, from 8pm wknds*

Logan

Accommodations

Glenlaurel—A Scottish Country Inn [GS,NS,WC] 14940 Mt Olive Rd (off State Rte I-80), Rockbridge **740/385-4070, 800/809-7378** *full brkfst, hot tub*

Inn & Spa at Cedar Falls [GS,NS,WI,WC] 21190 State Rte 374 **740/385-7489, 800/653-2557**

Lazy Lane Cabins [GF,NS] **740/385-3475, 877/225-6572** *secluded cabins sleep 2-8, hot tubs, fireplaces*

Mansfield

Bars

Sami's [MW,NH,D,DS] 178 Wayne St **419/522-1500** *open Th-Sat*

Monroe

Bars

Old Street Saloon [MW,NH,D,K,DS] 13 Old St (at Elm St) **513/539-9183** *8pm-2am Th-Sat, clsd Sun-Wed*

Niles

Erotica

Niles Books 5970 Youngstown Warren Rd (off Rte 46) **330/544-4940** *10am-10pm, till midnight Sat, non-9pm Sun*

Oberlin

Accommodations

Hallauer House B&B [GF,SW,WI] 14945 Hallauer Rd **440/774-3400, 877/774-3406** *eco-friendly historic inn 3 miles S of Oberlin*

Restaurants

The Feve [★TG,WI] 30 S Main St (at College St) **440/774-1978** *11am-midnight, popular weekend brunch, plenty veggie, full bar from 5pm*

Bookstores

MindFair Books 13 W College St (shares storefront w/ Ben Franklin) **440/774-5711** *10am-6pm, till 8pm Fri, noon-5pm Sun*

Oxford

Cruisy Areas

Hueston Woods State Park [AYOR] *mornings & at dusk*

Perrysville

Accommodations

Circle JJ Ranch [M,21+] 1104 Amsterdam Rd SE, Scio **330/627-3101** *open April-Oct, special events, theme wknds*

Quaker City

Erotica

Lion's Den 65799 Batesville Rd (exit 193, off I-70) **740/758-5210** *24hrs*

Sandusky

Nightclubs

Crowbar [MW,NH,D,K,GO] 206 W Market St (at Jackson St) **419/624-0109** *6pm-2:30am*

Restaurants

Mona Pizza Gourmet 135 Columbus Ave (at Market St) **419/626-8166** *11am-10pm, till 3am wknds*

Cruisy Areas

Boeckling Boat Dock [AYOR]

Springfield

Nightclubs

Diesel [★MW,D,E,K,DS] 1912-14 Edwards Ave (at N Belmont Ave) **937/324-0383** *9pm-2:30am, clsd Sun-Mon, patio*

Cruisy Areas

Clarence J Brown Reservoir Beach [AYOR]

Toledo

Info Lines & Services

AA Gay/ Lesbian 3205 Glendale Ave (First Unitarian Church) **419/380-9862** *8pm Wed*

Bars

McCune's Other Side Bistro [MW,F] 5038 Lewis Ave **419/476-1577** *3pm-2am, from 11am Sun*

Mojo [M,DS] 115 N Erie St **567/315-8333** *11pm-2:30am*

R House [M,DS,S] 5534 Secor Rd (btwn Laskey & Alexis) **419/984-3015** *4pm-2:30am, patio*

Warren

Nightclubs

The Funky Skunk [M,D,DS,K] 143 E Market St (at Park Ave) *9pm-2:30, clsd Sun-Tue*

West Lafayette

Restaurants

Lava Rock Grill at Unusual Junction [WC,GO] 56310 US Hwy 36 **740/545-9772** *'50s-style diner in restored railroad station*

Yellow Springs

Restaurants

Winds Cafe & Bakery [WC] 215 Xenia Ave (at Cory St) **937/767-1144** *lunch & dinner, Sun brunch, clsd Mon, full bar*

Youngstown

Bars

Mineshaft [M,NH,F] 1105 Poland Ave **330/207-6437** *5pm-midnight, till 2am Fri-Sat, from 3pm Sun*

Nightclubs

Utopia Video Nightclub [MW,D,DS] 876 E Midlothian Blvd (at Zedaker St) **330/781-9000** *7pm-2:30am*

Entertainment & Recreation

The Knox Bldg [F,BW,E] 110 W Federal Plaza W **330/744-7683** *11:30am-2am, events, movies, art, also bar*

Oklahoma

Bartlesville

Cruisy Areas

Johnstone Park [AYOR]

Grand Lake

Accommodations

Southern Oaks Resort & Spa [GF,SW,NS,GO] 2 miles S of Hwy 28/ 82 Junction, Langley **918/782-9346** *19 cabins on 30 acres*

Restaurants

The Artichoke Restaurant & Bar 35896 S Hwy 82, Langley **918/782-9855** *5pm-10pm, clsd Sun-Mon*

Frosty & Edna's Cafe Highway 28, Langley **918/782-9123** *6am-9:30pm*

Lighthouse Supper Club Highway 85 & Main, Ketchum **918/782-3316** *5pm-9pm,, clsd Sun-Tue*

Lawton

Cruisy Areas

The Strip [AYOR] Fort Sill Blvd, near Cache Rd *by car*

McAlester

Bars

Fat Mary's [GS,DS,K] 1561 W Brewer Rd *5pm-2am, from 7pm Fri-Sat, clsd Sun-Mon*

Oklahoma City

Info Lines & Services

AA Live & Let Live 3405 N Villa **405/947-3834** *5:30pm Mon*

Accommodations

➤**Habana Inn** [★MW,SW,NS,WC] 2200 NW 39th St (at Youngs) **405/528-2221, 800/988-2221 (reservations only)** *gay resort, also 2 bars, gift shop*

Renaissance Waterford Oklahoma City Hotel [GF,SW,WI] 6300 Waterford Blvd (at Pennsylvania) **405/848-4782** *also restaurant & bar*

Bars

Alibi's [GS,NH,TG,GO] 1200 N Pennsylvania (at NW 11th) **405/604-3684** *3pm-2am*

The Boom [MW,NH,F,K,DS,WI,WC] 2218 NW 39th St (at Pennsylvania) **405/601-7200** *4pm-2am, from 11am Sun, clsd Mon*

Edna's [GF,NH,F] 5137 N Classen Blvd (at NW 51st) **405/840-3339** *2pm-2am, from noon wknds, dive bar*

The Finishline [MW,NH,D,CW,WC] at Habana Inn **405/525-2900** *noon-2am, poolside bar*

Hi-Lo Club [MW,NH,D,E,DS] 1221 NW 50th St (btwn Western & Classen) **405/843-1722** *noon-2am, live bands*

Partners 4 Club [W,NH,D,E,K,WC] 2805 NW 36th St (at May Ave) **405/602-2030** *5pm-2am, from 7pm Sat, from 11am Sun, clsd Mon & Wed*

OKLAHOMA CITY'S

HABANA INN

The Southwest's Largest All Gay Resort

175 Guest Rooms ★ Two Swimming Pools
Poolside Rooms ★ Suites ★ Cable TV

Park Once And Party All Night!
Located In The Habana Inn Complex

2200 NW 39th Expressway, Oklahoma City, OK 73112

Call for rates and information
(405) 528-2221 Reservations only: 1-800-988-2221
Website: www.habanainn.com

Partners Too [MW,D,WC] 2807 NW 36th St (at May Ave) **405/942-2199** *5pm-2am, clsd Sun-Tue*

Phoenix Rising [M,NH,D,CW,B,L,GO] 2120 NW 39th St (at Pennsylvania Ave) **405/601-3711** *4pm-2am, from 2pm Sun, patio*

Tramps Patio [M,D,S,WI,WC] 2201 NW 39th St (at Barnes) **405/521-9888** *noon-2am, from 10am wknds*

Nightclubs

Apothecary 39 OKC [M,E,WC] 2125 NW 39th St (at Pennsylvania) **405/605-4100** *5pm-2am, upbeat jazz*

The Copa [★MW,D,E,DS,K,S,WC] at Habana Inn **405/525-0730** *9pm-2am, clsd Mon, male dancers Fri-Sat*

Wreck Room [★MW,D,DS,S,YC] 2127 NW 39th St (at Pennsylvania) **405/525-7610** *10pm-close Fri-Sat only, [18+] after 1am*

Cafes

The Red Cup [F,E,NS,WI] 3122 N Classen Blvd (at NW 30th St) **405/525-3430** *7am-3pm, from 9am wknds, vegetarian*

Restaurants

Bricktown Brewery Restaurant 1 N Oklahoma Ave (at Sheridan) **405/232-2739** *11am-10pm, till midnight Sat, from noon Sun, full bar*

Cheever's Cafe [R] 2409 N Hudson Ave (at NW 23rd) **405/525-7007** *11am-9:30pm, 5pm-10:30pm Sat*

Earl's Rib Palace 216 Johnny Bench Dr, Ste BBQ (in Bricktown) **405/272-9898** *11am-9pm, till 10pm Fri-Sat, noon-8pm Sun*

Iguana Bar & Grill 9 NW 9th St (at N Santa Fe Ave) **405/606-7172** *lunch & dinner, Mexican*

Ingrid's Kitchen [GO] 3701 N Youngs (btwn Penn & May, on NW 36th) **405/946-8444** *7am-9pm, till 10pm Fri-Sat 9:30am-2pm Sun, German/ American bakery & deli*

Pops 660 W Hwy 66, Arcadia **405/928-7677** *brkfst, lunch & dinner, diner fare, look for the 66-foot tall soda bottle*

Rococo Restaurant & Fine Wine 2824 N Pennsylvania (at NW 27th St) **405/528-2824** *lunch Mon-Fri, dinner nightly, Sun brunch, full bar*

Someplace Else Deli & Bakery [★] 2310 N Western Ave **405/524-0887** *7am-6:30pm, 9:30am-4pm Sat, clsd Sun*

Sushi Neko 4318 N Western (btwn 42nd & 43rd) **405/528-8862** *11am-11pm, clsd Sun*

Ted's Cafe Escondido 8324 S Western Ave (at 84th St) **405/635-8337** *lunch & dinner, Tex-Mex*

Entertainment & Recreation

First Friday Gallery Walk from 28th at N Walker to 30th at N Dewey **405/525-2688** *open tour of Paseo Arts District galleries, first Fri-Sat*

Bookstores

Full Circle Bookstore [F] 50 Penn Pl, 1900 NW Expwy (in NE corner of 1st level) **405/842-2900, 800/683-7323** *10am-9pm, noon-5pm Sun, also cafe & coffee bar*

Retail Shops

Jungle Red [WC] at Habana Inn **405/524-5733** *novelties, leather, gifts*

Publications

Oklahoma Gazette 405/528-6000 *"Metro OKC's independent weekly"*

Erotica

Christie's Toy Box 7914 N MacArthur **405/720-2453** *multiple locations in OKC*

Cruisy Areas

Trosper Park [AYOR] *beware cops (!)*

Tulsa

Info Lines & Services

Dennis R Neill Equality Center [WC] 621 E 4th St (at Kenosha) **918/743-4297** *noon-9pm, till 6pm Sun, also Pride store*

Gay/ Lesbian AA 918/627-2224

Accommodations

The Mayo Hotel [GF,F,WI,WC] 115 W 5th St **918/582-6296**

Tulsa Hyatt [GF,F,SW,WI,WC] 100 E Second St (at 2nd St) **918/234-1234**

Bars

The ReVue [MW,NH,K,DS] 822 S Sheridan Rd **918/836-5272** *4pm-2am*

Tulsa Eagle [★M,NH,K,L,WI,WC] 1338 E 3rd (at Peoria) **918/592-1188** *2pm-2am*

The Yellow Brick Road [MW,NH,WC] 2630 E 15th St (at Harvard) **918/293-0304** *4pm-2am*

Nightclubs

Club Majestic [MW,D,DS,TG,YC,Wi,WC,GO] 124 N Boston (at Brady) **918/584-9494** *9pm-2am Th-Sun*

Cafes

Gypsy's Coffee House [E,WI] 303 MLK Jr Blvd **918/295-2181** *9am-11pm, till 2am Fri-Sat, from 10am wknds*

Restaurants

Cancun International [BW,WC] 705 S Lewis Ave (at 11th) **918/583-8089** *11am-9pm, from 10am Sat-Sun, clsd Wed*

Eloté [K,WC] 514 S Boston Ave **918/582-1403** *11am-10pm, till 2pm Mon, clsd Sun, fresh Mexican & full bar*

James E McNellie's Public House [WC] 409 E 1st St **918/382-7468** *11am-1am, great burgers & full bar*

White Lion Pub 6927 S Canton Ave (off 71st) **918/491-6533** *4pm-10pm, clsd Sun-Mon, British-style pub*

Wild Fork [E,WC] 1820 Utica Square **918/742-0712** *7am-9pm, till 11pm Th-Sat, 10am-3pm Sun*

Entertainment & Recreation

Gilcrease Museum 1400 N Gilcrease Museum Rd **918/596-2700, 888/655-2278** *one of the best collections of Native American & cowboy art in the US*

Philbrook Museum of Art 2727 S Rockford Rd (1 block E of Peoria, at end of 27th St) **918/324-7941** *clsd Mon, Italian villa built in the '20s oil boom complete w/ kitschy lighted dance flr, the gardens are a must in spring & summer*

Publications

The Tulsa Voice **918/585-9924** *"Tulsa Metro's only independent newsweekly"*

Erotica

Midtown Superstore 319 E 3rd St (at Elgin) **918/584-3112** *24hrs*

OREGON

Ashland

Info Lines & Services

Gay/ Lesbian AA **541/773-4848**

Accommodations

The Arden Forest Inn [GS,NS,SW,WI,WC,GO] 261 W Hersey St (at N Main) **541/488-1496, 800/460-3912** *full brkfst*

Ashland Creek Inn [GF,NS,GO] 70 Water St **541/482-3315** *gourmet brkfst*

Country Willows B&B Inn [GF,SW,NS,WI,WC] 1313 Clay St (at Siskiyou Blvd) **541/488-1590** *full brkfst*

Lithia Springs Resort [GS,NS,WI] 2165 W Jackson Rd (at N Main) **541/482-7128, 800/482-7128**

Romeo Inn B&B [GF,SW,NS,WI] 295 Idaho St **800/915-8899** *full brkfst, jacuzzi*

Restaurants

The Black Sheep Pub & Restaurant [E,WI] 51 N Main St (on the Plaza) **541/482-6414** *11:30am-1am*

Greenleaf Restaurant [BW] 49 N Main St (on The Plaza) **541/482-2808** *8am-8pm, creekside dining*

Bookstores

Bloomsbury Books 290 E Main St (btwn 1st & 2nd) **541/488-0029** *8:30am-8pm, 10am-6pm Sun*

Retail Shops

Travel Essentials 252 E Main St **800/258-0758** *10am-5:30pm, 11am-5pm Sun, luggage, books, accessories*

CRUISY AREAS

Keno Rock Quarry *take Dead Indian Memorial Rd past Howard Prairie Lake to mile marker 18, turn right at Keno Rd, when you see pile of gravel on your left, turn right into quarry*

Bend

ACCOMMODATIONS

Dawson House Lodge [GF,NS,WI] 109455 Hwy 97 N, Chemult **541/365-2232, 888/281-8375** *rustic inn w/ modern amenities, near Crater Lake*

RESTAURANTS

Blacksmith Restaurant 211 NW Greenwood Ave (at NW Harriman) **541/318-0588** *4:30pm-close, new American, upscale*

McKay Cottage 62910 O. B. Riley Rd **541/383-2697** *7am-2pm,1916 bungalow with tables on the lawn serving , great brkfst*

Wild Oregon Foods 61334 S Hwy 97 (in the Bend Factory Stores) **541/668-6344** *11am-8pm, from 9am wknds, till 4pm Sun, clsd Mon, farm-to-table diner*

CRUISY AREAS

Drake Park [AYOR] Riverside Dr *clsd winter*

Sawyer Park [AYOR] *evenings*

Eugene

INFO LINES & SERVICES

Gay/ Lesbian AA 1166 Oak St (at First Christian Church) **541/342-4113**

ACCOMMODATIONS

C'est La Vie Inn [GF,NS,WI] 1006 Taylor St (at W 10th) **541/302-3014, 866/302-3014** *full brkfst*

Valley River Inn [GF,SW,NS,WI,WC] 1000 Valley River Wy **541/743-1000, 800/543-8266**

BARS

Spectrum [MW,E,F] 150 Broadway **541/654-4424** *10am-midnight, till 2am Fri-Sat, clsd Mon*

RESTAURANTS

Glenwood Restaurant 1340 Alder St (at 13th Ave) **541/687-0355** *7am-9pm*

EROTICA

Spice Adult Emporium 1166 South A St (at 10th St), Springfield **541/726-6969** *24hrs*

CRUISY AREAS

Skinner Butte Park [AYOR]

Idleyld Park

ACCOMMODATIONS

Umpqua's Last Resort Wilderness RV Park & Campground [GS,WI,GO] 115 Elk Ridge Ln **541/498-2500**

Klamath Falls

CRUISY AREAS

Haglestein Park [AYOR] Hwy 97 (about 10 miles N of town, past Klamath Lake)

Moore Park [AYOR] *summers*

Medford

EROTICA

Castle Megastore 1601 N Riverside Ave **541/608-9540**

CRUISY AREAS

Jackson County Sports Park [AYOR]

Touvelle Park [AYOR] along Rogue River

Ontario

CRUISY AREAS

Ontario State Park [AYOR] on the Snake River

Portland

see also Vancouver, Washington

INFO LINES & SERVICES

Live & Let Live Club 1210 SE 7th Ave **503/238-6091** *12-step meetings*

Q Center [WI] 4115 N Mississippi Ave (at N Mason St) **503/234-7837** *LGBTQ community center*

Travel Gay Portland Visitors Center [WI] 800 SW Washington St #M1

Accommodations

The Ace Hotel [GS,NS,WI,WC] 1022 SW Stark St (at 11th) **503/228-2277** *hip hotel for "cultural influencers on a budget"*

Hotel deLuxe [GF,NS,WI] 729 SW 15th Ave (at SW Morrison) **503/219-2094**

Hotel Monaco Portland [GF,WI] 506 SW Washington (at 5th Ave) **503/222-0001, 888/207-2201** *also restaurant, gym*

Hotel Vintage Plaza [★GF,WI,WC] 422 SW Broadway (at SW Washington) **503/228-1212, 800/263-2305** *upscale, also restaurant*

Inn at Northrup Station [GF] 2025 NW Northrup St (at NW 21st) **503/224-0543, 800/224-1180** *cute, colorful boutique hotel*

Jupiter Hotel [GF,NS,WI,WC] 800 E Burnside **503/230-9200, 877/800-0004** *mid-century, renovated motor-inn-turned-boutique-hotel; also restaurant and lounge*

The Lion & the Rose [GS,NS,WI,GO] 1810 NE 15th Ave (at NE Schuyler) **503/287-9245, 800/955-1647** *in 1906 Queen Anne mansion*

The Mark Spencer Hotel [GF,NS,WI] 409 SW Eleventh Ave (near Stark) **503/224-3293, 800/548-3934**

McMenamins Crystal Hotel [GS,SW,WI] 303 SW 12th Ave (at Stark) **503/972-2670, 855/205-3930** *former bathouse, also restaurant & bar*

The Nines [GF,WI,WC] 525 SW Morrison St **877/229-9995** *great art, rooftop deck & bar with vew of the west side*

Portland's White House B&B [GS,NS,WI,GO] 1914 NE 22nd Ave (at NE Hancock St) **503/287-7131** *in 1911 Greek Revival mansion*

Riverplace Hotel [GF] 1510 SW Harbor Way **503/228-3233** *restaurant & bar*

Bars

CC Slaughter's [★M,D,F,DS,WI,WC] 219 NW Davis St (at 3rd) **503/248-9135** *3pm-2am, drag brunch Suni*

Chopsticks [GS,F,K,YC,WC] 3390 NE Sandy Blvd **503/234-6171** *4pm-2:30am, from 5pm wknds*

Crush [MW,E,F,WI,WC,GO] 1400 SE Morrison (at SE 14th) **503/235-8150** *noon-2am from 11am wknds, clsd midnight Sun*

Darcelle XV [GS,F,C,DS,S,WC,$] 208 NW 3rd Ave (at NW Davis St) **503/222-5338** *6pm-11pm, till 2am Fri-Sat, clsd Sun-Tue*

Eagle Portland [M,B,L,N,WC] 835 N Lombard St (at N Albina Ave) **503/283-9734** *2pm-2:30am*

Scandals [M,NH,K,E,F,WC,GO] 1125 SW Stark St (at SW 12th) **503/227-5887** *noon-2am, friendly bar*

SGbg [GS,NH,F,WC] 2512 NE Broadway (at NE 25th Ave) **503/287-4210** *4pm-2:30am, from 11am wknds*

Silverado [★M,D,F,K,S,WC,GO] 318 SW 3rd Ave (at SW Oak St) **503/224-4493** *9am-2:30am, strippers*

Stag PDX [M,DS,K] 317 NW Broadway (in the Pearl) **971/407-3132** *5pm-2am, from 7pm Mon-Tue, from 11am Sun for brunch*

Vault Martini Bar [GS,F,WC] 226 NW 12th Ave (btwn 12th & Davis Sts) **503/224-4909** *4pm-midnight, from 3pm Th-Sat, till 2am Fri-Sat, full menu*

Nightclubs

Holocene [GS,D,E,DS] 1001 SE Morrison (at SE 10th) **503/239-7639** *many gay theme nights*

Cafes

Blend [WI,WC] 2710 N Killingsworth (at Greeley) **503/473-8616** *7am-6pm, 8am-5pm Sun*

Cup & Saucer Cafe [★F,BW,WC] 3566 SE Hawthorne Blvd (at SE 36th) **503/236-6001** *8am-3pm, till4pm Fri-Sun*

Elephant's Delicatessen [WC] 115 NW 22nd Ave (at NW Davis) **503/224-3955** *7am-7:30pm, 9:30am-6:30pm Sun*

Marco's Cafe & Espresso Bar [BW,WC] 7910 SW 35th (at Multnomah Blvd), Multnomah **503/245-0199** *7am-9pm, 8am-9pm wknds*

Pix Pâtisserie [BW,WC] 2225 E Burnside St **971/271-7166** *4pm-midnight, from 2pm wknds, dessert*

Voodoo Doughnut 22 SW 3rd Ave **503/241-4704** *24hrs*

Restaurants

Andina 1314 NW Glisan St (at 13th Ave) **503/228-9535** *lunch, dinner & tapas, Peruvian, full bar*

Besaw's [WC] 1545 NW 21st Ave **503/228-2619** *brunch & dinner daily, comfort food*

Bijou Cafe [★WI,WC] 132 SW 3rd Ave (at Pine St) **503/222-3187** *8am-2pm, "farm-fresh breakfast"*

Bluehour [WC] 250 NW 13th Ave (at NW Everett St) **503/226-3394** *lunch Sun-Fri, dinner nightly, Sun brunch, extensive wine list*

Bread & Ink Cafe [★WI,WC] 3610 SE Hawthorne Blvd (at 36th) **503/239-4756** *brkfst, lunch & dinner, packed for brunch on Sun, full bar*

Dot's Cafe [WC] 2521 SE Clinton (at 26th) **503/235-0203** *noon-2am, full bar*

Genie's Cafe [WC] 1101 SE Division St (at 12th) **503/445-9777** *8am-3pm, house-infused vodkas*

Hobo's [P,WC] 120 NW 3rd Ave (btwn Davis & Couch) **503/224-3285** *4pm-2:30am*

Masu [WI,WC] 406 SW 13th Ave (at Burnside) **503/221-6278** *lunch Mon-Th, dinner nightly, sushi*

Mint [GO,WC] 816 N Russell St **503/284-5518** *4pm-11pm & lunch weekdays, also 820 Lounge*

Montage [★WC] 301 SE Morrison (at 3rd) **503/234-1324** *5pm-2am,till 4am Fri-Sat Louisiana-style cookin', full bar*

Nicholas' [WC] 318 SE Grand (btwn Oak & Pine) **503/235-5123** *11am-9pm, from noon Sun, Middle Eastern*

Nostrana [WC] 1401 SE Morrison **503/234-2427** *lunch Mon-Fri, dinner nightly; fresh, local, wood-fired Italian*

Old Town Pizza [WC] 226 NW Davis (at NW 3rd) **503/222-9999** *11:30am-11pm, above Shanghai Tunnels, supposedly home to 100-year-old ghost*

Oven & Shaker 1134 NW Everett St **503/241-1600** *11:30am-midnight, wood burning oven pizza, full bar*

Paley's Place 1204 NW 21st Ave (at NW Northrup St) **503/243-2403** *dinner nightly, Northwest cuisine*

Paradox Cafe [★WC] 3439 SE Belmont St (at SE 35th) **503/232-7508** *9am-3pm, from 8:30am wknds, mostly vegetarian diner, killer Reuben*

The Roxy [★WI,WC] 1121 SW Stark St (btwn 11th & 12th) **503/223-9160** *24hrs, clsd Mon, retro American diner*

Santa Fe Taqueria [★E,WC] 831 NW 23rd (at Kearney) **503/220-0406** *11am-midnight*

Saucebox [D,WC,GO] 214 SW Broadway (at Burnside) **503/241-3393** *5pm-close, pan-Asian, full bar*

Tasty n Sons [★] 3808 N Williams **503/241-1600** *brunch & dinner daily, full bar*

Vita Cafe [★WC] 3023 NE Alberta St (btwn 30th & 31st) **503/335-8233** *brkfst, lunch & dinner, mostly vegetarian/vegan*

Yakuza Lounge [WC] 5411 NE 30th Ave (at Killingsworth) **503/450-0893** *5pm-close, Japanese, full bar*

Entertainment & Recreation

Gay Skate 1 SE Spokane St (at Oaks Park Way, at Oaks Rink) **503/233-5777** *7pm-9pm 3rd Mon only*

Out Dancing [MW] 7981 SE 17th Ave **503/318-1031** *LGBT dance lessons*

Sauvie's Island Beach 25 miles NW (off US 30) *follow Reeder Rd to the Collins beach area, park at the farthest end of the road, then follow path to beach; also "Rooster Rock," 22 miles E on Columbia River*

Bookstores

Powell's Books [★WC] 1005 W Burnside St (at 10th) **503/228-4651, 800/878-7323** *9am-11pm, huge new & used bookstore, cafe, readings*

Retail Shops

Hip Chicks Do Wine 4510 SE 23rd Ave (SE Holgate & 26th) **503/234-3790** *11am-6pm, clsd Tue-Wed*

UnderU4men 800 SW Washington St **503/274-2555** *10am-7pm, till 9pm Fri, 11am-6pm Sun, designer underwear & in-store underwear models*

Publications

PQ Monthly 503/228-3139 *monthly print and daily online newspaper committed to representing LGBTQ communities in all their diversity*

Gyms & Health Clubs

Common Ground Wellness Center [GF,R] 5010 NE 33rd Ave (at Alberta St) **503/238-1065** *10am-11pm, wellness center, public hot tubs, call for men's & trans nights*

Men's Clubs

Hawks PDX 234 SE Grand Ave **503/946-8659** *10am-5am, 24hrs wknds*

Steam Portland [MO,PC,GO] 2885 NE Sandy Blvd **503/736-9999** *24hrs*

Erotica

Fantasy for Adults 1703 W Burnside (near 15th) **503/295-6969** *10am-3am*

Fat Cobra Video 5940 N Interstate Ave **503/247-3425** *9am-midnight, till 3am Fri-Sat*

She Bop [GO] 3213 SE Division St **503/688-1196** *11am-7pm, till 8pm Fri-Sat*

She Bop [GO] 909 N Beech St (off N Mississippi) **503/473-8018** *11am-7pm, till 8pm Fri-Sat*

Spartacus Leathers 300 SW 12th Ave (at Burnside) **503/224-2604** *10am-10pm, till midnight Th-Sat. noon-9pm Sun*

Taboo Video 237 SE MLK, Jr Blvd (at Pine) **503/239-1678** *24hrs*

Cruisy Areas

Kelly Point [AYOR] on Marine Dr *follow trail to left of parking lot*

Salem

Nightclubs

Southside Speakeasy [GS,NH,D,F,K,DS,WI,GO] 3529 Fairview Industrial Dr SE (at Madrona) **503/362-1139** *11am-2am, from 3:30pm wknds*

Restaurants

Davinci's 180 High St SE **504/399-1413** *dinner only, clsd Sun, full bar*

Word Of Mouth 140 NE 17th St **503/930-4285** *7am-3pm, clsd Mon-Tue*

Erotica

Bob's Adult Bookstore 3815 State St (at Lancaster) **503/363-3846** *9am-midnight, 10am-10pm Sun*

Cruisy Areas

Bush Park [AYOR] 12th & State Sts *days only*

Sauvie Island

Entertainment & Recreation

Collins Beach [N,AYOR] take Hwy 30 N from Portland, turn onto "Sauvie Island Bridge" (then take Gillihan Rd to Reeder Rd) *get a parking permit before you go (available at general store at base of Sauvie Island Bridge)*

Silverton

Accommodations

The Oregon Garden Resort [GF,F,SW,WI] 895 W Main St **800/966-6490** *boutique-style resort*

Pennsylvania

Abington

Bars

Kitchen Bar [GF,D,F,E] 1482 Old York Rd **215/576-9766** *noon-2am, from 8am wknds*

Restaurants

Vintage Bar & Restaurant [WC] 1116 Old York Rd **215/887-8500** *11am-2am*

Allentown

see also Bethlehem

Bars

Stonewall, Moose Lounge [★M,D,E,K,DS,S,V] 28 N 10th St (at Hamilton) **610/432-0215** *7pm-2am, clsd Sun- Mon*

Erotica

Adult World 880 S West End Blvd/ Rte 309, Quakerstown **215/538-1522**

Cruisy Areas

Union Terrace Park [AYOR] Union & St Elmo's Sts

Upper Macungie Park [AYOR] Rte 100 (1 mile N of the I-78 exit)

Altoona

Nightclubs

Escapade [MW,D,GO] 2523 Union Ave, Rte 36 **814/946-8195** *8pm-2am*

Erotica

Adult World Old Rte 220 (Bellwood exit, off I-99) **814/742-7781** *9am-midnight, till 1am Fri-Sat*

Beaver Falls

Erotica

Human Nature 18 7211 Big Beaver Blvd (on Rte 18) **724/847-3777** *10am-10pm, till midnight Fri-Sat, 1pm-9pm Sun*

Berwick

Cruisy Areas

Test Track Park [AYOR] S Eaton St (off Rte 11)

Bristol

Erotica

Bristol News World 576 Bristol Pike/ Rte 13 N **215/785-4770**

Cruisy Areas

Silver Lake Park [AYOR]

Butler

Nightclubs

M&J's Lounge [MW,NH,18+,PC,BYOB] 124 Mercer St **724/496-8955** *9pm-midnight Th, 9:30pm-3am Fri-Sat*

Cruisy Areas

Moraine State Park [AYOR] Bear Run area (south shore)

Easton

Bars

La Pazza [MW,D,F] 1251 Ferry St **610/515-0888** *1pm-closing, clsd Mon*

Edinboro

Cruisy Areas

Lakeside Commons [AYOR] Rte 6 N (behind the mall overlooking the lake), Waterford *days*

Elizabeth

Erotica

Adult Mart 931 Hayden (Rte 51) **412/384-6383** *10am-mignight, till 2am Fri-Sat*

Erie

Nightclubs

The Zone [MW,D,B,F,DS] 133 W 18th St (at Peach) **814/452-0125** *8pm-2am*

Restaurants

La Bella [BYOB,GO] 802 W 18th St **814/456-2244** *5pm-9pm, clsd Sun-Tue*

Publications

Erie Gay News 814/456-9833 *covers news & events in the Erie, Cleveland, Pittsburgh, Buffalo & Chautauqua County (NY) region*

Erotica

Adult Mart 1313 State St (btwn 13th & 14th) **814/459-7014** *10am-midnight, from 8am Fri-Sat*

Modern News 1113 State St (at 12th) **814/453-6932**

CRUISY AREAS

Glenwood Park [AYOR] park on the hill (overlooking the zoo)

Export

EROTICA

Murrysville Video - Adult Mart 6094 William Penn Hwy (Hwy 22) **724/733-2203** *10am-10pm, till midnight Fri-Sat*

Gettysburg

ACCOMMODATIONS

Battlefield B&B [GS,WI,WC,GO] 2264 Emmitsburg Rd (at Ridge Rd) **717/334-8804** *full brkfst, Civil War home*

Greensburg

CRUISY AREAS

Harrison Ave [AYOR] off Otterman St

Harrisburg

INFO LINES & SERVICES

LGBT Community Center Coalition of Central PA 1306 N 3rd St **717/920-9534**

BARS

Bar 704 [M,NH,OC,WC] 704 N 3rd St **717/234-4226** *4pm-2am*

The Brownstone Lounge [MW,NH,F,WC] 412 Forster St (btwn 3rd & 6th) **717/234-7009** *2pm-2am, from noon wknds*

NIGHTCLUBS

Stallions [★M,D,E,K,DS,S,V,WC] 706 N 3rd St (enter rear) **717/232-3060** *7pm-2am*

CRUISY AREAS

Riverfront Park [AYOR] Front & State Sts

Johnstown

NIGHTCLUBS

Lucy's Place [GS,D,K,DS,S] 520 Washington St (near Central Park) **814/539-4448** *6pm-2am, clsd Sun-Mon*

CRUISY AREAS

Central Park [AYOR]

Lancaster

ACCOMMODATIONS

Cameron Estate Inn [GS,F,NS,WC,GO] 1855 Mansion Ln, Mount Joy **717/492-0111**

Lancaster Arts Hotel [GF,F,WC] 300 Harrisburg Ave **717/299-3000, 866/720-2787**

BARS

Tally Ho [MW,D,K,DS,YC] 201 W Orange St (at Water) **717/299-0661** *8pm-2am*

RESTAURANTS

The Loft 201 W Orange St (above Tally Ho bar) **717/299-0661** *lunch and dinner, clsd Sun-Mon, contemporary American/ French*

EROTICA

The Den 53 N Prince St **717/299-1779**

CRUISY AREAS

Lancaster County Park [AYOR]

Long's Park [AYOR] Rte 30 at Harrisburg Pike

Lebanon

EROTICA

Hobbeze Lebanon Adult Gifts 1604 E Cumberland St/ Rte 422 (at 15th Ave) **717/273-6398** *10am-midnight*

CRUISY AREAS

Union Canal Tunnel Park [AYOR]

Milford

ACCOMMODATIONS

Hotel Fauchere [GF,NS,WI,WC] 401 Broad St (at Catharine St) **570/409-1212** *historic boutique hotel, also restaurant & bar*

Montgomery

EROTICA

Adult Playtime Boutique 737 Rte 15 (top of the mountain, near the rest area)) **570/547-2663** *10am-11pm, noon-8pm Sun*

New Hope

see also Lambertville & Sergeantsville, New Jersey

ACCOMMODATIONS

Ash Mill Farm B&B [GF,NS,WI] 5358 York Rd (at Rte 202), Holicong **215/794-5373**

BARS

Havana [GS,F,E,K] 105 S Main St **215/862-9897** *noon-2am*

The Raven [GS,F,E,SW] 385 W Bridge St **215/862-2081, 215/862.3868** *11am-2am, also accommodations, restaurant and shows*

Razz Room [GS,C,F] 6426 Lower York Rd (at the Clarion Hotel & Suites) **888/596-1027** *cabaret, food served*

RESTAURANTS

Karla's 5 W Mechanic St (at Main) **215/862-2612** *noon-11pm, till midnight Fri-Sat, from 11am Sat, full bar till 2am*

New Hope Star Diner [WC] 6522 Lower York Rd **215/862-5575** *6am-11pm*

EROTICA

Le Chateau Exotique 27 W Mechanic St **215/862-3810** *fetishwear*

New Milford

ACCOMMODATIONS

Hillside Campgrounds [★MO,D,SW,N,WI,21+GO] 948 Creek Rd **570/756-2007** *seasonal, campground, cabins, disco Fri-Sat*

Oneida Campground & Lodge [M,D,SW,N,WI,GO] **570/465-7011** *seasonal*

Philadelphia

INFO LINES & SERVICES

Mazzoni Center 1348 Bainbridge St **215/563-0652** *8am-9pm, till 5pm Fri, clsd wknds, dedicated to meeting the unique health and wellness needs of the LGBTQ communities*

William Way LGBT Community Center 1315 Spruce St (at Juniper) **215/732-2220** *11am-10pm, noon-5pm wknds*

ACCOMMODATIONS

Alexander Inn [GS,NS,WI,GO] Spruce (at 12th St) **215/923-3535, 877/253-9466**

The Gables B&B [GS,NS,WI,GO] 4520 Chester Ave **215/662-1918**

The Independent Hotel [GS,WI,WC] 1234 Locust St (at 13th) **215/772-1440**

Morris House Hotel [GF,NS,WI] 225 S 8th St **215/922-2446**

Palomar Philadelphia [GF,WI,WC] 117 S 17th St **215/563-5006, 888/725-1778**

BARS

Bike Stop [M,D,B,L,K] 204-206 S Quince St (btwn 11th & 12th) **215/627-1662** *4pm-2am, from 2pm wknds, cruisy*

Blaze's 2nd Story Loft Bar [M,D,DS,K] 2372 Orthodox St **267/339-1579** *6pm-2am, 3 bars*

Boxers PHL [M] 1330 Walnut St **215/735-2977** *4pm-2am from noon wknds, sports bar*

ICandy [M,D] 254 S 12th St (btwn Locust & Spruce) **267/324-3500** *4pm-2am*

Khyber Pass Pub [GF,F,E,WC] 56 S 2nd St (btwn Market & Chestnut) **215/238-5888** *10am-2am*

L'Etage [GS,D,C] 624 S 6th St (at Bainbridge) **215/592-0656** *7:30pm-1am, till 2am Fri-Sat, clsd Mon, also crepe restaurant downstairs*

North Third [GS,F] 801 N 3rd (at Brown) **215/413-3666** *4pm-2am, from 10am wknd brunch*

Rosewood [M] 1302 Walnut St **215/545-1893** *9pm-2am, from 5pm Fri, clsd Sun-Wed, cosy & elegant, easy way to get into Woodys*

Stir Lounge [MW,NH,D,V] 1705 Chancellor St (at Rittenhouse Sq btwn Walnut & Spruce) **215/732-2700** *4pm-2am*

Tabu Club & Sports Bar [★M,D,E,F,E,K] 254 S 12th St **215/964 -9675** *11am-2am, 3 levels & roof deck*

Tavern on Carmac [MW,D,C,P] 243 S Camac St (at Spruce) **215/545-1102** *5pm-midnight, clsd Tue, also restaurant*

Toasted Walnut [MW,D,F,K] 1316 Walnut St **215/546-8888** *open 4pm, clsd Mon*

U-Bar [★M,NH] 1220 Locust St (at 12th) **215/546-6660** *11am-2am*

Woody's [M,D,CW,F,K,S,WI,YC,WC] 202 S 13th St (at Walnut) **215/545-1893** *4pm-2am, Latin Th*

Nightclubs

Bob & Barbara's Lounge [GS,E,DS] 1509 South St **215/545-4511** *3pm-2am*

Voyeur [M,D,K,C,DS,PC] 1221 St James St (off 13th & Locust) **215/735-5772** *midnight-3am, from 11pm Th-Sat*

Cafes

Capogiro 119 S 13th St (at Sansom) **215/351-0900** *7:30am-11:30pm, till 1am Fri-Sat, gelato*

Capriccio 110 N 16th St (at Benjamin Franklin Pkwy) **215/735-9797** *6:30am-7pm, 8am-8pm wknds*

Green Line Cafe [F,E] 4239 Baltimore Ave (at 43rd) **215/222-3431** *7am-9pm, 8am-6pm Sun*

Restaurants

Cantina Feliz [WC] 424 S Bethlehem Pike, Fort Washington **215/646-1320** *11am-9pm, from 4pm Sat-Sun, till 11pm Sat*

Chef Tony's Kitchen 4320 Megargee St **215/624-7876** *11am-10pm, till 8pm Sat-Sun, classic American*

The Continental 138 Market St (at 2nd) **215/923-6069** *lunch, dinner, wknd brunch, also bar until 2am,*

Geno's Steaks [GO] 1219 S 9th St **215/389-0659** *24hrs, great cheesesteak*

Honey's [BYOB] 800 N 4th St **215/925-1150** *7am-4pm, till 5pm wknds*

Knock 226 S 12th St **215/925-1166** *lunch & dinner, Sun brunch, American, also bar*

Little Nonna's [GO] 1234 Locust (at The Independent Hotel) **215/546-2100** *lunch and dinner, dinner only Sun, casual Italian-American*

Lolita 106 S 13th St (at Sansom) **215/546-7100** *lunch & dinner, upscale Mexican*

Mercato [BYOB] 1216 Spruce St **215/985-2962** *dinner, Italian*

Mixto 1141 Pine St **215/592-0363** *lunch & dinner, brkfst wknds, Latin American*

My Thai 2200 South St (at 22nd) **215/985-1878** *5pm-10pm, full bar*

New Harmony 135 N 9th St (at Cherry) **215/627-4520** *11am-11pm, vegan/Chinese*

Paesano's 1017 S 9th St **215/440-0371** *11am-3pm, till 5pm Fri-Sat, great sandwiches*

Sabrina's 910 Christian St **215/574-1599** *8am-10pm, till 8pm Tue-Th, till 4pm Sun-Mon*

El Vez 121 S 13th St (at Sansom) **267/238-3649** *lunch Mon-Sat, dinner nightly, Sun brunch, full bar*

Entertainment & Recreation

The Walt Whitman House 328 Mickle Blvd, Camden, NJ **856/964-5383** *the last home of America's great & controversial poet, just across the Delaware River*

Bookstores

Big Blue Marble Bookstore [GO] 551 Carpenter Lane **215/844-1870** *10am-6pm, from 11am Mon, till 7pm Th-Fri*

Philly AIDS Thrift @ Giovanni's Room [★] 345 S 12th St (at Pine) **215/923-2960** *11am-8pm,till 9pm Fri-Sat, till 7pm Sun, all proceeds from thrift items to fund local HIV/AIDS organizations*

Retail Shops

Philadelphia AIDS Thrift 710 S 5th St **215/922-3186** *11am-8pm, till 9pm Fri-Sat, till 7pm Sun*

Publications

PGN (Philadelphia Gay News) 215/625-8501 *LGBT newspaper w/ extensive listings*

Gyms & Health Clubs

Optimal Sport 1315 [GO] 1315 Walnut St **215/735-1114**

Men's Clubs

Club Philly [NS,WI,PC] 1220 Chancellor St (at 12th & Walnut) **215/735-7671** *24hrs*

Philly Jacks [MO,18+,PC] 723 Chestnut St (btwn 7th & 8th) **215/618-1519** *5 sex parties per month, club only open during parties; call for dates*

Sansom Street Gym [★MO,V,PC] 2020 Sansom St **267/330-0151** *24hrs*

Erotica

Adonis Cinema Complex 2026 Sansom St (at 20th) **215/557-9319** *24hrs*

Condom Kingdom 437 South St (at 5th) **215/829-1668** *safer sex materials & toys*

Danny's 133 S 13th St (at Walnut) **215/925-5041** *24hrs*

Fantasy Island Adult Books 7363 State Rd **215/332-5454**

Passional Boutique 317 South St **215/829-4986, 877/826-7738** *noon-9pm*

Sexploratorium 317 South St **215/923-1398** *noon-10pm, till 9pm Sun-Tue, workshops and gallery*

Pittsburgh

Info Lines & Services

AA Gay/ Lesbian 412/471-7472 *call for times & location*

Gay/ Lesbian Community Center 210 Grant St **412/422-0114** *9am-9pm, noon-6pm Sun*

Accommodations

Arbors B&B [MO,NS,WI,GO] 745 Maginn St **412/231-4643**

Camp Davis [MW,D,SW] 311 Red Brush Rd, Boyers **724/637-2402** *1 hour from Pittsburgh, cabins & campsites, variety of events*

The Inn on Negley [GF,NS,WI,WC] 703 S Negley Ave (at Elmer St) **412/661-0631**

Morning Glory Inn B&B [GF,WI] 2119 Sarah St **412/431-1707** *in 1862 Italianate-style Victorian townhouse*

The Parador Inn [GF,WI,GO] 939 Western Ave **412/231-4800, 877/540-1443**

The Priory [GF,NS,WI,WC] 614 Pressley St (near Cedar Ave) **412/231-3338, 866/377-4679**

Bars

5801 [★MW,V,WC] 5801 Ellsworth Ave (at Maryland) **412/661-5600** *4pm-2am, from 2pm Sun, also restaurant*

The Backdraft Bar & Grill [GS,F,E,K] 3049 Churchview Ave **412/885-1239** *11am-2am, till midnight Sun*

Blue Moon Bar & Lounge [M,NH,TG,S] 5115 Butler St (in Lawrenceville) **412/781-1119** *5pm-2am, 4pm-1am Mon*

Cattivo [W,D,DS,E,K,F] 146 44th St, Lawrenceville **412/687-2157** *4pm-2am, clsd Sun-Tue,live music*

Cruze Bar [MW,D,E,GO] 1600 Smallman St (at 16th St) **412/471-1400** *4pm-2am, clsd Mon*

Element [MW,WC] 5744 Ellsworth Ave, Shadyside **412/727-8135** *5pm-2am*

Images [M,K,S,V] 965 Liberty Ave (at 10th St) **412/391-9990** *2pm-2am, go-go boys*

PTown [MW,D,K,DS,WI] 4740 Baum Blvd **412/621-0111** *5pm-am*

Real Luck Cafe [MW,NH,F,S,WC,GO] 1519 Penn Ave (at 16th) **412/471-7832** *4pm-2am*

Remedy [GS,NH,D,MR] 5121 Butler St **412/781-6771** *4pm-2am, from 12:30pm Sun, also restaurant upstairs*

There Ultra Lounge [MW,K,WC] 931 Liberty Ave (at Smithfield) **412/642-4435** *3:30pm-2am, from 7:30pm Sat-Sun*

NIGHTCLUBS

941 Saloon [MW,D,K] 941 Liberty Ave (at Smithfield St, 2nd flr) **412/281-5222** *2pm-2am*

The Link [MW,D,F,E,DS,S] 91 Wendel Rd, Herminie **724/446-7717** *7pm-2am, clsd Mon, patio*

Tilden [M,D,PC] 941 Liberty Ave (at Smithfield St, upstairs) **412/391-0804** *after-hours, from midnight Fri-Sat, membership required*

CAFES

Square Cafe [E,GO] 1137 S Braddock Ave **412/244-8002** *7am-3pm, from 8am Sun*

Zeke's Coffee 6012 Penn Ave **724/201-1671** *7am-8pm, clsd wknds*

RESTAURANTS

Dinette 5996 Centre Ave **412/362-0202** *dinner only, clsd Sun-Mon, plates to share, starters & thin-crust pizzas*

Double Wide Grill [E] 2339 E Carson St (at S 24th St) **412/390-1111** *lunch & dinner, wknd brunch, BBQ, plenty veggie/ vegan*

Eleven 1150 Smallman St (at 11th) **412/201-5656** *lunch & dinner, Sun brunch*

Harris Grill 5747 Ellsworth Ave **412/362-5273** *dinner nightly, wknd brunch, full bar*

Kaya 2000 Smallman St (at 20th) **412/261-6565** *lunch & dinner, Latin/ Caribbean, plenty veggie*

NOLA On the Square [E] 24 Market Sq **412/471-9100** *11am-11pm*

OTB Bicycle Cafe 2518 East Carson St (at S 26th) **412/381-3698** *11am-10pm, burgers, plenty veggie, also bar till 2am*

Pamela's Diner [★GO] 60 21st St **412/281-6366** *7am-3pm, from 8am Sun, also 5 other locations in Pittsburgh*

Point Brugge Cafe 401 Hastings (at Reynolds) **412/441-3334** *lunch & dinner, Sun brunch, clsd Mon, Belgian/ European*

Primanti Brothers [★] 46 18th St **412/263-2142** *24hrs, Pittsburgh's iconic sandwich shop, many locations*

Spoon 134 S Highland Ave **412/362-6001** *dinner nightly, Sun brunch, fresh "farm to table" menu, also lounge*

Zenith [WC] 86 S 26th St **412/481-4833** *11:30am-8:30pm, Sun brunch 11am-2pm, clsd Mon-Wed, vegetarian/ vegan, also antiques store*

ENTERTAINMENT & RECREATION

Andy Warhol Museum 117 Sandusky St (at General Robinson) **412/237-8300** *10am-5pm, till 10pm Fri, clsd Mon, is it soup or is it art? see for yourself*

Burgh Bits & Bites Food Tour **412/901-7150** *explore the vivid history & culinary delights of the Steel City*

RETAIL SHOPS

Slacker [WC] 1321 E Carson St (btwn 13th & 14th) **412/381-3911** *noon-9pm, 11am-6pm Sun, magazines, clothing, leather*

Who New? [GO] 5156 Butler St **412/781-0588** *noon-6pm, clsd Mon-Tue, open Sun by chance, vintage modern design*

MEN'S CLUBS

Club Pittsburgh [★WI,PC] 1139 Penn Ave (enter side) **412/471-6790** *24hrs*

EROTICA

Adult Mart 2735 Stroschein Rd (off Rte 22), Monroeville **412/372-5477** *24hrs, 13 miles from Pittsburgh*

Adult Mart 346 Blvd of the Allies **412/261-9119** *8am-2am, 24hrs wknds*

CRUISY AREAS

Schenley Park [AYOR]

Poconos

Accommodations

Rainbow Mountain Resort [MW,D,TG,E,K,SW,WI,GO] **570/223-8484** *also restaurant & bar, DJ Fri-Sat*

The Woods Campground [MW,SW,18+] 845 Vaughn Acres Ln, Lehighton **610/377-9577**

Reading

Bars

The Peanut Bar & Restaurant [GF,NS,WI] 332 Penn St **610/376-8500, 800/515-8500** *11am-11pm, till midnight Fri-Sat, clsd Sun, a Reading landmark!*

Restaurants

Judy's On Cherry 332 Cherry St **610/374-8511** *lunch Tue-Fri, dinner Tue-Sat, clsd Sun-Mon, Mediterranean*

The Ugly Oyster [E] 21 S 5th St (at Cherry) **610/373-6791** *11:30am-2am, clsd Sun, traditional Irish pub*

Cruisy Areas

Mt Penn [AYOR] *btwn pagoda & fire tower & surrounding woodlands*

Scranton

Bars

Twelve Penny Saloon [MW,NH,L,TG,F,K,DS,WC,GO] 3501 Birney Ave, Moosic **570/941-0444** *6pm-2pm, from 4pm wknds*

Cruisy Areas

Court House Square [AYOR]

Shippensburg

Erotica

Lion's Den 8071 Olde Scotland Rd (Penn exit 24, off I-81) **717/530-8032** *24hrs*

State College

Accommodations

The Atherton Hotel [GF,WI,WC] 125 S Atherton St (at College Ave) **814/231-2100**

Bars

Chumley's [★M,NH,WC] 108 W College **814/238-4446** *5pm-2am, from 6pm Sun*

Nightclubs

Indigo [GS,D,V,YC] 112 W College Ave (at Hotel State College) **814/234-1031** *9pm-2am, clsd Mon-Wed, "Alternative" night Sun*

Cruisy Areas

The Wall [AYOR] 100 blk of College Ave

Sunbury

Cruisy Areas

Market St & Park [AYOR] downtown

Uniontown

Cruisy Areas

Dunlap Creek Park [AYOR]

West Chester

Cruisy Areas

Court House Wall [AYOR] *late nights*

Wilkes-Barre

Nightclubs

Heat [GS,D,DS] 69-71 N Main St (at E Union St) **570/266-8952** *8pm-2am, clsd Mon-Wed*

Erotica

Cinema 309 [AYOR] Rte 309 (Blackman St exit, off I-81) **570/822-2694** *about a half mile on Route 309*

Cruisy Areas

Nesbitt Park [AYOR] Susquehanna River (N of Pierce St bridge), Kingston

Williamsport

Cruisy Areas

Scenic Overlook [AYOR] 3 miles S, on Rte 15 N

Rhode Island

Newport

Info Lines & Services

Sobriety First 135 Pelham St (at Channing Memorial Church) **401/438-8860** *8pm Fri*

Accommodations

Architect's Inn [GF,NS,WI,GO] 2 Sunnyside Pl **401/845-2547** *fireplaces, near beach, shops & restaurants*

Francis Malbone House Inn [GF,NS,WI,WC] 392 Thames St (at Memorial Blvd) **401/846-0392, 800/846-0392**

Hilltop Inn [GF,NS,WI,GO] 2 Kay St **401/619-0054**

Hydrangea House Inn [★GS,NS,WI,GO] 16 Bellevue Ave **401/846-4435, 800/945-4667** *full brkfst, near beach*

Restaurants

Whitehorse Tavern 26 Marlborough St (at Farewell) **401/849-3600** *lunch & dinner, Sun brunch, upscale dining, patio*

Erotica

Newport Video 228 JT Connell Hwy **401/847-4480** *10am-11pm, till midnight Fri-Sat, arcade*

North Kingstown

Erotica

Amazing 6774 Post Rd/ Rte 1 **401/885-0209** *11am-9pm, till 11pm Fri, noon-5pm Sun*

Providence

Info Lines & Services

Brothers in Sobriety 372 Wayland Ave (at Community Church) **401/438-8860, 800/439-8860** *7:30pm Sat*

Accommodations

The Dean [GS,F,K] 122 Fountain St **401/45-3236** *historical building has been elegantly transformed into a 52-room hotel*

Edgewood Manor [GF,NS,WI] 232 Norwood Ave (at Broad) **401/781-0099** *1905 Greek Revival mansion*

Hotel Dolce Villa [GS] 63 De Pasquale Square (at Atwells) **401/383-7031**

The Hotel Providence [GS,F,WI] 139 Mathewson **401/861-8000, 800/861-8990**

NYLO Hotel [GS,WI,WC] 400 Knight St, Warwick **401/734-4460** *also restaurant & bar*

Renaissance Providence Hotel [GS,F,NS,WI,WC] 5 Avenue of the Arts (at Francis) **401/919-5000**

Bars

Alleycat [MW,NH,V,GO] 17 Snow St (at Washington) **401/272-6369** *3pm-1am, till 2am Fri-Sat*

The Point Tavern [GS,F] 302 Wickenden St **401/751-4900** *5pm-1am, from noon wknds*

The Providence Eagle [M,B,L,WC] 124 Snow St **401/421-1447** *2pm-1am, till 2am Fri, from noon wknds*

The Stable [MW,NH,V,WC] 125 Washington (at Mathewson) **401/272-6950** *2pm-1am, till 2am Fri-Sat, from noon Sat-Sun*

Nightclubs

Dark Lady [M,D,K,DS,V] 17 Snow St **401/272-6369** *9pm-1am, till 2am Fri-Sat, theme nights*

EGO Providence [M,D,DS] 73 Richmond St **401/383-1208** *check www.egopvd.com for events*

Mirabar [M,D,S,WC] 15 Elbow St **401/331-6761** *3pm-1am, till 2am Fri-Sat, male dancers*

Platforms Dance Club [GS,D,18+] 165 Poe St **401/781-3121** *8pm-2am*

Cafes

Coffee Exchange 207 Wickenden St **401/273-1198** *6:30am-11pm, deck*

Pastiche Fine Desserts 92 Spruce St **401/861-5190** *8:30am-11pm, 10am-10pm Sun, clsd Mon*

White Electric Coffee 711 Westminster **401/453-3007** *7am-6:30pm, 8am-4pm Sat, 9am-4pm Sun*

RESTAURANTS

Al Forno [★] 577 S Main St **401/273-9760** *dinner only, clsd Sun-Mon*

Bacaro 262 S Water St **401/751-3700** *dinner only, clsd Sun-Mon, Cicchetti (small plates) and wine bar*

Bravo Brasserie 123 Empire St **401/490-5112** *lunch Tue-Sat, dinner nightly, Sun brunch*

Cafe' Paragon 234 Thayer St **401/331-6200** *11am-1am, European Bistro/Café style atmosphere with a full bar*

Caffe Dolce Vita 59 DePasquale Plaza (at Spruce St) **401/331-8240** *8am-1am, till 2am wknds, wknd brunch, authentic Italian cafe, patio*

Camille's 71 Bradford St (at Atwell's Ave) **401/751-4812** *lunch & dinner, clsd Sun, full bar*

CAV 14 Imperial Pl **401/751-9164** *11am-10pm, till 1am Fri, wknd brunch*

Don José Tequilas Mexican 351 Atwells Ave **401/454-8951** *11:30-11pm, till 1am Fri-Sat*

Fellini Pizzeria [★GO] 166 Wickenden St **401/751-6737**

Julian's 318 Broadway (at Vinton) **401/861-1770** *9am-11pm, bar open till 1am*

Mill's Tavern 101 N Main St **401/272-3331** *dinner nightly*

Nicks on Broadway 500 Broadway **401/421-0286** *8:30-3pm & 5:30-11pm, clsd Mon-Tue*

ENTERTAINMENT & RECREATION

WaterFire Waterplace Park **401/272-3111** *May-Oct only, bonfire installations along the Providence River at sunset*

BOOKSTORES

Books on the Square 471 Angell St (at Wayland) **401/331-9097, 888/669-9660** *9am-9pm, 10am-6pm Sun, some LGBT*

PUBLICATIONS

Options Magazine 401/724-5428 *LGBT community magazine*

MEN'S CLUBS

Club Body Center [WI,PC] 257 Weybosset St, 2nd flr (at Richmond) **401/274-0298** *24hrs*

Gay Mega-Plex [PC,WC,GO] 257 Allens Ave (S of Public St) **401/780-8769** *24hrs*

EROTICA

Adult Video News 255 Allens Ave (at Bay) **401/785-1324** *9am-1am, till 3am Th-Sat, arcade*

Mister Sister 268 Wickenden St **401/421-6969** *fetishwear, sex toys, classes*

CRUISY AREAS

State House Circle Road [AYOR] *nights*

Warwick

CRUISY AREAS

Salter Grove Park [AYOR] Narragansett Pkwy (off Post Rd)

Westerly

CRUISY AREAS

Misquamicut State Beach [AYOR] go left before the bridge (at Fenway Beach)

SOUTH CAROLINA

Blacksburg

EROTICA

BedTyme Stories 145 Simper Rd (I-85, exit 100) **864/839-0007**

Bowman

EROTICA

Lion's Den 2269 Homestead Rd (exit 159, off I-26) **803/829-1781** *24hrs*

Charleston

INFO LINES & SERVICES

Acceptance Group (Gay AA) 45 Moultrie St (at St Barnabus Lutheran Church) **843/723-9633 (AA#)** *7pm Mon, Th & Sat*

Accommodations

Aloft Charleston Airport & Convention Center [GF,SW,WI,WC] 4875 Tanger Outlet Blvd (at International Blvd), N Charleston **843/566-7300, 877/462-5638**

Belmond's Charleston Place [GF,F] 205 Meeting St **843/722-4900, 888/635-2350** *famous for its traditional southern hospitality*

Bars

Dudley's on Ann [M,NH,K,18+,GO] 42 Ann St (at King St) **843/577-6779** *4pm-2am*

Nightclubs

Deja Vu II [W,D,F,E,DS,K,S,PC,WC,GO] 4628 Spruill Ave **843/406-5545** *5pm-2pm Th, from 8pm Fri-Sat, clsd Sun-Wed*

Cafes

Bear E Patch [WC] 1980-A Ashley River Rd **843/766-6490** *7am-9pm, 8am-8pm Sat, clsd Sun*

Restaurants

492 [E] 492 King St **843/203-6338** *5pm-10pm, later on Fri-Sat, 10am-3pm Sun,clsd Mon, swanky New American spot offering a daily-changing menu in a historic building from the late 1800s, must try sourdough sticky buns*

82 Queen 82 Queen St **843/723-7591** *lunch & dinner, Sun brunch, Lowcountry cuisine*

Fat Hen [★E,BW] 3140 Maybank Hwy, St Johns Island **843/559-9090** *dinner nightly, Sun brunch, French bistro, seafood*

Fig [WC] 232 Meeting St (near Hasell) **843/805-5900** *5:30pm-10:30pm, till 11pm Fri-Sat, clsd Sun, local ingredients*

High Cotton 199 E Bay St **843/724-3815** *dinner nightly, brunch wknds, Southern cuisine, full bar*

Hominy Grill 843/937-0930 *7:30am-3pm, from 9am wknds, great brkfst*

JohnKing Grill & Bar 428 King St (at John) **843/965-5252** *11am-2am*

Lewis Barbecue 464 N Nassau St **843/805-9500** *11am-10pm, clsd Mon, beef ribs that literally melt in your mouth*

Melvin's Legendary Bar-B-Que 538 Folly Rd **843/762-0511** *10:30am-9pm, clsd Sun*

The Park Cafe 843/410-1070 *7am-3am, from 9am wknds, fresh and tasty*

Prohibition 547 King St **843/793-2964** *4pm-2am from noon Fri, 11am Sat & 10am Sun, rustic-chic Modern American food with creative cocktails & a Jazz Age theme*

Virginia's On King 412 King St **843/735-5800** *7am-9pm, till 10pm Fri-Sat, 10am-3pm Sun, great brunch*

Entertainment & Recreation

Historic Charleston Foundation 40 E Bay St **843/723-1623** *call for info on city walking tours (March-April only)*

Old South Carriage Co [R] 12 Anson St **843/723-9712** *9am-7pm, till 9pm Fri-Sat, happy-golucky well cared for horses, some gay drivers*

The Real Rainbow Row 18 Anson St **843/722-8687** *walking tour of Charleston's rich, gay history and current LGBTQ community*

Cruisy Areas

Folly Beach [AYOR] western tip of island (make a right at the island's only traffic light & drive all the way to county park)

West Ashley Park [AYOR]

Columbia

Info Lines & Services

Harriet Hancock GLBT Community Center 1108 Woodrow St **803/771-7713** *community info, resources, HIV programs & more*

Primary Purpose Gay/ Lesbian AA 5220 Clemson (in the house behind St Martin's Church) **803/254-5301(AA#)** *6:30 Tue, 7pm Fri & Sun*

BARS

Art Bar [GS,D,K] 1211 Park St **803/929-0198** *5pm-2am, from 8pm wknds, live music*

Capital Club [M,NH,P,PC,WC] 1002 Gervais St **803/256-6464** *5pm-2am*

NIGHTCLUBS

PTS 1109 [MW,D,MR,TG,S,WI,PC,GO] 1109 Assembly St (at Gervais St) **803/253-8900** *5pm-2am, till 6am Fri, till 3am Sat-Sun*

CRUISY AREAS

Senate Street [AYOR] near the university

Greenville

BOOKSTORES

Out of Bounds 21 S Pleasantburg Dr **864/239-0106** *2pm- 8pm, till 6pm Sun, from 11am Fri-Sat*

Hilton Head

ACCOMMODATIONS

Sonesta Resort Hilton Head Island [GF,F,SW] 130 Shipyard Dr **843/842-2400**

CRUISY AREAS

Coligny Circle Beach [AYOR] S of the Holiday Inn (at the end of Pope Ave)

Pinckney State Park [AYOR] Hwy 278 *days*

Leesville

EROTICA

Lion's Den 2662 Ben Franklin (exit 139, off I-20) **803/657-5921** *24hrs*

Myrtle Beach

ACCOMMODATIONS

Rosewood Manor House B&B, Wedding Venue [GS,WI,GO] 900 Main St, Marion **336/312-9260** *1895 Anabellum private home, 1 hr from Mrytle Beach & 2.5 hrs to Charlston, recently updated interior with beautiful furnishings and decor*

BARS

Club Ultra Pulse [MW,D,F,K,DS,WC,GO] 2701 S Kings Hwy **843/315-0019** *4pm-4am*

St George [MW,K] 503 8th Ave N **843/712-1964** *4pm-4am*

RESTAURANTS

Carolina Roadhouse 4617 N Kings Hwy **843/497-9911** *11am-10pm*

Mr Fish 3401 N Kings Hwy **843/839-3474** *11am-9:30pm, full bar*

Sticky Fingers Smokehouse [WI,WC] 2461 Coastal Grand Cir **843/839-7427** *a chain, but a good one*

ENTERTAINMENT & RECREATION

Hurl Rock Park 82 Ave N (at Ocean Blvd , next to the Marriott) *lots of gays and lesbians Fri-Sun*

RETAIL SHOPS

Kilgor Trouts Music & More 708 8th Ave N **843/445-2800** *1am-8pm, noon-5pm Sun, gay pride items*

CRUISY AREAS

Huntington Beach State Park [AYOR] Hwy 17 S *Mon-Fri*

Hurl Rock Park [AYOR] at 21st Ave S (south end)

Rock Hill

BARS

Hideaway [MW,NH,K,DS,PC] 405 Baskins Rd **803/328-6630** *8pm-2am Th-Sat*

Spartanburg

NIGHTCLUBS

Club South 29 [M,D] 9112 Greenville Hwy (off I-85 exit 66 or I-26 exit 21a) **864/574-6087** *9pm-4am Fri-Sat only*

SOUTH DAKOTA

Murdo

ACCOMMODATIONS

Iversen Inn [GF,WI,GO] 108 E 5th St (on I-90 Business Loop) **605/669-2452**

Piedmont

ACCOMMODATIONS

Camp Michael B&B [M,NS,GO] 1683 Piedmont Meadows Rd **605/209-3503**

Pierre

CRUISY AREAS

LaFramboise Island [AYOR] off the causeway

Rapid City

INFO LINES & SERVICES

The Black Hills Center for Equality **605/348-3244** *call for hours, clsd Sun, LGBT resource center*

Sioux Falls

INFO LINES & SERVICES

The Center for Equality **605/610-9206** *support groups, counseling, library & more*

NIGHTCLUBS

Club David [GS,D,K,DS] 214 W 10th St (btwn Main & Dakota) **605/274-0700** *4:30pm-2am, patio*

EROTICA

Romantix Adult Superstore 311 N Dakota Ave (btwn 6th & 7th) **605/332-9316**

CRUISY AREAS

Sherman Park [AYOR] Kiwanis (btwn 12th & 26th Sts)

TENNESSEE

Bucksnort

EROTICA

Miranda's [GO] 4970 Hwy 230 **931/729-2006** *8am-3am, clsd Sun*

Chattanooga

NIGHTCLUBS

Alan Gold's [★MW,D,F,DS,YC,WC] 1100 McCallie Ave (at National) **423/629-8080** *4:30pm-3am*

Images [MW,D,F,DS,WC] 6005 Lee Hwy **423/855-8210** *5pm-3am Th-Sun, also restaurant*

EROTICA

Miranda's [GO] 2025 Broadway **423/266-5956** *8am-3am, from noon Sun, largest selection of LGBT products in TN*

Clarksville

EROTICA

Miranda's [GO] 19 Crossland Ave **931/648-0365** *8am-11:45pm, clsd Sun, largest selection of LGBT products in TN*

CRUISY AREAS

Fairground Park [AYOR]

Cleveland

BARS

Tbow's Tavern [GS,D,F,E,GO] 1585 Spring Place Rd SE **423/790-7403** *5pm-2am, clsd Sun-Mon*

Clifton

ACCOMMODATIONS

Bear Inn Resort [GS,WI,GO] 2250 Billy Nance Hwy **931/676-5552**

Gatlinburg

ACCOMMODATIONS

Big Creek Outdoors [GS,WC] 5019 Rag Mtn Rd, Hartford **423/487-5742, 423/487-3490** *cabins, camping, horseback riding*

Christopher Place, An Intimate Resort [GS,SW,NS,WC] 1500 Pinnacles Wy, Newport **423/623-6555** *full brkfst*

Mountain Vista Cabins [MW,NS,WI] 1805 Shady Grove Rd (at Old Birds Creek Rd), Sevierville **865/712-9897** *hot tub*

Stonecreek Cabins [GS,NS,GO] **865/429-0400** *private Smoky Mtn cabins*

Greeneville

Accommodations

Timberfell Lodge [MO,F,SW,N,NS,GO] 2240 Van Hill Rd (exit 36, off I-81) **423/234-0833, 800/437-0118** *also camping & RV hookups, full brkfst, hot tub*

Jackson

Erotica

Miranda's 186 Providence Rd, Denmark **731/424-7226** *8am-midnight, clsd Sun*

Cruisy Areas

Muse Park [AYOR]

Johnson City

Nightclubs

My Secret Closet [M,D,K] 2910 N Bristol Hwy (inside New Beginnings) **423/282-4446** *10pm-3am Wed-Sat only*

New Beginnings [★M,D,F,DS,WC] 2910 N Bristol Hwy **423/282-4446** *9pm-2am, from 8pm Fri-Sat, clsd Sun-Mon*

Kingsport

Cruisy Areas

Sullivan St [AYOR] near library

Knoxville

Nightclubs

Club XYZ [MW,D,DS,K] 1215 N Central **865/637-4999** *5:30pm-3am, from 9pm Sat, from 7pm Sun*

The Edge Knox [MW,D,F,K,DS,WC] 7211 Kingston Pike SW (at Cheshire Dr) **865/602-2094** *5pm-2:30am*

Erotica

Town & Country News 6927 Clinton Hwy **865/947-9153** *10am-midnight, clsd Sun*

West Knoxville News 5011 Kingston Pike **865/588-1972** *10am-midnight*

Cruisy Areas

The Block [AYOR] 100 Northview Dr (in Bearden area W of UT) *10pm-5am every night, hottest Fri-Sat after bars close*

Downtown [AYOR] btwn post office & library

IC King Park [AYOR] off Alcoa Hwy

Sharps Ridge [AYOR] off N Broadway

The Square [AYOR] intersection of Church, Market, Walnut & Union Sts

Memphis

Info Lines & Services

AA Intergroup 3540 Summer Ave #104 **901/726-6750**

Memphis Gay/ Lesbian Community Center 892 S Cooper (at Nelson) **901/278-6422** *2pm-9pm Mon-Fri*

Accommodations

Madison Hotel [GF,SW,NS] 79 Madison Ave (at Center Ln) **901/333-1200, 866/446-3674**

Talbot Heirs Guesthouse [GF,NS] 99 S 2nd St (btwn Union & Peabody Pl) **901/527-9772, 800/955-3956** *suites w/ kitchens, funky decor*

Bars

Dru's Place [W,NH,D,K,DS,BYOB] 1474 Madison (at McNeil) **901/275-8082** *1pm-midnight, till 2am Fri-Sat, beer & set-ups only*

Mollie Fontaine Lounge [GS,F] 679 Adams Ave (at Orleans) **901/524-1886** *5pm-2am, clsd Sun-Tue*

P&H Cafe [GS,F,E,K,BW,WC] 1532 Madison (at Adeline) **901/726-0906** *3pm-3am, from 5pm Sat, clsd Sun, dive bar*

Pumping Station [M,D,WC] 1382 Poplar (at Cleveland) **901/272-7600** *4pm-3am, from 3pm wknds, courtyard*

Cafes

Java Cabana [E,WI,WC] 2170 Young Ave (at Cooper) **901/272-7210** *6:30am-10pm, 9am-midnight Fri-Sat, noon-10pm Sun, clsd Mon, also art gallery*

Otherlands Coffee Bar [★F,E,WI,WC] 641 S Cooper (at Central) **901/278-4994** *7am-8pm, also gift shop*

Restaurants

Automatic Slim's Tonga Club [WC] 83 S 2nd St (at Union) **901/525-7948** *lunch & dinner, Sun brunch, Caribbean & Southwestern, full bar*

Cafe Eclectic 603 N McLean Blvd (at Faxon Ave) **901/725-1718** *6am-10pm, 9am-3pm Sun; also Harbortown location*

Cafe Society [WC] 212 N Evergreen St (at Poplar) **901/722-2177** *lunch Mon-Fri, dinner nightly, full bar*

Leonard's Pit Barbecue 5465 Fox Plaza Dr (at Mt Moriah Rd) **901/360-1963** *11am-9pm, till 2:30pm Sun-Wed*

Molly's La Casita 2006 Madison Ave (at N Morrison St) **901/726-1873** *lunch & dinner, Mexican*

Restaurant Iris [WC] 2146 Monroe Ave (at Cooper) **901/590-2828** *dinner Mon-Sat, French/ Creole, upscale*

RP Tracks 3547 Walker Ave (at Brister) **901/327-1471** *lunch & dinner, open till 3am, burgers, BBQ tofu*

Tsunami [WC] 928 S Cooper (at Young) **901/274-2556** *dinner only, clsd Sun, Pacific rim cuisine*

Entertainment & Recreation

Center for Southern Folklore [F] 119 S Main St (at Peabody Pl) **901/525-3655** *11am-6pm, from 2pm wknds, open later for shows, live music, gallery*

Graceland 3734 Elvis Presley Blvd **901/332-3322, 800/238-2000** *no visit to Memphis would be complete w/out a trip to see The King*

Memphis Rock 'N Roll Tours **901/359-3102** *historical tour of Memphis music scene*

Retail Shops

Inz & Outz [WC,GO] 1632 Union Ave **901/728-6535** *10am-8pm, noon-6pm Sun, pride items, books*

Erotica

Fantasy Zone [WC] 2532 N Watkins (at Overton Crossing) **901/357-8808** *9am-11pm, clsd Sun*

Romantix Adult Superstore 2220 E Brooks Rd **901/396-9050**

Romantix Airport Books 2214 Brooks Rd E (at Airways) **901/345-0657**

Nashville

Info Lines & Services

AA Gay/ Lesbian **615/831-1050** *call for info*

Accommodations

The Big Bungalow B&B [GF,E,NS,WI] 618 Fatherland St (at 7th) **615/256-8375** *full brkfst, live music, massage available*

Blythewood Inn B&B [GS,WI,WC] 109 Blythewood Drive, Columbia **931/982-0907** *spacious antebellum home constructed 1857-1859 in French Colonial Style Architecture just 45 minutes south of Nashville*

Hutton Hotel [GF,WI,WC] 1808 West End Ave (at 19th Ave) **615/340-9333**

Whispering Oaks Retreat Center [M,SW,N,WI,GO] 926 Walker Rd, Hampshire **931/709-1192**

Bars

Beyond the Edge [GF,F] 112 S 11th St **615/226-3343** *11am-2am, sports bar*

Canvas Lounge [M,D,K] 1707 Church St **615/320-8656** *4pm-3am*

The Patterson House [GS,F] 1711 Division St **615/636-7724** *5pm-1am, till 3am Th-Sat, great speakeasy vibe*

Stirrup Nashville [M,NH,MR,F,WC] 1529 4th Ave S (at Mallory) **615/782-0043** *4pm-3am, from noon wknds, patio*

Trax [M,NH,K,WI] 1501 Ensley Blvd (at Carney) **615/742-8856** *noon-3am*

Tribe [★MW,F,E,V,WC,GO] 1517 Church St (at 15th Ave S) **615/329-2912** *4pm-midnight, till 2am wknds, upscale, full restaurant*

Nightclubs

Bluebird Cafe [★GF,E] 4104 Hillsboro Pike (nr Warfield Dr) **615/383-1461** *live country music venue*

Play Nashville [M,D,MR,TG,E,DS,18+,WC] 1519 Church St (at 16th Ave) **615/322-9627** *9pm-3am, clsd Sun-Tue*

Cafes

Bongo Java [E,F] 2007 Belmont Blvd **615/385-5282** *7am-10pm, deck*

Fido [F] 1812 21st Ave S **615/777-3436** *7am-11pm*

Grins Vegetarian Cafe 2421 Vanderbilt Pl (at 25th Ave) **615/322-8571** *7am-9pm, till 3pm Fri, clsd wknds*

Restaurants

Battered & Fried [WC] 1008 Woodland St (at S 10th) **615/226-9283** *lunch & dinner, seafood, full bar, also Wave sushi bar*

Cafe Coco [E,BW] 210 Louise Ave (at State) **615/321-2626** *7am-midnight, 24hrs Wed-Sun, patio*

Calypso Cafe 3307 Charlotte Ave **615/321-3878** *11am-9pm, Caribbean*

Pancake Pantry 1796 21st Ave S (at Wedgewood Ave) **615/383-9333** *6am-3pm, till 4pm wknds, popular for brkfst*

Sky Blue Coffeehouse & Bistro 700 Fatherland St (at S 7th St) **615/770-7097** *brkfst & lunch*

Sole Mio [WC] 311 3rd Ave S **615/256-4013** *11am-10pm, till 11pm Fri-Sat, clsd Mon, Italian*

The Standard at the Smith House [R,WC] 167 Rosa Parks Ave (at Charlotte) **615/254-1277** *dinner Tue-Sat, clsd Sun-Mon, the only grand townhouse remaining in downtown Nashville*

Suzy Wong's House of Yum [GO] 1515 Church St (at 15th Ave S) **615/329-2913** *5pm-11pm, from 11am Sun*

Yellow Porch [WC] 734 Thompson Ln (at Bransford Ave) **615/386-0260** *lunch & dinner, clsd Sun, fresh Southern cuisine*

Entertainment & Recreation

NashTrash Tours [R] tours leave from the Farmers Market (900 8th Ave N) **615/226-7300** *campy tours of Nashville w/ the Jugg Sisters*

Publications

Out & About Newspaper **615/596-6210**

Erotica

Lion's Den 2807 Nolensville Pike **615/254-8891** *24hrs*

Miranda's [GO] 822 5th Ave S **615/256-1310** *8am-3am, from noon Sun, largest selection of LGBT products in TN*

Cruisy Areas

J Percy Priest Dam [AYOR]

TEXAS

Abilene

Erotica

Midnight Video 3305 E Hwy 80 **325/672-2000** *24hrs, more gay Wed*

Cruisy Areas

Kirby Park [AYOR]

Amarillo

Bars

212 Club [MW,NH,D,DS,WC] 212 SW 6th Ave (at Harrison) **806/372-7997** *4pm-2am*

R&R [GF,NH,WC,GO] 701 S Georgia St **806/342-9000** *4pm-2am*

Restaurants

Furrbie's [GO] 210 W 6th Ave **806/220-0841** *11am-7pm, till 3pm Sat, till 4pm Mon-Tue, clsd Sun, comfort food*

Erotica

Fantasy Gifts & Video 440 N Lakeside Dr **806/372-6500** *10am-11pm, till 1am Fri-Sat, noon-8pm Sun*

Arlington

see also Dallas & Fort Worth

Info Lines & Services

Tarrant County Lesbian/ Gay Alliance 817/877-5544

Nightclubs

The 1851 Club [MW,D,K,DS,V,WC] 931 W Division **817/642-5554** *3pm-2am*

Austin

Info Lines & Services

Lambda AA (Live & Let Live) [NS,WC] 6809 Guadalupe St (at Galano Club) **512/444-0071** *6:30pm & 8pm daily, 10am Sat, 11am Sun*

Q 2906 Medical Arts **512/420-8557** *2pm-10pm Tue-Sat, support & information for GBTQI men 18-29*

Accommodations

Austin Motel [GS,SW,WI] 1220 S. Congress Ave **512/441-1157** *great location, pets ok*

Brava House [GF,NS,WI] 1108 Blanco St (at W 12th) **512/478-5034** *close to downtown & 6th Street*

Crowne Plaza Hotel Austin [GF] 6121 North IH 35 **512/323-5466**

Hotel Saint Cecilia [GF,SW,WC] 112 Academy Dr **512/852-2400**

Hotel San Jose [★GS,SW,NS,WC,GO] 1316 S Congress Ave **512/852-2350, 800/574-8897**

Hotel Van Zandt [GF,F,SW] 605 Davis St **512/542-5300 877/202-2191** *in the thick of the City's hippest nightlife*

Kimber Modern [GS,WI,WO] 110 The Circle **512/912-1046** *Egyptian cotton sheets, all natural latex rubber queen beds, distinctive glass bathroom*

Mt Gainor Inn B&B [GS,NS,WI] 2390 Prochnow Rd (at Mt Gainor Rd), Dripping Springs **512/858-0982, 888/644-0982** *early 20th century German farmhouse*

Park Lane Guest House [GS,SW,GO] 221 Park Ln (at Drake) **512/447-7460, 800/492-8827** *full brkfst, also cottage*

Robin's Nest [GF,NS,WI] 1010 Stewart Cove **512/266-3413** *on Lake Travis, pets ok*

South Congress Hotel [★GF,F,SW] 1603 S Congress Ave **512/920-6405** *cool hotel*

Bars

'Bout Time II [MW,NH,D,TG,K,WI,WC] 6607 I-35 N **512/419-9192** *noon-3am*

Casino El Camino [GF,NH,F,WI,WC] 517 E 6th St (at Red River) **512/469-9330** *4pm-2am, psychedelic punk jazz lounge, great burgers*

Cheer Up Charlie's [MW,NH,E,F] 900 Red River *4pm-2am, live bands, shows*

The Iron Bear [M,B] 121 W 8th St **512/482-8993** *3pm-2am*

The Jackalope [GS,F] 404 E 6th **512/472-3663** *11am-2am, dive bar*

Nightclubs

The Belmont [GF] 305 W 6th St **512/457-0300** *live music venue*

Elysium [GS,D,A] 705 Red River (7th St) **512/478-2979** *9:30pm-2am, '80s Sun, '90s Tue, rest of the week goth, industrial & electronica club*

Highland Lounge [★MW,D,WC] 404 Colorado **512/522-4044** *7pm-2am*

Oilcan Harry's [★M,D,K,S,DS,18+,WI,WC] 211 W 4th St (btwn Lavaca & Colorado) **512/320-8823** *2pm-2am, patio*

Rain [M,D,K,S,WC] 217-B W 4th St (at Colorado St) **512/494-1150** *4pm-2am*

Cafes

Austin Java Cafe [F] 1608 Barton Springs Rd (at Kinney Ave) **512/482-9450** *7am-11pm, from 8am Sat-Sun; also 300 W 2nd St, 512/481-9400*

Bouldin Creek Coffeehouse [F] 1900 S 1st St **512/416-1601** *7am-midnight, from 9am wknds, vegetarian; occasional live music*

Joe's Bakery & Coffee Shop [WC] 2305 E 7th St (at Morelos & Northwestern) **512/472-0017** *6am-3pm, clsd Mon, Tex-Mex*

Spider House Cafe & Ballroom [E] 2908 Fruth St (at West Dr) **512/480-9562** *10am-2am, full bar, patio*

Restaurants

Changos 3023 Guadalupe **512/480-8226** *11am-8pm, taqueria*

Chez Nous [WC] 510 Neches St **512/473-2413** *lunch Tue-Fri, dinner nightly, clsd Mon*

Chuy's [WC] 1728 Barton Springs Rd **512/474-4452** *11am-10pm, till 11pm Fri-Sat, Tex-Mex, full bar*

Corazon at Castle Hill [WC] 1101 W 5th St (at Baylor) **512/476-0728** *lunch weekdays & dinner nightly, clsd Sun*

Eastside Cafe [BW,WC] 2113 Manor Rd (at Breeze Terrace) **512/476-5858** *11:30am-9:30pm, 10am-10pm wknds*

Fonda San Miguel 2330 W North Loop (at Hancock Rd) **512/459-4121** *dinner only, popular Sun brunch, Mexican, full bar*

Guero's [E] 1412 S Congress (at Elizabeth) **512/447-7688** *11am-11pm, from 8am wknds, great Mexican & people-watching, outdoor seating, live music outdoors on wknds*

Jo's Hot Coffee & Good Food [E,WC,GO] 1300 S Congress Ave (at James) **512/444-3800** *7am-9pm; also 242 W 2nd St, 512/469-9003*

Mother's Cafe & Garden [★BW,WC] 4215 Duval St (at 43rd) **512/451-3994** *11:15am-10pm, from 10am wknds, vegetarian*

Mr Natural 1901 E Cesar Chavez St **512/477-5228** *8am-8pm, vegetarian/vegan*

Polvos [WC] 2004 S 1st St (at Johanna) **512/441-5446** *7am-11pm, Mexican, outdoor seating*

Santa Rita Cantina 1206 W 38th St **512/419-7482** *lunch & dinner, wknd brunch*

Threadgill's [E] 6416 N Lamar **512/451-5440** *10am-10pm, till 9pm Sun, great chicken-fried steak; also 301 W Riverside Dr, 512/472-9304*

Wink [WC] 1014 N Lamar Blvd **512/482-8868** *dinner nightly, clsd Sun, upscale, also wine bar*

Zocalo Cafe 1000 W Lynn **512/472-8226** *11am-10pm, from 10am wknds, Mexican*

Entertainment & Recreation

Barton Springs [N] Barton Springs Rd (in Zilker Park) **512/867-3080** *natural swimming hole*

Bat Colony Congress Ave Bridge (at Barton Springs Dr) *colony of bats that flies out from under this bridge every evening March-Oct*

Hippy Hollow Park [N] *gay hangout*

Bookstores

Bookpeople 603 N Lamar Blvd (at 6th) **512/472-5050** *9am-11pm*

MonkeyWrench Books 110 E North Loop **512/407-6925** *noon-6pm,till 4pm Sat, till 8pm Sun,, independent, radical bookstore*

Retail Shops

Tapelenders [GO] 1114 W 5th St #501 (in back) **512/472-0844** *10am-10pm, till midnight Fri-Sat, LGBT*

Publications

Austin Chronicle 512/454-5766 *has extensive online gay guide (check out www.austinchronicle.com)*

Gyms & Health Clubs

Hyde Park Gym 4125 Guadalupe (at 41st St) **512/524-0450** *5am-10pm, 7am-7pm Sat, 8am-7pm Sun*

Milk + Honey Spa 100A Guadalupe St **512/236-1115** *9am-9pm*

Erotica

Adult Video Megaplexxx 7111 S Ih 35 **512/442-5430** *24hrs, arcade*

Forbidden Fruit 108 E North Loop **512/453-8090** *11am-7pm, till 9pm Fri-Sat, noon-6pm Sun*

New Video 7901 S IH 35 **512/280-1142** *24hrs, arcade*

Cruisy Areas

Hippie Hollow-Lake Travis [AYOR]

Bryan

Bars

Revolution Cafe & Bar [GF,NH,TG,F,E,WI,WC] 211 B S Main St (at 27th) **979/823-4044** *6pm-2am, from 8pm Sun-Mon, from 4pm Fri*

Nightclubs

Halo Bar [MW,D,K,DS,V,18+,WC] 121 N Main St (at William J Bryan Pkwy) **979/823-6174** *9:30pm-2am Th-Sat*

Corpus Christi

Info Lines & Services

Clean & Serene AA 3026 S Staples (at All Saints Episcopal Church in Pantry Building behind church) **361/992-8911, 866/672-7029** *8pm Fri*

Accommodations

Anthony's By The Sea [GS,SW,WI,NS,WC,GO] 732 S Pearl St, Rockport **361/729-6100, 800/480-2557**

Port Aransas Inn [GS,SW,WI,WC] 1500 S 11th St (at Ave G), Port Aransas **361/749-5937**

Bars

The Hidden Door [M,NH,D,DS,WC,GO] 802 S Staples St (at Coleman) **361/882-5002** *noon-2am, patio, also the Loft piano bar Fri-Sun*

Crawford

Accommodations

Homestead at 3218 [MO,SW] 3218 Canaan Church Rd **254/486-0032** *clothing-optional members-only retreat, RV/travel trailer pad sites, primitive camping sites and café/bar*

Dallas

see also Arlington, Fort Worth

Info Lines & Services

Lambda AA 2438 Butler #106 **214/887-6699**

Resource Center Community Center [WC] 5750 Cedar Springs Rd **866/657-2437** *9am-9pm, till 5pm Sat, noon-5pm Sun*

Accommodations

The Adolphus Hotel [GF,SW] 1321 Commerce St **214/742-8200, 844/432-3965** *a Dallas icon property since 1912. recently restored, restaurants and bars, spa and gym*

The Highland Dallas [GF,SW,WI] 5300 E Mockingbird Ln **214/520-7969**

Hotel ZaZa [GF,SW] 2332 Leonard St (at State) **214/468-8399, 888/880-3244**

Lumen [GF,F,SW,WI,WC] 6101 Hillcrest Ave **214/219-2400**

MCM Elegante' Hotel and Suites [GF,SW,WI] 2330 W Northwest Hwy **214/351-4477 , 877/351-4477**

Bars

Alexandre's [GS,E,K,WC] 4026 Cedar Springs Rd (at Knight St) **214/559-0720** *9am-2pm, from 2pm Sun, live music*

BJ's NXS [M,D,S,WC,GO] 3215 N Fitzhugh (at Travis) **214/526-9510** *6pm-2am from 4pm Sun-Mon, patio*

Dallas Eagle [M,B,L] 5740 Maple Ave (at Inwood Rd) **214/357-4375** *5pm-2am, from 4pm Fri-Sat, from 2pm Sun*

Grapevine [GS,WI,WC] 3902 Maple Ave (at Shelby) **214/522-8466** *3pm-2am, from 1pm Sun, classic dive bar*

The Hidden Door [M,NH,L,WC] 5025 Bowser Ave (at Mahanna) **214/526-0620** *7am-2am, from noon Sun, patio*

JR's Bar & Grill [★MW,F,E,V,YC,WI,WC] 3923 Cedar Springs Rd (at Throckmorton) **214/528-1004** *11am-2am, from noon Sun, from 1pm Mon*

The Mining Co [★M,D,L] 3903 Cedar Springs Rd (at Reagan) **214/521-4204** *5pm-4am, clsd Mon-Wed*

Pekers [MW,NH,E,K,C,DS,WC] 2615 Oak Lawn Ave, Ste 101 (btwn Fairmount & Brown) **214/528-3333** *noon-2am, from 10am Sat*

Pub Pegasus [M,NH,WI,WC] 3326 N Fitzhugh Ave (at Travis) **214/559-4663** *noon-2am, patio*

Sue Ellen's [★W,D,E,WC] 3014 Throckmorton (at Cedar Springs) **214/559-0707** *4pm-2am*

Tin Room [M,NH,D,S,WC] 2514 Hudnall St (at Maple Ave) **214/526-6365** *10am-2am, from noon Sun, patio*

Woody's [MW,K,V,WC] 4011 Cedar Springs Rd (btwn Douglas & Throckmorton) **214/520-6629** *2pm-2am, sports bar, patio*

Zippers [M,NH,S] 3333 N Fitzhugh (at Travis) **214/526-9519** *noon-2am*

Nightclubs

Club Los Rieles [M,D,DS,MR-L] 1707 S Lamar St **214/546-1109** *Latin club, wknds only*

Kaliente [M,D,MR-L,K,DS,WC] 4350 Maple Ave (at Hondo) **214/520-6676** *9pm-2am, salsa & Tejano*

Marty's Live [MW,D,S] 4207 Maple Ave (at Knight St) **214/599-2151** *5pm-2am*

Round-Up Saloon [★M,D,CW,K,WC] 3912 Cedar Springs Rd (at Throckmorton) **214/522-9611** *3pm-2am, from noon wknds*

Station 4 [★MW,D,C,DS,S,V,18+] 3911 Cedar Springs Rd (at Throckmorton) **214/526-7171** *9pm-4am Wed-Sun, also Rose Room cabaret, patio*

Cafes

Opening Bell Coffee [E,BW,WI] 1409 S Lamar St, Ste 012 **214/565-0383** *7am-10pm, from 9am wknds, till midnight wknds*

Restaurants

Ali Baba Cafe 1901 Abrams Rd (near La Vista Dr) **214/823-8235** *lunch & dinner*

Bangkok Orchid [GO,BYOB,WC] 331 W Airport Fwy (at N Beltline), Irving **972/252-7770** *lunch & dinner, clsd Mon, ask for Danny*

Black-Eyed Pea [WC] 7979 Belt Line Rd **972/490-1932** *11am-9pm*

Blue Mesa Grill 4866 Montfort Dr, Addison **972/934-0165** *11am-10pm*

Bread Winners [WC] 3301 McKinney Ave **214/754-4940** *7am-9pm*

Cafe Brazil 3847 Cedar Springs Rd **214/461-8762** *open 24hrs*

Cosmic Cafe [E,BW,WI] 2912 Oak Lawn Ave **214/521-6157** *11am-10:30pm, till 11pm Fri-Sat, noon-10pm Sun, veggie, also yoga & meditation*

Cremona Bistro 2704 Worthington St (at Howell) **214/871-1115** *lunch weekdays & dinner nightly, Italian, full bar, patio*

Dream Cafe [BW,WI,WC] 2800 Routh St (in the Quadrangle) **214/954-0486** *7am-9pm, till 10pm Fri-Sat, brkfst served till 5pm*

Hattie's [WC] 418 N Bishop Ave **214/942-7400** *lunch daily, dinner Tue-Sun, Southern*

Hunky's [★BW,WC,GO] 3940 Cedar Springs Rd (at Reagan) **214/522-1212** *11am-10pm, till 11pm Sat, from noon Sun, burgers & salads, patio*

Lucky's Cafe [WC] 3531 Oak Lawn **214/522-3500** *7am-10pm, classic comfort food, great brkfst*

Mario's [★] 5404 Lemmon Ave **214/599-9744** *11am-11pm, Mexican & Salvadorian*

Naga Kitchen & Bar 665 High Market St (Victory Park) **214/953-0023** *lunch Mon-Sat, dinner nightly, authentic Thai*

Stephan Pyles 2330 Flora St Ste150 **214/580-7000** *lunch Mon-Fri, dinner Mon-Sat, clsd Sun, Southwestern cuisine*

Taco Joint [WC] 911 N Peak St **214/826-8226** *6:30am-2pm, from 8am Sat, clsd Sun*

Thai Soon [WC] 101 S Coit, Ste 401 (at Belt Line) **972/234-6111** *lunch & dinner*

Ziziki's [WC] 4514 Travis St, #122 (in Travis Walk) **214/521-2233** *11am-10pm, Sun brunch, Greek & Italian, full bar*

Retail Shops

Tapelenders [GO] 3926 Cedar Springs Rd (at Throckmorton) **214/528-6344** *9am-midnight, LGBT*

Publications

Dallas Voice 214/754-8710 *LGBT newspaper*

Men's Clubs

Club Dallas [SW,PC,WI] 2616 Swiss Ave (at Good Latimer) **214/821-1990** *24hrs*

Erotica

Amazing 11311 Harry Hines Blvd #603 **972/243-2707**

Leather Masters 3000 Main St **214/528-3865** *noon-10pm, clsd Sun-Mon*

Lido Theatre 7035 John Carpenter Fwy (at Mockinbird Ln) **214/630-7127** *24hrs*

Mockingbird Video 708 W Mockingbird Ln (at I-35 & Halifax) **214/631-3003** *24hrs, bookstore w/ arcade*

New Fine Arts 1720 W Mockingbird Ln (at Hawes) **214/638-0765** *24hrs*

Paris Adult Book & Video Store 11118 Harry Hines Blvd **972/263-0774** *24hrs, bookstore w/ arcade*

Cruisy Areas

Reverchon Park [AYOR]

Tom Braniff Park [AYOR] off SH 114 (at Tom Braniff exit) *beware cops (!)*

Denison

Bars

Good Time Lounge [MW,E,K,DS,PC] 2520 Hwy 91 N **903/463-6086** *7pm-2am Wed-Sun*

El Paso

see also Ciudad Juárez, Mexico

Bars

8 1/2 [M,S] 504 N Stanton St **915/351-0262** *2pm-2am*

Briar Patch [MW,NH,K] 508 N Stanton St (at Missouri) **915/577-9555** *4pm-2am, from noon wknds patio*

Chiquita's Bar [MW,NH,MR-L,WC] 310 E Missouri Ave (at Stanton) **915/351-0095** *2pm-2am*

Epic [MW,D,E,DS] 510 N Stanton St (at Missouri) **915/525-0984** *9pm-2am, from 6pm Wed-Fri, from 7pm Sun, clsd Mon*

The Speak Easy [MW] 303 E Franklin Ave **915/351-0445** *2pm-2am*

The Tool Box [M,NH] 506 N Stanton St (at Missouri) **915/351-1896** *2pm-2am, patio*

Nightclubs

Touch Bar & Nightclub [M,D,DS,V,WC] 11395 James Watts Dr *5pm-2am*

Restaurants

The Little Diner [BW,WC] 7209 7th St, Canutillo **915/877-2176** *11am-8pm, clsd Wed, true Texas fare*

Erotica

Eros 4828 Montana (near Reynolds) **915/565-2929** *10am-midnight, from noon-10pm Sun*

Eustace

Accommodations

Circle J Ranch [M,18+,SW,N,WI,PC,GO] **903/479-4189** *campground (cabins, tents, RVs) 1 hour from Dallas*

Fort Worth

see also Arlington & Dallas

Info Lines & Services

Tarrant County Lesbian/ Gay Alliance **817/877-5544** *info line & newsletter*

Bars

Club Changes [MW,NH,D] 2637 E Lancaster Ave **817/413-2332** *2pm-2am*

Club Reflection [MW,NH,D] 604 S Jennings Ave **817/870-8867** *2pm-2am*

Urban Cowboy Saloon [MW,NH,D,F,K,DS] 2620 E Lancaster Ave **817/744-7765** *7pm-2am, from 3pm wknds, clsd Mon*

Cruisy Areas

Benbrook Dam [AYOR] *parking lot & woods*

Trinity Park [AYOR] *parking lot & woods*

Galveston

Accommodations

Hotel Galvez [GF,NS,WI] 2024 Seawall Blvd **409/765-7721**

Lost Bayou Guesthouse B&B [GF,NS,WI] 1607 Ave L (at 16th) **409/770-0688** *1890 Victorian home survived hurricane of 1900*

Bars

23rd Street Station [M,K] 1706 23rd St (at O Ave) **409/443-5678** *noon-midnight, strippers on wknds*

Robert's Lafitte [M,DS,WC] 2501 Q Ave (at 25th St) **409/765-9092** *10am-2am*

Rumors Beach Bar [MW,D,K,DS] 3102 Seawall Blvd **409/497-4176** *noon-2am*

Cafes

Mod Coffee & Tea House [F,E,BW,WI] 2126 Post Office St (at 22nd) **409/765-5659** *7am-10pm*

Restaurants

Eat Cetera [BW,WC] 408 25th St **409/762-0803** *11am-7pm, clsd Sun*

Mosquito Cafe [WC] 628 14th St (at Winnie) **409/763-1010** *8am-9pm, 8am-9pm Sat, till 3pm Sun, clsd Mon*

The Spot [WC] 3204 Seawall Blvd (at 32nd St) **409/621-5237** *good burgers, great view, also Tiki Bar*

Star Drug Store [WC] 510 23rd St **409/766-7719** *9am-3pm, old-fashioned drug store & soda fountain*

Cruisy Areas

The Dunes [AYOR] at East Beach off Hwy 87

Groesbeck

Accommodations

Rainbow Ranch Campground [MW,SW,NS,GO] 1662 LCR 800 **254/729-8484, 888/875-7596** *on Lake Limestone*

Gun Barrel City

Bars

Garlow's [MW,D,DS] 308 E Main St **903/887-0853** *4pm-close*

Houston

Info Lines & Services

Gay & Lesbian Switchboard Houston **713/529-3211** *24hr crisis hotline and resource directory*

Lambda AA Center [WC] 1201 W Clay (btwn Montrose & Waugh) **713/521-1243**

The Montrose Center 401 Branard **713/529-0037** *8am-7pm, wknds open for events,center space empowers our community, primarily lesbian, gay, bisexual and transgender individuals and their families, to enjoy healthier and more fulfilling lives*

Accommodations

Hotel Derek [GF] 2525 W Loop S (at Westheimer) **713/961-3000, 866/292-4100** *modern, chic hotel*

Hotel Sorella [GF] 800 W Sam Houston Pkwy N **713/973-1600, 855/596-3397**

The Houstonian [GF,WC] 111 N Post Oak Ln (near Woodway Dr) **713/680-2626, 800/231-2759**

La Maison [GS,WI] 2800 Brazos **713/529-3600, 877/529-3999**

The Lancaster Hotel [★GS] 701 Texas Ave **713/228-9500, 800/231-0336** *historic and newly renovated small luxury hotel downtown, restaurant & bar*

The Sam Houston [GF,F,WI] 1117 Prairie St (at Fannin) **832/200-8800**

Bars

Blur [MW,D,18+] 710 Pacific St (at Crocker) **713/529-3447** *10pm-2am, clsd Mon-Tue*

Cockpit Bar & Grill [GS,NH,K,WI,GO] 8101 Airport Blvd **713/640-9898** *4pm-2am, clsd Sun, lil ol' dive bar by Hobby Airport*

Crocker [MW,NH,K,WI] 2312 Crocker St **713/529-3355** *11am-2am*

Eagle Houston [M,NH] 611 Hyde Park Blvd (at Stanford) **713/523-2473** *noon-2am*

George Country Sports Bar [M,NH,CW,GO] 617 Fairview (at Stanford) **713/528-8102** *7am-2am, from 10am Sun, sports bar, patio*

Guava Lamp [★MW,K,V,WI,WC] 570 Waugh Dr **713/524-3359** *4pm-2am, from 2pm Sun*

JR's [★M,K,DS,S,V,WC] 808 Pacific (at Grant) **713/521-2519** *noon-2am, patio*

Mary's Alibi [MW,D] 2409 Grant St (at Hyde Park Blvd) **713/522-2867** *4pm-2am, clsd Mon*

Michael's Outpost [M,NH,E,OC] 1419 Richmond (at Mandell) **713/520-8446** *3pm-2am, from noon wknds*

Neon Boots [★MW,CW,K,GO] 11410 Hempstead Rd (in the Historic Esquire Ballroom) **713/677-0828** *4pm-midnight, from noon wknds, till 2am Fri-Sat*

Rich's [MW,D] 2401 San Jacinto **281/846-6685** *opens 10pm Th-Sat, from 5pm Sun*

Ripcord [M,L,WC] 715 Fairview (at Crocker) **713/521-2792** *1pm-2am, from noon wknds, till 3am Fri-Sat*

The Room Bar [MW,D,DS,V] 4915 FM 2920 Rd #148, Spring **281/907-6866** *2pm-2am*

Tony's Corner Pocket [MW,NH,K,S,WI] 817 W Dallas (btwn Arthur & Crosby) **713/571-7870** *noon-2am, from 7am Fri-Sunb, large deck*

Nightclubs

Club L2 Houston [MW,D,MR,18+] 2912 Wentworth St **713/227-9667** *10pm-4am Sat, mostly African American, hip hop*

Crystal [M,D,DS,MR-L] 6680 Southwest Fwy (at Colorado) **713/278-2582** *9pm-3am Wed-Sun, Latino club, theme nights*

The Eagle [M,D] 611 Hyde Park **713/236-8777** *4pm-2am from noon wknds*

F Bar Houston [MW,D,E,K] 202 Tuam St **713/522-3227** *5pm-2am, from 9pm Sat, 3pm Sun, clsd Mon*

Numbers [GF,D,E,V,YC] 300 Westheimer (at Taft) **713/526-6551** *80's Fri, also live music venue*

Ranch Hill Saloon [MW,NH,D,CW,K,DS,WC,GO] 24704 I-45 N, Spring **281/298-9035** *4pm-2am, from 2pm wknds, noon Sun during football season*

South Beach Nightclub [M,D,S] 810 Pacific **713/521-0107** *9pm-4am Fri-Sat*

Viviana's Nite Club [M,D,MR-L,DS] 4624 Dacoma St **713/681-4101** *9pm-5am, till 6am Sat, clsd Mon-Th*

Cafes

Empire Cafe [WI,WC] 1732 Westheimer Rd **713/528-5282** *7:30am-10pm, till 11pm Fri-Sat*

The Path of Tea [WC] 2340 W Alabama St (at Kirby) **713/252-4473** *10am-9pm, till 11pm Fri-Sat, 1pm-6pm Sun*

Restaurants

Aka Sushi House 2390 W Alabama St **713/807-7875** *noon-11pm*

Argentina Cafe [WC] 3055 Sage Rd (at Hidalgo St) **713/622-8877** *10am-9pm, from 11am Sun*

Baba Yega's [WC] 2607 Grant (at Pacific) **713/522-0042** *11am-9pm, till 10pm Fri-Sat, from 10am wknds, full bar, patio*

Barnaby's Cafe [BW,WC] 604 Fairview (btwn Stanford & Hopkins St) **713/522-0106** *11am-10pm, multiple locations*

Beaver's 6025 Westheimer Rd **713/714-4111** *11am-10pm, till 11pm Fri-Sat,, BBQ*

Bellagreen 2311 W Alabama **713/533-0777** *11am-10pm, organic & all-natural American*

Brasil [BW,WC] 2604 Dunlavy (at Westheimer) **713/528-1993** *8am-11pm, till midnight Th-Sat*

Chapultepec [WC] 813 Richmond (btwn Montrose & Main) **713/522-2365** *24hrs, Mexican*

El Tiempo Cantina [WC] 1308 Montrose Blvd **713/807-8996** *11am-9pm, till 10pm Wed-Th, till 11pm Fri-Sat, Mexican seafood*

House of Pies [★WC] 3112 Kirby Dr (btwn Richmond & Alabama) **713/528-3816** *24hrs*

Hugo's [WC] 1600 Westheimer Rd (at Mandell) **713/524-7744** *lunch & dinner, Mexican, popular brunch*

Kelley's Country Cookin' [WC] 8015 Park Pl (at Gulf Fwy) **713/645-6428** *6am-10pm, great brkfst*

Ninfa's [★] 2704 Navigation Blvd (at N Delano St) **713/228-1175** *11am-11pm, Mexican, full bar*

Sparrow Bar + Cookshop [GO] 3701 Travis St **713/524-6922** *lunch & dinner Tue-Sat, also bar*

Entertainment & Recreation

Beer Can House 222 Malone St **713/926-6368** *seasonal; 10am-2pm Wed-Fri; 50,000+ beer cans cover the building!*

Retail Shops

The Chocolate Bar [WC] 1835 W Alabama St **713/520-8599** *chocolate gifts & yummy desserts*

Hollywood Super Center 2409 Grant St (at Crocker St) **713/527-8510** *10am-1am, till 3am Fri-Sat*

Publications

abOUT Magazine PO Box 667626 **713/396-2688** *Texas LGBT entertainment news source*

OutSmart **713/520-7237** *monthly LGBT newsmagazine*

Gyms & Health Clubs

Houston Gym [GO] 1501 Durham Rd (at Washington & Eigel) **713/987-3897** *5am-10pm, 8am-8pm wknds*

Men's Clubs

The Club Houston [★SW,PC] 2205 Fannin St (at Webster) **713/659-4998** *24hrs*

Erotica

Loveworks 25170 I-45 N, Spring **281/292-0070**

Kilgore

Erotica

Venus 1907 Industrial Blvd **903/986-2090** *10am-11pm, till midnight Fri-Sat, noon-8pm Sun*

Longview

Nightclubs

Rainbow Members Club (RMC) [MW,D,DS, PC,WC] 203 S High (at Cotton) **903/753-9393** *5pm-2am Wed-Sat, from 3pm Sun*

Cruisy Areas

Hinsley Park [AYOR]

Teague Park [AYOR]

Lubbock

Info Lines & Services

AA Lambda 4501 University Ave (at MCC) **806/792-5562** *8pm Fri*

Accommodations

LaQuinta Inns & Suites North [GF,SW,WI,WC,GO] 5006 Auburn St (at Winston) **806/749-1600**

Nightclubs

Club Luxor [GS,D,K,DS,WC] 2211 Marsha Sharp Fwy **806/744-3744** *9pm-2am Fri-Sat*

Cruisy Areas

McKenzie Park [AYOR]

Marfa

Accommodations

El Cosmico [GS,WI,GO] 802 S. Highland Ave **432/729-1950, 877/822-1950** *vintage trailer, yurt & teepee hotel & campground*

McAllen

see Rio Grande Valley

Odessa/ Midland

Erotica

County Line 6947 Commerce, Odessa **432/552-0055** *24hrs*

Rio Grande Valley

Bars

PBD's [M,D,DS,S,WC] 2908 N Ware Rd (at Daffodil), McAllen **956/682-8019** *8pm-2am, clsd Mon*

San Antonio

Info Lines & Services

Lambda AA 980 Barnett (720 Club), Kerrville **210/828-6235** *8:15pm daily*

Accommodations

Arbor House Suites B&B [GS,NS,WC,GO] 109 Arciniega (btwn S Alamo & S St Mary's) **210/472-2005**

Brackenridge House [GF,SW,WI] 230 Madison (at Beauregard) **210/271-3442** *B&B in historic King William district*

Emily Morgan Hotel [GF,F,SW,WI] 705 E Houston St (at Ave E) **210/225-5100**

Hotel Havana [GS,GO] 1015 Navarro St **210/222-2008**

Bars

2015 Place [M,NH,K] 2015 San Pedro (at Woodlawn) **210/733-3365** *2pm-2am, pati*

The Annex [M,NH,WI,WC] 330 San Pedro Ave (at Euclid) **210/223-6957** *2pm-2am, cruise bar*

Essence [M,NH,K,S] 1010 N Main Ave (at E Euclid) **210/223-5418** *2pm-2am*

The Flying Saucer [GF, F] 11255 Huebner Rd #212 (at I-10) **210/696-5080** *11am-1am, till 2am Th-Sat, noon-midnight Sun, large beer selection*

Mix [GF,E] 2423 N St Marys St **210/735-1313** *4pm-2am, from 7:30pm Sat-Sun, dive bar*

Pegasus [★M,K,L,S] 1402 N Main Ave (btwn Laurel & Evergreen) **210/299-4222** *2pm-2am*

Silver Dollar Saloon [MW,D,CW,K] 1818 N Main Ave (at Dewey) **210/227-2623** *5pm-2am, clsd Mon*

Sparky's Pub [M,NH] 1416 N Main Ave (at Evergreen) **210/320-5111** *3pm-2am*

Nightclubs

The Bonham Exchange [★MW,D,V,18+,GO] 411 Bonham St (at 3rd/ Houston) **210/224-9219** *8pm-2am*

Heat [M,D,S] 1500 N Main Ave (at Evergreen) **210/227-2600** *9pm-2am, clsd Mon-Tue*

The Industry [GS,D] 8021 Pinebrook Dr (at Callaghan) **210/366-3229** *10pm-2am Th, from 8pm Fri-Sat*

Cafes

Candlelight Coffeehouse & Wine Bar [E,WI,WC] 3011 N St Mary's (at Rte 281) **210/738-0099** *4pm-11pm, from 10am wknds, clsd Mon*

Restaurants

Chacho's [E,K,WC] 7870 Callaghan Rd (at I-10) **210/366-2023** *24hrs, Mexican*

Guenther House 129 E Guenther (at S Alamo St) **210/227-1061, 800/235-8186** *7am-3pm, located in restored Pioneer Flour Mills founding family home*

Lulu's Bakery & Cafe [WC] 918 N Main (at W Elmira) **210/222-9422** *24hrs, Tex-Mex*

Luther's Cafe [K,E,WC,GO] 1503 N Main Ave (at Evergreen) **210/223-7727** *11am-3am, great burgers, live music*

Madhatter's Tea House [BYOB,WI,WC] 320 Beauregard **210/212-4832** *8am-9pm, till 3pm Sun, patio*

El Mirador [BW,WC] 722 S St Mary's St (at Durango Blvd) **210/225-9444** *8am-9pm, till10pm Fri-Sat, patio*

Taco Taco Cafe 145 E Hildebrand **210/822-9533** *7am-2pm*

WD Deli 3123 Broadway St **210/828-2322** *10:30am-4pm, clsd Sun*

Retail Shops

ZEBRAZ.com 1608 N Main Ave (at E Park Ave) **210/472-2800, 800/788-4729** *9am-midnight, till 10pm Sun-Tue, LGBT dept store*

Men's Clubs

Alternative Club Inc [SW,PC] 827 E Elmira St (at St Mary's) **210/223-2177** *noon-9am, 24hrs wknds*

Erotica

Dreamers 2376 Austin Hwy (at Walzem) **210/653-3538** *24hrs*

Cruisy Areas

Please Note: All cruisy areas for San Antonio have been removed because the San Antonio Park Rangers aggressively police these areas.

San Marcos

Bars

Stonewall Warehouse (MW,D,DS) 141 E Hopkins St *6pm-2am, clsd Sun-Mon*

South Padre Island

Bars

Upper Deck Hotel and Bar [GS,F] 120 E Atol St **956/761-5953** *5pm-2am, from 8am wknds & daily during summer*

Terrel

Erotica

Dreamers 6086 W Hwy 80 (Frontage Rd exit) **972/524-1449** *24hrs*

Tyler

Info Lines & Services

Tyler Area Gays/ TAG 903/321-2081 *social events & LGBT resources*

Accommodations

Cross Timber Ranch B&B [GS,SW,NS,WI,GO] 6271 FM 858 (at Hwy 64), Ben Wheeler **903/833-9000**

Cruisy Areas

Bergfeld Park [AYOR]

Waco

Cruisy Areas

Midway Park [AYOR]

Wichita Falls

Bars

Krank It Karaoke Kafe [GF,D,K,18+,WC] 1400 N Scott Ave (at Old Iowa Park Rd) **940/761-9099** *8:30pm-2am, from 7pm Fri-Sat, clsd Mon-Tue*

Cruisy Areas

Lucy Park [AYOR]

Wimberley

Accommodations

Bella Vista [GS,SW,NS,GO] 2121 Hilltop **512/847-6425**

Utah

Bryce Canyon

Accommodations

Hatch Station [GF,WI,WC] 177 S Main, Hatch **435/735-4015** *also operates a diner, convenience store*

The Red Brick Inn of Panguitch B&B [GF,WI] 161 N 100 West (at 200 North), Panguitch **435/690-1048** *full brkfst*

Logan

Cruisy Areas

Logan Canyon [AYOR] *Zanavoo loop*

Millcreek

Restaurants

Rawtopia 3961 S Wasatch Blvd **801/486-0332** *11am-9pm, till 10pm Fri-Sat, till 8pm Sun, raw food*

Moab

Accommodations

Castle Valley Inn [GF] 424 Amber Ln **435/259-6012**

Mt Peale Resort Inn, Lodge & Cabins [GS,NS,WI,GO] 1415 E Hwy 46 (at mile marker 14), Old La Sal **435/686-2284, 888/687-3253** *B&B & cabins, hot tub, aso Animal Sanctuary and Healing center*

Red Cliffs Lodge [GF,SW,NS,WC] Hwy 128 (at mile marker 14) **435/259-2002, 866/812-2002** *resort, on Colorado River, hot tub*

Park City

Restaurants

Loco Lizard Cantina [WC] 1612 Ute Blvd (in Kimball Jct Shopping Ctr) **435/645-7000** *11:30am-close, brunch wknds, Mexican, full bar*

Provo

Bars

City Limits Tavern [MW,DS] 440 W Center St **801/374-2337** *2pm-2am*

Salt Lake City

Info Lines & Services

Utah Pride Center 1380 S Main St **801/539-8800, 888/874-2743** *info, resource center, meetings, coffee shop, programs, youth activity center & much more*

Accommodations

Anniversary Inn [GF,WI] 460 S 1000 E (at 400) **801/363-4900, 800/324-4152** *elaborate, kitschy theme rms*

Hotel Monaco Salt Lake City [GF,F,WI,WC] 15 W 200 S (at S Main) **801/595-0000**

Peery Hotel [GF,F,NS,WI,WC] 110 W 300 S **801/521-4300, 800/331-0073**

Under the Lindens [★M,NS,WI,GO] 128 S 1000 E (downtown) **801/355-9808** *mention Damron for a discount*

Bars

Club Try-Angles [M,NH,D,F,PC,GO] 251 W 900 S (at 300 W) **801/364-3203** *4pm-2am, from 6pm Sat, from 2pm Sun*

The Sun Trapp [MW,D,K,CW,WI,WC] 102 S 600 W (at 100 S) **801/235-6786** *1pm-2am, patio*

The Tavernacle Social Club [GF,F,K,P,NS,PC] 201 E 300 South (at 200 E) **801/519-8900** *5pm-close, from 8pm Sun-Mon, "Duelin' Pianos"*

Nightclubs

Area 51 [GS,D] 451 South 400 West (at 400 S) **801/534-0819** *9pm-2am, clsd Sun-Tue*

Cafes

Coffee Garden [WC] 878 E 900 S **801/355-3425** *6am-11pm*

Restaurants

Bambara 202 S Main St **801/363-5454** *lunch Mon-Fri, brkfst & dinner daily, upscale American*

Blue Plate Diner 2041 S 2100 E **801/463-1151** *7am-9pm, till 10pm Fri-Sat*

Cafe Trio Downtown 680 S 900 E **801/533-8746** *11am-10pm, Italian*

Cedars of Lebanon [WI,E] 152 E 200 South (at State St) **801/364-4096** *lunch & dinner, Lebanese, veggie/ vegan-friendly*

Citris Grill 3977 S Wasatch Blvd **801/466-1202** *8am-9pm, till 10pm Wed-Sat*

Finn's 1624 S 1100 East (at Logan) **801/467-4000** *7:30am-2:30pm*

Himalayan Kitchen 360 S State St (at 400 S) **801/328-2077** *lunch & dinner, dinner only Sun, Indian/Himalayan, plenty veggie*

Market St Grill [WC] 48 W Market St **801/322-4668** *11:30-9pm, from 9am Sun, fresh seafood, full bar*

The Med 420 E 3300 South **801/493-0100** *lunch & dinner, Mediterranean*

The New Yorker Restaurant [WC] 60 W Market St **801/363-0166** *dinner nightly, clsd Sun, fine dining*

Red Iguana [★] 736 W North Temple **801/322-1489** *lunch & dinner, Mexican*

Sage's Cafe 368 E 100 S **801/322-3790** *lunch & dinner, brkfst wknds, clsd Mon-Tue, vegan/ vegetarian*

Stoneground 249 E 400 South **801/364-1368** *lunch & dinner weekdays, from 5pm wknds*

Vertical Diner [E,WI,WC] 234 W 900 S **801/484-8378** *10am-9pm,vegetarian diner*

Zest Kitchen & Bar 275 S 200 W **801/433-0589** *11am-11pm, till 1am Fri-Sat, full cocktail menu, healthy vegetarian, 100% gluten-free kitchen*

Entertainment & Recreation

Plan-B Theatre Company 138 West 300 South (at Rose Wagner Performing Arts Center, btwn W Temple & 200 West) **801/355-2787** *at least one LGBT-themed production each season*

Tower Theatre 876 E 900 South **801/321-0310** *alternative films, many LGBT movies*

Bookstores

Golden Braid Books [WI] 151 S 500 E **801/322-1162** *10am-9pm, till 6pm Sun*

Weller Book Works 607 Trolley Sq **801/328-2586** *10am-9pm, noon-5pm Sun*

Retail Shops

Cahoots [WC,GO] 878 E 900 S (at 900 E) **801/538-0606** *10am-9pm, unique gift shop*

Publications

Q Salt Lake 801/649-6663, 800/806-7357 *bi-weekly LGBT newspaper*

Erotica

All For Love [TG,WC] 3072 S Main St (at 33rd St S) **801/487-8358** *clsd Sun, lingerie & S/M boutique*

Blue Boutique 1383 E 2100 South **801/485-2072** *also piercing*

Mischievous 559 S 300 W (at 6th St S) **801/530-3100** *clsd Sun*

Cruisy Areas

Memory Grove [AYOR] Canyon Rd (below the Capitol, on the E side)

Sugarhouse Park [AYOR] 21st S *also btwn 13th & 17th E*

Zion Nat'l Park

Accommodations

2 Cranes Inn - Zion [GS,WI,GO] 125 East Main St, Rockville **435/216-7700** *contemplative whimsical eco-conscious inn for all your Zion Canyon explorations*

Canyon Vista Lodge B&B [GF,NS] 2175 Zion Park Blvd (at Hwy 9), Springdale **435/772-3801**

Red Rock Inn [GS,NS,WC] 998 Zion Park Blvd, Springdale **435/772-3139** *cottages w/ canyon views, full brkfst, hot tub*

Under The Eaves Inn [GS,GO] 980 Zion Nat'l Park Blvd, Springdale **435/772-3457**

Cafes

Cafe Soleil [BW,GO] 205 Zion Nat'l Park Blvd, Springdale **435/772-0505** *6am-8pm seasonal*

Vermont

Statewide

Info Lines & Services

Vermont Gay Tourism Association *Vermont's official office to promote gay & lesbian travel throughout the state, see www.vermontgaytourism.com*

Brattleboro

Accommodations

Frog Meadow Farm [M,NS,WI,GO] 34 Upper Spring Hill Rd, Newfane **802/365-7242, 877/365-7242**

Nutmeg Inn [GS,WI,WC] 153 Rte 9 W, Wilmington **802/380-6101**

Bookstores

Everyone's Books [WC] 25 Elliot St **802/254-8160** *9:30am-6pm, till 8pm Fri, till 7pm Sat, 11am-5pm Sun*

Burlington

Info Lines & Services

Pride Center 55 S Champlain St # 12 **802/860-7812** *drop-in & cybercenter, support & advocacy, events*

Accommodations

The Inn at Essex [GF,SW,WI,WC] 70 Essex Way, Essex **802/878-1100, 800/727-4295** *culinary resort*

Lang House on Main Street B&B [GF,WI] 360 Main St **802/652-2500, 877/919-9799** *exquisite rooms, gourmet breakfast and personal service, kids ok*

One of a Kind B&B [NS,WI] 53 Lakeview Terrace **802/862-5576** *2-rm suite & cottage*

Nightclubs

Metronome/ Nectar's [GF,D,F,E] 188 Main St **802/658-4771**

Cafes

Muddy Waters [BW] 184 Main St **802/658-0466** *7:30am-10pm*

Radio Bean Coffeehouse [F] 8 N Winooski Ave (at Pearl) **802/660-9346** *8am-midnight, till 2am Th-Sat, 10am-11pm Sun,also bar*

Restaurants

Daily Planet 15 Center St (at College) **802/862-9647** *4pm-close, also bar till 2am*

Leunig's Bistro & Cafe [GO] 115 Church St **802/863-3759**

Shanty on the Shore 181 Battery St **802/864-0238** *11am-9pm, seafood, views of Lake Champlain*

Silver Palace 1216 Williston Rd **802/864-0125** *11:30am-9pm, 5pm-9pm Sun, Chinese, full bar*

Retail Shops

Peace & Justice Store 60 Lake St (at College St) **802/863-2345** *10am-6pm, limited hrs in winter, fair trade retail store*

Cruisy Areas

The Loop [AYOR] downtown Bank, College & St Pauls Sts

Chester

Accommodations

Chester House Inn [GS,WI,WC,GO] 266 Main St **888/875-2205** *inn circa 1780*

Dorset

Cruisy Areas

Dorset Quarry [AYOR] on Rte 30 & Kelly Rd

Jay Peak

Accommodations

Phineas Swann B&B [GS,NS,WI,GO] **802/326-4306** *restored Victorian on Trout River, full brkfst*

Killington

Accommodations

Huntington House Inn [GF,WI,WC,GO] 19 Huntington Pl, Rochester **802/767-9140** *located on the park, restaurant & lounge*

Killington Mountain Lodge [GF,SW,WI,WC] 2617 Killington Rd **802/422-4302** *full brkfst, jacuzzi*

Manchester

Accommodations

Hill Farm Inn [GF,NS,WI] 458 Hill Farm Rd (at Historic Rte 7-A), Arlington **802/375-2269** *full brkfst*

Cafes

Little Rooster Cafe Rte 7-A (at Hillvale Dr), Manchester Center **802/362-3496** *7am-2:30pm, down-home breakfast & lunch dishes*

Restaurants

Bistro Henry [R] 1942 Depot St (.5 mile E of Rte 7), Manchester Center **802/362-4982** *dinner only, clsd Mon, Mediterranean, also bar*

Chantecleer 8 Read Farm Lane , E Dorset **802/362-1616** *call for hours, seasonal*

Bookstores

Northshire Bookstore 4869 Main St, Manchester Center **802/362-2200, 800/437-3700** *10am-7pm, till 9pm Fri-Sat*

Marshfield

ACCOMMODATIONS

Marshfield Inn & Motel [GF,WI,NS,GO] 5630 US Rte 2 **802/426-3383** *country lodging in a serene mountain setting, pets ok*

Montpelier

RESTAURANTS

Julio's [WI] 54 State **802/229-9348** *11am-9pm, till 10pm Fri-Sat, Mexican*

Sarducci's [WC] 3 Main St **802/223-0229** *11:30am-9:30pm, from 4:30pm Sun, Italian, full bar*

Wayside Restaurant [WC] 1873 Rte 302 **802/223-6611** *6:30am-9:30pm*

Richmond

RESTAURANTS

The Kitchen Table Bistro 1840 W Main St **802/434-8686** *5pm-9pm, clsd Sun-Mon, seasonal menu, local food*

Rutland

ACCOMMODATIONS

Lilac Inn [WC] 53 Park St, Brandon **802/247-5463** *full brkfst*

Saxtons River

ACCOMMODATIONS

The Saxtons River Inn [GF,NS,WI] 27 Main St (at Academy Ave) **802/869-2110** *historic Victorian inn w/ charming pub & restaurant, located in quaint New England village*

St Johnsbury

ACCOMMODATIONS

Comfort Inn & Suites [GF,SW,WI,WC] 703 US Rte 5 S (at I-91) **802/748-1500**

Fairbanks Inn [GF,SW,WI,WC] 401 Western Ave **802/748-5666**

Stowe

ACCOMMODATIONS

Fitch Hill Inn [GS,WI,NS] 258 Fitch Hill Rd (at Rte 15/100), Hyde Park **802/888-3834, 800/639-2903** *full brkfst*

The Green Mountain Inn [GF,F,SW,NS,WI,WC] 18 Main St **802/253-7301, 800/253-7302**

Northern Lights Lodge [GF,SW,WI,GO] 4441 Mountain Rd **802/253-8541** *full brkfst, hot tub, sauna*

The Old Stagecoach Inn [GF,NS,WI] 18 N Main St (at Stowe St), Waterbury **802/244-5056** *historic village inn, full brkfst, also full bar*

Timberholm Inn [GS,NS,WI] 452 Cottage Club Rd **802/253-7603, 800/753-7603** *full brkfst, hot tub*

Waterbury

ACCOMMODATIONS

Grünberg Haus B&B & Cabins [GS,NS,WI] 94 Pine St, Rte 100 S **802/244-7726, 800/800-7760** *full brkfst, also cabins*

Moose Meadow Lodge [GS,NS,WI,GO] 607 Crossett Hill **802/244-5378**

Wells River

ACCOMMODATIONS

The Gargoyle House [M,N,NS,WI,GO] 3351 Wallace Hill Rd (at US 302 & I-91) **802/429-2341**

West Dover

ACCOMMODATIONS

Deerhill Inn [GS,SW,NS,WI] 14 Valley View Rd **802/464-3100** *inn w/ restaurant*

Inn at Mount Snow [GF,NS,WI,GO] 401 Rte 100 **802/464-8388** *at the base of Mt Snow*

Winooski

BARS

The Bridge Club 45 Main St **802/448-3740** *open 5pm, clsd Sun-Mon*

Woodstock

ACCOMMODATIONS

The Ardmore Inn [GF,NS,WI] 23 Pleasant St **802/457-3887** *1867 Greek Revival, full brkfst*

Deer Brook Inn [GF,NS,WI] 4548 W Woodstock Rd **802/672-3713**

The Lincoln Inn & Restaurant at the Covered Bridge [GS,WI,WC,GO] 2709 W Woodstock Rd **802/457-7052** *Country Inn on the Ottauquechee River*

The Woodstocker Inn B&B [GS,WI] 61 River St **802/457-3896** *eclectic, indulgent and contemporary*

VIRGINIA

Alexandria

see also Washington, District of Columbia

ACCOMMODATIONS

Lorien Hotel & Spa [GF,F,WC] 1600 King St **703/894-3434, 877/956-7436**

Morrison House [GF,F] 116 S Alfred St **703/838-8000**

Arlington

see also Washington, District of Columbia

INFO LINES & SERVICES

Arlington Gay/ Lesbian Alliance *monthly meetings & outreach events (see: www.agla.org)*

BARS

Freddie's Beach Bar & Restaurant [MW,F,E,K,DS,WC] 555 S 23rd St (at Fern St) **703/685-0555** *4pm-2am, from 11am Fri, fron 10an wknds for brunch, patio*

CAFES

Java Shack [MW] 2507 N Franklin Rd (at Wilson Blvd & N Barton) **703/527-9556** *7am-5pm, 8am-5pm Sun*

CRUISY AREAS

Seabee Memorial [AYOR] Memorial Dr

Cape Charles

ACCOMMODATIONS

Cape Charles House B&B [GF] 645 Tazewell Ave (at Fig) **757/331-4920** *1912 colonial revival home w/ antiques*

Sea Gate B&B [GF,WI,GO] 9 Tazewell Ave **757/331-2206** *full brkfst*

Charlottesville

ACCOMMODATIONS

The Inn at Court Square [GF,NS] 410 E Jefferson St **434/295-2800, 866/466-2877**

NIGHTCLUBS

Impulse Gay Social Club [MW,D,K,DS] 1417 Emmet St N **434/973-1821** *10pm-4am Fri-Sat only*

RESTAURANTS

Escafe [E,GO] 215 W Water St **434/295-8668** *lunch & dinner,clsd Mon*

CRUISY AREAS

Chris Green Lake [AYOR] Rte 29 to Airport Rd

Danville

CRUISY AREAS

Ballou Park [AYOR]

Hampton

CRUISY AREAS

Grandview Beach [AYOR] nude beach past rock mounds

Harrisonburg

CAFES

Artful Dodger Coffeehouse [D,E,WC] 47 W Court Square **540/432-1179** *8:30am-2am, from 9:30am wknds, also bar*

Lynchburg

CRUISY AREAS

Blackwater Creek area [AYOR]

Peaks View Park [AYOR]

Norfolk

Info Lines & Services

Saturday Night Live Gay/ Lesbian AA 1301 Colley Ave (at First Lutheran Church) **757/625-1953** *8pm Sat*

Accommodations

B&B at Historic Page House Inn [GF,NS,WI] 323 Fairfax Ave **757/625-5033, 800/599-7659** *1899 mansion*

Nightclubs

The Wave [M,D,S,WC] 4107 Colley Ave (at 41st St) **757/440-5911** *10pm-2am, clsd Sun, Mon & Wed*

Restaurants

Charlie's American Cafe [E] 4024 Granby St **757/962-7701** *7am-2pm, 5pm-2am, full bar*

Tortilla West 508 Oropax St **757/440-3777** *dinner only, Sun brunch, open till 1am, Mexican, plenty veggie/ vegan*

Petersburg

Restaurants

Wabi-Sabi [GO] 29 Bollingbrook St **804/862-1365** *11am-12:30am, till 9am Mon-Tue, till 1:30am Fri-Sat, tavern downstairs with DJ*

Richmond

Info Lines & Services

Diversity Richmond 1407 Sherwood Ave **804/622-4646** *community place where LGBTQ+ citizens are treated with respect and dignity*

Accommodations

Omni Richmond Hotel [GF,SW,WI,WC] 100 S 12th St (at Cary St) **804/344-7000** *views of city & James River*

Bars

Babes of Carytown [MW,D,CW,DS,F,E,K,WC] 3166 W Cary St (at Auburn) **804/355-9330** *11am-2am, from noon Sat, 10am-8pm Sun*

Barcode [M,NH,F,K,WI] 6 E Grace St (btwn 1st & Foushee Sts) **804/648-2040** *4pm-2am*

Godfrey's [MW,D,F,K,DS] 308 E Grace St (btwn 3rd & 4th) **804/648-3957** *10pm-close, clsd Mon-Tue, drag brunch wknds from noon*

Nightclubs

Club Colours [MW,D,MR-AF,F,S,WC] 536 N Harrison St (at Broad) **804/353-9776** *9pm-3am Sat*

Restaurants

Galaxy Diner 3109 W Cary St **804/213-0510** *11am-midnight, some veggie, full bar*

The Village 1001 W Grace **804/353-8204** *8am-2am, bar till 2am, American*

Entertainment & Recreation

Richmond Triangle Players 1300 Altamont Ave (at W Marshall St) **804/346-8113** *LGBT-themed plays, films & cabaret*

Venture Richmond 804/788-6466 *tour the James River, lots of shops, restaurants, etc*

Erotica

Quality Books 8 S Crenshaw Ave **804/257-7146**

Cruisy Areas

Deep Run Park [AYOR]

Forest Hill Park [AYOR] at 42nd St

Texas Beach/ North Bank Park [AYOR] *also Great Shiplock Park*

Roanoke

Bars

Backstreet Cafe [MW,NH,F] 356 Salem Ave (off Jefferson) **540/345-1542** *7pm-2am, clsd Sun-Mon*

Cuba Pete's [GF,NH,F,K,WC] 120 Church Ave SW (at First St SW, inside Macado's) **540/342-7231** *11am-2am, more gay wknds, also Macado's restaurant*

Shenandoah Valley

Accommodations

Frog Hollow B&B [GS,GO] 492 Greenhouse Rd (at Rte 11), Lexington **540/463-5444** *full brkfst*

The Olde Staunton Inn [GS,WI] 260 N Lewis St, Staunton **540/886-0193** *B&B, hot tub*

Piney Hill B&B [GS,NS,GO] 1048 Piney Hill Rd (at Mill Creek Crossroads), Luray **540/778-5261, 800/644-5261** *country B&B, full brkfst*

Virginia Beach

Accommodations

Capes Ocean Resort Hotel [GF,SW,NS,WI,WC] 2001 Atlantic Ave (at 20th St) **757/428-5421, 800/456-5421** *oceanfront rooms, private balconies*

Ocean Beach Club [GF,F,WC] 3401 Atlantic Ave (at 34th St) **757/213-0601, 800/245-1003**

Bars

Rainbow Cactus [M,D,CW,F,DS,WC] 3472 Holland Rd (at Diana Lee) **757/368-0441** *7pm-2am, clsd Mon-Tue*

Erotica

Nancy's Nook 1301 Oceana Blvd **757/428-1498** *24hrs*

Washington

Accommodations

Gay Street Inn [GF,NS,WI] 160 Gay St **540/316-9220**

WASHINGTON

Auburn

Cruisy Areas

Isaac Evans Park [AYOR] Green River Rd (off 104th Ave SE)

Bainbridge Island

Bookstores

Eagle Harbor Book Co 157 Winslow Wy E **206/842-5332** *10am-6pm*

Bellevue

see also Seattle

Bellingham

Bars

Rumors [MW,D,WC] 1119 Railroad Ave (at Chestnut) **360/671-1846** *4pm-2am*

Cafes

Tony's Coffee House [WC] 1101 Harris Ave (at 11th), Fairhaven **360/738-4710** *7am-6pm*

Restaurants

The Bourbon Bar & Grill [E,K,WC] 108 W Main St (Washington Ave), Everson **360/746-8285** *11am-10pm*

Skylark's Hidden Cafe [E] 1308 11th St (at McKenzie) **360/715-3642** *7am-midnight, outdoor seating, full bar, live jazz wknds*

Bookstores

Village Books 1200 11th St (at Harris) **360/671-2626** *10am-7:30pm, till 7pm Sun, new & used*

Erotica

Great Northern Bookstore 1308 Railroad Ave (at Holly) **360/733-1650** *11am-midnight, 1pm-10pm Sun*

Cruisy Areas

Teddy Bear Cove [AYOR]

Bender Creek

ACCOMMODATIONS

Triangle Recreation Camp [MW,PC] PO Box 1226, Granite Falls 98252 *members-only camping on 80-acre nature conservancy; www.camptrc.org*

Bremerton

INFO LINES & SERVICES

AA Gay/ Lesbian 360/830-6283

Centralia

CRUISY AREAS

Fort Borst Park [AYOR] Harrison Ave

Edmonds

CRUISY AREAS

Edmonds City Park [AYOR] by ferry dock

Everett

INFO LINES & SERVICES

AA Gay/ Lesbian 2624 Rockefeller **425/252-2525** *7pm Sun*

EROTICA

Airport Video 11732 Airport Rd (1 block W of Hwy 99, at 128th St) **425/290-7555** *24hrs*

CRUISY AREAS

Forest Park [AYOR] off 41st St

Issaquah

CRUISY AREAS

Sammamish State Park [AYOR] I-90 & SR 900

Kennewick

CRUISY AREAS

Columbia Park [AYOR] *days only, cops & bashers after dark*

Kent

EROTICA

The Fantasy Shop 604 Central Ave S **253/850-8428** *videos, toys, clothing*

La Conner

ACCOMMODATIONS

The Wild Iris [GF,NS,WI,WC,GO] 121 Maple Ave **360/466-1400, 800/477-1400**

Long Beach Peninsula

ACCOMMODATIONS

The Historic Sou'wester Lodge, Cabins & RV Park [GF,NS] Beach Access Rd (38th Pl), Seaview **360/642-2542** *inexpensive suites, cabins w/ kitchens & vintage trailers*

Mt Vernon

RESTAURANTS

Skagit Food Co-op [WI,WC] 202 S 1st St (at Memorial Hwy) **360/336-3886** *8am-9pm, from 9am Sun*

CRUISY AREAS

Lions Park [AYOR] Freeway Dr (along the river)

Oak Harbor

CRUISY AREAS

Joseph Whidbey Park [AYOR] Swantown & Crosby

Olympia

INFO LINES & SERVICES

Free at Last AA 360/352-7344 *call for info*

ACCOMMODATIONS

Swantown Inn B&B [GF,NS,WI] 1431 11th Ave SE (at Central St) **360/753-9123**

BARS

Hannah's Bar & Grille [GS,NH] 123 5th Ave SW (at Columbia) **360/357-9890** *11am-2am*

NIGHTCLUBS

Jakes on 4th [MW,D,K,F] 311 E 4th **360/956-3247** *noon-2am*

RESTAURANTS

Saigon Rendez-Vous 117 5th Ave SW (btwn Columbia & Capitol Wy) **360/352-1989** *Vietnamese, really good fake meat*

Retail Shops

Dumpster Values 302 4th (at Franklin) **360/705-3772** *11am-8pm, noon-6pm Sun, clothing, zines, records, toys*

Cruisy Areas

Capitol Lake Marathon Park *take 5th Ave E to the parkway, follow signs to park*

Packwood

Accommodations

Packwood Lodge [GS,WI,GO] 13807 US Hwy 12 **360/496-5333** *small boutique lodge 7 miles from the entrance to Mt Rainier National Park, pets/kids ok*

Pasco

Nightclubs

Out & About Restaurant & Lounge [MW,D,F,K,C,DS,WC] 327 W Lewis **509/543-3796** *6pm-2am, clsd Sun-Tue, 18+ Fri, also restaurant*

Redmond

Restaurants

Teapot Vegetarian House 15230 NE 24th St **425/747-8881** *11am-10pm, vegan*

Cruisy Areas

Marymoor Park [AYOR] *days (cops evenings)*

San Juan Islands

Accommodations

Inn on Orcas Island [GF,NS,GO] **360/376-5227** *waterfront, full brkfst*

Lopez Farm Cottages & Tent Camping [GS] 555 Fisherman Bay Rd, Lopez Island **360/468-3555, 800/440-3556** *hot tub, also camping*

Entertainment & Recreation

Western Prince Whale & Wildlife Tours 2 Spring St (at Front), Friday Harbor **360/378-5315, 800/757-6722** *whale-watching & wildlife tours April-Oct*

Seattle

Info Lines & Services

Seattle Area Support Groups and Community Center [WC] 115 15th Ave E #201 **206/322-2437** *9am-9pm, recovery meetings for the GLBTQ community*

Accommodations

The Ace Hotel [GS,NS,WI,GO] 2423 1st Ave (at Wall St) **206/448-4721**

Alexis Hotel [GF,WI,WC] 1007 1st Ave (at Madison) **206/624-4844, 866/356-8894** *luxury hotel w/ Aveda spa*

Bacon Mansion [GS,NS,WI,WC] 959 Broadway E (at E Prospect) **206/329-1864**

Gaslight Inn [★GS,SW,NS,WI,GO] 1727 15th Ave (at E Howell St) **206/325-3654** *B&B in Arts & Crafts home*

Hotel 1000 [GF,WI] 1000 First Ave **206/957-1000**

Hotel Monaco [GF,F,WI,WC] 1101 4th Ave (at Spring St) **206/621-1770, 800/715-6513** *gym, also restaurant & bar*

Inn at the Market [GF] 86 Pine St **206/443-3600, 800/446-4484** *in Pike Place Market*

MarQueen Hotel [GS] 600 Queen Anne Ave N (btwn Roy & Mercer) **206/282-7407, 888/445-3076** *in Theater District, kitchenettes*

The Sorrento Hotel [GF,F,WI] 900 Madison St **206/622-6400, 800/426-1265**

Bars

The Baltic Room [GS,E] 1207 Pine St (at Melrose) **206/625-4444** *9pm-2am*

The Bottleneck Lounge [GS,GO] 2328 Madison St (at John St) **206/323-1098** *4pm-2am, bar snacks*

CC Attle's [★M,NH,F,V,WC] 1701 E Olive Way **206/323-4017** *3pm-2am, patio, also Veranda Room & Men's Room*

Cha Cha Seattle [GF,NH,E,GO] 1013 E Pike St (at 11th Ave) **206/322-0703** *5pm-2am, hipster lounge, big burritos*

Changes In Wallingford [★M,NH,F,K,V,WC] 2103 N 45th St (at Meridian) **206/545-8363** *noon-2am*

The Crescent Lounge [GS,NH,K,WC] 1413 E Olive Wy (at Bellevue) *noon-2am, karaoke nightly*

The Cuff [★M,D,CW,B,WIWC] 1533 13th Ave (at Pine) **206/323-1525** *2pm-2am, after-hours wknds, T-dance Sun, levi crowd, patio*

Diesel [★M,NH,B,WC] 1413 14th Ave (at Madison) **206/322-1080** *2pm-2am, from noon wknds*

Hula Hula [GF,K] 501 E Olive Way **206/284-5003** *4pm-2am, tiki bar*

Madison Pub [★M,NH,WI,WC] 1315 E Madison St (at 13th) **206/325-6537** *noon-2am*

OutWest [MW,NH,E,K] 5401 California Ave SW **206/937-1540** *4pm-midnight, til 2am Th-Sat*

Poco Wine Room [GS,F] 1408 E Pine St (at 14th Ave) **206/322-9463** *4pm-2am,*

Pony [★M] 1221 E Madison St (at 13th Ave) **206/324-2854** *5pm-2am*

queer/bar [MW,D,F,DS] 1518 11th Ave **206/687-7491** *4pm-2am*

R Place [M,NH,D,F,K,S,V,WI] 619 E Pine St (at Boylston Ave) **206/322-8828** *4pm-2am, from 2pm wknds*

Rendezvous [GF,C,E] 2322 2nd Ave (at Battery) **206/441-5823** *3pm-2am, live shows, also restaurant*

The Seattle Eagle [M,L,WC] 314 E Pike St (at Bellevue) **206/621-7591** *2pm-2am, patio, rock 'n' roll, theme nights*

Temple Billiards/ The Pharmacy [GF,F] 126 S Jackson **206/682-3242** *11am-2am, from 3pm wknds*

NIGHTCLUBS

The Can Can [GS,F,C] 93 Pike St #307 (in the Pike Place Market) **206/652-0832** *6pm-2am*

Contour [GF,D,F,E] 807 1st Ave (at Columbia) **206/447-7704** *3pm-2am, till 6am Fri-Sat, fire performances, also bar & restaurant*

Dimitriou's Jazz Alley [GF,F,E,NS,$] 2033 6th Ave (at Lenora) **206/441-9729** *call for events & reservations*

Neighbours Dance Club [★MW,D,YC,WC] 1509 Broadway (btwn Pike & Pine) **206/324-5358** *9pm-2am, till 3am Th, till 4am Fri-Sat, 2 flrs, also [18+] room Th-Sat*

Re-bar [★GS,D,E,C] 1114 Howell (at Boren Ave) **206/233-9873** *10pm-2am, clsd Mon, DJ Wed-Sun*

CAFES

The Allegro [WI] 4214 University Wy NE (at NE 42nd St) **206/633-3030** *7am-10pm*

Cafe Besalu 5909 24th Ave NW **206/789-1463** *7am-3pm, great pastries*

Espresso Vivace [WI] 532 Broadway Ave **206/860-5869** *6am-11pm*

Fuel Coffee [WI] 610 19th Ave E **206/329-4700** *6am-9pm*

Kaladi Brothers Coffee [WI] 517 E Pike St **206/257-1688** *6:30am-10pm, from 8am wknds*

RESTAURANTS

Bamboo Garden 364 Roy St (at Mercer St) **206/282-6616** *11am-10pm, Chinese vegetarian & kosher*

Cafe Campagne 1600 Post Alley **206/728-2233** *10am-10pm, from 8am wknds*

Cafe Flora [BW,WC] 2901 E Madison St **206/325-9100** *vegetarian & vegan*

Canlis 2576 Aurora Ave N **206/283-3313** *dinner only, fancy seafood*

Dahlia Lounge 2001 4th Ave (at Virginia) **206/682-4142** *lunch Mon-Fri, dinner nightly, wknd brunch, full bar*

Dick's Drive In 115 Broadway E (at Denny) **206/323-1300** *10:30am-2am, excellent fries & shakes*

Flying Fish 300 Westlake Ave N **206/728-8595** *lunch Mon-Fri, dinner nightly, full bar*

Fresh Bistro 4725 42nd Ave SW (btwn Alaska St & Edmunds) **206/935-3733** *dinner Mon-Sat, wknd brunch*

Glo's [★] 1621 E Olive Wy (at Summit Ave E) **206/324-2577** *7am-3pm, midnight -4pm wknds, brkfst only*

Grim's Provisions & Spirits [E] 1512 11th Ave **206/324-7467** *4pm-midnight, 6pm-2am Fri-Sat, clsd Sun-Mon, Capitol Hill's most unique three level Restaurant*

Julia's [C,DS] 300 Broadway E (at Thomas) **206/860-1818** *9am-11pm, till midnight Fri-Sat, full bar*

Kabul 2301 N 45th St **206/545-9000** *5pm-9:30pm, clsd Tue, Afghan*

Lola 2000 4th Ave (at Virginia) **206/441-1430** *6am-11pm, till midnight wknds, popular brunch*

Paseo 4225 Fremont Ave N (at N 43rd St) **206/545-7440** *11am-9pm, clsd Mon, Cuban*

Queen City Grill [★WC] 2201 1st Ave (at Blanchard) **206/443-0975** *5pm-10pm, clsd Sun, fresh seafood, full bar*

Saint John's Bar & Eatery 719 E Pike St (at Harvard Ave) **206/245-1390** *11am-2am, from 10am wknds*

Snappy Dragon 8917 Roosevelt Wy NE **206/528-5575** *11am-9:30pm, 4pm-9pm Sun, Chinese*

Spinasse 1531 14th Ave E **206/251-7673** *5pm-10pm, till 11pm Fri-Sat, traditional cuisine of the Piedmont region of Northern Italy*

Sunlight Cafe [BW,WC] 6403 Roosevelt Wy NE (at 64th) **206/522-9060** *8am-9pm, vegetarian*

Tamarind Tree 1036 S Jackson St **206/860-1404** *10am-10pm, till midnight Fri-Sat, Vietnamese*

Thaiger Room 206/632-9299 *11am-10pm, from noon wknds, Thai*

Wild Ginger Asian Restaurant & Triple Bar [★] 1401 3rd Ave (at Union) **206/623-4450** *lunch Mon-Sat, dinner nightly, bar till 1am*

Wild Mountain 1408 NW 85th St **206/297-9453** *7:30am-3pm*

Entertainment & Recreation

Alki Beach Park 1702 Alki Ave SW, West Seattle *popular on warm days*

Garage [★F,21+] 1130 Broadway **206/322-2296** *3pm-2am, way-cool pool hall, full bar, also bowling alley*

Hugo House [C,WC] 1021 Columbia St **206/322-7030** *noon-6pm, till 5pm Sat, clsd Sun; Zine Archive & Publishing Project*

Northwest Lesbian & Gay History Museum Project *exhibits & publication*

The Vera Project [GF] corner of Warren Ave N & Republican St (in Seattle Center) **206/956-8372** *queer-friendly all-ages music arts center*

Bookstores

Elliott Bay Book Company 1521 10th Ave **206/624-6600, 800/962-5311** *10am-10pm, till 11pm Fri-Sat, till 9pm Sun*

Left Bank Books 92 Pike St (at 1st Ave) **206/622-0195** *10am-7pm*

Retail Shops

Lifelong Thrift 312 Broadway Avenue E **206/329-5792** *all sales from donated items fund Lifelong AIDS*

UnderU4men 709 Broadway E (at Roy) **206/324-6446** *11am-7pm, till 8pm Fri, till 6pm Sun, designer underwear & swimwear & in-store models*

Publications

SGN (Seattle Gay News) 206/324-4297 *weekly LGBT newspaper*

The Stranger 206/323-7101 *queer-positive alternative weekly*

Men's Clubs

Club Z [PC] 1117 Pike St (at Boren) **206/622-9958** *24hrs*

Steamworks [★WI,PC] 1520 Summit Ave (btwn Pike & Pine) **206/388-4818** *24hrs*

EROTICA

Castle Megastore 206 Broadway Ave E **206/204-0126**

Fantasy Unlimited 2027 Westlake Ave (at 7th) **206/622-4669** *24hrs*

Hollywood Erotic Boutique 12706 Lake City Wy NE **206/363-0056** *24hrs, theater*

Taboo Video 9813 16th SW Ave **206/767-4855** *8am-midnight*

CRUISY AREAS

Arboretum [AYOR] *days*

Green Lake Park [AYOR] 5500 blk of W Green Lake Wy (btwn putting course & aqua theater) *evenings*

Spokane

INFO LINES & SERVICES

AA Gay/ Lesbian 1700 W 7th Ave #100 **509/624-1442** *call for meeting times*

ACCOMMODATIONS

The Davenport [GF,SW,WI] 10 S Post St **509/455-8888**

RESTAURANTS

Mizuna [R] 214 N Howard **509/747-2004** *11am-10pm, from 4pm Sun, full bar*

BOOKSTORES

Auntie's Bookstore [WC] 402 W Main Ave (at Washington) **509/838-0206** *9am-9pm, 11am-6pm Sun-Mon*

Suquamish

INFO LINES & SERVICES

Kitsap Lesbian/ Gay AA 18732 Division Ave NE (at Congregational Church of Christ) **360/830-6283** *7pm Sun*

Tacoma

INFO LINES & SERVICES

AA Gay/ Lesbian 253/474-8897

Rainbow Center 2215 Pacific Ave **253/383-2318** *1pm-5pm Mon-Fri, till 4pm Sat, community & resource center*

ACCOMMODATIONS

Chinaberry Hill [GF,NS,WI] 302 Tacoma Ave N **253/272-1282** *full brkfst, jacuzzis, bay views, fireplaces*

Hotel Murano [GF,WI,WC] 1320 Broadway Plaza (at S 15th) **253/238-8000** *restaurants & bars*

BARS

The Mix [MW,K] 635 St Helens Ave **253/383-4327** *2pm-2am*

NIGHTCLUBS

Club Silverstone [MW,NH,D,F,K] 739 1/2 St Helens Ave (at 9th) **253/404-0273** *11am-2am*

CAFES

Shakabrah Java Cafe [WC] **253/572-2787** *7am-4pm, from 8am Sun*

EROTICA

Castle Megastore 6015 Tacoma Mall Blvd **253/471-0391**

CRUISY AREAS

Wright Park [AYOR] 6th & G Sts

Vancouver

see also Portland, Oregon

Walla Walla

CRUISY AREAS

Fort Walla Walla Park [AYOR]

Pioneer Park [AYOR]

Wenatchee

CRUISY AREAS

River Walk [AYOR] at 19th St

Whidbey Island

ACCOMMODATIONS

Whidwood Inn [GS,NS,GO] **360/720-6228** *near historic Coupeville, hot tub*

Winthrop

ACCOMMODATIONS

Chewuch Inn [GF,NS,WI,WC] 223 White Ave **509/996-3107** *E of N Cascades Mtns*

Yakima

Erotica

X Spot 1111 N 1st St **509/248-8598** *9am-1am*

West Virginia

Bluefield

Cruisy Areas

East River Mountain Overlook [AYOR] off Rte 460 (take lane nearest mtn & turn off, go all the way up mtn)

Charleston

Bars

Broadway [M,D,DS] 210 Leon Sullivan Wy (at Lee) **304/343-2162** *3pm-3am, from 1pm wknds*

Nightclubs

Atmosphere Ultra Lounge [MW,D,DS] 706 Lee St **304/343-3737** *5pm-2am, clsd Mon*

Entertainment & Recreation

Living AIDS Memorial Garden corner of Washington St E (at Sidney Ave) **304/346-0246** *in memory of those who have died of AIDS, provide a place of reflection for those who are living with AIDS, and for those who are survivors*

Bookstores

Taylor Books [WI] 226 Capitol St **304/342-1461** *7:30am-8pm, till 10pm Fri, 9am-10pm Sat, till 3pm Sun, also cafe*

Erotica

Bookmart Video 4100 Maccorkle Ave SE (at 41st St SE) **304/925-9000** *11am-11pm, noon-8pm Sun*

Cruisy Areas

Coonskin Park [AYOR] Greenbriar St (take Greenbriar St exit from I-77 heading from Beckley)

Daniel Boone Park [AYOR] Kanawha Blvd (just N of Capitol) *evenings*

Fairmont

Cruisy Areas

Morris Park [AYOR] Pleasant Valley Rd

Ghent

Erotica

Lion's Den 302 Odd Rd (exit 28 off I-77) **304/787-3333**

Huntington

Accommodations

Pullman Plaza Hotel [GF,SW,NS,WI,WC] 1001 3rd Ave (at 10th St) **304/525-1001, 866/613-3611**

Bars

Club Deception [M,D,B,K,DS,PC,WC] 1037 7th Ave (at 11th St) **304/522-3146** *5pm-2am*

The Stonewall [★MW,D,K,DS,18+,WC,GO] 820 7th Ave (enter in alley) **304/523-2242** *8pm-3am, clsd Mon-Tue*

Nightclubs

Sharkey's [GS,D,E,K] 410 10th St **304/523-3200** *7pm-2am*

Cruisy Areas

Rotary Park [AYOR] near 8th Ave & 29th St (off Rte 60 E, take 29th St exit)

Lewisburg

Cruisy Areas

Tuckwiller Park [AYOR] off Rte 60 (from I-64 take exit 161 & head E for 1 mile)

Logan

Cruisy Areas

Chief Logan State Park [AYOR] *daylight till 10pm*

Lost River

Accommodations

Guest House at Lost River [MW,F,SW,NS,WI,GO] 288 Settlers Valley Wy (at Mill Gap Rd) **304/897-5707** *full brkfst, hot tub, restaurant & bar*

Cafes

Lost River Trading Post 295 E. Main St, Wardensville **304/874-3300** *9am-5pm, till 6pm Fri-Sun, antiques and cafe*

Restaurants

Lost River Grill & Motel [WI] St Rd 259 **304/897-6482** *11:45am-9pm, 8am-10pm Sat, 4pm-9pm Mon, full bar*

Martinsburg

Erotica

Variety Books & Video 255 N Queen St (at Race) **304/263-4334**

Cruisy Areas

I-81 Rest Area 1/2 mile past exit 20 (in closed weigh station) *evenings*

Milton

Erotica

Lion's Den 325 Summers Addition (exit 28, off I-64) **304/743-0190** *24hrs*

Mineral Wells

Erotica

Lion's Den State Rte 14 & I-77 (exit 170, off I-77) **304/489-9690** *24hrs*

Morgantown

Nightclubs

Vice Versa [MW,D,K,DS,S,PC,18+,WC] 335 High St (enter rear) **304/292-2010** *8pm-3am Th-Sun*

Cruisy Areas

Cooper's Rock State Park [AYOR] 10 miles E of town (off I-68, take Cooper's State Park exit) *parking lot & woods*

Marilla Park [AYOR] E Brockway Ave (btwn Morgantown & Sabraton) *midday & evenings*

Parkersburg

Cruisy Areas

Corning Boat Ramp [AYOR] Staunton Ave (off I-77)

Pliny

Erotica

Route 35 Adult Video & Books 1651 US Rte 35 N (near Buffalo) **304/937-4900** *24hrs*

Princeton

Erotica

Exotic Illusions Adult Bookstore 853 Frontage Rd/ Rte 460 (btwn Bluefield & Princeton) **304/487-2170** *24hrs*

Proctor

Accommodations

Roseland Guest House & Campground [MO,F,SW,N,NS,GO] **304/455-3838** *222 secluded acres w/ campsites, theme wknds*

Wheeling

Erotica

Market St News 1437 Market St (at 14th St) **304/232-2414**

Wisconsin

Appleton

Bars

Rascals Bar & Grill [MW,F] 702 E Wisconsin Ave (at Lawe) **920/954-9262** *5pm-2am, from noon Sun, fish-fry Fri, patio*

Erotica

Eldorado's 2545 S Memorial Dr (at Hwys 47 & 441) **920/830-0042**

Cruisy Areas

Lutz Park [AYOR]

Ashland

Cruisy Areas

Prentice Park [AYOR]

Eau Claire

Info Lines & Services

LGBT Community Center of the Chippewa Valley 800 Wisconsin St, Bldg D02 #409 **715/495-7941** *drop-in 7pm-10pm Fri, call for other hours, library & variety of events*

Nightclubs

Scooters [MW,D,K,DS,WC] 411 Galloway (at Farwell) **715/835-9959** *3pm 2am*

Erotica

Adult Video Unlimited 1518 Bellinger St **715/834-3393**

Green Bay

Info Lines & Services

Gay AA 920/432-2600 *call for times & locations*

Bars

Napalese Lounge [M,NH,F,DS,WC] 1351 Cedar St **920/432-9646** *11am-close, DJ Fri-Sat*

No Limits [MW] 500 N Baird St **920/544-4963** *3pm-2am*

Roundabout [MW,K] 1264 Main St **920/544-9544** *2pm-2am*

Nightclubs

Club XS [MW,D] 1106 Main St *7pm-2am*

Erotica

Lion's Den 836 S Broadway (at 5th) **920/433-9640** *8am-midnight*

Kenosha

see also Racine

Bars

Club Icon [MW,D,K] 6305 120th Ave (on E Frontage road of I-94) **262/857-3240** *7pm-2am, from 3pm Sun, clsd Mon*

La Crosse

Accommodations

Rainbow Ridge Farms B&B [GF,NS,WI] N 5732 Hauser Rd (at County S), Onalaska **608/783-8181, 888/347-2594**

Bars

Chances R [MW,NH] 417 Jay St (at 4th) **608/782-5105** *3pm-close*

My Place [MW,NH,GO] 3201 South Ave (at East Ave) **608/788-9073** *3pm-close, from noon wknds*

Players [★MW,D,MR,TG,WC,GO] 300 S 4th St (at Jay St) **608/784-4200** *5pm-2am, from 3pm Fri-Sun, clsd Mon& Wedt*

Erotica

Pleasures 405 S 3rd **608/784-6350**

Cruisy Areas

Pettibone Park [AYOR] on the Mississippi River (off of North Beach, across from the Holiday Inn) *days only*

Madison

Info Lines & Services

OutReach, Inc 2701 International Lane #101 **608/255-8582** *10am-7pm, noon-4pm Sat, clsd Sun*

Bars

Five Nightclub [★MW,D,K,DS,V,TG] 5 Applegate Ct (btwn Fish Hatchery Rd & W Beltline Hwy) **608/271-1768** *4pm-2am, from 2pm Sun*

Green Bush [GF] 914 Regent St (at Park) **608/257-2874** *4pm-midnight, clsd Sun, also Sicilian restaurant*

Shamrock Bar & Grill [★MW,F] 117 W Main St (at Fairchild) **608/259-8480** *11am-2am*

Woof's [MW,NH,B,D,L,F] 114 King St (on Capitol Sq) **608/204-6222** *4pm-2am, from noon Sun*

Nightclubs

Plan B [MW,D,K] 924 Williamson St **608/257-5262** *4pm-2am, from 9pm Sun, clsd Mon*

Sotto [★MW,D] 303 N Henry St *9pm-2am, clsd Sun-Wed, best sound system in the city*

Cafes

Java Cat [F,WI] 3918 Monona Dr (at Cottage Grove Rd) **608/223-5553**

Restaurants

Fromagination 12 S Carroll (on Capital Sq) **608/255-2430** *10am-6pm, till 5pm Sat, till 4pm Sun, cheese shop, sandwiches*

Monty's Blue Plate Diner [BW,WC] 2089 Atwood Ave (at Winnebago) **608/244-8505** *7am-9pm, till 10pm wknds*

Publications

Our Lives *LGBT publication, www.ourlivesmadison.com*

Erotica

Red Letter News 2528 E Washington (btwn North & Milwaukee) **608/241-9958**

Cruisy Areas

Burrows Park [AYOR]

Olin Park [AYOR] W shore of Lake Monona (parking lot near Sheraton) *afternoons*

Mazomanie

Cruisy Areas

Mazo Nude Beach [AYOR] Madison *30 miles NW on Hwy 4, then 14 miles N to Laws Dr, turn left & go 1/2 mile to gravel rd*

Milwaukee

Info Lines & Services

AA Galano Club 7210 W Greenfield Ave **414/276-6936**

Milwaukee LGBT Community Center [WI] 1110 N Market St, 2nd Fl **414/271-2656** *10am-10pm, from 6pm Sat, till 5pm Mon, clsd Sun*

Accommodations

Ambassador Hotel [GS,WI,WC] 2308 W Wisconsin Ave (at N 24th) **414/345-5000, 888/322-3326**

The Brumder Mansion [GF,NS,WI] 3046 W Wisconsin Ave (at N 31st) **414/342-9767** *B&B, full brkfst, fire-places, live music*

Hotel of the Arts/ Days Inn [GF,NS,WI] 1840 N 6th St (at Reservoir Ave) **414/265-5629**

The Iron Horse Hotel [GF] 500 W Florida St (at S 5th St) **888/543-4766** *friendly hotel geared toward motorcycle enthusiasts*

The Milwaukee Hilton [GF,F,SW,WI,WC] 509 W Wisconsin Ave (at 5th St) **414/271-7250, 800/445-8667**

Bars

Art Bar [GS,E,WI,GO] 722 E Burleigh St (at Fratney) **414/372-7880** *3pm-2am, from 10am wknds*

D.I.X. [M,V] 739 S 1st St (at National) **414/231-9085** *4pm-2am, from noon Sun*

Fluid [M,NH,V] 819 S 2nd St (at W National) **414/643-5843** *5pm-close, from 3pm Fri, from 2pm wknds*

Hamburger Mary's Milwaukee [MW,F,DS,K] 730-734 S 5th St **414/488-2555** *11am-10pm, till midnight wknds*

Harbor Room [M,L,F,V] 117 E Greenfield Ave (at S 1st St) **414/672-7988** *6am-2am*

Hybrid Lounge [M,F,K] 707 E Brady (at Van Buren) **414/810-1809** *4pm-close, from 10am Sat-Sun*

Kruz [M,L] 354 E National Ave (at S Water St) **414/272-5789** *3pm-close, patio, cruisy*

The Nomad [GF] 1401 E Brady St (at Warren) **414/224-8111** *2pm-2am, from noon wknds, soccer pub*

Taylor's [GS,NH,D,WC,GO] 795 N Jefferson St (at Wells) **414/271-2855** *4pm-close, patio*

This Is It [M,OC] 418 E Wells St (at Jefferson) **414/278-9192** *3pm-2am*

Two [GS] 718 E Burleigh St (at Fratney) *7pm-close Wed-Sat*

Woody's [M,NH,WI] 1579 S 2nd St (at Lapham St) **414/672-0806** *4pm-close, from 2pm wknds, sports bar*

Nightclubs

La Cage/ ETC/Montage Lounge [★M,D,S,V,YC,WC] 801 S 2nd St (at National) **414/383-8330** *6pm-close, from 10pm Fri-Sat*

Cafes

Bella Caffe 189 N Milwaukee St **414/273-5620** *6am-9pm, till 11pm Fri-Sat, 8am-6pm Sun*

Fuel Cafe [WI,WC] 818 E Center St **414/374-3835** *7am-10pm,from 8am wknds*

Restaurants

Beans & Barley 1901 E North Ave (at Oakland Ave) **414/278-7878** *8am-9pm, vegetarian cafe & deli*

Harvey's [E] 1340 W Towne Sq Rd, Mequon **262/241-9589** *dinner nightly, clsd Sun*

Honeypie Cafe 2643 S Kinnickinnic Ave (at Potter) **414/489-7437** *10am-10pm, from 9am wknds, till 9pm Sun, homemade midwestern classics*

The Knick [★WC] 1030 E Juneau Ave (at Waverly) **414/272-0011** *11am-midnight, from 9am wknds, full bar*

Lulu [E] 2261 & 2265 S Howell Ave **414/294-5858** *11am-10pm, also bar till late, live music wknds*

Meritage [WC] 5921 W Vliet St **414/479-0620** *5pm-9pm, till 10pm Fri-Sat, clsd Sun-Mon*

Range Line Inn [R] 2635 W Mequon Rd, Mequon **262/242-0530** *4:30pm-10pm, clsd Sun-Mon*

Sanford Restaurant 1547 N Jackson St **414/276-9608** *dinner only, clsd Sun, Milwaukee fine dining Euro-style*

Entertainment & Recreation

Boerner Botanical Gardens 9400 Boerner Dr (in Whitnall Park), Hales Corners **414/525-5655** *8am-dusk, 40-acre garden & arboretum, garden clsd in winter*

Harley-Davidson Museum [F] 400 Canal St (at N 6th St) **877/287-2789**

Mitchell Park Domes 524 S Layton Blvd (27th St, at Pierce) **414/257-5611** *botanical gardens*

Off the Wall Theatre 127 E Wells St **414/327-3552** *alternative theatre group*

Riverwest Public House Cooperative [GS,D,F,K] 815 E Locust St **414/562-9472** *3pm-2am, frrom 11am wknds, community gathering space*

Bookstores

OutWords Books, Gifts & Coffee [WC] 2710 N Murray Ave (at Park Pl) **414/963-9089** *11am-7pm, till 8pm Fri, clsd Sun, pride items*

Woodland Pattern 720 E Locust St **414/263-5001** *11am-8pm, noon-5pm wknds, clsd Mon*

Publications

Wisconsin Gazette 3956 N Murray Ave **414/961-3240** *Milwaukee's most honored alternative publication*

Erotica

Booked Solid 7035 W Greenfield Ave (at 70th), West Allis **414/774-7210**

Cruisy Areas

Juneau Park [AYOR] *beware after 10pm*

Neenah

Bars

ReMixx [MW,NH,D,GO] 8386 State Road 76 **920/725-6483** *4pm-11pm, till 2:30am Fri-Sat, from 11am Sun, clsd Mon-Tue*

Oshkosh

Bars

Deb's Spare Time [MW,NH,F,E,18+,GO] 1303 Harrison St (btwn Main & New York) **920/235-6577** *11am-2am, from 9am wknds*

Erotica

Lion's Den 1650 Plainview Dr (at Hwys 41 & 26) **920/235-9040** *24hrs*

Racine

Info Lines & Services

LGBT Center of SE Wisconsin 1456 Junction Ave **262/664-4100** *11am-5pm, till 3pm Sat, clsd Sun*

Bars

Brass Monkey [GS,NH] 1436 Junction Ave *2pm-2am*

Sheboygan

Bars

The Blue Lite [MW,NH,D] 1029 N 8th St (off Rte 143) **920/457-1636** *7pm-close, from 3pm Sun*

Cafes

Paradigm Coffee & Music [E,F] 1202 N 8th St **920/457-5277** *7:30-10pm, from 8am wknds, clsd Mon*

Sturgeon Bay

Accommodations

The Chanticleer Guest House [★GS,SW,NS,WI,WC,GO] 4072 Cherry Rd **920/746-0334, 866/682-0384** *on 70 acres*

Superior

Bars

The Flame [MW,D,E,K,DS,WI] 1612 Tower Ave **715/395-0101** *3pm-2:30am*

The Main Club [M,D,L,B,DS,WC] 1217 Tower Ave (at 12th) **715/392-3335** *3pm-2am*

Wausau

Nightclubs

Oz [M,D,K,DS,V] 320 Washington **715/842-3225** *7pm-close*

Wyoming

Casper

Erotica

Emporium Video Exchange 1210 East F St **307/265-9726** *10am-11pm*

Cruisy Areas

Morad Park [AYOR]

Cheyenne

see also Fort Collins, Colorado

Info Lines & Services

Wyoming Equality/ United Gays & Lesbians of Wyoming 307/778-7645 *10am-2pm Mon-Fri, info, referrals & newsletter, social activities*

Cruisy Areas

I-25 Rest Area Southbound [AYOR] *parking lot & woods, late nights*

Lions Park [AYOR] near skating pond

Etna

Retail Shops

Blue Fox Studio & Gallery [GO] 107452 N US Hwy 89 **307/883-3310** *open 7 days, hours vary, pottery, jewelry & mask studio, local travel info*

Evanston

Erotica

Romantix Adult Superstore 1939 Harrison Dr **307/789-0800**

Gillette

Cruisy Areas

Camplex Park [AYOR] Garner Lake Rd (off I-90, Garner Lake Rd exit, go S 1 mile) *parking lot & woods*

Lander

Cruisy Areas

City Park 3rd St (at City Park Ave)

Laramie

Accommodations

Cowgirl Horse Hotel [W] 32 Black Elk Trail **307/745-8794** *specializing in women travelers & their horses, men welcome*

Bookstores

The Second Story 105 Ivinson Ave **307/745-4423** *10am-6pm, clsd Sun, independent*

Cruisy Areas

I-80 Rest Area [AYOR] Happy Jack Rd (13 miles E, take Happy Jack Rd exit off I-80) *afternoons, late evenings*

Sheridan

Cruisy Areas

Sheridan Information Center [AYOR] take 5th Ave exit off I-90 *parking lot & woods*

Canada

Alberta

Calgary

Accommodations

11th Street Lodging [GS,NS,WI,GO] **403/209-1800** *"no shoe" policy inside*

Calgary Westways Guest House [GS,NS,WI,GO] 216 25th Ave SW **403/229-1758, 866/846-7038** *full brkfst*

Bars

The Back Lot [M,WC] 209 10th Ave SW (at 1st St SW) **403/265-5211** *2pm-2am, martini lounge, patio*

Ming [GF] 520 17th Ave SW **403/229-1986** *4pm-2am, martini lounge*

Texas Lounge [MO] 308B 17th Ave SW (enter rear) **403/229-0911** *11am-2am*

Nightclubs

Lolita's [GS,C] 1413 9th Ave SE **403/265-5739** *cabaret/ performance club, also restaurant*

Twisted Element [M,D,K,DS,S,WI] 1006 11th Ave SW **403/802-0230** *9pm-close*

Cafes

Caffe Beano [WC] 1613 9th St SW (at 17th Ave) **403/229-1232** *6am-10pm, from 7am wknds*

Restaurants

Thai Sa-On 351 10th Ave SW (at 4th) **403/264-3526** *lunch & dinner, clsd Sun*

Bookstores

Daily Globe News Shop 1004 17th Ave SW (at 10th St) **403/244-2060** *9am-10pm*

Publications

Gay Calgary & Edmonton Magazine **888/543-6960** *monthly LGBT publication*

Men's Clubs

Goliath's Saunatel [F,PC] 308 17th Ave SW (enter rear) **403/229-0911** *24hrs, cocktails*

Cruisy Areas

North Glenmore Park [AYOR] S end of Crowchild *down the ravine*

Edmonton

Info Lines & Services

Pride Centre of Edmonton 10608 105 Ave **780/488-3234** *noon-9pm, 2pm-6:30pm Sat, clsd Sun-Mon*

Accommodations

Labyrinth Lake Lodge [GS,NS,WI,GO] **780/905 9827** *lodge on private lake, hot tubs*

Northern Lights B&B [MW,SW,NS,GO] **780/483-1572** *full brkfst*

Nightclubs

Evolution [M,D,DS,K] 10220 103 St NW **780/424-0077** *9pm-3am, 6pm-2am Th, clsd Mon-Wed*

Publications

Gay Calgary & Edmonton Magazine Calgary **888/543-6960** *monthly LGBT publication*

Men's Clubs

Steamworks [WI] 11745 Jasper Ave (at 118th St) **780/451-5554** *24hrs*

Westerose

Accommodations

Pine Trails Getaway [MW] RR1 **780/975-9133** *gay campground & cabins, pets ok*

British Columbia

Birken

Accommodations

Birken Lakeside Resort [GF,SW,GO] 9179 Portage Rd **604/452-3255** *cabins & campsites, hot tub, lesbian-owned*

Chilliwack

Restaurants

Bravo Restaurant & Lounge [WC,GO] 46224 Yale Rd (at Nowell St) **604/792-7721** *5pm-close, clsd Sun-Tue, Pacific NW cuisine, martinis*

Gulf Islands

Accommodations

Hummingbird Lodge B&B [GF,NS] 1597 Starbuck Ln (at Whalebone Dr), Gabriola **250/247-9300, 877/551-9383** *private, luxurious atmosphere, close to beaches and kayaking*

Kamloops

Cruisy Areas

Mission Flats Beach [AYOR] off Mission Flats Rd (15 miles W of town) *popular nude beach*

Okanagan County

Accommodations

Eagles Nest B&B [M,NS,WI,GO] 15620 Commonage Rd (at Carrs Landing Rd), Kelowna **250/766-9350, 866/766-9350** *full brkfst, hot tub, overlooking Lake Okanagan*

Watermark Beach Resort [GF,SW] **250/495-5500, 888/755-3480** *restaurant & bar*

Cafes

Bean Scene [WC] 371 Bernard Ave, Kelowna **250/763-1814** *6am-10pm, 7am-9pm wknds*

Port Alberni

Accommodations

Eagle Nook Wilderness Resort & Spa [GF] 4715 Gertrude St **800/760-2777** *private log cabins, gourmet meals, health spa*

Prince George

Erotica

Doctor Love 1412 Patricia Blvd **250/614-1411**

Surrey

Cruisy Areas

Green Timbers Park [AYOR] 144th St & 100th Ave

Tofino

Accommodations

Beachwood [GF,NS,GO] 1368 Chesterman Beach Rd **250/725-4250** *private apt, steps to the beach*

BriMar B&B [GS] 1375 Thornberg Crescent **250/725-3410, 800/714-9373** *on the beach, full brkfst*

Vancouver

Info Lines & Services

AA Gay/ Lesbian 604/434-3933

QMUNITY: BC's Resource Centre 1170 Bute St (btwn Davie & Pendrell Sts) **604/684-5307, 800/566-1170** *10am-6pm, clsd wknds*

Accommodations

Barclay House B&B [GS,NS,WI,GO] 1351 Barclay St (at Jervis) **604/605-1351, 800/971-1351** *full brkfst*

Blue Horizon Hotel [GF,SW,NS,WI,WC] 1225 Robson St **604/688-1411**

Granville B&B [GF,WI] 5050 Granville St (at 34th Ave) **604/739-9002, 866/739-9002**

L' Hermitage Hotel [GS,SW,WI] 788 Richards St (at Robson) **778/327-4100**

The Listel Hotel [★GS,F,SW,NS,WI] 1300 Robson Street (at Jervis) **604/684-8461, 800/663-5491** *boutique hotel, gym*

The Loden [GS] 1177 Melville St **604/669-5060, 877/225 6336** *unique luxury boutique hotel, pets ok*

Moda Hotel [GS,WI] 900 Seymour St (at Smithe) **604/683-4251, 877/683-5522** *also 3 bars [M,S]*

"O Canada" House B&B [GS,WI,GO] 1114 Barclay St (at Thurlow) **604/688-0555, 877/688-1114** *full brkfst*

Opus Hotel [GF,WC] 322 Davie St (at Hamilton, Yaletown) **604/642-6787, 866/642-6787** *also bar and restaurant*

The Sutton Place Hotel [GF,NS,WI,SW] 845 Burrard St (at Smithe) **604/682-5511, 866/378-8866**

The West End Guest House [GS,NS,GO] 1362 Haro St (at Broughton) **604/681-2889, 888/546-3327**

Bars

1181 [M] 1181 Davie St (at Bute) **604/687-3991** *6pm-3am, upscale cocktail lounge*

The Fountainhead Pub [MW,NH,TG] 1025 Davie St (at Burrard) **604/687-2222** *11am-midnight, till 2am Fri-Sat, wknd brunch, patio*

Guilt and Company [GS,F,E] 1 Alexander St (downstairs) **604/288-1704** *7pm-1am, infused drinks and homemade beef jerky*

The PumpJack Pub [M,NH,L,WC] 1167 Davie St (off Bute) **604/685-3417** *1pm-1am, till 2am Fri-Sat*

Score [MW,NH,F] 1262 Davie St (at Jervis St) **604/632-1646** *11am-late, from 10am wknds, sports bar & restaurant*

Nightclubs

816 Granville/ The World [M,D] 816 Granville St *midnight-6am Fri-Sun*

The Junction [M,D,F,DS] 1138 Davie St **604/669-2013** *3pm-3am*

Numbers [★M,D,K,V] 1042 Davie (btwn Thurlow & Burrard) **604/685-4077** *8pm-3am, cruisy*

Cafes

Coming Home [GO] 753 6th St (at 8th Ave), New Westminster **604/544-5018** *9am-2:30pm, clsd Mon*

Delaney's 1105 Denman St **604/662-3344** *6am-9pm, from 6:30am wknds, coffee shop*

Small Victory 1088 Homer St **604/899-8892** *7am-6pm, from 8am wknds, great coffee and bakery*

Sweet Revenge [GO] 4160 Main St (at 26th) **604/879-7933** *7pm-midnight, till 1am Fri-Sat, patisserie*

Restaurants

Brioche 401 W Cordova (at Homer, in Gastown) **604/682-4037** *7am-9pm, from 8am wknds,*

Cafe Deux Soleils 2096 Commercial Dr **604/254-1195** *8am-11pm, from 9am wknds, vegetarian*

Cascade Room 2616 Main St (at 10th) **604/709-8650** *4pm-1am, till 2am wknds, modern take on the classic British pub*

The Dish [GO] 1068 Davie St **604/689-0208** *7am-10pm, 9am-9pm Sun, veggie fast food*

Elbow Room Cafe 560 Davie St (at Seymour) **604/685-3628** *8am-4pm, great brkfst*

Havana [★] 1212 Commercial Dr **604/253-9119** *11am-11pm, Cuban fusion, full bar, patio*

Lickerish 903 Davie St (at Hornby) **604/696-0725** *5pm-1am, till 2am Fri-Sat, hip hop resto lounge*

Lift Bar & Grill 333 Menchions Mews **604/689-5438** *11:30am-midnight, upscale fare with amazing rooftop bar*

Maenam 1938 W 4th Ave **604/730-5579** *lunch Tue-Sat, dinner 5pm-10pm, clsd Mon, Thai*

Martini's Whole Wheat Pizza 151 W Broadway (btwn Cambie & Main) **604/873-0021** *11am-2am, from 2pm Sat, till midnight Sun, great pizza & full bar*

Naam [E,WC] 2724 W 4th St (at MacDonald) **604/738-7151** *24hrs, vegetarian*

Seasons in the Park Cambie St & W 33rd Ave (Queen Elizabeth Park) **604/874-8008** *from 11:30am, 10:30am Sun, best panoramic view from every seat in the house*

Entertainment & Recreation

Capilano Suspension Bridge 3735 Capilano Rd, N Vancouver **604/985-7474**

Cruisey T leaves from N foot of Denman St (at Harbor Cruises) **604/551-2628** *Pride weekend and some Sun (seasonal), 4-hour party cruise around Vancouver Harbour*

Lotus Land Tours [$] 1033 Marinaside Crescent #1606 **604/684-4922, 800/528-3531** *orca-watching safari, guided kayaking day trip & beach BBQ*

Rockwood Adventures 6342 Bruce St, West Vancouver **604/913-1621** *rain forest walks & city tours for all levels w/ free hotel pickup*

Sunset Beach Beach Ave, right in the West End (near Burrard St Bridge) *home of Vancouver AIDS memorial*

Wreck Beach [N] below UBC *lots of fun events, check www.WreckBeach.org*

Bookstores

Little Sister's [★WC] 1238 Davie St (btwn Bute & Jervis) **604/669-1753, 800/567-1662 (in Canada only)** *10am-11pm, LGBT*

People's Co-op Bookstore 1391 Commercial Dr (btwn Kitchener & Charles) **604/253-6442, 888/511-5556** *LGBT section*

Retail Shops

Cupcakes 2887 W Broadway **604/974-1300** *9:30am-5:30pm, till 7pm Fri-Sun, clsd Tues*

Mintage 1714 Commercial Dr **604/646-8243** *vintage & future fashions*

Next Body Piercing 1068 Granville St (at Nelson) **604/684-6398** *noon-6pm, 11am-7pm Fri-Sat, also tattooing*

Top Drawers 809 Davie St **604/684-4861** *men's underwear & swimwear*

Publications

Xtra! **604/684-9696** *LGBT newspaper*

Gyms & Health Clubs

Fitness World 1214 Howe St (at Davie) **604/681-3232** *day passes*

Spartacus Gym 1522 Commercial Dr **604/254-6267**

Men's Clubs

Fahrenheit 212° [PC,WI] 1048 Davie St (at Burrard) **604/689-9719** *24hrs*

Steam1 430 Columbia St (across from the Columbia Sky Train station), New Westminster **604/540-2117** *30 minutes from Vancouver*

Steamworks 123 W Pender St (at Beatty St) **604/974-0602** *24hrs*

Erotica

The Love Nest 119 East 1st St, North Vancouver **604/987-1175** *10am-6pm, till 8pm Th-Fri. noon-5pm Sun*

Womyn's Ware [GO] 896 Commercial Dr (at Venables) **604/254-2543** *11am-6pm, till 7pm Th-Fri, till 5:30pm Sun, toys for men too*

Cruisy Areas

Central Park [AYOR] S side of the Boundary & Kingsway intersection *on the Vancouver/ Burnaby border*

Harbor Quay Promenade [AYOR] Port Alberni

Richmond Nature Park [AYOR] Richmond /
Stanley Park [AYOR] Lee's Trail

Wreck Beach [AYOR] below UBC

Victoria

Accommodations

Dashwood Manor Seaside B&B Inn [GS,WI,GO] 1 Cook St (at Dallas Rd) **250/385-5517** *heritage designated 1912 British Arts and Crafts Tudor Revival home with great views of the ocean*

Inn at Laurel Point [GF,F,SW,WI,WC] 680 Montreal St (at Quebec St) **250/386-8721, 800/663-7667** *edge of Victoria's Inner harbour within walking distance of downtown Victoria, great views, pets OK*

Oak Bay Guest House [GF,NS] 1052 Newport Ave **250/598-3812** *1912 Tudor-style house, full brkfst, near beaches*

Bars

Paparazzi [MW,D,K,DS,V,WC] 642 Johnson St (enter on Broad St) **250/388-0505** *4pm-2am*

Restaurants

Green Cuisine 560 Johnson St #5 (in Market Square) **250/385-1809** *10am-8pm, vegan, also juice bar, bakery*

Santiago's Cafe [GO] 660 Oswego St **250/388-7376** *11am-9pm, tapas bar, patio*

Entertainment & Recreation

Butchart Gardens 800 Benvenuto Ave, Brentwood Bay **250/652-5256, 866/652-4422**

Bookstores

Bolen Books 1644 Hillside Ave #111 (in shopping center) **250/595-4232** *8:30am-9pm, LGBT section*

Retail Shops

Oceanside Gifts [WC] 812 Wharf St, Ste 102 (across from Empress Hotel on the lower causeway) **250/380-1777** *8am-10pm, gifts from across Canada*

Cruisy Areas

Albert Head Beach [AYOR] Colwood

Beacon Hill Park [AYOR] Dallas Rd, near totem pole

Island View Beach [AYOR] Saanichton

Saxe Point Park [AYOR] take Esquimalt Rd to Fraser St, Esquimalt

Thetis Lake Park [AYOR] Highland Rd exit, toward Duncan (off Hwy 1) *look for parked cars & pathway to "Blowjob Hill"*

Whistler

Accommodations

Coast Blackcomb Suites at Whistler [GF,SW,NS,WC] 4899 Painted Cliff Rd **604/905-3400** *bar & restaurant*

Four Seasons Resort Whistler [GF,SW,NS,WC] 4591 Blackcomb Wy **604/935-3400** *luxury resort & spa*

The Listel Hotel [GF,SW,NS,WI,WC] 4121 Village Green (at Whistler Way) **604/932-1133, 800/663-5472** *hotel w/ pool, sauna & outdoor hot tub*

Westin Whistler [GF,SW,NS,WI,WC] 4090 Whistler Wy **604/905-5000, 888/627-8979** *full-service resort hotel, full bar & restaurant*

Restaurants

Araxi 4222 Village Square **604/932-4540** *lunch & dinner, local ingredients, also seafood bar & lounge*

The Bearfoot Bistro [R] 4121 Village Green **604/932-3433** *6pm-midnight, excellent wine cellar*

Quattro 4319 Main St **604/905-4844** *dinner nightly, Italian*

Sachi Sushi 106-4359 Main St **604/935-5649** *lunch & dinner*

Southside Diner 2102 Lake Placid Rd (off Hwy 99) **604/966-0668** *7am-midnight, hosts occasional Gay Social*

Trattoria di Umberto [R] 4417 Sundial Pl **604/932-5858** *lunch & dinner*

Entertainment & Recreation

Ziptrek Ecotours PO Box 734 V0N 1B0 **604/935-0001, 866/935-0001** *ziplines crisscross the Fitzsimmons Creek btwn Whistler & Blackcomb*

Cruisy Areas

Lost Lake *from the parking lot, walk 1 km counter-clockwise around the lake to Dick Dock*

White Rock

Cruisy Areas

Marine Dr/ White Rock Beach [AYOR] walk E toward Crescent Beach

Manitoba

Winnipeg

Info Lines & Services

Rainbow Resource Centre 170 Scott St (at Wardlaw) **204/474-0212, 855/437-8523** *call for hrs, clsd wknds, also info line, many social/ support groups*

Bars

Club 200 [MW,K,DS,S,WC] 190 Garry St (at St Mary Ave) **204/943-6045** *4pm-2am, 6pm-midnight Sun*

Fame [MW,D,DS,TG] 279 Garry St **204/414-9433** *9pm-2am Fri-Sat only*

Restaurants

Buccacino's Cucina Italiana [E] 155 Osborne St **204/452-8251** *11am-10pm, till 11pm Fri-Sat, from 10am Sun, full bar, patio*

Bookstores

McNally Robinson [WC] 1120 Grant Ave #4000 (in the mall) **204/475-0483, 800/561-1833** *9am-10pm, till 11pm Fri-Sat, noon-6pm Sun*

Men's Clubs

Adonis Spa [MO] 1060 Main St (at Burrows) **204/589-6133** *24hrs*

Erotica

Dominion News 262 Portage Ave (btwn Garry & Smith) **204/942-6563** *8am-7pm, till 9pm Fri-Sat Sat, noon-5pm Sun*

Cruisy Areas

Assiniboine Ave [AYOR] parking lot (btwn Main & Smith Sts) *nights by car*

Assiniboine Park [AYOR] parking lot of central picnic area (1/4 km W of pavilion) *weekday afternoons*

Bonnycastle Park [AYOR]

Osborne St Village [AYOR]

New Brunswick

Fredericton

Nightclubs

boom! [MW,D,K] 474 Queen St **506/206-8999** *8pm-2am, 4pm-7pm Sun, clsd Mon-Wed*

Restaurants

Molly's Cafe 554 Queen St **506/457-9305** *10am-11pm, noon-midnight wknds, full bar, garden patio*

Erotica

Pleasures N' Treasures 558 Queen St **506/458-2048** *11am-10pm, till 11pm Th-Sat*

Cruisy Areas

The Green [AYOR]

Grand Manan Island

Restaurants

ODD Rainbow Restaurant [BW,WI,WC,GO] 1 Ferry Wharf Rd (at Rt 776) **506/662-9894**

Moncton

Accommodations

Auberge Au Bois Dormant Inn [GF,NS,WI,GO] 67 rue John (at Birch) **506/855-6767** *affordable luxury inn, full brkfst*

Nightclubs

Triangles [MW,NH,D,K] 234 St George St (at Archibald) **506/857-8779** *10pm-2am Th-Sat only*

Restaurants

Calactus Cafe 125 Church St (at St George) **506/388-4833** *11am-10pm, vegetarian*

Cruisy Areas

The Block [AYOR] Main St (btwn Highland & Fleet Sts)

Champlaine Place [AYOR]

St John

Accommodations

Mahogany Manor [GS,NS,WC,GO] 220 Germain St **506/636-8000, 800/796-7755** *full brkfst*

Bars

Happinez Wine Bar [GF] 42 Princess St **506/634-7340** *4pm-midnight, till 2am Fri-Sat*

Restaurants

East Coast Bistro 60 Prince William St **506/642-2822** *lunch & dinner*

Cruisy Areas

Rockwood Park [AYOR] at beach & on trails

Nova Scotia

Annapolis Royal

Accommodations

Bailey House B&B [GF,WI] 150 St George St (at Drury Ln) **902/532-1285, 877/532-1285** *circa 1770 historic waterfront home*

Digby

Accommodations

Harbourview Inn [GF,SW,NS,WI,WC,GO] 25 Harbourview Rd (at Hwy 1), Smith's Cove **902/245-5686, 877/449-0705** *century-old country inn*

Halifax

Bars

Menz & Mollyz Bar [MW,NH,DS,K,P] 2182 Gottingen St, Level 2 (btw Cunard & Agricola) **902/446-6969** *4pm-2:30am*

Reflections Cabaret [MW,D,E,C,DS,WC] 5187 Salter St **902/422-2957** *10pm-4am, clsd Tue-Wed*

Cafes

Coburg Coffee House [WI] 6085 Coburg Rd **902/429-2326** *7am-8pm, cozy, vibrant cafe located on the edge of Dalhousie campus*

The Daily Grind [WI] 1479 Birmingham **902/407-0876** *9am-8pm, till 10pm Fri-Sat, also art market*

Restaurants

Bistro Le Coq 1584 Argyle St **902/407-4564** *noon-10pm, till 11pm Fri-Sat, Parisian charm and cuisine*

Brooklyn Warehouse 2795 Windsor St **902/446-8181** *lunch & dinner, clsd Sun, bistro providing seasonal New Canadian cuisine in a warm, low-lit space, full bar*

Chives Canadian Bistro [GO] 1537 Barrington St **902/420-9626** *5pm-9:30pm*

Heartwood 6250 Quinpool Rd **902/425-2808** *10am-8pm, clsd Sun, vegetarian*

Entertainment & Recreation

The Khyber 1588 Barrington St **902/422-9668** *visual & performing arts center*

Bookstores

Atlantic News 5560 Morris St (at Queen) **902/429-5468** *8am-9pm, from 9am Sun*

Trident Booksellers & Cafe [WI] 1256 Hollis St (at Morris St) **902/423-7100** *8am-5:30pm, 10am-5pm Sun, used, popular cafe*

Retail Shops

Venus Envy 1598 Barrington St **902/422-0004, 877/370-9288**

Publications

Wayves PO Box 34090 Scotia Square B3J 3S1 **902/889-2229** *monthly magazine "for the rainbow community of Atlantic Canada"*

Men's Clubs

Torpedo Sauna & Spa [MO,V,18+,WI,PC,GO] 2199 Gottingen St (at Cunard St) **902/406-3005** *4pm-11pm, till 9pm Mon, from 4pm Fri-Sun*

Cruisy Areas

Citadel Hill [AYOR] *evenings*

Crystal Crescent Beach [N,AYOR] 45 minutes from Halifax *for nude beach, head S from parking lot; 20-minute walk*

Tangier

Accommodations

Spry Bay Campground & Cabins [GS] 19867 Highway #7 **902/772-2554, 866/229-8014** *also restaurant & convenience store*

Ontario

Belleville

Cruisy Areas

Zwick's Park [AYOR]

Grand Valley

ACCOMMODATIONS

The Ridge [MW,F,SW,GO] Country Rd 109 (at Hwy 25 S) **519/928-3262** *trailers & tents, restaurant, dance hall, day visitors welcome, seasonal*

Hamilton

ACCOMMODATIONS

Cedars Campground [MW,D,SW,GO] 1039 5th Concession W Rd, Millgrove **905/659-3655** *seasonal, private campground, also bar, restaurant wknds*

MEN'S CLUBS

Central Spa [GO] 401 Main St W (at Poulette) **905/523-7636** *10am-midnight*

Karel's Steambaths [PC] 12 Holton Ave N (at King St) **905/549-9666** *noon-10pm, till midnight Fri-Sat, till 6pm Sun*

EROTICA

Stag Shop 58 Centennial Pkwy N **905/573-4242** *10am-9pm, noon-6pm Sun, also 980 Upper James St, 905/385-3300*

CRUISY AREAS

Jackson St [AYOR] from Catherine to City Hall

Kingston

CRUISY AREAS

Little Cataraqui Conservation Area [AYOR] King St W

MacDonald Park [AYOR]

Kitchener

EROTICA

Stag Shop 10 Manitou Dr **519/895-1228** *10am-9pm, noon-6pm Sun, also at 1585 Victoria St., N Kitchener 519/742-3859*

London

ACCOMMODATIONS

DoubleTree by Hilton Hotel [GF,SW,WI,WC] 300 King St **519/439-1661** *onvenient location in the heart of downtown*

NIGHTCLUBS

Club Lavish [GS,D,K] 238 Dundas St **519/667-1222** *10pm-2am, clsd Sun-Wed, rooftop patio*

RESTAURANTS

Blackfriars Bistro [★] 46 Blackfriars (2 blocks S of Oxford) **519/667-4930** *lunch & dinner, Sun brunch, full bar*

MEN'S CLUBS

Central Spa [F] 722 York St (at rear, Complex 722) **519/438-2625** *10am-2am, 24hrs Fri-Sat, also bar*

EROTICA

Stag Shop 1548 Dundas St E **519/453-7676** *10am-9pm, noon-6pm Sun, also 371 Wellington Rd S, 519/668-3334*

Minden

ACCOMMODATIONS

Buttermilk Falls Resort [GS] 16941 Hwy 35 (at Hwy 118) **705/489-1904, 888/368-3147** *housekeeping cottages on the banks of crystal clear Boshkung Lake*

Niagara Falls

ACCOMMODATIONS

Absolute Elegance B&B [GS,NS] 6023 Culp St (at Main & Ferry) **289/296-9473**

Angels Hideaway [GS,NS] 4360 Simcoe St (at River Rd) **905/354-1119** *full brkfst*

Stone Boutique Suites [GF,NS] 5225 River Rd (at Otter St) **905/357-2271** *3 self-contained cottage suites, 10 minutes to falls*

CRUISY AREAS

Clifton Hill [AYOR]

Oshawa

Nightclubs

Club 717 [MW,D,DS,K,WI] 717 Wilson Rd S #7 **905/434-4297** *7pm-midnight, 9pm-2am Fri-Sat, clsd Mon-Wed*

Erotica

Forbidden Pleasures 1268 Simcoe St N **905/728-0834** *10am-9pm, noon-6pm Sun*

Ottawa

Info Lines & Services

Kind Space 222 Somerset Street W #104 **613/563-4818** *3pm-9pm, We believe everyone on the human sexuality and gender spectrum should be celebrated and supportedOttawa Pride*

Accommodations

Brookstreet [GF,SW] 525 Legget Dr **613/271-1800, 888/826-2220** *golf, also restaurant*

Lord Elgin Hotel [GF,SW] 100 Elgin St **613/235-3333, 800/267-4298** *also restaurant & bar*

Rideau Inn [GS,NS,GO] 177 Frank St **613/688-2753**

Bars

The Lookout [MW,F,WC,GO] 41 York, 2nd flr (in Byward Market) **613/789-1624** *2pm-2am, till 9pm Sun, men's night Th*

Swizzles [MW,D,K,WI] 246 Queen St **613/232-4200** *3pm-2am, till 11pm Mon-Tue*

T's Pub [MW,D,F,DS] 323 Somerset St W **613/233-7375** *2pm-2am*

Nightclubs

Mercury Lounge [GS,D,E,F,WI] 56 Byward Market Sq (side door upstairs) **613/789-5324** *8pm-3am, clsd Sun-Tue,*

Cafes

Bridgehead Coffee [WI,GO] 366 Bank St (at Gilmour) **613/569-5600** *7am-9pm*

Restaurants

Ahora Mexican Cuisine [GO] 307 Dalhousie St (below Sweet Art) **613/562-2081** *noon-10pm*

The Buzz 374 Bank St **613/565-9595** *dinner nightly, Sun brunch, clsd Mon, also bar*

Johnny Farina [WC] 216 Elgin St **613/565-5155** *11:30am-10pm, from 4pm Sun, Italian*

Kinki [★E] 41 York St **613/789-7559** *11:30-1am. till 2am Th-Sat, Asian fusion, full bar, DJ & gay night Wed*

La Dolce Vita 180 Preston Street **613/233-6239** *11:30am-9pm, till 10pm Fri-Sat, except Mon dinner only, gluten-free menu available*

Shanghai Restaurant [K] 651 Somerset St W (at Bronson Ave) **613/233-4001** *5pm-10pm, till 2am Sat, clsd Sun-Tue, also bar, DJ*

Bookstores

The Gifted Type 254 Elgin St (btwn Somerset & Cooper) **613/233-9651** *gay magazines*

Retail Shops

Stonewall Wilde's Gallery 370 Bank St **613/233-5258** *11am-6pm, till 4pm Sun, Canadian art for everyday living*

Venus Envy 226 Bank St **613/789-4646**

Men's Clubs

Central Spa [PC] 1069 Wellington St **613/722-8978**

Erotica

One in Ten 256 Bank St (2nd Fl) **613/563-0110** *noon-8pm. clsd Sun*

Wicked Wanda's 382 Bank St **613/820-6032** *10am-9pm, till 10pm Wed-Sat, from 11am Sun*

Cruisy Areas

Elgin St [AYOR]

Remic Rapids Lookout [AYOR] *parking spot along Ottawa river*

Stratford

Cruisy Areas

Shakespeare Memorial Gardens [AYOR]

Toronto

INFO LINES & SERVICES

519 Church St Community Centre [WC] 519 Church St (on Cawthra Park) **416/392-6874** *9am-10pm, till 5pm wknds, LGBT info center & cafe*

AA Gay/ Lesbian 416/487-5591

Canadian Lesbian/ Gay Archives 34 Isabella **416/777-2755** *7:30pm-10pm Tue-Th & by appt*

ACCOMMODATIONS

Bonnevue Manor B&B [GS,NS,WI] 33 Beaty Ave (at Queen St & Roncesvalles) **416/536-1455** *full brkfst, kids ok, great location*

Drake Hotel [GF,NS] 1150 Queen St W (at Beaconsfield) **416/531-5042, 866/372-5386** *popular Corner Cafe for brkfst, also roof bar*

The Gladstone Hotel [★GS,NS,WI] 1214 Queen St W (at Gladstone Ave) **416/531-4635**

Hazelton Hotel [GF,NS,WI] 118 Yorkville Ave (at Avenue Rd) **416/963-6300** *luxury property*

Hotel Le Germain [GF,WI,WC] 30 Mercer St (at Peter St) **416/345-9500, 866/345-9501** *kids/ pets ok, also restaurant & bar*

BARS

The Beaver [MW,D,F,GO] 1192 Queen St W (at Northcote Ave) **416/537-2768** *5pm-2am, patio*

Bistro 422 [GS,F] 422 College St (at Bathurst St) **416/963-9416** *5pm-2am, dive bar*

The Black Eagle [M,B,L,F] 457 Church St (btwn Maitland & Alexander) **416/413-1219** *3pm-3am, heated rooftop patio*

Boutique Bar [MW] 506 Church St (at Maitland) **647/705-0006** *2:30pm-2am, from 4:30 Mon-Th during winter, in the Village, offering a variety of martinis, classic cocktails and inventive drinks & great patio*

The Cameron House [GS,E] 408 Queen St W (at Cameron St) **416/703-0811** *4pm-2am, from 6pm Sun, also theater*

The Churchmouse & Firkin [MW,NH,F] 475 Church St (at Maitland) **416/927-1735** *11am-2am, English pub*

Dakota Tavern [GF,CW,F] 249 Ossington Ave (at Dundas) **416/850-4579** *6pm-2am, live country music, bluegrass brunch from 10am wknds*

Flash [MO,S,PC] 463 Church St **416/925-8363** *5pm-2am, sex club featuring male dancers*

Hair of the Dog Pub [GS,F] 425 Church St **416/964-2708** *11:30am-midnight, till 2am Sat, from 10:30am wknds, great patio*

The House on Parliament Pub [GS,NH,F] 456 Parliament St (at Carlton) **416/925-4074** *11:30am-2am, rooftop patio*

Melody Bar [GS,E] 1214 Queen St W (at Gladstone Hotel) **416/531-4635** *5pm-1am, 6pm-2am Fri-Sat, clsd Sun-Wed*

O'Grady's [GS,F,DS] 518 Church St (at Maitland) **416/323-2822** *9am-2am, huge patio*

Pegasus [MW,NH] 489-B Church St (at Wellesley, upstairs) **416/927-8832** *11am-2am*

The Raq [GS,D,F] 739 Queen St W, 2nd flr (at Palmerston) **416/504-9120** *5pm-1am, till 2am Fri-Sat, clsd Sun-Tue, upscale pool hall*

Remington's Men of Steel [M,S,WC,GO] 379 Yonge St (at Gerrard) **416/977-2160** *5pm-2am, strip bar*

Smiling Buddha [GS,E,YC] 961 College St (at Dovercourt) **416/519-3332** *7pm-2am, dive bar & event venue hosting live metal punk & hardcore music, plus comedy shows*

Sneaky Dee's [GF,F,E] 431 College St (at Bathurst) **416/603-3090** *11am-3am, from 9am Sun*

WAYLA (What Are You Looking At) Lounge [GS,K] 996 Queen St E **406/901-5570** 8pm-2am, from 6pm Sun

Woody's/ Sailor [★M,NH,E,DS,V,18+,WC] 465-467 Church (at Maitland) **416/972-0887** *1pm-2am*

Nightclubs

Club 120 [M,F,TG,S] 120 Church St, 2nd flr (at Club 120) *10pm-close, clsd Mon-Tue, trans-themed club on Th called Goodhandy's*

Crews and Tangos [M,D,K,DS] 508 Church St **647/349-7469** *8pm-2am, great drag shows*

El Convento Rico [★GS,D,MR-L,TG,DS] 750 College St (at Crawford) **416/588-7800** *9pm-4am, clsd Mon-Th*

Fly Toronto [★GS,D,$] 8 Gloucester St (2 streets N of Yonge & Wellesley) **416/925-6222** *Sat only*

Ink Events [GS,D] **416/869-9444** *visiting big-name DJs, check www.inktickets.com for dates and location*

Lee's Palace/ Dance Cave [GS,D,E] 529 Bloor St (at Albany) **416/532-1598** *dance cave Mon, Th-Sat*

The Mod Club [GS,D] 722 College (at Crawford) **416/588-4663** *10pm Fri-Sat*

Cafes

Fuel Plus [GO] 471Church St **647/352-8807** *7:30am-6pm, til 7pmFri-Sat, 9am-5pm Sun, providing good fuel*

JetFuel [WI] 519 Parliament St **416/968-9982** *7am-8pm*

Restaurants

AFT Kitchen & Bar 686 Queen St E **647/346-1541** *11am-2am, BBQ, nice patio*

Black Hoof 938 Dundas St W **416/551-8854** *6pm-midnight, clsd Tue-Wed, charcuterie & cheese, not for vegetarians!*

Cafe 668 885 Dundas St W **416/703-0668** *5pm-9pm, till 10pm Fri-Sat, vegetarian*

Cafe Diplomatico [★WI] 594 College (at Clinton, in Little Italy) **416/534-4637** *8am-1am, till 2am Fri-Sat, Italian*

Drake's Corner Cafe [WI] 1150 Queen St W (at Drake Hotel) **416/531-5042** *8am-6pm, till 9pm Wed-Th,till 11pm Fri-Sat, popular brkfst spot*

Easy Restaurant 1645 Queen St W **416/537-4893** *9am-5pm, hole in the wall great greasy spoon*

Flo's Diner [GO] 70 Yorkville Ave (near Bay St) **416/961-4333** *7:30am-4pm Mon till 9pm Th-Sat, from 8am-4pm Sun*

Kalendar 546 College St **416/923-4138** *11:30am-11pm, till 2am Th-Sat, from 10:30am wknds, patio*

Kanpai Snack Bar 252 Carlton St **416/968-6888** *5pm-11pm,cool spot serving Taiwanese snacks, beer, cocktails, sake & wash it down w/ol school hip hop*

La Hacienda 640 Queen St W (near Bathurst) **416/703-3377** *noon-11pm, from 11am wknds, Mexican*

Lee Restaurant 601 King S W **416/504-7867** *5:30pm-10:30pm, till 11:30pm Fri-Sat, Asian fusion*

Lola's 634 Church St **416/966-3991** *11am-10pm, organic comfort food*

Nota Bene 180 Queen St W **416/977-6400** *lunch Mon-Fri, dinner nightly, clsd Sun, Mediterranean*

Smith 553 Church St (at Dundonald) **416/926-2501** *lunch, dinner & wknd brunch, clsd Mon-Tue*

Supermarket [E] 268 Augusta Ave (at College) **416/840-0501** *5pm-1am, from 1pm Sat, from 11:30am Sun, clsd Mon, Asian menu, also bar w/ DJs*

Urban Herbivore 64 Oxford St (at Augusta) **416/927-1231** *10am-7pm, vegetarian/vegan*

ENTERTAINMENT & RECREATION

AIDS Memorial in Cawthra Square Park

The Bata Shoe Museum 327 Bloor St W **416/979-7799** *10,000 shoes from over 4,500 years—including the platforms of Elton John & the pumps of Marilyn Monroe*

Buddies in Bad Times Theatre 12 Alexander St (at Yonge) **416/975-8555** *LGBT theater; also Tallulah's cabaret*

BOOKSTORES

Glad Day Bookshop [★] 499 Church St **416/901-6600** *10am-7pm, from noon Sun, great selection of LGBT books, coffee shop & bar 9am-late*

RETAIL SHOPS

Out on the Street 551 Church St **416/967-2759** *10am-8pm, till 9pm Th-Sat, 11am-7pm Sun*

Take a Walk on the Wild Side 161 Gerrard St E (at Jarvis) **416/921-6112, 800/260-0102** *noon-5pm, clsd Sun-Mon, "hotel, boutique & club for cross-dressers, transvestites, transexuals & other persons of gender"*

PUBLICATIONS

Xtra! 416/925-6665, 800/268-9872 *LGBT newspaper*

MEN'S CLUBS

Cellar 78 Wellesley St E (at Church) **416/975-1799** *24hrs, no sign, enter through black door*

Spa Excess [★] 105 Carlton St (at Jarvis) **416/260-2363, 877/867-3301** *24hrs*

Splash Steam and Sauna 1610 Dundas St W (at Brock) **416/588-6191** *11am-9pm*

Steamworks [WI] 540 Church (at Wellesley, level 2) **416/925-1571** *24hrs*

EROTICA

North Bound Leather [WC] 7 St Nicholas St **416/972-1037** *10am-7pm, till 9pm Th-Fri, till 6pm Sat, noon-5pm Sun, toys & clothing*

Seduction 577 Yonge St **416/966-6969** *10am-midnight, 1pm-9pm Sun*

Stag Shop 239 Yonge St **416/368-3507** *also 532 Church St, 416/323-0772*

CRUISY AREAS

Balfour Park [AYOR]

Cawthra Park [AYOR] Church St *summer sunbathing*

Hanlan's Pt Beach [AYOR] Toronto Islands *summers*

High Park [AYOR]

Yonge Street Walkway [★AYOR]

Turkey Point

ACCOMMODATIONS

The Point Tent & Trailer Resort [MO,L,SW,N,GO] 906 Charlotteville Rd #2, RR 1, Vittoria **519/426-7275** *on 50 acres*

Waterloo

ACCOMMODATIONS

Colonial Creekside [GS,SW,WI,GO] 485 Bridge St W (at Lexington) **519/886-2726** *suites with private in-room dining*

RESTAURANTS

Ethel's Lounge 114 King St N (at Spring) **519/725-2361** *11:30am-2am, full bar, patio*

EROTICA

Stag Shop 7 King St N **519/886-4500** *10am-9pm, noon-5pm Sun*

Windsor

BARS

Phog [GF,F,E] 157 University Ave W (at Church St) **519/253-1605** *5pm-2am, from 8pm Sun-Mon, art & events*

Vermouth [GF] 333 Ouellette **519/977-6102** *8pm-2am Fri-Sat only, popular martini lounge*

CAFES

The Coffee Exchange [WI] 266 Ouellette **519/971-7424** *7am-11pm, 8am-midnight wknds*

Erotica

Stag Shop 2950 Dougall Ave **519/967-8798** *10am-9pm, 11am-7pm Sun*

Cruisy Areas

Jackson Park [AYOR] area at Ouelette Overpass

River Front Park [AYOR] at foot of Ouelette St *evenings*

Prince Edward Island

Charlottetown

Accommodations

The Great George [GF,NS,WI,WC] 58 Great George **902/892-0606, 800/361-1118** *located in center of historic Charlottetown*

The Hotel on Pownal [GF,WI] 146 Pownal St **902/892-1217, 800/268-6261** *unique designed rooms*

Rodd Charlottetown Hotel [GF,SW,WI] 75 Kent St (at Pownall) **902/894-7371, 800/565-7633** *also restaurant & lounge*

Shipwright Inn Heritage B&B [GF,NS,WI] 51 Fitzroy St **902/368-1905, 888/306-9966** *full brkfst*

Bars

Baba's Lounge [GF,F,E] 181 Great George St **902/892-7377** *11am-11pm, till midnight Fri-Sat from 5pm Sun; also Cedars Lebanese restaurant*

Entertainment & Recreation

Blooming Point north end, Blooming Point *nude beach*

Bookstores

Book Mark 172 Queen St (in mall) **902/566-4888** *9am-8pm, till 9pm Th-Fri, till 5:30pm Sat, clsd Sun*

Hermanville

Accommodations

Johnson Shore Inn [GS,WC,GO] 9984 Rte 16 **902/687-1340, 877/510-9669** *full brkfst, seasonal*

North Rustico

Accommodations

Around The Sea [GS,WI] 130 Lantern Hill Dr **866/557-8383** *the world's first rotating house with luxury condo rental suites*

Province of Québec

Hull

Cruisy Areas

Meech Lake Beach [AYOR]

Laurentides (Laurentian Mtns)

Accommodations

Le Septentrion B&B [MW,SW,NS,WI,GO] 901 chemin St-Adolphe, Morin-Heights/ St-Sauveur **450/226-2665**

Magog

Accommodations

Au Gîte du Cerf Argenté B&B [GS,NS,GO] 2984 chemin Georgeville Rd (off Hwy 10) **819/847-4264** *renovated century-old farmhouse*

Auberge aux Deux Pères [GF,SW,WI,GO] 680 chemin des Peres **819/769-3115** *near golf, biking & other outdoor activities*

Montréal

Note: M°=Metro station

Info Lines & Services

AA Gay/ Lesbian 514/376-9230

Gay/ Lesbian Community Centre of Montréal 2075 rue Plessis #110 (at Ontario) **514/528-8424** *1pm-6pm, clsd wknds • library till 8pm Mon & Wed*

Interligne / LGBTQ+ Helpline 514/866-5090 (English) *24hrs*

Accommodations

Alexandre Logan [GF,WI] 1631 rue Alexandre DeSeve (at Logan) **514/598-0555, 866/895-0555** *a quiet and charming bed and breakfast, with a beautiful Victorian style*

Alexandrie Hostel [GF,F,NS,WI,GO] 1750 Amherst (at Robin) **514/525-9420** *rooms and apts in the Village, kids/ pets ok*

Auberge le Pomerol [GF,F,NS,WI] 819 boul de Maisonneuve E (at St-Christophe) **514/526-5511 , 800/361-6896** *great location*

Aubergell B&B [MO,NS,WI,GO] 1641 Amherst (at de Maisonneuve) **514/597-0878** *full brkfst, rooftop terrace*

Aux Studios Montcalm—Guesthouse [M,WI,GO] 1303 rue Montcalm (at Ste-Catherine St) **514/815-6195**

B&B Le Cartier [GS,NS,WI,GO] 1219 rue Cartier (at Ste-Catherine Est) **514/917-1829, 877/524-0495** *private studio*

B&B Le Terra Nostra [GF,NS,WI] 277 rue Beatty (at Lasalle) **514/762-1223** *affordable luxury on St-Lawrence river, near city life; stylish rms w/ spacious bathrooms, heated floor, award-winning garden, full brkfst*

BBV (B&B du Village) [M,WI] 1279 rue Montcalm (at Ste-Catherine) **514/522-4771, 888/228-8455**

Les Bons Matins [MW,NS,WI] 1401 Argyle Ave **514/931-9167, 800/588-5280** *full brkfst*

Le Chasseur B&B [GS,GO] 1567 rue St-André (at Maisonneuve) **514/521-2238, 800/451-2238** *Victorian row house, summer terrace*

La Conciergerie Guest House [★M,N,NS,WI,GO] 1019 rue St-Hubert (at Viger) **514/289-9297** *hot tub, gym & sundeck*

L' Escogriffe B&B [MO,WI,GO] 1264 rue Wolfe (at rue Ste-Catherine E) **877/523-6105** *full brkfst*

Hôtel Dorion [GS,WI] 1477 rue Dorion (at Maisonneuve) **514/523-2427** *low-key budget hotel in the Gay Village*

Hôtel Gouverneur Montréal Place Dupuis [GF,SW,WI] 1415 rue St-Hubert (at Maisonneuve) **888/910-1111** *also restaurant & bar, pets ok*

Hotel Lord Berri [GF,WC] 1199 rue Berri (at Ste-Catherine) **514/845-9236, 888/363-0363** *also Italian resto-bar*

Jade Blue B&B [GS,NS,WI] 1225 de Bullion St (at Ste-Catherine) **514/878-9843, 800/878-5048** *theme rooms, full brkfst*

L Hotel Montreal [GF,NS,WI] 262 rue St-Jacques W (at St Nicolas) **514/985-0019, 877/553-0019** *also bar & lounge, in the heart of Old Montreal*

Loews Hotel Vogue [GF,WC] 1425 rue de la Montagne (near Ste-Catherine) **514/285-5555, 844/834-7848**

La Loggia Art & Breakfast [GS,NS,WI,GO] 1637 rue Amherst (at Maisonneuve) **514/524-2493, 866/520-2493** *in Gay Village, sundeck*

Sir Montcalm B&B [M,NS,WI,GO] 1453 Montcalm (at Ste Catherine St) **514/522-7747**

Turquoise B&B [GS,GO] 1576 rue Alexandre DeSève (at Maisonneuve) **514/523-9943** *shared baths*

BARS

Bar Le Cocktail [MW,NH,K] 1669 Ste-Catherine Est (at Champlain) **514/597-0814** *11am-3am*

Bar Rocky [M,DS,OC] 1673 rue Ste-Catherine Est (at Papineau) **514/521-7865** *8am-3am*

Black Eagle Bar (Aigle Noir) [M,L,PC] 1315 Ste-Catherine Est (at Visitation) **514/529-0040** *8am-3am, theme nights*

Cabaret Mado [★MW,D,K,C,DS,WC] 1115 rue Ste-Catherine Est (at Amherst, below Le Campus) **514/525-7566** *11am-3am, theme nights, owned by the fabulous Mado!*

Le Campus [M,S] 1111 rue Ste-Catherine Est, 2nd flr (at Amherst) **514/526-3616** *3pm-3am, from 1pm wknds, nude dancers, ladies night Sun*

Club Bolo [MW,D,CW,$] 2093 rue de la Visitation (at Association Sportive) **514/849-4777** *9:30pm-12:30am Fri, special events Sat, T-dance from 3:30pm Sun, also lessons*

Club Date Piano Bar [MW,NH,K,P,S] 1218 rue Ste-Catherine Est (at Beaudry) **514/521-1242** *8am-3am*

Foufounes Electriques [GF,D,E] 87 Ste-Catherine Est (at St-Laurent) **514/844-5539** *4pm-3am, patio*

Fun Spot [MW,NH,D,TG,K,DS,WI] 1151 rue Ontario Est (at Wolfe) **514/522-0416** *11am-3am, poker machines*

Normandie [MW,NH,K] 1295 Amherst (at Ste-Catherine) **514/522-2766** *10am-3am, terrace, popular happy hour*

Play [M,YC] 1450 rue Ste-Catherine Est *4pm-3am*

La Relaxe [M,NH] 1309 rue Ste-Catherine Est, 2nd flr (at Visitation) **514/523-0578** *noon-3am, open to the street—as the name implies, a good place to relax & people-watch*

St-Sulpice [GS,K,WI] 1680 rue St-Denis (at Ontario) **514/844-9458** *11am-3am, till midnight Sun, terrace*

Le Stud [MO,D,B,L] 1812 rue Ste-Catherine Est (at Papineau) **514/598-8243** *10am-3am*

NIGHTCLUBS

Circus After Hours [GS,D] 915 rue Ste-Catherine Est **514/844-3626** *2am-8am Th & Sun, 1am-10pm Fri-Sat*

Cirque du Boudoir [GS,D,E] **514/398-0669** *opulent quarterly theme parties*

Complexe Sky [★MW,D,SW,L,F,C,DS,S] 1474 rue Ste-Catherine Est **514/529-6969** *noon-3am*

Red Lite (After Hours) [★GF,D,$] 1755 rue de Lierre, Laval **514/660-7335** *Fri-Sun only 2am-10am*

Stéréo [★GS,E,$] 858 rue Ste-Catherine Est (at St-Andre) **514/658-2646** *after-hours Fri-Sun only*

Stock Bar [★MO,S] 1171 Ste-Catherine (at Montcalm) **514/842-1336** *shows start at 8pm nightly, nude dancers*

Unity II [★MW,D,S,YC] 1171 rue Ste-Catherine Est (at Montcalm) **514/523-2777** *9pm-close Fri-Sat only, great rooftoop terrace*

CAFES

Cafe Santropol [WC] 3990 St-Urbain (at Duluth) **514/842-3110** *11am-10pm, unique sandwiches*

Cafe Titanic [★WI] 445 St-Pierre (in Old Montréal) **514/849-0894** *8am-4pm, clsd wknds, salads & soups*

RESTAURANTS

L' Anecdote [GO] 801 rue Rachel Est (at St-Hubert) **514/526-7967** *9am-10pm, till 11pm Th-Sat, brkfst all day*

Au Pain Perdu 4489 rue de la Roche **514/527-2900** *7am-3pm, charming brunch spot in renovated garage*

Bangkok [WC] 1616 rue Ste-Catherine Ouest **514/935-2178** *11:30am-9:30pm, from 5pm Sun*

Beauty's [★] 93 Mont-Royal Ouest **514/849-8883** *7am-3pm, 8am-4pm wknds, diner/ Jewish deli, worth the wait*

La Binerie 367 Mt-Royal **514/285-9078** *6am-2pm Tue-Wed & 5pm-9pm Th-Sat, 7:30am-3pm Sun, clsd Mon, Québecois*

Le Cagibi [E] 5490 boul St-Laurent **514/509-1199** *9am-midnight, from 10:30am wknds, from 6pm Mon, vegetarian, also live music & events*

La Colombe [BYOB] 554 Duluth Est **514/849-8844** *5:30pm-midnight, clsd Sun-Mon, French*

L' Express [★R,WC] 3927 rue St-Denis (at Duluth) **514/845-5333** *8am-2am, from 10am Sat-Sun, French bistro & bar, great pâté*

Fantasie [GO] 1355 rue Ste-Catherine Est **514/523-3466** *dinner only, Thai/Southeast Asian cuisine*

Le Nouveau Palais 281 rue Bernard W **514/273-1180** *5pm-11:30pm. till 3am Th-Sat, from 10am wknds, old school diner*

Resto du Village [WI,GO] 1310 rue Wolfe **514/524-5404** *9am-midnight, "cuisine canadienne"*

Saloon Cafe [★] 1333 rue Ste-Catherine Est (at Panêt) **514/522-1333** *11:30am-10pm, big dishes & even bigger drinks*

Schwartz's Deli 3895 boul St-Laurent **514/842-4813** *8am-12:30am, till 1:30am Fri, till 2:30am Sat*

Entertainment & Recreation

Ça Roule 27 rue de la Commune Est **514/866-0633, 877/866-0633** *join the beautiful people skating up & & biking down Ste-Catherine*

Prince Arthur Est at boul St-Laurent, not far from Sherbrooke Métro station *closed-off street w/ tons of outdoor restaurants & cafés—it's touristy but oh-so-European*

Retail Shops

Chez Priape [★] 1311 Ste-Catherine Est (at Visitation) **514 /521-8451, 800/461-6969** *10am-9pm, till 10pm Wed & Th-Sat, till 11pm Fri-Sat, leather, BDSM, menswear & toys*

Cuir Mont-Royal 1126 Ave du Mont-Royal Est **514/527-0238** *leather, fetish*

Publications

Fugues 514/848-1854, 888/848-1854 *glossy LGBT bar/ entertainment guide*

Men's Clubs

Le 5018 Sauna [M] 5018 boul St-Laurent (at St-Joseph) **514/277-3555** *24hrs, hot tub*

Colonial Bath 3963 av Coloniale (at Napoléon) **514/285-0132** *noon-midnight, 10am-10pm Sun*

GI Joe 1166 Ste-Catherine Est (at Montcalm) **514/528-3326** *24hrs*

L' Oasis [★V,PC] 1390 Ste-Catherine Est (at Plessis) **514/521-0785** *24hrs, hot tub*

Sauna 1286 [M] 1286 chemin de Chambly (at Breggs), Longueuil **450/677-1286** *24hrs*

Sauna Centre-Ville [★V,WI] 1465 rue Ste-Catherine Est (at Plessis) **514/524-3486** *24hrs*

Sauna Pont-Viau [M] 1-A rue de Nevers (at boul de Prairies), Laval **450/663-3386** *24hrs*

Erotica

La Capoterie 2061 St-Denis **514/845-0027** *11am-7pm, till 10pm Fri-Sat, noon-6pm Sun*

Il Bolero 6846 St-Hubert (btwn St-Zotique & Bélanger) **514/270-6065** *fetish & clubwear emporium, ask about monthly fetish party*

Cruisy Areas

Angrignon Park [AYOR]

De Maisonneuve Park [AYOR]

Parc Mont-Royal [AYOR] Park Ave *summer nights*

Quebec City

Restaurants

Vertige 540 Ave Duluth E **514/842-4443** *5pm-10pm, clsd Sun-Mon, try the tapas menu*

Accommodations

ALT Hotel Québec [GF,NS,WI,WC] 1200 av Germain des Prés (at Laurier Blvd), Sainte-Foy **418/658-1224, 800/463-5253** *restaurant*

Auberge Place D'Armes [GF,NS,WI] 24 rue Ste-Anne (at St-Louis) **418/694-9485, 866/333-9485** *also restaurant, pets ok*

Le Château du Faubourg [GF,NS,GO] 429A rue St-Jean (at Claire Fontaine) **418/524-2902** *B&B in château, also beauty salon*

Dans les Bras de Morphée [GF,SW,WI,GO] 225 chemin Royal, St-Jean-De-L'Ile d'Orléans **418/829-3792** *full brkfst, near beach, shared baths*

Domaine de l' Arc-en-Ciel [MO,SW,18+] 1878 rang 5 Ouest (exit 266, off Rte 20), Joly **418/728-5522** *camping, full brkfst, also bar & restaurant*

Gite TerreCiel [GS,WI,GO] 113 rue Sainte Anne, Baie-Saint-Paul **418/435-0149** *charming spot near the center of the village, wonderful brkfst*

Hotel Hippocampe [MO,GO] 31 rue McMahon (at Ste-Angèle) **418/692-1521, 888/388-1521** *nice small hotel within the walls of Old Quebec*

Hotel Le Clos Saint-Louis [GS,NS,WI] 69 St-Louis (at St-Ursule) **418/694-1311, 800/461-1311**

Hôtel Le Germain Dominion 1912 [GF,WI,WC] 126 rue St-Pierre (at Marché Finlay) **418/692-2224, 888/833-5253** *boutique hotel in city's 1st skyscraper*

Hôtel-Motel Le Voyageur [GS,SW,WI] 2250 boul Ste-Anne (at Estimauville) **418/661-7701, 800/463-5668** *restaurant & bar*

Le Moulin de St-Laurent Chalets [GS,SW,NS] 6436 chemin Royal, St Laurent, Ile d' Orleans **418/829-3888, 888/629-3888** *cottages, also restaurant*

Bars

Bar Le Drague [★M,NH,D,F,K,C,DS,WC] 815 rue St-Augustin (at St-Jean) **418/649-7212** *10am-3am, terrace*

Bar St Matthew's [MW,NH] 889 côte Ste-Geneviève (at St-Gabriel) **418/524-5000** *11am-3am, patio*

ForHom [MO,OC,PC] 221 rue St-Jean (entrance at 225) **418/522-4918** *5pm-1am, till 3am Fri-Sat, good place for quiet conversation*

Restaurants

Le Hobbit 700 rue St-Jean (at Ste-Geneviève) **418/647-2677** *8am-10pm*

La Piazzetta 3100 De-la-Forest **418/521-4393** *11am-10:30pm, thin-crust pizza & more*

Entertainment & Recreation

Fairmont Le Château Frontenac 1 rue des Carrières **418/692-3861, 800/257-7544** *this hotel disguised as a castle remains the symbol of Québec, come & enjoy the view from outside*

Ice Hotel /Hôtel de Glace [GF] 75, Montée de l'Auberge, Pavillon Ukiuk, Sainte-Catherine-de-la-Jacques-Cartier **418/875-4522, 877/505-0423** *sometimes getting put on ice isn't a bad thing—check it out before it melts away, 9 km E of Québec City in Montmorency Falls Park (Jan-March only)*

Men's Clubs

Bloc 225 [PC] 225 St-Jean (at Turnbull) **418/523-2562, 877/523-2562** *24hrs*

Sauna Backboys [V] 264 rue de la Couronne (at Prince Edward) **418/521-6686, 877/523-6686** *24hrs*

Sauna Hippocampe [★V] 31 rue McMahon (at Ste-Angèle) **418/692-1521** *24hrs, bar, also small hotel*

Erotica

Importation André Dubois [TG,WC] 46 côte de la Montagne (at Frontenac Castle) **418/692-0264**

Cruisy Areas

Rue St-Denis [AYOR]

St-Alphonse-de-Granby

Accommodations

Bain de Nature [MO,SW,N,GO] 127 rue Lussier **450/375-4765** *B&B & free-form camping, beautiful small lake, all meals included, hot tub, day visitors welcome*

St-François-du-Lac

Accommodations

Domaine Emeraude [MO,F,SW,N,GO] **450/568-3634** *seasonal, cabins, camping, RV spots & rental condos, also restaurant & bar*

St-Hubert

Men's Clubs

3481 Sauna [GS] 3481 Montee St-Hubert **450/462-3481** *24hrs*

Ste-Julienne

Accommodations

Camping de la Fierté [MO,SW,N,18+] 2905 Montée Hamilton **450/834-2888** *theme wknds summers, tent & RV spots, cabin, also bar/ restaurant/ rec hall*

Ste-Marthe

ACCOMMODATIONS

Camping Plein Bois [MO,D,SW,N,WI,GO] 550 chemin St-Henri **450/459-4646** *seasonal, DJ Fri-Sat, also restaurant & bar, volleyball, 350 campsites & 200 trailer sites*

SASKATCHEWAN

Ravenscrag

ACCOMMODATIONS

Spring Valley Guest Ranch [★GS,F,NS,GO] **306/295-4124** *1913 character home, also cabin, full brkfst*

Regina

INFO LINES & SERVICES

Gay & Lesbian Community of Regina 2070 Broad St (at Q Nightclub & Lounge) **306/569-1995** *opens 5pm, clsd Sun*

NIGHTCLUBS

Q Nightclub & Lounge [MW,D] 2070 Broad St (at Victoria) **306/569-1995** *opens 5pm, clsd Sun, owned by Gay & Lesbian Community of Regina*

RESTAURANTS

Abstractions Cafe [E] 2161 Rose St **306/352-5374** *9am-5:30pm, from 11am Sat, clsd Sun*

The Creek in Cathedral Bistro 3414 13th Ave **306/352-4448** *lunch & dinner, clsd Sun*

CRUISY AREAS

Douglas Park [AYOR]

Wascana Park [AYOR] at College Dr & Lorne St

Saskatoon

INFO LINES & SERVICES

Gay/ Lesbian AA 877/254-3348

Out Saskatoon 201-320 21st St W **306/665-1224, 800/358-1833** *queer community center, 9am-4:30pm, till 9pm Wed-Fri, clsd wknds, library, many social/ support groups, gift store*

NIGHTCLUBS

Diva's [MW,D,DS,K,WI,PC] 220 3rd Ave S #110 (alley entrance) **306/665-0100** *8pm-2am, till 5am Sat,, clsd Mon-Tue*

Pink Lounge & Nightclub [MW,D] 69 24th St E **306/665-6863** *7am-2am, clsd Mon-Tue*

RESTAURANTS

2nd Ave Grill 123 2nd Ave S **306/244-9899** *11am-10pm, till 11pm Fri-Sat, clsd Sun, nice atmostphere with good wine list*

2nd Ave Grill 830 Valley Rd **306/244-9899** *views of river*

Prairie Ink 3130 8th St E **306/955-3579** *9am-10pm, till 11pm Fri-Sat, 10am-6pm Sun, located within a bookstore*

ENTERTAINMENT & RECREATION

AKA Gallery 424 20th St W **306/652-0044** *noon-6pm, till 4pm Sat, clsd Sun-Mon, contemporary art & performance*

BOOKSTORES

Turning the Tide 615 Main St **306/955-3070** *noon-8pm, till 10pm Th-Sat, Saskatoon's alternative book-store*

CRUISY AREAS

Lakewood Park [AYOR] *nights*

Caribbean

British Virgin Islands

Tortola

Accommodations

Fort Recovery Villa Beach Resort [GF,SW,WC] West End, Road Town, Tortola **284/541-0955, 855/349-3355** *private beachfront villas*

Dominican Republic

Las Terrenas

Accommodations

Hotel Residence Playa Colibri [GF,SW,WI] Francisco Camaño Deño 301 **809/240-6434** *restaurant & bar, beach terrace*

Puerto Plata

Accommodations

Tropix Hotel [GF,SW,GO] **809/571-2291** *garden setting near center of town & beach, full brkfst*

Santiago

Bars

Monaco Bar [MW,D] Av 27 de Febrero #40 (Frente Al Banco Santa Cruz), Santo Domingo **809/226-1589**

Santo Domingo

Accommodations

Caribe Colonial Hotel [GF,WI] Isabel Catolica 159 **809/688-7799** *boutique hotel*

Bars

Esedeku [MW,D] **809/763-8292** *8pm-close, from 5pm Sun, clsd Mon*

Fogoo Discotec [M,D,DS] 67 Calle Arzobispo Nouel (btw Espaillat & Santome) **809/401-8559**

Restaurants

El Conuco 152 Casimiro de Moya (behind Jaragua Hotel) **809/686-0129** *touristy local landmark*

Onno's Bar [M,DS] 157 Calle Hostos (at El Conde) **809/689-1183** *clsd Mon-Wed, DJ on the wknds; also two other locations in Cabarete and Altos de Chavon*

Entertainment & Recreation

Parque Duarte Calle Duarte (at Calle Padre Billini) *Th-Sun nights, this park is the gathering place for young gay Dominicans*

Men's Clubs

Apolo Spa 108 Calle Arzobispo Noue (btw 19 de Marzo & Calle Duarte) **829/689-0599** *2pm-11pm*

Erotica

Cine Lido [AYOR] 342 Avenida Mella **809/764-0537** *0:30pm-10:30pm*

Cruisy Areas

Avenida el Conde [AYOR] *pedestrian mall*

Dutch & French West Indies

Aruba

Accommodations

Little David Guest House [M,SW,N,GO] Seroe Blanco 56L, Oranjestad **297/583-8288**

Bars

Jimmy's Place [★GS,NH,D,F] Windstraat 32, Oranjestad **297/582-2550** *5pm-1am, till 3am Fri-Sat, clsd Sun-Mon*

The Paddock [GS,NH,F] LG Smith Blvd #13, Oranjestad **297/583-2334, 297/583-2606** *10am-2am*

Restaurants

Cafe the Plaza Seaport Marketplace, Oranjestad **297/583-8826** *8am-1am, patio*

CRUISY AREAS

Eagle Beach [AYOR] btwn La Quinta Resort & Dutch Village Hotel, Oranjestad *afternoons*

Barbados

ACCOMMODATIONS

Gemini House B&B [GF,WI] 70 Plover Court, Inch Marlow, Christ Church **246/428-7221** *close to beach great brkfst*

Inchcape Seaside Villas [GF,WI] **246/428-7006** *private villa rentals tucked away from the touristy areas*

ENTERTAINMENT & RECREATION

Baxter's Road Bridgetown *many cafés & bars, also cruisy area in the car park after 10pm Fri-Sat*

Curacao

INFO LINES & SERVICES

Pink House Incastraat 16, Willemstad **5999/462-6616** *LGBT community center, health & rights organization; also events*

ACCOMMODATIONS

The Avila Beach Hotel [GF] 130 Penstraat, Willemstad **800/747-8162 , 599-9/461-4377** *downtown luxury beachfront hotel, restaurants, bars & spa on site*

Floris Suite Hotel [M,SW,WI,WC,GO] Piscadera Bay **5999/462-6111, 800/411-0170**

Kura Hulanda [GF] Langestraat 8, Willemstad **888/264-3106 , 5999/434-7700** *also Jacob's Bar*

Papagayo Beach Resort [GF] Willemstad **5999/747-4333** *luxury, versatility and modern design, restaurant and beach club*

BARS

Grand Cafe De Heeren [GS,E] Zuikertuintjeweg 1 **5999/736-0491** *9am-1am, till 2:30am Th-Fri, clsd Sun, also restaurant*

Mundo Bizarro [GF,E] Nieuwestraat 12 (in the Pietermaai quarter) **5999/461-6767** *weird & wonderful eatery & café*

Rainbow Lounge [MW] at Floris Suite Hotel, Piscadera Bay **5999/462-6111** *5pm-midnight*

NIGHTCLUBS

Cabana Beach [GF,D] at Seaquarium Beach **599/946-5158** *open Wed-Sat, also restaurant*

RESTAURANTS

O Mundo [E] Zuikertuintje Shopping Mall, Willemstad **5999 /738-8477** *10am-10pm*

ENTERTAINMENT & RECREATION

Cas Abao Beach *popular local beach*

Dolphin Academy Curaçao Sea Aquarium, Bapor Kibra z/n (east of Willemstad, at Sea Aquarium Park) **5999/465-8900, 5999/465-8300** *swim w/ dolphins!*

Jan Thiel Beach *good people-watching*

Mambo Beach Boulevard Sea Aquarium Beach *shops, restaurants and more*

Museum Kura Hulanda Klipstraat 9, Willemstad **5999/434-7765** *African history & culture, Antillean art*

Saba

ACCOMMODATIONS

Juliana's Hotel [GS,SW,WI] Dutch West Indies, Windwardside **599/416-2269, 866/783-3319** *full brkfst, ocean & garden views, also Saban-style cottages & restaurant*

St Barthelemy

ACCOMMODATIONS

Cheval Blanc St-Barth Isle de France [GF,F] Plage des Flamands **590-590 /275 -666, 800/810-4691** *ultraluxe hotel*

Hotel le Village St-Jean [GF,SW] St-Jean Hill **590-590/27-61-39, 800/651-8366** *hotel & cottages*

BARS

Le Sélect [GF,F] 132 Rue de France (Gustavia) **590-590/27-86-87** *oldest and best meeting place in St Barths, good burgers*

Restaurants

Le Grain de Sel [★] Grand Saline Beach **590/524-605** *lunch & dinner, clsd Mon, relaxing setting, ideal before & after sunbathing*

Entertainment & Recreation

Anse Gouverneur St-Jean Beach [N] *perfect beach*

Anse Grande Saline Beach [N] *gay section on the left side of Saline*

St Maarten

Accommodations

Blue Ocean Villas [GF] **804/714-8290** *private villa rentals*

Holland House [GF] 43 Front St, Philipsburg **721/542-2572, 800/370-1329** *on the beach, restaurant, bar*

St Martin

Accommodations

Villa Rainbow [MO,SW,NS,WI,GO] Pic Paradis *stone villa w/ view of Caribbean, info@villarainbow.fr*

Nightclubs

Eros [M,D] Rue Victor Maurasse, Marigot **590/690-881-930** *11pm Sat & some other nights, spectacular view from top of the club*

Lotus [GS,D] 111 Welfare Rd (Simpson Bay) **599/545-2861** *10pm-4am, clsd Sun-Tue*

Restaurants

L' Escapade [R] 94 Blvd de Grand Case **590-590/87-75-04** *French*

Le Pressoir 30 Blvd de Grand Case **590-590/87-76-62** *dinner nightly, clsd Sun*

Entertainment & Recreation

Orient Beach on the northeast side of the island *gay-friendly nude beach*

Cruisy Areas

Cupecoy Beach [AYOR] park at established lot w/ blue & white "Cupecoy Beach" sign (near French border) *gay beach, take a friend & avoid if beach is secluded*

Jamaica

Montego Bay

Accommodations

Half Moon [GF,SW] **800/626-0592** *upscale resort*

Negril

Accommodations

Seagrape Villas [GS] The Cliffs, West End Rd **831/625-1255 (US#)** *3 lovely seafront villas*

Ocho Rios

Accommodations

Golden Clouds Villa [GF,SW,WC,GO] North Coast Rd, Oracabessa **876/544-9497, 800/516-4353** *private estate, full brkfst, fully staffed*

Port Antonio

Accommodations

Hotel Mocking Bird Hill [GF,F,SW,WC,GO] **876/993-7267, 876/993-7134**

Martinique

Les Trois Ilets

Accommodations

Le Carbet B&B [MW,N,GO] 18 rue des Alamandas (in Anse Mitan district) **596/596-66-0331** *quiet & private location; rooftop jacuzzi, near beach, restauraunts & water sports; 20 minutes from airport*

PUERTO RICO

Please Note: For those with rusty or no Spanish, "carretera" means "highway" and "calle" means "street."

Baja Sucia

ENTERTAINMENT & RECREATION

Playa Sucia/ La Playuela S of Cabo Rojo Nat'l Wildlife Refuge, Guanica *beautiful, secluded beach*

Bayamon

BARS

Start Night Club [MW,DS] 31 Ongay St (behind Clendo lab) **787/536-3579** *9pm-2am Th, 10pm-4am Fri-Sat only*

Guanica

ENTERTAINMENT & RECREATION

Gilligan's Island take Rd 333 to Copamarina Resort, then take ferry to island **787/821-4941 (ferry info)** *beautiful beach located in a biosphere on Southern coast of PR*

Rincon

ACCOMMODATIONS

The Horned Dorset [GS,SW] Apartado 1132 **787/823-4030** *luxury living and hotel accommodations*

Lemontree Oceanfront Cottages [GS,NS,WI,WC] Carr 429, km 4.1 (at Carr 115) **787/823-6452** *kids ok*

San Juan

INFO LINES & SERVICES

Centro Communitario LGBTTPR/ LGBT Community Center 37 Calle Mayaguez **787/294-9850** *1pm-9pm, clsd wknds, psychosocial services, support groups, activities*

ACCOMMODATIONS

Acacia Seaside Inn [GF,SW,WI] 8 Taft St (at McLeary) **787/727-0668, 787/727-0626**

Andalucia Guesthouse & Vacation Rentals [M,WI,GO] 2011 McLeary Ave (at San Miguel St, Ocean Park) **787/309-3373**

Casa del Caribe Guest House [GF,NS,WI] Calle Caribe 57, Condado (at Magdalena) **787/722-7139, 877/722-7139**

La Concha [GS] 1077 Ashford Ave, Condado **787/721-7500** *retro urban showcase & architectural landmark*

Coqui del Mar Guesthouse [GF,GO] 2218 Calle General del Valle (at General Patton, Ocean Park) **787/220-4204**

Hotel El Convento [GF,SW,WI] Calle Cristo 100, Old San Juan (btwn Caleta de las Monjas & Calle Sol) **787/723-9020, 800/468-2779**

Miramar Hotel [GF,WI] 606 Ave Ponce de Leon (at Miramar) **787/977-1000** *also restaurant & bar*

Numero Uno on the Beach [GS,SW,WC] Calle Santa Ana 1, Ocean Park (near Calle Italia) **787/726-5010, 866/726-5010** *also Pamela's restaurant & bar*

The San Juan Water & Beach Club Hotel [GF,SW,NS,WI,WC] 2 Tartak St (Isla Verde), Carolina **787/728-3666, 888/265-6699** *boutique hotel on beach, restaurant & lounge*

BARS

Atlantic Beach Bar & Hotel [GS] 1 Calle Vendig, Condado **787/721-6900** *10am-2am, great beach location*

Batucada [GS,NH,K] 15 Ave Carlos Chardon, Hato Rey **787/993-1291** *sports bar & grill*

Oasis [★M] Av Condado 6 (in Condado, next to the San Juan Marriot) **787/721-7145** *1pm-close, near beach*

SX [M,D,S] 1204 Ponce de Leon (at RH Todd Ave) *stripper bar*

Tia Maria's [MW,NH] 326 Ave Jose de Diego, Parada 22 (at Ponce de León), Santurce **787/724-4011** *noon-2am, also liquor shop*

Nightclubs

Circo Bar [★M,D,K,DS] Calle Condado 650, Parada 18, Santurce **787/725-9676** *9pm-5am, beware of the neighborhood*

Polo Norte Gay Lounge [M] 261 Calle Tetuan **787/469-5147**

Cafes

Cafe Berlin [★] Calle San Francisco 407, Plaza Colón, Old San Juan (btwn Calles Norzagary & O'Donnel) **787/722-5205** *11am-11pm, espresso bar*

Kasalta Bakery 1966 McLeary Ave (at Teniente Matta) **787/727-7340** *6am-10pm, bakery & deli*

Restaurants

Aguaviva [WC] 364 Calle La Fortaleza, Old San Juan (at Calle O'Donnell) **787/722-0665** *dinner nightly, fresh seafood & ceviche*

Ajili Mojili 1052 Ashford Ave, Condado (at Aguadilla) **787/725-9195** *local specialties, live music, great ambiance*

Bebo's Cafe 1600 Calle Loiza (at Del Parque) **787/268-5087** *cheap & delicious, cafeteria-style Puerto Rican favorites*

Cafe Puerto Rico 208 O'Donnell, Old San Juan **787/724-2281** *noon-11pm, great mofongo, patio*

La Casita Blanca 351 Calle Tapia (off Ave Eduardo Conde, near Laguna Los Corozas) **787/726-5501** *11am-4pm, till 6pm Th, till 9pm Fri-Sat, amazing local cuisine, best reached by car, no English spoken, beware of neighborhood*

Colombo [WI] 1024 Ashford Ave (at Aguadilla St) **787/725-1212** *8am-3am, American, also bar*

Dragonfly 364 S Fortaleza St, Old San Juan (across from Parrot Club) **787/977-3886** *opens 5:30pm daily, full bar*

Fleria 1754 Calle Loiza, Santurce **787/268-0010** *lunch & dinner, clsd Sun-Mon, Greek*

El Jibarito Calle Sol 280 **787/725-8375** *Puerto Rican/ criolla, also bar*

Oceano Restaurant & Lounge 2 Calle Vendig, Condado **787/724-6400** *great location on the beach, Sun gay party*

Perla 1077 Ashford Ave, at La Concha Resort, Condado **787/721-7500** *enjoy an upscale dining experience inside a gigantic conch shell*

Vidy's Cafe [K] Ave Universidad 104 (Rio Piedras) **787/767-3062** *10am-1am, plenty veggie*

Entertainment & Recreation

Atlantic Beach in front of Atlantic Beach Hotel *very gay-friendly beach*

Nuyorican Cafe San Francisco 312 (by El Callejon) **787/977-1276, 787/366-5074** *live music & arts venue*

Ocean Park Beach E of Condado *adult-oriented (less kids)*

La Placita/ Plaza del Mercado Santurce *open-air market by day, street-party by night; lots of bars & restaurants*

Gyms & Health Clubs

Muscle Factory Avenida Ashford (at Vendig, Condado) **787/721-0717** *gay gym, fun shower activity*

Men's Clubs

Xteamworks Bath House 1752 Ave Fernandez Juncos **787/728-7674** *6pm-midnight, till 4am Fri-Sat*

Cruisy Areas

Parque Central [AYOR] at Interstate PR-1 & PR-2 *popular evenings*

La Playita [AYOR] Av Muñoz Rivera (in front of capitol bldg in Old San Juan) *afternoons*

Scenic Overlook [AYOR] off Muñoz Rivera Dr *observation parking area near capitol bldg*

Las Uvas [AYOR] E of Condado (at Ocean Park Beach, W of Calle Yardley Pl) *mixed gay/ straight by day, cruisy by night*

Bars

Temptation [M,D,F] 608 Calle Bolivar (Santruce) **787/309-8888** *10pm-3am, from 5pm Fri*

Vieques Island

Accommodations

Bravo! [GS,SW,GO] North Shore Rd (at Lighthouse) **787/741-1128, 939/260-0110** *Vieques' "first true beachside designer hotel" w/ beautiful ocean views*

Hacienda Tamarindo [GF] just west of the village of Esperanza **787/741-8525** *is perched on a Vieques hilltop with spectacular 180 degree views of the Caribbean, full brkfst and many activities*

Hix Island House [GS,SW,NS,WI,WC] **787/435-4590** *open-air lofts, private terraces, yoga*

Trinidad & Tobago

Tobago

Accommodations

Grafton Beach Resort [GF,F,SW] **868/639-0191** *oceanfront resort on 5 acres*

Kariwak Village Hotel & Holistic Haven [GF,F,SW,WI,WC] Store Bay Local Rd, Crown Point **868/639-8442** *holistic hotel*

Virgin Islands

St Croix

Accommodations

Sand Castle on the Beach [★M,SW,WI,GO] 127 Smithfield, Frederiksted **340/772-1205** *gay resort (from rooms to beachfront villas), also restaurant & bar*

St John

Accommodations

Gallows Point Suite Resort [GF,F,SW,WC] Cruz Bay **340/776-6434, 800/323-7229** *beachfront resort*

Hillcrest Guest House [GF,NS,WI] **340/776-6774, 340/998-8388** *vacation rental suites*

St John Inn [GF,SW,NS,WI] **340/693-8688** *affordable, small boutique hotel*

Restaurants

Asolare Rte 20, Cruz Bay **340/779-4747** *5:30pm-9:30pm, Asian/ French fusion, hip and elegant with great views*

Entertainment & Recreation

Salomon Bay *20-minute hike on Salomon Beach Trail*

St Thomas

Accommodations

Pavilions & Pools Hotel [GF,SW] 6400 Estate Smith Bay **340/718-9150, 800/524-2001** *1-bdrm villas each w/ own private swimming pool*

Restaurants

Mafolie Hotel & Restaurant 7091 Estate Mafolie **340/774-2790** *great place for lunch w/ a view*

Oceana Restaurant & Wine Bar Historic Pointe at Villa Olga **340/774-4262** *dinner only, on the water's edge, owned by renowned chef Patricia LaCorte*

Virgilio's 18 Dronningens Gade **340/776-4920** *11:30am-10pm, clsd Sun, great Italian, full bar*

Entertainment & Recreation

Beach at Emerald Beach Resort up hill (near airport runway) *walking distance from cruise ship dock*

Little Magens Beach *gay nude beach, near main beach at Magens Bay*

Morning Star Beach *popular gay beach*

Mexico

MEXICO

Please Note: Mexican cities are often divided into districts or "Colonias," which we abbreviate as "Col." Please use these when giving addresses for directions.

Acapulco

ACCOMMODATIONS

Casa Condesa [M,SW] Bella Vista 125 **52-744/484-1616, 800/816-4817** *full brkfst*

Hotel Boca Chica [GF,SW] Punta Caletilla (Fraccionamiento las Playas) **833/422 3238** *1950s retro-cool hotel, restaurant & bar*

Hotel Encanto [GF,F,SW,WI] Jacques Cousteau 51 (Fraccionamiento Brisas Marques) **52-744/446-7101**

Las Brisas [GF,SW,WC] Carretera Escenica 5255 **52-744/469-6900** *luxury resort, private pools, kids ok*

BARS

Picante [★GS,D,S,AYOR,$] Privada Piedra Picuda 16 (behind Demas) **52-744/484-2209** *9pm-5am, popular male dancers, hustlers*

NIGHTCLUBS

Baby 'O [GS,D] **52-744/484-7474** *10:30pm-5am, till midnight Sun*

Demas Factory/ Pink [★MO,D,S,$] Ave de los Deportes #10 **52-744/484-1800** *10:30pm-3am*

Relax [★MW,D,K,DS,YC] Calle Lomas de Mar 4 (Zona Dorada) **52-744/287-1000** *1pm-4am*

RESTAURANTS

100% Natural Av Costera Miguel Alemán 200 (near Acapulco Plaza) **52-744/485-3982** *24hrs, fast (healthy) food, plenty veggie*

Becco al Mare 52-744/446-7402 *6pm-midnight, Italian, nice views*

Beto's Restaurant [★] Av Costera Miguel Alemán 99 (at Condesa Beach) **52-744/484-0473** *11am-midnight, full bar, seafood, palapas*

El Cabrito Av Costera Miguel Alemán 1480 **52-744/484-7711** *2pm-11pm, local favorite, you must try the roasted goat*

Carlos & Charlie's [E] Blvd de las Naciones #1813 (in La Isla Shopping Village) **52-744/462-2104** *lunch & dinner*

Kookaburra 3 Fracc (at Marina Las Brisas) **52-744/446-6039** *lunch & dinner, int'l, expensive*

La Cabaña de Caleta Playa Caleta Lado Oriente s/n (Fracc. las Playas) **52-744/469-8553, 52-744/469-7919** *9am-9pm, seafood, right on Playa Caleta, great magaritas*

La Tortuga [GO] Calle Lomas del Mar 5 **52-744/484-6985** *noon-midnight, clsd Mon, full bar, patio*

Shu Blvd de las Naciones 1813 (Centro Comercial La Isla) **52-744/462-2001** *Japanese*

Su Casa Av Anahuac 110 **52-744/484-1300** *5pm-midnight, seafood, tasty margaritas, great views*

Suntory de Acapulco Costera Miguel Alemán 36 **52-744/484-8088** *2pm-midnight, Japanese, gardens*

El Zorrito's Av Costera Miguel Alemán (at Anton de Alaminos) **52-744/485-3735** *traditional Mexican, several locations along Costera, some all night*

CRUISY AREAS

Playa Condesa & Beto's Beach near Hotel Fiesta Americana *cruisy by the rocks, at sundown*

Plaza Alvarez/ Zócalo [AYOR] *hustlers (chichifos)*

San Diego Fort [AYOR] along the Costera

Aguascalientes

Cruisy Areas

Plaza Principal [AYOR]

Cabo San Lucas

Accommodations

Cabo Villas Beach Resort [GF,SW] Callejon del Pescador s/n (Col. El Medano) **52-624/143-9166, 866/962-2268** *resort on Medano Beach*

Solmar Suites [GF,SW] Av Solmar 1 **800/344-3349** *oceanfront suites at southernmost tip*

Nightclubs

Las Varitas [GF,D,E] Calle Vallentin Gomez Farias (at Camino Viejo a San Jose) **52-624/143-9999** *9pm-3am, clsd Mon*

Restaurants

Mi Casa [R] Av Cabo San Lucas (at Lazarus Cardenas) **52-624/143-1933** *lunch & dinner, great chicken mole*

Cancun

Entertainment & Recreation

see also Cozumel & Playa del Carmen

Accommodations

Rancho Sak Ol [GF] Puerto Morelos **52-998/292-896** *beachfront palapa-style B&B, 30 minutes from Cancún*

Bars

11:11 [M,D,K] Avenida Tulum, El Centro (M22 M5 Lotes 33 y 35) **52-998/135 2243** *10pm-6am Fri-Sat*

Picante Bar [★M,D,DS,S,YC] Av Tulúm 20, Centro (E of Av Uxmal, next to Plaza Galerías) *9pm-5am, hustlers, [DS,S] Wed-Sat*

Restaurants

100% Natural Sunyaxchen 62 **52-998/884-0102** *healthy fast food*

Perico's Av Yaxhilan 61 **52-998/887 -884** *noon-1am, traditional Mexican served up w/ huge theatrical flare*

Entertainment & Recreation

Chichén Itza *the must-see Mayan ruin 125 miles from Cancún*

Playa Delfines in the Hotel Zone (next to Hilton's beach) *gay beach*

Cruisy Areas

Avenida Tulúm [AYOR] Centro *take a stroll & take your pick, late*

El Mirador (Ruinas del Rei) [AYOR] next to Hilton Hotel (near the lighthouse)

Parque de las Palapas [AYOR] opposite Cinema Blanquita *near the Cine Blanquita*

Playa Delfines [AYOR] at S end of hotel zone *afternoons, beware cops (!) back in the bushes*

Chihuahua

Accommodations

Hacienda Huiyochi [MW] Copper Canyon **51-1/625-121-8101** *first and only hotel in Copper Canyon that caters to the LGBT community, full brkfst, kids/pets ok*

Ciudad Juárez

see also El Paso, Texas, USA

Bars

Club La Escondida [GS,NH] Calle Ignacio de la Peña 366 W **52-656/612-0234**

Club Olímpico [M,NH,P] Av Lerdo 210 S (city center) **52-656/612-5742** *noon-2am*

Nightclubs

G-Life Club [M,D] 16 de septiembre 119 (at Constitucion) **52-656/304-4513** *4pm-9pm Th-Fri and 9am-3pm Sat only*

Men's Clubs

Baños Roma Calle Ignacio Mejía 881 E (at Calle Constitución) **52-656/612-7732** *9am-9pm*

Cruisy Areas

Plaza de la Constitución [AYOR] Plaza Hidalgo

Cordoba

Cruisy Areas

Mercado Juárez [AYOR] btwn Calles 7 & 9

Sidewalk Cafes [AYOR] El Portal Zevallos

Cozumel

see also Cancún & Playa del Carmen

Accommodations

Flamingo Hotel [GF] Calle 6 Norte #81 (at Ave 5) **954/351-9236, 800/806-1601**

Cuernavaca

Accommodations

Casa del Angel [GS,NS,GO] Calle Clavel 18, Col. Satelite (at Begonia) **52-777/512-6775** *contemporary guesthouse on hill overlooking 16th-c city of Cuernavaca, hot tub, full brkfst*

Las Mañanitas [GF,SW] Ricardo Linares 107 **52-777/362-0000** *a Relaix & Chateaux-award-winning resort, gardens, restaurant, peacocks!*

La Nuestra [GS,SW,NS,WI,GO] Calle Mesalina 18 (at Calle Neptuno) **52-777/315-2272, 404/806-9694**

Bars

Barecito [MW,F,GO] Comonfort 17 (at Morrow) **52-777/314-1425**

La Casa del Dictador [M,D] Jacarandas 4 (at Av Emiliano Zapata) **52-777/317-3186, 52-777/317-2377** *wknds only, garden*

Restaurants

La India Bonita Dwight Morrow 15 (btwn Morelos & Matamoros) **52-777/312-5021** *9am-9pm, till 5pm Sun-Mon*

La Maga [E] Calle Morrow #9 Altos **52-777/310-3871** *1pm-9pm, till 11pm Th-Sat, clsd Sun, buffet style*

Marco Polo Calle Hidalgo 30 (in front of cathedral, 2nd flr) **52-777/312-3484, 52-777/318-4032** *1pm-close, Italian (pasta & pizza), overlooking cathedral*

Entertainment & Recreation

Diego Rivera Murals Plaza de Museo (in Cuauhnáhuac Regional Museum)

Men's Clubs

Banos San Carlos Amado Nervo 111 (Col. Carolina) **52-777/317-2796** *6am-8am, clsd Sun*

Tepoz Spa [18+,SW] Carretera San Andres de la Cal #69 (next to Gallaecia), Tepoztlan, Morelos **739/395-8457** *11am-9:30pm Sat-Sun only, also apt rental*

Cruisy Areas

Mercado [AYOR] *Sun*

Plaza Morelos [AYOR]

Zócalo [AYOR] *also adjacent bar, Fri-Sat only*

Guadalajara

Accommodations

Casa Alebrijes Hotel [M,WI,GO] Libertad 1016, Zona Centro **52-33/3614-5232** *boutique hotel in historic center, two blocks from gay nightlife area*

Casa de las Flores B&B [GS,WI,GO] Santos Degollado 175, Tlaquepaque **52-33/3659-3186** *15 minutes from downtown Guadalara, wonderful breakfasts-and margaritas!*

Casa Venezuela [GS,NS,WI,GO] Calle Venezuela 459 (at Col. Americana) **52-33/3826-6590** *B&B in 100-year-old colonial house, full brkfst*

Casa Vilasanta [GS,WI] Calle Rayon 170 **52-33/3124-1277** *great little boutique hotel/hostel in an awesome location*

Hostel Lit [GF,WI] Degollado 413 **52-33/1200-5505** *great location*

Hotel San Francisco [GF,F] Degollado 267 **52-33/3613-3256** *hotel with Old World charm, balconies and courtyards, close to many gay bars, also restaurant*

Old Guadalajara B&B [GS,NS,GO] Belén 236 (Centro Histórico) **52-33/3613-9958** *elegant private 16th-century home; in downtown historic district; quiet, peaceful and discreet; perfectly safe; gay owners always available*

La Perla B&B [GS,NS,WI,GO] Prado 128, Col. Americana (Vallarta y Lopez Cotilla) **317/534-2661** *full breakfast, "B&B in the heart of Guadalajara" that once belonged to Gloria Marin: "our theme is the 'Golden Age of Mexican Cinema'"*

La Villa del Ensueño [GS,NS] Florida St 305, Tlaquepaque **52-33/3635-8792** *beautiful little and colorful boutique hotel, great brkfst*

BARS

California's [M] Pedro Moreno 652 (at 8 de Julio, Col. Centro) **52-33/3614-3221** *9pm-3am, clsd Mon-Tue*

Caudillos Bar [★M,D,F,YC] Calle Prisciliano Sánchez 305, Centro (at Ocampo) **52-33/3613-5445** *5pm-3am, dancing from 9pm, friendly bar, also restaurant*

El Ciervo [M,D] 20 de Noviembre 797 (at Los Angeles, Sector Reforma) **52-33/3619-6765** *cruisy*

Club YeYe [MW,V,F] Prisciliano Sánchez 395 (Zona Centro) **52-33/1337-5253** *5pm-3am, chic video lounge*

Condado [MO,CW] Colon 434 (btwn Leandro Valle & Nueva Galicia) **52-33/1400-1159** *6pm-3am Wed-Sun*

Dolce Veele [MW,F,K,WI] Enrique González Martínez 177 **52-33/1523-9593** *4pm-3am*

Equilibrio [GS,D,$] Ocampo 293 (at Miguel Blanco) **52-33/3658-3988** *1pm-4am*

Maskaras [MW,NH,F,E] Calle Maestranza 238 (at Prisciliano Sánchez) **52-33/3614-8103** *noon-3am, colorful atmosphere, live music*

Voltio [MO,L,B,S] Mexicaltzingo 1521 (Av Enrique Diaz de Leon) *theme nights*

NIGHTCLUBS

Babel [M,D] Morelos 741 **52-33/3146-1520** *Fri-Sat only*

CAFES

Vida Caffe [MW] Av.Juarez 604 (Centro histórico) **52-33/3825-4195** *5pm-midnight*

GYMS & HEALTH CLUBS

Renacer Day Spa [★MO] Amado Nervo 106 (Col. Ladrón de Guevara) **52-33/3616-4441** *noon-10pm, European-style day spa, sauna, steam room, , solarium*

MEN'S CLUBS

Baños Guadalajara Federalismo Sur #634 **52-33/3826-4149** *6:30am-8:30pm, till 2:30pm Sun, 3 steam rooms, bar, massage, popular afternoons*

Banos Santa Terecita Andres Teram #462 (btwn Manuel Acuna & Herrara y Cairo Sts, Colonia Santa Terecita) **52-33/3825-1464** *7am-8:30pm, popular evenings, four steam rooms*

Riilax [MO] Venustiano Carranza 313 (at Angulo) **52-33/3331-1062**

CRUISY AREAS

Parque Revolución [AYOR] Av Juárez at Av Federalismo

Plaza Tapatía [AYOR] near Degollado Theater *days*

Isla Mujeres

ACCOMMODATIONS

Casa Sirena [GF,GO] Av Miguel Hidalgo, Centro (at Bravo y Allende) *Isla Mujeres is a short, 20-minute ferry ride from Cancun. rooftop bar*

La Paz

ACCOMMODATIONS

Hotel Mediterrane [GS,F,NS,WI,GO] Allende 36 (at Malecón) **52-612/125-1195** *sundeck, also bar & restaurant*

CAFES

Zoe [GO] Allende 36 (at Hotel Mediterrane) **52-612/125-1195** *opens 7am*

CRUISY AREAS

Malecón (Seawall) [AYOR] *afternoon & early evening*

León

NIGHTCLUBS

La Madame [M,D,DS] Mariano Escobedo #2903 **52-477/763-3086** *10pm-3am, clsd Mon-Wed, go-go boys*

Manzanillo

ACCOMMODATIONS

Las Hadas [GF,SW] Av Vista Hermosa s/n (Fracc. Península de Santiago) **52-314/331-0101, 888/559-4329** *great resort & location*

Red Tree Melaque Inn [GF,SW,NS,WI,GO] Primaveras 32 (30 miles N of Manzanillo), Melaque-Villa Obregon **52-315/355-8917, 480/389-5786 (US)** *bungalows, near ocean*

CRUISY AREAS

Santiago Beach [AYOR]

Mazatlán

ACCOMMODATIONS

El Cid Resort [GF,SW] **888/733-308**

The Pueblo Bonito Emerald Bay [GF,SW] Ave Ernesto Coppel Compaña 201 **52-669/989-0525, 800/990-8250** *also piano bar*

Ramada Mazatlán [GF,SW] Av Playa Gaviotas 100 (Zona Dorada) **52-669/983-5333, 800/528-8760 (US#)** *resort, also popular Joe's Oyster Bar*

BARS

Vitrolas Bar [MW,F,K,DS,S] Heriberto Frías 1608 (in Centro Historico) **52-669/985-2221** *3pm-1am, clsd Mon, lunch menu*

RESTAURANTS

Roca Mar [★] Av del Mar (at Calle Isla de Lobos, Zona Costera) **52-669/981-6008** *seafood, full bar*

MEN'S CLUBS

Baños Mazatlan Sodomas [AYOR] Calle Genaro Estrada 712 (btwn Benito Juarez & Arquiles Serdan) **52-669/209-8953** *1pm-10pm, busy after 5pm, sleazy*

Mérida

ACCOMMODATIONS

Angeles de Mérida [GF,SW,NS] Calle 74-A, #494-A (at Calle 57 & Calle 59) **52-999/923-8163** *restored 18th-c home, full brkfst, spa services available*

Los Arcos B&B [GF,SW,GO] Calle 66 **52-999/928 0214** *colonial home from 1800s, in heart of Mérida's Centro, courtyard*

Casa Ana B&B [GF,SW,NS] Calle 52 #469 (btwn 51 & 53) **52-999/924-0005**

La Casa Lorenzo [GF,SW,WI,GO] Calle 41 #516 A (btwn 62 & 64) **954/302-3273 (US#), 844/493-5974** *great location and brkfst*

Gran Hotel [GF,F] Calle 60 #496 (nr Parque Cepeda Peraza) **52-999/924-7730 & 923-6963** *historic turn-of-the-century hotel, courtyard with balconies, also restaurant*

Posada Santiago Guesthouse [GS,SW,NS,WI,WC,GO] Calle 57 No 552 (between Calle 66 & 68, Centro Historico) **52-999/2902-7008** *blend of Yucatán culture & North American ambiance; near Zocalo; kitchenettes*

NIGHTCLUBS

Pride Disco [M,D,S] Campeche A (200 meters del Puente de Ulman), Anillo Periferico **52-999/946-4401** *south of town, take a taxi*

Restaurants

Cafe La Habana Calle 59 #511-A (at Calle 62) **52-999/928-6502** *24hrs, also bar & café*

Cafeteria Pop [BW] Calle 57 (btwn Calle 60 & 62) **52-999/928-6163** *brkfst, lunch & "light dinner"*

La Bella Época Calle 60 #447 (upstairs in the Hotel del Parque) **52-99/928-1928** *4pm-1am, Yucatécan, try for a balcony table*

Men's Clubs

La Banana Azul [M,WI,NS,GO] 514 Calle 70 (btwn 65 & 67, 3 blocks from Parque Santiago) **52-999/923-3957** *3pm-8pm, steam room, massage, gym*

Cruisy Areas

Calle 60 [AYOR] btwn the Zócalo & Santa Lucia park

Santa Lucia Park [AYOR] *late afternoons & evenings*

Zócalo [AYOR] near corner of Calle 60 & 61

Mexico City

Note: M°=Metro station

Note: Mexico City is divided into "Zonas" (ie, Zona Rosa) & "Colonias" (abbreviated here as "Col."). Remember to use these when giving addresses to taxi drivers.

Info Lines & Services

Cálamo (LGBT AA) Av de Chapultepec 465, desd 202 (Col. Juárez) **52-55/5574-1210** *8pm Mon-Fri, 7pm Sat, 6pm Sun*

Centro Cultural de la Diversidad Sexual Colima 267 (Col. Roma Norte) **52-55/4414-2565** *Mexico City's LGBT center, also cafe*

Accommodations

Las Alcobas [★GS,WI] Presidente Masaryk 390A **52-55/3300-3900** *a former apartment complex, this masterfully designed boutique hotel has evolved from a series of private 'homes' into a collection of meticulously crafted, intimate alcoves, two restaurants on site and spa*

Best Western Majestic Hotel [GF,WC] Ave Madero 73, Col. Centro **52-55/5521-8600** *on the Zócalo Plaza, rooftop restaurant*

Condesa Haus [GF,WI,GO] Cuernavaca 142 (at Campeche) **52-55/5350 8744** *great location and yummy brkfst*

Downtown México [GF,SW] 30 Isabel la Católica **52-55/5130-6830** *magnificent 17th century building, rooftop bar*

Hostal Central Historico Regina [GF,F,YC,WI] 5 de Febrero #53 (Col. Centro) **52-55/5434-5817** *rooftop bar and free brkfst*

Hotel Casa Blanca [GF,F,SW] Lafragua 7 (Col. Tabacalera) **52-55/5096-4500** *also restaurant & bar*

Hotel Gillow [GF,F,WI] Isabel la Católica 17 (Col. Centro) **52-55/5518-1440** *close to Zócalo and museums, moderately priced, also restaurant and bar*

Hotel Principado [GF,F,WI] Londres 42 (Col Juarez) **52-55/5533-2944** *Hotel Principadogood location, no frills*

El Patio 77 [GF,WI] Icazbalceta 77 (Col. San Rafael) **52-55/5455-0332**, **52-55/5592-8452** *eco-friendly B&B*

The Red Tree House [GF,GO] Culiacan 6 (at Avenida Amsterdam) **52-55/5584-3829** *stylish B&B*

W Mexico City [★GF,WI] Campos Eliseos 252 **52-55/9138-1800** *in trendy Polanco, 2 restaurants & bar*

Bars

Bar Lili [MW,NH] Calle 65 #5 (Col. Puebla) **52-55/4551-0414**

Boy Bar [M,S] Amberes 14 (Zona Rosa) **52-55/3011-1059**, **52-55/5207-5591** *10pm-close Th-Sat only*

Drrama by 42 [M,DS,K] Amberes 4 (Zona Rosa) **52-55/5208-0352** *open 6pm, clsd Sun-Mon*

La Gayta/ Pussy Bar [MW,NH,YC] Amberes 18 (Zona Rosa) **52-55/1406 4016** *1pm-2am*

Kinky Bar [GS,DS,V] Amberes 1 (at Paseo de la Reforma, Zona Rosa) **52-55/5514-4920** *clsd Sun-Wed, lounge, more gay Fri-Sat*

El Marrakech Salón [MW,NH] Republica de Cuba 18 (Col. Centro) **52-222/362 2627** *6pm-2:30am, clsd Sun-Wed*

Oasis [M,K,DS,$] República de Cuba 2 (Centro Historico) **52-55/5511-9740** *3pm-1am, till 3am Fri-Sat*

Papi Fun Bar aka King [MW,NH,YC] Amberes 18 (Zona Rosa) **52-55/5208-3755** *2pm-1:30am*

El Taller/ El Almacen [MO,D,B,L,S,V] Av Florencia 37-A, Zona Rosa (basement, no sign so look for big nuts & bolts above door) **52-55/5207-0727** *5pm-3am, clsd Mon, cruisy leather/ levi crowd, also sex shop*

Tom's Leather Bar [★M,B,L,S,V,$] Av Insurgentes 357 (Col. Condesa) **55-84/5564-0728** *9pm-2:30am, clsd Mon*

Viena Bar [★M] República de Cuba 3 (Centro Historico) **52-55/5512-0929** *11am-11pm, clsd Mon-Tue, beer bar*

Nightclubs

Bearmex [MO,B] Calle Londres 182 *open 8pm, clsd Sun*

Cabaré-Tito Fusion [MW,18+] Londres 77 (Zona Rosa) **52-55/5511-1613** *open 4pm, clsd Mon-Tue, drag shows Th*

Cabaré-Tito Neón [MW,D,DS,S] Calle Londres 161, Local 20-A, Plaza del Angel (Zona Rosa) **52-55/644-6259** *6pm-close*

Envy [GS,D] Av. Pdte. Masaryk 393 (Col Polanco) **52-55/5280-5646** *11pm-4am Fri only*

Hibrido [MW,D,S] Florencia 56 (Zona Rosa) **52-55/5511-1197** *Th-Sun*

Restaurants

Azul Historico 30 Isabel la Católica **52-55/5510-1316** *9am-11pm, on the first floor of an open building with trees inside, great food and cocktails*

El Cardenal Calle de Palma 23 **52-55/5521-8815** *8am-6:30pm, incredible pastries*

Casa Merlos Victoriano Zepeda 80 (at Obsevatoria) **52-55/5277-4360** *1pm-6pm, clsd Mon-Wed, traditional poblano food, definitely try the molé*

La Nueva Opera [P] Ave Cinco de Mayo 10 (Centro Historico) **52-55/5512-8959** *1pm-midnight, clsd Sun, legendary cantina since Pancho Villa fired a bullet into the ceiling*

Xel-Ha **52-55/5553-5968** *1pm-midnight, till 7pm Sun, traditional cuisine of the Yucatan*

Entertainment & Recreation

Museo de Arte Carrillo Gil Av Revolución 1608 (Col San Angel) **52-55/5550-6260, 52-55/5550-3983** *10am-6pm, clsd Mon, contemporary art*

Museo de Frida Kahlo Calle Londres 247 (Coyacán) **52-55/5554-5999** *10am-5:45pm, clsd Mon, also garden & café*

Museo Templo Mayor Calle Seminario 8 (at República de Guatemala, enter on plaza, near Cathedral) **52-55/4040-5600** *9am-5pm, clsd Mon, artifacts from the central Aztec temple at Tenochtitlán*

Bookstores

El Armario Abierto Agustín Melgar 25 (Col. Condesa) **52-55/5286-0895** *Mexico's only bookstore specializing in sexuality, some LGBT titles*

Retail Shops

Rainbowland Estrasburgo 31 (Zona Rosa) **52-55/5207-0432** *1pm-10pm, flags, accessories, souvenirs, movies, books, underwear & swimwear and much more LGBTIQ items*

Publications

Revista G *magazine*

Gyms & Health Clubs

Qi Wellness Center Amsterdam 317 (in Condesa) **52-55/5564-5888** *gym w/ spa*

Men's Clubs

Baños Finisterre [AYOR] Manuel Maria Contreras 11, Col. San Rafael (4 blocks W of M° San Cosme) **52-55/5555-3543** *6am-9pm, till 4pm Sun, traditional bathhouse where men go, hang out, and get a massage; not "anything goes" like in US or Europe*

Baños San Juan [AYOR] Calle López 120 (N of M° Salto de Agua, in Centro Historico) **52-55/5510-4602** *6:30am-8:30pm*

Baños Señorial [AYOR] Calle Isabel la Católica 92 (Centro Historico) **52-55/5709-3120**

La Casita II [AYOR,18+] Insurgentes S 228 (Col. Roma) **52-55/5514-4639** *24hrs*

Club San Francisco Calle Rio Tiber 36 **52-55/5525-0936** *6am-11pm, 10am-3pm Sat, clsd Sun, more of a gym*

So Do Me [★] **52-55/5250-6653** *noon-10pm, till 1am Fri, 24hrs wknds*

La Toalla Obregon [AYOR,18+] Álvaro Obregón 259 (Col. Roma) **52-55/5511-0686** *24hrs*

Cruisy Areas

Alameda Central [AYOR] W side of park (Centro Historico) *afternoons & early evenings, dangerous later*

Bosque de Chapultepec [AYOR] either side of gate to monument (Zona Rosa) *afternoons*

Zona Rosa [AYOR] *nights, anywhere & everywhere, but especially Calle Florencia btwn Reforma & Liverpool, also Calles Génova, Hamburgo & Londres*

Monterrey

Accommodations

Travohotel Monterrey Histórico [GF,SW] Av Padre Mier 194 N (at Garibaldi, Centro) **52-81/8228-5100** *also restaurant, near Zona Rosa*

Bars

Akbal [GS,K] Abasolo 870B, 2nd flr, Casa del Maíz **52-81/1954-5628** *more gay Sun*

Nightclubs

Between Bar [M,D,DS] 2121 Eugenio Garza Sada Ave **52-81/1495-6710** *9pm-4am Fri-Sat only*

Men's Clubs

Baños Orientales Calle Hidalgo 310 Oriente, Guadalupe **52-81/8367-1768** *10am-11pm, sauna, steam bath, hustlers, in SE Monterrey*

Sparta Sauna Gym 107 Álvaro Obregón **52-81/1739-3111** *noon-midnight*

STIC Baños de Vapor & Spa Av de los Héroes 47 (at Av Francisco I Madero) **52-81/8375-7690** *6am-10pm, till 2pm Sun*

Cruisy Areas

Avenida Juárez [AYOR] btwn Calle Matamoros & Calle Padre Mier (Centro) *part of "El Circuito," hustlers*

Plaza Hidalgo [AYOR] Zona Rosa *late afternoons & early evenings*

Morelia

Accommodations

Hotel de la Soledad [GF,WI] Ignacio Zaragoza 90 **52-443/312-1888** *in converted convent, also restaurant & bar*

Bars

Sak Bar [M,] Av Morelos Nte 128 (Centro Histórico) **52-44/3312-6225** *6:30pm-2am, clsd Sun-Tue*

Nightclubs

Con la Rojas [M,D,$] Aldama 343 (Centro), Queretaro **52-442/212-4795** *9pm-3am, clsd Sun-Wed*

Con la Rojas [M,D,$] Calle Aldama 343 (Centro) **52-443/312-1578** *10pm-2:30am, clsd Sun-Tue*

Mamá no lo sabe [M,K] Aldama 116 (at García Obeso) **52-44/3258-7448** *10pm-3:30am, clsd Sun-Wed*

Restaurants

Fonda Las Mercedes [★] Calle Leon Guzmán 47 **52-443/312-6113** *inside beautiful colonial home*

Men's Clubs

Baños Mintzicuri Calle Vasco de Quiroga 227 (enter through the Hotel Mintzícuri) **52-443/312-0664** *gay area through door marked "Ruso General"*

Baños Valladolid Eduardo Ruiz 605 **52-44/3312-9985** *6am-10pm*

Erotica

Cine Arcadia Eduardo Ruiz 870 **52-44/3484-1583** *noon-midnight*

Cruisy Areas

Escalinatas de Santa María [AYOR]

Oaxaca

Accommodations

Casa Adobe B&B [GS,WI,GO] Independencia 801 (at Matamoros), Tlalixtac de Cabrera **52-951/517-7268** *15 minutes from center of Oaxaca*

Casa Colonial [GF,WI,WC] Calle Miguel Negrete 105 (Division Poniente) **52-951/516-5280**

Casa Machaya Oaxaca B&B [GF] Sierra Nevada 164, Col. Loma Linda **52/951-1328203**

Casa Mona Oaxaca B&B [GS,WI,GO] Calzada Porfirio Diaz (at Belisario Dominguez) **52-951/351-5643** *3 blocks to the Central Historic District*

Casa Sol Zipolite [M,SW,WI,GO] 6 Arco Iris, Col. Arroyo Tres **52-95/8100-0462** *300 meters from famous Playa Zipolite*

Posada Arigalan [GS,WI] **52-958/111-5801, 956/280-2165 (US)**

Nightclubs

Club Privado 502 (aka El Número) [GS,D,K,PC,$] Calle Porfirio Díaz 502 (Centro, ring to enter) **52 951 /514-8552** *10pm-close, clsd Sun-Tue*

La Costa [M,D,S] Av 16 de Septiembre #517 (Col. Cinco Señores) **52-951/511-2908** *wknds only 9pm-close*

Gavana Dance Club [GS] Calzada Porfirio Diaz #216 (Col. Reforma) *9pm-close Th-Sat*

Restaurants

El Asador Vasco [★] Portal de Flores 10-A (Centro) **52-951/514-4755** *great views & authentic Oaxacan cuisine (can you say ¡mole!)*

Casa Crespo Allende 107 **52-951/516-0918** *lunch & dinner, also cooking classes*

Men's Clubs

Baños del Jardin Melchor Ocampo 509 **52-951/516-5668**

Cruisy Areas

Parque Alemeda & Zócalo [AYOR] *early evenings*

Playa del Carmen

see also Cancún & Cozumel

Accommodations

Aventura Mexicana Hotel [GF,SW,N] Av 10 (at Calle 24) **52-984/873-1876, 800/455-3417**

Hotel Copa Cabana [GS,WI,WC] 5ta Av Norte **52-984/873-0218**

Luna Blue Hotel & Bar [GS,SW,WI] Calle 26 (at 5th Av) **52-984/873-0990** *adults-only boutique hotel*

Reina Roja Hotel [GS,SW,WI] 22 Street (btwn 5th & 10th Ave) **52-984/877-3800** *luxury urban style boutique hotel in the heart of Playa del Carmen, pets ok*

Nightclubs

Playa 69 [M,D,GO] Av 5 (btwn Calle 4 & Calle 6, ground flr) **52-916/271-3458** *8pm-4am, clsd Sun-Mon,dangerous area*

Playa Palms [GS,SW,WI] 1st Avenue Bis (btwn 12 & 14th N St) **52-984/803-3908, 888/676-4431** *directly in front of a pristine, white sandy beach in downtown Playa del Carmen*

Restaurants

100% Natural Calle Quinta Avenida 209 Mz 28 **52-984/73-2242** *7am-11pm, vegetarian*

Puebla

Bars

La Cigarra [M,S,V] Ave 5 Poniente 538 (at Calle 7, Centro) **52-222/246-6356** *6pm-3am, beer bar*

Men's Clubs

Baños Las Termas Av 5 de Mayo 2810, Centro **52-222/232-9562** *8am-8pm, open later wknds, till 3pm Sun, clsd Mon, popular afternoons*

Cruisy Areas

Zócalo/ Main Park [AYOR] at cathedral *late evenings*

Puerto Vallarta

INFO LINES & SERVICES

Community Center GLBT SETAC Aldanaca 178-4A y 4B (Versalles) **52-322/224-1974** *noon-8pm, 9am-2pm Sat, clsd Sun, AA meetings, movie nights, HIV testing & Spanish classes*

ACCOMMODATIONS

Almar Resort Luxury LGBT Beach Front Experience [M,F,SW,WI] 380 Amapas **52-322/222-4888** *Mantamar Beach Club on site*

Blue Chairs Beach Resort [MW,SW,WI,WC] **52-322/222-5040 , 888/302-3662** *direct beachfront access*

Boana Torre Malibu Condo Hotel [GS,F,SW,GO] Calle Amapas 325 **52-322/222-0999, 52-322/222-6695** *near gay beach*

Casa Cúpula [MW,SW,NS,WI,WC,GO] Callejon de la Igualdad 129, Col. Amapas **52-322/223-2484, 866/352-2511**

Casa de las Flores [GO] Calle Santa Barbara #359 **503 /314-444(US), 52-3222/120-5242** *condos is located on a bluff overlooking the Blue Chairs on Los Muertos Beach*

Casa Fantasía [GS,SW,NS,WC,GO] Pinot Suarez 203, Col. Emiliano Zapata (near the Rio Cuale) **52-322/223-2444** *B&B made up of 3 haciendas, terrace*

Casa Tranquila [GS,WI,GO] Morelos #7-A (at Lázaro Cárdenas), Bucerias, Nayarit **52-329/298-1767, 322/728-7519** *apartments w/ kitchens, near beach, massage*

Hotel Emperador [GS,WI] Amapas 114 **52-322/222-1767 , 800/523-1158** *located right on "Los muertos" beach*

Hotel Mercurio [MW,SW,WI,GO] **52-322/222-4793, 866/388-2689** *gay/ lesbian hotel in Vallarta's Gayborhood, 1 1/2 blocks from beach*

Villas David B&B [MO,SW,NS,WI,GO] Calle Galeana 348 (at Calle Miramar) **877/832-3315 (US#), 52-322/223-0315** *located in the heart of beautiful Old Puerto Vallarta, rooftop jacuzzi and pool, balconies*

BARS

Los Amigos Bar [MW,NH] Calle Venustiano Carranza 237 (upstairs, next to Paco's Ranch) **52-322/222-7802** *6pm-4am, Mexican cantina, patio*

Anonimo [M,NH] Rodolfo Gomez 157 **52-322/206-4439** *4pm-2am*

Apaches [★GS,F,GO] Olas Altas 439 (at Rodriguez) **52-322/429-8885** *5pm-2am, clsd Sunn, classy cocktail bar, martinis & margaritas, tapas*

Blondies Loft & Slushbar [M] Amapas (at Pulpito) *11am-2am, Loft from 4pm*

La Cueva Calle Olas Altas 414 (2nd Fl) **52-322/171-2090** *3pm-2am, Mexican cantina*

Divas [MW,NH] 388 Francisco L Madero (E of Insurgentes) **52-322/222-7774** *12:30pm-4am*

Frida [GS,B,F,GO] 301-A Insurgentes (at Venustiano Carranza) **52-322/222-3668** *1pm-2am, from 7pm Mon-Tue, Mexican cantina, more gay later in evening*

Garbo [M,E,P,GO,18+] Pulpito 142 (at Olas Altas) **52-322/223-5753** *6pm-2am, upscale martini lounge, live music*

Luna Azul [M] Lazatro Cardenas 308 **52-322/113-0322** *1pm-2am*

Mr Flamingos [M] Ignacio L Vallarta *2pm-3am*

La Noche [MW] Lázaro Cárdenas 257 (Zona Romantica) **52-322/222-3364** *7pm-2am, cocktail lounge & rooftop garden*

The Palm Cabaret [M,D,C] Olas Altas 508 (at Rodolfo Gomez) **52-322/223-4818** *4pm-4am*

Reinas [M,NH] Lazaro Cardenas 361 **52-322/205-0433** *4pm-2am*

Signature Lounge [GS] Púlpito 180 (at Signature by Pinnacle) **52-322/113-0342** *1pm-9pm, great sunset views*

StreetBar [M] 136 Francisca Rodriguez **52-322/222-8609** *opens 4pm*

Twisted Palms [★M] Ignacio Vallarta 228-18 (at Plaza Romy) **52-322/223-8019** *6pm-midnight, clsd Wed, rooftop deck*

Nightclubs

La Alhambra [M,D] Lazatro Cardenas 240-1 **52-322/356-6851** *7pm-2am, from 4pm Sun*

Antropology [MO,DS,S,YC,$] Calle Morelos 101, Plaza Río (at Plaza Rio Cuale) **52-322/167-6556** *9pm-4am*

CC Slaughter's [M,D] Lazaro Cardenas 254 Emiliano (Zapata) **52-322/222-3412** *10pm-6am*

La Margarita [M] Lazatro Cardenas 257 **52-322/222-1367** *7pm-2am2pm-3am*

Open Vallarta [M,D] Venustiano Carranza 212 **52-322/148-7645** *10pm-6am Th-Sun*

Paco's Ranch [M,D,DS,GO,$] 237 Ignacio Vallarta **52-322/222-1899** *10pm-6am, also rooftop terrace*

Wet Dreams [MO,S] Lazaro Cardenas 312 (Col Emiliano Zapata) **52-322/222-8112** *8pm-3am, strippers*

Cafes

A Page in the Sun 179 Plaza Lázaro Cárdenas (in Zona Romantica) **52-322/222-3608** *7am-11pm, coffee shop & English bookstore*

Cafe San Angel [★] Olas Altas 449 (at Francisco Rodreguez) **52-322/294-0417** *8am-midnight, sidewalk cafe, also crepes, smoothies, salads and sandwiches*

The Coffee Cup [GO] Puesta del Sol L-14 (Marina Vallarta) **52-322/221-2517** *7am-10pm, clsd Sun in summer*

Restaurants

El Arrayan [GO] Allende #344 (at El Centro) **52-322/222-7195** *6pm-11pm, clsd Tue*

The Blue Shrimp Olas Altas 366 (Zona Romantica) **52-322/222-4246** *11am-midnight*

El Brujo [★] Venustiano Carranza 510 (at Naranjo) **52-322/223-3026** *1pm-9:30pm, clsd Mon, Mexican/ seafood, worth the wait*

Cafe Bohemio [MW,GO] Rodolfo Gómez 127 (at Olas Altas) **44-322/134-2436** *5pm-2am, clsd Sun, open-air cafe, late-evening happy hour*

Cafe de Olla [★] Calle Basilio Badillo 168 **52-322/223-1626** *10am-11pm, clsd Tue, Mexican, wait list an hour*

Cafe des Artistes [★R] Calle Guadalupe Sánchez 740 (at Leona Vicario) **52-322/226-7200** *6pm-11:30pm, upscale French w/ a Mexican twist*

Chez Elena [GO] Matamoros 520, Centro (at Los Quatro Vientos Hotel) **52-322/222-0161** *6pm-11pm, seasonal, also rooftop bar & B&B*

Daiquiri Dick's [★] Olas Altas 314 (on Playa Los Muertos) **52-322/222-0566** *9am-11pm*

De Santos [E] 2479 Francisco Medina Ascencio **52-322/688-1602** *1pm-3am*

El Dorado Pulpito 102, Playa de los Muertos **52-322/223-5568** *10am-4pm beach club & restaurant*

Memo's Casa de los Hotcakes [★] Calle Basilio Badillo 289 **52-322/222-6272** *8am-2pm, long lines for cheap & good brkfst*

Mezzogiorno Ristorante Italiano Avenida del Pacifico 33 (North Beach Bucerias Nayarit) **52-329/298-0350** *6pm-11pm, clsd Mon off season, also beach bar*

El Mole de Jovita 220B Basillo Badillo **52-322/223-3065** *noon-11pm, 3pm-10pm Sun, authentic mole*

La Palapa Pulpito 103, Col Emiliano Zapata **52-322/222-5225** *brkfst, lunch & dinner, beachside dining*

La Piazzetta Rodolfo Gomez #143 (at Olas Atlas, Romantic Zone) **52-322/222-0650** *4pm-11pm, Italian*

Planeta Vegetariano Iturbide 270 (Centro) **52-322/222-3073** *8am-10pm, clsd Sun, buffet-style*

Red Cabbage [GO] Calle Rivera del Rio 204-A (at Basilio Badillo) **52-322/223-0411** *5pm-11pm, clsd Sun & summers, on Rio Cuale w/ great kitschy decor*

The Swedes/ Crows Nest Bar [MW,GO] Púlpito 154 (at Olas Altas) **52-322/223-2353** *4pm-2am, Swedish/ European, also bar upstairs*

Tre Piatti [★] Lázaro Cárdenas 292 (Emiliano Zapata) **52-322/222-2773** *clsd Tue, great Italian owner is the former chef of Quince in San Francisco*

Trio [★E] Guerrero 264 (Centro) **52-322/222-2196** *6pm-midnight, clsd Sun*

Entertainment & Recreation

Boana Tours Calle Amapas 325 (at Casa Boana Torre Malibu) **52-322/222-0999, 52-322/222-6695** *horseback tours daily*

Diana's Cruise the Bay Tour [MW,F] meet at Los Muertos pier *9:30am-5pm Th, open bar*

Mantamar Beach Club Bar & Grill [★] Malecón #169 Col Emiliano Zapata **52-322/222-6260** *great beach scene*

Ocean Friendly Paseo del Marlin 510-103, Col. Aralias **52-322/225-3774, 044-322/294-0385 (cell)** *whale-watching tours, Dec 15-March 31*

Playa Los Muertos/ Playa del Sol [★] S of Rio Cuale *the gay beach, now spans "Blue Chairs" & "Green Chairs"*

Publications

Gay PV 52-322/113-0224 *great gay magazine for PV*

Men's Clubs

Spartacus Spa Ignacio L Vallarta 264 **52-322/178-4299** *4pm-2am, till 8am Fri-Sat*

Cruisy Areas

Malecón (Seawall) [AYOR] facing Calle Morelos (esp near benches across from Presidencia Municipal at Iturbide) *evenings*

Playa Los Muertos [AYOR] near green chairs at The Beach Café & further S by the rocks *afternoons*

Plaza Caracol Mall [AYOR]

Querétaro

Cruisy Areas

Alameda Parque [AYOR]

El Jardín Guerrero [AYOR] 3 blks from Centro Historico

Plaza de Armas [AYOR]

Zócalo/ Obregón Plaza [AYOR]

San Jose del Cabo

Accommodations

El Encanto Inn [GF,SW] **210/858-6649, 52-614/142-0388** *spa and restaurant, pets ok*

One & Only Palmilla [GF,SW] Apartado Postal 52, 23400 **52-624/146-7000, 855/878 5831 (US#)** *upscale resort*

San Miguel de Allende

Accommodations

Casa de Sierra Nevada [GF,SW] Calle Hospicio 35 (Centro) **52-415/152-7040, 800/701-1561 (US#)** *suites with fireplaces, horseback riding, also restaurant & spa*

Casa Schuck Boutique B&B [GF,SW,WI] Garita 3, Centro **52-415/152-0657, 937/684-4092 (US)** *luxury boutique hotel with colonial charm and private gardens and rooftop deck*

Dos Casas [GF] Calle Quebrada 101 (Guanajuato) **52-415/154-4073** *luxury B&B 3 blocks from main square; rent one of the deluxe rooms (including room with jacuzzi, sauna, and private terrace) or the whole house*

Las Terrazas San Miguel [GS,NS,WI,GO] Santo Domingo 3 **52-415/152-5028, 707/534-1833 (US#)** *4 rental homes*

Restaurants

La Azotea Umaran 6 **52-415/152-8265** *1pm-midnight, delicious tapas & drinks*

San Miguel Deli & Bistro Cuna de Allende 11 (at Hotel Vista Hermosa) **52-415/152-2799**

Tepic

Men's Clubs

Banos America Jesus Garcia #37 (Fraccionamiento Simancas) **52-311/213-3747** *7am-10pm, till 5pm Sun, two steam rms, bar, popular afternoons*

Tijuana

Bars

Bar Hawaii [M,DS,S] Zona Centro *24hrs*

Latinos Bar [M,DS] Avenida Revolución,509 **52-664/504-1023** *24hrs*

Luna Sol Lounge [GS,GO] Av Pacifico 640, Playas de Tijuana **52-664/609-4977** *2pm-midnight, beach bar*

El Ranchero Bar [★M,NH,D,F,AYOR] Plaza Santa Cecilia 769 (btwn Calles 1, 2, Revolución & Constitución) *24hrs, cruisy cantina, hustlers, use caution in bathrooms*

Villa Garcia [M,D] Plaza Santa Cecilia 751 *10am-late, small dance flr, cruisy*

Nightclubs

Club Fusion [M,D,K,DS] Calle Larroque 8806 **52-664/264-6781** *8pm-3am Fri-Sun*

Colibri Lounge [M,D,S] 2020 Avenida Revolución **52-664/638 1274** *9pm-3am, clsd Mon-Wed*

Extasis [★M,D,S,$] Larroque 213 (in Plaza Viva Tijuana, next to the border) **52-664/682-8339** *8pm-late, clsd Mon-Wed, go-go boys*

Mike's Disco [MW,D,DS,V,18+] Av Revolución 1220 (at Calle 6A) **52-664/116-2526** *9pm-5am*

Premier [M,S] Av Revolución 645 (btwn 1st & Coahuila) **52-664/688-0821** *9pm-5am, clsd Mon*

Cafes

D'Luna Cafe Calle 8 #8380 (Miguel Hidalgo 8391) **52-664/321-9735** *8am-11pm*

Men's Clubs

Banos Vica [GS] Gustavo Díaz Ordaz 1535 **52-664/622-0386**

Erotica

Sexy Rosa Boutique Romantica & Sex Shop [WI] 712 Ave Revolucion (Baja California Norte Tijuana) **52-664/685-4948, 619/632-6580** *store is clean and english is spoken*

Todos Santos

Accommodations

The Todos Santos Inn [GS,SW,NS,GO] Calle Legaspi #33 (Topete) **52-612/145-0040** *colonial inn w/ bar*

Tulúm

Accommodations

Azulik [GF,WI] Carretera Tulum Ruinas Km 5 **54-115/984-1575, 866 /471-3472** *beautiful location, excellent restaurant, spa & beach access*

Casa de las Olas B&B [GF,WI] 10.6km Tulum Beach Rd **52-004/007 3009** *sustaianable beach villa, very secluded that has 5 beautiful ocean front suites*

Kore Tulum Retreat and Spa Resort [GS,SW] Carretera Tulum Boca Paila Km 3.8 **52-984/161-0001** *gourmet all inclusive resort located in a fascinating corner of Mexico*

Om Tulum [GF,WI] Caraterra Ruinas Punta -Allen Km 9.5 **521-98/425-3108** *cabanas and restaurant is an eco-tourism style small hotel*

Posada Luna del Sur [GF] Calle Luna Sur 5 **52-984/182-9696** *family-run small delightful hotel, centrally situated in Tulum, full brkfst*

Veracruz

Accommodations

Hotel Villa del Mar [GF,SW] Blvd Miguel Ávila Camacho 2431 (across street from Playa del Mar beach) **52-229/989-6500** *hotel with separate motel and bungalows, close to aquarium, moderate price, on the beach*

ENTERTAINMENT & RECREATION

San Juan de Ulua Fortress **52-229/938-5151** *9am-4:30pm, clsd Mon, impressive early colonial-era floating fortress*

Veracruz Aquarium Blvd Avila Camacho (at Xicolencat) **52-229/932-7984** *10am-7pm, one of the largest & best in the world; don't miss it!*

MEN'S CLUBS

Baños El Edén [AYOR] Miguel Hidalgo 1113 (Centro) **52-229/932-3360** *buy tickets at rear counter of music store*

CRUISY AREAS

Plaza de Armas/ Zócalo [AYOR]

Waterfront & Av República [AYOR]

Zacatecas

ACCOMMODATIONS

Quinta Real Zacatecas [GF] Av Ignacio Rayón 434 (Col. Centro) **52-492/1105-1010, 800/500-4000** *5-star hotel built into grandstand of bullfighting ring*

CRUISY AREAS

Av Juárez [AYOR] E from Av Hidalgo for 2 blks

Zihuatanejo

ACCOMMODATIONS

Las Palmas Luxury Villas [GF,SW] Carretera a Playa Blanca 5 (Playa Blanca) **52-755/114-6376**

RETAIL SHOPS

Tequila Town Cuauhtemoc 14 (Col Centro) **52-755/554-2725** *tequlla experts also nightclub*

Central America

COSTA RICA

Alajuela

BARS

Rick's Bar & Restaurant [MW] Calle 2 Obispo Tristan, Ave 5 **506-2/441-3213** *6pm-close, from 4pm Sun*

Chirripó Nat'l Park

ACCOMMODATIONS

Monte Azul [GS,F,GO] Contiguo al puente de Chucuyo, Chimirol **506/2742-5222**

Guanacaste

ACCOMMODATIONS

Villa Decary [★GF] Nuevo Arenal, 5717 Tilaran **506-2/694-4330, 800/556-0505 (from US & Canada)** *former coffee farm on 7 acres overlooking Lake Arenal, great brkfst and environment*

Manuel Antonio, Quepos

INFO LINES & SERVICES

www.gaymanuelantonio.com Puntarenas **403/246-8941** *travel information source for gay travellers*

ACCOMMODATIONS

Casa de Frutas [GS,GO] Puntarenas Province, **506/4001-5878, 800/936-9622** *luxury villa in Tulemar Gardens*

Costa Verde [GS,SW,GO] **506-2/777-0584, 866/854-7958 (from US & Canada)** *bungalows, apts & studios, 4 restaurants on site*

Gaia Hotel & Reserve [GF,SW,WI,GO] km 2.7 Carretera Quepos a Manuel Antonio **506-2/777-9797, 800/226-2515** *luxury boutique hotel & Eco-friendly resort surrounded by wildlife refuge; spa, gym & restaurant, full brkfst*

Hotel Parador [GF,SW,WI] **506-2/777-1414, 877/506-1414** *large luxury resort*

Hotel Villa Roca [M,SW,NS,GO] **506-2/777-1349** *great ocean views, near beaches*

La Mansion Inn [GS,F,SW,GO] **506-2/777-3489, 800/360-2071** *luxury hotel, bar, in room spa, ocean views*

Moonshine Inn [SW,GO] **202/321-3867** *rainforest retreat villa rental, walking distance to beach and many restaurants, bars, and boutiques*

Paraiso Vista al Mar [GF,WI] de la plaza de Manuel Antonio **506/2777-7616** *ocean view adult only apt rentals with brkfst included, pets ok*

La Posada [GF,SW,GO] **506-2/777-1446** *4 bungalows & 2 guest rooms, borders national park, near beach*

Si Como No [GF,SW,WC] **506-2/777-0777, 888/742-6667** *25-acre wildlife refuge, also restaurant & spa*

Bars

Karma Lounge [M,D] under Victoria's Restaurant (Cockatoo Building on main road) **506/8703-7483** *6pm-2:30am, clsd Mon, outside seating*

MoGamBo BarCafe at Raphael's Terrazas [GS,D,E,F,K] 500 meters past Villa Roca (next to Hotel Arboleda) **506-2/7076 2043** *4pm-midnight, best margaritas and sunset happy hour*

Cafes

El Patio de Café Milagro Manuel Antonio Main Rd **506-2/2777-2272** *world famous fresh roasted coffees & live music nightly*

Restaurants

El Barba Roja [★] Ruta 618, Barba Roja **506-2/777-0331** *noon-10pm, American, great sunset location*

Emilio's Cafe top of the Manuel Antonio hill (near Hotel Mariposa) **506-2/2777-6807** *7am-9pm, spectacular views of the Manuel Antonio beach and bay*

El Gran Escape & Fish Head Bar Av 1 Quepos Centro **506-2/2777 7850** *11am-11pm, great beach bar with fresh seafood*

Rico Tico [★E] in Hotel Si Como No *brkfst, lunch & dinner, Tex/ Mex, includes use of pool bar, also Claro Que Si (seafood)*

Entertainment & Recreation

Playa Espadilla *gay beach at the far end of the beach, just to the left of the large rock, or in front of the surfing area*

Playa Playitas *gay area at the far end point over the far rocks of this beach*

Osa Peninsula

Accommodations

Blue Osa Yoga Sanctuary & Spa [GS,SW,NS,WI,GO] **506/8704-7006** *all meals included*

Playa Sámara

Accommodations

Casitas LazDívaz B&B [GS,WI,WC,GO] **506/2656-0295** *beachfront cottages, full brkfst, lesbian diva-owned*

Puerto Viejo

Accommodations

Banana Azul [M,WI,GO] 200 meters N of Perla Negra Hotel **506/2750-2035, 305 /846-8220 (US#)** *bar & restaurant, full brkfst*

Restaurants

Koki Beach Restaurant Bar & Lounge [WI] Main St (town center across from water) **506/8305-0747** *5pm-11pm, clsd Mon, Latin fusion cuisine*

Puntarenas

Accommodations

Villa Caletas [GS,F,SW] Garabito **506/2630-3000** *luxury boutique hotel in the Pacific Coast of Costa Rica with inspiring ocean views and decor*

Cruisy Areas

Beach [AYOR]

San Jose

BARS

Zona Rosa [MW,D,K] Calle 2 (250m norte del Correo Central) **506/8354-0547** *11am-2am*

ENTERTAINMENT & RECREATION

Gay Tours Costa Rica 309-2200 Coronado **506-2/305-8044** *daily events & excursions*

ACCOMMODATIONS

Colours Oasis Resort [MW,F,E,SW,WI,GO] El Triangulo Noroeste, Blvd Rohrmoser (200 meters before end of blvd) **506-2/296-1880, 866/517-4390 (US & Canada)** *full brkfst*

Hotel Kekoldi [GS,WI,GO] Av 9 (btwn Calles 5 & 7, Barrio Amón) **506-2/248-0804** *in art deco bldg in downtown, secluded garden*

NIGHTCLUBS

La Avispa [MW,D] 834 Calle 1 (pink house btwn Avs 8 & 10) **506-2/223-5343** *8pm-2am, popular T-dance from 5pm Sun, clsd Mon-Wed*

El Bochinche [MW,D,V] Calle 11 (btwn Avs 10 & 12, Paseo de los Etudiantes), San Pedro **506-2/221-0500** *7pm-2am, till 5pm Fri-Sat, clsd Sun-Tue, also full restaurant, Mexican, dancing/DJ after 10pm*

Club Energy [MW,DS] Paseo Colon (near 30th, by Pizza Hut) **506/2223-7594** *clsd Sun-Mon*

Puchos [M,DS,S] Calle 11 & Av 8 (knock to enter) **506-2/222-7967** *8pm-2:30am, clsd Sun*

RESTAURANTS

Cafe Mundo [GO] Av 9 & Calle 15 (200 meters E of parking lot for INS, Barrio Amón) **506-2/222-6190** *11am-11pm, 5pm-midnight Sat, clsd Sun, garden seating, bar*

Mirador Ram Luna from center of Aserrí, go 4 kilometers on the road toward Tabarca, Aserri **506-2/230-3022** *dinner nightly, lunch & dinner wknds, clsd Mon, hillside restaurant w/ amazing views*

Olio [★] Escalante, Bario California (N of Baselman's, San Pedro/ Los Yoses) **506-2/281-0541** *lunch & dinner, clsd Sun, Spanish, also full bar*

Vishnu Vegetarian Restaurant Av 1 (btwn Calles 3 & 1) **506-2/256-6063** *7am-9:30pm*

ENTERTAINMENT & RECREATION

Mercado Central/ Central Market Central Avenida (btwn Calles 6 & 8) *bustling market selling food, clothing, souvenirs & more*

MEN'S CLUBS

Paris Sauna corner of Calle 7 & Av 7 (1 block from Morazan Park) **506-2/248-9744** *noon-7pm*

Sauna Hispalis [★V] Av 2 #1762 (E of the Plaza de la Democracia, btwn Calles 17 & 19) **506-2/256-9540** *noon-10pm*

CRUISY AREAS

Parque La Sabana [AYOR] next to Municipal Stadium (btwn airport & San José) *evenings & wknds*

Parque Nacional [AYOR] N of Av 1 (btwn Calles 15 & 19)

Plaza de la Cultura [★AYOR] in front of the Nat'l Theater (btwn Calles 3 & 5) *late afternoons & early evenings*

San Ramon

ACCOMMODATIONS

Angel Valley Farm B&B [GS,NS,WI,WC] 200m N & 300m E of Iglesia de Los Angeles (at Autopista to Arenal Volcano) **506-2/456-4084, 707/260-2904 (US#)** *full brkfst, kids over 5 and small pets ok, on a farm in Costa Rica's central valley, "relax & re-energize your body & soul!"*

Cerro Coyote [GS,GO] Calle San Francisco 3 **506-2/383-0544** *full brkfst*

Santa Clara

ACCOMMODATIONS

Tree Houses Hotel Costa Rica [GS,NS,GO] **506-2/475-6507** *private treehouses in canopy of trees on wildlife refuge*

Tamarindo

ACCOMMODATIONS

Los Altos de Eros [GF,SW,WI,WC] **506/8850-4222, 800/931-1944** *5-Star luxury boutique hotel & excellent spa, meals included & no kids allowed*

Cala Luna Hotel & Villas [GF,SW] Playa Langosta (at Playa Tamarindo) **506-2/653-0214, 855/774-3767**

Hotel Sueño del Mar [GF,SW,NS,WI] Playa Langosta **506-2/653-0284** *private hacienda on the beach, full brkfst*

GUATEMALA

Antigua

ENTERTAINMENT & RECREATION

George's Travel Club of Guatemala [GO] **202/436-9983** *catering to the gay traveller visiting Guatemala*

Antigua Guatemala

CAFES

Sabe Rico 7 6th Ave S (btwn 5 & 6 calle) **502/7832-0648** *10am-10pm*

RESTAURANTS

Restaurante Fridas [E,GO] 5a Avenida Norte #29 **502/7832-1296** *noon-1am, best mexican cuisine & margaritas in town*

Sobremesa [★] Cuarta Calle Oriente 4 **502/7832-3231** *11am-10pm, clsd Tue, unique and delicious save room for dessert*

South America

ARGENTINA

Buenos Aires

INFO LINES & SERVICES

Comunidad Homosexual Argentina Tomas Liberti 1080 **54-11/4361-6382**

ACCOMMODATIONS

1555 Malabia House [GF,WI] Malabia 1555, Palermo Viejo (at Honduras) **54-11/4833-2410** *one of Buenos Aires leading boutique hotels*

The Cocker [GF,WI,GO] Av Juan de Garay 458 (at Defensa) **54-1/4362-8451**

Faena Hotel [GS,WI] 445 Martha Salotti St **54-11/4010-9000** *luxury hotel, restaurants and bars & live shows at El Cabaret*

Home Hotel [GF,WI,SW] Honduras 5860 **54-11/4778-1008** *boutique hotel, loft apts available*

Hotel Intercontinental Buenos Aires [GF,WI] Moreno 809 **54-11/4340-7100** *near commercial/ financial district, fitness center, bar, restaurants*

Hotel Vitrum [GF] 5641 Gorriti (Palermo) **54-1/4776-5030** *stylish boutique hotel*

Lugar Gay B&B [MO,WI,GO] Defensa 1120 **54-11/4300-4747** *located downtown in historical quarter of city (San Telmo, bohemian and chic), near most places on the gay scene*

Palermo Viejo B&B [GS,NS,WI,GO] Niceto Vega 4629 (at Av Scalabrini Ortiz) **54-11/4773-6012** *near shopping & gay nightlife*

Rooney's Boutique Hotel [GF,WI] Sarmiento 1775, Piso 3 **54-11/5252-5060** *exceptional location & free tango classes*

Solar Soler B&B [GF,NS] Soler 5676 (at Bonpland) **54-11/4776-3065** *located on a quiet street in Palermo Hollywood area*

Telmho Hotel Boutique [GF,WI] 1086 Defensa St (at Humberto Primo) **54-11/4307-9898** *good value and great location*

Bars

Flux Bar [MW,D,WI] Marcelo T de Alvear 980 (at 9 de Julio) **54-11/5252-0258** *7pm-close, from 8pm wknds, clsd Sun*

KM Zero [MW,D,DS,S,V] Av Santa Fe 2516 **54-11/3174-4603** *midnight-7am*

Sitges [★MW] Córdoba 4119 **54-11/4861-3763** *10:30pm-4am, till 6am Fri-Sat, clsd Mon-Tue*

Tom's [MO] Viamonte 638, in basement **54-11/4322-4404** *noon-4am, 24hrs wknds, dark room*

Zoom [M,L,B$] Uriburu 1018 **54-11/4827-4828** *2pm-5am, 24hrs Fri-Sun, maze, lounge, cruisy*

Nightclubs

Amerika [★M,D] Gascón 1040 (at Cordoba) **54-11/4865-4416** *midnight-7am, clsd Tue-Th, darkroom*

Bach Bar [MW,E,K,V] Antonio Cabrera 4390 **54-11/5184-0137** *from 11pm Fri-Sat & 10pm Sun only*

Bahrein [GS,D] Lavalle 345 **54-1/4315-2403** *5pm-11pm, till 7am Fri-Sat, from 11pm Sat, clsd Sun*

Club 69 [GS,D,DS] Niceto Vega 5510 (btwn Humboldt & Fitzroy, Palermo) **54-1/4779-9396** *11:30pm Th only, over-the-top theme parties*

Cocoliche [GS,D] Rivadavia 878

Contramano [MO,D,B] Rodriguez Peña 1082 (at Av Santa Fe) *midnight-6am Fri-Sat only, hustlers*

Fiesta Dorothy [MW,D] Alsina 940 (near Plaza de Mayo, at Palacio Alsina) **54-11/4334-0097** *huge dance bi-monthly dance party*

Fiesta Eyeliner [MW,D,A,DS] Sarmiento 1272 (at Salon Real) *monthly queer/ alternative dance party, check web for dates*

Fiesta Plop [MW,D] Av Federico Lacroze 3455 (at Alvarez Thomas, at El Teatro) *Fri only, young, alternative mixed crowd*

Fiesta Puerca [M,D] Federico Lacroze (at Alvarez Thomas)

Glam [★M,D] Cabrera 3046 **54-11/4964-9406** *midnight-close wknds, darkroom, patio*

Human Club [M,D] Coronel Marcelino Freyre (at Av Infanta Isabel) **54-11/5153-1060** *midnight Sat only, huge dance party*

Rheo [M,D] Marcelino Freyre S/N, Arco 17 (at Crobar) **54-1/3430-2711** *midnight Sat only*

Sub Club [MW,D] Cordoba 543 **54-11/2519-1162** *Fri-Sat only*

Cafes

Gout Cafe [GO] Juncal 2124 **54-11/4825-8330** *sandwiches, pastries, gluten free*

Pride Cafe [E] Balcarce 869 (in San Telmo) **54-11/4300-6435** *10am-10pm, live show Th night*

Restaurants

Bio Humbolt 2192 (Palermo Viejo) **54-11/4774-3880** *lunch & dinner, vegetarian, organic market*

La Cabana Alicia Moreau de Justo 380 **54-11/4314-3710** *brkfst, lunch & dinner, upscale steak house*

Casa Cruz 1658 Uriarte **54-11/4833-1112** *8:30pm-3am, later Fri-Sat, upscale, trendy restaurant, also bar*

Cumana Rodriguez Pena 1149 (at Arenales) **54-11/4813-9207** *low key restaurant at decent prices, plenty veggie & empanadas are great*

El Palacio de la Papa Frita [★] Av Corrientes 1612 **54-11/4374-8063** *8am-12:30am, hearty traditional meals*

Filo San Martin 975 **54-11/4311-0312** *noon-2am, Italian, t also art gallery*

Il Materello [★] Martin Rodriguez 517 (in la Boca nr socccer stadium) **54-11/4307-0529** *lunch & dinner, very good Italian and everyone loves the lasagna, beware of neighborhood after 4pm*

Mark's Deli & Coffeehouse El Salvador 4107 (in Palermo) **54-11/4832-6244** *11am-8pm, till 9pm Sun, clsd Mon*

Naturaleza Sabia Balcarce 958 (at Carlos Calvo) **54-11/4300-6454** *lunch & dinner, clsd Mon, vegetarian*

Rave Gorriti 5092 **54-11/4833-7832** *11am-2am, from 5pm Sun, great food & good prices*

Sucre Sucre 676 **54-11/4782-9082** *lunch & dinner, upscale contemporary*

Entertainment & Recreation

La Marshall Maipu 444 **54-11/4912-9043** *8:30pm Wed, exclusively gay tango lessons*

Museo Evita Peron Lafinur 2988 (in Palermo) **54-11/4807-9433** *2pm-7:30pm, clsd Mon*

Out & About Pub Crawl [MW] **54-911/3678-0170** *make new friends on a tour of the local gay bars*

Bookstores

Otras Letras Soler 4796, Palermo **54-1/2060-2942** *2pm-8pm, from 3pm Sat, clsd Sun, LGBT books & culture*

Men's Clubs

A Full Spa [MO,V,GO] Viamonte 1770 (at Av Callao) **54-11/4371-7263** *noon-midnight, 24hrs wknds*

Grupo Los Fiesteros Cerrito 1058 **54-11/6735-5783**

Homo Sapiens Gascon 956 **54-11/4862-6519** *noon-midnight*

Nagasaki Aguero 427 **54-1/4866-6335** *1pm-midnight*

Erotica

American Top Video Av Cabildo 2230 (Galeria Las Vegas) **54-11/4781-5343** *noon-8:30pm, from 10:30am Sat, clsd Sun*

Cine ABC Esmeralda 506 (at the Microcentro) **54-11/4393-4805** *theater with 3 screens*

Eden Av Santa Fe 1833 (gal Bozzini, B Norte) *cinema*

Cruisy Areas

Avenida Santa Fe [AYOR] btwn Callao & Coronel Diaz

Bosques de Palermo [AYOR] Figueroa Alcorta & Dorrego St

Costanera Sur [AYOR] near Puerto Madero Spain

Plaza Las Heras [AYOR] Coronel Dias & Av Las Heras

BRAZIL

Búzios

Accommodations

Casas Brancas [GF,SW] Alto do Humaitá 10 **55-22/2623-1458** *terrace, ocean views, spa, also restaurant*

Florianópolis

Info Lines & Services

Brazil Ecojourneys [GO] Estrada Rozália Paulina Ferreira 1132, Armação **55-48/3389-5619** *South Brazil specialists*

Accommodations

Majestic Palace [GF,SW] Avenida Beira-Mar Norte 2786 **55-48/3231-8000**

Ponta Dos Ganchos [GF,SW,WI] Gov Celso Ramos (off SC 410 on the Emerald Coast), Santa Catarina **55-48/3262-5000, 800/643-3346** *bungalows, private beach, canoe access, tennis, gym, massage, diving on request*

Bars

Bar Do Deca [★GS] Praia Mole (last bar on left side of beach) **55-48/3232-2052** *beach bar, popular in summer (Dec-April)*

Floribar [★] Rua Durval Melchiades de Souza 638 **55-48/3322-2550** *6pm-close Wed-Sat only, cafe & lounge*

Lagoa's Cafe [GS] at Texaco Station, Lagoa da Conceição *popular meeting place after the beach, also cafe*

Nightclubs

Concorde Club [★GS,D] Avenida Rio Branco 729 **55-48/3222-1981**

RESTAURANTS

Bistro Isadora Duncan Rodovia Jornalista Manoel de Menezes 2658, Barra da Lagoa **55-48/3232-7210** *7pm-1am, clsd Sun, seafood, amazing views*

Bob's Rua Trajano 205 **55-48/3224-6600** *popular fast food*

MEN'S CLUBS

Oceano [B,V] Rua Luiz Delfino 231 **55-48/3222-4547** *sauna, also bar, darkroom*

NIGHTCLUBS

Barbarella Lounge [GS,D] Rua Saldanha Marinho 351

Rio de Janeiro

Note: M°=Metro station

INFO LINES & SERVICES

Grupo Arco-Iris Rio de Janeiro Rua do Senado 230 **55-21/2222-7286** *1pm-7pm, till 11pm Sat, clsd Sun, LGBT community center*

Rainbow Kiosk/ Quiosque Atlantic Av (in front of Copacabana Palace Hotel) *24hrs, tourist info*

ACCOMMODATIONS

Casa Cool Beans [GS,SW,WI,GO] Rua Laurinda Santos Lobo 136 **55-21/2262-0552** *located in Rio de Janeiro's Santa Teresa artist district*

Casa Dois Gatos [M,SW,WI,GO] Rua Rosalina Terra 6, Cabo Frio **561/282-0023, 55-22/2645-5806** *free transportation from Rio airport*

Goiden Tulip Ipanema Plaza [GS,SW] Rua Farme Amoedo (at Rua Prudente de Morais) **55-21/3687-2000, 800/358-0846** *near gay beach, rooftop pool, also restaurant*

MyRioCondo.com [GS,WI,GO] 3150 Avenida Atlantica, Apt 901 (Copacabana) **215/847-2397 (US#)** *views of Copacabana Beach, near Le Boy & gay nightlife of Rio*

BARS

TV Bar [M,NH] Av Nossa Senhora de Copacabana 1417 **55-21/2267-1663** *10pm-5am, 9pm-3am Sun, clsd Mon-Wed*

NIGHTCLUBS

Boite 1140 [MW,D,DS] 1140 Rua Capitao Menezes **55-21/7830-8867** *11pm-5am, clsd Mon-Wed*

Le Boy [★MW,D,S,YC] Rua Raul Pompeia 102 (Copacabana) **55-21/2513-4993** *11pm-close, clsd Mon, also sauna*

Casa da Matriz [GS,D,K,18+] Rua Henrique de Novaes 107 **54-11/2226-9691** *11pm-5am clsd Sun-Tue,es*

La Cueva [M,D,B,L] Rua Miguel Lemos 51 (Copacabana) **55-21/2267-1364**

Fosfobox [GS,D] Rua Siqueira Campos 143 **55-21/2548-7498** *11pm-6am*

Galeria Cafe [GS,D] Rua Teixeira de Melo 31 (Ipanema) **55-21/2523-8250** *11pm-5am, clsd Sun-Tue, also gallery*

Papa G [MW,D,DS] 42 Almerinda Freitas **55-21/2450-1253** *11pm-5am, clsd Mon-Tue*

Turma OK [M,DS] Rua dos Inválidos 39 **55-21/3177-0181** *9pm-2am Sat, 7pm-midnight Sun only*

Up Turn [MW,D,F] 2000 Av das Americas **55-21/3387-7957** *lunch daily, club 11pm-5am Sat, outdoor seating*

The Week [GS,D] 154 Rua Sacadura Cabral **55-21/2253-1020**

CAFES

Cafeína Rua Farme de Amoedo 43 (Ipanema) **55-21/2521-2194** *8am-11:30pm*

RESTAURANTS

Gringo Cafe Rua Barao da Torre 240 **55-21/3813-3972** *8:30am-10pm, American classics*

Maxim's Av Atlantica 1850 **55-21/2255-7444** *noon-1:30am, outdoor seating with beach view*

Pizzaria Guanabara 1228 Ave Ataulfo de Paiva, Leblon **55-21/2294-0797** *11am-5am, great paellas, pizza & beer*

To Nem Ai [MW] Rua Farme de Amoedo 57 **55-21/3083-6510** *noon-3am, popular bar with outdoor seating*

Via Sete 55-21/2512-8100 *noon-midnight, plenty veggie*

Entertainment & Recreation

Copacabana Beach at Rua Rodolfo Dantas *gay across from Copacabana Palace Hotel*

Farme de Amoedo/ Farme Gay Beach across from Rua Farme de Amoedo *see & be seen at this popular gay beach*

Ipanema Beach *E of Rua Farme Amoedo*

Publications

Rio For Partiers 55-21/2523-9857 *great guide book*

Men's Clubs

Bonsucesso Sauna Rua Bonsucesso 252 **55-21/2260-9385** *1pm-10pm, till 11pm wknds*

Club 29 [WI] Rua Professor Alfredo Gomes 29 **55-21/2537-6822** *1pm-2am, till 4am Fri-Sat from 3pm Sun*

Copacabana Sauna [B] Rua Dias da Rocha 83 **55-21/2235-5563** *noon-midnight, popular w/ bears*

Estação Rua Tonelero 217 (Copacabana) **55-21/2547-9953** *3pm-close*

Gaylígola Rua Ubaldino do Amaral 50 (downtown) **55-21/9259-5625, 55-21/2224-6144** *2pm-6am, 24hrs wknds*

Point 202 Rua Siqueira Campos 202 **55-21/3816-1757** *3pm-1am, also bar, massage, shows*

Projeto SB [WI] Rua 19 de Fevereiro 162 (M° Botafogo) **55-21/2244-4263** *cafe & bar*

Rio G Spa Rua Teixeira de Melo 16 (at Prudente de Moraes) **55-21/2523-5092** *3pm-midnight, also bar, darkroom, massage*

Termas Catete [M] Rua Correia Dutra 34 **55-21/2265-5478** *1pm-1am, tilkl 6am Fri-Sat, darkrooms, cabins*

Termas Kabalk [M] Rua Santa Luiza 459 (near Varnhagem Square) **55-21/2572-6210** *3pm-11pm, bar, darkroom, very clean*

Cruisy Areas

Avenida Copacabana & Av Atlantica

Barra Beach *across street from beach; look for flags & go past building into woods*

São Paulo

Bars

Z Carniceria [GS,E] **55-11/2936-0934** *8pm-1am Th-Sat only*

Nightclubs

Aloka Club [★GS,D] Rua Frei Caneca 916 (in Cerqueira Cesar) **55-11/945-409-699** *11pm-6am, clsd Mon-Wed, underground nightclub*

Blue Space [M,D,DS,S] Rua Brigadeiro Galvao Bueno 723 (in Barra Funda) **55-11/3666-1616** *from 11pm Sat, from 7pm Sun, clsd Mon-Fri*

Bubu Disco Lounge [M,D] Rua dos Pinheiros 791 **55-11/3081-9659**

Las Vegas [GS,D] *10pm-4am Sat*

The Week [M,D,SW] Rua Guaicurus 324 (in Barra Funda) **55-11/3872-9966**

Cafes

Cafe Vermont Itaim [MW,E] Rua Pedroso Alvarenga 1192 (in Itaim Bibi) **55-11/3707-7721**

Restaurants

Bella Paulista Rua Haddock Lobo 354 (in Cerqueira Cesar) **55-11/3214-3347** *delicious baked goods and more*

O Pedaco de Pizza Rua Augusta 1463 **55-11/2619-8408** *noon-4am, till 11pm Sun-Mon, grab a slice just like NYC*

Spot Al Ministro Rocha Azevedo 72 (in Cerqueira Cesar) **55-11/3284-6131** *also bar*

Men's Clubs

Labrintus Club Rua Frei Caneca 328 (in Cerqueira Cesar) **55-11/992-558-349** *24hrs*

Chile

Santiago

Note: M°=Metro station

Info Lines & Services

Acciongay - Corporacion Chilena de Prevencion del SIDA San Ignacio 165 **56-32/672-0000** *AIDS info, testing & workshops*

Accommodations

The Aubrey Hotel [GF,SW,WI] Constitución 299-317, Bellavista **56-2/940-2800** *hip boutique hotel, piano lounge*

Lastarria Hotel [GF,SW,WI] Coronel Santiago Bueras 188 **56-2/840-3700** *luxury boutique hotel, bar & restaurant*

Le Reve Hotel [GF,WI] Orrego Luco 023 (Providencia) **56-2/757-6000, 56-2/757-6011** *luxury boutique hotel, brkfst buffet*

Bars

Bar 105 [MW] Bombero Nuñez 105 **56-2/403-2990** *10pm-late Th-Sat*

Bar de Willy [MW,E,S] Av 11 de Septiembre 2214 (Común Providencia) **56-2/381-1806** *10pm-4am, till 5am wknds, strippers on 1st flr*

Farinelli [M,DS] Bombero Nuñez 68 (Recoleta) **56-9/4537-2815** *10:30pm-3am Satl*

Pub Friend's [MW,E,DS] Bombero Nuñez 365 (at Dominica, barrio Bellavista) **56-2/777-3979** *9:30pm-4am, till 5am Fri-Sat*

Vox Populi [M,F] Ernesto Pinto Lagarrigue 364 (Bellavista) **56-2/738-0562** *9:30pm-3am, clsd Sun-Mon, also restaurant, garden patio*

Nightclubs

Blondie [GS,D,A] Alameda 2879, loc 104 **56-2/681-7793** *theme nights*

Bunker [MW,D,F,E] Bombero Nuñez 159 (Bellavista) **56-2/2737-1716** *11pm-close Fri-Sat*

Club Principe [M,D] Pio Nono 398 **56-2/777-6381**

Fausto [M,D,DS] Av Sta Maria 832 **56-2/777-1041**

Nueva Cero [M,D,DS] Euclides 1204 par 2 Gran Avenida **56-2/255-1729** *Fri-Sat only*

Cafes

Tavelli [★] Andrés de Fuenzalida 34 (Providencia) **56-2/3223-8420** *8:30am-9pm, from 10am Sat*

Restaurants

La Pizza Nostra Av Providencia 1975 & Pedro de Valdivia **56-2/231-8941** *Italian*

Santo Remedio [D] 152 Roman Diaz, Providencia **56-2/235-0984** *1pm-3:30pm & 6pm-2am, tapas, full bar*

El Toro [★GO] Loreto 33 **56-2/2761-5954** *1pm-1:30am, clsd Sun*

Gyms & Health Clubs

Sauna Mi Tiempo Bombero Nuñez 230 **56-2/735-3949** *3pm-10pm*

Men's Clubs

Baños 282 Bellavista 282 **56-2/777-1709** *1pm-midnight*

Banos Metro [V] Almirante Montt 471 (in the Bellas Artes district) **56-2/633-1321** *1pm-midnight, dark-room*

Erotica

Japi Jane Luis Thayer Ojeda 059, Oficina 11 **56-2/234-4917** *11am-8pm, till 4pm Sat, clsd Sun*

Cruisy Areas

Paseo Las Palmas [AYOR] in Providencia neighborhood

Plaza de Armas [AYOR]

Europe

AUSTRIA

Vienna

INFO LINES & SERVICES

Hosi Zentrum Heumuhlgasse 14 **43-1/216-6604** *clsd Mon, Wed-Th, LGBT political organization, many groups and events, cafe*

ACCOMMODATIONS

Altstadt [GF,WI] Kirchengasse 41 **43-1/522-6666** *located centrally in Vienna's ancient artist quarter Spittelberg*

Arcotel Wimberger [GF] Neubaugürtel 34-36 (at Goldschlagstr) **43-1/521-650** *4-star hotel, restaurant & bar on premises*

Art Hotel [GF] Brandmayergasse 7-9 **43-1/544-5108** *modern, art-filled hotel*

Boutique Hotel Stadthalle [GS] Hackengasse 20 **43-1/982-4272** *eco-friendly boutique hotel*

Gay At Home [MW,GO] **43-664/442-8049** *rental apts around Vienna*

Guesthouse Bakul [GF,WI] Stolberggasse 51 **43 650 /890-0713** *simple budget guesthouse*

Le Méridien Wien [GF,SW] Robert-Stolz-Platz 1 **43-1/588-900** *sauna, hot tub, also restaurant & bar*

Pension Wild [M,F,GO] Lange Gasse 10 (off Lerchenfelder Str) **43-1/406-5174** *small, friendly pension in the heart of Vienna, close to "gay area"*

Das Tyrol [GF] Mariahilfer Str 15 **43-1/587-5415** *small luxury hotel*

BARS

Cafe Rifugio [M] Schönbrunner Str 10 **43-699/109-77-891** *10am-10pm*

Cafe Savoy [★MW,F] Linke Wienzeile 36 (at Köstlergasse) **43-1/581-1557** *noon-2am, from 9am Sat-Sun, upscale cafe-bar*

Eagle Bar [★M,L,V] Blümelgasse 1 (at Gumpendorfer Str, U3-Neubaugasse) **43-1/587-2661** *9pm-4am, darkroom, also sex shop*

Felixx [MW,F,WI] Gumpendorferstr 5 **43-1/920-4714** *6pm-2am*

Mango Bar [★M,YC,GO] Laimgrubengasse 3 (U4-Kettenbrückengasse) **43-1/920-4714** *9pm-6am*

Peter's Operncafé Hartauer [GS,F] Riemergasse 9 (at Singer) **43-1/512-8981** *6pm-2am, clsd Sun-Mon, terrace*

Red Carpet [MW,D,YC] Magdalenenstr 2 **43-1/676-782-2966** *theme nights*

Sling [M,L] Kettenbrückengasse 4 (at Grüngasse, U4-Kettenbrückengasse) **43-1/586-2362** *3pm-4am, darkroom, private rooms, sling, erotic shop, "piss cinema"*

Studio 67 [GS,D] Gumpendorferstr 67 **43-1/966-7182** *10am-4am Th-Sat, upscale lounge & dance club*

Village Bar [★M,YC] Stiegengasse 8 (near Naschmarkt) **43-1/676-3848977** *8pm-3am*

Wiener Freiheit [MW,D,TG,F,V] Schönbrunner Str 25 (U4-Kettenbrückengasse) **43-1/931-9111** *8pm-midnight, clsd Sun-Mon, 3 flrs, disco 10pm-4am Fri-Sat*

NIGHTCLUBS

BallCanCan [MW,D] Schwarzenberg Platz 10 (at Ost Klub) *monthly queer Balkan club*

Heaven Gay Night [★M,D,TG,S,YC] **43-1/402-1022** *check www.heaven.at for events*

Meat Market [MW,D] *queer electro dance party, FB for dates & locations*

Pitbull [M,D,B,L] Lerchenfelder Gürtel 37 (upstairs) *10pm 2nd Fri only*

Queer Beat [M,D] Landstr Hauptstr 38 (at the Viper Room) *2nd & 4th Sat only*

Le Swing [M,TG,V,$] Hannovergasse 5 (at Wallensteinstr) **43-1/332-1670** *gay 9pm-2am Tue only for Transnight, also sauna*

Why Not? [M,D,S,V,WI] Tiefer Graben 22 (at Wipplinger, U-Schottentor) **43-1/925-3024** *10pm-close Fri-Sat & before public holidays, darkroom*

CAFES

Cafe Central Herrengasse 14 (at Strauchgasse) **43-1/533-37-63-61** *7:30am-10pm, from 10am Sun & public holidays, "world's most famous coffee-house"*

Cafe Standard Margaretenstr 63 **43-1/581-0586** *8am-9pm, from 11am Sat, clsd Sun*

Cafe Stein [GF,F,WI] Währinger Str 6-8 (near U-Schottentor) **43-1/319-7241** *8am-1am, from 9am Sun, terrace*

Das Möbel [WI] Burggasse 10 (Spittelberg) **43-1/524-9497** *10am-1am, trendy, also art gallery*

SMart Cafe [GS,F] Kostlergasse 9 **43-1/585-7165** *6pm-2am, till 4am Fri-Sat, clsd Sun-Mon, S/M & fetish cafe*

RESTAURANTS

Aux Gazelles Rahlgasse 5 **43-1/585-6645** *French/ Moroccan restaurant 6pm-midnight; Arabian-style lounge, cafe & deli 11am-2am*

Bin Im Leo [BW] Servitengasse 14 **43-1/391-7763** *4pm-midnight, from noon wknds, plenty veggie*

Cafe Raimann [★] Schönbrunner Straße 285 **43-1/813-5767** *8am-midnight, clsd Sun, great brkfst & coffee*

Cafe-Restaurant Willendorf Linke Wienzeile 102 (near Hofmuhlgasse, U4-Pilgramgasse) **43-1/587-1789** *6pm-2am, food served till midnight, full bar, terrace, located in the Gay/Lesbian Center of Vienna*

Florentin Berggasse 8 (at Wasagasse, U2-Schottentor) **43-676 /735-5625** *8am-11pm, Middle Eastern cuisine, great brkfst*

Halle Museumsquartier 1 **43-1/523-7001** *10am-2am, modern bistro, artsy crowd*

Mi Barrio [E] Münzwardeingasse 2 (U4-Pilgramgasse) **43-1/587-6125** *5pm-12:30am, till 2am Fri-Sat, 11am-4pm Sun, Latin American food, also full bar*

Motto [★R] Rüdigergasse 1 **43-1/587-0672** *6pm-2am, till 4am Fri-Sat, trendy, also nightclub, patio*

Santo Spirito [E] Kumpfgasse 7 **43-1/512-9998** *5pm-2am, hidden classical music delight*

Sly & Arny Lackierergasse 5 **43-1/405-0458** *6pm-1am, till 2am Fri-Sat, great cheap cocktails*

Stöger Ramperstorffergasse 63 **43-1/544-7596** *11am-midnight, clsd Sun, Viennese*

ENTERTAINMENT & RECREATION

Haus der Musik/ House of Music [F] Seilerstätte 30 **43-1/516-4810** *10am-10pm, interactive museum of sound, also cafe*

Kunsthistorisches Museum Maria Theresien-Platz (enter Heldenplatz) **43-1/525-240** *10am-6pm, till 9pm Th, clsd Mon, not to be missed*

BOOKSTORES

Löwenherz Berggasse 8 (next to Cafe Berg, enter on Wasagasse, U2-Schottentor) **43-1/317-2982** *10am-7pm, till 8pm Fri, till 6pm Sat, clsd Sun, LGBT, large selection of English titles*

RETAIL SHOPS

Tiberius [WC] Lindengasse 2 (at Stiftgasse, U3-Neubaugasse) **43-1/522-0474** *clsd Sun, designer fetish-wear*

PUBLICATIONS

Xtra *gay magazine*

MEN'S CLUBS

Apollo City Sauna [SW,V] Wimbergergasse 34 **43-660 /67-36-133** *2pm-2am, bar, darkroom, gym equipment*

Hard On [MO,L] Hamburgerstr 4 *fetish club; hangout for LMC (Leather & Motorbike Community)*

Kaiserbründl [F,V,SW] Weihburggasse 18-20 (at Grünangergasse, U1-Stephansplatz) **43-1/513-3293** *2pm-midnight, till 2am Fri-Sat, 3 flrs, 2 bars, darkroom maze, gym equipment*

Kino Labyrinth [M,TG,V] Favoritenstr 164 **43-1/920-4088** *[MO] Wed, gay & [TG] Fri, darkrooms, cabins, huge cruising area*

Sport Sauna [★F,V,YC] Lange Gasse 10 (at Pension Wild, U2-Lerchenfelderstr) **43-1/406-7156** *3pm-1am, 24hrs wknds, bar, gym equipment*

Erotica

Man for Man Hamburgerstr 8 (at Rechte Wienzeile, U-Kettenbrückengasse) **43-1/585-2064** *11am-11pm, from 2pm Sun-Mon, books, toys, videos, DVDs, private rooms*

Sexworld XXL Store [V] Mariahilfer Str 49 **43-1/587-6656** *clsd Sun, cabins, darkroom, cruisy, special gay section*

Wiscot Center Lerchenfelder Gürtel 45 **43-1/402-7822** *noon-midnight, till 3am Th & Sat*

Cruisy Areas

Rathauspark [AYOR] *evenings only*

Schweizer Garten [AYOR] next to Südbahnhof

Czech Republic

Prague (Praha)

Note: M°=Metro station

Prague is divided into 10 city districts:
Praha—1
Praha—2, etc.

Praha—Overview

Info Lines & Services

Czech AIDS Help Society Dům Světla, Malého 3, Praha 8 **420/800-800-980 (Helpline #), 420/224-814-284** *Czech org for AIDS prevention*

Accommodations

Apartments in Prague [GS,WI,WC] **420/775-588-508, 303/800-0858** *beautiful apartments in historic buildings in center of Prague*

Entertainment & Recreation

Letna Park & Beer Garden *great view of the city*

Websites

Gay Prague Scene

Praha—1

Accommodations

Buddha Bar Hotel [GS,WI] Jakubská 649/8 **420 /221-776-300** *small sexy hotel*

Hotel Leonardo [GS,F,WI] Karolíny Svetle 27 **420 /239-009-239** *great location*

Hotel Metropol [GS] Narodni 33 (at Na Perstyne) **420/246-022-100**

The ICON Boutique Hotel [★GS,F,WI,WC] V Jame 6 (at Vodickova) **420/221-634-100** *restaurant & bar*

Bars

Café Bar Flirt [M,D,B,F,K] Martinská 5/419 **420/224-248-592** *cafe open 10am-2am, bar open 10pm-2am Fri-Sat, bears meet 7pm Wed*

Friends Bar [★M,NH,D,V,WI] Bartolomejská 11 **420/226-211-920** *7pm-6am*

K.U. Bar [GS,D,E] Rytirská 13 (at Perlová, near Oldtown Square) **420/724-695-910** *7pm-4am, upscale & trendy*

Loca Cafe Bar [MW,D,F] Smetanovo náb e í 24 **420/212-240-967** *5pm-2am, till 3am Wed-Th, 4am Fri-Sat*

U Rudolfa [M,BW,OC] Mezibranská 3 **420/605-872-492** *2pm-2am, from 4pm wknds*

Nightclubs

Escape Club [MO,D,F,S,$] V Jame 8 (off Wenceslas Square) **420/702-059-994** *9pm-4am, go-go boys, also hustlers*

Cafes

Cafe Cafe [★WI] Rytirská 10 (at Perlová, near Oldtown Square) **420/224-210-597** *10am-11pm*

Cafe Louvre [GS,F,NS] Národni 22 (M° Narodni Trida) **420/224-930-949** *9am-11:30pm, the favorite hangout of Albert Einstein & Franz Kafka*

Cafe Muzeum [★] Mezibranska 19 **420/774-454-304** *10am-11pm, from 1pm wknds*

Q Cafe Opatovická 166/12 **420/776-856-361** *noon-midnight*

Restaurants

Campanulla Cafe Restaurant Velkoprevorske namesti 4 **420/257-217-736** *set in the beautiful garden of The Grand Priory of Bohemia Palace*

Lehka Hlava Borsov 2/280 **420/222-220-665** *noon-11:30pm, vegetarian*

Maitrea Tynska 6/1064 (nr Old Town Square) **420/221-711-631** *noon-11:30pm, vegetarian*

Noi [GO] Ujezd 19 **420/257-311-411** *11am-1am, Thai*

Petrinské Terasy [GO] Seminarská Zahrada 393, Malá Strana **420/257-320-688** *noon-11pm, in a former monastery, great view*

Restaurant Dlouhá Dlouhá 23 (basement) **420/222-329-853** *11am-11pm*

Staromestska Restaurace Staromestske namesti 19 **420/224-213-015** *11am-midnight, local Czech specialties, great spot outdoor dining right on the main square*

Entertainment & Recreation

NoD Gallery/ Roxy Dlouhá 33 *experimental theater, dance & performance; also cafe & live music venue*

Sex Machines Museum Melantrichova 18 **420/227-186-260** *10am-11pm*

Bookstores

Globe [E,F] Patrossova 6 **420/224-934-203** *English-language bookstore*

Men's Clubs

Sauna Babylonia [★WI] Martinská 6 (at Na Perstyne) **420/224-232-304** *2pm-3am, till 5am wknds, popular with tourists, gym equipment, bar*

Erotica

Erotic City Zitna 43 **420/737-221-264**

Praha—2

Accommodations

Balbin Penzion [GF,WI] Balbinova 26 (near Wenceslas Square) **420/222-250-660**

Prague Saints [MW,GO] Polska 32 (office location) (at Trebizkeho, at Saints Bar) **420/775-152-041, 420/775-152-042** *apts in gay Vinohrady district*

Bars

The Bourgeois Pig Coffee Bar & Vinyl [MW] Legerova 43 **420/607-075-765** *10am-2am (summer) from 6pm, clsd Sun (winter), cool spot*

Club Strelec [M,B] Anglicka 2 **420/606-947-613** *5pm-2am, till midnight Sun, more bears on Wed & Sat*

JampaDampa [★W,D,K] V Tunich 10 (at Zitna) **420/604-774-959** *6pm-2am, till 4am Wed, 6pm-6am Fri-Sat, clsd Sun-Mon*

Klub 21 [MW,F,YC] Rimska 21 **420/222-364-720** *7pm-close, clsd Sun, cellar bar/ gallery, mostly Czechs*

Saints [MW] Polska 32 (at Trebizkeho) **420/222-250-326** *7pm-2am, till 4am wknds*

Nightclubs

Club Saigon [GS,WI] Trebizskeho 9a **420/776-205-880** *5pm-1am, clsd Sun-Mon*

Empire [GS] Trebizskeho 1391/8 **420/776-000-808** *5pm-4am, cozy front bar*

Radost FX [GS,D] Belehradska 120, Vinohrady (at Radost FX) **420/224-254-776, 420/603-193-711** *open Th-Sat*

Termax [★M,D] 40 Vinohradska **420/222-710-462** *10pm-6am Fri-Sat onlye*

Termix [★MW,D,K] Trebizskeho 4 (at Vinohradska) **420/222-710-462** *10pm-6am, clsd Sun-Tue*

Restaurants

Celebrity Cafe Vinohradska 40 (in Vinohrady) **420/222-511-343** *8am-2am, noon-3am Sat, noon-midnight Sun, also bar*

Céleste Restaurant & Bar Rasalnovo nabrezi 1981/80 (at Dancing House) **420/2219-84160** *lunch & dinner, clsd Sun, French dining with great views of the river*

Radost FX Belehradska 120, Vinohrady **420/224-254-776, 420/603-193-711** *fabulous wknd brunch, vegetarian cafe, also nightclub [GF] w/ popular bi-monthly gay party Lollypop*

Erotica

Heaven [★] Gorazdova 11 **420/224-912-282** *cinema, toys, magazines, DVDs, darkroom, also bar & accommodations*

Praha—3

Bars

Little Temple Bar [M,DS,S,AYOR] Seifertova 3 (at Pribenicka) **420/222-710-773** *2pm-10pm, only gay venue open in the afternoon, hustlers, also sex shop, rent boys & hotel*

Piano Bar [MW,F,OC] Milesovská 10 (at Ondrickova) **420/775-727-496** *5pm-close, mostly Czech*

Nightclubs

Club Temple [★M,DS,S,AYOR] Seifertova 3 (at Pribenicka) **420/222-710-773** *8pm-4am, hustlers, also sex shop, rent boys & hotel*

Restaurants

Mozaika Burger Nitranská 13 **420/224-253-011** *noon-11:30pm*

Entertainment & Recreation

TV Tower Mahlerovy sady 1 **420/724-251-286** *get a bird's-eye view of the city from the top of this tower*

Men's Clubs

Alcatraz [MO,L,V,S] Borivojova 58 (off Seifertova, in Zizhkov) **420/222-711-458** *9pm-5am, clsd Mon-Tue, S/M club, theme nights*

Praha—5

Accommodations

Andel's Hotel [GF] Stroupeznickeho 21 (at Pizenska) **420/296-889-688** *restaurant & bar*

Men's Clubs

Drake's [F,WI] Zborovska 50 (at Petrinska) **420/257-326-828** *24hrs, full bar, darkroom, maze, sex shop*

Praha—6

Cruisy Areas

Sarka Lake [AYOR] by metro to Dejvicka & tram 26 to end station *nude bathing, summers*

Praha—7

Nightclubs

OMG/ Oh My Gay Party [M,D] U Pruhonu 3 (at Mecca) *3rd Sat only*

Praha—8

Accommodations

G Club Hotel [M,WI,GO] Stepnicná 9, Liben (at Na Malem Klinu) **420/777-839-733** *also nightclub 3pm-midnight, clsd Sun*

Men's Clubs

Sauna David [WI] Sokolovská 44, Karlin (at Vitkova) **420/222-317-869** *9am-11pm, from 11am wknds*

Sauna Labyrint [★MO] Pernerova 4 (at Peckova) *2pm-7am, sauna, steam room, dark room, also bar*

Praha—10

Accommodations

Arco Guest House [M,WI,GO] Donská 3 **420/271-740-734**

Ron's Rainbow Guest House [GS,WI,GO] Bulharska 4 (at Finská) **420/271-725-664, 420/731-165-022 (cell)**

Men's Clubs

Sauna Bonbon Cernomorska 6 (at Charkovska) **420/777-146-068** *3pm-1am, till 2am Fri-Sun*

Praha—11

Cruisy Areas

Seberak Lake [AYOR] *from endstation in Seberak, go to opposite side of lake to nude beach, summers*

Denmark

Copenhagen

Info Lines & Services

Kafe Knud Skindergade 21 **45/3332-5861** *4pm-10pm Tue & Th only, HIV resource center, cafe open Tue & Th only*

Sabaah Onkel Dannys Plads 1 *community center for LGBT ethnic minorities*

Wonderful Copenhagen Convention & Visitors Bureau Vesterbrogade 4A **45/7022-2442 (tourist info)** *"official tourism site of Copenhagen," extensive listings and resources*

Accommodations

66 Guldsmeden [GF,WI] Vesterbrogade 66 **45/3322-1500** *urban bohemian hide-away in the heart of Copenhagen s Montmartre area, cafe & lounge, buffet brkfst*

Copenhagen Admiral Hotel [GF,WI] Toldbodgade 24-28 **45/3374-1414** *restaurant & bar on site, great views*

First Hotel Kong Frederik [GF] Vester Voldgade 25 **45/3312-5902** *located central in Copenhagen*

First Hotel Skt. Petri [GF,F,WI,WC] Krystalgade 22 **45/3345-9100** *hotel embodying the ultra-coolest of Scandinavian design, great bar*

First Hotel Twentyseven [GF,WI] Løngangstræde 27 **45/7027-5627** *in the historical part of Copenhagen*

Hotel Kong Arthur [GF] Norre Sogade 11 **45/3345-7777** *full gym/spa, restaurants & bar on site*

Hotel Windsor [M,GO] Frederiksborggade 30, 1360 **45/3311-0830** *near gay scene, shared baths*

Radisson Collection Hotel Royal [GF] Hammerichsgade 1 **45/3342-6000** *full gym, restaurants & bar on site*

The Square [GF] Rådhuspladsen 14 **45/3338-1200** *central location with the serenity of tranquil, stylish surroundings, lobby bar & roof terrace*

Bars

Amigo Bar [MW,NH,K] Schønbergsgade 4 (Frederiksberg) **45 5/3321-4915** *10pm-6am*

Cafe Intime [GF,P] Allegade 25, Frederiksberg **45/3834-1958** *4pm-2am, cafe-bar*

Centralhjørnet [M,WI] Kattesundet 18 **45/3311-8549** *noon-2am*

Cosy Bar [★M] Studiestræde 24 (in Latin Quarter) **45/3312-7427** *10pm-6am, till 8am Fri-Sat*

Masken [★MW,F,WI] Studiestræde 33 **45/3391-0937** *2pm-3am, till 5am Fri-Sat*

Men's Bar [MO,L] Teglgårdsstræde 3 **45/3312-7303** *4pm-2am*

Never Mind [M] Nørre Voldgade 2 **45/3311-8886** *10pm-6am*

Oscar Bar Cafe [★M,F,WI] Radhuspladsen 77 **45/3312-0999** *noon-2am, great happy hour*

Nightclubs

SLM (Scandinavian Leather Men)Copenhagen [MO,L,PC] 17-C Lavendelstraede (in back building) **45/3332-0601** *10pm-close Fri-Sat, strict dress code, Th from 5:30pm & Sun from 4pm, no dress code*

Cafes

Jernbanecafeen [WI] Reventlowsgade 16 **45/3321-6090** *7am-2am, patio*

Restaurants

Jailhouse Restaurant & Bar [★M,B,F] Studiestraede 12 **45/3315-2255** *3pm-2am, till 5am Fri-Sat*

Luna's Diner Sankt Annæ St **45/3254-2000** *11am-11pm, till midnight Fri-Sat, American comfort food*

Tight Hyskenstraede 10 **45/3311-0900** *11:30am-11pm, from 5pm Sun, Canadian, French & Australian*

Entertainment & Recreation

Amager Strandpark *beach 5 km from city center*

Bellevue Beach *mostly gay beach, left end is nude*

Tisvildeleje Beach N of the city (take S-train to Hillerød, then local train to beach) *gay beach*

Warehouse 9 Halmtorvet 11A-F **45/3322-2847** *queer art, music, performance & more*

Men's Clubs

Amigo Sauna [★V] Studiestræde 31 **45/3315-2028** *noon-7am, sauna, steam, tanning, cabins, mazes*

Body Bio [TG,V,WI] Kingosgade 7 (basement) *noon-midnight, till 1am wknds, cabins, sauna, cruisy, mostly gay men, but open to all genders*

Erotica

Men's Shop Viktoriagade 24 **45/3325-4475** *magazines, books, toys, leather/ rubber gear, videos*

Cruisy Areas

Ørstedsparken [AYOR] btwn Nørre voldgade & Nørre farimagsgade *mainly at night*

Utterslev Mose [AYOR] off hwy toward Farum

Zigøjnerpladsen (Gypsy Square) [AYOR] near Arillerivej & Lossepladsvej

Websites

Out & About 45/4093-1977 *Denmark's LGBT media focusing on news, culture, city-fabric and lifestyle, www.oaonline.dk*

England

London

London is divided into 6 regions:
London—Overview
London—Central
London—West
London—North
London—East
London—South

London—Overview

Nightclubs

Exilio [MW,D,MR-L] Temple Pier Victoria Embankment (Victoria Embankment) **44-(0)79/5698-3230** *9:30pm-2:30am 2nd & last Sat*

Torture Garden 44-020/7700-1441 *the worlds largest fetish/ body art club; visit www.torturegarden.com for events*

Restaurants

Torture Garden [GS,D,E] **44-020/7500-7730** *world's largest Fetish / Body Art Club. Events Attract 800 - 2500 people monthly to various London venues,check www.torturegarden.com for dates*

Publications

Boyz 44-020/7025-6100 *newspaper w/ extensive club & event listings*

Gay Times 44-020/7424-7400 *glorious gay glossy*

London—Central

London—Central includes Soho, Covent Garden, Bloomsbury, Mayfair, Westminster, Pimlico & Belgravia

Accommodations

Dover Hotel [GF,WI] 42/44 Belgrave Rd **44-020/7821-9085** *near Victoria Station in the heart of Central London offers quality inexpensive accommodations*

Fitz B&B [MW,NS,WI,GO] 15 Colville Place (btwn Charlotte & Whitfield) **44-(0)78/3437-2866** *18th-c townhouse on pedestrian-only street*

George Hotel [GF] 58-60 Cartwright Gardens (N of Russell Square) **44-020/7387-8777** *full brkfst, some shared baths*

Hazlitt's [GF,WI] 6 Frith St (Soho Sq) **44-020/7434-1771** *3 historic Georgian buildings furnished w/ antiques*

Lincoln House [GS,WI,WC] 33 Gloucester Pl, Marble Arch (at Baker St) **44-20/7486-7630** *B&B, full brkfst*

Marble Arch Inn [GF,WI] 49-50 Upper Berkeley St **44-020/7723-7888** *located at the very heart of London*

Z Hotel [GS,WI] 17 Moor St **44-020/3551-3701** *a designer conversion of twelve Georgian town-houses, great Soho location*

BARS

Note: "Pub hours" usually means 11am-11pm Mon-Sat and noon-3pm & 7pm-10:30pm Sun

The Admiral Duncan [★MW,NH,TG,DS] 54 Old Compton St (Soho) **44-020/7437-5300** *pub hours*

Bar Soho [GS] 23-25 Old Compton St (at Frith St) **44-020/7439-0439** *noon-1am, till 3am Fri-Sat, from 2pm Sun*

Circa [M,D] 62 Frith St **44-020/7734-6826** *1pm-1am, from 4pm Mon, dance club 10pm-4am Fri-Sat*

City of Quebec [M,NH,OC] 12 Old Quebec St (at Marble Arch) **44-020/7629-6159** *pub hours, DJs Fri-Sat*

Compton's of Soho [★M,F,WC] 51-53 Old Compton St (at Dean St) **44-020/7479-7961** *noon-midnight, till 10:30pm Sun, cruisy*

Dog & Duck [GS,NH,F] 18 Bateman St (at Frith St) **44-020/7494-0697** *10am-11:30pm*

Duke of Wellington [GS,F] 77 Wardour (Soho) **44-020/7439-1274** *pub hours*

Freedom Bar [MW,D,DS] 66 Wardour St (off Old Compton St) **44-020/7734-0071** *4pm-3am, from 2pm wknds, till midnight Sun*

Friendly Society [MW,YC] 79 Wardour St (the basement at Old Compton, enter Tisbury Ct) **44-020/7434-3805** *4pm-11:30pm*

G-A-Y Bar [MW,F,V] 30 Old Compton St (at Frith) **44-020/7494-2756** *noon-midnight*

Green Carnation [★MW,D,F] 4-5 Greek St (Soho Sq) **44-020/8123-4267** *4pm-2am, inspired by the time & life of Oscar Wilde*

Halfway to Heaven [M,NH,K,C,OC,GO] 7 Duncannon St (at Charing Cross, West End) **44-020/7484-0736** *noon-midnight, till 2am Fri-Sat, till 10pm Sun*

King's Arms Soho [M,NH,B,F,K,V] 23 Poland St (at Noel, Soho) **44-020/7734-5907** *noon-11pm, till 1am Fri-Sat, 1pm-midnight Sun, popular bear hangout*

Ku Bar/ Ku Klub [MW,K,YC,WI] 30 Lisle St (Leicester Sq) **44-020/7437-4303** *noon-3am, till midnight Sun*

The New Bloomsbury Set [GS] 76 Marchmont St (at Tavistock Pl) **44-020/7383-3084** *4pm-11:30pm, till 10:30pm Sun, cozy basement oasis*

The Retro Bar [MW,NH,D,K] 2 George Ct (at Strand) **44-020/7321-2811** *pub hours*

Rupert Street [★MW,F,WC] 50 Rupert St (off Brewer) **44-020/7494-3059** *pub hours, upscale "fashiony-types"*

Star at Night [MW,D,F,E] 22 Great Chapel St (at Hollen St) **44-020/7494-2488** *6pm-11:30pm, clsd Sun-Mon*

Vault 139 [M] 139-143 Whitfield St (Warren St) **44-020/7388-5500** *1pm-1am, theme nights/dress codes*

The Village Soho [★M,D,18+,YC] 81 Wardour St (at Old Compton) **44-020/7478-0530** *5pm-2am*

The Yard [★M,F,E,YC,WC] 57 Rupert St (off Brewer) **44-020/7437-2652, 871/426-2243** *pub hours*

NIGHTCLUBS

G-A-Y Club [★M,D,E,YC,$] Under the Arches, Villers St (at Heaven) **44-020/7494-2756** *11pm-3am*

Heaven [★M,D] 9 The Arches (off Villiers St) **44-020/7930-2020** *the mother of all London gay clubs and live music venue*

KU Bar Frith St [M,D] 25 Frith St (at Old Compton St, Soho) **44-020/7287-7986** *noon-11pm, till midnight wknds, 3 floors*

The Shadow Lounge [M,D,PC] 5-7 Brewer St (Soho) **44-020/7317-9270** *10pm-3am, clsd Sun*

CAFES

Balans Cafe [★] 34 Old Compton St **44-020/7439-3309** *24hrs, terrace*

Caffe Nero 43 Frith St **44-020/7434-3887** *cruisy cafe7am-2pm, till 4pm Sat, cruisy cafe*

Flat White 17 Berwick St **44-020/7734-0370** *8am-6pm, from 9am wknds, Australian-style cafe*

Milk Bar [WC] 3 Bateman St **44-020/7734-0370** *8am-5:30pm, 9:30am-6pm wknds*

RESTAURANTS

The Gay Hussar [WC] 2 Greek St (on Soho Square) **44-020/7437-0973** *lunch & dinner, clsd Sun, Hungarian*

Mildred's [★] 45 Lexington **44-020/7494-1634** *noon-11pm, clsd Sun, vegetarian, plenty vegan*

Randall & Aubin 16 Brewer St (at Walkers Court) **44-020/7287-4447** *noon-11pm, casual French, good people-watching*

Wagamama Noodle Bar [NS] 81 Dean St **44-020/3198-2984** *noon-11pm, Japanese; many locations throughout city*

BOOKSTORES

Gay's the Word 66 Marchmont St (near Russell Sq Underground) **44-020/7278-7654** *10am-6:30pm, 2pm-6pm Sun, , "the most comprehensive collection of gay and lesbian books in the UK housed in this friendly independent bookstore"*

RETAIL SHOPS

Prowler Soho [★] 5-7 Brewer St (behind Village Soho bar) **44-020/7734-4031** *11am-9:30pm, till10pm Th-Sat, noon-8pm Sun, large gay dept store*

GYMS & HEALTH CLUBS

Soho Gyms 12 Macklin St (Holborn) **44-020/7242-1290** *many locations*

Sweatbox [18+,GO] 1-2 Ramilies St, Soho **44-020/3214-6014** *24hrs, gym & sauna*

MEN'S CLUBS

Saunabar Portsea 2 Portsea Pl (at Connaught St, Marble Arch) **44-020/7402-3385** *11:30am-10:30pm*

The Stable [F] 29 Endell St (at Betterton) **44-020/7836-2236** *sauna, steam, jacuzzi, holistic services, also bar*

EROTICA

Clone Zone Soho 35 Old Compton St **44-020/7234-3438** *11am-10pm, till 11pm Fri-Sat, noon-9pm Sun, other London locations*

London — West

London—West includes Earl's Court, Kensington, Chelsea & Bayswater

ACCOMMODATIONS

Cardiff Hotel [GF,WI] 5, 7, 9 Norfolk Sq (Hyde Park) **44-020/7723-9068** *B&B hotel in 3 Victorian townhouses, some share baths*

Millennium Bailey's Hotel [GF] 140 Gloucester Rd (at Old Brompton Rd, Kensington) **44-020/7373-6000** *also restaurant & bar*

Myhotel Chelsea [GF,WI] 35 Ixworth Place (at Elystan St, Chelsea) **44-020/7225-7500** *stylish boutique hotel in Chelsea*

Parkwood Hotel [GF,NS.WI] 4 Stanhope Pl (Marble Arch) **44-020/7402-2241** *central location, full brkfst*

BARS

West Five (W5) [MW,C,P] 6 Popes Ln (South Ealing) **44-020/8579-3266** *7pm-close, clsd Mon-Tue*

RESTAURANTS

The Churchill Arms 119 Kensington Church St **44-020/7727-4242** *inexpensive, fantastic Thai, also pub*

The Gate 51 Queen Caroline St, Hammersmith **44-020/8748-6932** *lunch & dinner, lunch only Sun, vegetarian*

Entertainment & Recreation

Walking Tour of Gay SOHO 56 Old Compton St (at Admiral Duncan Pub) **44–020/7437–6063** *2pm Sun, world-famous historical walking tour covering over 600 years of gay history in London's "square mile of sin"*

Retail Shops

Clone Zone [GO] 266 Old Brompton Rd (Earl's Court) **44–020/7373–0598** *10am-8pm, till 10pm Fri-Sat, noon-6pm Sun*

London—North

London—North includes Paddington, Regents Park, Camden, St Pancras & Islington

Accommodations

Ambassadors Bloomsbury [GF,WI,WC] 12 Upper Woburn Pl (at Euston Rd) **44–020/7693–5400** *near Kings Cross St Pancras and Euston Stations, Italian restaurant on site, full brkfst*

Roseate House London [GF,WI] 3 Westbourne Terr (Hyde Park) **44–020/7479–6600** *an English luxury lifestyle and boutique hotel*

Bars

G-A-Y Late [M,D] 5 Goslett Yard (Camden Town) *11pm-3am*

King William IV (KW) [★MW,F] 77 Hampstead High St (Hampstead) **44–020/7435–5747** *pub hours, beer garden, also hotel*

Nightclubs

Central Station [★MW,D,TG,F,C,DS,S,V,WI] 37 Wharfdale Rd (King's Cross) **44–020/7278–3294** *noon-1pm, complex includes B&B, terrace*

Club Kali [★MW,D,MR-A,TG,E,$] 1 Dartmouth Park Hill (at The Dome) **44–020/7272–8153 (Dome #)** *10pm-3am 3rd Fri, South Asian music*

East Bloc [M,D] 217 City Rd (at Shepherdess Walk, Old Street) **44–020/7735–5934** *10pm-4am, till 6am Fri-Sat, clsd Mon-Wed, electro dance club in funky basement space*

Egg [GS,D] 200 York Way (Kings Cross) **44–020/7871–1111** *check www.egglondon.co.uk for events*

Cafes

Dream Bags Jaquar Shoes 32-36 Kingsland Rd **44–020/7683–0912** *10am-1am, jam-packed club in a former shoe shop, also art exhibts, cafe & bar*

Restaurants

Manna [R] 4 Erskine Rd (at Ainger Rd, Camden) **44–020/7722–8028** *lunch & dinner, clsd Mon, vegetarian*

Providores and Tapa Room 109 Marylebone High St (at New Cavendish St) **44–020/7935–6175** *upstairs Asian fusion; more casual Tapa room downstairs open for brkfst, lunch & dinner, tapas*

Entertainment & Recreation

Rosemary Branch Theatre 2 Shepperton Rd **44–020/7704–2730 (bar), 44–020/7704–6665 (theatre)** *also restaurant & bar, many gay-themed plays*

Men's Clubs

The Underground Club 37 Wharfdale Rd (King's Cross, at the Underground Club (below Central Station bar)) **44–020/7278–3294** *noon-6pm, clsd Wed & Sun, theme days*

Underground Club [★MO] 37 Wharfdale Rd (King's Cross, below Central Station bar) **44–020/7278–3294** *sex parties, theme nights, check web for events*

Cruisy Areas

Clapham Common [AYOR] *west side of the common near to the south circular road in the wooded area*

Earls Court Graveyard *summers,watch out for the bobbies*

Hampstead Heath [★AYOR]

Highgate Hill take Archway Tube *male sun bathing area at the Highgate Ponds*

London – East

London–East includes City, Tower, Clerkenwell & Shoreditch

Accommodations

Andaz Liverpool Street [GS,F] 40 Liverpool St (near Bishopsgate, at Liverpool Street Station) **44-020/7961-1234**

The Hoxton [GF,NS,WI] 81 Great Eastern St **44-020/7550-1000** *also restaurant*

Bars

Bethnal Green Working Men's Club [MW,DS,C,TG] 42-44 Pollard Row (at Squirries St, Bethnal Green) **44-020/7739-7170** *performance art & cabaret*

BJ's White Swan [M,D,TG,F,DS,WC] 556 Commercial Rd (near Bromley St) **44-020/7780-9870** *8pm-2am, clsd Sun-Mon*

Dalston Superstore [★GS,NH,F,D,WI] 117 Kingsland High St (at Sandringham Rd) **44-020/7254 2273** *noon-2am, from 10am wknds, from 5pm Mon*

The Macbeth [GS,D,E,WI] 70 Hoxton St (at Crondall St, Old St) **44-020/7749-0600** *8pm-1am, roof terrace*

The Old Ship [MW,NH,C,WC] 17 Barnes St (Stepney) **44-020/7791-1301** *noon-midnight, till 11pm Mon-Tue*

Nightclubs

Backstreet [MO,L,PC] Wentworth Mews, Burdett Rd (at Mile End Rd, Bow) **44-020/8980-8557, 44-020/8980-7880** *10pm-2am, till 3am Fri-Sat, till 1am Sun, clsd Mon-Wed, strict leather/ rubber dress code*

Kaos [GS,TG,D,PC] *monthy parties, check www.kaoslondon.com*

Unskinny Bop [W,D,E] 42-44 Pollard Row (Bethnal Green Club) *9pm 3rd Satonly*

Urban Desi [MW,D,MR-A] *check www.ubnwld.com for events*

Way Out Club [MW,D,TG,S,PC,$] 64-73 Minories (enter through the garden) **44-(0)20/7264-1910** *9pm-3am Sat only, TV/TS & their friends*

Restaurants

Bistrotheque 23-27 Waderson St **44-020/8983-7900** *dinner nightly, wknd brunch • expensive & glamorous, also cabaret shows after dinner*

Cafe Spice Namaste 16 Prescott St **44-020/7488-9242** *lunch Mon-Fri, dinner nightly, clsd Sun, Indian*

Canteen 2 Crispin Pl (Spitalfields) **44-(0)84/5686-1122** *place to be for brkfst*

Hoxton Square Bar & Kitchen [E] 2-4 Hoxton Square **44-020/9613-1171** *great dark spot for brkfst*

Royal Oak 73 Columbia Rd (at Hackney Rd, Old St) **44-020/7729-2220** *6pm-10pm, from10am wknds, popular Sun for the Columbia Rd Flower market*

Men's Clubs

E15 Club 6 Leytonstone Rd **44-020/8555-5455** *9am-9pm, till 8pm Sat, from 10am Sun, jacuzzi, steamroom, garden, also bar*

Sailors Sauna [F,WI] 570-574 Commercial Rd (near Limehouse tube) **44-020/7791-2808** *11am-11pm, till 8am wknds*

Erotica

Gear London 75 Great Eastern St (Shoreditch) **44-020/7739-0292** *noon-8pm, till 5pm Sun, leather/ rubber*

London – South

London–South includes Southwark, Lambeth, Kennington, Vauxhall, Battersea, Lewisham & Greenwich

Accommodations

Griffin House [MW,WI,GO] 22 Stockwell Green **44-020/7096-3332** *2 rental apts near Vauxhall Gay Village & West End*

Bars

BackCOUNTER [GS,NH,D,DS,F,WI,WC] 7-11 S Lambeth Rd (Vauxhall) **44-020/3693-9600**

The Cambria [GS,E,F] 40 Kemerton Rd (Denmark Hill) **44-020/7737-3676** *4pm-1am, upmarket eclectic pub, beautiful back garden*

The Eagle London [M,L,E] 349 Kennington Ln (Vauxhall) **44-020/7793-0903** *8pm-2am, 9pm-4am Fri-Sat, 1pm-3am Sun, clsd Mon*

George & Dragon [MW,C] 2 Blackheath Hill (Greenwich) **44-020/8691-3764** *4pm-2am, till 4am Fri-Sat*

Prince of Greenwich [M,NH,F,E,DS] 72 Royal Hill (Greenwich) **44-020/8692-6089** *4pm-11:30pm, from noon wknds, clsd Mon*

The Two Brewers [MW,D,K,C] 114 Clapham High St (Clapham) **44-020/7819-9539** *5pm-2am, till 4am Fri-Sat*

Nightclubs

Black Sheep Bar [GS,D,A] 68 High St (at S Norwood Hill, Croydon) **44-020/8680-2233** *10pm-3am*

Bootylicious [MW,MR] 66 Albert Embankment (at Union) *11pm last Sat, popular black gay club*

Fire [GS,D,$] 47B S Lambeth Rd (Vauxhall) **44-020/3242-0040** *after-hours, Sat mornings & Sun afternoons*

Hard On [MW,D,PC] 66 Albert Embankment (at Union, in Vauxhall) **44-020/7533 402 985** *3rd Sat only, fetish party, large play area with equip-ment*

The Hoist [M,L] Railway Arch 47b&c, S Lambeth Rd (Vauxhall) **44-020/7735-9972** *S/M club w/ strict dress code, theme nights*

Horse Meat Disco [MW,D,TG] 349 Kennington Ln (at the Eagle) **44-020/7793-0903** *8pm Sun only, popular queer dance party*

Royal Vauxhall Tavern [M,D,TG,F,WC] 372 Kennington Ln (Vauxhall) **44-020/7820-1222** *8pm-late, 9pm-3am Fri-Sat, 2pm-midnight Sun*

Union Club [M,D] 66 Albert Embankment (Vauxhall) **44-020/7278-3294** *11pm-8am Fri, till 5am Sat & 9am Sun, cruise mazes, dark corners, popular last Fri & 3rd Sat*

XXL [MO,D,B] 1 Invicta Plaza (South Bank, at Pulse) **44-(0)78/7261-0981** *10pm-7am Sat, 9pm-3am Wed, "one club fits all"*

Restaurants

COUNTER Vauxhall Arches 7-11 S Lambeth Rd (Vauxhall) **44-020/3693-9600** *7am-midnight, bar and brasserie in the centre of Vauxhal*

Entertainment & Recreation

Battersea Barge [GF,F,E,C,GO] Riverside Walk Nine Elms Ln (Vauxhall) **44-020/7582-1066** *call for events, cabaret, comedy on the Thames River!*

Oval Theatre Cafe Bar [F] 52-54 Kennington Oval **44-020/7582-0080** *6pm-11pm Tue-Sat (cafe), inquire about current theatre & art*

Men's Clubs

Chariots Vauxhall [F,WI] Rail Arches 63-64 (Albert Embankment) **44-020/7247-5333** *noon-8am, 24hrs wknds*

The Locker Room 8 Cleaver St (Kennington) **44-020/7735-6064** *10am-midnight,, 24hours wknds*

Pleasuredrome [F,V,NS,GO] 124 Cornwall Rd (at Alaska St, Waterloo) **44-020/7633-9194** *24hrs*

Cruisy Areas

Hyde Park [AYOR] *Southeast cornor of Hyde Park in the Rose Garden*

FRANCE

PARIS

Note: M°=Métro station

Paris is divided by arrondissements (city districts); 01=1st arrondissement, 02=2nd arrondissement, etc

Paris—Overview

Note: When phoning Paris from the US, dial the country code + the city code + the local phone number

INFO LINES & SERVICES

Centre Gai et Lesbien 63 rue Beaubourg **33-1/4357-2147** *3:30-8pm, 1:30pm-7pm sat, clsd Sun, many groups/ events*

Gay AA 7 rue Auguste Vacquerie (at St George's Anglican) **33-1/4634-5965** *7:30pm Tue, see calendar for other times*

PUBLICATIONS

Têtu 33-1/5680-2080 *stylish & intelligent LGBT monthly (en français)*

Paris—01

ACCOMMODATIONS

Hotel Louvre Richelieu [GS,NS,WI] 51 rue de Richelieu (M° Palais-Royal) **33-1/4297-4620** *located near the Louvre, Opera House and shopping; "one of the best value hotels in this prestigious area"*

Hotel Louvre Saint-Honoré [GS,WI,WC] 141 rue Saint-Honoré (at rue du Louvre) **33-1/4296-2323**

BARS

Le Banana Cafe [★MW,D,E,P,S,YC,WC] 13-15 rue de la Ferronnerie (near rue St-Denis, M° Châtelet) **33-1/4233-3531** *6pm-dawn, go-go boys Th-Sat terrace*

Le Tropic Cafe [MW,D,TG,F,YC,WC] 66 rue des Lombards (M° Châtelet) **33-1/4013-9262** *4pm-5am, tapas, terrace*

Le Velvet [MW] 43 rue Saint Honore **33-1/4221-2926** *5pm-2am, till 4:30am Fri-Sat, clsd Sun-Mon*

RESTAURANTS

L' Amazonial [★C,DS,WC,GO] 3 rue Ste-Opportune (at rue Ferronnerie, M° Châtelet) **33-1/4233-5313** *lunch & dinner, brunch wknds, Brazilian/ int'l, heated terrace*

Au Diable des Lombards 64 rue des Lombards (at rue St-Denis, M° Châtelet) **33-1/4233-8184** *9am-2am, American, full bar, terrace*

La Poule au Pot 9 rue Vauvilliers (M° Les Halles) **33-1/4236-3296** *7pm-5am, clsd Mon & Aug, bistro, French*

ENTERTAINMENT & RECREATION

Forum des Halles 101 Porte Berger (M° Châtelet-Les Halles) **33-1/4476-9656** *underground sports/ entertainment complex w/ museums, theater, shops, clubs, cafes & more*

GYMS & HEALTH CLUBS

CMG Sports Club One 147 rue St-Honoré (M° Louvre) **33-1/4020-0303** *day passes available, many locations throughout city*

MEN'S CLUBS

Le Next 87 rue St Honoré (at rue du Roule, M° Chatelet-Les Halles) **33-06/8195-0587** *24hrs wknds*

Til't [M] 41 rue Ste-Anne (near av de l'Opera, M° Pyramides) **33-1/4296-0743** *noon-7am, bar*

EROTICA

Boxxman [WI] 2 rue de la Cossonnerie (M° Châtelet) **33-1/4221-4702** *10am-midnight, from noon Sun, videos, toys and fetish gear, also sex club*

CRUISY AREAS

Quai des Tuileries [AYOR] on bank of The Seine (M° Louvre) *aka Tata Beach*

Paris—02

BARS

L' Impact [MO,N,V] 18 rue Grenéta (M° Châtelet) **33-1/4221-9424** *8pm-3am, 10pm-6am Fri-Sat, from 3pm Sun, 100% naked, backroom, theme nights, free brkfst wknds*

NIGHTCLUBS

Chez Carmen [GS,D] 53 rue Vivienne **33-1/4236-4541** *midnight-8am, till 10am Fri-Sat, clsd Sun-Mon, beware of scamming bouncers*

Rex Club [GF,D,E,$] 5 blvd Poissonière (M° Bonne Nouvelle) **33-1/4236-1096** *call for events, clsd August*

RESTAURANTS

Le Lezard Cafe 32 rue Etienne Marcel **33-1/4233-2273** *8am-2am, clsd Sun, charming location and atmosphere with outdoor seating, full bar*

RETAIL SHOPS

Galerie au Bonheur du Jour 11 rue Chabanais **33-1/4296-5864** *2:30pm-7:30pm, clsd Sun-Mon, gay art*

MEN'S CLUBS

Euro Men's Club [V,SW,OC] 10 rue St-Marc (M° Bourse) **33-1/4233-9263** *11am-10pm*

Paris—03

ACCOMMODATIONS

Absolu Living [MW,GO] 236 rue St Martin **33-1/4454-9700** *fully furnished apts in central Paris, short & long-term stays*

Adorable Apartment in Paris [★GF,NS,GO] (M° Rambuteau) **415/287-0306 (US#)** *truly charming 2-bdrm flat in heart of the Marais; sleeps 4-6; near the Picasso Museum, Carnavalet and Pompidou Center*

Hôtel du Vieux Saule [GF] 6 rue de Picardie **33-1/4272-0114** *great location, good breakfast*

Hotel Jules & Jim [GS,GO] 11 rue des Gravilliers **33-1/4454-1313** *small boutique hotel with a bar in the Marais*

BARS

Le CUD Club [★M,D,YC] 12 rue des Haudriettes **33-1/4277-4412** *11pm-6am, till 7am wknds*

Le Dépôt [MO,D,S,YC,$] 10 rue aux Ours (btwn bd de Sébastopol & rue St-Martin, M° Rambuteau) **33-1/4454-9696** *2pm-8am, huge cruise bar on 3 flrs, big backroom*

Le Duplex [MW,NH,S,WI] 25 rue Michel-Le-Comte (at rue Beaubourg, M° Rambuteau) **33-1/4272-8086** *8pm-2am, till 4am Fri-Sat*

L' Enchanteur [MW,K] 15 rue Michel Lecomte (M° Rambuteau) **33-1/4804-0238** *10pm-7am, clsd Mon-Tue*

One Way [M,NH,B,L,F,V,OC] 28 rue Charlot (at rue des 4 Fils, M° République) **33-1/4887-4610** *5pm-2am, cruisy, darkroom, tapas*

Le Tango/ La Boite à Frissons [★MW,F] 13 rue au Maire (M° Arts-et-Métiers) **33-1/4272-1778** *10:30pm-5am, clsd Mon*

CAFES

La Perle 78 rue Vieille du Temple **33-1/4272-6993** *6am-2am, Parisian hipster dive bar*

MEN'S CLUBS

Sun City [SW] 62 Blvd de Sébastopol (M° Rambuteau) **33-1/4009-2609** *noon-2am, 24hrs wknds, cruise bar & sauna, swimming, gym, private cabins*

EROTICA

Rex 42 rue de Poitou (at rue Charlot, M° St-Sébastien-Froissard) **33-1/4277-5857** *1pm-8pm, clsd Sun, leather & S/M accessories*

Paris—04

ACCOMMODATIONS

Historic Rentals [GF,NS,WI] **800/537-5408 (US#)** *1-bdrm apt*

Hôtel Beaubourg [GS,WI] 11 rue Simon le Franc (btwn rue Beaubourg & rue du Temple, M° Hôtel-de-Ville) **33-1/4274-3424** *next to Centre Pompidou*

Hôtel de la Bretonnerie [GF] 22 rue Ste-Croix-de-la-Bretonnerie (M° Hôtel-de-Ville) **33-1/4887-7763**

Hôtel du Vieux Marais [GF,WI] 8 rue du Plâtre (M° Hôtel-de-Ville) **33-1/4278-4722** *centrally located*

Paris At Home [MW,WI,GO] **33-06/2559-1069** *B&B & apts*

Bars

Au Mange Disque [M] 15 rue de la Reynie (at Boule de Sebastopol) **33-1/4804-7817** *11am-2am, from 5pm Sun-Mon*

Bears' Den [MO,D,B,V] 6 rue des Lombards (at rue St-Martin, M° Hôtel-de-Ville) **33-1/4271-0820** *4pm-2am, till 4am Fri-Sat, T-dance Sun, darkroom, terrace*

Cox [★M,D,V] 15 rue des Archives (at rue Ste-Croix-de-la-Bretonnerie, M° Hôtel-de-Ville) **33-1/4272-0800** *5:30pm-2am, from 4:30pm Fri-Sun, terrace*

Dandy's Cafe [GS] 9 rue Nicolas Flamel **33-1/4271-4542** *2pm-2am*

Le Feeling [MW,NH,YC] 43 rue Ste-Croix-de-la-Bretonnerie (M° Hôtel-de-Ville) **33-1/4804-7003** *3pm-2am*

Le Freedj [MW,D] 35 rue Ste-Croix-de-la-Bretonnerie (at rue du Temple, M° Hôtel-de-Ville) **33-1/4029-4440** *6pm-4am*

Full Metal [M,L] 40 rue des Blancs Manteaux (M° Rambuteau) **33-1/4272-3005** *5pm-4am, till 6am Fri-Sat, from 3pm Sun, well-stocked "hard backroom bar," theme parties, dress code*

Gossip Cafe [MW,F] 16 rue des Lombards (at bd de Sébastopol, M° Châtelet) **33-1/4271-3683** *noon-11pm, also restaurant*

L' Imprevu Cafe [GS,NH,F] 9 rue Quincampoix **33-1/4278-2350** *3pm-2am, from 5pm Sun, low key cafe/ bar*

Les Jacasses [★W] 5 rue des Ecouffes (M° St Paul) **33-1/4271-1551** *5pm-2am*

Krash [★MO,L,V] 12 rue Simon Lefranc (at rue du Renard, M° Rambuteau) **33-1/5041-1326** *3pm-5am, till 7am Fri-Sat, sex bar*

Le Mic-Man [M,NH,V] 24 rue Geoffroy-l'Angevin (at rue Beaubourg, M° Rambuteau) **33-1/4274-3980** *noon-2am, open later wknds, friendly bar w/ cruisy cave downstairs*

La Mine [M,L] 20 rue du Plâtre **33-1/4271-3039** *5pm-2am*

L' Open Cafe [★MW,F] 17 rue des Archives (at rue Ste-Croix-de-la-Bretonnerie, M° Hôtel-de-Ville) *11am-2am, till 3am Fri-Sat, sidewalk cafe-bar*

Quetzal [★M,NH,S,WI] 10 rue de la Verrerie (at rue des Archives, M° Hôtel-de-Ville) **33-1/4887-9907** *5pm-5am, cruise bar, darkroom, terrace*

Le Raidd [M,D,S] 23 rue du Temple (M° Hotel de ville) **33-1/4277-0488** *6pm-4am*

Secteur X [MO] 49 rue des Blancs-Manteaux (at rue du Temple, M° Rambuteau) **33-1-09/5039-5085** *3pm-4am, till 6am Fri-Sat, cruisy, back room*

Sly Bar [M,NH,D] 22 rue des Lombards **33-6/6284-6461** *5pm-3am, close to Notre Dame, the Pompidou and the Louvre*

Les Souffleurs [MW,D,YC] 7 rue de la Verrerie (M° Hôtel-de-Ville) **33-1/4478-0492** *6pm-2am, artsy*

Le Voulez-Vous [MW,F] 18 rue du Temple (M° Hôtel-de-Ville) **33-1/8362-2220** *11am-2am, lounge & restaurant, terrace*

Woo Bar [M] 14 rue Saint-Merri **33-1/4272-7597** *4pm-5am, from 11am wknds, also restaurant*

Yono [M,D,E,F] 37 rue Vieille du Temple **33-1/4274-3165** *6pm-2am, clsd Sun-Mon, cozy basement bar*

Ze Baar [M,NH,F] 41 rue des Blancs Manteaux (at rue du Temple) **33-1/4271-7508** *5pm-2am, also restaurant*

Cafes

La Fronde 33 rue des Archives **33-1/4272-2734** *6:30am-2am, cool neighborhood small café*

Restaurants

4 Pat [D,GO] 4 rue St Merri **33-1/4277-2545** *noon-2am, Italian menu and festive staff*

L' Alimentari [★] 6 Rue des Ecouffes **33-1/4277-2459** *lunch & dinner, clsd Mon, very good small trattoria*

Le Chant des Voyelles 4 rue des Lombards (M° Châtelet) **33-1/4277-7707** *9am-1am, traditional French, terrace*

Le Gai Moulin [GO] 10 rue St-Merri (at rue du Temple, M° Hôtel-de-Ville) **33-1/4887-0600** *noon-midnight*

Les Piétons 8 rue des Lombards (M° Châtelet) **33-1/4887-8287** *noon-2am, Spanish/ tapas, also bar*

Who's 14 rue Saint Merri (M° Rambuteau) **33-1/4272-7597** *noon-6am, more gay when they open the dance floor at the back of the dining area and at brunch*

ENTERTAINMENT & RECREATION

Gay Beach E end of Ile St-Louis *sunbathing*

BOOKSTORES

Les Mots à la Bouche 6 rue Ste-Croix-de-la-Bretonnerie (near rue du Vieille du Temple, M° Hôtel-de-Ville) **33-1/4278-8830** *11am-11pm, 1pm-9pm Sun, LGBT, English titles*

EROTICA

BMC Store 21 rue des Lombards **33-1/4027-9809** *videos, DVDs, toys*

IEM Marais 16 rue Ste-Croix-de-la-Bretonnerie (M° Hôtel-de-Ville) **33-1/4274-0161** *noon-8pm, leather, latex, uniforms & fetish gear*

Menstore 8 Square Ste-Croix de la Bretonnerie **33-1/4454-5115** *11:30am-10pm, 1pm-7pm Sun*

oB Paris 8 Square Ste-Croix de la Bretonnerie **33-1/4805-1448** *11:30am-10pm, 1pm-7pm Sun, leather/ fetish*

CRUISY AREAS

Square du Pont de Sully [AYOR] at the end of Ile St-Louis (M° Sully-Morland) *along the side paths at night*

Paris—05

RESTAURANTS

Le Petit Prince [★] 12 rue de Lanneau (M° Maubert-Mutualité) **33-1/4354-7726** *7:30pm-midnight, French*

ENTERTAINMENT & RECREATION

Open-Air Sculpture Museum Quai Saint-Bernard *along the Seine btwn the Jardin des Plantes & the Institut du Monde Arabe*

Paris—06

ACCOMMODATIONS

The Hotel Luxembourg Parc [GS,WI] 42 rue de Vaugirard **33-1/5310-3650** *charming intimate hotel, excellent location, brkfst buffet, bar & gym*

RESTAURANTS

HD Diner 25 Rue Francisque Gay **33-1/329-6707** *9am-midnight, 50's style diner, other locations as well*

Paris—07

CRUISY AREAS

Champs de Mars [AYOR] (M° Pont-de-l'Alma)

Paris—08

ACCOMMODATIONS

François 1er [GF,WI] 7 rue Magellan **33-1/4723-4404** *boutique hotel near les Champs-Elysées, also bar*

Hôtel le Lavoisier [GF,WI] 21 rue Lavoisier **33-1/5330-0606** *19th-c townhouse*

Prince de Galles [GF,WI] 33 Avenue George V **33-1/5323-7777** *legendary jewel of the Parisian Art Deco movement near les Champs-Elysées, restaurant & bar*

Paris—09

ACCOMMODATIONS

The Grand [GF,WI] 2 rue Scribe **33-1/4007-3232, 888/424-6835 (US#)** *ultraluxe art deco hotel*

BARS

Mec Zone [M,L,V] 27 rue Turgot (M° Anvers) **33-1/4082-9418** *9pm-5am, 2pm-6am wknds, cruisy, theme nights, darkroom*

Rosa Bonheur [GF,D,F] 2, allée de la Cascade **33-1/4200-0045** *more gay Sun, arrive before 6pm to avoid the line*

Nightclubs

Escualita [M,D,TG] 77 Rue Pigalle (at Rouge Pigalle) *midnight Sun only, fabulous tranny dance party, all are welcome*

Glass [GS,D] 7 rue Frochot (in Pigalle) **33-9/8072-9883** *7pm-2am, popular with locals Mon*

Men's Clubs

IDM [★V,WI] 4 rue du Faubourg-Montmartre (at bd St-Martin, M° Grand-Blvds) **33-1/4523-1003** *full gym, jacuzzi, bar*

Paris—10

Bars

Cafe Moustache [M,NH,F,B,V] 138 rue du Faubourg St-Martin (at bd de Magenta, M° Gare-de-l'Est) **33-1/4607-7270** *4pm-2am, darkroom, patio*

Men's Clubs

Key West Sauna [★SW] 141 rue Lafayette (M° Gare-du-Nord) **33-1/4526-3174** *noon-1am, till 2am Fri-Sat*

Erotica

Thaalam Video Vision 12 Rue Perdonnet **33-7/5350-8296** *10:30am-9:30pm*

Cruisy Areas

Canal St-Martin Jean-Jaurès [AYOR] (M° Jaurès) *on the quais btwn the Jean-Jaurès & Louis-Blanc bridges*

Paris—11

Accommodations

Le 20 Prieure Hotel [GS,WI] 20 rue du Grand Prieuré **33-1/4700-7414** *next to the Place de la République, at the crossroads of the Marais and Canal St Martin*

Le General Hotel [GF,WI,WC] 5/7 rue Rampon **33-1/4700-4157** *peace and quiet in the bustling city*

Hôtel Beaumarchais [GS,WI] 3 rue Oberkampf (btwn bd Beaumarchais & bd Voltaire, M° Filles-du-Calvaire) **33-1/5336-8686**

Hotel Exquis [GF,WI,WC] 71 rue de Charonne **33-1/5606-9513** *a few minutes from Bastille and in a popular district among artists and antique dealers*

Bars

Le Bataclan [GF,E] 50 blvd Voltaire (at Bataclan club, M° Saint Ambroise) **33-1/4314-0030** *live music venue, more gay for the Follivores & Crazyvores*

Follivores/ Crazyvores [MW,D] 50 blvd Voltaire (M° Saint Ambroise) **33-1/4314-0030** *monthly sing-along dance parties; Follivores is 1960s-1990s French pop, Crazyvores is English-speaking; kitsch factor very high!*

Nightclubs

Les Disquaires [GS,D,E] 6 rue des Taillandiers (M° Bastille) **33-1/4021-9460** *5pm-2am, dance bar, live bands*

Gibus Club [★M,D] 18 rue du Faubourg-du-Temple (M° République, at Gibus Club) **33-1/4700-5914** *midnight -7am, clsd Mon-Tue*

Cafes

Cannibale Café [WI] 93 Rue Jean-Pierre Timbaud **33-1/4929-9559** *8am-2am, an old-fashioned Parisian café in Belleville*

Le Pause Cafe 41 rue de Charonne **33-1/4806-8033** *7:30am-2am, 8am-8pm Sun, hang with the locals aka smoky*

Restaurants

Le Tabarin [P] Rue du Pasteur Wagner **33-1/4807-1522** *lunch Wed-Sun, dinner Wed-Sun, full bar*

Entertainment & Recreation

L' ArtiShow 3 cite Souzy **33-1/4002-1803** *cabaret, also lunch & dinner served*

Bookstores

Violette & Co [GO] 102 rue de Charonne (at boulevard Voltaire, M° Charonne) **33-1/4372-1607** *11am-8pm, 2pm-7pm Sun, clsd Mon, LGBT & feminist, English titles & art shows*

Men's Clubs

Bunker [M] 150 rue St-Maur (M° Goncourt) **33-1/5336-0116** *4pm-2am, till 11pm Sun*

Entre Deux Eaux 45 rue de la Folie Mericourt (at rue Oberkampf) **33-1/4357-7646** *naked sex club for men, theme nights*

Paris—12

Sex Clubs

Atlantide Sauna [GS,TG,V] 13 rue Parrot (M° Gare de Lyon) **33-1/4342-2243** *women & transgender welcome, cabins, tanning, also bar*

Cruisy Areas

Bois de Vincennes [AYOR]

Paris—13

Cruisy Areas

Quai d'Austerlitz [AYOR]

Les Sablières [AYOR] *along the quai d'Austerlitz, from library to blvds Perijheriques, at night only*

Paris—14

Entertainment & Recreation

Friday Night Fever [GS] Place Raoul Dautry (btwn Montparnasse office tower & Montparnasse train station) *10pm-1am Fri (weather permitting), meet 9:30pm, rollerblading*

Men's Clubs

Les Bains d' Odessa [SW,WI] 5 rue d'Odessa **33-1/4047-8343** *noon-10pm, sauna, massage, dark room & bar*

Paris—15

Accommodations

Platine Hotel [GS,WI,WC] 20 rue Ingénieur Robert Keller **33-1/4571-1515** *Marilyn Monroe and 1950's theme, located 15 minute walking from the Seine and the Eiffel Tower, pets ok*

Bars

Mix [GS,D,$] 24 rue de l'Arrivée **33-7/8200-1600** *midnight-6am Sat only*

Paris—16

Accommodations

Keppler [GF,WI] 10 rue Keppler **33-1/4720-6505** *intimate homelike oasis within a Haussmanian building from the 19th Century, near major tourist stops, also bar*

Cruisy Areas

Bois de Boulogne [AYOR] (M° Porte Dauphine)

Paris—17

Restaurants

Sans Gêne 112 rue Legendre **33-1/8515-2533** *10am-2am, also bar*

Men's Clubs

King Sauna [★] 21 rue Bridaine (near place de Clichy, M° Rome) **33-1/4294-1910** *1pm-6am, bar*

Paris—18

Bars

Karambole Cafe [GS,F] 10 rue Hegesippe Moreau (M° Place de Clichy or La Fourche) **33-1/4293-3068** *8am-midnight, 10am-2am Th-Sat, till 6pm Sun, artsy cafe by day, DJs by night*

Le Tagada Bar [★M,NH,F] 40 rue Trois-Frères (M° Abesses) **33-1/4255-9556** *6pm-2am*

Nightclubs

Beardrop [MO,D,B] 75 rue des Martyrs (at Le Divan du Monde club) *monthly bear party, check www.beardrop.com for events*

Restaurants

Aux Trois Petits Cochons [★MW,R,GO] 28, rue La Vieuville **33-1/4233-3969** *8pm-1am, gourmet French*

Entertainment & Recreation

Michou [F] 80 rue des Martyrs (at Blvd de Clichy, M° Pigalle) **33-1/4606-1604** *infamous drag cabaret, dinner show*

Men's Clubs

Sauna Mykonos 71 rue des Martyrs **33-1/4252-1546** *11am-11:30pm*

Paris—19

Cafes

Cafe Cherie [GS,E,WI] 44 Blvd de la Villette (M° Belleville) **33-1/4202-0205** *11am-2am, live music & DJs starting at 10pm*

Paris—20

Accommodations

Mama Shelter [GS,WI] 109 rue de Bagnolet **33-1/ 4348-4848**

Entertainment & Recreation

Père Lachaise Cemetery bd de Ménilmontant (M° Père-Lachaise) *perhaps the world's most famous resting place, where lie such notables as Chopin, Oscar Wilde, Sarah Bernhardt, Isadora Duncan, Gertrude Stein & Jim Morrison*

Men's Clubs

Le Riad [SW,V] 184 rue des Pyrénnées (M° Gambetta) **33-1/4797-2552** *noon-midnight, Middle Eastern-themed sauna, bar*

Germany

Berlin

Berlin is divided into 5 regions:
Berlin—Overview
Berlin—Kreuzberg
Berlin—Prenzlauer Berg-Mitte
Berlin—Schöneberg-Tiergarten
Berlin—Outer

Berlin—Overview

Info Lines & Services

Gay AA for English Speakers Bülowstr 106 (at Mann-O-Meter) **49-30/787-5188** *5pm Tue, also Gay AA 8pm Th*

Mann-O-Meter Bülowstr 106 (at Nollendorfplatz) **49-30/216-8008** *5pm-10pm, from 4pm Sat, clsd Sun, gay center, cafe and B&B referral service*

Sonntags Club Greifenhagener Str 28 (S/U-Schönhauser Allee) **49-30/449-7590** *info line 10am-6pm, LGBT info, also cafe-bar open 5pm-midnight*

Nightclubs

Nina's Bar [MW,D,DS,TG,V] *check www.ninaqueer.com for events*

Restaurants

Paris Bar Kantstrasse152 **49-30/313-8052** *bistro & bar*

Entertainment & Recreation

Berlin Music Tour **49-17/2424-2037** *visit the haunts of David Bowie, Nina Hagen, Iggy Pop & Rammstein, among other popular musi cal acts*

The Jewish Museum Berlin Lindenstr 9-14 **49-30/2599-3300** *10am-8pm, till 10pm Mon*

Schwules (Gay) Museum U6/U7 Mehringdamm 61 **49-30/6959-9050** *2pm-6pm, till 7pm Sat, clsd Tue, guided tours 5pm Sat (in German)*

Publications

Blu **49-30/443-1980** *free monthly gay magazine*

Siegessaule **49-30/235-5390** *free monthly LGBT city magazine (in German), awesome maps*

Berlin—Kreuzberg

Accommodations

Hotel Transit [GF] Hagelberger Straße 53-54 **49-30/789-0470** *hotel in restored 19th-c factory*

The Mövenpick Hotel [GF,F,WI] **49-30/230-060** *convenient location, space-agey bar*

Bars

Barbie Bar [MW] Mehringdamm 77 (at Kreuzbergstr) **49-30/6956-8610** *4pm-midnight, till 1am wknds, lounge, terrace*

Barbie Deinhoffs [MW,D,C,V] Schlesische Str 16 **49-173/434-6363** *7pm-close, till 6am Fri-Sat*

Bierhimmel [GS,YC] Oranienstr 183 (U-Kottbusser Tor) **49-30/615-3122** *9am-3am, from 1pm wknds*

Ficken 3000 [M,D,L,V,YC] Urbanstr 70 (at Hermannplatz) **49-30/6950-7335** *10pm-8am, till 10am wknds, cruisy, large darkroom*

Galander [GS] Grossbeerenstr 54 (nr Mehringdamm) **49-30/2850-9030** *6pm-2am, lovely 20's cocktail bar, small snacks served*

Mobel Olfe [★MW] Reichenbergerstrasse 177 (at Skalitzer) **49-30/2327-4690** *open 6pm, clsd Mon*

Rauschgold [MW,K] Mehringdamm 62 (U-Mehringdamm) **49-30/9227-4178** *8pm-4am*

Roses [★MW,TG,YC] Oranienstr 187 (at Kottbusser Tor) **49-30/615-6570** *10pm-close*

Sofia [MW] **49-178/501- 5534** *9am-3:30am, clsd Sun*

Nightclubs

SchwuZ (SchwulenZentrum) [★M,D,E,WC] Mehringdamm 61 (enter through Café Sundstroem) **49-30/629-088** *from 11pm Fri-Sat*

Serene Bar [MW,D] Schwiebusser Str 2 **49-30/6904-1580**

SO 36 [★GS,D,TG,S,V,YC,WC] Oranienstr 190 (at Kottbusser Tor) **49-30/6140-1306, 49-30/6140-1307** *theme nights, also live music venue*

Cafes

Melitta Sundström [MW,E,WC] Mehringdamm 61 (at Gneisenaustr, U-Mehringdamm) **49-30/692-4414** *1pm-6am, terrace, also gay bookstore & performances*

Sudblock [★MW,F,E] Admiralstrasse 1-2 **49-30/6094-1853** *11am-3am, from 10am Sun, beer garden*

Restaurants

Amrit Oranienstr 202 **49-30/612-5550** *noon-1am, Indian*

Jolesch Muskauer Strasse 1 **49-30/612-3581** *Austrian culture in Kreuzberg*

Restaurant Z Friesenstr 12 **49-30/692-2716** *5pm-1am, Greek/ Mediterranean*

Men's Clubs

Boiler Berlin Sauna [F] Mehringdamm 34 **49-30/5770-7175** *noon-6am, 24hrs wknds*

Böse Buben Sachsendamm 76-77 **49-30/6270-5610** *4pm-11pm Wed, 8pm-3am Fri-Sat, 4pm-10pm Sun*

Triebwerk [M,L,V,WC] Urbanstr 64 (at Leinestr, U-Hermannplatz) **49-30/6950-5203** *10pm-close, clsd Th, cruise bar w/ darkroom*

Sex Clubs

Club Culture Houze [GS] Görlitzer Str 71 (off Skalitzer Str) **49-30/6170-9669** *gay male theme nights Mon & Fri, open to all other nights*

Berlin—Prenzlauer Berg-Mitte

Accommodations

Arte Luise Kunsthotel [GF] Luisenstr 19 (Mitte) **49-30/284-480** *former palace w/ rooms re-imagined by local artists, near River Spree*

Schall & Rauch Pension [MW] Gleimstr 23 (at Schönhauser Allee) **49-30/339-723** *also bar & restaurant*

Bars

Bärenhöhle [M,B,BW,WI] Schönhauser Allee 90 **49-30/4473-6553** *4pm-6am, from 8pm Sat, from 6pm Sun*

Besenkammer Bar [MW] Rathausstr 1 (at Alexanderplatz, under the S-Bahn bridge) **49-30/242-4083** *24hrs, tiny "beer bar"*

Betty F*** [MW,NH] Mulackstrasse 13 (at Gormannstrasse)

DarkRoom [MO,L] Rodenbergstr 23 (at Schönhauser Allee) **49-30/444-9321** *10pm-6am, uniform bar, darkroom, theme parties wknds*

Flax [M,D,F,K] Chodowieckistr 41 (off Greifswalder Str) **49-30/2578-2573** *6pm-4am, clsd Mon*

Greifbar [MO,L,V] Wichertstr 10 (at Greifenhagener Str, S/U-Schönhauser Allee) **49-30/8975-1498** *10pm-5am, darkroom*

Grosse Freiheit 114 [MO] Boxhagener Str 114 (in Friedrichshain) **49-30/2977-6713** *8pm-6am, Th till 4am, Sun till 2am, darkroom, cruisy*

Marietta [MW,D] Stargarder Str 13 **49-30/4372-0646** *6pm-1am*

Perle [MW] Sredzkistrasse 64 **49-30/4985-3450** *7pm-close, clsd Sun-Mon*

Privatleben [MW] Rhinowerstr 12 (at Gleimstra) **49-30/4074-9563** *from 6pm, clsd Tue, small friendly bar*

Reingold [GS,F,E,GO] Novalisstr 11 (U-Oranienburger Str) **49-30/4985-3450** *from 7pm, clsd Sun-Mon, more gay Th*

Stahlrohr [MO] Paul Robeson Strasse 50 **49-70/803-7691** *9pm-5am, from 10pm Fri-Sat, 6pm-3am Sun, clsd Mon, sex parties*

Nightclubs

Berghain [★MW,D,E] Am Wrietzener Bahnhof (off Strasse der Pariser Kommune, near Ostbahnhof station) **49-30/2936-0210** *converted power station is now dance club*

Chantals House of Shame [MW,D] *11pm Th*

GMF [M,D,DS] Alexanderstrasse 7 (at Week End, U-Alexanderplatz) **49-30/2809-5396** *Sun only 11pm-close*

KitKat Club [GS,D,C] Kopenickerstrasse 76 (enter on Bruckenstrasse) **49-30/217-3680** *8pm-close Th, 11pm-8am Fri-Sat, also S/M club*

Cafes

Anna Blume Kollwitzstrasse 83 **49-30/4404-8749** *8am-10pm, great brkfst*

November Husemannstr 15 (at Sredzkistr) **49-30/442-8425** *10am-2am, cafe-bar, terrace*

Poor and Literate [E,BW,WI,GO] Kopenhagenerstr 77 **49-30/4403-9520** *4pm-9pm Th-Sun*

Restaurants

Anda Lucia Savignyplatz 2 **49-30/5471-0271** *6pm-10pm, tapas bar*

Boccacelli Winterfeldtstraße 34 **49-30/2191-7111** *noon-midnight, nice atmosphere for tasty Italian*

Cavallino Rosso Hannoversche Strasse 2 **49-30/2790-8314** *modern and cosy atmosphere*

Rice Queen Danziger Str 13 (U-Eberswalder Str) **49-30/4404-5800** *5pm-11pm, from 2pm wknds, Asian fusion*

Schall & Rauch Wirtshaus [MW] Gleimstr 23 (at Schönhauser Allee) **49-30/443-3970** *10am-close*

Thüringer Stuben Stargarder Str 28 (at Dunckerstr, S/U-Schönhauser Allee) **49-30/4463-3339** *4pm-1am, from noon Sun, full bar*

Men's Clubs

Lab.oratory Am Wrietzener Bahnhof (downstairs at Berghain nightclub) *clsd Mon-Wed, hardcore sex club*

Erotica

Blackstyle Seelower Str 5 (S/U-Schönhauser Allee) **49-30/4468-8595** *1pm-6pm, till 8pm Fri-Sat, clsd Sun, latex and rubber wear, also mail order*

Duplexx Schönhauser Allee 131 (U-Eberswalder Str) **49-30/4849-4200** *videos, cruisy*

Leathers Eisenacherstr 101 **49-30/442-7786** *noon-10pm, till 6pm Sat, clsd Sun-Mon*

XXL Bornholmer Str 7 **49-30/3289-8222** *noon-3am, large cruising cinema*

Cruisy Areas

Volkspark Friedrichshain [AYOR] (at Märchenbrunnen, in Friedrichshain)

Berlin—Schöneberg-Tiergarten

Accommodations

Arco Hotel [GS,WC,GO] Geisbergstr 30 (at Ansbacherstr, U-Wittenbergplatz) **49-30/235-1480** *B&B inn, centrally located, kids/ pets ok*

Art-Hotel Connection [MO,L,WI,WC,GO] Fuggerstr 33 (corner Welser Str, near U-Wittenbergplatz) **49-30/2102-18800** *also special "fantasy" apt for kink & S/M types*

Axel Hotel Berlin [M,WI] Lietzenburger Str 13/15 **49-30/2100-2893** *good location, small gym and nice brkfst*

Bananas Berlin [M,WI,GO] Geisbergstr 41 **49-151/1616-1614** *central location in a quiet area one mile from Kurfürstendamm, shared baths*

Hotel California [GF] Kurfürstendamm 35 (at Knesebeckstr, U-Uhlandstr) **49-30/880-120** *cafe/bar*

Hotel Hansablick [GF,WI] Flotowstr 6 (at Bachstr, off Str des 17 Juni) **49-30/390-4800** *full brkfst, kids/ pets ok*

Hotel Zu Hause [GS,WI,GO] Kleiststrasse 35 (at Eisenacher Str) **49-(0)30/2362-6522** *simple small hotel located in the heart of the gay district*

R&Co Apartments [MO,GO] Fuggerstr 19 (behind RoB Berlin shop) **49-30/2196-7400** *in the heart of Berlin's gay scene, playroom*

Tom's Hotel [M] Motzstr 19 (at Eisenacherstr, U-Nollendorfplatz) **49-30/2196-6604** *centrally located*

BARS

Ajpnia eV [MO] Eisenacher Str 23 (U-Eisenacher Str) **49-30/2191-8881** *sex parties*

Blond [★MW,WI] Eisenacher Str 3a (at Fuggerstr, U-Nollendorfplatz) **49-30/6640-3947** *4pm-4am, from 3pm wknds*

Blue Boy Bar [M,V] Eisenacher Str 3a (at Fuggerstr, U-Nollendorfplatz) **49-30/218-7498** *24hrs, ring bell, hustlers; also Fugger-Eck [GS,NH], 1pm-6am, clsd Sun, terrace*

CDL [MO] Hohenstauffenstr 58 **49-30/3266-7855** *open 7pm, from 9pm Fri-Sat, from 3pm Sun, sex club*

Green Door [GS] Winterfeldstr 50 **49-30/152-515** *6pm-3am, till 4am Fri-Sat, cute decor*

Hafen [★M,TG,S,YC] Motzstr 19 (at Eisenacher Str, U-Nollendorfplatz) **49-30/211-4118** *7pm-close*

HarDie's Kneipe [M,NH,F,OC] Ansbacherstr 29 (in Wittenberplatz) **49-30/2363-9842** *noon-midnight, till 2am wknds*

Heile Welt [★MW] Motzstrasse 5 **49-30/2191-7507** *8pm-1am, small on the outside but big on the inside*

Incognito [MW,TG,DS] Hohenstauffenstr 53 (off Luther Str, U-Viktoria Luise Platz) **49-30/2191-6300** *6pm-4am*

Mutschmann's [MO,L] Martin-Luther-Str 19 (at Motzstr, U-Nollendorfplatz) **49-30/2191-9640** *10pm-close, from 11pm Fri-Sat, clsd Sun-Mon, darkroom*

Neues Ufer [MW,OC] Haupstrasse 157 (U-Bahn Kleistpark) **49-30/7895-7900** *2pm-2am, till midnight Mon-Tue, city's oldest gay bar & David Bowie's favorite cafe*

New Action [★MO,L] Kleiststr 35 (at Eisenacherstr, U-Nollendorfplatz) *10pm-5am, till 7am Fri-Sat, from 5pm Sun, fetish/ cruise bar*

Pinocchio Musikcafe [M] Fuggerstr 3 (at Schönhauser Allee, U-Nollendorfplatz) **49-30/2362-0333** *2pm-2am, till 4am wknds*

Prinzknecht [★M] Fuggerstr 33 (U-Nollendorfplatz) **49-30/236-27444** *3pm-2am*

Reizbar [M] Motzstr 30 (Kalckreuthstr) **49-30/2363-7981** *9pm-2am, clsd Mon, theme nights & darkroom*

Scheune [★MO,L,V] Motzstr 25 (at Nollendorfplatz) **49-30/213-8580** *9pm-7am, till 9am Fri-Sat, uniform bar, theme nights*

Tabasco [M,F,AYOR] Fuggerstr 3 (at Schönhauser Allee, U-Nollendorfplatz) **49-30/214-2636** *6pm-6am, 24hrs wknds, hustlers*

Tom's Bar [MO,L,V] Motzstr 19 (at Eisenacherstr, U-Nollendorfplatz) **49-30/213-4570** *10pm-6am, open later Fri-Sat, very cruisy, downstairs maze*

Tramps [M,NH,B,L] Eisenacher Str 6 (atFuggerstr) *24hrs*

Woof [M,B,WI] Fuggerstr 37 (at Ansbacherstr) **49-30/2360-7870** *10pm-4am*

NIGHTCLUBS

Kumpelnest 3000 [GF,D,TG,YC] Lützowstr 23 (at Potsdamer Str, U-Kurfürstenstr) **49-30/261-6918** *7pm-6am, popular wknds*

Cafes

Cafe Berio [★WC] Maaßenstr 7 (at Winterfeldtstr, U-Nollendorfplatz) **49-30/216-1946** *6am-3am, brkfst all day, terrace, also bar*

Cafe Savigny Grolmanstr 53-54 (at Savignyplatz) **49-30/4470-8386** *9am-midnight, full bar, terrace*

Restaurants

Diodata Goltzstrasse 51 **49-30/2191-7884** *11am-11pm, 10am-3pm Sun, Viennese*

Gnadenbrot Martin-Luther-Str 20a **49-30/2196-1786** *3pm-1am, cheap & good*

Les 3 Veuves de Wilmersdorf Fechnerstrasse 30 **49-30/8600-8251** *excellent burgers*

More [★] Motzstrasse 28 (at Martin-Lutherstrasse) **49-30/2363-5702** *9am-midnight*

Ottenthal Kantstrasse 153 **49-30/313-3162** *cuisine of Austria*

Sissi Motzstr 34 **49-30/2101-8101** *great Austrian food, terrace & location*

Witty's Organic Food Wittenbergplatz *organic snack bar, look for the rainbow flags*

Entertainment & Recreation

Xenon Kino Kolonmenstr 5-6 **49-30/7800-1530** *gay & lesbian cinema*

Bookstores

Prinz Eisenherz Buchladen [★WC,GO] Motzstrasse 23 **49-30/313-9936** *10am-8pm, clsd Sun, LGBT books, comics and magazines in German, French & English, also a gallery*

Retail Shops

Bruno's Maaßenstr 14 (U-Nollendorfplatz) **49-30/3466-5333** *10am-10pm, clsd Sun, fashion, magazines, books, toys, condoms and lubricants*

Erotica

City Men Fuggerstr 26 **49-30/218-2959** *11am-1am, videos, magazines, toys*

The Jaxx Club [V] Motzstr 19 (U-Nollendorfplatz) **49-30/213-8103** *noon-3am, movies, mags and toys & darkroom*

Pool Berlin [V] Schaperstr 11 (at Joachimsthaler Str, in Wilmersdorf, U-Kurfürstendamm) **49-30/214-1989** *clsd Sun, gay emporium*

RoB Berlin Fuggerstr 19 **49-30/2196-7400** *clsd Sun, leather/fetish shop*

Cruisy Areas

Tiergarten [AYOR] along Str de 17 Juni (near the Siegessäule monument)

Berlin—Outer

Accommodations

ART-Hotel Charlottenburger Hof [GF] Stuttgarter Platz 14 (at Wilmersdorfer Str) **49-30/329-070** *also cafe & bar*

Novum Hotel Kronprinz Berlin [GF,WC] Kronprinzendamm 1 (at Kurfürstendamm, in Halensee) **49-30/896-030** *affordable, cute & tidy, great brkfst*

Bars

Himmelreich [MW] Simon Dach Str 36 (off Warschauer Str, in Friedrichshain, U-Frankfurter Tor) **49-30/2936-9292** *from 6pm, from 4pm Sun*

Monster Ronsons [★MW,K] Warschauerstr 34 **49-30/8975-1327** *7pm-6am*

Silver Future [MW] Weserstr 206 (Neukölln) **49-30/2390-0855** *5pm-2am, "Kings And Queens And Criminal Queers"*

Nightclubs

Die Busche [★MW,D,S,$] Warschauer Platz 18 **49-30/296-0800** *10pm-5am Fri-Sat only*

Cafes

Schrader's [GO] Malplaquetstr 16b (at Utrechter Str, Wedding) **49-30/4508-2663** *9:30am-1am, popular Sun brunch, also bar*

Restaurants

Cafe Rix Karl-Marx-Str 141 (in Neükolln) **49-30/686-9020** *9am-midnight, till 1am Fri-Sat, Mediterranean, also bar*

Kurhaus Korsakow Grunbergerstrasse 81 (in Friedrichshain) **49-30/5473-7786** *5pm-close, from 9am wknds, clsd Mon*

Cruisy Areas

Volkspark Wilmersdorf [AYOR]

Ireland

Dublin

Info Lines & Services

AA 105 Capel St (at Outhouse) **353-1/873-4999** *6pm Tue & 7:45pm Fri*

Gay Switchboard Dublin **353-1/872-1055** *6:30pm-9:30pm, 4pm-6pm wknds*

Outhouse 105 Capel St **353-1/873-4999** *LGBT community center, cafe, library, meetings*

Accommodations

The Arlington Hotel Temple Bar [GS] 16 Lord Edward St **353-1/670-8777** *conveniently located with restaurant & bar*

The Clarence [GF,WI,WC] 6-8 Wellington Quay **353-1/407-0800** *owned by Bono & The Edge of U2*

The Dylan [★GS] Eastmoreland Place **353-1/660-3000** *restaurant & bar*

Fitzwilliam Hotel [GF,WI] St Stephen's Green **353-1/478-7000** *lovely hotel right in the heart of Dublin, bar & restaurant*

Inn On the Liffey [MW,WI,GO] 21 Upper Ormond Quay **353-1/677-0828**

The Merchant House [GS,WI,GO] 8 Eustace St (Temple Bar Area) **353-1/633-4477** *free access to Basic Instincts Cruise Zone*

Waterloo House [GS,F] 8-10 Waterloo Rd **353-1/660-1888** *restaurant & bar*

Bars

Front Lounge [★MW,D,TG,K] 33 Parliament St **353-1/670-4112** *noon-11:30pm, till 2am Sat*

The George aka Bridies [★MW,D,K,DS,E] 89 S Great George St **353-1/478-2983** *2pm-2:30am, till 11:30pm Mon-Tue, till 1am Sun*

Oscars Cafe & Bar [GS] **353-1/555-1442**

Panti Bar [MW,D,F,DS,WC] 7-8 Capel St **353-1/874-0710** *5pm-close, theme nights*

Nightclubs

Mother [MW,D] Exchange St (at Copper Alley, Arlington Hotel) *10:30pm Sat only*

Nimhneach [GS] *fetish & BDSM party, strict dress code, see www.nimhneach.ie for dates & location*

Cafes

3Fe 54 Middle Abbey St (Twisted Pepper Bldg) **353-1/661-9329** *10am-7pm, noon-6pm Sun, run by barista champion*

Irish Film Institute Bar & Restaurant 6 Eustace St (in Temple Bar) **353-1/679-5744** *lunch & dinner, next to independent cinema*

Lovinspoon Cafe 13 N Frederick St **353-1/804-7604** *7am-6pm, clsd Sun (except summers)*

Restaurants

Brasserie Sixty6 [WI] 66 S Great Georges St **353-1/400-5878** *lunch, dinner, brkfst wknds*

La Cave 28 S Anne St **353-1/679-4409** *12:30pm-close, from 5pm Sun, French*

The Chameleon 1 Lower Fownes St **353-1/671-0362** *5pm-11pm, from 3pm Sun, clsd Mon, Indonesian*

Cornucopia 19 Wicklow **353-1/677-7583** *8:30am-9pm, till 10:30pm Sat, from noon Sun, affordable vegetarian*

DavyByrnes 21 Duke St **353-1/677-5217** *11am-11pm, famous pub frequented by James Joyce*

L' Ecrivain [P,R] 109A Lower Baggot St **353-1/661-1919** *lunch Mon-Fri, dinner Mon-Sat, clsd Sun*

Eden 7 South William St **353-1/670-6887** *lunch & dinner, wknd brunch, patio dining*

F.X. Buckley 2 Crow St **353-1/671-1248** *5:30pm-close, steak & seafood*

Fire Restaurant Mansion House, Dawson St **353-1/676-7200** *5:30pm-close, noon-3pm jazz lunch Sat, clsd Sun*

Odessa [★DS] 14 Dame Court **353-1/670-7634** *also nightclub*

Shack 24 E Essex St **353-1/679-0043** *lunch & dinner*

Trocadero 4 Saint Andrew St **353-1/677-5545** *5pm-midnight, clsd Sun*

The Winding Stair Restaurant [YC] 40 Lower Ormond Quay **353-1/872-7320** *lunch & dinner, Irish, also bookshop*

Entertainment & Recreation

Dublin Bears [M,B] *check www.dublinbears.ie for events*

Bookstores

Chapters Bookstore Ivy House, Parnell St **353-1/872-3297**

The Winding Stair Bookshop 40 Lower Ormond Quay **353-1/872-7320** *10am-6pm, till 7pm Th-Sat, from noon Sun, also restaurant*

Publications

GCN (Gay Community News) Unit 2 Scarlet Row, Essex St W, Temple Bar, 8 **353-1/675-5025** *monthly LGBT newspaper, many resources*

Men's Clubs

The Boilerhouse [★F,V] 12 Crane Ln **353-1/677-3130** *noon-6am, 24hrs wknds*

The Dock Sauna [WI] 21 Upper Ormond Quay (at the Inn On the Liffey) **353-1/677 0828** *10am-4am, 24hrs wknds; also gay B&B*

Italy

Rome

Note: M°=Metro station

Info Lines & Services

Gay Help Line 800/713-713 *4pm-8pm, clsd Sun*

Accommodations

2nd Floor B&B [MW,WI,GO] via San Giovanni in Laterano 10 **39-06/9604-9256** *in the heart of Rome's gaylife*

Albergo Del Sole al Pantheon [GF,WI] Piazza della Rotonda 63 **39-06/678-0441** *4-star hotel, "oldest hotel in Rome"*

Ares Rooms [GF] Via Domenichino 7 **39-334 /959-2057** *some shared baths, a 5-minute walk from Santa Maria Maggiore Basilica*

Daphne Trevi [GF,NS] Via degli Avignonesi 20 **39-06/8953-8471** *18th-century building on a quiet cobblestone street*

Discover Roma [MW] Via Castelfidardo 50 **39-06/4470-3154**

Domus Valeria B&B [MW,WI,GO] Via del Babuino 96, Apt 14 (Spanish Square) **39-339/232-6540** *cozy B&B for gays, lesbians & hetero friends, located in central Rome*

Franklin [GF,WI] Via Rodi 29 **39-06/3903-0165** *music-themed hotel w/ CD library*

Gayopen B&B [GS,GO] Via dello Statuto 44, Apt 18 (at Via Merulana, Piazza Vittorio) **39-06/482-0013** *full brkfst*

Hilton Garden Inn Rome Claridge [GF] Via Liegi 62 **39-06/845-441** *near Borghese park, gym w/ sauna & Turkish bath*

Hotel Altavilla [GF,WI] Via Principe Amedeo 9 **39-06/4782-5568** *central location and budget rates*

Hotel Edera [GF,WI] Via A Poliziano 75 **39-06/7045-3888** *simple but great location, in a quiet area close to the Coliseum*

Hotel Labelle [GS,WI] Via Cavour 310 **39-06/679-4750** *near the Roman Forum*

Hotel Welcome Piram [GS] Via Giovanni Amendola 7 **39-06/4890-1248** *exclusive hotel near Rome's Termini train station, cocktail bar & spa*

Le Petit Real [GS,NS,WI,WC] Via Cavour 58, 4th flr (near Colosseum) **39-06/482-3566** *B&B inn a few steps from Colosseum*

Nicolas Inn [GF,NS,WI] Via Cavour 295 (at Via dei Serpenti) **39-328/555-3004** *near the Colosseum & Roman Forum*

Pensione Ottaviano [GF] Via Ottaviano 6 **39-06/3973-8138** *in quiet area near St Peter's Square, hostel*

The Rainbow B&B [MW,WI] Viale Giulio Cesare 151 **39-06/347-507-0344 (cell)** *a few steps from St. Peter's and the Vatican Museums, right above Ottaviano*

Relais Conte di Cavour de Luxe B&B [GF,WI] Via Farini 16 (at Via Cavour) **39-06/482-1638** *great location, minutes from the Coliseum*

Relais le Clarisse [GS,NS,WI,GO] Via Cardinale Merry del Val 20 (at Viale Trastevere) **39-06/5833-4437** *Mediterranean garden, on historic site in central Rome*

Scalinata di Spagna [GS,NS,WI] Piazza Trinità dei Monti 17 (M° Piazza di Spagna) **39-06/6994-0896, 39-06/679-3006 (booking #)** *great rooms, fantastic location and a very nice breakfast terrace overlooking entire Rome*

Scott House Hotel [GF,WI] Via Gioberti 30 **39-06/446-5379** *unique atmosphere close to Termini railway station*

Valadier [GF,WI] Via della Fontanella 15 **39-06/361-1998** *luxury 4 star in Rome Centre, 2 restaurants & piano bar*

BARS

Coming Out [★MW,D,TG,F,E,K,V,GO] Via San Giovanni in Laterano 8 (near Colosseum) **39-06/700-9871** *7:30pm-2am*

Garbo [MW,F,GO] Vicolo di Santa Margherita 1a (in Trastevere, Tram 8) **39-06/581-2766, 39-34/9815-1446** *10pm-3am, clsd Mon, cocktail bar*

Skyline [M,L,F,S,WI,PC] Via Pontremoli 36 **39-06/700-9431** *10:30pm-3am, till 4am Fri-Sat, clsd Mon, 2-floor American bar, backroom, darkroom, monthly sex parties*

NIGHTCLUBS

L' Alibi [★MW,D,S,YC] Via di Monte Testaccio 40-44 (M° Piramide) **39-320/354-1185** *11:30pm-5am, clsd Mon-Wed, theme nights, rooftop garden in summer*

Amigdala [MW,D] *Sat only, check site for dates & location, www.twitter.com/AMIGDALAroma*

Il Diavolo Dentro [M,L,N] Largo Itri 23-24 **39-398/419-298** *11pm-5am Fri-Sat, 6pm-3am Sun, clsd Mon-Th & month of August*

Frutta e Verdura [MW,D] Via Placido Zurla 68-70 (in Casilina) **39-347/879-7063** *4:30am-10am Sun & public holiday evenings, darkroom*

Gorgeous [M,D] Via del Commercio 36 (at Alpheus) **39-06/574-7826** *11pm-5am Sat*

Muccassassina [★MW,D,S,YC,$] via di Portonaccio 212 (at Qube) **39-06/541-3985** *10:30pm-5am Fri only (Sept-June)*

CAFES

Oppio Caffè [★MW,F,E] Via delle Terme di Tito 72 **39-06/474-5262** *brkfst, lunch & dinner, open 24hrs in Aug, full bar, terrace w/ great view*

RESTAURANTS

Aroma via Labicana 125 *one of the finest dining experiences in Rome*

La Carbonara Via Panisperna 214 **39-06/482-5176** *lunch & dinner, clsd Sun, classic Roman cuisine since 1906*

Cecilia Metella Via Appia Antica 125/127/129 *located in the center of the Appia Antica Park*

Città in Fiore Via Cavour 269 **39-06/482-4874** *lunch Th-Mon, dinner nightly, Chinese*

Ditirambo Piazza della Cancelleria 74-75 (near Campo dei Fiori) **39-06/687-1626** *Intimate trattoria serving seasonal & creative Roman classics*

La Focaccia Via della Pace 11 **39-06/6880-3312** *11am-2am, pizza*

Gelateria San Crispino Via Panetteria 42 (near Trevi Fountain) **39-06/679-3924** *noon-12:30am, till 1:30am Fri-Sat, gelato!*

Glass Hostaria Vicolo Del Cinque 58 *ultra-modern gem*

Il Pagliaccio Via Dei Banchi Vecchi 129 *cuisine that spans the globe in the fusion of flavors*

La Rosetta Via della Rosetta 8-9 *fish-only restaurant right in the heart of Rome*

Mater Matuta [★] Via Milano 47 (basement) **39-06/4782-5746** *lunch Mon-Fri, dinner nightly, also wine bar*

Osteria del Pegno [WC] Vicolo Montevecchio 8 (Plaza Navona) **39-06/6880-7025** *lunch & dinner, clsd Wed winter, large pizza selection*

ParmAromA Via del Pozzo delle Cornacchie 36 **39-06/6880-6729** *off the beaten path located in a cellar, must try risotto!*

Ristorante da Dino Via dei Mille 10 (at Piazza Indipendenza) **39-06/491-425** *clsd Wed*

La Taverna di Edoardo II [WC] Vicolo Margana 14 **39-06/6994-2499** *7:30pm-midnight, clsd Tue, full bar*

Entertainment & Recreation

Gay Village **39-06/753-8396** *gay summer festival*

Retail Shops

Hydra II [L] Via Urbana 139 **39-06/489-7773** *leather, vinyl, clubwear, western, vintage & more*

Men's Clubs

Apollion Sauna [V] Via Mecenate 59a (at Via Carlo Botta, M° Piazza Vittorio) **39-06/482-5389** *2pm-11pm, gym equipment, bar*

EMC-Europa Multiclub [V,YC,SW,PC] Via Aureliana 40 (M° Repubblica) **39-06/482-3650** *1pm-midnight, 24hrs wknds, fountain whirlpool, gym & bar*

K Sex Club [L,V,PC] Via Amato Amati 6-8 (at Via Dulceri), Casilina **39-06/587-6731** *10pm-3am, till 4am Fri-Sat, clsd Mon, S/M club and bar, maze, darkroom*

Mediterraneo Sauna [F,V,PC] Via Pasquale Villari 3 (btwn Via Merulana & Via Labicana, M° Manzoni) **39-06/7720-5934** *1pm-11pm, 3 floors, full bar, jacuzzi, maze*

Cruisy Areas

Colosseo Quadrato [AYOR] (near Palazzo della Civiltà del Lavoro park)

Monte Caprino Park [AYOR] Capidoglio Hill

Villa Borghese [AYOR] (in front of the Architecture Academy)

Travel Agents

Through Eternity Tours Italy [GO] Via Astura 2/B **39-06/700-9336** *walking tours of Rome, get 10% off by using the code "Damron10"*

NETHERLANDS

AMSTERDAM

Amsterdam is divided into 5 regions:
Amsterdam—Overview
Amsterdam—Centrum
Amsterdam—Jordaan
Amsterdam—Rembrandtplein
Amsterdam—Outer

Amsterdam—Overview

Info Lines & Services

COC-Amsterdam Rozenstraat 14 (at Prinsengracht, in the Jordaan) **31-20/626-3087** *info line 10am-5pm, also cafe 8pm-11:30pm Wed-Fri*

Gay/ Lesbian Switchboard **31-20/623-6565** *noon-10pm, 4pm-8pm wknds, English spoken*

Pink Point Westermarkt (Raadhuisstraat & Keizersgracht, in the Jordaan by Homomonument) **31-20/428-1070** *10am-6pm; info on Homomonument & general LGBT info; friendly volunteers; queer souvenirs & gifts*

Nightclubs

Fuckin' Pop Queers/ Ultrasexi/ Multisexi [MW,D,TG,A] *monthly queer dance parties at different clubs around the city, check web for details*

Rapido [M,D] *popular monthly dance parties, check clubrapido.com for dates & locations*

Entertainment & Recreation

The Anne Frank House Prinsengracht 263-267 (in the Jordaan) **31-20/556-7105 (recorded info), 31-20/556-7100** *the final hiding place of Amsterdam's most famous resident*

Boom Chicago Leidseplein 12 (Leidseplein Theater) **31-20/423-0101 (tickets)** *English-language improv comedy; distributes free Boom! guide*

Gay and Lesbian History Walks 31-20/628-689-775 *mention Damron & you get 10% off*

MacBike Stationsplein 12 (next to Centraal Station) **31-20/620-0985** *rental bikes & map for self-guided tour of Amsterdam's gay points of interest, also 4 other locations*

The van Gogh Museum [WC] Paulus Potterstr 7 (on the Museumplein) **31-20/570-5200** *under renovations, check www.vangoghmuseum.nl for updates*

Publications

Attitude Magazine NL 31-20/788-1360 *monthly bilingual entertainment paper w/ club listings*

Gay News Amsterdam 31-20/679-1556 *bilingual paper, extensive listings*

Amsterdam—Centrum

Info Lines & Services

Personal Guide To Amsterdam's Gay Red Light District [MO,GO] **31-6-21/36 40 21** *expat American living in Amsterdam's GAY Red Light District available as personal guide to visiting gay American men coming to Amsterdam for the first time, www.terminal99.com*

Accommodations

Amsterdam B&B Barangay [GS,NS,WI,GO] **31-6/2504-5432** *near tourist attractions*

Amsterdam Central B&B [MW,WI,GO] Oudebrugsteeg 6-II (at Warmoesstraat) **31-62/445-7593** *in 16th-c guest-house, also apts, full brkfst*

Anco Hotel-Bar [MO,L,N,NS,WI,GO] OZ Voorburgwal 55 (across from the Oude Kerk) **31-20/624-1126** *1640 canal house, also bar*

Crowne Plaza Amsterdam City Centre [GF,F,SW,WI,WC] NZ Voorburgwal 5 **31-20/620-0500, 877/227-6963 (US#)**

Hotel The Exchange [GS,WI,WC] Damrak 50 **31-20/523-0080** *an independent design hotel in central Amsterdam that playfully weaves together fashion and architecture in unique rooms*

Mauro Mansion [GS] Geldersekade 16 (at OZ Kolk)

NH City Centre Hotel [GF,WI,WC] Spuistraat 288-292 **31-20/420-4545** *Amsterdam School-style architecture, rooms specially adapted for disabled*

NH Grand Hotel Krasnapolsky [GF,WI,WC] Dam 9 (at Warmoesstraat) **31-20/554-9111**

Park Plaza Victoria Amsterdam [GF,SW,WI,NS,WC] Damrak 1-5 (opposite Centraal Station) **31-20/623-4255**

Winston Hotel and Nightclub [GF] Warmoesstraat 129 **31-20/623-1380** *hipster hotel w/ alt-rock bar & decor*

Bars

De Barderij [M,NH,OC] Zeedijk 14 (at OZ Kolk) **31-20/420-5132** *4pm-midnight, till 3am Fri, from noon Fri & Sun, clsd Mon,Wed & Sat, large brown café*

Boys Club 21 [MO,S] Spuistraat 21 **31-20/622-8828** *from 5pm, boys' house (escorts) w/ full bar & live strip shows*

Cafe Mandje [GS] Zeedijk 63 (at Stormsteeg) **31-20/622-5375** *4pm-1am, till 3am Sat, clsd Mon, originally opened in 1927 as Amsterdam's first gay bar by dyke-on-bike Bet van Beeren*

The Cuckoo's Nest [MO,L,V,18+] NZ Kolk 6 (at NZ Voorburgwal) **31-20/627-1752** *1pm-1am, till 2am Fri-Sat, cruisy, large play cellar*

Dirty Dick's [MO,L] Warmoesstraat 86 (at Oudebrugsteeg) **31-20/627-8634** *4pm-3am, till 4am Fri-Sat, very cruisy, darkroom*

Getto [★MW,F,K,WI] Warmoesstraat 51 (at Nieuzel) **31-20/421-5151** *4pm-1am, from 7pm Tue, 1pm-midnight Sun, clsd Mon, also restaurant*

Hot Spot [M,NH] Jonge Roelensteeg 4 **31-20/770-4037** *5pm-1am, till 3am Fri-Sun, clsd Mon-Wed*

Prik [★MW,F] Spuistraat 109 **31-20/320-0002** *4pm-1am, till 3am Fri-Sat, patio*

Queen's Head [M,DS,S] Zeedijk 20 (off Nieuwmarkt) **31-20/420-2475** *4pm-1am, till 3am Fri-Sat, bingo Tue*

The Web [★MO,B,L,F,V] St Jacobsstraat 6 (btwn Nieuwendijk & NZ Voorburgwal) **31-20/623-6758** *1pm-1am, till 2am Fri-Sat, darkroom, [B] Sat, rooftop patio*

Cafes

Dampkring/ Coffeeshop Amsterdam Haarlemmerstraat 44 **31-20/427-6739** *8am-1am, smoking coffeeshop, great fresh OJ*

Gary's Late Night [★] TT Vasumweg 260 **31-20/637-3643** *noon-3am, till 4am Fri-Sat, fresh muffins & bagels*

Puccini Bomboni [★] Staalstraat 17 **31-20/626-5474** *If you love chocolate, do we have a cafe for you!*

Restaurants

Cafe de Jaren Nieuwe Doelenstraat 20-22 **31-20/625-5771** *8:30am-1am, till 2am Fri-Sat, int'l, some veggie, full bar, terrace on Amstel River*

Cafe Latei [WI] Zeedijk 143 (in Red Light District) **31-20/625-7485** *8am-10pm, from 9am Sat, from 10am Sun, till 6pm Mon-Wed; Indian food; great coffee hangout*

Greenwoods Singel 103 (near Dam Square) **31-20/623-7071** *8:30am-4pm, English-style breakfast and tea snacks*

Hemelse Modder [★WC,GO] Oude Waal 11 **31-20/624-3203** *6pm-10pm, popular w/ lesbians & gay men, full bar*

Japans Restaurant An Weteringschans 76 (at Vijzerstraat) **31-20/624-4672** *6pm-10pm, clsd Sun-Mon, full bar, patio, cash only*

Krua Thai [WC] Staalstraat 22 **31-20/622-9533** *5pm-10:30pm*

Het Land van Walem [WC,GO] Keizersgracht 449 **31-20/625-3544** *9am-midnight, int'l, local crowd, canal-side terrace*

Maoz Muntplein 1 **31-20/420-7435** *11am-1am, vegetarian*

't Sluisje [★MW,TG,DS] Torensteeg 1 **31-20/624-0813** *6pm-close, steak house, full bar, drag shows nightly, cash only*

Song Kwae Kloveniersburgwal 14 (near Nieuwmarkt & Chinatown) **31-20/624-2568** *1pm-10:30pm, Thai, full bar, terrace*

Entertainment & Recreation

PERSONAL GUIDE TO AMSTERDAM'S GAY RED LIGHT DISTRICT [MO,GO] **31-6-21/36 40 21**

Bookstores

The American Book Center [WC] Spui 12 **31-20/625-5537** *10am-8pm, till 9pm Th, 11am-6:30pm Sun, large LGBT section*

Retail Shops

Gays & Gadgets Spuistraat 44 **31-20/330-1461** *noon-7pm, gifts, gadgets, clothing, cards*

Magic Mushroom Spuistraat 249 **31-20/427-5765** *11am-7pm, till 8pm Fri-Sat, "smartshop": magic mushrooms & more*

Gyms & Health Clubs

Splash Looiersgracht 26-30 **31-20/624-8404** *gym & wellness center*

Erotica

4men Spuistraat 21 **31-20/625-8797** *cinema, darkroom, all-day ticket, private cabin, large sexshop*

Adonis [M] Warmoesstraat 92 **31-20/627-2959** *10am-1am, till 3am wknds*

Alfa Blue Nieuwendijk 26 **31-20/627-1664** *porn store & video theater*

Black Body [WC] Kerkstraat 173 **31-20/626-2553** *11am-7pm, 10am-6pm Sun,, rubber clothing specialists, also leather, toys, DVDs & more*

Christine Le Duc Spui 6 **31-20/624-8265**

Condomerie Het Gulden Vlies Warmoesstraat 141 **31-20/627-4174** *11am-6pm, clsd Sun, condoms in every size or color or configuration*

DeMask Zeedijk 64 **31-20/423-3090** *11am-7pm, clsd Sun, rubber & leather clothing*

Drake's of LA [★] Damrak 61 **31-20/627-9544** *videos & magazines, video cabins, cinema upstairs*

Mr B [WC] Warmoesstraat 89 **31-20/788-3060** *11am-7pm, till 10pm Th-Sat,till 6pm Sun, leather and rubber, also tattoo and piercing*

RoB Accessories Warmoesstraat 71 **31-20/428-3000** *leather, rubber, toys*

Le Salon Nieuwendijk 20-22 (near the Spui) **31-20/622-6565** *10m-10pm, sex supermarket, cinema*

Amsterdam—Jordaan

Accommodations

Chic and Basic Amsterdam [GF,NS,WI] Herengracht 13-19 (at Brouwersgr) **31-20/522-2345** *"the quiet hotel," full brkfst*

The Dylan [GF,WI] Keizersgracht 384 (at Runstraat) **31-20/530-2010** *sleep in high style, also restaurant*

Hotel Pulitzer [GF,F,WI] Prinsengracht 315-331 (at Reestraat) **31-20/523-5235** *luxury 5-star hotel, occupies 24 17th-century bldgs; also art gallery and cafe/bar/restaurant*

Hotel Rembrandt Centrum [GS,WI] Herengracht 255 (at Hartenstraat) **31-20/622-1727** *canalside hotel near Dam Square*

Marnixkade Canalview Apartments [MW,NS,WI,GO] **31-6/1012-1296** *spacious apartments in 19th-c canal house on a quiet canal in heart of Amsterdam's historic Jordaan district—a vibrant area with many shops and restaurants*

Bars

Cafe de Gijs [GF,TG,K] Lindengracht 249 (at Lijnbaansgr) **31-20/694-2353** *1pm-1am*

Nightclubs

de Trut [★MW,D,YC] Bilderdijkstraat 165 (at Kinkerstraat) **31-20/612-3524** *10pm-3am Sun only, hip underground party in legalized squat, doors close when it's full (btwn 11:30pm-midnight) so come early*

Cafes

Cafe 't Smalle Egelantiersgracht 12 **31-20/623-9617** *10am-1am, till 2am wknds, cute little pub , full bar, outdoor seating*

Lab111 [E] Arie Biemondstrat 111 **31-20/616-9994** *open 1pm-close, lab turned cafe, cult cinema and restaurant for film lovers and cinephiles in the centre*

Restaurants

Balthazar's Keuken Elandsgracht 108 **31-20/420-2114** *open plan kitchen gives the feeling of an intimate dinner*

Bojo [★] Lange Leidsedwarsstraat 49-51 (near Leidseplein) **31-20/622-7434** *4pm-midnight, Indonesian, inexpensive and large portions*

De Bolhoed Prinsengracht 60 (at Tuinstr) **31-20/626-1803** *vegetarian/ vegan*

Burger's Patio 2e Tuindwarsstr 12 **31-20/623-6854** *6pm-1am, Italian, plenty veggie*

Foodism Nassaukade 122 (at Hugo de Grootstraat) **31-20/486-8137** *5pm-10pm, good Mediterranean food; funky & fun*

Freud [E] Spaarndammerstraat 424 **31-20/688-5548** *lunch & dinner, clsd Mon*

Granada [E] Leidsekruisstraat 13 **31-20/625-1073** *noon-1am, til 3am Fri-Sat, Spanish, tapas, also bar*

Entertainment & Recreation

Homomonument Westermarkt (Raadhuisstraat/Keizersgracht) *moving sculptural tribute to lesbians & gays killed by Nazis*

Retail Shops

Dare to Wear Buiten Oranjestraat 15 **31-20/686-8679** *piercing, jewelry & accessories*

House of Tattoos Haarlemmerdijk 130c **31-20/330-9046** *11am-6pm, from 1pm Sun, great tattoos, great people*

Sex Clubs

Sameplace [GS,TG,D] Nassaukade 120 **31-20/475-1981** *[MO] Mon night only, theme nights, darkroom*

Amsterdam—Rembrandtplein

Accommodations

Amsterdam House [GF] 's Gravelandseveer 7 (at Kloveniersburgwal) **31-20/626-2577 (office), 31-20/624-6607 (hotel)** *hotel, apts & houseboats*

Dikker & Thijs Fenice Hotel [GF] Prinsengracht 444 (at Leidsestraat) **31-20/620-1212** *beautiful canal hotel; great location, nonsmoking rms; also bar & restaurant*

Eden Hotel [GF,WI,WC] Amstel 144 **31-20/530-7878** *3-star hotel overlooking Amstel River, brasserie*

Hotel Amistad & Apts [★M,NS,WI,WC,GO] Kerkstraat 42 (at Leidsestraat) **31-20/624-8074**

Hotel de l'Europe [GF,SW,WI] Nieuwe Doelenstraat 2-8 **31-20/531-1777** *grand hotel on the River Amstel*

Hotel Monopole [GF] Amstel 60 (at Kloveniersburgwal) **31-20/624-6271** *centrally located, kids ok, also apartments*

ITC Hotel [GS,WI,GO] Prinsengracht 1051 (at Utrechtsestraat) **31-20/623-0230** *18th-c canal house, great location, also bar & lounge*

Quentin Golden Bear Hotel [GS,WI] Kerkstraat 37 (at Leidsestraat) **31-20/624-4785**

Seven Bridges [★GF] Reguliersgracht 31 (at KeizersGracht) **31-20/623-1329** *small & so elegant, canalside, view of 7 bridges (surprise!), brkfst brought to you*

Bars

Amstel Fifty Four [M,NH,D,DS] Amstel 54 (at Kloveniersburgwal) **31-20/623-4254** *5pm-1am, till 3am Fri-Sat, classic brown cafe gone gay*

Cafe Dwarsliggertje [M,NH] Reguliersdwarsstraat 105 **31-20/611-497-034** *2pm-1am, till 3am wknds*

Het Dwarsliggertje Cafe [M,NH] Reguliersdwarsstraat 105 **31-61/1149-7034** *2pm-3am*

Fame [MW] Amstel 50 (at Kloveniersburgwal) *4pm-3am*

Lellebel [★M,NH,TG,F,K,DS] Utrechtsestraat 4 **31-20/427-5139** *8pm-3am, till 4am Fri-Sat, drag bar, very trans-friendly*

Mankind [MW,F,WI] Weteringstraat 60 (at Weteringschans) **31-20/638-4755** *noon-11pm, clsd Sun, cafe-bar, canal-side terrace*

Le Montmartre [★M,NH,YC] Halvemaansteeg 17 (at Reguliersbreestr) **31-20/625-5565** *5pm-3am, very Dutch*

Reality [M,NH,MR-L] Reguliersdwarsstraat 129 **31-20/639-3012** *8pm-3am, till 5am Fri-Sat, Surinamese*

Soho [★MW,D,YC] Reguliersdwarsstraat 36 (at St Jorisstraat) **31-20/422-3312** *6pm-3am, till 4am Fri-Sat, from 4pm Sun, afterwork cocktails and dance club*

Spijker [★MO,NH,L,V] Kerkstraat 4 (at Leidsegracht) **31-20/233-8665** *4pm-1am, till 3am Fri-Sat, darkroom*

Taboo [★MW,NH] Reguliersdwarsstraat 45 **31-20/775-3963** *5pm-3am, from 4pm wknds, great atmosphere*

Het Wapen van Londen [★M,YC] Amstel 14 (at Vijzelstraat) **31-6/1539-5317** *3pm-1am, 2pm-2am Fri-Sat, from 4pm Sun, cafe-bar, terrace*

Nightclubs

Church [MO,D] Kerkstraat 52 (at Leidsestraat) *clsd Mon, theme nights w/ dress code, open to all on Th for Blue party*

Cafes

Betty Boop Reguliersdwarsstraat 29 (at Leidsestraat) *9am-1am, occasional gay events*

Happy Feelings Kerkstr 51 **31-20/423-1936** *11am-1am, smoking coffeeshop, publisher's choice*

Lunchroom [GO] Reguliersdwarsstr 31 (at Koningsplein) **31-20/622-9958** *10am-7pm, till 9pmTh-Sa, terrace open in summer*

The Other Side [M,GO] Reguliersdwarsstr 6 (at Koningsplein) **31-72/625-5141** *11am-1am, gay smoking coffeeshop*

Restaurants

Fred's Steak & Ribhouse Amstel 32 **31-20/689-5651** *Argentinean steaks, seafoods, all grilled specialities*

Garlic Queen [R] Reguliersdwarsstr 27 **31-20/422-6426** *6pm-close, clsd Mon-Tue, even the desserts are made w/ garlic!*

Golden Temple [NS] Utrechtsestr 126 **31-20/626-8560** *5pm-9:30pm, vegetarian & vegan*

De Huyschkaemer Utrechtsestraat 137 **31-20/627-0575** *9am-1am, till 3am wknds, from 11am Sun, great brkfst*

Red Keizersgracht 594 **31-20/320-1824** *informal and warm ambiance*

Rose's Cantina [★] Reguliersdwarsstr 40 (near Rembrandtplein) **31-20/625-9797** *5pm-11pm, Tex-Mex, full bar*

Saturnino [GO] Reguliersdwarsstr 5 **31-20/639-0102** *noon-midnight, Italian, full bar*

Erotica

B1 Cinema Reguliersbreestraat 4 **31-20/623-9546** *9:30am-11pm, from noon Sun, cinema, booths, labyrinth*

The Bronx Kerkstraat 53-55 (near Leidseplein) **31-20/623-1548** *huge gay shop for sex supplies*

Amsterdam—Outer

Accommodations

Between Art & Kitsch [GF,WI] Ruysdaelkade 75-2 (at Daniel Stalpertstraat) **31-20/679-0485** *near the museums of Museumplein*

The Collector B&B [GF,WI,GO] De Lairessestr 46 hs (in museum area) **31-6/1101-0105 (cell)**, **31-20/673-6779** *full brkfst*

Conscious Hotel Vondelpark [GS,WI,WC] Overtoom 519 **31-20/820-3333** *eco-conscious hotel, 3 other locations in Amsterdam*

Freeland Hotel [GF,WI,GO] Marnixstraat 386 (at Leidsegracht) **31-20/622-7511** *full brkfst*

Hotel Arena [★GF,WI] Gravesandestraat 51 (at Mauritskade) **31-20/850-2400** *hotel in former orphanage, popular nightclub in restored chapel*

Hotel Kap [GS,GO] Den Texstraat 5 **31-20/624-5908** *bikes available to rent, also self-catering apt*

Hotel Rembrandt [GF,NS,WI] Plantage Middenlaan 17 (at Plantage Parklaan) **31-20/627-2714** *beautiful brkfst rm w/ 17th-c art, near Rembrandtplein*

Lloyd Hotel [★GF,F,WI] Oostelijke Handelskade 34 **31-20/561-3607** *hip hotel for all budgets in cool Eastern Harbor area*

NL Hotel [GS,WI,GO] Nassaukade 368 (at B Toussaintstraat) **31-20/689-0030** *design hotel in Amsterdam on the Singel Gracht, surrounded by museums, shops, cafés, restaurants, and gallerie*

Prinsen Hotel [GF] Vondelstraat 36-38 (near Leidseplein) **31-20/616-2323**

Nightclubs

Melkweg [GS,E] Lijnbaansgracht 234 (at Leidseplein) **31-20/531-8181** *popular live-music venue, also restaurant/ cafe, cinema, theater*

Restaurants

Het Bosch Jollenpad 10 **31-20/644-5800** *French cuisine with modern twists*

De Peper Overtoom 301 **31-20/412-2954** *6pm-1am, clsd Wed,Sat & Mon, sliding scale, volunteer-run vegan cafe, also monthly queer parties*

Rijsel Marcusstraat 52b **31-20/463-2142** *classic meets '60s interior with a modern industrial feel*

De Waaghals Frans Halsstraat 29 **31-20/679-9609** *5pm-9:30pm, vegetarian*

Cruisy Areas

Oosterpark [AYOR] at Linnaeusstr (behind the Tropenmuseum)

Sarphatipark [AYOR] *near baseball field*

Vondelpark [AYOR] at Vondelstr *in the rose garden*

Westerpark [AYOR] *at night, N of lake*

SCOTLAND

Edinburgh

Info Lines & Services

LGBT Centre for Health & Wellbeing 9 Howe St **44-0131/523-1100** *support services and information*

The LGBT Healthy Living Centre [WI] 9 Howe St **44-0131/523-1100** *open when we are running groups and events, which is usually in the evenings and at weekends*

Accommodations

94DR [GS,WI,GO] 94 Dalkeith Rd **44-131/662-9265** *boutique guest-house, central location, full brkfst*

Alva House [M,NS,GO] 45 Alva Pl **44-0845/257-1475** *near gay bars & nightlife*

Averon Guest House [GF,NS,WI] 44 Gilmore Pl **44-0131/229-9932** *comfortable guesthouse in city center*

Ayden Guest House [GS,NS,WI,GO] 70 Pilrig St **44-0131/554-2187** *in-house chef cooks fabulous brkfst*

Garlands [GS,NS,WI,GO] 48 Pilrig St (off Leith Walk) **44-0131/554-4205** *Georgian town house, full brkfst*

Sheraton Grand Hotel and Spa [GF,SW,NS,WI] 1 Festival Sq **44-131/229-9131** *restaurant & bar*

Tigerlily [GF,WI] 125 George St **44-131/225-5005** *glamorous bar & restaurant*

Village Apartments [MO,GO] 5 Broughton Market **44-0131/556-5094** *located right in the heart of the gay quarter*

The Witchery by the Castle [GF] Castlehill (The Royal Mile) **44-0131/225.5613** *theatrical suites at the gates of Edinburgh castle*

BARS

The Auld Hoose [GS,NH,F] 23-25 St Leonards St **44-0131/668-2934** *noon-1am, from 12:30pm Sun*

Cafe Habana [MW,WI] 22 Greenside Pl **44-0131/558-1270** *1pm-1am, theme nights, popular pre-clubbing*

CC Bloom's [M,S,D,GO] 23 Greenside Pl (at Leith Walk) **44-0131/556-9331** *11am-3am, theme nights*

Planet [★MW,F] 6 Baxter's Pl (at Leith Walk) **44-0131/556-5551** *4pm-1am*

The Regent [M,F,WI] 2 Montrose Terrace **44-0131/661-8198** *noon-1am, from 12:30pm Sun*

The Street [GS,D,F,WI] 2 Picardy Pl **44-0131/556-4272** *noon-1am, patio*

Theatre Royal Bar [GF,F] 25-27 Greenside Pl **44-0131/557-2142** *noon-midnight*

Woodland Creatures [GS,F,E] 260 - 262 Leith Walk **44-0131/629-5509** *noon-1pm, from 5pm Mon, cool café bar*

NIGHTCLUBS

GHQ [M,D] 4 Picardy Pl **44-845/166-6024** *10pm-3am, clsd Mon-Tue, fashionable gay crowd, theme nights*

CAFES

Cafe Nom de Plume [GO] 60 Broughton St **44-0131/478-1372** *11am-11pm*

Filmhouse Cafe [BW] 88 Lothian Rd **44-0131/229-5932, 44-0131/228-2688 (cinema)** *9am-11:30pm, till 12:30am Fri-Sat, also cinema*

RESTAURANTS

Henderson's [BW] 94 Hanover St **44-0131/225-2131** *organic vegetarian, also deli & cafe*

Tower Restaurant & Terrace [WC] National Museum of Scotland, Chambers St (at George IV Brigde) **44-0131/225-3003** *lunch & dinner, panoramic views of Edinburgh's castle & historic skyline*

Valvona & Crolla [★] 19 Elm Row **44-0131/556-6066** *clsd Sun, oldest Italian deli in Scotland*

ENTERTAINMENT & RECREATION

Black Kilt Tours [GO] 125b Grange Loan **44-786/416-5362** *tailor-made driver/guided tours of Scotland for the LGBT community and friends*

BOOKSTORES

Word Power Books 43-45 W Nicolson St **44-0131/662-9112** *10am-6pm, noon-5pm Sun, independent & radical, events*

NATIONAL PUBLICATIONS

ScotsGay 44-0131/539-0666

MEN'S CLUBS

No 18 18 Albert Pl **44-0131/553-3222** *noon-10pm, till 11pm Fri-Sun, sauna club*

Steamworks [WI] 5 Broughton Market (btwn Barony & Dublin) **44-0131/477-3567** *11am-11pm, cafe,labyrinth*

EROTICA

Q Store 5 Barony St **44-0131/477-4756**

SPAIN

Barcelona

Note: M°=Metro station

INFO LINES & SERVICES

Casal Lambda Av Marquès de l'Argentera, 22 **34/93-319-5550** *5pm-9pm, community center & cafe, archives & library, also publish magazine*

Col-Lectiu Gai de Barcelona (CGB) 34/934-534-125 *7pm-9:30pm, till 3am Fri-Sat, clsd Sun-Mon*

ACCOMMODATIONS

California Hotel [GS] Rauric 14 (at Ferran, M° Liceu) **34/93-317-7766** *next to the Ramblas and Plaza Catalunya*

Catalonia Diagonal Centro [GF,F,WI,WC] Balmes 142-146 **34/93-415-9090**

Catalonia Portal de l'Àngel [GF,SW,WI] Avenida Portal de L'Angel 17 **34/93-318-4141** *3-star hotel, brkfst buffet*

Fashion House [GS,WI] Bruc 13 Principal **34/63-790-4044** *shared baths*

HCC Regente [GF,SW,WI,WC] Rambla de Catalunya 76 **34/93-487-5989** *in 1913 art nouveau bldg*

HCC Taber [GF,WI] Arago 256 **34/93-487-3887** *in art nouveau bldg designed by Doménech i Montaner, next to Rambla de Catalunya*

Hostal Baires [GF] **34/93-319-7774** *in Barrio Gótico*

Hostal Medea [GS,WI] Mallorca 290 (at Bruch) **34/93-459-2366** *10-minute walk away from Plaça Catalunya*

Hotel Axel [MW,SW,WI,WC] Aribau 33 (at Consell de Cent) **34/93-323-9393** *full brkfst, rooftop bar*

Hotel Colon [GF] Avenida Catedral 7 **34/93-301-1404** *right in the plaza, easy walking to most things*

Hotel Majestic Barcelona [GF,SW,WC] Paseo de Gracia 68 (in city center) **34/93-488-1717** *5-star hotel, rooftop pool*

Pension Eos [MW,GO] Gran Via de los Corts Catalanes 575 (M° Universitat) **34/93-451-8772, 34/617-931-439** *B&B in gay district*

Room Mate Emma [GF,WI] Carrer Rosselló 205 **855/471-2739** *nightclub vibe*

Bars

Aire/ Sala Diana [GS,D,F,S,YC] Valencia 236 (btwn Enriq. Granados & c/ Balmes) **34/93-451-8462**

Átame [M,E,DS] Consell de Cent 257 (at M° Universidad) **34/93-454-9273** *8:30pm-2:30am, clsd Mon*

Bacon Bear Bar [M,B] Casanova 64 (M° Urgell) *6pm-3am, theme nights*

Bar Plata [M] Consejo de Ciento 233 (at Urgell) **34-934 /524-636** *8pm-2am, great people-watching, outdoor seating*

Berlin Dark [M,L] Pasage Prunera 18 (at de la Font Honrada) *10pm-3am Tue-Sun, also Berlin Day 5pm-9pm Mon-Fri*

El Cangrejo [MW,D] Villarroel 86 *10:30pm-3am, clsd Mon-Tue*

La Chapelle [M] Muntaner 65 **34-9/3453-3076** *cafe by day, patio*

La Cueva [MW,DS] Calàbria 91 *open 4pm, clsd Mon*

Moeem [MW] Muntaner 11 **34/659-229-033** *6pm-3am, cheap drinks*

New Chaps [M,L,S,V] Av Diagonal 365 (M° Diagonal) **34/93-215-5365** *9pm-3am, till 3:30am Fri-Sat, from 7pm Sun, darkroom*

Night Barcelona [MO,S] Diputación 161 (M° Urgell) **34/935-031-701** *6pm-3am, darkroom & cabins*

People Lounge [M,E,F] Villarroel 71 (M° Urgell) **34/93-451-5986** *8pm-3am*

Punto BCN [★M,WC] Muntaner 63-65 (at Y Aragón, Metro, M° Universitat) **34-93/451-9152** *6pm-2:30am, upscale cafe-bar*

SkyBar [MW] Aribau 33 (at Hotel Axel) **34/93-323-9393**

Zelig [GS,D,F] **34/931-250-135** *11am-1am, till 3am Fri-Sat*

Nightclubs

Arena Classic [★M,D,S,V,YC,$] Diputació 233 (at Balmes, M° Universitat) **34/93-487-8342** *2:30am-6am Sat-Sun only, Spanish music*

Arena Sala Madre [★M,D,F,S,V,YC,$] Balmes 32 (at Diputació, M° Universitat) **34/93-487-8342** *12:30am-5am, clsd Mon (except in Aug), darkroom*

Metro [★MO,D,L,DS,V,YC,$] Sepúlveda 185 (M° Universitat) **34/93-323-5227** *12:15am-5:30am*

Souvenir Barcelona [★GS,D] Noi del Sucre 75 (Viladecans) *after-hours club 6am-1pm Sat-Sun & holidays*

Cafes

La Concha del Barrio Chino [GS,D,TG] Guardia 14 (M° Liceu) **34/93-302-4118** *4pm-3am*

Restaurants

7 Portes Passeig d'Isabel II, 14 **34/93-319-3033** *1pm-1am, Catalan*

El Berro Diputació 180 **34/933-236-956** *8am-1:30am,from 9am wknds, inexpensive diner-style restaurant, also bar*

Botafumeiro [R] El Gran de Gràcia 81 **34/932-184-230** *1pm-1am, Galician seafood, full bar*

dDivine [MW,DS,R] Balmes 24 (M° Universitat) **34/93-317-2248** *8am-4pm & 8pm-midnight, dinner show hosted by "Divine"*

Little Italy [E] Carrer del Rec 30 (near Passeig del Born) **34/93-319-7973** *1pm-4pm & 8pm-midnight, live jazz*

Entertainment & Recreation

Chernobyl Beach take the Metro to Sant Roc *popular gay beach*

Museu Picasso Montcada 15-23 **34/93-256-3000** *works of Picasso before he went to Paris*

Parc Guell Mount Tibidado *mosiacs & sculpture by Gaudi*

Playa Mar Bella *popular gay beach*

Sant Sebastiàn *popular gay beach*

Bookstores

Antinous [WC] Josep Anselm Clavé 6 (btwn Las Ramblas & Ample, M° Drassanes) **34/93-301-9070** *LGBT, books & gifts, also cafe*

Cómplices Cervantes 2 (at Avinyó, M° Liceu) **34/93-412-7283** *10:30am-8:30pm, from noon Sat, clsd Sun, LGBT, Spanish & English titles*

Men's Clubs

Bruch C/ Pau Claris 87 **34/93-487-4814** *11am-10pm*

Casanova [★F,V] Casanova 57 (at Diputació, M° Universitat) **34/93-323-7860, 34/65-016-5078** *24hrs, gym equipment, also bar*

Club Black Hole Sepúlveda 81 (btw Calabria and Viladomat) *6pm-midnight, 11pm-6am Fri-Sat, clsd Sun-Mon, fetish club and playground*

Condal [F,V,SW] Espolsasacs 1 (at Carrer Condal, M° Catalunya) **34/93-317-6817** *24hrs*

Galilea Sauna [F,V,WI] Calabria 59 (M° Rocafort) **34/93-426-7905** *24hrs wknds*

Open Mind Arago 130 **34/934-510-479** *11pm-4am, till 7am Fri-Sat, clsd Mon-Tue, cruising, fetish and SM club*

Sauna Barcelona [V,SW,WI] Tuset 1 (at Av Diagonal) **34/93-200-7716** *24hrs wknds*

Thermas [SW] Diputación 46 (at Entenza, M° Rocafort) **34/93-325-9346** *24hrs, hustlers*

Sex Clubs

Dalila [TG] Carrer del Consell de Cent, 185 **34/934-511-028** *24hrs, rent of rooms to independent and major transvestites of age*

Erotica

Boyberry Calàbria 96 (M° Rocafort) **34/93-426-2312** *noon-11pm, from 3pm wknds, darkroom, videos*

Erotic Museum of Barcelona Ramblas 96 **34/93-318-9865** *10am-midnight (seasonal hours)*

Kitsch Muntaner 17-19 (at Gran Via) **34/93-453-2052** *10am-10pm, clsd Sun*

Nostromo Diputació 208 (downstairs, M° Universitat) **34/93-451-3323** *noon-10pm, video cabins, darkroom*

Sestienda Rauric 11 (at Farran, M° Liceu) **34/93-318-8676** *clsd Sun*

Zeus Gay Shop Riera Alta 20 (M° Sant Antoni) **34/93-442-9795** *clsd Sun*

Cruisy Areas

Parc de Montjuïc [AYOR] btwn Avs del Estadio & Rius y Taulet *behind the archaeology museum, by the cascade*

Parc Sagrada Familia [AYOR]

Playa de la Mar Bella [AYOR] *on the beach & in the park*

Las Ramblas [AYOR]

Travel Agents

Rainbow Barcelona Tours Via de les Corts Catalanes 581 USA **34-63/318-553**

Madrid

Note: M°=Metro station

Info Lines & Services

COGAM (Colectivo de Lesbianas, Gays, Transexuales, y Bisexuales de Madrid) Puebla 9 (Bajo) **34/915-230-070** *5pm-9pm, LGBT center, groups, library, also cafe-bar*

Accommodations

Chueca Pension [MW,WI] Gravina 4 **34/91-523-1473** *hostel*

Hostal CasaChueca [MW,WI,GO] Calle San Bartolomé 4 (at San Marcos) **34/91-523-8127**

Hostal La Fontana [MW,WI] Valverde 6, 1° (M° Gran Vía) **34/91-521-8449**

Hostal la Zona [M,WI,GO] Calle Valverde 7, 1 & 2 (at Gran Vía) **34/91-521-9904** *full brkfst, private balconies*

Hostal Puerta del Sol [GS,WI,WC,GO] Plaza Puerta del Sol 14, 4° (at Calle de Alcalá, M° Sol) **34/91-522-5126** *centrally located*

Hotel Catalonia Gaudí [GF,F,WI] Gran Vía 7-9 (at Alcalá) **34/91-531-2222** *4-star hotel in the heart of the city*

Hotel Urban Madrid [GF,SW,WI] Carrera de San Jerónimo 34 **34/91-787-7770** *upscale hotel w/ 3 restaurants*

Pensión Madrid House [GS,WI,GO] Barbieri 1 **34/651-387 535** *one block from Chueca Square*

Bars

Attack Fun SX Bar [M,V] Calle de Lavapiés 12 (at Plaza Tirso de Molina) **34-91/115-4290** *9pm-late, clsd Mon, sex club, darkroom,naked & underwear nights*

Bear's Bar [★MO,B,L,V] Calle Pelayo 4 (M° Chueca, ring to enter) **34/91-521-7358** *7pm-2am, till 3:30am wknds, darkroom, cruisy*

Black & White (Blanco y Negro) [M,D,S,AYOR] Libertad 34 (at Gravina, M° Chueca) **34/91-531-1141** *8pm-5am, hustlers*

Coto Cruising Bar [M,D] Calle Hernan Cortes 21 **34-915/230-363** *5pm-3:30am*

Enfrente [M,B,L] Infantas 12 (M° Gran Vía) **34/68-779-1462** *8pm-3am, DJs Th & Sun*

Fulanita de Tal [W,D] Calle de Regueros 9 **34/913-195-069**

Gris [MW,E] **34/647-262-693** *9pm-3:30am, clsd Sun-Mon, reduced drink prices until 11:30pm*

Hot Bar [M,B,L,V] Infantas 9 (M° Chueca, ring to enter) **34/972-251-426** *1pm-3am, cruising in the basement*

Leather [MO,D,L,S,V,OC] Pelayo 42 (at Gravina, M° Chueca) **34/91-308-1462** *7pm-3pm [S] Th-Sat, darkroom*

Museo Chicote [GS,F,E] Calle Gran Via 12 **34/915-326-737** *7pm-3am, 50s style lounge*

La Ochenta (80) [MW,D,GO] Calle de la Sombrerería 8 (in Lavapies area) **34/609-779-793** *8pm-3am, 80's music*

The Paso [★M,V] Calle Costanilla de los Capuchinos 1 (M° Gran Via) **34/91-522-0888** *8pm-3am*

Rick's [★M,D,YC] Calle del Clavel 8 (at Infantas, M° Gran Vía, ring to enter) **34/915-413-500** *midnight-5:30am*

Rimmel [M,NH,V,YC] Calle de Luis de Góngora 2 (M° Chueca) *7pm-3am, darkroom, hustlers*

El Rincón Guay [MW,NH,F,WI] Embajadores 62 (Lavapiés quarter) **34/914-683-700** *9am-2am*

Sixta [GS,GO] Calatrava 15 (M° La Latina) **34/913-663-018** *10:30pm-2am, 4pm-midnight Sun, clsd Mon-Wed, packed on Sun afternoon*

Truco [★W,D] Calle de Gravina 10 (at Plaza de Chueca) **34/91-532-8921** *8pm-close, clsd Mon-Tue, dance bar, seasonal terrace*

Why Not [M,D] San Bartolomé 6 (M° Gran Vía) *10pm-3am*

Nightclubs

Boite [GS,D] Calle Tetuan 27 (Plaza del Carmen) **34/91-522-9620** *check listings for gay club nights*

Dark Hole [GS,D] Calle Valverde 10 *1am -6am Sat, gay goth club*

Griffin's [★M,D,DS,E] Marqués de Valdeiglesias 6 (M° Banco de España) **34/91-522-2079** *11pm-late*

Joy Eslava [★GS,D,DS,S] Arenal 11 (M° Sol) **34/91-366-3733** *11:30pm-6pm Sat only, fabulous crowd*

LL [★M,D,S,DS,V] Pelayo 11 (M° Chueca) **34/91-523-3121** *8:30pm-3am, darkroom, cruisy, 2 flrs*

Odarko [MO,D] *Electrodance gay-fetish party, once a month, only for men into masculine attitude and dress-codes, check FB page for details*

Ohm [★GS,D,S] Plaza de Callao 4 (at Sala Bash, M° Callao) **34/915-413-500** *midnight-close Fri-Sat*

Strong Center [M,D,L,S,V,$] Trujillos 7 (M° Santo Domingo) **34/91-541-5415** *11pm-6am, cruisy, huge darkroom*

CAFES

Cafe Acuarela [MW] Gravina 10 (M° Chueca) **34/915-249-935** *3pm-3am, from 11am Sat-Sun, bohemian cafe-bar*

D'Mystic [★] Gravina 5 (M° Pelayo) **34/91-308-2460** *9:30am-2am hip cafe-bar in Chueca area*

Mama Inés [★] Hortaleza 22 (M° Chueca) **34/91-523-2333** *9am-2am, sandwiches, pies*

RESTAURANTS

Al Natural Zorrilla 11 (M° Sevilla) **34/91-369-4709** *lunch & dinner, no dinner Sun, vegetarian*

Antigua Taqueria [GO] Calle Cabestreros 4 (in Lavapies area) **34/915-308-270** *11am-midnight, till 2am Fri-Sat, Tex-Mex*

Artemisa Ventura de la Vega 4 (at Zorrilla) **34/91-429-5092** *vegetarian; also Tres Cruces 4 location*

Barandales Menorca, 31 **34-91/557-2152** *specialize in castilian food from two castilian provinces*

La Berenjena [GO] Calle Marqués de Toca,7 (in Lavapies area) **34/914-675-297** *1:30pm-2am, till midnight Sun, clsd Mon*

Botin **34/91-366-4217** *one of the oldest restaurants in the world*

Cafetín La Quimera Sancho Davila, 34 *offers a typical flamenco show*

Ecocentro Esquilache 2, 4, y 6 (at Pablo Iglesias, M° Rios Rosas) **34/91-553-5502** *open till midnight, vegetarian, natural foods, also shop, herbalist school*

La Gastrocroqueteria de Chema Calle del Barco 7 **34/913-642-263** *dinner nightly from 9pm, lunch wknds from 2pm*

Gula Gula [★MW,E,DS,R] Gran Via 1 (M° Gran Via) **34/910-133-747** *lunch & dinner, buffet/ salad bar*

La Gamella Calle Alfonso XII, 4 *Spanish and American cuisine*

La Gloria Paseo Infanta Isabel, 5 *fine seasonal dishes*

Mercado de la Reina Calle Gran Vía 12 **34/915 -213-198** *9am-2am, hip and happening with high quality food*

Momo [NS,GO] Calle de la Libertad 8 **34/915-327-348** *lunch and dinner, clsd Sun, charming staff*

ORIO Madrid C/ Fuencarral 49 **34-93/342-5411** *great tapas*

Shikku Lagasca, 5 **34-91/344-1664** *chic Japanese*

Taberna La Bola Calle Bola, 5 **34/9157-6930** *best of the castillan cuisine*

Vegaviana Pelayo 35 **34/913-080-381** *lunch & dinner, clsd Mon, vegetarian*

Villa Cazorla Calle Castillo 14 **34-91/665-7578** *surrounded by Parque del Castillo and Bosque Pinar*

BOOKSTORES

A Different Life Pelayo 30 (M° Chueca) **34/91-532-9652** *11am-10pm, LGBT, books, magazines, music, videos, sex shop downstairs*

Berkana Bookstore [WC] Hortaleza 64 **34/91-522-5599** *10:30am-9pm, from noon Sat-Sun, LGBT, ask for free gay map of Madrid*

Publications

Shangay Express 34/91-445-1741 *free bi-weekly gay paper, also publishes Shanguide*

Gyms & Health Clubs

Energy Gym [★] Hortaleza 19 (M° Gran Via, Chueca) **34/91-531-1029, 34/91-522-3073** *8:30am-11:30pm, 10am-6pm Sun, crowded after 6pm, wet area is cruisy*

Holiday Gym Princesa [SW] Serrano Jover 3 (M° Argüelles) **34/916-216-000** *central location*

Men's Clubs

Adán [SW] San Bernardo 38 (M° Noviciado) **34/91-532-9138** *old and not very clean, visited mostly by rent boys and their clientss*

Club Baco Calle del Olmo 31 **34/655-873-991** *9pm-2am Th-Fri, 11pm-6am Sat, 6pm-1am Sun, clsd Mon-Wed, fetish club*

Into the Tank [★D,L] Diputació 94 **34/91-521-7734** *check www.intothetank.org for party dates*

Octopus [V,SW] Churruca 10 (at Apodaca, M° Tribunal/ Chueca) **34/91-183-2832** *10am-midnight, 24hrs wknds, darkroom, bar*

Paraíso [★SW,V] Norte 15 (at San Vicente F, M° Noviciado) **34/915-225-899** *noon-midnight, 24hrs wknds, gym equipment, also bar, darkroom*

Sauna Center [D] Cuesta de Santo Domingo 1 **34/915-424-570** *24hrs, busiest on Sunday morning when the guys come from the clubs and parties*

Sauna Lavapiés Zurita 3 **34-911/232-652** *24hrs, clean but reported to be not very busy*

Sauna Olimpo Calle de Valverde 32 **34-915/229-956** *noon-midnight, 24hrs wknds*

Sauna Príncipe [F,V] Travesia de las Beatas 3 (M° Opera) **34/915-590-259** *2pm-midnight, also bar, darkroom*

Sauna Puerta de Toledo **34/913-659-095** *2pm-11pm*

Erotica

Amantis Pelayo 46 **34/91-702-0510** *10am-10pm, till 9pm Sun*

City Sex Store c/ Hortaleza, next to #18 (in Chueca) **34/91-181-2723** *11am-10pm, noon-9pm Sun*

Cruisy Areas

Casa de Campo [AYOR] *at night on top of hill—travel along only road going up from lake*

El Corte Ingles [AYOR] Puerta del Sol *large department store, men's lounge on 3rd & 5th flrs*

Parque del Campo de las Naciones [AYOR] *by the bridge leading to the auditorium*

Parque El Retiro [AYOR] (M° Atocha) *at night in garden around statue of fallen angel*

Plaza de Toros [AYOR] *car cruising at night*

Sitges

Accommodations

Antonio's Guesthouse [MW,WI,GO] Passeig Vilanova 58 **34/93-894-9207** *also apts*

Los Globos [MW,WI,WC,GO] Avda Ntra Sra de Montserrat 43 **34/93-894-9374** *also bar*

Hotel Antemare [GF,SW] Verge de Montserrat 48-50 **34/93-894-7000** *1 block from beach*

Hotel Liberty [★MW,NS,WI,WC,GO] Isla de Cuba 45 (at Artur Carbonell) **34/93-811-0872** *seasonal*

Hotel Medium Renaixença [GS] Illa de Cuba 13 , 08070 **34/938-948-009** *some shared baths, bar*

Hotel Medium Romàntic [GS] Sant Isidre 33 **34/938-948-375** *full brkfst, some shared baths, seasonal, also bar*

Hotel Santa Maria [GS] Paseo de la Ribera 52 **34/93-894-0999** *clean & modest, great restaurant*

Medium Sitges Park Hotel [GS,SW,WI,WC] Calle Jesus 16 **34/938-940-205** *restaurant, bar & garden*

Parrot's Hotel [MW,WI] Joan Tarrida 16 **34/93-894-1350** *also bar, restaurant & sauna*

Sitges Royal Rooms [★GS,WI] **34-93/811-1515** *lovely rooms, rooftop terrace, garden restaurant and great brkfst*

URH Hotel Sitges Playa [GF,SW,NS,WC] Port Alegre 53 **34/938-948-676** *also bar/restaurant*

Bars

Barcode [★M,NH,V] Sant Bonaventura 10 **34/93-894-7634** *9pm-3am*

Bears' Bar [M,B,V] Bonaire 17 **34/93-894-6296** *10pm-3am (Fri-Sat only off-season), also rooms to rent*

Dark/ DSB [M] Bonaire 14 *10pm-3am, friendly bar*

El Horno [★M,B,L,F,V] Joan Tarrida Ferratges 6 **34/93-894-0909** *5:30pm-3am, darkroom*

Mojito & Co [M] Plaza Industrial 2 *5pm-3am, breezy lounge w/ outdoor seating*

Parrot's Pub [★MW,S] Plaza Industria 2 (at Primero de Mayo) **34/93-894-7881** *5pm-close, seasonal, patio, also restaurant*

El Seven [M,D,S,V] Calle Nou 7 **34/938-948-718** *10pm-2:30am (wknds only off-season), clsd Nov-Feb, terrace, darkroom*

XXL [★M,D,L,V] Joan Tarrida Ferratges 7 *11pm-3:30am (wknds only off-season), darkroom*

Nightclubs

Bourbon's [★M,D,V,YC] Sant Bonaventura 13 **34/93-894-3347** *10pm-2am, darkroom*

Comodín [M,D,DS] Tacó 4 **34/605-115-243** *10pm-3am, clsd Mon, darkroom*

Organic [M,D,TG,S,$] Bonaire 15 **34/627-536-235** *opens 2:30am (wknds only off-season)*

El Piano [MW,C,P] Bonaventura 37 **34/93-814-6245** *10pm-3am*

Privilege [M,D] Bonaire 24 *11pm-3:30am, seasonal, darkroom*

Queenz [M,D,DS,C] Bonaire 17 **34-938/940-712** *10pm-3:30am, seasonal*

Ricky's [GS] *midnight-6am, clsd Mon, more gay Fri*

Ruby's Bar At Queenz [M,D] Carrer Bonaire 12 **34-627 /536-235** *2am-6am (in season)*

Ruby's Bar At Queenz [M,E,DS] Carrer Bonaire 17 **34/938-940-712** *10:30pm-3am*

Cafes

33 Sitges Carrer Major 33 **34/93-811-3307** *7pm-midnight & 1pm-3pm wknds*

Mont Roig Cafe [★WI] Marques de Montroig 11-13 **34/93-894-8439** *9am-3am, patio, also full bar*

Restaurants

Beach House [GO] Paseo Ribera 33 **34-935 /168-136** *brkfst & dinner, full bar*

Ma Maison [★MW] Bonaire 28 **34/93-894-6054** *lunch & dinner, French, full bar, terrace*

Pic Nic [WI] Paseo de la Ribera **34/93-811-0040** *in front of gay beach*

So Ca/ Southern California Sant Gaudenci 9 **34/93-894-3046** *1pm-close, also bar*

El Trull [★MW] Mossèn Felix Clará 3 (off Major) **34/93-894-4705** *dinner nightly, lunch wknds,, French/ int'l*

Entertainment & Recreation

Gay Beach (Platja de la Bassa Rodona) *in front of Calipolis Hotel & Picnic cafe*

Playa De Las Balmins *turn left then pass a long beach strip and then climb a hill past a cemetery, great beach with cafe*

Playa del Muerto *exclusively gay beach 50 minutes walk from the center of Sitges, also beach bar*

Retail Shops

Laguna Beach Shop Sant Josep 25 **34/938-947-204** *10:30am-2pm, 5pm-9pm*

Men's Clubs

Parrots Sauna Joan Tarrida 16 **34/93-894-1350** *seasonal*

Sauna Sitges Espalter 11 **34/662-074-192** *4pm-10am, also bar & theme parties*

Erotica

The Mask 34/93-811-2214 *24hrs wknds*

Cruisy Areas

Espigon Beach [AYOR] *beware of cops!*

L' Estanyol Beach [AYOR] *nights, go right, past gay beach—beware of cops!*

Gay Beach [AYOR] La Playa De La Bossa Rodona *in front of Calipolis Hotel & Picnic cafe (beware of cops!)*

Playa del Muerto [AYOR] *in woods near Terramar Hotel, daytime (beware of cops!)*

Asia

Japan

Tokyo

Accommodations

24 Kaikan [M,F,V] Shinjuku 2-13-1 **81-3/3354-2424** *hotel & sauna*

The Capitol Hotel Tokyu [GF,WI] 10-3 Nagata-cho 2-chome (Chiyoda-ku) **81-3/3503-0109** *restaurant, bar, spa & gym on site*

HI Tokyo Central Hostel [GF] 18F Central Plaza (1-1 Kagurakashi, Shinjuku-ku) **81-3/3235-1107** *11pm curfew*

Hotel Century Southern Tower [GF] 2-2-1 Yoyogi (Shibuya-ku) **81-3/5354-0111** *near gay district, multiple restaurants in building*

Hotel Chinzanso Tokyo [GF,SW,WC] 10-8 Sekiguchi 2-chome (Bunkyo-ku) **81-3/3943-1111** *surrounded by historic Japanese garden*

Hotel Sunroute Plaza Shinjuku [GF] 2-3-1 Yoyogi (Shibuya-ku) **81-3/3375-3211** *near gay district*

Keio Plaza Hotel [GF,SW] 2-2-1 Nishi Shinjuku **81-3/3344-0111** *restaurants & bars*

Park Hyatt [GF,SW] 3-7-1-2 Nishi Shinjuku **81-3/5322-1234** *luxury hotel featured in Lost in Translation; also restaurants & lounge*

Shinjuku Prince Hotel [GF,WI] 30-1 Kabuki-cho 1-chome (Shinjuku-ku) **81-3/3205-1111** *located in the center of Kabuki-cho, one of Japan's best entertainment districts, restaurant & bar*

Shinjuku Washington Hotel [GF,WI] 2-9 Nishi-Shinjuku, 3 chrome (Shinjuku-ku) **81-3/3343-3111** *in the heart of the gay district, also restaurant & bar*

Tokyu Stay [GF] 5-9-8 Nishi Shinjuku **81-3/3370-1090** *great location*

Bars

Advocates Cafe [★MW,YC] 1-F, Dai-7 Tenka Bldg (Shinjuku 2-18-1) **81-3/3358-3988** *6pm-4am, till 1am Sun, cafe-bar*

Alamas Cafe [MW,D] 1/F Garnet Bldg, Shinjuku 2-12-1 **81-3/6914-9215** *6pm-2am, till 5am Fri-Sat, 3pm-midnight Sun*

The Annex [M,F,OC] 1/F Futami Bld (2-14-11 Shinjuku Ni-Cho) **81-3/3356-5029** *8pm-4am*

Arty Farty [★M,D,YC] 2F, #33 Kyutei Bldg (Shinjuku 2-11-7), Shinjuku-ku **81-3/5362-9720** *6pm-1am*

Base [M,B,YC] 10-16 Maruyamacho (Shibuya) **81-3/5728-1233** *a warm den for young bears*

Bridge [MW] Shinjuku Ni-chome 13-16 (Sensho Building 6F) *8pm-5am*

Campy! Bar [MW,DS] Shinjuku Ni-chome 12-10 (Musashino Building 1F) *8pm-5am*

Cholesterol [M] Shinjuku-ku

The Dock [★M,D] B1, Dai-2 Seiko Bldg (Shinjuku 2-18-5), Shinjuku-ku **81-3/3226-4006** *9pm-4am*

Fuji [M,K,OC] St Four Bldg, B104 (Shinjuku 2-12-16), Shinjuku-ku **81-3/3354-2707** *8pm-3am, till 5am wknds*

GB [★M] B1, Shinjuku Plaza Bldg (Shinjuku 2-12-3), Shinjuku-ku **81-3/3352-8972** *8pm-2am, till 3am Fri-Sat, 7pm-midnight Sun, clsd Mon, great spot before going to the clubs*

Gold Finger [MW,K] Shinjuku Ni-chome 12-11

Keivi [M,NH] 4F Yoshino Bldg, 17-10 Sakuragaoka **81-3/3462-9200** *7pm-midnight*

Kinsmen [MW] 2F Shinjuku 2-12-16 (near Shinjuku Sanchome Station) **81-3/3354-4949** *8pm-1am, till 3am Fri-Sat, clsd Mon*

Poplar [M,OC] B1 St Four Bldg (Shinjuku 2-12-16) **81-3/3350-6929** *6pm-2am*

Shibuya 246 [MO,WI,GO] 3/F Tozaki Bldg, 2-7-4 Dougen-zaka Shibuya **81-3/6277-5023** *6pm-2am, till midnight Sun*

Tac's Knot [MW,GO] Block A 2/F, 3-11-12 #202 (near Shinjuku 3-Chome Station (Exit C6)) **81-3/3341-9404** *8pm-2am, also art exhibitions*

Usagi [M] on lock U facing block V, 5th Fl (up the narrow stairs) **81-3/3464-4111** *great balcony*

Wordup Bar [M,D] 2-10-7 2F TOM Bld Shinjuku **81-3/3353-2466** *11pm-close*

Yo Chan Chi Shinjuku 2 *Tokyo's oldest and smallest gay bars*

NIGHTCLUBS

Agit [W,K,GO] **81-3/3350-8083** *8pm-5am*

Club Dragon [★MO,D,L,V] 1/F Stork Nagasaki Building (2-11-4 Shinjuku) **81-3/3341-0606** *6pm-3am, till 5am Fri-Sat*

Shangri-La [★M,D] **81-3/5534-2525** *bi-monthly party, www.facebook.com/shangrila.agh for dates and location*

CAFES

Ore no Yome [M] 3 Chome-9-13 (Iwashita Building, Higashi Ikebukuro) **81-3/6331-1533** *6pm-11pm, secret club for tranny, cross dressing with clothes available to try on for the experi-ence*

RESTAURANTS

Angkor Wat 1-38-13 Yoyogi (Shibuya-ku) **81-3/3370-3019** *lunch & dinner, Cambodian*

Ban Thai 1-23-14 Kabuki-cho, 3rd flr (Shinjuku) **81-3/3207-0068** *lunch & dinner*

Chin-ya 1-3-4 Asukusa **81-3/3841-0010** *lunch & dinner, serving shabu-shabu & sukiyaki since 1880*

Edogin [★] 4-5-1 Tsukiji (Chuo-ku) **81-3/3543-4401** *lunch & dnner, clsd Sun, sushi*

Gonpachi 1-13-11 Nishiazabu, 1F, 2F (Minato-ku) **81-3/5771-0170** *11:30am-3:30am, multiple locations*

Kakiden 3-37-11 Shinjuku, 8th flr **81-3/3352-5121** *lunch & dinner, upscale Japanese*

Kitchen Five 4-2-15 Nishi-Azabu (Minato-ku) **81-3/3409-8835** *6pm-9:45pm, Mediterranean*

Las Chicas Jingumae 5-47-6 (off Shibuya), Shibuya-ku **81-3/3407-6865** *11:30am-11pm, English spoken*

Maisen 4-8-5 Jingu-mae (Shibuya-ku) **81-1/2042-8485** *11am-10:45pm, specializes in tonkatsu*

Moti 3F Roppongi Hama Bldg (6-2-35 Roppongi) **81-3/3479-1939** *1130am-11pm, Indian*

New York Grill [R] 3-7-1-2 Nishi Shinjuku (at Park Hyatt Hotel, 52nd flr) **81-3/5323-3458** *lunch & dinner*

New York Grill [R] 3-7-1-2 Nishi Shinjuku (at the Park Hyatt) **81-3/5323-3460**

The Pink Cow 2-7-5 Bright Bld. B (Minato ku Akasaka) **81-3/6441-2998** *6pm-late, clsd Mon*

Sasa-no-yuki 2-15-10 Negishi (Taito-ku) **81-3/3873-1145** *11am-9pm, clsd Mon, serving homemade tofu for 300 years*

Tenmatsu 1-8-2 Muromachi (Nihonbashi, Chuo-ku) **81-3/3241-5840** *lunch & dinner, tempura*

Bookstores

Okamalt Shin-Chidorigai 2F (2-18-10 Shinjuku) *1pm-8pm, clsd Th-Sat, Tokyo's only shop dedicated to LGBT-lit*

Retail Shops

Isetan Men's 3-14-1 Shinjyuku 1-11-15 **81-3/3352-1111** *popular place for men's fashion, cruisy*

Gyms & Health Clubs

Gold's Gym Harajuku 6-31-17 Jingumae (Shibuya-ku) **81-3/5766-3131** *24 hrs, except Sun, many gay members*

Shinjuku Tipness Kaleido Bldg 5-7F (Nishi-Shinjuku 7-1), Shinjuku-ku **81-3/3368-3531** *many locations throughout city*

Men's Clubs

24 Kaikan [M,F,V] Asakusa-2-29-16 (Taitoku) **81-3/3354-2424** *24hrs, darkroom, sauna, restaurant, hotel*

HX [YC] 1F, UI Bldg (Shinjuku 5-9-6) **81-3/3226-4448** *3pm-10am, 24hrs wknds, long-haired men are not permitted*

King of College 2F Sakagami Bldg (2-14-5, Shinjuku-ku) **81-3/3352-3930** *6am-10pm, rent boys*

Cruisy Areas

Hibiya Park [AYOR] near Yurakucho Station

Shin Kiba Park [AYOR] near Shin Kiba Station

Ueno Park near Tokyo Metropolitan Festival Hall

Southeast Asia

Thailand

Bangkok

Info Lines & Services

Gay AA 43 Soi Sathorn Soi, 6th Fl #C67 (above Vincent's restaurant) **66-087/815-3563** *7pm Th, in English*

Accommodations

Baan Saladaeng [GF,WI] 69/2 Soi Saladaeng 3, Saladaeng Rd (Silom, Bangrak) **66-2/2636-3038** *near gay scene and subway, no lift*

The Babylon Bangkok [MO,SW,WI] 34 Soi Nandha, Sathon Soi 1, S Sathon Rd **66-2/679-7984** *also spa & saunas, foam party last Sat*

Bangkok Rama Place, City Resort & Hotel [GF,SW,WI,WC,GO] 1546 Pattanakarn Rd (in Suan-Luang District) **66-2/722-6602-5** *full brkfst, also restaurant*

Best Comfort Residential Hotel [M,SW,WI] 49 Soi Sukhumvit 19 (Wattana) **66-2/651-1310** *residential hotel in the heart of Bangkok*

D&D Inn [GF,SW] 68-70 Khaosan Rd (Phranakorn) **66-2/629-0526** *"life's little luxuries at a price you can afford," central location*

Elephantstay [GS,GO] Royal Elephant Kraal & Village (74/1 M3 Tumbol Suanpik), Phra Nakhon Si Ayutthaya **66-80/668-7727, 66-87/116-3307** *live w/, care for & learn about elephants; near Lopburi River; 1 hour to Bangkok*

Furama Silom [GF,SW] 533 Silom Rd **66-2/688-6888** *also gym, restaurant & bar*

Heaven@4 Hotel [GS,WI] 20/3-4 Sukhumvit Soi 4 **66-2/656-9450** *also bar*

Hostel Na Nara [GS,NS,WI] 72-74 Naratiwat Rd Silom **66-2/635-0169** *full brkfst, kids ok, also restaurant*

Hotel de Moc [GF,SW,WI,WC] 78 Prajatipatai Rd, Pra-Nakorn **66-2/629-2100-4** *central location near sightseeing destinations, restaurant & cafe on site*

Lub d [GF] 4 Decho Rd (Silom, Bangrak) **66-2/634-7999** *hostel with some private rooms; also Siam Sq location*

Luxx [GF,WI] 6/11 Decho Rd **66-2/635-8800** *style-conscious, minimalist design hotel, full brkfst*

Old Capital Bike Inn [GF,NS] 607 Pra Sumen Rd (at Rajdamnern Ave, in Pra Nakhon) **66-2/629-1787** *fun ambience, funky rooms, eager to please staff, and a fantastic breakfast*

Pinnacle Lumpinee Park Hotel [GS] 17 Soi Ngam Duphli, Rama 4 Rd, Sathorn **66-2/287-0111**

Regency Park Hotel [GF,SW] 12/3 Sukhumvit 22, Soi Sainamthip **66-2/259-7420** *located in heart of Bangkok, full brkfst*

Sheraton Grande Sukhumvit [GF,SW,WI,WC] 250 Sukhumvit Rd **66-2/649-8888**

Tarntawan Place Hotel [MW,WI,WC] 119/ 5-10 Thanon Surawong Rd **66-2/238-2620** *centrally located, modern amenities, bar & lounge*

Bars

The Balcony Pub & Restaurant [★M,F,K] 86-88 Silom Soi 4 (off Silom Rd) **66-2/235-5891** *5:30pm-close*

Bed Supperclub [GS,D,F] 26 Soi Sukhumvit 11, Sukhumvit Rd, Klongtoey-nua, Wattana **66-2/651-3537** *7:30pm-close*

Club Cafe [M] 8/5 Silom Soi 2 (Bang Rak) **66-86/978-5221** *3pm-3am, Moroccan-styled, chill-out bar with a relaxed atmosphere enhanced by water underneath the glass floor*

Club Love Remix [GS,D,YC] 89/2 Lamsali Rd (Khlong Chan, Bang Kapi) **66-2/378-4345** *9pm-2am*

Expresso [M] 8/10-11 Silom Rd, Soi 2 (Bang Rak) *relaxed café-bar*

G Bangkok [M,D] **66-2/632-8033** *11pm-3am, "guys on display"*

Golden Cock [M] 39/27 Soi Rajanakarindra 1, Surawong Rd (Bang Rak) **66-2/236-3859** *1pm-1am*

Jupiter 2018 [M,S] Silom Rd Soi 4 **66-02/266-3682** *9pm-1am*

Maxi's Bar & Restaurant [M] 38/1-2, Soi Pratuchai, Surawong Rd **66-2/2266-4225** *5pm-2am*

Tawan [★M,S] 2/2 Soi Thantawan, Silom Soi 6 (off Suriwong Rd) **66-2/634-5833** *8pm-1am, specializing in muscular go-go boys*

Telephone Pub & Restaurant [★MW,F,K,WI] 114/ 11 Silom Rd, Soi 4 **66-2/234-3279** *6pm-2am*

Nightclubs

Disco Disco [M,D] 8/12-13 Silom Rd, Soi 2 (Bang Rak) **66-2/234-6151** *10pm-2am*

DJ Station [★MW,D] 8/6-8 Silom Rd, Soi 2 (Bang Rak) **66-02/266-4029** *9pm-2am, 3 levels & outdoor terrace*

Dream Boy [★M,S] 38/3-6 Duangthawee Plaza (at 38 Surawong Rd, Bang Rak) **66-2/233-2121** *9pm-1am, go-go boy shows nightly*

Ick [M,D,E] 3581/13 Ramkhamhaeng Soi 89/2 **66-93/519-6456** *10pm-2am*

Joob Bar & Bistro [MW,D,S] Ladphrao Soi 85, Wang Thonglang **66-81/875-9123** *10:30pm-2am, large stage, state-of-the-art lighting and sound system*

X Boom [M,D,S] Soi Anuman Ratchathon, Suriwong, Bangkok *opens at 8pm, popular 'after-hours' place, go-go dancers*

Cafes

Bug & Bee 18 Silom Rd, Suriyawong (Bang Rak) **66-2/233-8118** *24hrs*

Rocket Coffeebar Sukhumvit Soi 49 **66-2/662-6638** *nice terrace*

Restaurants

Cabbages & Condoms 6 Soi 12 Sukhumvit Rd (at Birds & Bees Resort) **66-2/229-4611** *11am-10pm, Thai food w/ safe-sex education*

Crêpes & Co 59/4 Langsuan Soi 1 (Ploenchit Rd, Lumpini) **66-2/015-3388** *9am-11pm, lounge, full bar*

Eat Me [E] Soi Pipat 2 (off Soi Convent) **66-2/238-0931** *3pm-1am, upscale, also gallery, live music*

Fork & Cork [★K,GO] 100 Silom Soi 4 **66-2/234-7249** *5pm-2am, Thai & Western, full bar, terrace*

Full Moon 614 Ladprao Rd, Plaza Ladprao (Khwaeng Lat Phrao, Khet Lat Phrao,) **66-89/985 3344** *5pm-2am, terrace & bar*

Indigo 6 Convent Rd (off Silom Rd) **66-2/235-3268** *noon-1am, clsd Sun, patio, full bar, French*

Loy Nava Dinner Cruises [R] 37 Charoen Nakorn Rd, Klongsan **66-2/437-4932** *traditional Thai cuisine on rice barge on Chao Phraya River*

Mango Tree [★R] 37 Soi Tantawan 6, Khwaeng Suriya Wong (off Suriwong Rd) **66-2/236-2820** *11:30am-midnight, traditional Thai food, live music nightly*

May Kaidee 111 Tanao Rd, Bang-lamphu (behind Burger King) **66-9/137-3173** *9am-10pm, innovative vegetarian; also 33 Samen Rd*

Once Upon a Time 32 Soi Petchaburi 17, Pratunam **66-2/252-8629** *11am-11pm, located down a little side street with a lovely garden*

Entertainment & Recreation

Calypso Cabaret [GS,F,C,DS] 296 Phaya Thai Rd, Pathumwan (at Asia Hotel) **66-2/261-6355** *shows nightly at 8:15pm & 9:30pm*

Mambo [F,C] 59/28 Sathu-phararam 3 Rd **66-2/294-7381-2** *shows nightly at 7:15pm & 10pm*

Men's Clubs

Adonis Massage 44/11 Convent Rd (Silom) **66-2/236-7789** *1pm-11pm*

Arena 491/23-24, 3/F, Silom Plaza **66-2/635-3645** *Thai massage*

Banana Club [F] 41/9 Sukhumvit Soi 11 **66-2/651-0002** *3 flrs, massage, also restaurant*

Body Club 4/24-25 Sukhumvit Soi 8 **66-89/171-9009** *noon-10pm*

Chakran [F,K,V,SW] 32 Soi Ari 4, Phaholyothin Soi 7, Phayathai **66-2/279-1359** *darkroom, gym, pool-side bar*

Chakran Sauna [★SW] 32 Ari Alley 4, Phaholyothin Soi 7 **66-2/279-1359** *3pm-11pm, 2pm-2am Fri-Sun, multi story upscale spa with restaurant & bar*

Heaven Sauna [B] 4F Warner Bldg, 119 Soi Mahesak **66-2/266-9092** *1pm-11:30pm, rooftop garden*

Sauna Mania 35/2 Soi Pipat 2 (off Soi Convent, Silom) **66-2/636-8129** *noon-midnight, enter on 2nd flr*

V Club 7 [F] 32 Chakran Bldg, Soi Paholyothin 7 (Soi Ari 4) **66-02/279-3322** *2pm-midnight*

Australia

New South Wales

Sydney

Info Lines & Services

The Gender Centre **61-2/9519-8200** *9am-4:30pm Mon-Fri, free services for transgender/ transsexual people & their partners/ friends/ families*

Twenty 10 (Lesbian & Gay Counselling Service) **61-2/8594-9555** *9:30am-5pm, info & support*

Accommodations

1831 Boutique Hotel [GF,WI] 631-635 George St (at Goulburn St) **61-2/9265-8888** *close to the Capital theatre*

Best Western Hotel Stellar [GS,WI] 4 Wentworth Ave (at Oxford St) **61-2/9264-9754** *kitchenette in each room, also cafe & bar*

Brickfield Hill B&B Inn [GS,WI,GO] 403 Riley St (at Foveaux), Surry Hills **61-2/9211-4886** *in gay district, near beaches*

Governors on Fitzroy B&B [M,WI,GO] 64 Fitzroy St (at Bourke), Surry Hills **61-2/9331-4652** *3 blocks from Oxford St, full brkfst, hot tub, shared baths, garden*

Kirketon Boutique Hotel [GF,WI] 229 Darlinghurst Rd (at Farrell Ave) **61-2/9332-2011** *also restaurant & bar*

Medusa [GF,WI] 267 Darlinghurst Rd (at Liverpool), Darlinghurst **61-2/9331-1000** *modern boutique hotel*

Nomads Westend [GF,NS,WI,WC] 412 Pitt St (at Goulburn St) **61-2/9211-4588, 1800/013-186** *budget/ backpacker's accommodations*

Bars

Bar Cleveland [GS,D,F,YC] 433 Cleveland St (at Bourke), Surry Hills **61-2/9698-1908** *10am-4am, till midnight Sun, cocktail lounge, DJ*

The Beauchamp [★GS,NH,F,GO] 265 Oxford St (at S Dowling), Darlinghurst **61-2/9331-2575** *noon-2am*

Beresford Sundays [MW] 354 Bourke St (at Albion St), Surry Hills **61-2/9357-1111** *from noon Sun, fun in the sun*

The Colombian [★MW,D] 117-123 Oxford St (at Crown St), Darlinghurst **61-2/9360-2151** *9am-6am, trendy pub & cocktail bar, 2 levels, theme nights*

Green Park Hotel [GS] 360 Victoria St (at Liverpool), Darlinghurst **61-2/9380-5311** *10am-2am, noon-midnight Sun, very gay Sun, stylish bar*

The Imperial [MW,D,F,K,DS,S] 35 Erskineville Rd, Newtown **61-2/9519-9899** *11:30am-midnight, till 3am Fri-Sat*

The Oxford [★MW,D,F,E] 134 Oxford St (at Bourke St, Taylor Square), Darlinghurst **61-2/8080-7080** *10am-close, 3 bars*

The Palms On Oxford [★M,D] 124 Oxford St (at Bourke St, Taylor Square), Darlinghurst **61-2/9357-4166** *8pm-late, clsd Mon-Wed*

The Stonewall [★M,D,K,DS,S] 175 Oxford St (at Bourke), Darlinghurst **61-2/9360-1963** *11am-4am, 3 bars*

Websters Bar [GF,F] 323 King St (at Phillips St), Newtown **62-2/9519-1511** *10am-4am, till midnight Sun, 3 floors, including a rooftop terrace*

Nightclubs

ARQ [★M,D,DS,$] 16 Flinders St (at Taylor Square), Darlinghurst **61-2/9380-8700** *9pm-late Th-Sun, clsd Mon-Wed, drag shows Th*

Heaven Social Dance [M,DS] Corner Ulverstone St & Lawson St (at Mounties Bowling Club), Northmead **61-204/3323-2425** *bi-monthly drag shows, proceeds go to local charity organizations, check www.heavensocial-dance.com for dates*

Home [★GF,D,$] Tenancy 101, Cockle Bay Wharf (at Wheat Rd, Darling Harbour) **61-2/9266-0600** *open Fri-Sun*

Slide [MW,D,F,E,C] 41 Oxford St (at Pelican) **61-2/8915-1899** *6pm-3am, 5pm-4am Fri, 7pm-4am Sat-Sun, clsd Mon-Tue*

Sly Fox [MW,D,E] 199 Enmore Rd, Enmore **61-2/9557-2917** *6pm-3am*

Cafes

Fratelli Fresh [★] 211 Bent St, Moore Park (Entertainment Quarter) **61-2/8099 7069** *11:3-am-10pm, Italian vegetarian*

Victoire 660 Darling St **61-2/9818-5529** *7:30am-4pm, great bread*

Restaurants

10 William Street 10 William St **61-2/9360-3310** *5pm-midnight, from noon Fri-Sat, Italian quirky wine bar*

Bentley Restaurant & Bar 320 Crown St (Surry Hills) **61-2/9332-2344** *lunch weekdays, dinner nightly, clsd Sun, tapas & small plates, excellent wine*

Bertoni Cafe 281 Darling St **61-2/458-011-404** *6am-6:30pm, Italian*

Bills Surry Hills 359 Crown St (Surry Hills) **61-2/9360-4762** *7am-10pm, great ricotta pancakes*

Billy Kwong [★R,WC] 28 Macleay St #1 (Potts Point) **61-2/9332-3300** *dinner nightly from noon Sun, sustainable local and organic Chinese*

The Boathouse on Blackwattle Bay [R] 123 Ferry Road (Glebe) **61-2/9518-9011** *lunch & dinner Tue-Sun, gourmet seafood, some veggie, great view*

Fu Manchu [NS] 249 Victoria St, Darlinghurst **61-2/9360-9424** *5pm-10pm, chic noodle bar, cash only*

Iku Wholefood Kitchen [NS] 25a Glebe Point Rd, Glebe **61-2/9692-8720, 800/732-962** *lunch & dinner, creative vegan/ macrobi-otic fare, outdoor seating*

Kujin 41b Elizabeth Bay Rd, Elizabeth Bay **61-2/9331-6077** *lunch & dinner, clsd Sun,*

Queen Victoria Hotel/ Razors Bistro [WI] 167 Enmore Rd, Enmore **61-2/9517-9685**

Sean's Panaroma 270 Campbell Parade, Bondi Beach **61-2/9365-4924** *open 6pm , from noon Sat-Sun, clsd Mon-Tue*

Thai Kanteen [★GO] 541 Military Rd (at Harbour St), Mosman **61-2/9960-3282** *dinner nightly, clsd Sun, modern Thai*

Thai Pothong [WC] 294 King St (Newtown) **61-2/9550-6277** *lunch & dinner*

Entertainment & Recreation

Bondi Beach Bondi Beach *Sydney's most popular beach, more gay at north end*

Bronte Beach *check out the pool above the cliffs*

Lady Jane Beach/ Lady Bay Beach [M,N] Watsons Bay

Obelisk Beach [M,N] Middle Head Rd (at Chowder Bay Rd)

Sydney Gay/ Lesbian Mardi Gras 94 Oxford St, Darlinghurst 2010 **61-2/9383-0900** *the wildest party under the rainbow on this planet (see www.mardigras.org.au)*

Bookstores

The Bookshop Darlinghurst 207 Oxford St (near Darlinghurst Rd), Darlinghurst **61-2/9331-1103** *10am-10pm, Australia's oldest LGBT bookstore, staff happy to help w/ tourist info*

Gertrude & Alice 46 Hall St (Bondi Beach) **61-2/9130-5155** *second-hand books, also coffee shop*

Retail Shops

Bang 4 Flinders St, Darlinghurst **61-2/9357-3362** *designer labels, clubwear*

Bang 4 Flinders St (Darlinghurst) **61-02/9357-3362** *11am-7pm, designer labels, clubwear*

House of Priscilla 47 Oxford St, Darlinghurst **61-2/9286-3023** *wigs, costumes & more*

Publications

DNA 61-2/9764-0200, 888/263-2624 (US #) *monthly gay men's magazine*

SX Weekly 61-2/9360-8934 *free gay/ lesbian weekly*

Sydney Star Observer 61-2/8263-0500 *weekly newspaper w/ club & event listings*

Gyms & Health Clubs

City Gym 107-113 Crown St (at William St), E Sydney **61-2/9360-6247** *day passes available*

Men's Clubs

357 aka Sydney City Steam [F,WI,GO] 357 Sussex St (Darling Harbour) **61-2/9267-6766** *10am-6pm, 24hrs wknds, 4 levels, cafe/bar*

Bodyline Spa & Sauna [★V] 10 Taylor St, Darlinghurst **61-2/9360-1006** *11am-1am, till 5am Fri-Sat*

Headquarters [V,NS,WI] 273 Crown St (at Goulburn, near Oxford), Darlinghurst **61-2/9331-6217** *24hrs wknds, 3pm-7pm Mon-Th, theme rooms, theme nights*

Signal [V,WI] at Riley & Arnold Sts (upstairs), Darlinghurst **61-2/9331-8830**

Sydney Sauna [F,WI] 38-42 Oxford St, Darlinghurst **61-2/9360-3431** *24hrs*

Sex Clubs

Aarows [MW,TG,18+] 17 Bridge St (at Pitt St), Rydalmere **61-2/9638-0553** *24hrs, men only Sun*

Erotica

Gay Exchange 44 Park St **61-2/9267-6812**

Pleasure Chest 705 George St (at Ultimo Rd), Haymarket **61-2/9212-6440** *24hrs*

Sax Fetish [GO] 110a Oxford St (Taylor Square) **61-2/9331-6105** *leather and fetish, clothing, accessories, toys*

Toolshed 81 Oxford St, Darlinghurst **61-2/9332-2792** *clothing, fetishgear, toys, pride items and more*

Cruises

Men Only

SAILORdudes Admiraly Quay, ZH 3063EE Rotterdam, Netherlands **3165/133-1459** fun, affordable, active gay sailing holidays (clothing optional) for fit dudes • www.sailordudes.com

Mostly Men

Atlantis Events 9200 Sunset Blvd, Ste 500, West Hollywood, CA 90069 **310/859-8800, 800/628-5268** largest LGBT tour operator in the world • all-gay cruise, resort & tour vacations • www.atlantisevents.com

Pied Piper Tours 70-50 Austin St. Ste. 112UL, Forest Hills, NY 11375 **718/261-4596, 800/874-7312** gay group cruises • www.gaygroupcruises.com

RSVP Vacations 310/432-2300, 800/328-7787 gay & lesbian cruise vacations • www.rsvpvacations.com

Gay/Lesbian

Aquafest 4801 Woodway #400-W, Houston, TX 77056 **800/592-9058** LGBT groups mingle w/ mixed clientele on major cruise lines • www.aquafestcruises.com

Port Yacht Charters 9 Belleview Ave, Port Washington, NY 11050 **516/883-0998, 877/DO-A-BOAT** custom charters worldwide, specializing in the Caribbean • commitment ceremonies • gourmet cuisine • www.portyachtcharters.com

R Family 5 Washington Ave, Nyack, NY 10960 **917/522-0985** family-friendly vacations designed especially for the LGBT community • www.rfamilyvacations.com

Rainbow Charters Kewalo Basin, Honolulu, HI 96814 **808/347-0235** gay & lesbian weddings • custom sailing cruises • whale-watching • snorkeling • sunset cruises • www.RainbowChartersHawaii.com

Luxury Tours

Mostly Men

HE Travel 626 Josephine Parker Dr #206, Key West, FL 33040 **305/294-8174, 800/825-9766** worldwide adventures for the uncommon traveler • Peru, India, Morocco, South Africa, Greece, Turkey, Italy, Egypt & more • www.hetravel.com

Gay/Lesbian

DavidTravel 310 Dahlia Pl, Ste A, Corona del Mar, CA 92625-2821 **949/427-0199** full-service travel agency & tour operator • small luxury group departures & customized travel for individuals & groups • milestone events, including honeymoons! • www.DavidTravel.com

Steele Luxury Travel New York City, NY 10011 **646/688-2274** unique & top-rated travel experiences to exotic destinations worldwide • www.steeletravel.com

Great Outdoors Adventures

Men Only

Adventure Bound Expeditions 711 Walnut St, Boulder, CO 80302 **303/449-0990, 877/440-0990** outdoor adventure worldwide • hiking, kayaking, safaris, wildlife viewing • www.adventureboundmen.com

Mostly Men

Saltyboys gay & naturist sailing cruises • www.saltyboys.com

Scuba Scotty San Francisco, CA **760/974-6477** scuba instruction • local & exotic destinations • gay-owned • www.scubascotty.com

Gay/Lesbian

Out in Alaska 1819 Dimond Dr, Anchorage, AK 99507 **907/339-0101** adventure travel throughout Alaska for LGBT travelers • your best bet for a fun & authentic Alaska vacation! • www.outinalaska.com

OutWest Global Adventures PO Box 2050, Red Lodge, MT 59068 **800/825-9766** specializing in gay/ lesbian active & adventure travel • worldwide • www.outwestadventures.com

Undersea Expeditions 758 Kapahulu Ave #100-1188, Honolulu, HI 96816 **858/270-2900, 800/669-0310** gay & lesbian scuba adventures worldwide • www.UnderseaX.com

Gay/Straight

GoNorth Alaska Adventure Travel Center 3713 South Lathrop St, Fairbanks, AK 99709 **907/479-7271, 855/236-7271** guided tours throughout Alaska & the Arctic • air taxis & transportation • www.GoNorth-Alaska.com

Himalayan High Treks 241 Dolores St, San Francisco, CA 94103 **415/551-1005** experience indigenous Buddhist & Hindu cultures • www.hightreks.com

Natural Habitat Adventures PO Box 3065, Boulder, CO 80307 **303/449-3711, 800/543-8917** up-close encounters w/ the world's most amazing wildlife in its natural habitat • www.nathab.com

Open Eye Tours PO Box 324, Makawao, HI 96768 **808/572-3483** customized private land tours of Maui & other islands • visit popular spots or places seldom seen, walking or not • sharing Maui's best-kept secrets since 1983 • www.openeyetours.com

Paddling South & Saddling South 2100 Bridgeway, Sausalito, CA 4965 **415/332-8494** sea-kayak trips in Baja • www.tourbaja.com

Puffin Fishing Charters PO Box 1169, Seward, AK 99664 **907/224-4653, 800/978-3346** guided charter fishing • almost 30 years of experience • halibut, salmon & rockfish on vessels custom-built for Alaskan waters • www.puffincharters.com

Voyageur North Outfitters 1829 E Sheridan, Ely, MN 55731 **218/365-3251, 800/848-5530** canoe outfitting & trips • www.vnorth.com

Spiritual/Health Vacations

Gay/Lesbian

Spirit Journeys 428 Riverview Dri, Ashville, NC 28806 **828/475-2581** spiritual retreats, workshops & adventure trips throughout the US & abroad • www.spiritjourneys.com

Thematic Tours

Mostly Men

Coda International Tours, Inc 12794 Forest Hill Blvd #1A, West Palm Beach, FL 33414 **561/791-9890, 888/677-2632** culturally focused travel programs • www.codatours.com

Gay/Lesbian

Brazil Fiesta Visa Service 268 Bush St #3531, San Francisco, CA 94104 **415/986-1134** expedited Brazilian visa service • www.brazilfiesta.net

CM by Carlos Melia 630 5th Ave #2207, 10011 New York City **917/754-5515** boutique gay travel to Argentina, Uruguay & New York City • all services tested by me • "Been There Done That" • www.carlosmelia.com

Gay Bali Tours Jl. Braban No. 67, Seminyak, 80361 Bali, Indonesia **62-361/736-818, 62-361/788-6627** premier & professional tour operator permanently based in Bali • www.baligay.net

Kuyay Travel Puerto Rosales 46, 5550000 Puerto Varas, Los Lagos, Chile **56-652/801-265, 56-97/519-3259** gay-owned/run travel planner & tour host in Patagonia • www.gaypatagonia.com

National Gay Pilots Association 4931 W. 35th Street Ste 200, St. Louis Park, MN 55416 **866/800-6472** several annual gatherings • call for more info • www.ngpa.org

Planetdwellers Shop 1 113-115 Oxford St, Darlinghurst , NSW 2010 , Australia **61-2/9357-2900** | LGBT tours of Australia • come to OZ! • www.planetdwellers.com.au

Toto Tours 1326 W Albion Ave #3W, Chicago, IL 60626 **773/274-8686** unique worldwide adventures for gay men, lesbians, their friends & adult family members • www.tototours.com

Venture Out 575 Pierce St #604, San Francisco, CA 94117 **415/626-5678** high-end, escorted, small-group tours for gay & lesbian travelers to countries around the world • www.venture-out.com

Gay/Straight

Alaska Railroad 327 West Ship Creek Ave, Anchorage, AK 99510 **907/265-2399, 800/544-0552** rail & tour packages • www.alaskarailroad.com

Amazon Nature Tours PO Box 128, Jamestown, RI 02835 **401/423-3377, 800/688-1822** small group boat tours of the Amazon & more • call for color catalog • www.naturetours.com

Aria Tours PO Box 159, Little Bridge St, Almonte, ON K0A 1A0, Canada **613/461-1299, 866/686-1288** luxury travel for opera & the arts to the most spectacular destinations in the world • www.ariatours.com

Brazil Ecojourneys Estrada Rozalia Paulina Ferreira 1132, Armação, 88063-555 Florianopolis, Brazil **55-48/3389-5619** lesbian-owned Brazil tour operator • www.brazilecojourneys.com

Heritage Tours Private Travel 121 W 27th St #1201, New York, NY 10001 **212/206-8400, 800/378-4555** custom private trips to Morocco, Spain, Portugal, Turkey, Southern & East Africa • htprivatetravel.com

Holbrook Travel 3540 NW 13th St, Gainesville, FL 32609 **352/377-7111, 800/451-7111** natural history tours in Central America, South America & Africa • small groups • www.holbrooktravel.com

Lima Tours Jr De la Union 1040, Lima, Peru **51-11/619-6976** personalized, gay-friendly tours to Peru • www.limatours.com.pe

New England Vacation Tours PO Box 560, West Dover, VT 05356 **802/464-2076, 800/742-7669** gay/ lesbian tours (including fall foliage) conducted by a mainstream tour operator • www.newenglandvacationtours.com

Pacha Tours 36 W 44th St # 1208, New York City, NY 10036 **800/722-4288** trips to Turkey, Spain, France & Greece • www.pachatours.com

Sublime Journeys Albrook Plaza, no. 31, Panama City, Panama **507/315-1305** progressive, diverse & extraordinary travel experiences in South & Central America • www.discoversublime.com

VIP Tours of New York 320 W 38th St, New York, NY 10018 **212/247-0366, 800/300-6203** private, custom-designed tours of New York • specializing in theater, architecture, gay life & more • groups from one to 100+ • www.viptoursny.com

Way To Go Costa Rica, Panama, Nicaragua & Belize 5171 Glenwood Ave # 111, Raleigh, NC 27612 **800/835-1223** custom itineraries for individuals & groups to Costa Rica, Belize,
Nicaragua & Panama • www.waytogocostarica.com

Welcome Rajasthan Jaipur, Rajasthan 30216, India **91-141/220-5527 , 91-141/491-4416** tours & car rentals for Rajasthan, India • www.welcomera-jasthan.com

Wild Rainbow African Safaris 85 Tunnel Road, 12A Box 233 , Asheville, NC 28805 **800/423-1945** bespoke African safaris lead by Jody Cole • www.wildrainbowsa-faris.com

Custom Tours

Costa Rica Experts 3166 N Lincoln Ave #424, Chicago, IL 60657 **773/935-1009, 800/827-9046** • www.costaricaexperts.com

Travel & Culture Dubai 201 Al Habbai Building (opposite Deira city center), Dubai, United Arab Emirates **971/56-495-4061** tours, safaris & hotel reservations in Dubai • www.dubai.travel-culture.com

Travel & Culture Pakistan 702 Panorama Center Office Plaza, 75530 Karachi, Pakistan **0321/242-4778** tours, safaris & hotel reservations in Pakistan • www.travel-culture.com

Travel & Culture Sri Lanka 07-1B, E Tower, World Trade Ctr, Colombo, Sri Lanka **94/777-864-479** tours, safaris & hotel reservations in Sri Lanka • www.srilanka.travel-culture.com

Various Tours

Mostly Men

Detours Gay Travel 800/680-8066 boutique gay tour operator specializing in group adventures to the world's most exotic destinations • www.detourstravel.com

Source Events PO Box 530988, Miami, FL 33153 **305/672-9779, 888/768-7238** specializing in all-gay Windstar cruises • luxury adventures around the world • www.sourceevents.com

Out In The Vineyard 6926 Eveton Lane, Sonoma, CA 95476 **707/495-9732** LBGT Wine weekend in Somoma annually and some tours abroad • www.outinthevineyard.com

Gay/Lesbian

Brand g Vacations 3333 Republic Ave, Minneapolis, MN 55426 **952/405-9309, 800/433-4303** The LGBT River Cruise Experts • www.brandgvacations.com

Friends of Dorothy Travel® 1177 California St #B, San Francisco, CA 94108 **415/864-1600** unique gay & lesbian adventures • individual & group arrangements • www.fodtravel.com

Ishpingo Tours 954/636-2822, 866/456-3325 LGBT tour specialists for Ecuador & the Galapagos • www.ishpingotours.com

Out & About Travel 161 Federal St, Providence, RI 02903 **800/842-4753** full-service travel agency specializing in gay & lesbian tours, cruises, adventure travel, ski trips, honeymoons, customized packages & more • serving the GLBT community since 1999! • www.gaytravelpros.com

Zoom Vacations Chicago, IL **773/772-9666** takes gay group travel to the next level • experience the best of a destination w/ surprises, insider events & a sense of magic • www.zoomvacations.com

GET IT ON
Google Play

Download on the
App Store

Tan Line Optional
Photo by: Cliff Baker